LET THE TRUMPET SOUND

Books by Stephen B. Oates

BIOGRAPHY

The Civil War Quartet
I. The Fires of Jubilee (Nat Turner)
II. To Purge This Land with Blood (John Brown)
III. With Malice Toward None (Abraham Lincoln)
IV. Let the Trumpet Sound (Martin Luther King, Jr.)

ESSAYS

Our Fiery Trial: Abraham Lincoln, John Brown,
and the Civil War Era

HISTORY

Confederate Cavalry West of the River
Rip Ford's Texas
The Republic of Texas
Visions of Glory
Portrait of America (2 vols.)

Let the Trumpet Sound

THE LIFE OF
MARTIN LUTHER KING, Jr.

STEPHEN B. OATES

1817

HARPER & ROW, PUBLISHERS, New York
Cambridge, Philadelphia, San Francisco, London
Mexico City, São Paulo, Sydney

Portions of this book originally appeared, in somewhat different form, in *American Heritage* and the *Massachusetts Review*.

LET THE TRUMPET SOUND. Copyright © 1982 by Stephen B. Oates. All rights reserved. Printed in the United States of America. No part of this book may be used or reproduced in any manner whatsoever without written permission except in the case of brief quotations embodied in critical articles and reviews. For information address Harper & Row, Publishers, Inc., 10 East 53rd Street, New York, N.Y. 10022. Published simultaneously in Canada by Fitzhenry & Whiteside Limited, Toronto.
FIRST EDITION
Designer: Sidney Feinberg

Library of Congress Cataloging in Publication Data

Oates, Stephen B.
  Let the trumpet sound.
  Includes bibliographical references and index.
  1. King, Martin Luther. 2. Afro-Americans—Civil
rights. 3. Afro-Americans—Biography. I. Title.
E185.97.K5O18 1982   323.4′092′4 [B]   81-48046
ISBN 0-06-014993-0   AACR2

82 83 84 85 86 10 9 8 7 6 5 4 3 2

To the memory of

Addie Mae Collins
Denise McNair
Carol Robertson
and
Cynthia Wesley

For it was to restore the beloved community, so
that the children of the world might inherit a
legacy of peace, that he came down out of the
academy, down from his pulpit, and marched his
way to glory.

For the trumpet shall sound, and the
dead shall be raised incorruptible,
and we shall be changed.

I Corinthians 15:52

CONTENTS

PRELUDE

THIS IS THE FOURTH in a quartet of "lives" I have written about Americans profoundly affected by the moral paradox of slavery and racial oppression in a land based on the ideals of the Declaration of Independence. The other biographies are of Nat Turner, John Brown, and Abraham Lincoln. King, though struggling in a subsequent century, was both historically and symbolically linked to these figures of the Civil War era. For King perceived that the civil-rights movement was an extension of the Civil War, that Negroes of his day were striving to realize the promise of Lincoln's Emancipation Proclamation. In truth, as this biography attempts to demonstrate, King did more than any other leader in his generation to help make emancipation a political and social fact in the racially troubled South. King also mounted a personal crusade to convert President John F. Kennedy into a modern Lincoln in the theater of civil rights, only to become in many ways (in his sense of history, his brilliant oratory, his defense of the moral example of American democratic principles) another Lincoln himself. In the end, King fell in Memphis, a victim of the same conflict over racial tensions and national destiny that had claimed Lincoln's life in another April long before—and that had claimed the lives of Brown and Turner, too. Though *Let the Trumpet Sound* can be read entirely on its own, it is part of a larger biographical tapestry.

It is also part of a personal literary odyssey which began that tragic day in 1968 when King was assassinated. I was working on my life of John Brown then, narrating the genesis of the 1859 raid on Harpers Ferry—Brown's messianic attempt to free the slaves by inciting them to revolt. At this juncture, Brown was arguing furiously that peaceful resistance to slavery was useless, that only violence could remove that "sin against God" and force America to fulfill the promise of the Declaration. I could scarcely believe that King, the modern apostle of *non-violent* resistance, had been murdered when I was at this point in Brown's life. As I huddled near my television set, staring at those calamitous scenes in Memphis, hearing highlights of King's most famous orations, I was stricken with the revelation that 1859 was really only yesterday, that past and present were indeed a continuum. My biography of Brown was not about some remote figure in a distant historical era, for many of the fundamental problems he dealt with still had not been solved.

I cannot claim that I vowed at that moment to write a life of King one day. But my biography of Brown led inevitably to sequels about the slave rebel Nat Turner and about Abraham Lincoln. All three were driven, visionary men, all were inextricably caught up in the slave and race issues of their day, and all in their separate ways embraced violent solutions to the egregious wrong of Negro bondage. My life of King, another impassioned and spiritual man, grew logically out of the other three volumes, extended them to a biographical quartet on the Civil War epoch and its century-old legacies, and afforded yet another view of how Americans have tried to combat racial injustice in their country. Thus I ended as I began, recounting in *Let the Trumpet Sound* the very scenes that had so haunted me in 1968.

It has taken me five years to prepare this book. The first new life of King to appear in eleven years (and the first written by a professional biographer), it is also the first to utilize the indispensable Martin Luther King Collection at Boston University, the extensive King and SCLC collections at the Martin Luther King, Jr., Center for Nonviolent Social Change in Atlanta (material that only recently became available), the pertinent records in the John F. Kennedy and Lyndon B. Johnson presidential libraries, the Ralph J. Bunche Oral History Collection at Howard University, the holdings of the Horace Mann Bond Center for Equal Education at the University of Massachusetts, and other public and private sources, not to mention a cornucopia of government documents and published memoirs, autobiographies, oral histories, monographs, and other works bearing on the King story that have come out during the last eleven years. In order to gain a three-dimensional sense of the man, I sequestered myself in the National Archives for part of one June, studying tapes, newsreels, and television recordings that featured King and his campaigns; reviewed Eli Landau's incomparable *King: A Filmed Record, Montgomery to Mem-*

phis; and listened over and over to tapes of his speeches. I also visited the historical sites of King's life and campaigns, which gave me a special feel for him I could have acquired in no other way. I drew, too, from interviews with members of King's inner circle and many others who were involved with him and the civil-rights movement. Their willingness to tell their stories has been invaluable, for they reveal a very human King with universal appeal.

Because of all the new materials it uses, *Let the Trumpet Sound* is the most complete account of King's life to be published thus far. While some people tried to discourage me from delving into the personal King, fearful that I might somehow tarnish his image, I have attempted to depict all sides of this complicated, creative, and divided man—the public figure and private individual, the outer and inner selves. I have no interest in adding to the deification of King as a flawless immortal. It seems obvious to me that only by viewing the whole man—and viewing him realistically—can we truly comprehend, appreciate, and identify with him.

Like everybody, King had imperfections: he had hurts and insecurities, conflicts and contradictions, guilts and frailties, a good deal of anger, and he made mistakes. I have tried to relate his human flaws with sympathy and understanding. I have tried to do the same in describing his achievements, which were astounding for a man who was cut down at the age of only thirty-nine and who labored against staggering odds—not only the bastion of segregation that was the American South of his day, but the monstrously complex racial barriers of the urban North, a hateful FBI crusade against him, a lot of jealousy on the part of rival civil-rights leaders and organizations, and finally the Vietnam War and a vengeful Lyndon Johnson. King was all things to the American Negro movement—advocate, orator, field general, historian, fund raiser, and symbol. Though he longed to be a teacher and scholar on the university level, he became instead a master of direct-action protest, using it in imaginative and unprecedented ways to stimulate powerful federal legislation that radically altered southern race relations.

By 1967 and 1968, despite declining popularity at home and a deepening personal depression, he stood as a global champion of love and nonviolence in a world racked by war and plagued by hate. Regardless of his own shattered dreams, he insisted to the very end that he was still an optimist, that he still believed that one day all of God's children would live together in a symphony of brotherhood. In those distressing final months, he was getting up a remarkable class movement with revolutionary overtones, a movement whose origins and objectives until now have never been fully revealed. His speeches and sermons were widely published, and his books on nonviolence and the Negro movement were translated into more than fifteen languages, including the Gujarati, Oriya, and Hindi languages of India. King liked to ruminate on the fertile cross-pollination of ideas that had engendered the philosophy of nonviolence to which he had committed his life (Thoreau had been inspired by sacred Hindu writings and doctrine, Gandhi by Thoreau, and King and his colleagues by both of them). Through his own writings, King contributed to that cross-pollination. A preeminent voice in the quest for human rights during his era, King reached more blacks—more Americans, more citizens of the world—than any other U.S. reform leader in his century. He marched and orated before a global audience, summoned his long-suffering people to a great historical destiny, and in the process won the Nobel Prize for peace. He was one of the most learned social and religious activists to emerge in his embattled nation, a scholarly and yet passionate young minister—the grandson of a slave—who forged a world view of striking insight. Yet that world view was born out of painful struggle against inner and outer adversity.

A word about the form in which this book is written. For me, true biography—the best biography—remains a storytelling art, whose mission (in the words of Paul Murray Kendall) is "to perpetuate a man as he was in the days he lived, a spring task of bringing to life again." It is "the art of human portrayal in words," as Leon Edel has reminded us, and "the biographer who respects his craft makes his figure speak in its own voice and stance." The storytelling approach is the one I have taken in *Let the Trumpet Sound* and the other volumes in my quartet—an old and honorable genre too often disparaged in our analytical time. Not that true biography lacks analysis. Virtually everything said in good life-writing is the result of painstaking research, selection, and study. When it comes to composition, though, I celebrate the fact that true biography is not abstract, is not an explanation of lifeless data and impersonal force, is not an author-dominated lecture in which the biographer pompously upstages his own subject, but is a form of literature which conveys the warmth and immediacy of a life being lived. It belongs to what Barbara W. Tuchman has termed "the literature of actuality." Unlike the writer of fiction, the writer of lives is limited to what really happened and cannot, must not, invent anything. As Edel has said, "a biographer fashions a man or woman out of seemingly intractable materials of archives, diaries, documents, dreams, a glimpse, a series of memories." The true biographer recounts his story sequentially, suggesting the essence of his subject through graphic scenes, character development, interpersonal relationships, telling quotations, revealing details, and dramatic narrative sweep. At the same time, the true biographer must have a sense of history and a thorough knowledge of the era in which his subject lived and died. In sum, the true biographer must be a historian who is steeped in his material and an artist who wields a deft and vivid pen. If he is successful, as Justin Kaplan has noted, his book "is dramatically and psychologically coherent—it makes sense, it is believable, it is a good story." I have endeavored to make *Let the Trumpet Sound* a good story, one that captures all the passion and drama of King's life and the spirit of his turbulent, extraordinary time.

For me, biography has not only been high literary and historical adventure, but deep personal experience as well. I have lived through four human lives besides my own, something that has enriched me beyond measure as a writer and a man. In the sixteen years it has required to create my quartet, I have come to believe—as Yeats suggested—that "nothing exists but a stream of souls, that all knowledge is biography."

*In times like the present, men should utter nothing
for which they would not willingly be responsible
through time and eternity.*

ABRAHAM LINCOLN, *1862*

*One day historians will record this movement as one
of the most significant epics of our heritage.*

MARTIN LUTHER KING, JR., *1962*

PART ONE

ODYSSEY

Tell me, muse, of the man of many resources
who wandered far and wide after he sacked the
holy citadel of Troy, and he saw the cities
and learned the thoughts of many men, and on
the sea he suffered in his heart many woes.

HOMER, *The Odyssey*

H<small>E WOULD ALWAYS REMEMBER</small> the day he joined the church. It was a spring Sunday in 1934, and an evangelist down from Virginia was conducting a spirited revival in the packed sanctuary of Ebenezer Baptist Church in Atlanta. In the King family pew, five-year-old M. L.—for that was how he went in his youth—sat with his grandmother and his older sister Christine. Up behind the pulpit, with its exquisite gold cross, Reverend King—the boy's father—reposed in imperial splendor in the pastor's chair. Behind him, Mother toiled at the organ near the singing choir. All about M. L., all about the church, people in their Sunday finest clapped and shouted and sang. Presently, as M. L. squirmed and glanced, the evangelist gesticulated at the pulpit, expatiating on the glories of salvation and membership in the House of God. When he invited people to join the church, M. L.'s sister took off for the pulpit—the first person that morning to offer a pledge. At once M. L. ran after her, determined that Christine was not going to "get ahead of me." And so he joined God's House, not because of any "dynamic conviction" (as he later claimed), but because of "a childhood desire to keep up with my sister." Even at his baptism, he was "unaware of what was taking place." Hence conversion for him was never an abrupt religious experience, never "a crisis moment." It was simply a gradual assimilation of religious ideals from his church and family environment.

The church was M. L.'s second home. All his close friends were in his Sunday-school classes. In those classes, unlettered women in bright dresses and high-heeled shoes, smelling of sweet perfume, instructed him in fundamentalist precepts, exhorting him to accept the literalness and infallibility of the Scriptures. After Sunday school came regular worship in the sanctuary, a voltage-charged affair in which the congregation swayed and cried (*amen, yes!, that's right, well?*) as Reverend King preached in remarkable oratorical flourishes, his voice ranging from a booming baritone to a near shriek. M. L. looked up to his father with a mixture of awe, respect, intimidation, and embarrassment. He thought Daddy awfully emotional.

After worship came Sunday dinner at church—succulent fried chicken, ham, black-eyed peas, and watermelon—and then more devotionals and religious activities that lasted into the night. The boy was at church all day on Sunday and part of the afternoons and evenings on weekdays. The church defined his little-boy world, gave it order and balance, taught him how to "get along with people." Here M. L. knew who he was—"Reverend King's boy," somebody special.

Home was only three blocks away on Auburn Avenue, in a sedate neighborhood in a middle-class section of black Atlanta. The house was a two-story Victorian dwelling with a banister M. L. and little brother A. D. liked to slide down. One day M. L. was leaning against the banister and suddenly fell over it head first, plunging twenty feet to the floor and bouncing through an open door into the cellar. As though by a miracle, he wasn't hurt. He seemed to have a propensity for accidents: twice cars knocked him down and once A. D. clubbed him in the head with a baseball bat. Later M. L. decided that he survived such mishaps because God was looking out for him.

Physically, M. L. was small for his age, but healthy all the same. At his birth, he wrote later, the doctor pronounced him "a one hundred percent perfect child from a physical point of view." True, Mother often said he had given her a difficult time in childbirth. It was on a cold and cloudy Saturday, January 15, 1929, that M. L. entered the world, so quiet that the doctor feared him stillborn and had to spank him several times before he cried. The elder King, of course, wanted his first son named after him. Since he was called Mike (his mother's name for him), the doctor entered Michael King, Jr., on the baby's birth certificate. Five years later—the year M. L. joined the church—Daddy officially corrected both their names to Martin Luther King, Sr. and Jr. But Daddy still went by Mike, his son by M. L. In the big house on Auburn Avenue, there was room for only one Mike King.

To his father's gruff delight, M. L. was an active, athletic child. He played baseball in an open field in back of the King home, flew kites and model airplanes, and pedaled a bicycle about the neighborhood. Neighbors sometimes saw him bouncing a ball off the side of the King home, lost in solitary reverie. As at church, though, the rhythms of home life centered on worship, and days began and ended with family prayer. On Daddy's orders, M. L., Chris, and little A. D. recited Scripture at evening meals in the dining room, with its fireplace and white lace curtains. After dinner, Grandmother Williams regaled the children with vivid Biblical stories. "She was very dear to each of us," M. L. wrote later, "but especially to me. I sometimes think that I was her favorite grandchild." He thought her "a saintly grandmother" and called her "Mama." Because she was warm and sympathetic and never hurt him, he loved her more than anyone.

Not that he lacked affection for his mother, Alberta. She was a short, subdued woman, quiet and deliberate and slow to anger. The children called her Mother Dear, their father Daddy. Family friends described Alberta as a perfect preacher's wife, who dressed fashionably, knew everybody at Ebenezer by name, and tried to have a smile for every person she met. M. L. remembered that his parents lived together "very intimately" and seldom argued—"my father happens to be the kind who just won't argue." In any case, Mother Dear was content to let her husband have his way and be a placid ally in his decisions and judgments, setting forth her "motherly cares" behind the scenes.

M. L. greatly admired his Daddy, who always provided for the family and who set a "noble" example for the boy. In truth, Reverend King was fiercely protective of his children, determined that they should not suffer as he had. Raised on a sharecropping farm on a central Georgia plantation, he had spent his youth plowing behind a mule. Because he had to curry the animal every morning, he smelled like a mule and school chums teased him so much that he said he got "a mule complex." "I may *smell* like a mule," he cried one day, "but I don't *think* like a mule." Early on, of course, he learned what it was like to be a "nigger" in Dixie. He observed the vast discrepancy between the way white folks and black folks lived. He saw his mama toil as a cleaning "girl" for a white banker's family in nearby Stockbridge, and he often went with her to their house, where he ran his fingers over soft drapes and luxurious chairs. "Why," he asked, "do *they* have things and *we* don't?" He saw his papa get cheated at the plantation commissary, saw whites beat black people and even hang one from a tree, and he vowed to hate white people until the day he died. Once a white man struck him for refusing to bring him a pail of water. Enraged, his mama whipped that man herself. But don't tell your papa, she said, or he'll "take it up" with the white man and get himself lynched.

Mike's papa was a troubled fellow, an alcoholic who beat Mike's mother after Saturday-night binges, taking out his rage on her and on himself. When papa abused her one awful Saturday night, Mike, then fifteen, grabbed his papa and wrestled him furiously around the room, finally pinning him to the floor with an arm locked around his neck. The next day, his father apologized and promised never to hurt mama again. But King had taken enough of rural Georgia life and set off for Atlanta with only a pair of shoes slung over his shoulder. As he passed the white banker's house, he promised himself, "Some day I'm going to have a brick house as big as that—bigger. Someday I'm even going to be a director of a bank like that man."

In Atlanta, Mike worked as a mechanic's helper in a repair shop, then as a railroad fireman—one of the best jobs unskilled blacks could secure at that time. But it was the ministry that appealed most to him: in church, Mike King was captivated by the powerful and emotional preachers he heard. He discerned that they were the natural leaders of the black community, proud men who even commanded the respect of Atlanta whites. Feeling called to the ministry, Mike became pastor of two small churches—he preached in them on alternate Sundays—and attended night classes to earn his high-school diploma. In 1926, he entered Morehouse College, a privately endowed Negro school in Atlanta, to work on a bachelor's degree in divinity. He drove around town in a Model T Ford, a stubborn, independent man who was quick with figures and alert to business deals.

Meanwhile he'd started courting Alberta Williams, daughter of the pastor of Atlanta's Ebenezer Baptist Church, Reverend Adam Daniel Williams. Born in 1863, the year of Lincoln's Emancipation Proclamation, Williams had literally come up from slavery. He had taken over Ebenezer in 1894, in the dawn of the modern Jim Crow era, and with irrepressible zeal had built it into one of black Atlanta's most prestigious Baptist churches. He served in various offices of the National Baptist Convention, received an honorary doctorate from Morehouse (his alma mater), and inspired his congregation with his "sulfurous evangelism." Mike King very much admired Dr. Williams, a man's man who charmed the women in his congregation and stood up resolutely to white people. After the Atlanta race riot of 1906, he became a charter member of a strong local chapter of the National Association for the Advancement of Colored People and served as its president. When an inflammatory white newspaper attacked Atlanta Negroes as "dirty and ignorant," Dr. Williams helped lead a boycott that eventually closed the paper down. In addition, he was one of the leaders of a Negro citizens group that pressured Atlanta into building Booker T. Washington High School, the city's only high school for blacks. By the 1920s, Dr. Williams was a visible member of Atlanta's black elite, an eloquent and elegant man who refused to let segregation cow him.

An affectionate, paternalistic father, Dr. Williams sent his daughter Alberta to the best available schools and tried to protect her from "the worst blights of discrimination." By the early 1920s, Mike King was calling at the Williams home on Auburn Avenue and taking Alberta for drives in his Model T. There was a mutual attraction between this shy and diffident young woman and her explosive, gesticulating beau, and their courtship led inevitably to marriage. They were wedded on Thanksgiving Day, 1926, and moved into the upstairs of her parents' house, a twelve-room structure with a garden in a respectable black neighborhood. Not long after, Mike King became assistant pastor at Ebenezer, and he and Alberta began to build a family in the house on Auburn Avenue: first came Willie Christine, then M. L., Jr., and finally Alfred Daniel, or A. D., named partly after Dr. Williams.

In the spring of 1931, Dr. Williams died suddenly of an apoplectic stroke. That fall, Mike King became pastor of Ebenezer, embarked on an ambitious building program that led to a renovated church, and eventually raised membership from six hundred to several thousand, complete with six choirs. Meanwhile, he continued to take courses at Morehouse, earned his degree while the children were growing up, and later won a doctor of divinity degree at Atlanta's Morris Brown College. Because he had come up the hard way, he loved respectability and was attracted to wealth and power. As he'd vowed, he became a director of a Negro bank and amassed interests in other enterprises, thus earning himself a place in Atlanta's black middle class.

By the 1930s, his hatred for whites had eased some, and he was one of several Negro spokesmen white city officials called on in times of crisis. Like Dr. Williams, Reverend King was active in the NAACP at a period when white America regarded it as dangerously radical. He served not only on the NAACP's Executive Board, but also on its Social Action Committee, which ultimately won a legal battle to equalize teachers' salaries in Atlanta. He went down to City Hall and challenged the tangle of Jim Crow laws and practices that systematically disenfranchised Negroes in Atlanta and everywhere else in Dixie. He put up with insult and evasion, paid his poll tax, passed Georgia's severe "literacy" test for blacks, and finally secured his right to vote in national elections. In 1936, fed up with political discrimination, he led several hundred Atlanta Negroes on a voting-rights march to City Hall, a spectacle, he said, that "no living soul in that city had ever seen."

As head of the house, Daddy was a frugal man who never squandered money. His constant prayer was "God, grant that my children will not have to come the way I did." Thanks to his care and industry, the children never lacked necessities, never knew hunger or squalor or want. Daddy even gave them each a weekly allowance for ice cream and sodas, and he praised them for excelling at tasks he set for them.

In all, Reverend King ruled his home like a fierce Old Testament patriarch, certain that he alone knew what was best for the children and intolerant of dissent or rival viewpoints. In fact, he could be a tyrant, and Alberta and Grandmother Williams never dared dispute him. When the children broke a rule, became sassy or sullen, Daddy took a strap to them. He even made them thrash one another, to demonstrate that chastisement was personal.

Of course, stern discipline for children was nothing unusual in America in the 1930s; parents and principals alike spanked them as a matter of course. Still, M. L. was an extremely sensitive boy, and it hurt him deeply to be whipped by his awesome father; it aroused such guilt in him, such anger. Sometimes his anger found an external target: once when A. D. pestered Christine to tears, M. L. grabbed a telephone and clubbed him on the head, knocking A. D. cold. But most of the time M. L. endured his father's strap without a word, relying on "stoic impassivity" to control the vortex of feelings it provoked in him. "He was the most peculiar child whenever you whipped him," Daddy remarked. "He'd stand there, and the tears would run down and he'd never cry. His grandmother couldn't stand to see it." In fact, she would go off to another room and sob uncontrollably, unable to bear M. L.'s mute suffering. It was no wonder that he loved her so.

One day when the King boys were playing upstairs, A. D. slid down the banister and accidentally knocked Grandmother down. She did not move. M. L. stood there in shock, certain that Mama was dead—that he and A. D. had killed her. M. L. was so distraught that he ran upstairs and hurled himself out a window, falling twelve feet to the ground. He lay there motionless as his relatives screamed his name. When he heard that Mama was all right, though, he got up and walked away as though nothing had happened. But his parents and family friends were incredulous: the boy had apparently tried to kill himself.

T HE ADULTS REMARKED about how intelligent he was, how he could see and feel things beyond the understanding of most children, how he could drive you to distraction with all his questions. When his family rode through Atlanta, he observed all the Negroes standing in bread-lines and asked his parents about them. It was the middle of the De-pression, and 65 percent of Atlanta's black population was on public relief. M. L. was deeply affected by the sight of those tattered folk, worried lest their children not have enough to eat.

Yes, the adults said, he was a brilliant child, a gifted child, who could talk like he was grown sometimes. My, how that boy loved lan-guage. "You just wait and see," he once told his parents. "When I grow up I'm going to get me some big words." "Even before he could read," his Daddy boasted, "he kept books around him, he just liked the idea of having them." And his memory was phenomenal. By age five, he could recite whole Biblical passages and sing entire hymns from memory. His parents and grandmother all praised him for his precocious ways, making him flush with self-esteem. In fact, he was so bright that his parents slipped him into grade school a year early. Daddy recalled what happened next. "He was always a talkative chap, you know. So he shot his mouth off and told them he was only five while the other children were six, so they booted him right out of that class."

At six, he began singing hymns at church groups and conventions, accompanied by Mother Dear on the piano. Now he belted out a rol-licking gospel song, now groaned through a slow and sobbing hymn. He sang his favorite with "a blues fervor." It was "I Want to Be More and More Like Jesus." People often wept and "rocked with joy" when he performed for them. But he "didn't get puffed up," his Daddy related, and sat down quietly when he was finished. Frankly, all the fuss embarrassed him.

In his preschool years, M. L.'s closest playmate was a white boy whose father owned a store across the street from the King home. In September, 1935, the two chums entered school—separate schools, M. L. noticed. He attended Younge Street Elementary School with Christine, and there was not a single white child there. Then the parents of his friend announced that M. L. could no longer play with their son. But *why?* he sputtered. "Because we are white and you are colored."

Later, around the dinner table, he confided in his parents what had happened, and for the first time they told him about "the race problem." They recounted the history of slavery in America, told how it had ended with Abraham Lincoln and the Civil War, explained how whites eventually maintained their superiority by segregating Negroes and making them feel like slaves every day of their lives. But his mother counseled him, "You must never feel that you are less than anybody else. You must always feel that you are *somebody*." He did feel that he was somebody. Everyone told him how smart and sensitive he was, praised him for his extraordinary ways. Yes, he had an idea he was somebody. Still, this race trouble was disturbing. "As my parents discussed some of the tragedies that had resulted from this problem and some of the insults they themselves had confronted on account of it, I was greatly shocked, and from that moment on I was determined to hate every white person."

So it was that M. L. began his real education in Atlanta, Georgia. Oh, he studied arithmetic, grammar, and history at school, passing easily through the lower grades and transferring in the sixth grade to David T. Howard Colored Elementary School, where he was deferential to teachers, considerate of his peers, precocious and diligent as always. But as with other Negro children, his true education was to learn in countless painful ways what it meant to be black in white America. He found out that he—a preacher's boy—could not buy a Coke or a hamburger at the downtown stores. He could not even sit at the lunch counters there. He had to drink from a "colored" water fountain, relieve himself in a rancid "colored" restroom, and ride a rickety "colored" freight elevator. White drugstores and soda fountains, if they served him at all, made him stand at a side window for ice cream, which came to him in a paper cup. White people, of course, got to eat their ice cream out of dishes. If he rode a city bus, he had to sit in the back as though he were contaminated. If he wanted to see a new movie in a downtown theater, he had to enter through a side door and sit in the "colored section" in the back balcony. Of course, he could always go to the decrepit "colored" movie house, with its old films and faded and fluttering screen.

He learned, too, how white Atlantans loved their Confederate heritage, cherished the halcyon days when plantations and slavery flourished in the surrounding countryside. He witnessed all the fanfare that attended the world première of the motion picture *Gone With the Wind,* which opened in Atlanta on December 15, 1939, when he was ten. White Atlanta quivered with excitement when Clark Gable, Olivia de Havilland, Vivien Leigh and her husband Laurence Olivier, all came to town for the opening. There was a gala parade downtown, then a grand ball at the auditorium, festooned with Rebel flags. Here white Atlantans reveled in songs like "Suwanee River," "Carry Me Back to Old Virginny," and "My Old Kentucky Home," and danced waltzes like southerners of old. The next night more than 2,000 white Atlantans crowded into Lowe's Grand Theater to see what they fantasized was the world of their ancestors portrayed in living color, a world of cavalier gentlemen and happy darkies, of elegant ladies and breathless belles in crinoline, a world that was lost forever in the Civil War. With its coveted myths and racial stereotypes (a good "nigger" was a loyal and obsequious slave, a bad "nigger" was an uppity and impudent black who rode in the same buckboard with a Yankee carpetbagger), *Gone With the Wind* became one of the most popular motion pictures ever produced in America, playing to millions of whites all over the land.

This too M. L. learned: a good nigger was a black who minded his own business and accepted the way things were without dissent. And so his education went. He discovered that whites referred to Negroes as "boys" and "girls" regardless of age. He saw WHITES ONLY signs staring back at him almost everywhere: in the windows of barber shops and all the good restaurants and hotels, at the YMCA, the city parks, golf courses, and swimming pools, and in the waiting rooms of train and bus stations. He found that there were even white and black sections of Atlanta and that he resided in "nigger town."

Segregation caused a tension in the boy, a tension between his mother's injunction (remember, you are *somebody*) and a system that demeaned and insulted him every day, saying, "You are less than, you are not equal to." He struggled with that tension, struggled with the pain and rage he felt when a white woman in a downtown store slapped him and called him "a little nigger" . . . when he stood on the very spot in Atlanta where whites had lynched a Negro . . . when he witnessed nightriding Klansmen beat Negroes in the streets there . . . when he saw "with my own eyes" white cops brutalize Negro children. When his parents admonished him to love whites because it was his Christian duty, M. L. asked defiantly: "How can I love a race of people who hate me?"

Besides, he didn't think his Daddy really loved them either. His Daddy stood up to whites, the way Grandfather Williams used to do. Yes, Daddy was always "straightening out the white folks." He would not let white agents make collections at his house. He would not ride the city buses and suffer the humiliation of having to sit in a colored section. He would not let whites call him "boy." One day when M. L. was riding with his Daddy in the family car, a white patrolman pulled him over and snapped, "Boy, show me your license." Daddy shot back, "Do you see this child here?" He pointed at M. L. "That's a *boy* there. I'm a *man*. I'm Reverend King."

"When I stand up," King said, "I want everybody to know that a *man* is standing." "Nobody," he asserted, "can make a slave out of you if you don't think like a slave." "I don't care how long I have to live with the system, I am never going to accept it. I'll fight it until I die."

Yes, M. L. said, Daddy was "a real father to me." He set a powerful example for M. L. He demanded respect. But if his father exemplified manly strength, it was Grandmother Williams M. L. turned to for support in these dispiriting years. She was a tremendous source of warmth in a world that menaced and hurt him. He relied on Mama so much that his love for her, he said, was "extreme."

One day when he was supposed to be studying, M. L. stole away from home to watch a parade in the Negro business section. It was May 18, 1941, a warm spring day with a scent of magnolias in the air. While M. L. was enjoying the parade, a messenger brought him terrible news from home. Something had happened to his grandmother. But what could have happened to Mama? She was supposed to be at Mount Olive Baptist Church, speaking on a Woman's Day program. M. L. ran home with his heart pounding, only to find a lot of people there—his parents, people from the church. Mama had suffered a heart attack and had died on the way to the hospital. God had come for her and taken her away.

M. L. was stunned. But why? Why had God taken Mama from him? Was God punishing his family because he had sinned, because he had left the house without telling anyone, because he had run off to watch a parade? Grief-stricken, racked with guilt, the boy raced upstairs and leaped out the window after his Mama, trying to follow her from this world. He struck the ground in a painful heap. Again shouting people ran up to him. He was still alive: bruised and shaken, but still in this world. Afterward, in his bedroom, he shook with sobs, unable to bear the hurt he felt inside.

He cried off and on for days and couldn't sleep at night. "Don't blame what has happened to your grandmother on anything you've done," Daddy told him in his bedroom. "God has His own plan and His own way, and we cannot change or interfere with the time He chooses to call any of us back to Him." But M. L. was tormented by doubts, and he pressed his parents about the doctrine of immortality. They tried to explain it, tried to reassure the boy that Grandmother was in Heaven. But how could they know for sure? What if she had not ascended like Jesus and was lost somewhere? What if she were just dead? Was it possible that people just died and never again saw those who loved them? He felt so miserable and so alone without Mama. Who would cry for him now when Daddy had to whip him?

NOT LONG AFTER MAMA DIED, Daddy bought another house on nearby Boulevard. The old place was "running down," Daddy claimed, and the new house was a better one in a higher-class neighborhood. And so the boy left the house of his birth—Mama Williams's house— and moved into a place that held no memories for him. It was poised on a bluff that overlooked downtown Atlanta; from the windows, M. L. could see tall buildings move against the clouds. The new house was a two-story brick dwelling—precisely the kind Daddy had promised to own one day. He was now "a major force" in Atlanta's black community, a man with considerable business interests and political and social clout. He belonged to a small interracial coalition and was prominent in the Negro Voters League. Because he was a Negro on the climb, he received abusive letters and phone calls from the Ku Klux Klan.

As the children entered their teens and developed wills of their own, Daddy tried to temper his domineering impulses and even en- \couraged them to express their views at the dinner table. But in a clash of wills he still overrode them. Christine tended to submit and let Daddy have his way, A. D. to rebel outright (and get thrashed as a consequence), and M. L. to waver in between. Still grieving for his grandmother, he tried to avoid collisions with his father, for whom he had such mixed and powerful feelings. But when he did incite Dad-dy's wrath, he too suffered the indignity of his strap. He recalled that his father whipped him until he was fifteen.

M. L. struggled with himself over his father, torn between his re-spect and love for the man and his desperate need for independence. Ambivalent about confronting him face to face, M. L. rebelled in sub-tle, indirect ways. Ever "the precocious and questioning type," as he put it, he mounted an insurrection in Daddy's church, no longer uncrit-ically accepting the literalist teachings he received there. At thirteen, "I shocked my Sunday School class by denying the bodily resurrection of Jesus." From then on, "doubts began to spring forth unrelentingly," and he grew skeptical of Sunday-school Christianity, with its legends and stories. At the same time, he became disillusioned with the unbri-dled emotionalism—all the stamping and shouting—that went on in his father's church. "I didn't understand it," he said later, "and it embarrassed me." He came to doubt that religion could ever be "emo-tionally satisfying" or "intellectually respectable."

But how to tell his father about his doubts? The elder King was pressuring him to become a minister and succeed him at Ebenezer, thus keeping its pastorship in the family. In discreet ways M. L. let it be known that he would not become a minister, would not follow in his Daddy's footsteps. At one point in his mid-teens, he did feel a call to preach, but fought it off. An emotional, fundamentalist ministry had little relevance to the modern world, he thought, and he wanted nothing to do with it. He would *not* be a preacher, would *not* be like Daddy.

He had a lot of anger in him. In sandlot games, he competed so ferociously that friends could not tell whether he was playing or fight-ing. In basketball, he refused to pass and shot every time he got the ball. In backyard football, the neighborhood boys started him as quarterback because of his "shrimpy size." "But he wound up as fullback," a friend recalled, "because he ran over anybody who got in his way."

He also had his share of fights, excelling in what an associate termed "middle-class combat." He never battled with knives and stones, as lower-class boys often did. And he preferred negotiation to fisticuffs. But if negotiation failed, M. L.'s ritual remark was "let's go to the grass," and he tore into his adversary. "He could outwrestle anybody in our gang," a chum said, "and he knew it." In all, young King was "a bit of a hellion" and subject to "violent swings in mood."

Meanwhile he sailed through school, skipping grades as he went, and entered Booker T. Washington High School at thirteen. It was the fall of 1942, and Atlanta's black community hummed with war news. Blacks were serving in America's armed forces—half of them overseas in segregated outfits. On the home front, A. Philip Randolph—the celebrated Negro labor leader—had threatened to lead a massive protest march if President Roosevelt did not employ blacks in the defense industry. Roosevelt responded with an executive order that prohibited racial discrimination in defense plants and government agencies alike. In 1941, Negroes up in Harlem had conducted a successful bus boycott; and the next year a new organization called the Congress of Racial Equality (CORE) staged sit-ins in Chicago retail stores, testing racial discrimination in employment practices through direct-action protest.

At Booker T. Washington, King enjoyed history and English. But overall the curriculum did not challenge him, and he compiled a B-plus average with a modicum of effort. He and Christine often studied together until she graduated: he helped her with mathematics, and she corrected the spelling in his English compositions. "I can't spell a lick," he complained. But he possessed a remarkable vocabulary that dazzled teachers and peers alike.

At fourteen, M. L. was a sensuous youth who played a violin, liked opera, and relished soul food—fried chicken, cornbread, and collard greens with ham hocks and bacon drippings. Physically he was small and plump-faced, with almond-shaped eyes, a mahogany complexion, and expressive hands. But the most memorable thing about him was his voice. It had changed into a rich and resonant baritone that commanded attention when he spoke in class or held forth in a nearby drugstore.

He discovered something else about his voice: girls blushed and flirted when he spoke to them in his mellifluent drawl. A natty dresser, nicknamed "Tweed" because of a fondness for tweed suits, he became a connoisseur of lovely young women, many of them from the best Negro families in Atlanta. A. D. could not remember a time when his big brother was not interested in girls, and M. L. himself laughed that women and food were always his main weaknesses. "He kept flitting from chick to chick," A. D. said later, "and I decided I couldn't keep up with him. Especially since he was crazy about dances, and just about the best jitterbug in town."

But he had a serious side, too, an introspective side that made him seem aloof sometimes. He liked to read alone in his room, to study the way authors and orators put words together. He asserted later that his "greatest talent, strongest tradition, and most constant interest was the eloquent statement of ideas."

In the eleventh grade, he entered an oratorical contest sponsored by the Negro Elks in a distant Georgia town. A "dear" female teacher accompanied him on what proved a memorable occasion. Speaking on "The Negro and the Constitution," King captured a prize with the force of his presentation. That night, heading back to Atlanta on a crowded bus, he and his teacher reviewed the exciting events of the day. Presently the bus stopped and some whites got on. There were no empty seats. The white driver came back and ordered King and the teacher to surrender theirs, but King refused to budge. The driver threatened him, called him "a black son-of-a-bitch," until at last he heeded his teacher's whispers and reluctantly got up. They stood in the aisle all the way home, jostled and thrown about as the bus sped down the highway. "That night will never leave my mind," King said later. "It was the angriest I have ever been in my life."

Because the war was drawing off Negro college students, Atlanta's Morehouse College started admitting exceptional high school juniors to fill its depleted student ranks. In the spring of 1944, M. L. passed the college's entrance examinations, graduated from Booker T. Washington after the eleventh grade, and made plans to enroll in Morehouse that fall. He was only fifteen years old.

Through the college, King secured summer employment on a Connecticut tobacco farm. It was not his first job—he'd delivered papers for years. But it was the first time he'd been away from home, and he enjoyed it immensely. Sure, he and other Morehouse students put in long hours in the hot and humid tobacco fields. But on weekend trips to Hartford they found to their joy that they could eat in high-class restaurants just like white folks. They could also enter theaters by the front door and sit freely in the main auditorium. Perhaps M. L. noticed Hartford's ramshackle black tenements, observed all the black cooks and menials in town. Nevertheless, he spoke of "the exhilarating sense of freedom" he felt in Connecticut, where he could go and do pretty much as he pleased.

But on the train trip back to Atlanta, the reality of segregation smote him like a physical blow. As the forests of Virginia hurtled by outside, King made his way to the dining car and started to sit down anywhere, as he had done on the way through New York and New Jersey. But the train was in Dixie now, and the waiter led him to a rear table and pulled a curtain down to shield the white passengers from his presence. He sat there, staring at that curtain, unable to believe that others could find him so offensive. "I felt," he said, "as though the curtain had dropped on my selfhood."

THAT SEPTEMBER HE ENTERED MOREHOUSE in search of a useful profession that might enable him to help his people. He felt a burning need to heal blacks, to break their bonds, to emancipate them. He considered becoming a physician, then a lawyer. "I was at that point where I was deeply interested in political matters and social ills," he recalled. "I could see the part I could play in breaking down the legal barriers to Negroes." Envisioning himself an attorney, he practiced giving trial speeches before a mirror in his room.

At first King remained aloof from the main currents of Morehouse life. Younger and smaller than his classmates, he lived at home and commuted to school for classes, still wrestling with himself over a vocation. He dated high school girls, telling them how their beauty caused the Rubicon to part and men to meet their Waterloos. Eventu-

ally, though, he became more involved in college life: he joined the
football team, sang in the glee club, and went out with fashionable
young women from contiguous Spelman College. Like his fellow students, all four hundred of them, he was proud to be "a Morehouse
man" and felt at home on campus, with its leisurely air, stately magnolias, and undulating lawns.

Unable to decide on a profession, he chose sociology as his major
and English as his minor. As he began his studies, he was shocked to
learn that he read only at the eighth-grade level—and his schooling
had hardly been deprived. Later he spoke bitterly about the inferior
education he'd received in Atlanta's colored schools. But thanks to his
intelligence, he rapidly overcame his deficiencies and earned an impressive number of A's in English, history, philosophy, and sociology.
But he was disappointed in many of his sociology courses, repelled by
their emphasis on abstract data and impersonal force. Why study theories and numbers without seeking the human processes that lay behind
them? he wanted to know. He objected to the reduction of people to
mere numbers and grumbled about the "apathetic fallacy of statistics."

But he found guidance and inspiration from several brilliant professors. There was Walter Chivers, his sociology adviser, who taught
that capitalism exploited black people, pointing out that "Money is not
only the root of evil; it is also the root of this particular evil—racism."
There was Gladstone Lewis Chandler, professor of English, whom
King and the other students affectionately referred to as "G. L. C." A
native of the British West Indies, with a B.A. from Middlebury and an
M.A. from Harvard, Chandler was a spare, balding man who sported a
pipe and a tweed jacket. Stern and caustic in the classroom, he respected his students and demanded as much of them as he did of
himself. "Clarity, unity, coherence and emphasis were his word-gods,"
recalled an appreciative student; "like a devout disciple, he prodded
his pupils with a passion that made them conscientious converts."
"Gentlemen," he would announce on the first day of English composition, "we are going to establish a 'GLC Word Bank.' You deposit some
new words each class session, invest them in congenial conversation
and withdraw rich dividends." King loved Chandler's word games.
When asked, "How are you," King would reply with a grin, "Cogitat-
ing with cosmic universe, I surmise that my physical equilibrium is
organically quiescent." But Chandler also taught King the art of lucid

and precise exposition, and King later described him as "one of the most articulate, knowledgeable and brilliant professors" at Morehouse, "one of those rare unique individuals who was so dedicated to his work that he forgot himself into immortality." Under Chandler's supervision, King polished his forensic style and in his sophomore year won second place in the Webb Oratorical Contest.

Then there was Professor George D. Kelsey, director of the Department of Religion, who became King's favorite classroom teacher. Before he encountered Kelsey, he was increasingly skeptical of religion, troubled by the discrepancy between his earlier fundamentalist instruction—King's term for it—and what he was learning in history and philosophy. But Kelsey helped him work through his problems with fundamentalism. In his course on the Bible, Kelsey challenged King "to see that behind the legends and myths of the Book were many profound truths which one could not escape." Kelsey also contended that pulpit fireworks were both useless and obsolete and that the modern minister should be a philosopher with social as well as spiritual concerns. Kelsey's views set King ablaze. Thanks to him, "the shackles of fundamentalism were removed from my body," and he began to rethink his religious attitudes.

Finally, he fell under the spell of Dr. Benjamin Mays, the college president and "a notorious modernist" in the eyes of the orthodox. As a preacher and theologian, Mays was out to renew the mission of the black church, charging in his books that too many preachers encouraged "socially irrelevant patterns of escape." At Morehouse chapel, this tall and erudite man, with his iron-gray hair and hypnotic voice, mesmerized his young disciples by preaching stewardship, responsibility, and engagement. "Do whatever you do so well," he counseled, "that no man living and no man yet unborn could do it better." Here at Morehouse, he was not turning out doctors or lawyers or preachers, Mays said. He was turning out *men*.

Mays challenged the traditional view of Negro education as "accommodation under protest" and championed it instead as liberation through knowledge. Education, he told his students, allowed the Negro to be intellectually free; it was an instrument of social and personal renewal. Unlike most other Negro educators, Mays was active in the NAACP and spoke out against racial oppression. He lashed the white church in particular as America's "most conservative and hypocritical institution."

King was enormously impressed. He saw in Mays what he wanted "a real minister to be"—a rational man whose sermons were both spiritually and intellectually stimulating, a moral man who was socially involved. Thanks largely to Mays, King realized that the ministry could be a respectable force for ideas, even for social protest. And so at seventeen King elected to become a Baptist minister, like his father and maternal grandfather before him. "I came to see that God had placed a responsibility upon my shoulders," he recalled a few years later, "and the more I tried to escape it the more frustrated I would become." Committed to the pulpit and God the Father, King also resolved a lingering question he had about his grandmother's death: he became, he said, "a strong believer in personal immortality."

With "no little trepidation," he approached his Daddy and told him about his decision to become a preacher. Though secretly overjoyed, Daddy growled that he wanted to be "reassured." M. L. would first have to preach a trial sermon in one of Ebenezer's smaller auditoriums. When the prescribed day came, King felt very much on trial, what with his Daddy present as both judge and jury. Mustering his courage, he grasped the pulpit and launched into his sermon. "He was just seventeen," the elder King said, "and the crowds kept coming, and we had to move to the main auditorium." The sermon was a resounding success. But if young King expected accolades from his father, he was disappointed, for the old man was too reserved to show his satisfaction before his son. That night, though, Daddy got down on his knees and thanked God for giving him such a boy.

That same year, 1947, young King was ordained and made assistant pastor at Ebenezer. As God and fate would have it, he was following in his Daddy's footsteps after all. But he was wrong if he thought this might ease his father's dogmatic ways. One night after he'd begun preaching King went to a dance. When Daddy found out, he was furious. Did M. L. not understand that Baptist doctrine *frowned* on dancing, especially by a preacher? The following Sunday, Daddy made M. L. stand up before the entire congregation and apologize.

During summer breaks from Morehouse, King worked as a manual laborer in Atlanta so that he could pay some of his expenses. Daddy, of course, objected to such employment, for fear that white bosses would exploit and degrade his son. Besides, as Reverend King's boy, M. L. could secure a respectable job at any number of Negro businesses in town. But young King wanted to find out what life was like for the underprivileged, to "learn their plight and to feel their feelings." So, against Daddy's wishes, he hired on at the Railway Express Company, unloading trucks and trains in torrid summer heat. He quit, though, when the white foreman called him a nigger. He took a similar job on the loading platform of the southern Spring and Mattress Company. As he struggled there in mindless physical toil, he noticed that he and other Negro laborers earned less money than their white counterparts even though they did the same work. King was beginning to understand what Professor Chivers meant when he said that capitalism exploited blacks and encouraged racism.

Because he could blame racism in part on the system, King felt less antagonistic toward white people now. Back at Morehouse, he served on the Atlanta Intercollegiate Council, an interracial student group, and learned that contact on fairly equal terms could alleviate racial hostility. "As I got to see more of white people," he said of his experience on the council, "my resentment softened and a spirit of cooperation took its place." At the same time, Morehouse professors inspired him with their frank discussions about race. They "encouraged us in a positive quest for solutions to racial ills," King remembered, "and for the first time in my life, I realized that nobody was afraid."

He realized, too, that he could never be "a spectator in the race problem," that he wanted to be involved in "the very heat of it." He hoped, of course, to be involved through the church. But how, by what method and means, were black folk to improve their lot in a white-dominated country? In his study of American history—and King was developing an acute sense of the past—he observed that Negroes since emancipation had searched in vain for that elusive path to real freedom, too often finding themselves on a dead-end street without an exit sign. In the 1890s, with Jim Crow segregation practices sweeping Dixie, Booker T. Washington advised Negroes to "let down your buckets where you are" and accept segregation, which the U.S. Supreme Court in *Plessy* v. *Ferguson* (1896) upheld as the law of the land. Washington admonished his people to forget about political and social equality for now and to learn skills and trades to support themselves. By imitating white standards and values, perhaps they could earn white people's friendship and preserve racial peace. But in King's judgment it was "an obnoxious negative peace" in which "the Negro's mind and soul were enslaved."

As Washington preached accommodation and Negro self-help, W. E. B. Du Bois, a brilliant scholar whose militancy and race pride were reminiscent of Frederick Douglass's, summoned the Negroes' "talented tenth" to take the lead and find solutions to the misery of the black masses. In 1905, against a backdrop of spiraling racial violence, Du Bois led a small band of well-educated, bold, and unhappy Negro professionals who met in the city of Niagara Falls and issued a blazing manifesto to white America. They vowed to stand up and battle for the Negro's "manhood rights," denounce and defeat oppressive laws, and "assail the ears" and the conscience of white Americans "so long as America is unjust." The Niagara Platform became a blueprint for the NAACP, established in 1909 in the centennial of Lincoln's birth, with Du Bois and seven other Niagara leaders joining nineteen white racial progressives on the NAACP's original board. The first nationwide organization dedicated to gaining Negroes their rights as citizens, the NAACP concentrated on legal action and court battles, winning its first victory in 1915—the same year the twentieth-century Klan was founded on Stone Mountain in Georgia—when the U.S. Supreme Court outlawed the grandfather clauses in the state constitutions of Oklahoma and Maryland.

The next year, flamboyant Marcus Garvey, wearing a braid-trimmed uniform and preaching racial pride, launched a "Back to Africa" movement that reached from one to four million Negroes until Garvey's downfall in 1923, when he was convicted and imprisoned for mail fraud. Still, in King's view, his message had little appeal to millions of other Negroes who had roots in American soil that went back for generations. Du Bois dismissed Garvey's version of the old colonization schemes as "spiritual bankruptcy and futility." But Du Bois himself became disillusioned with America, resigned from the NAACP, and advocated "voluntary segregation" rather than integration.

For American Negroes, the road to freedom's land was elusive indeed. The NAACP, fighting segregation through case-by-case litigation in the federal courts, continued to mark up hard-earned victories against southern white primaries and segregated law schools in the border states. But the masses of black folk in the South and the teeming ghettoes of the North languished in searing poverty. With white America largely indifferent to their suffering, in fact insisting that "niggers" were happy with their lot, voices of violence—of retaliation and doom—rang out from ghetto and "nigger town" soap boxes. At the same time, Negro ministers everywhere in the republic tended to preach Washington's doctrine of accommodation and to promise their congregations that all would be gladness once they reached God's Kingdom.

King shuddered at such a negative approach to the race problem. Yet Du Bois and Garvey hadn't found the solution either. How indeed were Negroes to combat discrimination in a country ruled by the white majority? A class assignment in Thoreau's "Civil Disobedience" offered a clue, introducing King to the idea of passive resistance. King was probably aware of the Negro civil disobedience then taking place in America: in 1947, A. Philip Randolph threatened to lead a protest march if the armed services were not desegregated (President Truman subsequently did desegregate them), and CORE conducted little-publicized "stand-ins" and "freedom rides." But whether he knew about these or not, King first encountered the theory itself in "Civil Disobedience." He was infatuated with Thoreau's provocative argument that a creative minority—even a minority of "one honest man"—could set in motion a moral revolution.

After his classes, King often visited President Mays's office to discuss his studies and air his thoughts. It was Mays's turn to be impressed. "I perceived immediately that this boy was mature beyond his years; that he spoke as a man who should have had ten more years' experience than was possible. He had a balance and a maturity that were far beyond his years and a grasp of life and its problems that exceeded even that."

IN THE SPRING OF 1948, at nineteen, King graduated from Morehouse with a degree in sociology and elected to study for his B.A. in divinity at Crozer Seminary in Pennsylvania. "You're mighty young to go to

Crozer," his Daddy said. But King was determined to attend Crozer. It was one of the best seminaries in the country; besides that, he wanted to get out of Atlanta—out of Dixie—and attend an integrated northern school as many another southern Negro was doing. Also, he'd been dating a young woman on a fairly regular basis, and both families assumed that they would marry. Daddy was especially keen on the idea, pointing out what "a fine girl" she was and what a prominent family she came from. He urged his son to marry her. He would help take care of her as long as M. L. was in school. Then he could assume the pastorship of Ebenezer when Daddy retired.

But young King was not ready for marriage. He longed to be free of his Daddy and entangling family alliances. Happily for him, Daddy did not object to his son's continuing his education. And so he fled Atlanta that fall and headed for Crozer Seminary, situated in Chester, Pennsylvania, on the banks of the Delaware River just southwest of Philadelphia. Here King could pursue an independent life, relish the excitement of intellectual discovery, enjoy the freedom to seek and question without fatherly intrusions. Here for the first time he could truly be a man on his own.

He found Crozer a cloistered, tree-shaded campus located on a hilltop, seemingly a world apart from the smoky industrial city that surrounded it. Fewer than one hundred students—twelve of them women, six of them black—attended this private, nondenominational school, with its polished corridors and uncluttered walkways. Here King resided in a private room in a landscaped dormitory and matriculated in an atmosphere of quiet solemnity.

Still, he was terribly tense, unable to escape the fact that he was a Negro in a mostly white school. He was painfully aware of how whites stereotyped the Negro as lazy and messy, always laughing, always loud and late. He hated that image and tried desperately to avoid it. "If I were a minute late to class," he said, "I was almost morbidly conscious of it and sure that everyone noticed it. Rather than be thought of as always laughing, I'm afraid I was grimly serious for a time. I had a tendency to overdress, to keep my room spotless, my shoes perfectly shined and my clothes immaculately pressed."

He was just as intense in his studies, earning an A in every course he took in the curriculum—in Biblical criticism and church history, in the lives and works of the major prophets, in ethics, social philosophy, and the philosophy of religion. He even journeyed up to Philadelphia to take special philosophy classes at the University of Pennsylvania. His professors were vastly impressed with his academic zeal. The president of the seminary invited him out to his home and even left "this very bright young man" in charge of his class. Professor Kenneth Lee Smith, a bachelor who lived in King's dormitory, recalled him as an animated student, ready to argue with anybody on theological matters and the role of the church in modern life.

For the role of the church concerned him deeply. As a potential minister, he was more determined than ever to be like Benjamin Mays and serve God and humanity from his pulpit. As a consequence, King was not content simply to follow Crozer's prescribed course of study. On his own, he began a serious quest for a philosophical method to eliminate social evil, a quest that sent him poring over the works of the great social philosophers, "from Plato and Aristotle," as he wrote later, "down to Rousseau, Hobbes, Bentham, Mill, and Locke."

While he gained something from each of these thinkers, it was the theologian Walter Rauschenbusch who initially influenced him the most. In the turbulent 1890s, this tall, deaf, bearded scholar had taught church history at Rochester Theological Seminary, embroiled in ecclesiastical controversies of a bygone time. Beyond his study, a Social Gospel movement blazed in industrial America, as modernist Christians attacked the evils of unbridled capitalism and sought to make their religion relevant to the problems of the modern world. As the new century dawned, educated young clergymen across America demanded that social justice be defined in Christian terms.

Swept up in this tempest of reform, Rauschenbusch abandoned recondite scholarship and became the leading prophet of the new Social Gospel. In *Christianity and the Social Crisis* and other impassioned books, he blamed capitalism for all the squalor and want that plagued the land. Damning business as "the last entrenchment of autocracy," capitalism as "a mammonistic organization with which Christianity can never be content," Rauschenbusch summoned Christians to build a new social order—a true Christian commonwealth—in which moral law would replace Darwin's law of the jungle. Such a commonwealth had been the original mission of Christianity, Rauschenbusch contended, since Christ had called for a kingdom of God on earth, a whole way of life dedicated to the moral reconstruction of society. Theologians and ecclesiastics, however, had misconstrued Christ's teachings and founded not a kingdom but a church, which then amassed interests of its own. But what really shattered Christ's dream was the industrial revolution, which spawned capitalism and a whole era of competition, greed, and plunder. Still, Rauschenbusch did not attribute such evil to man himself, for man was basically good, intrinsically perfectible, able to become like Christ. No, sin was the product of an evil society—in this case, capitalist society. Exploitation, prostitution, crime—all were inherent in a social system that exalted profit over virtue, selfishness over brotherhood. The time had come, Rauschenbusch asserted, for Christians to eradicate capitalism, socialize vital economic resources, and establish God's kingdom as Christ originally intended. The time had come to usher in "the glad tomorrow," when man would inhabit a sinless Christian commonwealth based on love, cooperation, and solidarity.

At Crozer, King read Rauschenbusch in a state of high excitement. Here was the Christian activism he longed for. While he thought Rauschenbusch perilously close to equating God's kingdom with a specific social and economic system, which no Christian should ever do, King nevertheless became an ardent disciple. As he said later, Rauschenbusch provided him with a theological foundation for social concerns he'd had since he was a boy. And he engaged in spirited debates with anybody—professors and preachers alike—who held that man had only a limited capacity for improvement and that the church should confine itself to matters of the soul. A socially relevant faith must deal with the whole man—his body and soul, his material and spiritual well-being. It must work for the kingdom "down here" as well as "over yonder." Any religion that stressed only the souls of men and not their social and economic conditions was "a spiritually moribund religion awaiting burial."

What was more, Rauschenbusch's denunciation of capitalism struck a sensitive nerve in him. He remembered growing up in the Depression and asking his parents about all the Negroes he saw in Atlanta's breadlines. He remembered the exploitation he'd personally witnessed at the Southern Spring and Mattress Company and the lessons about capitalism pressed on him in Chivers's sociology course. As a consequence, he came to have distinct "anti-capitalist feelings."

During the Christmas holidays of 1949, King spent his spare time reading Karl Marx. He "carefully scrutinized" *Das Kapital* and *The Communist Manifesto* and several interpretive studies of Marx and Lenin. King came away from his inquiries frowning with Christian concern. Communism, he believed was profoundly and fundamentally evil, "a Christian heresy" that had bound up certain Christian principles in a web of practices and concepts no true Christian could ever accept. First, he objected to Communism's materialistic interpretation of history. The Communist contemptuously dismissed God as a figment of man's imagination, religion as a product of fear, ignorance, and superstition. Class and economic conflict, not divine will, were the forces operating on man. He did not need a God or a Jesus. Man could save himself and create a better world alone.

King pronounced this "a grand illusion." It was "cold atheism wrapped in the garments of materialism." Reality, he maintained, could not be explained in terms of "matter in motion," of the push and pull of economic forces. This left out too many "complexities." It arrogantly ignored Christian thought, which affirmed that "at the heart of reality is a Heart," King said, "a loving Father who works through history for the salvation of his children." Man could never save himself because man was not the measure of all things. He *needed* God. He *needed* a Savior. Communism was egregiously wrong in denying man's spiritual necessities.

Secondly, King could not accept the Communist tenet that the ends justified the means. He underscored Lenin's directions on how to achieve the new classless society: "we must be ready to employ trickery, deceit, lawbreaking, and withholding and concealing truth." Alas, King observed, modern history had witnessed "many tortuous nights and horror-filled days" because Lenin's followers took him at his word, resorting to perfidy and murder to build the Soviet state. As a Christian, King could never tolerate such "ethical relativism." "Immoral means," he stated flatly, "cannot bring moral ends."

King also disdained Communism's "crippling totalitarianism," which he felt stripped man of his inalienable rights and shackled him to the state. In theory, the state was an "interim reality," King noted, and was to "wither away" when the classless society emerged. But until then the state was omnipresent, with everything—religion, art, music, science—subordinated to its "gripping yoke." The state thus robbed man of the one quality that Paul Tillich said made him a man: his freedom, which he expressed through his ability to think and respond. By denying him that right, Communism deprived man of all conscience, all reason, and reduced him to "a depersonalized cog in the ever-turning wheel of the state." Communism was just "all mixed

up," a confusing anthropology that was wrong about God and therefore about man. True, Communism started with "men aflame with a
passion for social justice." Yet it had betrayed its original impulse:
while Communism trumpeted the glories of a classless society, it "created new classes and a new lexicon of injustice."

Still, King worried that "Communism may be in the world because
Christianity hasn't been Christian enough," and he prepared a sermon
called "The Challenge of Communism to Christianity," which he
preached one summer at Morehouse. A latter-day Rauschenbusch
summoned to battle a new evil, King enjoined the church to stop
mouthing "pious irrelevancies and sanctimonious trivialities," cease
being "the opium of the people" (as Marx described it), and concern
itself anew with social justice—with the creation of "a world unity in
which all barriers of caste and color are abolished."

As it happened, King's critique of Communism only intensified his
dislike of capitalism. In truth, he thought Marx correct in much of his
criticism in *Das Kapital*, which underscored for King the danger of
constructing a system on the sole motive of profit. This encouraged
"cut-throat competition and selfish ambition that inspire men to be
more concerned about making a living than making a life." It made
men so "I-centered" that they were no longer "thou-centered," and
led them into "tragic exploitation" and a concentration of wealth
among the few. Moreover, people in a capitalist system—people here
in America, even black people—too often judged a man's worth by the
size of his income, car, and home rather than his concern for humanity. Thus capitalism fostered a materialism just as evil as Communism.
It lulled individual men into the illusion that they could grow and live
in their own self-centered worlds—like the rich man in the parable,
the man whom God called a fool. Regardless of what the capitalist
claimed about rugged individualism, King thought John Donne had it
right when he declared that no man is an island unto himself. As King
liked to put it, all people in this world are "tied into a single garment
of destiny. Whatever affects one directly, affects all indirectly. We are
made to live together because of the interrelated structure of reality."

D URING BREAKS FROM HIS STUDIES at Crozer, King often visited J.
Pius Barbour, a local minister who knew his Daddy and told him to
"make yourself at home here, any time." In the Barbours' home, King
watched television—a remarkable device that brought world events
right into the living room—and savored Mrs. Barbour's "down-home"
cooking. Her specialty was a steak simmered in a spicy brown sauce.
"He could eat more than any little man you ever saw in your life,"
Mrs. Barbour declared. On Sundays, King sometimes preached in Barbour's church, imparting the gospel in a restrained, almost scholarly,
style. Among the church members were several young ladies who
swooned over that handsome M. L. King, with his sartorial elegance
and fetching smile. Walter McCall, a Crozer classmate and fellow
Morehouse man, often accompanied King to the church, and they cat-
egorized the young women according to their looks: "a light sister"
was not very pretty, but "a doctor" was a knockout.

One day the two friends took a car trip with a couple of young
women, heading across the Delaware River into New Jersey. Presently
they came to a roadside café in Maple Shade, just east of Camden, and
stopped to get something to eat. They were the only Negroes in the
place, though, and the waitress ignored them. At last King and McCall
hailed the proprietor. "The best thing would be for you to leave," he
said. They tried to reason with him: New Jersey law prohibited racial
discrimination in a public place, they said. "I want you out of here,"
the man cried. When they refused to move, he drew a pistol—"I'll kill
for less"—and drove them out, firing the gun overhead to make his
point.

Well, King and his companions were not going to let the matter
rest. They went to the police; the proprietor was arrested and a suit
filed against him by the Camden chapter of the NAACP. But the case
fell through when the witnesses—three white students from the University of Pennsylvania—declined to testify.

Back at the seminary, King had another brush with violence when
a North Carolina white student came banging on his door one day.
The student was well known for his racial views: he couldn't accept
Negroes as his schoolmates and called them "darkies." Somebody had
messed up his room—a prank called a "room raid"—and he blamed

King. He was in a tirade, shouting at King, hurling maledictions at him. Then he drew a pistol and threatened to shoot King dead. But King would not be rattled. Looking the maddened student in the eye, he calmly denied having anything to do with the room raid. By now the racket had attracted other students: they yelled at the North Carolinian, made him put his gun down. Afterward they brought the matter before the student government; but to everybody's surprise King refused to press charges. With students and faculty alike clamoring against him, though, the North Carolinian publicly admitted he was wrong and extended King an apology.

After that King became the most popular student at Crozer, widely admired not only for his scholarship, but for his courage and grace as well. Certain of acceptance now, he began to relax some and get more involved in campus social life. What was more, he and the North Carolina student eventually became friends. The entire episode seemed a valuable lesson in how to convert a foe into a comrade.

COMMITTED THOUGH HE WAS to the social gospel, King had reservations at Crozer about the power of Christian love, brotherly love, to effect social change. He'd read extensively in history, and it had revealed to him how impotent love could be. It had not ended slavery in antebellum America. No, it took the holocaust of Civil War to root out that abominable institution. Nor had the champions of brotherly love brought about an integrated America in this century, or stopped Hitler from plunging Europe into an inferno. The more King examined history, the more he wondered whether he could be a pacifist.

During his stay at Crozer, he attended a lecture on pacifism by Dr. A. J. Muste, executive secretary of the Fellowship of Reconciliation. Though deeply moved by Muste's strong moral convictions, King was dubious about his Christian pacifist position that all war is evil. Maybe war could never be a positive good, an absolute good. But perhaps it could serve as "a negative good" to combat the spread of evil. Terrible though it was, war might be preferable to Nazi—or Communist—totalitarianism.

In this frame of mind, King took up Nietzsche's *The Genealogy of Morals* and *The Will to Power*, which shook his faith in love more than anything he had read. Writing mostly in the 1880s, Nietzsche proclaimed God dead and warned that mass man—the moronic herd—was about to rise up and plunge the world into barbarism. Troubled and brooding, Nietzsche glorified war and preached the will to power. He raged against democracy and parliaments, assailed liberalism, socialism, and Communism, and flayed away at Christianity for encouraging servility and impotence with its "slave morality." What was the alternative to mob rule? Nietzsche prophesied the coming of a master race—a superman who would control the masses and govern the earth.

King put Nietzsche's work aside a little depressed. Though repelled by his obsession with power and race, King wondered if Nietzsche was not right about the weaknesses of Christian love. Maybe it could not change and purify the world. In fact, it seemed to King that the Christian injunctions to "love your enemies" and "turn the other cheek" were valid only in relationships between individuals, not in conflicts between nations or racial groups. Such conflicts needed a more realistic approach—though he wasn't sure what that entailed. He still greatly admired Rauschenbusch's compelling vision of a Christian commonwealth based on love. But how to bring that about? How to improve the lot of the masses—how to ameliorate the condition of his own dispirited people—without force and violence? King's study of slavery—especially of Nat Turner's rebellion in 1831—convinced him that it was impractical, even suicidal, for a minority to strike back against a heavily armed majority. It was also morally wrong. Yet if love was an ineffective tool for social change, how was meaningful reform to be accomplished?

One Sunday in Philadelphia, King attended a lecture by Dr. Mordecai W. Johnson, president of Howard University. Johnson had just spent fifty days in India, and his lecture was a stirring presentation of the life and teachings of Gandhi. As King sat rooted to his chair, Johnson explained how Gandhi had forged Soul Force—the power of love or truth—into a mighty vehicle for social change. Gesturing from the lectern, Johnson argued that the moral power of Gandhian nonviolence could improve race relations in America, too.

King was spellbound. "I had heard of Gandhi," he said, but Johnson's "message was so profound and electrifying that I left the meeting and bought a half-dozen books on Gandhi's life and works"—chief among them, Louis Fischer's *Life* and Gandhi's own *Autobiography*. King was deeply moved by Gandhi's March to the Sea, fascinated by his simple and celibate life, inspired by his inner struggles. As Fischer pointed out, Gandhi had embraced nonviolence in part to subdue his own violent nature. As a young lawyer in South Africa, he shouted at his wife and in one memorable scene tried to drive her from their home. Fischer maintained that the celebrated mahatma calm of later years derived from long training in temper control: Gandhi had become "a self remade man." This was a revelation for King, who had felt a lot of hatred in his life, especially toward whites. Now Gandhi showed him a means not only of harnessing his anger, but of channeling it into a positive and creative force.

Nonviolent resistance, Gandhi taught, meant noncooperation with evil, an idea he got from Thoreau, whose essay on civil disobedience "left a deep impression on me." Thoreau, in turn, had studied the *Bhagavad-Gita* and several of the sacred Hindu *Upanishads*, which for King further illustrated the interconnected structure of reality. Gandhi, for his part, took Thoreau's theory and gave it practical application in the form of strikes, boycotts, and protest marches, all conducted nonviolently and all predicated on love for the oppressor and a belief in divine justice. Gandhi's goal was not to defeat the British in India, but to redeem them through love, so as to avoid a legacy of bitterness. His term for this—Satyagraha—reconciled love and force in a single, powerful concept.

With barely restrained enthusiasm, King embraced Satyagraha as the theoretical method he had been searching for. True, there were differences between Gandhi's situation in India and the Negroes' in America. Gandhi had led a majority against a small minority, and antagonisms between Indians and the British were scarcely so deep and bitter as black-white conflicts in this country. Nevertheless, King was convinced that Gandhi's was the only moral and practical way for oppressed people to struggle against social injustice.

King thought Gandhi one of the great men of all time. "He was probably the first person in history to lift the love ethic of Jesus above mere interaction between individuals to a powerful effective social force on a large scale." King rejoiced that Christ had furnished him with the spirit; now Gandhi had showed him how it could work. Even in conflicts between groups and nations, you could love your enemies, turn your other cheek. Even if you were viciously beaten (as were Gandhi and his followers), your suffering could redeem your adversaries and purge you, too, of hatred. "The chain of hatred must be cut," King reflected. "When it is broken, brotherhood can begin."

After reading Gandhi, King sought a definition for the kind of love meant in Satyagraha. In the Greek language, he noted, there were three words for love: *eros*, which connoted romantic love; *philia*, which expressed intimate affection between friends or a man and a woman; and *agape*, which was defined as "understanding, redeeming good will for all men." Neither Jesus nor Gandhi intended that he should love his enemies as friends or intimates. That was absurd. *Agape* was the kind of love they meant—a disinterested love for all humankind, a love that saw the neighbor in everyone it met. King was delighted with this definition and enjoyed explaining it to his friends and professors, even to his dates. *Agape* was the love in Christ's teachings that took one to any length to restore "the beloved community," to forgive (as Jesus told Peter) seventy times seven to preserve community. But reacting to hatred with hatred only added to the bitterness and divisions in the world. Through *agape*, though, one perceived all human life as interrelated, all men as brothers, all humanity as a single process. With that love, King believed, the broken community could be "cemented" together again, and the kingdom of God on earth—the mission of true Christianity—attained at last. Gandhi had shown King how that, too, could be done.

By HIS SENIOR YEAR AT CROZER, King was an unabashed exponent of Protestant liberalism, which gave him an intellectual satisfaction he had never found in fundamentalism. He cherished what he considered liberalism's dedication to truth, its insistence on an open and analytical mind—which King thought the hallmark of an educated man. "I was absolutely convinced of the natural goodness of man," he recalled, "and the natural power of human reason."

Then he became involved with a young white woman, evidently the daughter of Crozer's superintendent of buildings and grounds. They fell in love and spoke tentatively of marriage. At this juncture,

Reverend Barbour intervened and gave King "a long, fatherly talk" about the terrible problems intermarriage would create for him in this country. Reluctantly, King broke off the relationship. When the woman's parents learned of her affection for King, they sent her away from Chester. It was a painful experience for King, a sobering experience. Years later, in the company of close friends, he would still discourse on "the *weltschmerz* of prejudice."

Perhaps the episode influenced his theological views, for in the same period he began having doubts about the natural goodness of man. He turned to Reinhold Niebuhr, whose ideas he'd studied in Crozer classes, and undertook a serious study of his theology and social ethics. A professor of religion at Union Theological Seminary, Niebuhr had pioneered neo-orthodoxy, the "new theology" that was the rage at American seminaries in midcentury. In works like *Moral Man and Immoral Society* and *The Nature and Destiny of Man*, Niebuhr mounted an all-out attack against liberalism, accusing it of "a false optimism" about man's essential nature. As history voluminously demonstrated, evil flourished ineradicably at all levels of human existence. It resided not only in man's fallibility, but in his sinful denial of that fallibility, which derived from his innate pride and selfishness. It was, Niebuhr asserted, an absurd and wicked faith which held that sinful man could perfect himself and his world. In claiming that he could, Protestant liberals were naïve victims of the nineteenth-century "cult of inevitable progress," which blinded them to man's basic evil. On that score, though he had once been a pacifist, Niebuhr castigated pacifism as a simplistic position, resting as it did on the sectarian rubbish that man was intrinsically good and that divine grace could lift him from the contradictions of history. For Niebuhr, there was no fundamental moral difference between nonviolent and violent resistance. In fact, in the presence of a totalitarian menace like the Nazis, pacifism could be irresponsible—almost collusion with evil. Can we really believe, Niebuhr asked, that conscientious objectors to a military society could have softened Hitler's heart and dissuaded him from invading Poland?

Though in class debates King had once rejected Niebuhr and defended Rauschenbusch, Niebuhr's "realistic" and "prophetic" analysis now appealed to him. Alas, King too had been naïve and sentimental about human nature. This had caused him, like Rauschenbusch, to overlook the fact that reason was "darkened by sin," as his examination of history should have indicated. Reflecting on history, King considered the vacillations of America's Founding Fathers—enlightened men in the Age of Reason—when it came to slavery and race on these shores. And he considered the rationalizations and histrionics of the southern proslavery apologists. "The more I observed the tragedies of history and man's shameful inclination to choose the low road," King said, "the more I came to see the depth and strength of sin." And the more he realized how man's tragic inclination to sin made him use his mind to rationalize his actions. Protestant liberals, for their part, had failed to understand that reason alone was little more than an instrument for justification—that reason devoid of "the purifying power of faith" could never free itself from "distortion and rationalization."

King was indebted to Niebuhr for clarifying this. By making him realize that evil was "stark, grim, and colossally real," Niebuhr had saved King from the trap of an illusory optimism about the capacity of man for good. Above all, Niebuhr helped King perceive "the glaring reality of collective evil"—the kind of group evil that caused otherwise decent men to kill, persecute, and crucify.

Too many pacifists, King decided, failed to recognize the existence of collective evil. He thought the pacifist nurtured a superficial idealism about human nature that made him unconsciously self-righteous, made him claim "to be free from the moral dilemmas that the Christian non-pacifist confronts." Repelled by such an attitude, King refused to join any pacifist organization.

As for pacifism itself, Niebuhr's critique left King in "a state of confusion" as to whether it could be a realistic and responsible position. Moreover, if Protestant liberalism was utterly wrong about the character of man, did this mean that neo-orthodoxy—with its echoes of fundamentalism—was utterly right? King was still grappling with such questions when he graduated from Crozer in June, 1951, with a B.A. in divinity. He finished at the top of his class, gave its valedictory address, and won a $1,300 scholarship to the graduate school of his choice. His choice was Boston University's prestigious School of Theology, where he planned to pursue a Ph.D. in systematic theology and work under Dr. Edgar Sheffield Brightman, an eminent scholar in the philosophy of personalism whose texts King had read since Morehouse days.

The elder King approved of his son's plans. He'd toiled long and hard to earn his own degrees, and he appreciated M. L.'s scholarly achievements. As in other summers, King returned to Atlanta and assumed his duties at Ebenezer, where he was now an associate pastor. At such times, Daddy "took a vacation" and let his son do much of the preaching. Young King saw something of "the Atlanta girl" Daddy wanted him to marry, heard more of his father's plans for him at Ebenezer. In the fall, he loaded his possessions into a new green Chevrolet—a graduation present from his Daddy—and set out for Boston. He drove through Washington, D.C., at a time when McCarthyism was gripping the capital and fears of Communist conspiracies were sweeping the land. On the racial front, the United States Supreme Court had ordered the law schools of the University of Texas and the University of Oklahoma to admit Negroes. And the NAACP Legal Defense Fund had elected to attack segregation in all public schools as unconstitutional. Out in Illinois, a Negro couple had moved into all-white Cicero, a Chicago suburb, only to be driven out by a nigger-yelling mob.

I N HIS FIRST SEMESTER AT BOSTON UNIVERSITY, King took Dr. Brightman's course in the philosophy of religion and under his tutelage began a study of Hegel, tackling the monumental *Phenomenology of Mind.* A gentle, white-haired fellow who peered out through small, round-rimmed glasses, Brightman thought King a "uniformly courteous young theologian" and an A student. On his part, King idolized Brightman, whose erudition was awe-inspiring. Alas, though, Brightman was extremely ill. In fact, he was dying. He managed to finish the term, but it was a terrible struggle for him. When he could no longer leave his home in Newton, King and other graduate students went there to see him, and he gave them all he could. He died during King's second year, and the young scholar would get tears in his eyes when he spoke of this man who had given him "so much" and helped to shape his character.

King's new adviser was forty-seven-year-old L. Harold DeWolf, a Brightman protégé who hailed originally from Nebraska. He had pastored there for a time and then come east to attend Boston University, where he earned his Ph.D. in 1935 and joined the faculty of systematic theology. A distinguished scholar in his own right, meticulous, learned, and exacting, DeWolf took King's measure and liked what he saw. "He was very self-contained and resourceful," DeWolf remembered, and always well prepared for their conferences, coming in with a list of questions and his own proposed answers. DeWolf noticed "a gentle kind of humor" in King and observed that he was "universally liked" among his classmates.

Under DeWolf's guidance, King plunged into the most rigorous and stimulating curriculum in his academic career. He took seminars in personalism and systematic theology, in the religious teachings of the New Testament, in the history of ancient, medieval, and modern philosophy, in Christian ethics and the psychology of religion. Writing at a feverish pace, he turned out technical compositions on "A View of the Cross Possessing Biblical and Spiritual Justification," on "The Christian Pertinence of Eschatological Hope," on "A Comparison of Friedrich Schleiermacher's Christology with that of Albrecht Ritschl," and on "The Place of Reason and Experience in Finding God." At the same time, he explored the lofty heights of comparative religions, perusing texts on Hinduism, Jainism, Buddhism, Sikhism, Zoroastrianism, Taoism, Confucianism, Shintoism, and Mohammedanism, and noting their mutal concern with the eternal conflict between good and evil. In traditional Judaism and Christianity, of course, the struggle was between God and Satan; in Zoroastrianism, between the God of light and the God of darkness; in Hinduism, between illusion and reality.

In his course on the psychology of religion, King encountered the theories of Sigmund Freud and John B. Watson. At first he scorned them both, rejecting psychology for the same reason that he spurned Communism and modern humanism: psychology, too, left out the spiritual and the divine in man. But on reflection he admitted that psychology offered useful insights into the dangers of repression, escapism, and irrational fear. Psychoanalysis, he decided, could help people understand the causes of their failures and fears, though the only cure for fear itself was "positive religious faith." He also conceded that behaviorists like Watson made him aware of environmental influences on the growth of personality. In fact, in an "Autobiography of Religious Development," prepared for a course in the religious development of personality, King applied Watsonian theory to his own life: he traced the influences of his childhood world on his anticapitalist sentiments, social and racial concerns, and deep religious faith. He said nothing, however, about his two suicide attempts. He simply stated that he had grown up in a family of loving relationships and that ever since childhood, even during periods of skepticism, "religion has been real to me and closely linked to life. In fact the two cannot be separated; religion for me *is* life."

In search of the meaning of life, King drove across the Charles River to take additional philosophy courses at Harvard, where he read existentialists like Jaspers, Kierkegaard, Heidegger, and Sartre, and discussed their "perception of the anxiety and conflict produced in man's personal and social life by the perilous and ambiguous structure of existence." In and out of class, he could impress audiences with his encyclopedic knowledge of philosophy, theology, and history and his remarkable ability to quote a host of thinkers to illustrate his points.

In the meantime he tried desperately to bring order to his vast accumulation of knowledge, to provide coherent answers to questions that still perplexed him—questions about Niebuhr, pacifism, and the nature of God and man. In his spare time, he turned back to Hegel, reviewing the *Phenomenology of Mind* and poring over *The Philosophy of History* and *The Philosophy of Right*. He pondered Hegel's contention that "world historical individuals" served as agents for "the will of the world spirit." Endowed with superior vision, such figures sensed the spirit and truth of the age—the Zeitgeist—and made it their own aim and destiny. "World-historical men—the Heroes of an epoch—must therefore be recognized as its clearsighted ones," Hegel asserted: "*their* deeds, *their* words are the best of the time." While King had reservations (Hegel's "absolute idealism" seemed to King "rationally unsound" because it "tended to swallow up the many in the one"), he admired "world-historical men" himself—from Plato and Aristotle to Lincoln and Gandhi—and incorporated the notion of the Zeitgeist into his understanding of history.

On other points, Hegel proved a revelation for him. For one thing, Hegel's analysis of the dialectical process showed King that growth came through pain and struggle, and persuaded him anew that the course of world history moved toward universal justice. For another thing, Hegel convinced King that the higher level of truth was found in a synthesis that reconciled an assertible proposition (the thesis) with another and seemingly contradictory proposition (the antithesis). Hegel's "truth as a whole" thus freed King from an either-or choice in his social and theological concerns and furnished him "a philosophical method of rational coherence." This meant forging "a creative synthesis of opposites in fruitful harmony." In economics, for instance, King observed that neither capitalism nor Communism possessed the full truth. "Historically capitalism had failed to see the truth in collective enterprise and Marxism failed to see the truth in individual enterprise. Nineteenth-century capitalism failed to see that life is social and Marxism failed and still fails to see that life is individual and personal." The kingdom of God, King concluded, was a synthesis that reconciled these two truths.

Eventually, Hegel helped King out of his dilemma over pacifism and neo-orthodoxy. But this came after he had been exposed to the pacifist teachings of Dean Walter Muelder and Professor Allan Knight Chalmers of the Boston University School of Theology. Their passion for social justice came not from a false idealism but from an abiding faith in man's ability to adapt and reform himself when he became "a co-worker with God." Thanks to their influence and that of other advocates of nonviolence at Boston University, King realized that Niebuhr had overemphasized man's corruption. "He was so involved in diagnosing man's sickness of sin that he overlooked the cure of grace," King wrote. If Protestant liberals were too optimistic about human nature, Niebuhr and the neo-orthodoxists were too pessimistic. Their revolt against liberalism had carried them too far the other way, so that they lapsed into a mood of antirationalism and semifundamentalism, which exaggerated the utter hopelessness of the world and man's incapacity to change it or himself. King deemed this "inadequate both for the church and personal life."

As with capitalism and Communism, King decided that the full truth about man was not found in either theological interpretation. The true explanation was a Hegelian synthesis of both: that man was capable of both good and evil, with an eternal civil war between the two raging within him. The nonviolent reformer, King believed, must appeal to the good in man, by asking man to open himself to the possibility God had given him for brotherhood.

As for Niebuhr's critique of pacifism, King saw that it tended to equate pacifism with complete nonresistance to evil, which naïvely trusted in the power of love. Reviewing his books on Gandhi, particularly Richard Gregg's *The Power of Nonviolence*, King now judged Niebuhr's position "a serious distortion." True pacifism, Gandhi had taught, was not "nonresistance to evil, but nonviolent resistance to evil." Had Gandhi not confronted evil with as much force, vigor, and strength as the violent resister? True pacifism was not some unrealistic submission to evil; it was, King noted, "a courageous confrontation of evil by the power of love, in the faith that it is better to be a recipient of violence than an inflictor of it." By appealing to the good in the oppressor, loving resistance (*agape* resistance) could bring about a transformation in the human heart and take man a long step closer toward the universal justice Hegel anticipated.

By 1953, King's analysis had led him to reject war, any kind of war. Since both the Soviet Union and the United States now possessed the atomic bomb, King sided with all those who condemned war as obsolete. In a day of potential atomic annihilation, war could no longer serve even as "a negative good" to arrest the spread of an evil force. No, "wisdom born of experience" dictated that man must now find an alternative to war—and that of course was love and nonviolence. In today's perilous world, King believed, we must love our enemies—or else.

In his graduate work, meanwhile, King was writing technical compositions on the radical idealism of George Berkeley, the ethical relativism of Charles Renouvier, and the personalism of Borden P. Bowne and Brightman himself. Under DeWolf's patient supervision, King sought to reconcile the conflict between relativism and idealism that bitterly divided the thinkers he studied. He was satisfied that he found such a synthesis in his examination of the philosophy of personalism, which held that a personal God operated in and on every human life and that the clue to "the meaning of ultimate reality" was thus found in personality. This "personal idealism," King said, became "my basic philosophical position. Personalism's insistence that only personality—finite and infinite—is ultimately real, strengthened me in two convictions: it gave me metaphysical and philosophical grounding for the idea of a personal God, and it gave me a metaphysical basis for [my belief] in the dignity and worth of all human personality."

As a student of personalism, King was certain that man could cast out evil from the world—by confronting his own sinfulness and opening himself to the Father's incandescent love and good will. Thus he not only rejected Niebuhr's argument that evil could never be eliminated; he also disagreed with Rauschenbusch that evil was social rather than personal. Evil was essentially personal, but it could be conquered—and social salvation attained—through "man's willing acceptance of God's mighty gift." Hence all men were "potential sons of God."

By now, things were falling together for him. From divergent intellectual currents, he had fashioned the rudiments of a coherent "synthesis" theology and a positive social philosophy, one predicated on nonviolence and an awareness of the complexity of human existence. He hadn't all the answers, by any means. He realized how much more he had to learn. But how he enjoyed intellectual inquiry. He would love to do this for the rest of his life, to become a scholar of personalism, the Social Gospel, and Hegelian idealism, inspiring young people as his own mentors had inspired him. Yes, that would be a splendid and meaningful way to serve God and humanity.

Ever solemn and serious in his studies, King was loquacious and debonair in his social life. "I'm an ambivert," he claimed, a cross between an extrovert and an introvert. He liked to quote what a French philosopher once said: "No man is strong unless he bears within his character antitheses strongly marked." Jesus too had recognized the need for blending opposites when he commanded men to be both tough-minded and tender-hearted. And if King was tough-minded as an intellectual, he was tender-hearted as always when it came to romances. "Apparently you are still meeting these girls who are one-time wreckers," a friend wrote. "Watch the Doctor don't let one catch you with your shoes off." Another associate marveled at his "gallivanting around Boston, the most eligible bachelor in town." But he cautioned King: "Remember, M. L., 'we are expecting great things from you.' The only element to restrain our expectations from bearing fruit will be M. L. himself."

King's best friend in Boston was a fellow Morehouse man named Philip Lenud, who was a Ph.D. candidate at Tufts University and whose father was also a Baptist minister. Lenud could perform the impressive feat of jumping in the air and clicking his heels together. He and King ate at the Western Lunch Box, which served down-home food, and frequented hot night spots like the Totem Pole in Boston's Negro section, which rocked with brassy jazz.

Because they found one another congenial, King and Lenud moved in together, renting a four-room apartment in a largely Negro neighborhood. Lenud cooked most of the meals, and King washed the dishes. After setting up house, the two bachelors organized a Philosophy Club that met on weekends "to solve the problems of the world." A dozen or so black students—male and female—would gather in the living room to drink coffee, chat, and critique a paper someone would present. Sometimes professors from area colleges would give talks; DeWolf himself spoke on "the meaning of the kingdom and how it will come."

Still, King was bored with bachelor life. If the right woman came along, he might like to settle down. One day he was having lunch with a married friend named Mary Powell. "Mary," he said, "I am about to get cynical. I have met quite a few girls here, but none that I am particularly fond of. Do you know any nice, attractive young ladies?"

She knew two and named one King had already met. "Who is the other one?" King asked.

"Coretta Scott," Mary said. "She is really a nice girl—pretty and intelligent." Mary paused. "But I don't think Coretta is really right for you. She doesn't attend church very often."

King was not bothered about that: he didn't want to date anyone too set in her religious beliefs. He persuaded Mary to give him Coretta's telephone number and to put in a good word for him.

He phoned her on a cold February evening in 1952. "This is M. L. King, Jr,." he announced. There was an embarrassing silence on the other end. "A mutual friend of ours told me about you and gave me your telephone number," King went on. "She said some very wonderful things about you and I'd like very much to meet you and talk to you."

"Oh yes"—now she remembered—"I've heard some very nice things about you, also." She had heard some bad things, too, like the fact that he was a Baptist preacher. She thought preachers were all pious stuffed shirts. Still, M. L. didn't sound like some narrow fundamentalist on the phone. In fact, he was smooth and easy. In fact, she had never heard anybody talk like him in her life. "You know every Napoleon has his Waterloo," King drawled. "I am like Napoleon at Waterloo before your charms." Coretta tutted, "Why, that's absurd. You haven't seen me yet."

King was unflappable. "Your reputation has preceded you," he said. "I'd like to meet you and talk some more. Perhaps we could have lunch tomorrow or something like that." She said she was free between classes from twelve to one. "I'll come over and pick you up," he said. "I have a green Chevy that usually takes ten minutes to make the trip from B.U., but tomorrow I'll do it in seven."

They had lunch in a cafeteria, with a cold rain falling outside. She thought "how short he seems," how unimpressive. He looked her over so intently—his eyes like shining pools—that she became self-conscious. He liked her hair—it was cut in bangs with a natural curl—and her shy and pretty smile. Though she seemed quiet, almost diffident, he could sense a degree of self-esteem. She was studying music at the New England Conservatory on a scholarship, had attended Antioch College before that, and had grown up on a farm just outside Marion, Alabama. He really did like her hair. As she touched it, he talked about his own life, about his classes at Boston University, about Communism and capitalism. As she listened to him, she no longer thought about how short he was. He was so sincere, so eloquent. And so sure of himself. And such a brain. To his searching statements, she attempted "some half-way intelligent replies." "Oh," he said, surprised. "You can think, too." And he smiled.

On the way back to the conservatory, he fell silent. Then: "Do you know what?" He looked at her. "You have everything I have ever wanted in a wife. There are only four things, and you have them all."

"I don't see how you can say that," she declared in astonishment. "You don't even know me."

"Yes, I can tell. The four things that I look for in a wife are character, intelligence, personality, and beauty. And you have them all. I want to see you again. When can I?"

She said she would have to check her schedule. "You may call me later."

ON SATURDAY NIGHT, he took her to a party in suburban Watertown. She seemed preoccupied. She was hoping he wasn't serious about marriage, because she was determined to become a singer and wanted nothing to stand in her way; also, she had been in love once and it had not worked out. She had promised never to become emotionally involved again unless she was certain she would marry. He could tell that her defenses were up, but sensed that she liked him a great deal.

At the party, young women made a great fuss over him. "Oh, so you are M. L. King, Jr. Oh! We've heard so much about you." He appeared to take it all in stride, with a relaxed and easy air about him. How come he was so popular? "You know," he said with a laugh, "women are hero worshipers."

When he took Coretta home, she was warm and affectionate toward him (those coquettish women had made her jealous). In his arms, she felt something tender between them. "He had taken me to the party," she thought, "and I was his girlfriend."

After that he pursued her aggressively ("not that I ran very hard"). He drove her out to the shore to buy clams and walk along the ocean, with its lapping waves and cawing gulls. He took her to the Boston Symphony Hall to hear Artur Rubinstein perform his magic on the piano. He saw her for lunch, went ice skating with her, walked with her in Boston's parks, teased her about another girl who had caught his eye (and laughed when it made her jealous), and talked on about things in an endless poetic flow. He talked about Rauschenbusch, Gandhi, *agape* love, Nietzsche, Hegel, and Marx. "I could never be a Communist," he said. "My father is a thorough-going capitalist, but I could not be that either." He talked about preaching—he preached some in area churches—and about how much he wanted to help humanity. Then he got around to the Atlanta girl his father intended him to marry. "But I am going to make my own decisions," he said; "I will choose my own wife."

And his choice, he said, was her. Would she marry him? Now, in all honesty he was concerned about her music career. Frankly, he couldn't marry a woman who would not be there when he came home. He would encourage her to have ideas and activities of her own, of course. He didn't want a wife he could not communicate with. But he believed that a woman's place was in the home, raising children. The problem with the American family was not infidelity, he contended, but the struggle to get ahead, to buy a big car and a big house, which required more and more couples to become working parents and short-shrift the children. Somebody had to work and somebody had to stay at home with them. "And biologically and aestheti-

cally women are more suitable than men for keeping house." Like his
father, King wanted to be the head of his house.

Well, he was certainly direct. Though his attitudes were no different from those of most other men in the 1950s, Coretta went through a
difficult time giving him an answer. If she married him, she would
have to forget a career and become a homemaker. If he entered the
ministry, she would have to be a *preacher's* wife, which was not at all
the kind of life she had set for herself. On the other hand, she adored
him. He made her feel "like a real woman." Still, he came from a
better background than she, and it bothered her. She had grown up in
culturally deprived rural Alabama, attending an impoverished "colored" school with outdoor toilets. She loved and respected her father,
an intrepid man who had built up his farm and become economically
independent of whites. But she felt inferior in comparison to Martin—
that was the name he used in her company—and what in her eyes was
an upper-class, big-city background.

He wanted her to meet his family, but she had reservations. "If
you don't want to come," he snapped, "just forget everything. Forget
it. Forget the whole thing." At last she relented, and in Atlanta that
summer he introduced her to his entire family. She found Daddy King
"a big man, bigger than I expected." He paid her little mind, since he
expected M. L. to marry the Atlanta girl and soon. But King made it
clear to Daddy that he was going to marry Coretta and nobody else:
Daddy was *not* going to rule him in matters of the heart. And Coretta
stuck up for herself, too. "I have something to offer, Daddy King," she
said during a subsequent visit. Finally, Daddy came around and gave
the couple his blessings. And so it was decided: she would marry Martin and let her career "take care of itself." But you realize, her sister
told her, that "you will not be marrying any ordinary young minister."

In June, 1953, a motorcade of Kings pulled up at the Scotts' new
house in Marion, Alabama, and Coretta introduced Martin to her family and friends. They all liked the young reverend because he didn't
"put on airs." On June 18, Daddy King married Martin and Coretta
on the lawn of her parents' home, with A. D. as best man. Because
there were no bridal suites for Negroes in the South, the couple spent
their wedding night in the home of a Scott family friend, an undertak-
er. "Do you know," King quipped, "we spent our honeymoon at a
funeral parlor?"

Back in Boston, the newlyweds rented a four-room apartment and resumed their respective studies. She would become his full-time wife after she earned her degree at the New England Conservatory, which would be in June, 1954. Still, she did not complain. She found that her husband was "a real man in every respect," and she surrendered herself to him, making his life her own. Though he wanted her to respect him as head of the house, he believed that marriage should be "a shared relationship." Because she had to take thirteen courses that year to graduate, he cleaned the apartment and washed the clothes, hanging them in the kitchen during recesses from his own studies. On Thursdays he even cooked the evening meal: his speciality was smothered cabbage, pork chops, and pigs' feet, which were tasty and cheap. Like his father, he budgeted family expenses with meticulous care, dutifully recording in a three-ring notebook what they spent money for, from laundry and parking to "Nodoze," "Xmas presents," "Drive in," and " Kotex."

By the summer of 1953, he was hard at work on his Ph.D. thesis, dividing his time between the apartment and the Boston University library. He had finished his course work in the spring term and passed his qualifying examinations without mishap (his only trouble was with German, his second language: he flunked the German test and had to petition the faculty for a re-exam, which he won and passed). To deepen his understanding of personalism, he chose to write his thesis on the divergent theisms of Paul Tillich and Henry Nelson Wieman, both celebrated theologians. Tillich, a monist, argued that God was transcendent and hence outside of things. Wieman, a pluralist, stressed God's immanence—His involvement in all things. In 1935, the two theologians had monopolized a Vermont religious retreat with their disagreements over the nature of God. And King used this real-life encounter as the starting point for his thesis. He wrote Tillich and other theologians for information (Tillich was beyond reach, away in Scotland), examined a veritable library of published writings, and recorded his findings on three-by-five cards, which he collated in his living room. He discovered that he partially disagreed with both of his subjects and sought to synthesize their antipodal interpretations, as he had done with Rauschenbusch and Niebuhr. By year's end, he had reached his principal conclusion: "Wieman's ultimate pluralism fails to satisfy the rational demand for unity. Tillich's ultimate monism swallows up finite individuality in the unity of being. A more adequate view is to hold a quantitative pluralism and a qualitative monism. In this way oneness and manyness are preserved."

Since he was finished with his residential requirements at Boston University, King elected to find employment and complete his thesis on the job. But should he go directly into teaching or first secure a pastorship? DeWolf urged him to find an academic position, for he considered King a "scholar's scholar" of great intellectual potential. DeWolf subsequently rated him one of the best five or six graduate students he had taught in his thirty-one years at Boston University. Because King possessed unusual initiative and intellectual curiosity, "a wide, probing concern with the relevance of the Christian faith to both the thought and life of humanity," DeWolf believed him capable of "quite creative and prominent scholarship."

For his part, King was immensely happy in the world of ideas and said he hoped ultimately to teach theology at a university or a seminary, to enjoy a life of the mind. As it turned out, several institutions offered him attractive posts—his old mentor and teacher, Benjamin Mays, tried to lure him back to Morehouse. But should he not preach before going into academe? Mays and DeWolf, not to mention Rauschenbusch, Niebuhr, and Tillich, had all been working ministers before settling into teaching and scholarship, and King thought he should follow their examples.

Several churches expressed an interest in him. But his firmest offer came from Dexter Avenue Baptist Church in Montgomery, Alabama, which was looking for a new pastor and invited him down to give a trial sermon. In January, 1954, he flew to Atlanta and then set out for Montgomery by car, enjoying a radio performance of his favorite opera—Donizetti's *Lucia di Lammermoor*. He thought: it really is lovely country down here—the rich and fertile farmlands, the sky a wintry silver. When he drove into Montgomery, which sprawled along a bend in the Alabama River, it occurred to him that this was his first visit to the Alabama capital.

The Dexter people were cordial and solicitous. They showed him the parsonage and the church, a red-brick building situated across the street from the whitest capitol King had ever seen. In fact, the church was surrounded by white state buildings, a Negro outpost in the old white square. He learned that Dexter had been built during the Reconstruction period after the Civil War and that it stood as a symbol of Negro aspirations in downtown Montgomery, drawing its members from the outlying Negro sections.

He was anxious about his sermon. Yes, he had preached plenty of times in Boston and Atlanta. But now he was on trial for his own job. How would he impress the Dexter congregation? Though a small church, Dexter counted mostly middle-class folk among its membership, and it had a long tradition of an educated ministry, which King liked. Should he give the Dexter people a display of scholarship, or rely on inspiration from God's spirit? Perhaps he recalled what he had written in a course on preaching back at Boston University. "You don't preach knowledge; you use knowledge to preach." Finally he told himself: "Keep Martin Luther King in the background and God in the foreground and everything will be all right. Remember you're a channel of the gospel, not the source."

On Sunday morning he stood at the pulpit of Dexter, surrounded by stained-glass windows, and gazed out over a packed sanctuary. He preached on "The Three Dimensions of a Complete Life," based on Revelation 21:16. "Love yourself, if that means healthy self-respect. That is the length of life. Love your neighbor as yourself; you are commanded to do that. That is the breadth of life. But never forget that there is an even greater commandment, 'Love the Lord thy God with all thy heart, and with all thy soul, and with all thy mind.' This is the height of life."

The sermon was a great success. The members came up to congratulate him, the men to shake his hand and the women to fawn over him. He was just twenty-five, hardly more than a boy to them, and just as smart and nice as he could be. Though reputed to be "snooty" and "ice-cold," they seemed warm to King this Sunday. As the pulpit committee shepherded him around the church, he heard stories about former pastor Vernon Johns, "a militant guy" who had exhorted the congregation like "a whirlwind" to get involved in social issues. But people at Dexter were "scared people" who tended to accept the racial status quo. At some point that day the pulpit committee asked King if he would accept a call to the pastorship. "I'll give it my most prayerful and serious consideration," he said.

He returned to Boston and in March, 1954, received a telegram from Dexter's pulpit committee, informing him that he had been unanimously chosen as pastor. The church offered him an annual sala-ry of $4,200—the highest of any Negro minister in Montgomery.

The offer threw King into a quandary. He was prepared to forgo an academic job and pastor for a few years to gain practical experi-ence. But did he really want to live in the Deep South, with all its racial woes? Coretta was hardly enthusiastic about returning to the South, especially to Montgomery. After all, she had grown up near there, and she knew what a rigidly segregated city it was. As it hap-pened, King had a preaching engagement in Detroit that Sunday, and on the flight out he sat by a window, looking down at the sunlit clouds and brooding over his dilemma. He thought about how much and how long he had resented segregation. He recalled the episodes that had hurt him so—the white parents who would not let him play with their son because he was "colored" . . . the white woman who had slapped him and called him "a little nigger" . . . the white bus driver who had called him a "black son-of-a-bitch" . . . the waiter who had pulled the curtain around him in the dining car. He shifted in his seat, pained by the memories. Could he endure all that again? Could he endure all the WHITES ONLY signs and the countless daily insults of being black in Dixie? He had never adjusted to separate accommodations because it "did something to my sense of dignity and self-respect." Now as the plane bore him toward Detroit, he thought: "I have a chance to escape from the long night of segregation. Can I return to a society that con-dones a system I have abhorred since childhood?"

When he returned from Detroit, he talked the matter over with Coretta. They considered how difficult it would be to raise children in the bonds of segregation and how inferior their education would be in the South in contrast to the North. Still, the South was their home, and they loved it despite its racial difficulties. In fact, King had felt a driving desire to do something about them since his youth. Here was a chance to practice the Social Gospel among his own downtrodden peo-ple, to return home where he was needed. He believed, too, that southern Negroes who received part of their education in the North ought to go back to the South and work to improve race relations there. After he put in several years as Dexter's pastor, he could go into academe as Mays and his other mentors had done.

On April 14, 1954, King accepted the Dexter offer, with the stipu-lation that the church furnish the parsonage and grant him time and expenses to finish his Ph.D. thesis. The church readily agreed. He would become official pastor in September, in the meantime commuting to Montgomery by plane.

King now flew to Atlanta to deal with his father. Predictably, Daddy King was not happy about his boy's decision, not happy at all. Here he was, an associate pastor at Ebenezer and marked for the pastorship one day. Why would he want to take over a little church like Dexter? Moreover, why would he want to live in Montgomery, where trouble with white folks was worse than in Atlanta? But young King would not be dissuaded. Patiently he heard his father out and then headed for Montgomery to preach his first sermon as Dexter's pastor. He did so on a May Sunday in 1954.

That same month the United States Supreme Court handed down an epochal decision that rocked the Jim Crow South to its foundations. In *Brown* v. *Board of Education,* the court outlawed segregated public schools, thus reversing the doctrine of "separate-but-equal" that had prevailed since *Plessy* v. *Ferguson* fifty-eight years earlier. "Separate educational facilities are inherently unequal," the court ruled, and created "a feeling of inferiority" in Negro students "that may affect their hearts and minds in a way unlikely ever to be undone." Thanks to the NAACP Legal Defense Fund, which had argued against school segregation before the court, American Negroes had won their most spectacular victory in this century. In one historic blow, the Supreme Court had smashed the whole legal superstructure for the idea of racial separateness, knocking down a century and a half of devious rationalizations in defense of the creed that blacks must be kept apart because they were inferior.

King was "elated" with the decision. It seemed to betoken a speedy end to the hated Jim Crow system in which he had grown up. He pronounced the Brown case "a world-shaking decree," a "noble and sublime decision" that would help right his troubled land with its own ideals. It seemed an auspicious time to be going home to the South, a time when good things seemed about to happen there.

But then came the southern reaction. Across Dixie, segregationists raged at the "tyrannical" court and branded the day of the Brown decision as "black Monday." In Mississippi, a former football star named Tut Patterson stormed: "There won't be any integration in Mississippi. Not now, not 100 years from now, maybe not 6,000 years from now—maybe never." And he helped form the South's first White Citizens' Council to preserve the "Southern way of life." Meanwhile fiery crosses burned against Texas and Florida skies, and random Klan terrorism broke out against blacks in many parts of Dixie. In Georgia, a gubernatorial candidate stood in ninety-degree heat and expounded his "three school" plan to defeat integration: one for whites, another for colored ("the way they want it"), and a third for those insane enough to want their children in integrated schools. In Montgomery, Alabama, the State Board of Education voted unanimously to continue segregated facilities through the 1954–1955 school year; and the state legislature "nullified" the court decision, vowing to preserve white supremacy come what may.

With the white South mobilizing against school desegregation, King took Coretta down to Montgomery, to show her the church and the parsonage and to tour the Negro section where they would have to live. It was truly another world from Boston. With falling hearts, they saw black people riding in the backs of buses and realized that Coretta would have to sit there, too, if she wanted to shop while he had the car. Coretta, who had wanted badly to remain in the North, tried to be brave. "If this is what you want," she told King, "I'll make myself happy in Montgomery." It was what he wanted. But he had no idea whether they could ever be happy here.

PART TWO

ON THE STAGE
OF HISTORY

THE PARSONAGE STOOD ON A SHADED STREET in a Negro district, several blocks southwest of the capitol. It was a white frame house, with seven rooms and a railed-in front porch, and tall oaks hovered about it like sentries. Inside, the pastor's wife had added personal touches to the furnishings provided by the church: a television set and a baby grand piano resided in the living room, two African "heads" hung on the wall there, and West Indian gourds and art pieces decorated the mantel above the close-in fireplace.

Each morning the young pastor arose at 5:30, made coffee, and went through the painful ordeal of shaving. Because his whiskers were tough and ingrown, he could only remove them with an old-fashioned English straight razor and a special shaving powder that gave off a terrible odor. The face in the mirror had a neat mustache now, small ears, and immaculately clipped hair, and lit up in a boyish grin when he remembered something humorous. Ready for the day, he secluded himself in a book-lined den, with its scholarly disarray, and wrote for three hours on his thesis. At nine he breakfasted with his wife and then drove downtown to Dexter Church. He felt a special fondness for the old red-brick church, with its twin doorway lamps and bell tower. It stood on the corner with an aura of unembellished dignity, unintimidated by the white government buildings that loomed across the street.

Here the young pastor ministered to the brothers and sisters of his congregation, who came to him with all manner of spiritual and secular needs. He served as their character witness, negotiated with whites in their behalf, married and buried them. He cautioned any Negro who harbored violent impulses that the strong man was the man who could stand up without striking anybody. He counseled couples with marital troubles that maybe they could not get along because they didn't understand one another and were afraid. They must get behind appearances, he said, must "discover the meaning of soul beauty before they can really discover the meaning of love." For him, divorce was "a court of last resort," but if it was unavoidable he would do what he could to help both parties adjust to "this unfortunate break in their marriage." He also did what he could for unwedded young mothers, but "it is always a frustrating experience," he said of the problem. "I feel so helpless." When the parents of such a girl came to him, he would explain that "her emotions are fraught with deep hurt, shame and pride. Hurt because the boy does not want to share the same responsibility as she is sharing; shame because she feels that she has done something that society looks down upon." But he did not encourage a forced marriage, because the baby "would be the victim of a set of parents who did not love each other and would probably be brought up in an atmosphere of strife and tension which would play more havoc on its personality than if it had to face the fact that it had no legal father." It was best that the baby receive "a double amount of love from its mother and her relatives." Still, he was never satisfied with such advice, and when the opportunity came he joined a committee of the Planned Parenthood Federation, which disseminated literature on unwanted pregnancies.

At prescribed hours during the week, he closed his office door and devoted himself to his sermon for the next Sunday. On Tuesday he would sketch an outline, on Wednesday do research and decide what illustrations and life situations to use, and on Friday and Saturday write the sermon on lined yellow pages. His breadth of historical references might range from Plato, Aristotle, and St. Thomas Aquinas to Alfred the Great, Thomas Carlyle, James Russell Lowell, Lincoln and Frederick Douglass, Niebuhr, Freud, and Gandhi. Then on Sunday he would preach without notes for thirty-five to forty minutes, quite as though he were extemporizing, and his congregation would clap and cry in appreciation.

• At first his sermons tended to be sober and intellectual, like a classroom lecture. But he came to understand the emotional role of the Negro church, to realize how much black folk needed this precious sanctuary to vent their frustrations and let themselves go. And so he let himself go. The first "Amen!" from his congregation would set him to "whooping" with some old-fashioned fireworks, in which he made his intellectual points with dazzling oratory. For what was good preaching if not "a mixture of emotion and intellect"? As a preacher in his own right, free from entanglements with his father, King learned to appreciate the southern Negro church as never before. Here in their church—the only place that was truly their own—black people could feel free of the white man, free of Jim Crow, free of everything. Here they could be spiritually reborn and emotionally uplifted, exhorting their preacher as he in turn exhorted them, both engaging in a call-and-response dialogue that went back to their African ancestry. And young King, observing this at Dexter, seeing now what he had been blinded to in his youth, became a master at call-and-response exhortation: "And I tell you [*tell it, doctor*] that any religion that professes to be concerned with the souls of men [*well awright*] and is not concerned with the slums that damn them [*amen, brother*] and the social conditions that cripple them [*oh yes*] is a dry as dust religion [*well*]. Religion deals with both heaven and earth [*yes*], time and eternity [*uh-huh*], seeking not only to integrate man with God [*clapping, clapping*], but man with man."

His congregation adored him. He was "suave, oratorical, and persuasive," said one member. And he was such a young man to be so smart and confident. "You mean that little boy is my pastor?" said one woman the first time she saw him. "He looks like he ought to be home with his mamma." In truth, women members tended to mother him. For them, he was an idealized son, so educated, charming, and handsome. "I love Dr. King like my own son," said one elderly matron. "His own mother couldn't possibly love him any more than I do."

His reputation as a preacher spread beyond Montgomery, and invitations to speak fell on his desk from as far away as Pennsylvania. "I understand you are developing into a good preacher in your own right," a family friend wrote him. "Remain careful of your conduct. Steer away from 'trashy' preachers. Be worthy of the best. It may come to you some day." The friend teased Daddy King: "They tell me you have a son that can preach rings around you any day you ascend the pulpit. How about that? If it is so, it is a compliment to you." "Every way I turn people are congratulating me for you," Daddy wrote King in December. "You see young man you are becoming very popular. As I told you you must be much in prayer. Persons like yourself are the ones the devil turns all of his forces loose to destroy."

Determined to practice what he preached, King launched an ambitious social-action program at Dexter. Under his supervision, committees formed to tend the sick and needy, help artists with promise, and administer scholarship funds for high-school graduates. At the

same time, a social and political action committee held forums on political developments and kept members apprised of NAACP activity in
Dixie. Soon Dexter was contributing more to the NAACP than any
other Negro church in town.

Within a year, King had earned himself a reputation as a social
activist. He was elected to the executive committee of the NAACP's
Montgomery chapter, comprising mostly professional and business
people whose incomes were independent of whites and who had little
fear of economic reprisals for their "radical" NAACP work. King also
belonged to the Alabama Council on Human Relations, the only interracial group in town. But he observed that overall "the vital liaison
between Negroes and whites was totally lacking. There was not even a
ministerial alliance to bring white and colored clergymen together."

It was clear why. White people wanted no contact on an equal
basis with blacks. In this complacent Deep South city, 90,000 whites
and 50,000 Negroes largely went their separate ways, kept apart by a
rigid racial caste system that relegated Negroes to the gutters of the
social order. A local statute even forbade blacks and whites to play
cards, dice, checkers, or dominoes together. Yet the two races entered
inexorably into one another's lives—most black adults, for instance,
toiled as maids and menials in white homes, public accommodations,
and other businesses. Montgomery whites, of course, told themselves
that "our niggers are happy and don't want integration." In their barber shops and beauty salons, their clubs and restaurants, white folks
damned integration as the work of Communists, called the NAACP
"the National Association for the Advancement of the Communist
Party," and denounced the U.S. Supreme Court as a tool of Moscow.
They expected "niggers" to know their place and the mass of them to
stay away from the polls and out of politics.

To King's dismay, most local Negroes accepted all this with appalling apathy. The majority of educated blacks seemed complacent and
terribly afraid of angering the white man. And domestics and day
laborers seemed as passive as stone. Some of them, King understood,
feared white retaliation if they stood up to the system. But many others suffered from a "corroding sense of inferiority, which often expressed itself in a lack of self-respect." As a consequence, many poor
Negroes really did think themselves inferior, really did think they belonged in the gutters of Southern life. And then there were the black
preachers—historically the natural leaders of the Negro community.
There were fifty Negro churches in and around Montgomery, and yet

most of their pastors practiced "dry-as-dust religion," contending that their job was to get people into Heaven, not change things down here.

What a defeatist and distressing attitude this was. Yet the attitudes of the activist leadership troubled King, too. There was, he noted, "an appalling lack of unity among the leaders," as too many committees worked at cross purposes and without cooperation, which resulted in a "crippling factionalism." About the only thing the black leadership seemed to agree on was the need to observe Emancipation Day on January 1, when prominent Negroes would talk eloquently about Lincoln and Negro rights—and then do nothing about gaining them. As King surveyed Montgomery's divided and phlegmatic Negro community, he doubted that meaningful social reform could ever occur in this old Confederate city.

Still, his social activism was not without rewards. He became fast friends with Ralph Abernathy, pastor of the First Baptist Church and an activist preacher, too. Socializing together in their churches and homes, they and their wives talked about building a new Christian order somehow, someday. Now twenty-nine, four years older than King, Abernathy was short and stocky, with "the wily charm of a hand-shaking, Black-belt politician," as an acquaintance later put it. He was born in black-belt Marengo County, about ninety miles southwest of Montgomery, and was one of twelve children from a sharecropping family with mixed-blood ancestry. Abernathy tickled people with stories about his first "goggle-eyed and breathless" visits to nearby Selma, the biggest town he'd ever seen as a boy. He jocularly called himself "the barefoot boy from Marengo County."

His father was a proud, perceptive man who realized that a Negro had to own his land before he could be free of whites. Plowing the white man's field all day, he saved money so that he could buy his own. Once he did, he became one of the leading black citizens of the county: he was a church deacon and the first Negro there to vote and serve on a grand jury. He also built the county's first Negro school and furnished its firewood himself. He was soon so prosperous that he had black tenants working his own place. But he died when Abernathy was sixteen—a shattering loss from which Abernathy never fully recovered. Behind his witty, unruffled façade, Abernathy was an extremely sensitive man who needed recognition and approval. Yet he never forgot two things his father always told him: that "if I ever saw a fight to get in it" and that "preaching was a job of a man and not a boy." Unlike King, he had come to the ministry by way of Negro schools in the South—Alabama State in Montgomery and Atlanta University.

To a lot of people, King and Abernathy seemed an odd pair. Largely northern educated and a scion of Atlanta's black middle class, King was learned, fastidious, and urbane. Abernathy, by contrast, came from a bucolic background and was so slow and earthy that some thought him crude. How could two such dissimilar individuals become friends?

The truth was that they complemented one another, each providing something the other needed. In King's friendship, Abernathy found an acceptance he yearned for—the acceptance of a brilliant and educated member of the black middle class. In Abernathy, King found a country boy who had risen from an impoverished background and had earned his right to champion Negro improvement. In point of fact, Abernathy personified Negro improvement. And King, who was born into a privileged Negro life, felt something special in the companionship of a man who had worked his way up to King's position entirely on his own. Even their styles were complementary. "King would strike a deft, graceful jab," one observer said, "while Abernathy slugged and walloped."

What was more, the two men shared a keen sense of humor. Friends recalled how they could cut up at the dinner table, swapping jokes until they had each other and everyone else in tears. "I declare," one woman told them, "you two could be on stage." King, for his part, was an expert at mimicking other preachers, recounting their follies in one hilarious parody after another. Once, during a birthday party, he and Abernathy took the floor to imitate a swinging gospel show that came over the radio. They dedicated their first number to Miss Coretta King, "a dear sister over there in Montgomery," and swayed and pranced about arm in arm, slurring their words and singing off-key until they collapsed from laughter.

And so King passed his first year in Montgomery, fraternizing with Abernathy, tending his flock, getting involved in life's adversities. Over the winter, he completed his thesis—"A Comparison of the Conception of God in the Thinking of Paul Tillich and Henry Nelson Wieman"—and successfully defended it at Boston University. He received his doctorate at the end of the spring term in 1955. DeWolf pronounced the thesis "quite a searching philosophical and theological study," a difficult comparison ably done. Later, King preached to an interracial congregation in Boston, with his former teachers from the Boston University School of Theology sitting in the front row of the balcony. "He called them by name, one by one," a white woman re-membered. "He thanked them individually, told them how much he owed them, how he would never have been where he was without them, how grateful he was for their loving concern."

King reached another milestone in the spring of 1955: Coretta broke the news that he was going to be a father. There had been some question as to whether they could have children, and King had vowed to adopt if they could not. Now he was beaming. He wanted *eight* children before they were through, he gushed. "We'll compromise and have four," Coretta said.

King hoped the baby would be a boy. If it were, he would christen him Martin Luther King III.

STILL, IT WAS NOT AN AUSPICIOUS TIME. From Virginia to Texas, White Citizens' Councils were springing up to block school desegrega-tion, and southern state capitals were ringing with cries of interposition and nullification. Faced with stiffening white resistance, the Supreme Court shied away from immediate compliance with the Brown decision and called instead for action "with all deliberate speed." Like many other Negroes, King was deeply disappointed, for the new court order seemed to invite indefinite postponement. And that was precisely what the white South had in mind. Mustering its own legal forces, white officialdom promised to tie up the Brown decision in "a century of litigation."

White reaction was voluble and violent for another reason, too. Since World War II, the number of black voters in Dixie had risen dramatically, thanks to NAACP victories in the federal courts that re-moved one obstacle after another to Negro enfranchisement. With more and more Negroes trying to vote and go to school with whites, southern segregationists caught a glimpse of the apocalypse: if the "nigger-loving" federal courts got their way, "niggers" would soon be taking away white jobs and copulating with white daughters. The white man's South—the South of Robert E. Lee and Jefferson Davis—would disappear in an orgy of interracial violence and sex in which the "niggers" would come out on top.

King was well aware of such anxieties. He read white newspapers. He overheard white people talk. He thought them victims of irrational fears—fear of economic and social loss, fear of intermarriage, fear of somebody different. Some whites, he noticed, practiced escapism, pretending that nothing was going on. Others flocked to meetings of the White Citizens' Councils, often held in sporting arenas. And still others joined the Klan and resorted to nightriding terrorism. And it was all futile, King said, because violence, resistance, and escapism only instilled deeper and more pathological fears.

And those fears, in turn, often led to macabre atrocities. An example was the case of Emmett Till, a fourteen-year-old Negro who came down from Chicago that summer to visit relatives in Greenwood, Mississippi. One August night three white men dragged him away from a Negro home and flung him into the Tallahatchie River with a seventy-pound cotton gin fan tied to his neck with barbed wire. The whites murdered him because of a rumor that he had whistled at a white woman. The Brown decision, and the southern white reaction to it, had made national news out of southern racial matters, and numerous outside reporters came to Mississippi for the trial of two of the killers, who of course went free. Why all this fuss over a dead "nigger" in the Tallahatchie? complained one Mississippi white. "That river's full of niggers."

Montgomery, meanwhile, had a similar case, and King became involved in it as an NAACP leader. Back in 1952, a white woman had accused a teenage Negro of raping her. His name was Jeremiah Reeves, and he was a drummer in the Negro high school band. When an all-white court found him guilty of rape and sentenced him to hang, Reeves appealed with the help of local Negro activists and the NAACP. After a bitter legal battle that consumed five years, Reeves was executed.

The Reeves case stirred Montgomery's Negro community like a whirlwind. Here was one more example of white man's justice, of the legal double standard that Negroes had to live by in Dixie. In the early 1950s alone, plenty of white men had sexually abused Negro women in Montgomery, but none of them had ever been arrested and brought to trial. One white man had beaten his Negro lover to death: there were grisly reports that he had found her messing around with a black man and had poured lighter fluid into her vagina and set it afire. Yet nothing happened to him. A white cop forced a black girl into his patrol car and raped her in a cemetery, but nothing happened to him either. Two other cops forced a black woman to ride with them to a vacant lot in a railroad yard. Here they made her perform "unnatural acts" on them, raped and beat her, after which she ran "wet and crying" to a local preacher, who tried to rally the Negro community behind her. But what was the use? An all-white grand jury dismissed the charge against the policemen. On another occasion, a white father raped a fifteen-year-old Negro girl, his babysitter. When a white judge declared him innocent, local blacks boycotted his store, which was situated in a black neighborhood, and drove him out of business. But it didn't help the young woman, who died of shock from the assault.

By the spring and summer of 1955, a flame of discontent was smoldering below the surface of passivity in black Montgomery. King himself sensed the stirrings—a growing resentment at white man's justice, sexual abuses, and endless daily harassment and humiliation. The most commonplace outrage occurred on the city buses, the only means of transportation for thousands of local Negroes. Though they comprised 70 percent of the bus clientele, white drivers—all drivers were white—went out of their way to insult Negro passengers, calling them "niggers," "apes," and "black cows." The drivers particularly singled out black women for abuse. They made Negroes pay at the front of the bus and then step off and reboard through the back door; sometimes the drivers roared away before the luckless blacks could get on again, leaving them stranded without their fares. Once a Negro was on the bus, he could not sit down in the first four rows, which a sign reserved for WHITES ONLY. If all the front seats were taken and more whites entered the bus, Negroes in the unreserved section had to turn their seats over to them. If a white took a seat beside a Negro, the Negro had to stand, because bus company regulations prohibited white and black passengers from sitting together. If a Negro found the unreserved section full and the white section empty, he had to stand in the aisle, gazing at the empty seats in front. A Montgomery city ordinance enforced the seating policy, and Negro violators could be fined and jailed.

By 1955, Montgomery blacks were becoming increasingly fed up with the Jim Crow buses and their insulting drivers—none more so than gruff and gravel-voiced E. D. Nixon, a regional official of the Brotherhood of Sleeping Car Porters and a leader of the Montgomery and Alabama chapters of the NAACP. Six feet three and coal black, Nixon spoke in a slurred, ungrammatical, excited style and was extremely sensitive about his want of education, though he boasted that he had more property and money in the bank than a lot of B.A.s, M.A.s, and Ph.D.s. "He was considered the most militant man in town," said his NAACP secretary, and he pointed to the buses as the worst example of racial insults to black folk. What he wanted, he said, was a test case to challenge the city bus ordinance in the courts.

In the space of ten months that year, three Negroes challenged the Jim Crow bus regulations, and the police arrested and hauled them all off to jail. But city authorities either dismissed their cases or charged them with disorderly conduct, thus denying Nixon an incident he could use to test the city segregation ordinance. Even so, one of the arrests—that of a fifteen-year-old high-school girl—so aroused the black community that there was talk of a bus boycott. King was in the thick of such talk. Why couldn't Montgomery Negroes mount a bus protest? It had been done in other cities: up in Harlem during World War II, down in Baton Rouge in 1953. King even served on a Negro citizens' committee that called on the police commissioner and the manager of the local bus lines, but nothing came of the meeting. Nothing came of the boycott either, and King despaired of ever getting Montgomery Negroes to put their words of hurt into action.

In November, 1955, several members of the Montgomery NAACP urged King to run for president. He started to do so, but changed his mind on the grounds that he needed to devote more time to his church work. That same month, Coretta presented him with a baby girl, whom they named Yolanda. King was proud of Yoki and said she came at a time when he needed a healthy diversion from the pressures of his work.

ON FRIDAY MORNING, DECEMBER 2, King was working at Dexter when he received a phone call from E. D. Nixon. "We got it!" Nixon exclaimed. "We got our case!" With unrestrained excitement, Nixon recounted what had happened late yesterday afternoon. Mrs. Rosa Parks, a tailor's assistant in a downtown department store, had gotten on a bus at Court Square and taken a seat behind the "lily-white section." When the bus filled up, the driver ordered Mrs. Parks to stand so that a white man could sit down. She refused to move. She'd gone shopping after work, and her feet hurt. She couldn't bear the thought of having to stand all the way home. The driver, of course, threatened to call the police. Go ahead and call them, Mrs. Parks sighed. And she thought how you spend your whole life making things comfortable for white people. You just live for their well-being, and they don't even treat you like a human being. Well, let the cops come. She wasn't moving.

Two patrolmen took her down to the police station, where officials booked her for violating the city bus ordinance. Her throat was dry, but they wouldn't let her drink from the whites-only fountain. She made a phone call, and Brother Nixon came on the run to post her bond. When he learned of her charge, he was quite beside himself. It was the first time a Negro had been charged with violating the city segregation code—a historic blunder and the test case Nixon had been waiting for. "We can go to the Supreme Court with this," he said in the Parks home that evening, "and boycott the bus line at the same time." Surely black Montgomery would rally behind Mrs. Parks, for she was no ordinary "colored." Honest, smart, and "morally clean," she had worked with Nixon as secretary of the Montgomery NAACP and enjoyed considerable respect in the black community.

All this Nixon told King. "We have took this type of thing too long already," Nixon said "We got to boycott the buses. . . . Make it clear to the white folks we ain't taking this type of treatment any longer."

King agreed. Had Nixon phoned Ralph Abernathy? Yes, Nixon said, and Abernathy was all for it. And so were a lot of other folks. What they needed was to call a leaders' conference that night and get organized. King offered his church as the meeting place.

He was astonished at the turnout that evening. From forty to fifty ministers and civic leaders gathered in his church, and all threw their support behind a boycott. True, some fretted about repercussions, but all realized that they had to act. Already rumors were abroad that Negro toughs were threatening to "beat the hell out of a few bus drivers" and were oiling guns and sharpening switch-blade knives. To ward off violent Negro retaliation and still stand up to the white man, the leaders agreed to launch a boycott on Monday, December 5. The ministers would alert their congregations on Sunday morning, and King and others would circulate leaflets throughout black Montgomery. Once the boycott was under way, they would hold a mass meeting

at Holt Street Baptist Church in the Negro district and there decide
how long the protest would last. When the meeting ended, King said,
"the clock on the wall read almost midnight, but the clock in our souls
revealed that it was daybreak."

The next day he and his church secretary mimeographed seven
thousand leaflets, and a veritable army of women and young people
took off to distribute them. Meanwhile King and other leaders contacted Montgomery's eight Negro taxi companies, with an operating fleet
of sixty to seventy cars, and persuaded them to haul black people for
the bus fare of ten cents apiece.

On Sunday, though, King received a shock. The Montgomery Advertiser carried a long article about the projected boycott (Nixon
claimed that he had leaked the story to help spread the word). The
piece not only accused the NAACP of planting "that Parks woman"
on the bus to stir up trouble, but likened the protest to the tactics of
the White Citizens' Councils, which often boycotted whites who resist-
ed them. Suddenly King was beset with doubts. Was the paper right—
were Negroes about to embrace the same "negative solutions" as the
hated Citizens' Councils? Was a boycott unethical? Even un-Chris-
tian? He brooded in his den, surrounded by his books. Finally he decided that "boycott" was the wrong term for what they were about to
do. They weren't out to strangle an isolated firm. No, they were withdrawing their cooperation from an evil system. In fact, the bus company was "an external expression of the system," and if it suffered that
could not be helped. Was this not what Thoreau summoned moral
men to do? They were telling whites: "We can no longer lend our
cooperation to an evil system." For "He who accepts evil without protesting against it is really cooperating with evil." And they were
through cooperating.

Exhausted, he went to bed early that night, but not to sleep. Two-
week-old Yoki started to cry, and the phone rang and rang. Condemned to lie awake, he worried that his people might not respond to
the leaflets and the exhortations of their ministers. What if they were
still too apathetic or too frightened to participate? The leaders hoped
for 60 percent cooperation, but what if they got only 30 percent—or
even less? What if the boycott fizzled on the first day? Would whites
not laugh at them? Would they not suffer an irreversible setback?

At last dawn came. In the kitchen, King made some coffee and sat
down to await the first bus on the South Jackson line, due to stop in

front of his house at 6 A.M. He was still in the kitchen when Coretta cried, "Martin, Martin, come quickly!" He ran to the front window just as the bus went by. It was empty. The South Jackson line carried more Negroes than any other in town; the first bus was usually jammed with Negro domestics on their way to work. In a state of high excitement, King awaited the second bus, due in fifteen minutes. It too was empty. And so was the third bus, save for a couple of white passengers. With spirits soaring, King fetched Abernathy in his car and they cruised the streets. All over town the buses were empty of black people. It looked as though the boycott would be almost 100 percent effective.

They thrilled at the drama unfolding in Montgomery. There were students happily hitchhiking to Alabama State, the city's all-black college. There were old men and woman walking as far as twelve miles to their dreary downtown jobs. There was a Negro riding a mule to work, another in a horse-drawn buggy. Not a single passenger stood at the bus stops—just bands of youths who cheered and sang, "No riders today," as the buses pulled away. Soon motorcycle cops were trailing them, dispatched by the city fathers to arrest Negro "goon squads" thought to be keeping "the coloreds" off the buses. The city fathers refused to believe that Negroes could do this thing by themselves. No, this had to be the work of the NAACP and other "outside agitators."

At nine, King and Abernathy drove to City Hall for Rosa Parks's trial. A large crowd of Negroes milled about the place, eying a squadron of police armed with sawed-off shotguns. "My Gawd," said Nixon when he came to City Hall with Mrs. Parks, "the black man is born again!" In her trial, the judge found Parks guilty of disobeying the Montgomery segregation ordinance and fined her $14, including court costs. As Nixon filed an appeal bond, King was amazed at the stupidity of white officials. Unwittingly they were inviting a federal court test of the kind of Jim Crow statutes on which the entire superstructure of segregation depended.

At three that afternoon, King and the other leaders met in a local church and set up a permanent organization to run the boycott and handle future racial difficulties as well. At Abernathy's suggestion, they called it the Montgomery Improvement Association, to stress the positive, uplift approach of their movement. The next order of business was the election of officers. "Mr. Chairman," said businessman Rufus Lewis, "I would like to nominate Reverend M. L. King for pres-

ident." Nixon vigorously supported the motion, and the group elected
King unanimously. Taken by surprise, King said he would like to think
it over. Only three weeks before, he had refused to run for the
NAACP presidency . . . But Nixon cut him short. "You ain't got much
time to think, 'cause you in the chair from now on."

At that King relented. "Somebody has to do it," he said, "and if
you think I can, I will serve."

Still, he wondered why they had selected him rather than one of
the established leaders like Nixon, Lewis, or Ralph Abernathy, who
was secretary of the black Ministerial Alliance. Later Nixon claimed
that King was "my man" and that he more than any other promoted
his candidacy. King could talk to people "from any direction," Nixon
said, and he hadn't been in Montgomery long enough "to be spoiled
by politicians—the city fathers. They couldn't get their hand on him
nohow. So many ministers accept a handout, and then they owe their
soul." But young King didn't owe white people anything.

But B. J. Simms, a history professor at Alabama State, thought
there was more to King's election than that. According to Simms,
many leaders feared that the boycott would fail, and they pushed
King as a sacrificial scapegoat, so that he would have to take all the
blame. Attorney Fred D. Gray, on the other hand, contended that
King was a compromise choice between two rival factions—one led by
Nixon, "the leader of the masses," and the other by "Coach" Lewis,
"the leader of the classes." Had either of them become MIA president,
Gray maintained, "we would have gotten bogged down in personalities." And so they all—Nixon and Lewis included—closed ranks behind King, "a nice young man" who hadn't "become identified with
any particular group." King himself decided that this was why he was
chosen president. "Somebody had to bell the cat," as another observer
put it, "so they gave him the bell."

Once they chose their officers, the group turned to the boycott and
the mass meeting scheduled that night. Afraid of white retaliation,
some ministers urged that they conceal their names and pass out secret
leaflets, so that whites would not know what was in the air. At that
Nixon was on his feet. "What the hell you people talkin' 'bout? How
you gonna have a mass meeting, gonna boycott a city bus line without
the white folks knowing it?" His voice rose. "You oughta make up
your mind right now that you gon' either admit you are a grown man
or concede to the fact that you are a bunch of scared boys."

King said he was "no coward" and agreed that they should protest out in the open, like men. After that there was no more talk of secrecy. With the mass meeting only an hour away, the group directed that a committee under Abernathy draft a set of demands and present it as a resolution that night.

King went home at six, nervous about telling Coretta about the MIA presidency. Since their marriage, she'd had to make a lot of difficult adjustments, giving up her career, coming south to Montgomery, learning the role of a young minister's wife, and then becoming a mother. She had scarcely regained her equilibrium from the enormous responsibility of a baby in her life. How would she respond to this latest intrusion, which was bound to take him away from home much of the time? But she was very supportive when he told her about the meeting and his election as MIA president. "You know that whatever you do, you have my backing," she said.

Reassured, he went into his study and closed the door. It was almost 6:30, and he had to leave at 6:50 to make the mass meeting. Only twenty minutes to prepare the most important speech of his life. Fear knifed through him. He had always taken at least fifteen hours to prepare a sermon. Now in only a few minutes—and they were ticking away—he had to devise a speech that would give his people "a sense of direction" and "a passion for justice." Worse, reporters and television newsmen were certain to be on hand to record and transmit his remarks across the country. He was overcome by feelings of inadequacy. He looked at his watch: he had already wasted five minutes just worrying. He prayed that God be with him and help him be strong. With minutes fleeing by, he began an outline with a trembling hand. Then he stared at the paper, blocked by another problem. How could he arouse the people to militant action and yet keep their fervor within controllable bounds? So many Negroes were victims of deadly bitterness and could easily be excited to violence. What could he say that would incite people to positive action, to action without hate?

His problem seemed clear now. He must combine two apparent irreconcilables—militancy and moderation. At Boston University, he had learned from Hegel how to synthesize opposites. But that had been in the realm of theory. This was the real thing. People's lives and destiny—his own life and destiny—were at stake now. He stared at the paper again, pondering the militant angle of his speech. At issue was black people's self-respect. If they took the Rosa Parks incident lying down, they would violate their own dignity, not to mention "the eternal edicts of God Himself." But he must balance this with an appeal to Christian love. . . .

By the time he had sketched a mental outline, he had to go. He had not eaten since breakfast, but there was no time for food. When he reached Holt Street Baptist a short while later, he was astonished at what he saw: police cars were circling the area, and hundreds of people, thousands of them, were milling about the church, unable to get inside. On the roof, a loudspeaker broadcast the proceedings from the sanctuary, and from time to time the throng outside broke into cheers.

It took fifteen minutes for King to park his car and make his way into the church. It had been packed since five that afternoon, and the other MIA leaders were transported with excitement. There was not an empty seat anywhere in the sanctuary; people spilled into the aisles and through the doorways in back. After preliminary songs and speeches, King stood at the pulpit, looking out over a row of television cameras at a sea of expectant black faces.

"We're here this evening for serious business," he said, speaking without notes. "We're here in a general sense because first and foremost, we are American citizens, and we are determined to acquire our citizenship to the fullness of its meaning. We are here also because of our deep-seated belief that democracy transformed from thin paper to thick action is the greatest form of government on earth." His implication was clear to everyone present: the critical element in race relations was the flagrant discrepancy between American ideals and practices so far as Negroes were concerned. But their protest was a revolt within the system, not against it. They were out to reform, not tear down.

"But we are here in a specific sense because of the bus situation in Montgomery. We are here because we are determined to get the situation corrected." He rehearsed what had happened to Rosa Parks, who sat behind him, a dignified, bespectacled woman and the heroine of the hour. After recalling the abuses and indignities blacks had suffered on the buses, he sounded his militant call to action. "But there comes a time when people get tired. We are here this evening to say to those who have mistreated us so long that we are tired—tired of being segregated and humiliated; tired of being kicked about by the brutal feet of oppression." The crowd was with him now, responding in bursts of shouts and applause. "We have no alternative but to protest. For many years, we have shown amazing patience. We have sometimes given our white brothers the feeling that we liked the way we were being treated. But we come here tonight to be saved, to be saved from patience that makes us patient with anything less than freedom and justice." There was a chorus of "well" and "amen."

He spoke of the divisions and apathy that had immobilized them in the past. "I want to say that in all of our actions we must stick together. Unity is the great need of the hour, and if we are united we can get many of the things that we not only desire, but which we justly deserve." And they were not wrong in what they were doing. "If we are wrong, the Supreme Court of this nation is wrong. If we are wrong, the Constitution of the United States is wrong. If we are wrong, God Almighty is wrong. If we are wrong, Jesus of Nazareth was merely a Utopian dreamer who never came down to earth. If we are wrong, justice is a lie." The crowd rode on the waves of his oratory, stamping and cheering in a frenzy of excitement.

Now that he had them aroused, though, he turned to caution. Theirs was not a violent movement, not a black counterpart of the White Citizens' Councils or the Ku Klux Klan. "In our protest, there will be no cross burnings. No white person will be taken from his home by a hooded Negro mob and brutally murdered. There will be no threats and intimidation. We will be guided by the highest principles of law and order." Their method was persuasion, not coercion. They would say to people, "Let your conscience be your guide." Moreover, "our actions must be guided by the deepest principles of our Christian faith. Love must be our regulating ideal." And he recited Christ's admonition: "Love your enemies, bless them that curse you, and pray for them that despitefully use you." He pleaded, "If we fail to do this our protest will end up as a meaningless drama on the stage of history, and its memory will be shrouded with the ugly garments of shame. In spite of the mistreatment that we have confronted we must not become bitter, and end up by hating our white brothers. As Booker T. Washington said, 'Let no man pull you so low as to make you hate him.'

"If we protest courageously, and yet with dignity and Christian love, when the history books are written in the future, somebody will have to say, 'There lived a race of people, of black people, of people who had the moral courage to stand up for their rights. And thereby they injected a new meaning into the veins of history and civilization.'"

It had all come pouring out in sixteen minutes of inspired extemporizing. It was as though he had been preparing for this speech all his life—as though his doubts and reaffirmations about the ministry, his courses and readings and reflections in college, had been intended for this ringing moment.

He sat down, trembling from his effort. Across the church, people were yelling and waving their arms, clapping and singing as he had never seen them do before. Imagine Martin Luther King, a twenty-six-year-old scholar, making people rock with such emotion. "It was the most stimulating thing I have ever heard," one man said. "Nobody dreamed of Martin Luther King being that sort of man under these conditions." Said Rufus Lewis: "This was the time that the people were brought face to face with the type of man that Martin Luther [King] was—not only the people who came to the mass meeting, but those who nominated him, too. That was the great awakening. It was astonishing, the man spoke with so much force."

Abernathy was standing at the pulpit now, reading the MIA's demands to the bus lines and the city officials. First, they must guarantee that bus drivers treat Negroes courteously. Second, passengers must be seated on a first-come, first-serve basis, Negroes sitting from the back forward and whites from the front backward. Third, Negro drivers must be employed at once on predominantly Negro routes. Until these demands were met, the Negroes of Montgomery would stay off the buses in a display of determination and solidarity.

"It has been moved and seconded that the resolution as read will be received and adopted," King sang out. "Are you ready for the question?" "Yes!" the crowd roared back. "All in favor let it be known by standing on your feet." Crying out in ecstasy, the great congregation rose en masse.

King had to leave now, to speak at a Negro YMCA banquet. But "my heart was full," he recalled, for he was convinced that no historian could ever describe the meeting this night. "The victory is already won," he reflected, "no matter how long we struggle to attain the three points of the resolution. The real victory was in the mass meeting, where thousands of black people stood revealed with a new sense of dignity and destiny." Still, he had to concede that their mild demands were only a "temporary alleviation" of the bus problem. In fact, they did not meet the NAACP's minimum standard for civil-rights demands, and the NAACP remained initially uninvolved. The truth was that the MIA seating arrangement could easily be accommodated within Montgomery's segregation ordinance. The MIA's chief hope was that the Parks case would ultimately result in a court order against bus segregation. Meanwhile Montgomery Negroes would continue to protest, applying pressure through direct action as well as through the courts. Above all, the boycott would give the people a sense of involvement and contribution. This had been lacking in the work of the NAACP, which favored legal battles over direct-action campaigns that involved the Negro people. Here in Montgomery, the MIA intended to combine NAACP-style legal action with grassroots protest.

King marveled at what was happening here. He called it "the miracle of Montgomery." A month before he would not have thought a bus boycott possible. Now he saw it as "the culmination of a slowly developing process." To be sure, Rosa Parks's arrest was "the precipitating factor" in the protest, but not the cause. No, it was really the story of 50,000 Negroes who just got tired of injustice and who "were willing to substitute tired feet for tired souls."

Yet there was "a divine dimension" at work here, too. As the Almighty labored to create "a harmony out of the discords of the universe," King mused, He had selected Montgomery, Alabama, "as the proving ground for the struggle and triumph of freedom and justice in America." And was this not symbolically significant? For Montgomery was the birthplace and first capital of the old slave-based Confederacy. How sublime it would be to transform this "cradle of the Confederacy" into a cradle of freedom and brotherhood.

What was more, King felt that he had been chosen as an instrument of God's will, to inspire his people and help effect this transformation. How else explain his speech this night? For the first time he understood what older preachers meant when they said, "Open your mouth and God will speak for you."

W̶ITH THE BOYCOTT UNDER WAY IN EARNEST, King assembled an MIA strategy committee that met for hours at a time in various Negro homes. They were an outspoken and animated lot—four ministers, three Alabama State professors, a businessman, and a lawyer, debating their next step in late-night sessions in someone's living room. They epitomized the professional and business class that had furnished Negro leadership since the formation of the NAACP. Of them all, Abernathy was the most influential, standing second only to King in power and influence. When the boycott began, Abernathy claimed that he could have become the leader. Instead, he said, he chose to stand with King "as Caleb stood with Moses."

On Thursday, December 8, King and a special MIA deputation filed into the commissioners' chamber in City Hall, to meet with Mayor W. A. "Tacky" Gayle, Commissioners Clyde Sellers and Frank A. Parks, and two representatives of the bus company, all of whom had reluctantly agreed to a hearing. As they sat in chairs in front of the commissioners' table, with reporters and television cameramen gathering around, King gazed on the city fathers with optimism. Surely they were basically decent men who would comprehend the rightness of the Negroes' complaints and accede to their demands.

"Who is the spokesman?" Mayor Gayle asked, opening the session. The other Negroes looked to King. "All right," the mayor said, "come forward and make your statement."

At the table, in the glare of television cameras, King explained to the white men why the boycott had begun. He cited the abuses of the drivers and other humiliations Negroes had to suffer on the buses, told how patient they had been, recalled how they had tried to negotiate in recent months but to no avail. Then he presented the MIA's three demands, pointing out that the first-come, first-serve seating arrangement was already in operation in Nashville, Atlanta, and Mobile, each of which remained as segregated as Montgomery. The Negroes were trying not to change the law, but to gain reforms within the law. As for driver courtesy, King said, "This is the least that any business can grant to its patrons." As for Negro drivers, "it seems to me that it would make good business sense for the company to seek employees from the ranks of its largest patronage." In closing, King promised that Negroes would conduct their protest on the highest level of restraint and dignity, thus gaining justice for whites as well as blacks.

He returned to his chair, certain that his rational and sensible statement would win the city fathers over. They talked among themselves, pressed "Preacher King" on certain points, and then nodded their assent when the bus company's attorney—a man named Crenshaw—maintained that the MIA seating arrangement would blatantly violate city law. At that Mayor Gayle adjourned the meeting, and the newsmen left.

The mayor summoned King to the table, said that he and a few of his people should stay behind and try to work something out with the men from the bus company. As the smaller group gathered around the table, Commissioner Parks told Crenshaw in a quiet voice, "I don't see why we can't arrange to accept the seating proposal. We can work it within our segregation laws." King glanced at Crenshaw. "But, Frank," Crenshaw said, "I don't see how we can do it within the law. If it were legal I would be the first to go along with it; but it just isn't legal. The only way that it can be done is to change your segregation laws." Parks said nothing. "If we granted the Negroes these demands," Crenshaw went on, "they would go about boasting of a victory that they had won over the white people; and this we will not stand for."

King protested that the MIA would do no such thing. But Crenshaw remained adamant and hostile. When King asked what the bus company would concede, Crenshaw said, "We will certainly be willing to guarantee courtesy. But we can't change the seating arrangement because such a change would violate the law. And as far as bus drivers are concerned, we have no intention now or in the foreseeable future of hiring 'niggras.'"

King left City Hall, disappointed and angry. How could he have been so naïvely optimistic about Crenshaw and the city fathers? They did not care if his position was sincere and reasonable. They were interested in only one thing: preserving the racial status quo. Even when Negroes sought justice within the system of segregation, the city fathers answered with an irrational no. Oh yes, King told himself, you have learned a hard lesson. You can never persuade the privileged to surrender their privileges on their own. You have to *make* them do it, keep resisting *until* they do it. Remember what Hegel said: growth comes through pain and struggle. Well, they would struggle on, then. The bus company could not continue to operate with nearly 70 percent of its patrons gone. If King's people remained united behind the boycott, whites sooner or later would have to negotiate, or capitulate.

Crenshaw and the city fathers, however, refused to take the boycott seriously. "Comes the first rainy day," the mayor said with a laugh, "and the Negroes will be back on the buses."

In fact, it rained the next day. But the Negroes stayed off the buses, most of them trudging to work under umbrellas and newspapers, bundled up against the wet cold. When he observed that, the mayor was certain that Communists were at work in Montgomery.

To FORCE NEGROES BACK ON THE BUSES, the police commissioner ordered Negro taxi companies to charge the legal minimum rate of forty-five cents per customer, thus ending cheap taxi fares for the boycotters. But King and the MIA moved quickly to meet the crisis. They devised an ingenious car pool—based on a similar operation used in the Baton Rouge boycott—which went into operation on Tuesday, December 13. Volunteer Negro drivers transported people to and from work, operating out of forty-eight dispatch and forty-two pickup stations established in key sections of the city. The car pool was so efficient that a local white judge later praised it as the best transportation system Montgomery had ever known.

In time B. J. Simms of Alabama State took command of the car pool and ran it with military precision. Because of their mutual interest in history and other intellectual concerns, King and Brother B. J. were fairly close and "talked shop" when they were together. Later the MIA added a fleet of new station wagons, registered as church property and known affectionately as "rolling churches" among the boycotters.

Not all Negroes would ride in Brother B. J.'s vehicles. Some preferred to "demonstrate with their feet" their desire for dignity and justice, and they walked to and from work every day, regardless of the weather. Once a car-pool driver chanced on an old woman hobbling along with great difficulty, and he offered her a ride. She waved him on. "I'm not walking for myself. I'm walking for my children and my grandchildren."

Then there was Old Mother Pollard. "Now listen," King told her at church one night, "you have been with us all along, so now you go on and start back to ridin' the bus, 'cause you are too old to keep walking."

"Oh, no," she protested, "I'm gonna walk just as long as everybody else walks. I'm gonna walk till it's over."

"But aren't your feet tired?" King asked.

"Yes," she said, "my feet is tired, but my soul is rested."

King was delighted. In her "ungrammatical profundity," he liked to say, Old Mother Pollard captured the very spirit of the "miracle of Montgomery."

The miracle was manifested in other ways too. When threatened by their white employers, boycotting domestics refused to be intimidated. "Pooh!" said one Negro maid. "My white lady ain't going to get down and mop that kitchen floor. I know that." One day an influential matriarch asked her maid, "Isn't this bus boycott terrible?" "Yes, ma'am," the black woman said, "it sure is. And I just told all my young 'uns that this kind of thing is white folks' business and we just stay off the buses till they get this whole thing settled."

As it happened, some whites were sympathetic and even supportive. "Would you believe," Brother B. J. said, "that many native-born members of prominent southern families with links that dated back to the cavaliers of Virginia helped and encouraged us and made anonymous contributions? They would call and say, 'Don't reveal my name but go to it. We're all for you.'" When a Negro domestic grew tired of the boycott and returned to the buses, her white employer fired her. "If you have no race pride—if your own people can't trust you—then I can't trust you in my house," the white woman said.

In mid-December, a white woman named Juliette Morgan published a letter in the Montgomery *Advertiser*. "The Negroes of Montgomery," she wrote, "seem to have taken a lesson from Gandhi—and our own Thoreau, who influenced Gandhi. Their own task is greater than Gandhi's, however, for they have greater prejudice to overcome.

"One feels that history is being made in Montgomery these days, the most important in her career. It is hard to imagine a soul so dead, a heart so hard, a vision so blinded and provincial as not to be moved with admiration at the quiet dignity, discipline and dedication with which the Negroes have conducted their boycott."

When King and his colleagues read this, they wanted to know who Juliette Morgan was. On investigation, they found that she was a young white librarian who came from an old Alabama family and who lived alone with her mother. Her comments about Gandhi set King to thinking. There were distinct parallels between the Montgomery bus boycott and Gandhi's struggle in India. What Gandhi accomplished there—freedom and justice without a legacy of bitterness— was precisely what King desired here in Montgomery. With the help

of several pacifists and Christian socialists, who hurried to Montgomery to contribute ideas about Gandhi and nonviolent direct action,
King set about fashioning a philosophy for the bus protest, one that
derived largely from the social philosophy he had forged at Crozer
and Boston University. Here at last was a chance to translate his own
theoretical concepts into practical action.

King imparted his philosophy at twice-weekly mass meetings,
black Montgomery's unique contribution to American Negro protest.
King himself stressed the significance of the mass meetings: they cut
across class lines, he said, and brought "the Ph.D.'s, the M.D.'s, and
the No D's" together in a common cause, binding the Negro community together as no other civil-rights action had ever done. For the
people, the mass meetings became the focal point of the protest, af-
fording them an opportunity, said one observer, "to give vent to what
they had felt so long." The meetings would begin at 7 P.M., with songs
and prayers and Scripture readings, committee reports, and pep talks
by the MIA ministers. Then King, the president of the movement, the
man everyone came to hear, would orate on nonviolence, indicating
what he had learned in his intellectual odyssey in college. As he spoke,
he would plant his short legs firmly apart and shift his weight from
one foot to another. To stress a point, he would rise up on the balls of
his feet and use his fingers "in little illustrative gestures."

"One of the great glories of American democracy is that we have
the right to protest for rights," King would say. "This is a nonviolent
protest. We are depending on moral and spiritual forces, using the
method of passive resistance." And this *is* resistance, he would insist, it
is not stagnant passivity, a "do-nothing" method. "It is not passive
nonresistance to evil, it is active nonviolent resistance to evil." And it is
not a method for cowards. Gandhi said that if somebody uses it because he's afraid, he's not truly nonviolent. Really, nonviolence is the
way of the strong.

We have to resist because "freedom is never given to anybody. For
the oppressor has you in domination because he plans to keep you
there. He never voluntarily gives it up. And that is where the strong
resistance comes. We've got to keep on keepin' on, in order to gain
freedom. It is not done voluntarily. It is done through the pressure that
comes about from people who are oppressed."

"I want young men and young women who are not alive today but
who will come into this world, with new privileges and new opportu-

nities, I want them to know and see that these new privileges and opportunities did not come without somebody suffering and sacrificing for them."

But to gain these principles "within the framework of the American democratic set-up," we must eschew violence at all costs. For us, violence is both impractical and immoral. Remember that "he who lives by the sword will perish by the sword." Moreover, "to meet hate with retaliatory hate would do nothing but intensify the existence of evil in the universe. Hate begets hate, violence begets violence; toughness begets a greater toughness. We must meet the forces of hate with the power of love; we must meet physical force with soul force. Our aim must never be to defeat or humiliate the white man, but to win his friendship and understanding." We are asking the white man to open himself to the gift that God has given him for brotherhood.

Our campaign is not against individuals but against the forces of evil in the world. The basic tension here is not between Negroes and whites, but between justice and injustice. "And if there is a victory, it will be a victory not merely for fifty thousand Negroes, but a victory for justice and the forces of light."

King would quote Gandhi: "Rivers of blood may have to flow before we gain our freedom, but it must be our blood." The same must be true of us, King would say, because "unearned suffering is redemptive." It avoids the "tragic bitterness" that comes from hate and transforms resister and oppressor alike. "Along the way of life, someone must have sense enough and morality enough to cut off the chain of hate. This can only be done by projecting the ethic of love to the center of our lives."

When we say "love your enemies," we do not mean to love them as a friend or an intimate. We mean what the Greeks called *agape*—a disinterested love for all mankind. This love is our regulating ideal and the beloved community our ultimate goal. As we struggle here in Montgomery, we are cognizant that we have cosmic companionship and that the universe bends toward justice. We are moving "from the black night of segregation to the bright daybreak of joy," "from the midnight of Egyptian captivity to the glittering light of Canaan freedom."

As King spoke in a singsong cadence, his followers would cry and clap and sway, carried along by the magic of his oratory. It was in the mass meetings that King discovered what extraordinary power he possessed as an orator. His rich religious imagery reached deep into the Negro psyche, for religion had been black people's main source of strength and survival since slavery days. Yet "he has that Baptist hum which makes what is said only as important as how it is said," as one writer put it. His delivery was "like a narrative poem," said a woman journalist who heard him. "His elocution has the beauty and polish of Roland Hayes singing a spiritual." She thought his voice had such depths of tenderness and sincerity that it could "charm your heart right out of your body." He was so sincere, in fact, that he could make unlettered folk respond to a quotation from Hegel or St. Thomas Aquinas. "I don't know what that boy talkin' about," said one woman, "but I sure like the way he sounds." To churchwomen, he seemed a saint sent by the Lord Himself. "When I hears Dr. King," one said, "I see angel's wings flying 'round his head." Soon the churchwomen were calling him "L. L. J."—"Little Lord Jesus."

Because of their enormous respect for King, most of the boycotters agreed to try nonviolence as an experiment. Inevitably there were those who argued that they should "kill off" a few whites because that was "the only language these white folks will understand." But King persuaded the vast majority of Negroes to try nonviolence as a method, even if they did not accept it as a way of life.

AFTER THE FIRST MEETING with the city fathers, King and his colleagues had wired the parent firm of the Montgomery bus lines, whose headquarters were in Chicago, and urged it to send down a representative; maybe he could induce the city fathers to listen to reason. The company president replied that an official would be in Montgomery in a few days. King heard nothing more about the matter until December 15, when a white friend told him that one C. K. Totten of the National City Lines had been in town for two days. He hadn't bothered to contact King or any other local Negro.

Still, King struggled not to be bitter. When the mayor called a second meeting on Saturday, December 17, King and his associates went to City Hall in good faith. Mayor Gayle marched into the room with a retinue of whites: Totten (who at first seemed friendly enough), the city commissioners, four representatives of the bus lines, and the mayor's all-white citizens' committee, which included Reverend E. Stanley Frazier of the St. James Methodist Church. To demonstrate their willingness to negotiate, King and the MIA had modified their demand about Negro drivers: the bus company need not hire them immediately. But it must promise to take them on as vacancies occurred.

Totten rose to speak for the bus company. To King's shock, he took Crenshaw's position, dwelling at length on how the MIA demands violated local law. Had the man had a southern accent, King would have sworn he *was* Crenshaw.

When Totten finished, King jumped up. "Mr. Totten has not been fair in his assertions. He has made a statement that is completely biased. In spite of the fact that he was asked to come to Montgomery by the MIA, he has not done the Negro community the simple courtesy of hearing their grievances. The least that all of us can do in our deliberations is to be honest and fair."

King's Negro colleagues chorused "amen." Totten shifted uncomfortably in his seat. Then Reverend Frazier began speaking, and King listened with morbid fascination. Frazier was one of the most outspoken segregationists in the Methodist Church, "a tall, distinguished-looking man," King thought, "the quintessence of dignity." He was lecturing the Negroes on the frailties of human nature and the error of their ways. They had strayed from the path of righteousness, he said, led into darkness by ministers of the gospel. The task of Christian preachers was to lead men's souls to God, not to sow confusion by getting enmeshed in social problems. With the Christmas season approaching, all of them—whites and Negroes alike—must focus their attention on the Babe of Bethlehem. This the Negro preachers must tell their flocks. They must tell them to end the boycott and guide them "to a glorious experience of the Christian faith."

When he finished, Gayle and the other whites looked smug and satisfied. How could the Negroes question the authority of the Scriptures? King stood and said. "We too know the Jesus that the minister just referred to. We have had an experience with him, and we believe firmly in the revelation of God in Jesus Christ. I can see no conflict between our devotion to Jesus Christ and our present action. In fact, I can see a necessary relationship. If one is truly devoted to the religion of Jesus he will seek to rid the earth of social evils. The gospel is social as well as personal. We are only doing in a minor way what Gandhi did in India; and certainly no one referred to him as an unrepentant sinner; he is considered by many a saint.

"We have been talking a great deal this morning about customs. It has been affirmed that any change in present conditions would mean going against the 'cherished customs' of our community. But if the customs are wrong we have every reason in the world to change them. The decision which we must make now is whether we will give our allegiance to outmoded and unjust customs or to the ethical demands of the universe. As Christians we owe our ultimate allegiance to God and His Will, rather than to man and his folkways."

To white men accustomed to dealing with obsequious Negroes, King must have seemed an aberration. When the talking was over, the mayor appointed an interracial committee of eight whites and eight Negroes to convene on Monday morning, then adjourned the meeting.

King drove home with his mind on Frazier. "How firmly he believed in the position he was taking," King thought. "He would probably never change now; time-worn traditions had become too crystallized in his soul. The 'isness' of segregation had for him become one with the 'oughtness' of moral law." Though King believed that history and religion both proved Frazier wrong, he could not help but admire the man's zeal and sincerity. "Why is it," King asked himself, "that the whites who believe in integration are so often less eloquent, less positive, in their testimony than the segregationists?" It was a tragedy of history that the "children of darkness" were often more determined and forceful than the "children of light."

It troubled him, too, that the children of darkness numbered so many white preachers. Because the boycott appealed to the Christian conscience, King had expected white ministers to become the Negroes' allies and even take their case to the white power structure. But only Robert Graetz, a slender, sandy-haired West Virginian who pastored Montgomery's Negro Lutheran Church, had joined the MIA. King thought how whites had called him a "nigger lover," slashed his automobile tires, poured sugar into his gas tank, and wished him a nigger brother-in-law. He thought about how Graetz had tried to reason with white preachers and priests in town—and about his own appeals to them. But "most folded their hands—and some even took stands *against* us," as Frazier had done. King felt "chastened and disillusioned." Expecting the support of white ministers, he decided, was "the most pervasive mistake I have ever made."

On Monday morning, King was on hand for the meeting of the mayor's interracial committee. A man was present he had not seen before. "That is Luther Ingalls," the Negroes whispered, "secretary of the Montgomery White Citizens' Council." King was indignant. "We will never solve this problem so long as there are persons on the committee whose public pronouncements are anti-Negro," he cried.

"He has as much right to be on the committee as you do," a white preacher snapped. "You have a definite point of view and you are on it."

The whites now ganged up on King. *You* are the main stumbling block to a resolution of this problem. *You* are causing all the trouble with your insults, accusing us of lacking open minds. King backpedaled. He was only referring to those on the committee who were anti-Negro. Why were his Negro colleagues not standing with him? He felt isolated and terrible. Then suddenly Abernathy was on the floor. *Dear Ralph.* Reverend King, Abernathy said, spoke for the entire Negro delegation in the matter of Mr. Ingalls. King noticed that the whites looked disappointed. So that was it. This had all been a ruse to divide the Negro leaders and perhaps sabotage the boycott. But Abernathy's statement had foiled the effort. There was some empty talk after that, then the white chairman closed the session, promising to call another. He never did.

King drove home knowing that negotiations were finished. He felt depressed, borne down by a heavy guilt for getting angry at the meeting. "You must not harbor anger," he admonished himself. "You must be willing to suffer the anger of the opponent, and yet not return anger. No matter how emotional your opponents are, you must be calm." He even phoned a white committee member and apologized for any misunderstanding he might have caused.

With the failure of negotiations, the city fathers grasped for scapegoats. The mayor officially charged that "outside agitators" were "stirring this thing up," and claimed in a burst of mendacity that he had offered the Negroes "equal accommodations and everything else. But they want integration—that's the whole thing." They "are fighting to destroy our social fabric." They "are laughing at white people behind their backs." Other white officials also maintained that "Negro radicals," "extremists," and "Communists" were running the boycott. And they had better watch out, editorialized the Montgomery *Advertiser,* because "the white man's economic artillery is far superior, better emplaced, and commanded by more experienced gunners."

Bob Graetz thought white leaders were flustered, unable to deal with "our love campaign." And King, once he considered the true meaning of the term, decided that he liked being called an extremist. Was not Christ an extremist for love? he asked. Were not the early Christians called "disturbers of the peace" and "outside agitators"? Still, he cautioned his followers to "steer clear of any Communist infiltration." It was a time of anti-Communist hysteria across the land, and the boycotters must always be on guard and "have no dealings with any Communists."

One day a white man came up to King. "For all these years we have been such a peaceful community," he said; "we have had so much harmony in race relations and then you people have started this movement and boycott, and it has done so much to disturb race relations, and we just don't love the Negro like we used to love them, because you have destroyed the harmony and the peace that we once had in race relations."

"Sir," King retorted, "you have never had real peace in Montgomery. You have had a sort of negative peace in which the Negro too often accepted his state of subordination. But this is not true peace. True peace is not merely the absence of tension; it is the presence of justice. The tension we see in Montgomery today is the necessary tension that comes when the oppressed rise up and start to move forward toward a permanent, positive peace."

Christmas came on. Across Montgomery, Christmas trees glimmered in white and Negro homes, and white and Negro churches rang with carols, stories about Bethlehem, and prayers for "Peace on Earth, good will toward men." In the bustle of last-minute shopping, boycotting blacks sang an official protest song composed by a Negro bandleader:

> Ain't gonna ride them busses no more
> Ain't gonna ride no more
> Why in the hell don't the white folk know
> That I ain't gonna ride no more.

AFTER CHRISTMAS, whites resorted to psychological warfare to break the boycott, hinting at violence, trying to sow dissension among leaders and followers alike. Whites circulated rumors that King himself was pocketing MIA money, that he had bought himself a big new Cadillac and his wife a Buick station wagon. Prominent whites also told older, more established Negro preachers that their positions had been usurped by "these young upstarts" and that they should be the protest leaders. By now, the boycott was commanding national attention and thrusting King into the headlines. And this reactivated the "self-defeating rivalries" that had afflicted the black community before the protest. Jealous of King and hostile to seminary-trained ministers in general, a lot of "anti-intellectual" preachers, who were called to the pulpit by divine inspiration, griped and groaned that King was using the movement to get attention and enrich himself.

"I almost broke down under the continual battering of this argument," King recalled. When other MIA leaders began repeating it themselves, King called an emergency meeting and offered his resignation. "I am willing to decrease so that others may increase," he told them. "Maybe a more mature person can bring about a speedier conclusion." His colleagues were shocked. Aware that the people probably would not follow anyone but King, they assured him that they were pleased with his leadership and unanimously urged him to remain. After the meeting, King drove to the parsonage "more at peace than I had been in some time."

As January passed, the city fathers turned to more devious tactics. They lured three unsuspecting Negro preachers to a city commission meeting, then on January 22 announced to the press that a settlement had been reached with Negro leaders and that the boycott was over. When King heard about the hoax, he was incredulous. Clearly he had more to learn about the sneakiness of segregationists. Quickly he sent word out to black Montgomery that the announcement was a lie. The next morning, Negro paperboys aroused their clients and warned them not to believe "that stuff about the boycott on the front page." King and others confronted the three ministers, who repudiated the newspaper story, and King himself publicly announced that the boycott was still on.

After that the mayor went on television and warned that the city commission was going to "stop pussy-footing around with the boycott." Then the police started harassing the car pool, threatening to arrest Negro drivers, revoke their licenses, and cancel their insurance policies. One dreary January evening, King was on his way home when two motorcycle cops arrested him for speeding. A patrol car came and took him away. Alone in the back seat, King panicked. The car was heading in the opposite direction from downtown, where he thought the jail was located. Presently the driver turned onto a dark and dingy street and headed under a bridge. King was certain that the cops were going "to dump me off" in some remote place. "But this can't be," he thought. "These men are officers of the law." But the law was white man's law, and he feared that a mob was waiting on the other side of the bridge. He was going to be murdered and mutilated. The cops would claim that the mob had overpowered them. . . .

As the car moved past the bridge, King braced himself, certain that he was approaching his doom. But when he looked up, he saw a light in the distance and gradually made out the sign: "Montgomery Jail." He let out a sigh of relief, for "going to jail at that moment seemed like going to some safe haven."

Inside, the jailer booked and threw him into a large cell with many others. As he stood there, "strange gusts of emotion swept through me like cold winds," King said. For the first time in his life, he was behind bars, and he felt profoundly disoriented, for his father had taught him to have an Old Testament respect for the law. But remember what Thoreau said. "Under a government which imprisons any unjustly, the true place for a just man is also a prison." "The real road to happiness," Gandhi said, "lies in going to jail and undergoing suffering and privations there in the interest of one's country and religion."

King found himself with drunks, vagrants, and thieves, all thrown together in democratic misery. They lay on cots with torn-up mattresses, relieved themselves in a naked toilet in the corner. The place reeked of urine and sweat. No matter what these men have done, King thought, "they shouldn't be treated like this."

The jailer came and led him down a long corridor into a small room at the front. Here the police fingerprinted him "like a criminal." Meanwhile Ralph Abernathy had tried to sign King's bond and a crowd of Negroes had gathered in front of the jail. Intimidated, the police released King on his own recognizance and told him his trial would be held on Monday morning. All this for a minor traffic violation! King would be found guilty, of course. But at home, in the company of his wife, church members, and MIA friends, King felt strong again, knowing that he did not stand alone.

By LATE JANUARY, King was receiving thirty to forty hate letters a day. Some were signed from the "KKK," warning him to "get out of town or else." Others were crudely lettered threats on his life. "You old son of a bitch," read one missive from a Montgomery white citizen, "did you know you only have a very short time to life if you dont quit your dam foolishness here in Montgomery? You old goddam son of a bitch when you think you are as good as white people you are sadly mistaken. . . . If you don't heed this warning it will be kayo for you and your gang." "You niggers are getting your self in a bad place," another letter said. "We need and will have a Hitler to get our country straightened out."

Then there were the obscene phone calls—as many as twenty-five a day now. Sometimes there was only the hawk of a throat, the sound of spit against the receiver. Other callers would curse and rave, accusing King of lusting after white women, of wanting to perform "incredible degeneracies." Still others threatened not only to murder King, but to wipe out his wife and daughter too. King could not bear such phone calls. He had no right to put his family in such danger. He saw how upset Coretta was, for she had to answer the phone when he was gone, and the threats were getting to her, too. But they did not dare take the phone off the hook lest they miss some urgent call about the boycott. It was getting so bad that they both jumped when the phone went off.

One day a friend reported from reliable sources that a plan was afoot to have King assassinated. King admitted that he was "scared to death," worn down by "the freezing and paralyzing effect" of fear. He found himself at a mass meeting, trying to give an impression of strength. "If one day you find me sprawled out dead, I do not want you to retaliate with a single act of violence. I urge you to continue protesting with the same dignity and discipline you have shown so far." A strange hush fell over the church. Afterward, Abernathy said, "Something is wrong. You are disturbed about something." But King was evasive. "Martin, you were not talking about some general princi- ple," Abernathy said. "You had something specific in mind." For the first time, King confided in Abernathy about the threats on his life and family. Abernathy tried to help, to say something comforting, but King was still afraid.

He found himself wishing that there might be "an honorable way out without injuring the cause." He would look at Coretta and Yoki and freeze with fear: *they can be taken away from me at any moment.*

One night he came home late from an MIA meeting. Exhausted, he crawled into bed and tried to sleep, knowing that he had to get up early "to keep things going." The phone rang. Steeling himself, he picked up the receiver. On the other end was a furious voice, "an ugly voice," and it cut through King like a dagger, "Nigger, if you aren't out of this town in three days we gonna blow your brains out and blow up your house." There was a click.

King rose and walked the floor. He thought about all the things he had studied in college, the philosophical and theological discourses on sin and evil, and realized that he couldn't take it any more: the calls, the threats, this awful fear. He went into the kitchen and put on a pot of coffee. Yes, he had to quit. There was no other choice. He watched the coffee perk, poured a cup, and sat down at the table. He brooded on how he could step down without appearing to be a coward. He thought about Coretta and Yoki—"the darling of my life"—and felt weak and terribly alone. Then he heard something say to him, "You can't call on Daddy now. He's up in Atlanta a hundred and seventy- five miles away. You can't even call on Momma now."

He put his head in his hands and bowed over the table. "Oh, Lord," he prayed aloud, "I'm down here trying to do what is right. But, Lord, I must confess that I'm weak now. I'm afraid. The people are looking to me for leadership, and if I stand before them without strength and courage, they too will falter. I am at the end of my pow- ers. I have nothing left. I can't face it alone."

He sat there, his head still bowed in his hands, tears burning his eyes. But then he felt something—a presence, a stirring in himself. And it seemed that an inner voice was speaking to him with quiet assurance: "Martin Luther, stand up for righteousness. Stand up for justice. Stand up for truth. And, lo, I will be with you, even unto the end of the world." He saw lightning flash. He heard thunder roar. It was the voice of Jesus telling him *still* to fight on. And "he promised never to leave me, never to leave me alone. No, never alone, No, never alone. He promised never to leave me, never to leave me alone. . . ."

He raised his head. He felt stronger now. He could face the morrow. Whatever happened, God in His wisdom meant it to be. King's trembling stopped, and he felt an inner calm he had never experienced before. He realized that "I can stand up without fear. I can face anything." And for the first time God was profoundly real and personal to him. The idea of a personal God was no longer some "metaphysical category" he found philosophically and theologically satisfying. No, God was very close to him now, a living God who could transform "the fatigue of despair into the buoyancy of hope" and who would never, ever, leave him alone.

On the night of January 30, Gandhi's birthday, King was speaking at a mass meeting when he received dreadful news. His house had been bombed. He sped home in a strange calm. A crowd of Negroes surged about the parsonage, white police trying to hold them back. The bomb had exploded on the porch, breaking it in two and showering the living room with broken glass. The house was full of people; Mayor Gayle and Police Commissioner Sellers had just arrived. King forced his way inside and found Coretta and Yoki at the back. He hugged them. "Thank God you and the baby are all right!" Quietly he told Coretta to get dressed, for she was still in her robe.

Gayle and Sellers told King they truly regretted "this unfortunate incident." But C. T. Smiley, chairman of Dexter's board of trustees and principal of Booker T. Washington High School, said in a cutting voice: "Regrets are all very well, but you are responsible. It is you who created the climate for this."

Outside the crowd was getting out of control. A Negro man confronted a policeman: "You got your thirty-eight, and I got mine. Let's shoot it out." Even Negro boys were armed with broken bottles, and there were jeers at the cops. "Let us see Reverend King," a woman cried out. King stepped out onto the shattered porch, which still smelled of dynamite fumes, and surveyed his angry brothers and sisters on the lawn and in the street beyond. "He held up his hand," an observer said, "and they were suddenly silent . . . absolutely still."

"My wife and baby are all right," he said. "I want you to go home and put down your weapons. We cannot solve this problem through retaliatory violence. . . . We must love our white brothers, no matter what they do to us. We must make them know that we love them. Jesus still cries out across the centuries, 'Love your enemies.' This is what we must live by. We must meet hate with love." His voice was quivering. "Remember, if I am stopped, this Movement will not stop, because God is with this Movement."

Slowly his people dispersed, melting away in the night. Afterward a policeman told a reporter, "I'll be honest with you. I was terrified. I owe my life to that nigger Preacher, and so do all the other white people who were there."

King and his family spent the night at the home of a church member. King lay in a front bedroom, unable to sleep, a distant street lamp glowing in the curtained window. He thought about the viciousness of people who could bomb his home, and anger rose in him. His wife and daughter could have been killed. He thought about the city commissioners and all the vicious things they had said about him and the Negro. He was on the verge of real hatred when he caught himself again. You must not be bitter, must not hate. He tried to put himself in the position of the city fathers. "These are not bad men," he reflected. "They are misguided. They have fine reputations in the community. In their dealings with white people they are respectable and gentlemanly. They probably think they are right in their methods of dealing with Negroes. They say the things they say about us and treat us as they do because they have been taught these things. From the cradle to the grave, it is instilled in them that the Negro is inferior. Their parents probably taught them that; the schools they attended taught them that; the books they read, even their churches and ministers often taught them that; and above all the very concept of segregation teaches them that. The whole cultural tradition they have grown under—a tradition blighted with more than 250 years of slavery and more than 90 years of segregation—teaches them that Negroes do not deserve certain things. So these men are merely the children of their culture. When they seek to preserve segregation they are seeking to preserve only what their local folkways have taught them was right."

They were victims of the collective evil that Niebuhr stressed, the kind of evil that caused basically good men to be blind, ignorant, and hateful.

Aⁿfter the bombing, floodlights blazed all night at King's parsonage, and watchmen stood guard around the clock. Somebody had thrown dynamite on E. D. Nixon's lawn, and King was taking no chances. He let his sentries carry pistols and shotguns and even bring them inside his home. He told people this was only for self-defense, to protect his family. Of course he was still nonviolent. Of course he didn't want anyone shot and killed.

But the guns troubled him. He felt afraid with them in his house. He told himself, "I've got to be totally nonviolent because the guns here are going to attract guns." Again he had to face the question of death. Remember, if something happens, it is meant to be. Nothing can stop the cause. You don't need guns to protect yourself or your family. "Ultimately," he reasoned, "one's sense of manhood must come from within." He ordered the guns out of his house. Henceforth he would face any form of violence with only his faith in God and in the power of love.

February came with a rush of ominous events. In Montgomery, white officials refused to put Rosa Parks's case on the court dockets, thus blocking the MIA's hopes of taking it into the federal courts. Consequently, the MIA got five Negro women to file suit in the U.S. District Court in town, asking that the Alabama and Montgomery transportation laws be declared unconstitutional. Nine days later, the local White Citizens' Council—which now included all three city commissioners—held a rally in the Montgomery coliseum, where Senator James Eastland of Mississippi ranted against the NAACP, and racist handbills circulated by the thousands: "When in the course of human events it becomes necessary to abolish the Negro race, proper methods should be used. Among these are guns, bow and arrows, sling shots and knives. We hold these truths to be self evident that all whites are created equal with certain rights, among these are life, liberty and the pursuit of dead niggers. In every stage of the bus boycott we have been oppressed and degraded because of black, slimy, juicy, unbearably stinking niggers. The conduct should not be dwelt upon because behind them they have an ancestral background of Pygmies, Head hunter, snot suckers. . . . If we don't stop helping these African flesh eaters, we will soon wake up and find Reverend King in the white house."

In Washington, some one hundred southern congressmen signed a ringing denunciation of school integration called "The Southern Manifesto." In Birmingham, Alabama, Nat King Cole, the celebrated Negro singer, was performing in the city auditorium when a gang of whites leaped on stage and mauled him brutally. Afterward they grabbed a Negro pedestrian and mutilated his genitals. In Tuscaloosa, a Negro named Autherine Lucy tried to enter the University of Alabama, only to be expelled after whites attempted to murder her. Asked if she was connected with the Montgomery protest, a local judge said, "Autherine is just one unfortunate girl who doesn't know what she is doing, but in Montgomery it looks like all the niggers have gone crazy."

By February 21, the situation in Montgomery was extremely tense. "This is like war," one Negro said. "You can't trust anyone, black or white, unless you know him." "They can bomb us out and they can kill us," said E. D. Nixon, "but we are not going to give in." On February 21, in an effort to break the boycott once and for all, an all-white grand jury found the Negroes guilty of violating an obscure state antilabor law, which prohibited boycotts. The grand jury indicted eighty-nine leaders, including twenty-four ministers and all the drivers in the car pool.

King was in Nashville, giving a series of lectures at Fisk University, when the grand jury made its move. That night, he talked on the phone with Abernathy, who was certain that the arrests would start the next day and that he and King would be at the head of the list. Early the next morning, King flew home by way of Atlanta, where Coretta and Yoki were staying with his parents. The boycott was two months old now; his people were tired, worn down from all the intimidation. Would the mass arrests break their spirit? Would this end their movement?

In Atlanta he found another problem. Daddy King did not want him going back to Montgomery. He was sick with worry about M. L.; so was Momma, and she was subject to heart attacks. Daddy could scarcely talk about the danger to M. L. without getting tears in his eyes. "Although many others have been indicted," he told his son, "their main concern is to get you. They might even put you in jail without a bond." They might even kill him. Daddy had told Atlanta's Police Chief Herbert Jenkins, "They gon' kill my boy." And Jenkins agreed. "I think you're in great danger," he once warned King. "I think you're a marked man. I think if you don't leave Montgomery and come back to Atlanta, they gon' *bury* you over there."

As Daddy carried on about his safety, King was terribly distressed. It hurt his conscience that he should cause his parents such pain. But he had to go back to Montgomery. His conscience would hurt him far more if he did not go back. To his dismay, Daddy now summoned several close friends to try and reason with his boy. Here came gray-haired Dr. Mays, as elegant as always. Here came the president of Atlanta University, a prominent businessman, and several drugstore owners. Assembling them in the living room, Daddy announced that he had talked to a white lawyer who agreed that M. L. should not return to Montgomery. What about them? Didn't they think his boy should stay in Atlanta where he would be safe? There were murmurs of approval. Then all eyes fell on young King, who kept thinking, These are my elders, the leaders of my people. But he had to stand up to them and Daddy. "I must go back to Montgomery," he said with great earnestness. "My friends and associates are being arrested. It would be the height of cowardice for me to stay away. I would rather be in jail ten years than desert my people now. I have begun the struggle, and I can't turn back. I have reached the point of no return."

The men were silent. Then Daddy King broke down sobbing. King looked at Dr. Mays, desperate for support. Deeply moved by King's speech, Mays said, "Martin must do what he feels is right. No great leader runs away from the battle." The others nodded in agreement. One even phoned Thurgood Marshall, general counsel of the NAACP Legal Defense Fund, who promised King the best legal help available.

At last Daddy withdrew his objections, and King felt better. He had stood up for himself against the strongest man in his life. But, characteristically, Daddy insisted on going with him when he and his family returned to Montgomery the next morning. There King found out from Abernathy that many of the boycott leaders had turned themselves in yesterday, a spectacle that had set black Montgomery ablaze with excitement. Never had the leaders made such a show of defiance and solidarity. King resolved to give himself up, too, and drove to the jail with Abernathy and his father. At the jail, "an almost holiday atmosphere prevailed," King said, as other Negro leaders stood happily in line to get booked. King himself was photographed and fingerprinted and his trial set for March 19. At a mass meeting that night, standing before 5,000 clapping, stamping people, King cried that their movement could never be broken now.

Sometime that day or the next, King had "a wonderful talk" with Bayard Rustin, a Negro who worked for the Fellowship of Reconciliation (FOR), an old pacifist organization that had helped establish CORE and pioneer nonviolent direct action in the North. Rustin had come down from New York to advise the MIA on the organizational techniques of nonviolence. Forty-five now, he spoke with an elegant British accent and stood six feet three, with high cheekbones and vigorous gray hair that flared out of his head like a fountain. Born illegitimate in West Chester, Pennsylvania, he grew up in his grandparents' home and saw his father only twice before he died in an accident. Struggling against the currents of conformity, he became a Quaker and a socialist, and he read extensively in pacifist literature. In 1938, as a student at the City College of New York, he joined the Young Communist League, only to quit when it tried to restrict his integration efforts. During World War II, he served as FOR youth secretary, helped establish CORE chapters in the North, and went to prison for twenty-eight months for resisting the draft. After the war, again affiliated with FOR, he developed a philosophical pacifism that earned him recognition as a leading radical intellectual.

When he came to Montgomery that February, Rustin heard all the talk about Communist influences on the boycott, and he warned King that his own political history might hurt the movement. "Look," King said, "we need everybody who can come to help us." Besides, Rustin's brush with Communism had happened a long time ago; he was certainly no Communist now. He became King's adviser, helping him write speeches, filling him in on CORE and FOR direct-action operations in the North, and communicating with key figures across the country about the significance of Montgomery. King was very fond of Rustin, a bona-fide intellectual who could talk with him about philosophical matters, and enjoyed his company immensely. King had so little time to read and reflect these days, what with the boycott demanding almost all of his time, and he found Rustin a marvelous source of information on the latest studies of pacifism and nonviolence.

Rustin was worried about King, though. "Martin," he said one day, "I don't see how you can make the challenge you are making here without a very real possibility of your being murdered, and I wonder if you have made your peace with that." Rustin added: "I have the feeling the Lord has laid his hands on you, and that is a dangerous, dangerous thing."

According to Rustin, Daddy King made a final effort in this period to fetch his son home to Atlanta. He called King, Coretta, and Rustin to a prayer session and enlisted the Lord in his efforts to get King out of Montgomery, talking to God about how his boy had done his duty here and how the safety of his family was now the important thing. Rustin noticed that King was weeping. "Daddy," he said, "you ought not to do this to me." Then: "You know, I will have to pray this through myself."

But humiliating though it was, the prayer session proved a liberating moment in King's life, Rustin said. After that, he was firmer with his father than Rustin had seen him before. He would say, "Now, Daddy, I know how you feel. If you want to debate this with me, I'm willing to debate it. But I want you to know that this I've got to do."

ON MARCH 19, King's trial began in the old Montgomery County courthouse, with more than five hundred Negroes milling about outside. King entered the crumbling courtroom pursued by a gaggle of American and European reporters. He waved to Coretta, A. D., Christine, Daddy King, and friends and supporters from as far away as Michigan and New York. On the bench was Judge Eugene Carter, a stern man who taught a Bible class. Warning the mostly Negro audience that "this ain't no vaudeville," the judge ordered the hall cleared of spectators. But the courtroom was almost always filled with blacks, many wearing improvised white crosses that read, "Father, forgive them."

The first to be tried of the eighty-nine Negroes indicted by the grand jury, King sat at the front with MIA attorney Fred Gray and a battery of high-powered lawyers from Alabama and the New York office of the NAACP, which assumed King's legal costs. Though he and his counsel had little hope for justice in a southern court, they were still well prepared, for they wanted to prove that Negroes could argue as diligently and forcefully as whites.

In the defendant's chair, King watched transfixed as rival white and Negro lawyers haggled over the legality of the boycott. When Mayor Gayle took the stand, a Negro attorney cunningly asked if a black defendant worked for him as a maid. "No, sir, she don't," the mayor said. King and the other Negroes gave a smile: a black lawyer had made a white man say "sir" to him.

As the trial dragged on, the defense summoned a parade of witnesses to demonstrate that the Negroes had legal reason and just cause for boycotting a bus company that abused them so. One woman recounted how a policeman had shot and killed her husband after a run-in with a white driver. Another told how a driver had slammed the door on her blind husband and driven away with his leg caught in the door. The bus went some distance before the man got free. King felt a tender sadness as these "simple people—most of them unlettered—sat on the witness stand without fear and told their stories." Then it was King's turn to take the stand. He was self-possessed and forthright as the prosecution interrogated him. When he stepped down, the Negroes in the courtroom applauded so loudly that the judge had to pound his gavel for order.

On March 22 the rival lawyers gave their summations. At once the judge found King guilty and fined him $500 and court costs—equivalent of 386 days at hard labor. Surprised at the speed of the verdict, King's attorneys made it clear that they would appeal; and the judge entered a continuance for the other indicted Negro leaders, until final appeal action in King's case. When a reporter asked him about King and the boycotters, the judge grunted that "they didn't seem like Communists."

As King left the courtroom, newsmen bombarded him with questions: Would he call off the boycott? What were his plans now? King had pulled his hat down tightly on his head and clenched his right fist. "The judge's verdict will not increase or decrease in any way my interest in the protest. The protest goes on!" At sight of King, the crowd outside broke into cheers. "Hail King!" a Negro cried. "Hail *the* King!" someone else shouted. "King *is* King!" yelled another.

King was smiling when he drove away. He was proud to be a convicted criminal and proud of his crime. It was the crime of leading a nonviolent protest against injustice and trying to instill a new self-respect in his people. On this cloudy afternoon, he thought, Judge Carter had convicted more than Martin Luther King, Jr., case number 7399. He had convicted every Negro in Montgomery. For they were all bound together in a common purpose, drawn close by their shared trials and by the tactics of their opponents. Their opponents could not understand what was going on in Montgomery because their methods were aimed at the old Negro. But they were dealing with a new Negro in the South today, a Negro "with a new sense of dignity and destiny."

K ING'S ARREST AND TRIAL made the boycott national front-page news and brought reporters streaming into town to cover the Negro mass movement now rocking the cradle of the Confederacy. "This city became an international stamping grounds for newspapermen from everywhere," said B. J. Simms. They came from all over America, from England, France, and India, from China, Japan, Malaysia, and the Philippines.

The big story, of course, was King, and reporters and television people swarmed after him like hornets. King handled them with great eclat, for he understood the power of a favorable press. In one press conference, a reporter asked about the Communist charge, and King "proceeded to give a perfectly beautiful little thumbnail sketch of the development of Marxism and how he differed from this," said an adviser from FOR. "He used with ease and explained carefully the teachings of Feuerbach, Hegel, Marx, Engels, and so on, just very casually and easily. Then he said that he, himself, was a man of nonviolence." The reporters were enthralled. They had never met a Negro like King in their lives.

Neither had people who witnessed him on television. Neither had they seen a Negro speak with such eloquence and erudition about the promise of America and the aspirations of "her citizens of color" to gain their full citizenship. "We were then, without knowing it, into the era of electronic perception of the world and our own history," wrote a sensitive white journalist named Pat Watters, a southerner. King's ringing oratory, carried into millions of homes by the power of television, electrified an entire generation of Negro Americans, especially the young, who sent love letters cascading into his home and church office. "THANK YOU, THANK YOU, THANK YOU," wrote a young woman from the Bronx in New York. "You are truly a remarkable person; a great leader and a courageous fellow citizen. We are all very proud of you as our leader in the fight for human dignity." Everywhere she went in New York black people were talking about King. "For years to come—for centuries hence—as long as human existence—the name of Martin Luther King, Jr., will sing triumphantly in the hearts and souls of mankind." And whites wrote him, too, praising his "wise and statesmanlike leadership" and his "success in leading your people through one of the world's greatest tribulations." But it was the black masses that he touched the most, for he gave them (as Harry Belafonte phrased it) a "personal direction and . . . a personal sense of hope and identity."

But there was hate mail as always, a blizzard of racist diatribes from as far away as California and Maine. Clearly King was getting to American segregationists, or they would not have responded to him with such desperate bombast and at such length. Some of these letters ran from ten to twenty pages. Remarkably enough, King answered some of his hateful correspondents. He would thank them for taking the time to write him, though "I must confess that I am in total disagreement with your views." Then he would set their views straight with a calm and judicious argument, citing in particular New Testament passages which demonstrated "that segregation is a tragic evil that is unchristian."

But he was getting tired from all his work, extremely tired. "Frankly, I worry about him," Coretta told a reporter. "He never has a minute to himself. When he isn't in court, he is attending meetings of the MIA. When he's home, he's always on the phone. People call him from all over the country. I try to protect him as much as possible so that he can rest, but there is little that I can do." Though he had once required seven to eight hours of sleep, he now got by on a few hours a night. Sometimes he would get so tired that he would put his head on his desk for a catnap, or pull two chairs together and lie down for a few precious moments of oblivion. But most of the time, he wrote Rustin, "I find myself so involved I hardly have time to breathe."

His work was so overwhelming that he could no longer do it alone. Consequently the MIA provided him with a permanent office and an executive assistant and secretaries to answer his phone, deal with his voluminous correspondence, and account for contributions, which poured in from all over the world. The largest donors were church groups, especially Negro churches. But money came from various other organizations too—$2,000 from A. Philip Randolph's Brotherhood of Sleeping Car Porters, $1,000 from the National Negro Funeral Directors Association, and thousands of dollars from NAACP national and local chapters. King, for his part, was scrupulously honest in handling contributions. "In the position that I find myself in at this time," he wrote, "I am extremely vulnerable, and it is necessary to be extremely cautious."

In May and June there was a flurry of court activity about the buses. First, the Montgomery bus company dropped its segregated seating policy, only to be overruled by an order from an Alabama circuit court that segregation on the buses must continue. Two days later, on May 11, King was in federal court when a three-judge panel opened hearings on the case the MIA had filed in February, which claimed that bus segregation violated the Fourteenth Amendment. For King, it was a relief to be in a federal court, what with the "tragic sabotage of justice in the city and state courts of the South." But in the federal courts the Negro had an honest chance for justice. In June the federal panel ruled that the Alabama bus laws were unconstitutional, and lawyers for the city of Montgomery at once filed an appeal to the U.S. Supreme Court. Montgomery now operated under conflicting court orders—one from a federal court against segregated buses, another from a state court maintaining Jim Crow seating patterns. The issue would have to be settled by the U.S. Supreme Court, as Nixon had wanted all along.

Meanwhile King set out on a grueling coast-to-coast speaking tour that lasted through the spring and summer. His national fame brought people flocking to churches, auditoriums, and convention halls, to hear him relate "The Montgomery Story" and expound a world view of great historical and spiritual insight. The Negroes of Montgomery, he told his audiences, are proving how far we have come since the Negro first landed in America in 1619, only to end up as the white man's slave—as "a depersonalized cog in a vast plantation machine." In time Negroes lost faith in themselves and succumbed to the white-supremacist argument that they were nobody, a race of inferiors. "The tragedy of physical slavery was that it gradually led to the paralysis of mental slavery," King said; "the Negroes' mind and soul became enslaved." But there were whites who had a nagging conscience and realized what a monstrous moral contradiction it was that slavery should exist in a country based on the proposition that all men are created equal. There was Thomas Jefferson, who wrote of slavery that "I tremble for my country when I reflect that God is just." There was Abraham Lincoln—King's favorite white hero—who overcame his vacillations about slavery and issued the Emancipation Proclamation. But emancipation did not bring full freedom to the Negro, for "the pharaohs of the South," supported by the U.S. Supreme Court, shackled him with racial segregation, "a new form of slavery disguised by certain niceties of complexity." And too many Negroes accepted their "place" in the Jim Crow system, thus becoming a party to "a pagan peace" that lasted well into the twentieth century.

But then something happened to the Negro, King said. He renounced this pagan peace and started fighting for his rights in the federal courts. At the same time, Negro veterans returning from World War II demanded justice in a country that had fought a war in part against racism, and Negroes themselves battled for the right to vote. Then came the Montgomery bus boycott, a mass movement that ignited ordinary black people and brought them for the first time into the struggle for equality. Yes, something happened to the Negro, and it was the realization that he was *somebody*.

Still, King warned, we must be realistic in our movement. We must avoid extreme optimism—the notion that "we have come a long way" and have nothing to do but await the inevitable. We must also avoid extreme pessimism—the notion that "we have come nowhere" and can do nothing to alter our lives. We must say realistically that we have come a long way, but still have a long way to go. We must realize that change does not roll in "on the wheels of inevitability," but comes through continuous struggle. And so we must straighten our backs and work for our own freedom. A man can't ride you unless your back is bent. We stand today between two worlds—the dying old order and the emerging new. With men of ill will greeting this change with cries of violence, some of us may get beaten. Some of us may even get killed. But we're not going to stop until we've won our full freedom now—in this century—and redeemed the soul of America. Today, psychologists have a favorite word, and that word is maladjust-

64748

ed. I tell you today that there are some things in our social system to which I am proud to be maladjusted. I shall never be adjusted to lynch mobs, segregation, economic inequalities, "the madness of militarism," and self-defeating physical violence. The salvation of the world lies in the maladjusted. By resisting nonviolently, with love and unrelenting courage, we Negroes can speed up the coming of a new world "in which men will live together as brothers; a world in which men will beat their swords into ploughshares and their spears into pruning hooks; a world in which men will no longer take necessities from the masses to give luxuries to the classes; a world in which all men will respect the dignity and worth of all human personality."

But as he crisscrossed the country, there were grim reminders that Martin Luther King—orator, philosopher, and historian of love—was still a Negro in a white man's land. On his way to Nashville one day, he tried to board a train through the white waiting room, only to be accosted by a policeman who threatened to kill him if he ever came there again. On another trip, his plane was delayed in Atlanta, and the airlines gave him and the white passengers complimentary meals at a nearby restaurant. The host, though, refused to seat King in the main dining room with the other passengers, instead ushering him back to a dingy compartment that concealed him from view. King was livid. It was the train ride from Connecticut all over again. "I would rather go a week without eating before eating under such conditions," he protested, and demanded to see the management. Then he stalked out, threatening to sue the place for insulting him so.

By the fall, all the traveling and speechmaking were taking their toll on him. His doctor ordered him to slow up lest he damage his health. In late October, in between public appearances and a medical examination at Boston's Lahey Clinic, King found time to speak in a lecture series at Boston University. While there he managed to escape to Harold DeWolf's house for dinner and conversation. He confessed how badly he needed a rest, and he and DeWolf talked about arranging a retreat for him in Boston, a sanctuary where he could be alone for "spiritual renewal and writing."

Roland Emerson Haynes, a Negro friend and student in the Boston University School of Theology, heard him speak in the lecture series and wrote him that it was a "most powerful address (I call it a sermon)." But he could not forget how harried King looked. "One wonders how one can effectively play the role of Pastor, Husband, Father

and Public Leader when every role demands so much from the individual. . . . You have a rare talent and an ingenious mind. I guess I
sound like an old man talking to you in this fashion; but M. L., I am
still concerned in your health and the continued success of the movement."

King was back in Montgomery when the city struck again, this
time at the very heart of the bus protest. On October 30, city attorneys
asked Judge Carter to enjoin the car pool as "a public nuisance" and
"a private enterprise" operating without a franchise. If the judge
agreed, the Negroes would all have to walk.

King fell into gloom. Another winter was approaching, and his
people were really tired. "If the city officials get this injunction
against the car pool—and they will get it—I'm afraid our people will
go back to the buses," King told Coretta. "It's just too much to ask
them to continue if we don't have transportation for them."

On November 12, the day before the court hearing, King faced his
people in a subdued mass meeting. He "almost shrank" from speaking
to them. He didn't know what to say. "They had backed us up," he
said later, "and we had let them down. It was a desolate moment. I
saw, all of us saw, that the court was leaning against us." Was the
boycott going to fail then? Almost twelve months of protest done in
vain? "We have moved all of these months with the daring faith that
God was with us in our struggle," he told his followers that night.
"The many experiences of days gone by have vindicated that faith in
a marvelous way. Tonight we must believe that a way will be found
out of no way."

The next day King was in court again, listening in despair as the
city demanded $15,000 in damages for the boycott and argued that
the car pool be shut down. As chief defendant, King sat at the front
table with the defense and prosecution, certain that Judge Carter
would find for the city. "The clock said it was noon," he remembered,
"but it was midnight in my soul."

During a recess at noon, King noticed a commotion at the back of
the room. In a moment an Associated Press reporter ran up with a
piece of paper. "Here is the decision you have been waiting for," he
exclaimed. "Read this release." King glanced over it with his heart
pounding.

The United States Supreme Court today affirmed a decision of
a special three-judge U.S. District Court in declaring Alabama's

state and local laws requiring segregation on buses unconstitutional.

King could scarcely believe what he read. He hurried back to share the miraculous news with Nixon, Abernathy, and Coretta. "God Almighty," a bystander cried, "has spoken from Washington, D.C."

Visibly distressed, Judge Carter and the city officials nevertheless proceeded with the courtroom charade, with Carter enjoining the car pool as almost everyone expected. For his part, King thought it all ironic. On the same day that the local court dissolved the car pool, the United States Supreme Court removed the conditions that had made it necessary.

Segregationists, of course, reacted to the Supreme Court order with a fusillade of threats. "Any attempt to enforce this decision will inevitably lead to riot and bloodshed," warned a member of the White Citizens' Council. Other whites threatened to hang any Supreme Court Justice—especially "that damn Hugo Black"—who set foot in this sovereign state. "If you allow the niggers to go back on the buses and sit in the front seats," said a note that came to King, "we're going to burn down fifty houses in one night, including yours."

That night forty carloads of robed and hooded Klansmen rumbled into Montgomery's Negro section, determined to scare the residents back into behaving the way "niggers" were supposed to. Usually they locked themselves in their homes when the Klan rode through their neighborhoods. But not this night. With doors open and porch lights ablaze, black folk watched and even waved as the motorcade went by. "They acted as though they were watching a circus parade," King rejoiced. "No one fears the Klan or the White Citizens' Council."

The next night thousands of jubilant Negroes crowded into Holt Street Baptist Church, the church where the boycott had begun almost a year before. In the invocation, MIA official S. S. Seay started crying from happiness. All over the church people wept and shouted for joy. Then Bob Graetz created a sensation when he read from I Corinthians: "When I was a child, I spoke as a child, I understood as a child, I thought as a child: but when I became a man, I put away childish things." In the course of business, the people voted to stay off the buses until the Supreme Court mandate reached Montgomery. Then King stood before them, and the great throng fell silent. "I would be terribly disappointed," he said, "If any of you go back to the buses bragging, 'We, the Negroes, won a victory over the white people.' We must take this not as victory over the white man but as a victory for justice and democracy. Don't go back on the buses and push people around. . . . We are just going to sit where there's a seat."

But then he said: "In the past, we have sat in the back of the buses, and this has indicated a basic lack of self-respect. It shows that we thought of ourselves as less than men. On the other hand, the white people have sat in front and have thought of themselves as superior. They have tried to play God. Both approaches are wrong. Our duty in going back on the buses is to destroy this superior-inferior relationship. . . . It is our duty to act in the manner best designed to establish man's oneness."

All over the church black people were clapping now, singing and shouting in praise of their leader. "Look at the way they greet that guy," said a white reporter. "They think he's a Messiah."

"MAY GOD CONTINUE TO BLESS YOU that you may reach higher heights," an old family friend wrote King in the wake of victory. "Your future is unlimited. You have a Ph.D. degree. You are beautifully married. You are humble. You are sweet. You have forty fruitful years before you. There is no position in any church, religious body, University and etc., which you could not fill. I have picked you for three outstanding positions in our race. I will be glad to risk my prophecy on that."

"Your fight for the cause of justice is supported by the prayers of thinking people everywhere," wrote an anonymous white woman. "God is no respecter of persons, and He is on the side of right. You have shown that you are on that side, and the Montgomery Negroes are very fortunate to have your wise and sane counsel and leadership. The city of Montgomery should be grateful to have you in its midst." She added, "Please forgive me for making this an anonymous letter. Not all of us have your forthright courage."

Instead of being grateful to "nigger" King, the city fathers assured white Montgomery: "The City Commission, and we know our people are with us in this determination, will not yield one inch, but will do all in its power to oppose the integration of the Negro race with the white race in Montgomery and will forever stand like a rock against social equality, inter-marriage, and mixing of the races under God's creation and plan."

Despite their irrational fears, King kept trying to reach the city commissioners: he warned them that violence could break out over integrated buses and pleaded with them to make a public statement, urging whites to obey the law of the land. But the commissioners did nothing, nothing at all, to prepare white Montgomery for the Supreme Court mandate.

Then it is up to us to avoid racial incidents, King said. In church workshops on nonviolence, he and his associates led Negroes through role-playing "socio-dramas" in which they acted out potential black-white conflicts on integrated buses. At the same time, King reminded his people over and over to abide by the Gandhian faith he had instilled in them throughout the protest. And the MIA even got out leaflets that urged blacks to be courteous and dignified, relying on "moral and spiritual force" to protect them from potential white retaliation.

For a week in early December, King and the MIA hosted an Institute on Nonviolence, to commemorate the anniversary of the start of the boycott and to discuss the power of nonviolent resistance. From across the Republic came distinguished white and black social scientists, religious and cultural leaders, politicians and lawyers, to give papers and make proposals on how nonviolence could improve American race relations in the light of the Montgomery victory. In the keynote address, called "Facing the Challenge of a New Age," King reminded the delegates—and all Americans beyond—that they were living in "one of the most momentous periods of human history," a transitional era in which the old order of white supremacy and exploitation was dying out and a new era of world community fast approaching. Yes, it was a painful time—all periods of great change were painful—but what a glorious new world awaited them, a world of "geographical togetherness" in which all people would rise above the "narrow confines of our individualistic concerns to the broader concerns of humanity.".

Then he addressed himself to the dispirited poor in his ranks, the Negroes who toiled as America's domestics and common laborers. "Whatever your life's work is, do it well," King said. "A man should do his job so well that the living, the dead, and the unborn could do it no better. If it falls your lot to be a street sweeper, sweep streets like Michelangelo painted pictures, like Shakespeare wrote poetry, like Beethoven composed music; sweep streets so well that all the host of Heaven and earth will have to pause and say, 'Here lived a great street sweeper, who swept his job well.'" Then he quoted Douglas Malloch:

If you can't be a pine on the top of the hill
Be a scrub in the valley—but be
The best little scrub by the side of the hill.
Be a bush if you can't be a tree.

He went on to outline what the Negro must struggle for in the coming new age. We must seek the ballot, he said, so that we will no longer be the "convenient tools of unscrupulous politicians." With the ballot, Negroes could help break up the unholy coalition of southern segregationists and northern reactionaries that dominated Congress and whipped back civil-rights legislation introduced there. Second, Negroes themselves must work for positive social legislation, to guarantee their rights as U.S. citizens and to prevent white segregationists from lynching them. Third, Negroes must invest their own economic resources in their cause. Their annual income now stood at $16 billion—almost the size of Canada's—and could be profitably used to facilitate Negro freedom on these shores.

Above all, Negroes must unite in a true mass movement based on nonviolence. "Our defense is to meet every act of violence toward an individual Negro with the fact that there are thousands of others who will present themselves in his place as potential victims. Every time one school teacher is fired for standing up courageously for justice, it must be faced with the fact that there are four thousand more to be fired. If the oppressors bomb the home of one Negro for his courage, this must be met with the fact that they must be required to bomb the homes of fifty thousand more Negroes. This dynamic unity, this amazing self-respect, this willingness to suffer, and this refusal to hit back will soon cause the oppressor to become ashamed of his own methods." And this will lead to that new day when we in America can live together in Christian brotherhood, and "when this day finally comes, 'The morning stars will sing together and the sons of God will shout for joy.'"

On December 20, the Supreme Court mandate finally reached Montgomery, and early the next day King, Abernathy, Nixon, and Glenn Smiley, a southern-born white minister of the Fellowship of Reconciliation, climbed aboard the first integrated bus. King and Smiley sat together in the formerly all-white section, southern-born black and white preachers riding side by side in symbolic tribute to that new order King had prophesied. On the buses that day, King happily noted that most whites accepted integrated seating without incident. True, one old man stood in the aisle muttering, "I would rather die and go to hell than sit behind a nigger." And a white woman slumped imperviously beside a Negro, only to leap up when she saw who it was. "What," she cried, "are these niggers gonna do next?" On another bus, a white man actually slapped a Negro woman, but she refused to strike back. "I could have broken that little fellow's neck all by myself," she said afterward, "but I left the mass meeting last night determined to do what Reverend King asked."

Still, King was troubled that most Negro riders—especially old folk—flocked to the backs of the buses. "Reverend," an old woman told him, "I know I can sit in front but I just goes to my old place." King realized that it would take time for such people to overcome habitual servility, but he had faith that they would do so (and ultimately they did). But he was glad to see young people and professionals boldly sitting in front as he did.

So it was that desegregated buses came at last to Montgomery, Alabama, but at an enormous cost. So that a black human being could sit beside a white human being, the MIA had spent $225,000 in court, transportation, and other expenses, the bus company had lost more than $250,000 in revenues, the city several thousand dollars in taxes, and downtown merchants several million dollars in business. "Oh, it pains me deeply when I think of the brain power and the man hours that we have poured into this thing," lamented the wife of a Negro physician. "Think how many constructive things we could do for the city if they did not force us to spend every second struggling for basic dignity."

And though it catapulted him to national fame, the boycott had cost King, too. In his annual report to Dexter, he commented on how much his "unbelievable schedule" as protest leader had threatened his health and balance. "Almost every week—having to make so many speeches, attend so many meetings, meet so many people, write so many articles, counsel with so many groups—I face the frustration of feeling that in the midst of so many things to do I am not doing anything well." But he thanked his congregation for standing by him when his critics—Negro and white alike—had tried "to cut me down and lessen my influence."

B Y CHRISTMAS, 1956, Negroes in three other southern cities had launched bus protests like that in Montgomery, and King kept in close contact with the leaders. Reverend Fred Shuttlesworth headed a band of intrepid boycotters in Birmingham, Reverend C. K. Steele another down in Tallahassee, Florida, and several other Negro ministers still another in Mobile. With additional protests under way, Bayard Rustin approached King about the necessity of a permanent, southern-wide organization to unite the various protest groups and expand the movement across Dixie. King thought it a marvelous idea and urged Rustin to draw up plans. At that Rustin hurried back to New York to consult friends like attorney Stanley Levison about a permanent civil-rights organization "designed around Dr. King's charisma."

On December 28, a reign of terror erupted in Montgomery, as armed whites opened fire on buses all over town, shot a pregnant Negro woman in both legs, and pummeled a teenage Negro girl. The Klan marched in full regalia, and fiery crosses lit up the night sky. Someone reported seeing a little Negro boy warming his hands at a burning cross. Then on January 3, 1957, a white group invaded Negro neighborhoods, handing out leaflets allegedly signed by Negroes who were tired of "Liver Lip Luther King." "We get shot at while he walks," the leaflets said. "He is getting us in more trouble every day." He and his associates "ride high, eat good, stay warm and pilfer the funds." "Wake Up! Mess is His Business. Run Him Out of Town!"

As King knew, the white opposition hoped to frustrate the court's bus order through organized violence and psychological treachery, under the conviction that blacks would stop protesting and return to the old ways when confronted with white defiance. This convinced King all the more of the need for a southwide Negro organization to "extend and intensify the struggle." Summoning Rustin back from New York, he consulted with Shuttlesworth of Birmingham and Steele of Tallahassee. As they went over Rustin's plans, all agreed that the southern Negro church should be the initial point of organization, because it offered a powerful reservoir of leadership from which to draw and was overall the most widespread and effective institution in the black community through which to launch a mass movement. Supported by Shuttlesworth and Steele, King issued a call for a southern conference to meet in Atlanta on January 10 and 11 to plan organizational strategy.

Early in the morning of January 10, King and Abernathy were asleep in the King home in Atlanta when an urgent phone call came through from Abernathy's wife. His home and church had both been bombed. Subsequent calls indicated that other Negro dwellings had been dynamited and that all-out war seemed to have begun in Montgomery. King flew there with Abernathy and toured the bomb sites. All told, four churches and two parsonages lay smoking from terrorists' bombs, and angry crowds milled about in the debris. King begged them to remain nonviolent, but he too was appalled. What kind of people would do this anyway? "When they bomb the house of the Lord," said an old man, "we are dealing with crazy people."

Still, King took some consolation in the way white officialdom responded. The governor made a predawn inspection of the bombed-out churches and offered a $2,000 reward for the arrests of suspects. Moreover, whites for the first time went on record in defense of law and order: the editor of the Montgomery *Advertiser*, several white preachers, and the city's most influential business group all publicly condemned the bombings, the preachers calling them unchristian and uncivilized.

On January 11 King returned to the Atlanta meeting, more determined than ever to forge a powerful new regional organization that would inspire and unify his beleaguered people. Out of the Atlanta conference, attended by sixty Negro leaders from ten southern states, came a blazing manifesto that urged Negroes "to refuse further cooperation with the evil elements" and "no matter how great the obstacles and suffering . . . reject segregation." It summoned men of good will across the Republic to make America truly "the land of the free and the home of the brave," and implored President Eisenhower to visit the South and make a public statement that he would uphold the Supreme Court school and bus decisions (the White House replied that this was impossible). Then they made plans to meet again in New Orleans and set up a permanent southern organization centered around the church.

After the conference, King and Rustin got to talking about Gandhi and a statement he had made about American Negroes back in 1935. When asked to visit America and help blacks in their struggle for equality, Gandhi responded, "How I wish I could, but I must make good the message here before I bring it to you." Then he said, "It may be that through the American Negro the unadulterated message of nonviolence will be delivered to the world." For King, this was the mission of his long-suffering people, and he meant to carry it out.

Still, he returned to Montgomery in a deepening depression. It had started when he saw the wrecked churches and parsonages the previous Saturday in Montgomery. Now, home again, he heard his people talk in subdued and frightened voices: would the city use the bombings as a pretext to shut down the buses entirely and destroy all the gains of the protest? And whose churches and homes would be dynamited next? Whites had threatened several members of King's own congregation, and he worried that several of them might be bombed out, even killed.

King took all this personally, feeling a terrible guilt that the bombs and threats and anxieties of his people were *his* fault. On Monday night, he addressed a mass meeting, and for the first time broke down in public. Clutching the pulpit, his face contorted in pain, he invited the audience to join him in prayer—and then felt seized by an uncontrollable emotion. "Lord," he cried, "I hope no one will have to die as a result of our struggle for freedom in Montgomery. Certainly I don't want to die. But if anyone has to die, let it be me."

"No, no," his people chorused.

King could not continue his prayer. Two ministers came to the pulpit and tried to get him to sit down. For several minutes he stood with their arms around him, unable to move. Finally some friends helped him to a seat.

"Unexpectedly," King wrote later, "this episode brought me great relief." After the meeting, many people assured him that "we were all together until the end." But the incident was cathartic in another way too: by praying that he be killed if somebody must be, he freed himself from his guilt that *I am to blame, I have caused all this suffering.* He was ready to lead again. He felt strong again. He felt God beside him, and he did not fear to die. It was as though he had told the forces of evil in the universe: kill me if you will, but the forces of light shall never cease to struggle for righteousness.

Before dawn on Sunday, January 27, the forces of evil struck again, as terrorizing whites bombed a Negro home and a Negro service station and cab stand. Somebody found an unexploded bomb, consisting of twelve sticks of dynamite, still smoldering on King's own porch. In the chill morning, King addressed a gathering crowd from his porch, "Tell Montgomery that they can keep shooting and I'm going to stand up to them; tell Montgomery they can keep bombing and I'm going to stand up to them. If I had to die tomorrow morning I would die happy because I've been to the Mountaintop and I've seen the Promised Land, and it's going to be here in Montgomery."

Fearful that Montgomery might plunge into anarchy, the authorities indicted five whites for all the bombings that had rocked the city, and two even signed confessions and came to trial. On hand as a subpoenaed witness, King looked on as an all-white jury disregarded the confessions and found the two men innocent. Grinning, they walked out of the courtroom.

King feared that such a miscarriage of justice would lead to more bombings. Instead, the disturbances abruptly stopped, perhaps because most Montgomery whites accepted desegregated buses and deplored all the violence. Meanwhile, the city commissioners worked out a compromise with King regarding his appeal for violating the state anti-labor law: he agreed to pay his $500 fine and the city to drop the cases against the other 88 indicted Negro leaders (and against the other white bombing suspects too). King remarked to several Negro newsmen, "We decided the best thing to do was to pay the fine and move on to another phase of the struggle."

In the following weeks, as he spoke across the nation, people would often ask him, "How are things in Montgomery today?" And he would say, "Better; things are much better in Montgomery today." Not only were blacks and whites riding together wherever they liked, but a lot of whites there seemed to have gained respect for their black neighbors. "We've got to hand it to those Negroes," whites would say. "They had principles and they stuck to them and they stuck together. They organized and planned well." "We didn't think they had it in them." And whites had a grudging admiration for King, too. "Don't let anyone fool you," a taxi driver told a Texas writer. "That young colored preacher has got more brains in his little finger than the City Commissioners and all the politicians in this town put together."

Still, the boycott had hardly made Montgomery a paragon of racial justice. Apart from the buses, the city remained strictly segregated, with most whites clinging tenaciously to the traditional caste system and threatening intimidation and endless litigation to preserve segregated schools and prevent the coming of King's new order. What was more, the local press never tired of telling whites that civil war was still going on in Dixie—a civil war against "Yankees and race-mixing."

But if the boycott had not transformed the hearts of most whites, it had had a tremendous impact on Negroes themselves. As King said, the Negro in 1955 was "unarmed, unorganized, untrained, disunited and, most important, psychologically and morally unprepared for the deliberate spilling of blood." Then came the Montgomery way, which showed the mass of black folks a method that enabled them to shed their passivity without violence, for violence would only have gotten them killed. Thanks to the method of nonviolent resistance, thanks to King's own "tremendous facility," as Rustin put it, "for giving people the feeling that they could be bigger and stronger and more courageous than they thought they could be," an entire black community for the first time had mounted a sustained direct-action protest in Dixie, in the very heart of the Deep South. "We got our heads up now," said a Negro janitor in Montgomery, "and we won't ever bow down again—no, sir—except before God!" What was more, Montgomery demonstrated that the church—the supporting mechanism for the entire protest—"can be a great transforming power if it will be true to its mission," as King pointed out. In truth, said a Negro historian, King and his ministerial associates "are raising to new heights the historic role of the Negro minister as the leader in civil rights."

King himself was now immensely popular, hailed far and wide as one of the most learned and yet passionate social activists to emerge in his embattled nation up to that time. Yet "I am really disturbed how fast all this has happened to me," he confided in Coretta. "People will expect me to perform miracles for the rest of my life. I don't want to be the kind of man who hits his peak at twenty-seven, with the rest of his life an anticlimax. Neither do I want to disappoint people by not being able to pull rabbits out of a hat."

PART THREE

FREEDOM IS
NEVER FREE

King wondered if his life would ever slow down again. He received so many speaking invitations that it was almost impossible to answer them all. And job offers flooded in, too, tempting him with salaries up to $75,000 a year. When DeWolf wrote him about some faculty position, King replied that he was happy in the pastorate and had about decided that this was where he should serve. But "I can never quite get the idea out of my mind that I should do some teaching." Beyond solidifying the southern Negro leadership organization, he didn't know what he wanted to do for certain.

On February 18, 1957, *Time* magazine published a feature story about King called "Attack on the Conscience" and written by Lee Griggs of *Time*'s Atlanta office. The magazine ran King's picture on the cover and conveyed the name and message of this "scholarly Negro Baptist minister" to an enormous audience. "Personally humble, articulate, and of high educational attainment," Griggs wrote, "Martin Luther King Jr. is, in fact, what many a Negro—and, were it not for his color, many a white—would like to be." Noting that King wore conservative, funeral-gray suits, Griggs trailed him through a typically hectic day. At his MIA office, King toiled in a cramped back room with yellowed walls, laying plans for a Negro credit union and a voter-registration drive in Montgomery. All the while the telephone rang. After an exhausting day, King struck out for a mass meeting, where he spoke after a round of hymns: "If we as a people had as much religion in our hearts as we have in our legs and feet, we could change this world." Later that night, "the mass meeting a warm memory," King talked quietly about the principles on which his efforts were based: "Our use of passive resistance in Montgomery is not based on resistance to get rights for ourselves, but to achieve friendship with the men who are denying us our rights, and change them through friend-ship and a bond of Christian understanding before God." For a lot of people, Griggs wrote, this probably seemed impossible. "But so, only 14 months before, was the notion that whites and Negroes might be riding peaceably together on integrated buses in Montgomery, Ala."

Was King reaching the white South? Griggs quoted a white minis-ter and a former chaplain at the University of Mississippi: "I know of very few white Southern ministers who aren't troubled and don't have admiration for King. They've become tortured souls." King, too, thought Negroes were troubling the white southern conscience. In fact, even diehard white supremacists were disturbed; even they knew that segregation was an egregious sin against God. "If it weren't," as King later told *Playboy* magazine, "the white South would not be haunted as it is by a deep sense of guilt for what it has done to the Negro—guilt for patronizing him, degrading him, brutalizing him, de-personalizing him, thingifying him; guilt for lying to itself. This is the source of the schizophrenia that the South will suffer until it goes through its crisis of conscience."

In the heady aftermath of Montgomery, King tried to be realistic about the future. When the NAACP circled 1963 as the target year for the end of segregation in America, King declared this much too opti-mistic and designated 2000 as the more reasonable date.

I⊤ WAS MARCH 3, and King and Coretta were on an airplane bound for Ghana in West Africa. Ghana had recently won her independence from Great Britain, and Prime Minister Kwame Nkrumah had invited King and other American dignitaries to attend independence-day cer-emonies in Accra, Ghana's capital. On the trip over, King pondered the history of the world's "dark-skinned people"—there were 1.5 bil-lion of them—and how Europe had plundered and oppressed so many of them. But they were on the move now, everywhere "in revolt against social and political domination." This was the spirit of the age, King thought, and he equated the struggles of the American Negro with the independence movements of other dark-skinned folk in the world. In their own quest for full citizenship, black Americans were part of a global movement to throw off racial oppression.

The Kings reached Accra at night and stayed at a low stucco bungalow that belonged to an English professor and his wife. Here servants brought King breakfast and tended his every need, bowing and speaking in obsequious tones like American slaves of old. Their servile attitude disturbed and depressed him.

On March 5, he assembled with representatives of sixty-nine other nations in the square around the old British colonial building, to witness the official birth of independent Ghana. At last bells tolled midnight, and the flag of Ghana replaced the Union Jack as fifty thousand people cheered wildly. On a wooden platform stood Nkrumah, a tall man in the bright robe of his Akan tribe, proclaiming Ghana free at last of colonial rule. At that the crowd started chanting, "*Free*-dom, *free*-dom, *free*-dom!" And King was "struck by the idea of a new Jerusalem descending from God," "a new Heaven and a new earth" about to be born in this epochal time.

The next morning, King came down with a virus which made him violently ill. For a time he was certain he would die. As he lay in the bungalow, burning with fever, a celebrated Anglican clergyman named Michael Scott came for a visit. Dressed in flowing white robes, Scott knelt at King's bedside and prayed for his recovery. But sick as he was, King managed a dialogue with Scott: they both believed that Ghana was a model African state, irrefutable proof that Africans could manage their affairs and run their governments regardless of what European imperialists claimed. They also discussed apartheid in South Africa and compared it to the grim conditions in the American South. "At bottom," King said, "both segregation in America and colonialism in Africa were based on the same thing—white supremacy and contempt for life."

A few days later, King felt well enough to dine with Prime Minister Nkrumah, who had once been a student in the United States. King was one of his favorite Americans, he said, and the people who followed King in Montgomery had given him great hope.

At last it was time for the Kings to go, time to leave this memorable African land, and return to Montgomery by way of Nigeria, Rome, Paris, Geneva, and London. In Nigeria, King was shocked at the universal suffering he saw. He had never witnessed such squalor, not even in the rural American South. He "talked angrily" about the British exploitation of Africa and said he was glad that the sun no longer rose and set on the British empire. In Rome, at St. Peter's Cathedral, he was so overcome by all the history it symbolized that he fell to the floor and prayed.

Back in Montgomery, King said his visit to Africa—the "land of my father's fathers"—was one of the most vivid experiences of his life. It was "a nonviolent rebirth." And from that time on he remained passionately interested in African affairs. He did all he could to help educate African students in the United States, served with Eleanor Roosevelt and John Gunther on the American Committee on Africa, and amassed an impressive archive of clippings and magazine pieces about developments there. At the same time, he maintained a heavy correspondence with African leaders—among them, Chief Albert Luthuli of South Africa, who withstood abuse and persecution, King said, "with a dignity and calmness of spirit seldom paralleled in human history." As he studied that "vast and complex continent," he surely realized that not all of Africa's woes could be ascribed to European imperialism. Nigeria, for example, had internal stresses and strains that derived from its three very different regions, and other small emerging states suffered from endemic ills as well. But King didn't discuss this, at least not in his writings. He focused almost exclusively on the similarities between the American Negro movement and black Africa's own strivings against white oppression. "Although we are separated by many miles we are closer together in a mutual struggle for freedom and human brotherhood," he wrote dissenters in Southern Rhodesia. "We realize that injustice anywhere is a threat to justice everywhere. Therefore, we are as concerned about the problems of Africa as we are about the problems of the United States." He understood what they were going through and how difficult it was to challenge the racial status quo. "But in the final analysis it is such a creative minority that save history."

But concerned though he was about Africa, he emphatically opposed any modern back-to-Africa movement in the United States. When a Negro begged him to lead their people to Liberia or Ghana, King firmly replied: "To have a mass return to Africa would merely be running from the problem and not facing it courageously.... We are American citizens, and we deserve our rights in this nation. I feel that God has marvelous plans for this world and this nation and we must have the faith to believe that one day these plans will materialize."

On March 25, King was in New York, discussing plans for a Washington prayer pilgrimage with A. Philip Randolph and Roy Wilkins of the NAACP. It was a critical time for American Negroes, with segregationists in Dixie undertaking an all-out campaign to obliterate Negro voting gains over the last decade and to obstruct school desegregation in a variety of devious ways. In Congress, progressive forces were promoting a new civil-rights bill, drafted by Eisenhower's Justice Department (the catalyst was Attorney General Herbert Brownell, not the President), which among other things would protect Negro rights in voting, education, and housing. But southern segregationists and northern reactionaries vowed to annihilate the bill should it ever come to a vote. In the view of King and his colleagues, Negroes themselves must pressure Congress to enact the bill, as well as dramatize the overall plight of America's "citizens of color." And all three thought a prayer pilgrimage to Washington, drawing thousands of Negroes from across the land, could best accomplish that purpose.

Randolph and Wilkins were the two most powerful Negro leaders in America, and King found it hard to believe that he was meeting with them as an equal. Fifty-five now, Wilkins was NAACP executive secretary, a slim, brown-skinned man with a small mustache and a wry smile. A native of St. Louis, he had studied journalism at the University of Minnesota and gone on to edit the Kansas City *Call* during the 1920s. In 1931, he joined the NAACP and worked in the New York office, where he succeeded Du Bois as editor of *The Crisis*, the NAACP's official publication, and in 1955 became the leader of the national organization. Urbane though he was, Wilkins lacked charisma—he was a writer, not an orator—and King's enormous popularity. In truth, this able and educated man was jealous of King and fretful that his projected new organization would compete with the NAACP.

By contrast, Randolph genuinely admired young King and treated him with avuncular warmth. Head of the Brotherhood of Sleeping Car Porters, the strongest Negro union in the country, Randolph was sixty-eight now, a tall broad-shouldered man who spoke in a magnetic baritone. In his youth, he had wanted to be an actor and liked to recite Shakespeare in rolling cadences. Later, at the City College of New York, he read Marx, decided that economics was the basis of racial injustice, and mounted the soapbox to orate on "everything from the French Revolution and the history of slavery, to the rise of the working class." When the United States entered World War I, the Wilson administration branded him "the most dangerous Negro in America" because he had the temerity to question why Negroes should fight for a nation that oppressed them. After the war, Randolph became the irrepressible chief of the porters union and dedicated himself to the proposition that trade unionism was the best solution to the social problems of blacks and whites alike. "We never separated the liberation of the white workingman from the liberation of the black workingman," he said.

King all but idolized "Mr. Randolph" and considered him America's greatest living Negro. He rejoiced, too, that both Randolph and Wilkins agreed that "the spiritual undergirding of our common struggle" must be stressed in this darkening hour. At a subsequent meeting, they and seventy-four other Negro leaders issued a call for "a Prayer Pilgrimage for Freedom," to take place on May 17—the third anniversary of the Brown decision—at the Lincoln Memorial in Washington. Meeting there, King knew, would emphasize the historical and symbolic ties of the civil-rights movement and the Civil War era. He himself liked to point out that the movement was an extension of the Civil War, that Negroes of his day were struggling to realize the promise of Lincoln's Emancipation Proclamation.

When the celebrated event came, King was disappointed in the turnout. He had hoped for 75,000 Negroes to gather at the Lincoln Memorial, but the actual crowd was estimated at from 15,000 to 37,000. After a procession of other Negroes had sung and spoken, King treated the throng to the kind of rousing oratory for which he had become famous, his voice booming over the loudspeakers as the statue of Lincoln looked on. In fact, King launched into a defense of Negro suffrage that seemed to take up where Lincoln had left off in his last public address, given in Washington on April 11, 1865. In that speech, Lincoln had endorsed limited Negro suffrage in the conquered South and granted outright that the black man deserved the electoral franchise. Now, standing in Lincoln's "symbolic shadow," King proclaimed that "so long as I do not firmly and irrevocably possess the right to vote I do not possess myself. . . . So our most urgent request to the President of the United States and every member of Congress is to give us the right to vote." Then he took off on an oratorical flight that set the crowd to clapping and echoing him:

"Give us the ballot [*give us the ballot*] . . . and we will transform the salient misdeeds of bloodthirsty mobs into the abiding good deeds of orderly citizens.

"Give us the ballot [*give us the ballot*] . . . and we will fill our legislative halls with men of goodwill, and send to the sacred halls of Congress men who will not sign a southern manifesto because of their devotion to the manifesto of justice.

"Give us the ballot [*give us the ballot*] . . . and we will place judges on the benches of the south who will 'do justly and love mercy,' and we will place at the head of the southern states governors who have felt not only the tang of the human but the glow of the Divine. . . .

"We come humbly to say to the men in the forefront of our government that the Civil Rights issue is not an ephemeral, evanescent domestic issue that can be kicked about by reactionary guardians of the status quo; it is rather an eternal moral issue which may well determine the destiny of our nation in the ideological struggle with Communism. The hour is late. The clock of destiny is ticking out. We must act now, before it is too late."

The *Amsterdam News* of New York, a Negro journal, praised King effusively for his address and asserted that he "emerged from the Prayer Pilgrimage to Washington as the number one leader of sixteen million Negroes in the United States."

"AFTER LIVING IN THE SOUTH ALL MY LIFE," King wrote a Michigan congressman, "I have come to see through grim experience that the southern reactionaries will never fall in line voluntarily; it will only come through proper, moral, and legitimate pressure"—especially from Congress and the President.

But the President seemed indifferent to southern recalcitrance and aloof from the congressional debates now raging over the civil-rights bill. So far, he had even refused to make a public defense of the Brown decision. The President's inaction offended King, who believed that much of the South's current racial trouble could have been avoided had Eisenhower exercised strong executive leadership.

On June 13, King and Abernathy visited for two and a half hours with Vice-President Richard Nixon, in hopes that he might be persuaded to influence his boss. In graphic terms, King described the southern white opposition to school desegregation, Negro enfranchisement, and integrated transportation. Abernathy added that southern Negroes were determined to gain their full citizenship, that segregationists were equally dedicated to stopping them, and that most southern whites were strung out between the two positions. But if they preferred segregation, most southerners would obey the law if Eisenhower chose to enforce it.

Though Nixon stoutly defended the President, King thought he seemed concerned about civil rights. "His travels have revealed to him how the race problem is hurting America in international relations," King later told Nixon biographer Earl Mazo, "and it is altogether possible that he has no racial prejudice." Still, King had his suspicions about the Vice-President. "He is one of the most magnetic personalities that I have ever confronted," with "a genius for convincing one that he is sincere. When you are close to Nixon he almost disarms you with his apparent sincerity. You never get the impression that he is the same man who . . . made a tear jerking speech on television in the 1952 campaign to save himself from an obvious misdeed. . . . If Richard Nixon is not sincere, he is the most dangerous man in America."

As it turned out, the Nixon interview was a waste of time, since the President himself remained inert in the matter of civil rights. On Capitol Hill, meanwhile, Senator Lyndon Baines Johnson of Texas herded the civil-rights bill through a stormy Senate. But to do so he bartered away the most significant provision in it—one that would have given the U.S. Attorney General injunctive power to enforce school desegregation and various other civil rights. Among other things, the final version of the bill authorized the Attorney General to seek injunctions in the matter of voting rights, and it created an independent advisory agency called the Civil Rights Commission. Though it was the first civil-rights legislation enacted since Reconstruction, King and other Negroes were unhappy with the 1957 Civil Rights Act because it ignored the school problem and other crucial issues. To make matters worse, Eisenhower's Justice Department proceeded to enforce the measure "with all deliberate lethargy," as one writer phrased it.

With the white South obstructing school desegregation and wiping out Negro voting rights in one state after another, King called 115 Negro leaders to Montgomery to plan a counter-offensive. Meeting on

August 7 and 8, the delegates formed the Southern Christian Leadership Conference, which King and Rustin had been working on since January, and unanimously chose King as president. In fact, the new organization centered almost entirely on King's prestige and popularity—"King *was* the Southern Christian Leadership Conference," said one insider. Unlike the NAACP, which was a membership organization, SCLC consisted entirely of local affiliates, each of which would send five voting delegates to SCLC's conventions—held biannually at first, then annually. As King envisioned it, the organization would operate through the southern Negro church and function as a service agency to coordinate local civil-rights activity.

SCLC's main goal was to bring the Negro masses into the freedom struggle by expanding "the Montgomery way" across the South. In this respect, it differed significantly from the other major civil-rights organizations. The National Urban League, founded in 1911, concentrated on improving Negro life in northern cities, doing little for the black masses in Dixie. CORE, established in 1942, had applied Gandhian direct-action techniques to the American scene, mostly in northern cities. But apart from outposts in St. Louis and Washington, D.C., CORE had failed to penetrate the South and remained largely a northern operation. By 1957, in fact, CORE was at its nadir as an effective civil-rights organization, lacking even a field staff to coordinate its scattered and piecemeal efforts. The NAACP, of course, continued to concentrate on legal action and court battles. But many influential Negroes thought it had become complacent and elitist now, largely insensitive to the suffering of the Negro masses, especially in the South. In any case, since the national executive had failed to implement many of the NAACP's court victories, a strictly legal strategy seemed ineffectual. Now King and his ministerial associates hoped to offer an alternative: a nonviolent, grassroots movement in Dixie under SCLC's banners.

SCLC's initial project was a southern-wide voter registration drive called the Crusade for Citizenship, to commence on Lincoln's birthday, 1958, and to demonstrate once again that "a new Negro, determined to be free, has emerged in America." Because *the right to vote does not raise the issue of social mixing to confuse the main argument,"* King hoped the campaign would attract the support of southern white moderates. SCLC, for its part, would conduct voting clinics across Dixie, gather evidence on white obstructionism, and utilize the media to educate Americans on the plight of the southern Negro.

To assist King, SCLC's founders provided for a central office in Atlanta and planned to raise an operating fund of $250,000, mainly through donations. Prim and principled Ella Baker became temporary executive director, charged with running the Atlanta office and overseeing the voting-rights drive. She came at the recommendation of both Bayard Rustin and Stanley Levison, a King friend and financial adviser in New York. Several years older than King, Baker dreamed of creating a true mass movement through SCLC, one that would stress collective enterprise over individual initiative. She resented all the attention being put on King and complained that SCLC was much too leader-oriented rather than the mass organizational force she had in mind. King clashed with her over this, asserting that he was going to lead because "the people" wanted him to.

To keep harmony within civil-rights ranks, King hastened up to New York and had a long talk with Wilkins and other NAACP leaders, assuring them that SCLC's approach supported and supplemented theirs. While the NAACP focused on legal strategy, SCLC would concern itself with "spiritual strategy"—with raising the moral conscience of America. As King repeatedly said, there was no single road to the promised land. It was imperative that Negroes advance on a united front along several parallel paths—one led by SCLC, another by the NAACP, still others by CORE and the Urban League.

That September, newspapers screamed with headlines about a school crisis in Little Rock, Arkansas. A federal court had ordered Central High School there to admit nine Negro students. But Governor Orval Faubus deployed the Arkansas National Guard around the school with orders to keep the blacks out. A fifteen-year-old Negro named Elizabeth Eckford, wearing bobby socks and ballet slippers, approached the school with her notebook, only to confront taunting white spectators and a line of gun-toting soldiers. She retraced her steps and stood alone at a bus stop, surrounded by jeering whites.

Another attempt to enroll the students provoked such disorders that mob rule threatened Central High. Faced with the most serious challenge to federal authority since the Civil War, Eisenhower was obliged to nationalize the Arkansas National Guard and dispatch a thousand regular army paratroopers to Little Rock. With white parents shouting and waving Confederate flags, U.S. soldiers escorted

Elizabeth Eckford and eight other Negro students into the school and through the corridors to their classes. Thanks to southern white intransigence, Eisenhower became the first President since Reconstruction to send federal troops to enforce Negro rights in Dixie, a move that enraged the white South and polarized the region.

For King, Little Rock was "a tragic revelation of what prejudice can do to blind the visions of men and darken their understanding." Moreover, it demonstrated "that while the forces of good will in our nation remained silent, the forces of opposition mobilized and organized." Still, he thought Little Rock might be "a blessing in disguise." For the first time, the school issue had been taken before the conscience of the nation. Now maybe men of good will would realize that the problem had to be dealt with forthrightly.

K ING WAS SO BUSY WITH MEETINGS and speeches, not to mention his church work, that he had scarcely any time for his family. He did hurry home during the third week in October, when Coretta gave birth to a son. King named him Martin Luther King III. "Little Marty" cried with such fervor that King said he detected the voice of a future preacher.

Then it was back to his whirlwind schedule. In between SCLC conferences and public appearances, King even began a book on the Montgomery story, to be published by Harper & Brothers' religious department. He also planned a trip to India, to meet Prime Minister Jawaharlal Nehru and other disciples of Gandhi. But because of his multitude of commitments, King had to postpone the trip until the next year. In mid-November his frenetic pace caught up with him: he fell sick and took to bed for more than a week.

But in early December he felt well enough to attend the MIA's annual Institute on Nonviolence, held in Montgomery's now famous Holt Street Baptist Church, and to deliver a candid address on "some things we must do." He recalled an incident that happened to him in the Atlanta airport a few days before. The terminal had two restrooms for males, one labeled "Colored Men" and the other just "Men." "I thought I was a man," King related, "and I still think I am so I decided to go into the Men's room, not the Colored Men's room." Though none of the whites complained, a Negro custodian became very upset. "The colored room is over there!" he cried. "You belong over there, that's for the colored." King replied, "I'm gonna stay here, right here," and he did. "That fellow was so conditioned by the system that he didn't think of himself as a man," King told his audience. Well, Negroes must continue to resist that system and try to change it. At the same time, though, they must strive to improve themselves.

"Let's do as Gandhi did in South Africa," King said. "Let's consider what the whites say against us and consider whether they have any good arguments. They say we want our constitutional rights so we can marry their daughters. But that is nonsense so we don't have to pay any attention to that." "Amen!" his audience responded. "They say that we smell," he went on. "Well the fact is some of us do smell. I know most Negroes do not have money to fly to Paris and buy enticing perfumes, but no one is so poor that he can't buy a five cent bar of soap." There was applause at that.

"And we kill each other and cut each other too much," King said. Let them "face some facts." In New York City, Negroes constituted 10 percent of the population, yet committed 35 percent of its crime. In Missouri, they comprised 26 percent of the population, yet collected 76 percent of the aid to dependent children. What was more, Negroes generally had eight times as many illegitimate children as whites. Yes, all this was caused *by* racial oppression and was no excuse *for* racial oppression. But Negroes themselves must improve these conditions. They must avail themselves of the doors already opening to them and "be ready for integration."

"You don't need to speak good English in order to be good," he said. "Our people didn't know English very well but they knew God." "Amen!" somebody shouted. "But there is no excuse for our school teachers to say 'you is'—they're supposed to be teaching but they're crippling our children."

He was warming to his subject now. "And our doctors should not spend their time on big cars and clothes but in reading books and going to medical institutes. Too many Negro doctors have not opened a book since leaving medical school." And Negro ministers "can't just whoop and holler, we must be able to preach the Gospel of Jesus Christ. And for this we need to study and think more, and not worry about getting amens." "Amen," the crowd yelled. "I'm going to holler tonight," King cried, "because I want to get this over. I'm going to be a Negro tonight." And he hollered about how too many Negroes lived beyond their means. "Oh, I know why Negroes like to buy Cadillacs and ride in bigger cars than whites. We've been pushed around and if we can't have a big home we can at least have a big car. But it's time to end this foolishness. There are too many Negroes with $2,000 incomes riding around in $5,000 cars." And the problem with liquor was worse. "The money Negroes spend on liquor in Alabama in one year is enough to endow three or four colleges." All of these, King concluded, "are some things we have it in *our* power to change."

After King's speech, several people lingered to talk. Among them were two whites who had come down to run seminars in the institute: Paul Simon, a young Democratic state legislator from Illinois, and Harris Wofford, a prominent Washington attorney who had studied Gandhi and advised King on his projected trip to India. The group got to discussing King's enormous popularity. "Don't you worry about our deifying Martin," said a local Negro preacher. "He's a great leader but Jesus Christ is the captain [of] our ship."

"It would help, though," a King friend said, "if he did something to curtail this hero-worship, a few jokes to show that he knows he's not a messiah."

"He knows it," a third man said. "He has a sense of humility and awe at what has happened to him, but he also has a sense of destiny. He sees himself as an instrument of history—of God—and is very earnest about finding and doing his duty."

King joined his friends. He complained about the difficulties of being a leader. "I haven't read a book—really sat down and read a book—for a year." And all the requests and demands on his time were getting him down. "Sometimes I accept an engagement just to get people off my back because I know if I say No they will be inviting me again a month later." He had a secretary to screen his calls, but black leaders tended to resent this. Said one organizational head a few days before: "Don't talk with me through no secy-tary. I'm as big as you are, King."

"There's a lot of jealousy of Martin among Negro leaders," a friend added. "Negro leadership is still the barrel of crabs that Booker T. Washington described. King is the youngest crab and the others near the top are afraid he is going to pull them down on his way up. And then a lot of people honestly disagree with him. They don't like all the acclaim he is getting, because they oppose his religious approach. They want us to rely on good lawyers rather than to look for an American Gandhi."

On the way out of the church, Simon asked Coretta if King was always so electrifying a speaker. "Sometimes he's even better," she said, and smiled. But behind her cheerful veneer Coretta was worried about King's safety. She confessed to Mrs. Wofford that she had a recurring nightmare in which her husband was killed.

AFTER THE INSTITUTE, King tried desperately to make some headway on his Montgomery book. Now represented by Marie Rodell's New York literary agency, which negotiated his contract with Harper & Brothers, King discovered what it was like to do business with big-time commercial publishing. "We have been growing more and more concerned as no further copy from you has come in," Rodell wrote him in mid-December. "We had hoped to have the entire first draft long before this. I know your illness caused some delay beyond your control, but time is slipping by fast. It is of the utmost importance that the book come out by next September, while the memory of the Montgomery protest is still fresh on every one's mind, and when, with the opening of school, the whole integration problem will be front-page news. It would be a pity—and I think represent a sizable loss in sales—to bring it out any later than that." The agency must have the manuscript by March 15—only four months away.

Faced with such a horrendous deadline, King hid out in an Atlanta hotel and toiled on his book in a wilderness of paper. One night a friend brought a visitor by—novelist James Baldwin, heralded as the most talented Negro writer to appear since Richard Wright. King was quite taken with this delicate man, whose large, kind eyes took in everything. As they chatted about King's leadership, Baldwin found him "immediately and tremendously winning," but observed that King did not like to talk about himself. Baldwin felt as though King were "a younger, much-loved, and menaced brother," and thought him "very slight and vulnerable to be taking on such tremendous odds."

For now, the worst odds seemed to be the completion of his book.

With New York badgering him to distraction to get it done, King prevailed on Lawrence D. Reddick, an Alabama State history professor, to help him do background research and check facts. And he begged New York to understand the hell he was going through, what with trying to write a book and plan SCLC's Crusade for Citizenship all at the same time. "It would be a great pity," Reddick wrote Rodell in King's behalf, "if so many demanded so much of him that hassled and harried he will not be able to do anything well—and never fulfill his bright promise."

In February, 1958, King abandoned his composition and devoted his energies to the Crusade for Citizenship, designed to double the number of Negro voters by 1960, a presidential election year. "We feel that one of the most decisive steps that the Negro can take at this time is that short walk to the voting booth," King said.

The crusade began on Lincoln's birthday, 1958, with twenty mass meetings taking place simultaneously in major cities across Dixie. King himself turned up at a mass meeting in Miami, Florida, to give a hard-hitting speech on Negro voting rights. "Let us make our intentions crystal clear," he declared. "We must and we will be free. We want freedom now. We want the right to vote now. We do not want freedom fed to us in teaspoons over another 150 years. Under God we were born free. Misguided men robbed us of our freedom. We want it back."

He rapped Negroes for their own "shameless indifference" to voting and contended that Negro apathy today was "a form of moral and political suicide." He also castigated the federal government for hypocritically advocating free elections in Europe while tolerating Negro disenfranchisement at home. If democracy was to win its rightful place in the world, "millions of people, Negro and white, must stand before the world as examples of democracy in action, not as voteless victims of the denial and corruption of our heritage."

Then he appealed to southern white moderates, insisting that they and not the Senator Eastlands truly represented Dixie. "We Southerners, Negro and white, must no longer permit our nation and our heritage to be dishonored before the world," King said. "We have a moral obligation to carry out. We have the duty to remove from political domination a small minority that cripples the economic and social institutions of our nation and thereby degrades and impoverishes everyone."

It was a fitting speech for Lincoln's birthday, recalling as it did

Lincoln's own defenses of popular government as a noble experiment marred by slavery and threatened by southern reactionaries of his time.

And so the Crusade for Citizenship was on, with SCLC exhorting affiliate churches to run voting clinics and canvass Negro neighborhoods, urging all eligible Negroes to turn out for voter registration. Alas, the crusade added few new Negro voters that spring, but it did stimulate local groups already in the field. Later Atlanta blacks launched a voter-registration campaign, and King lent his support, his heart "throbbing for joy" because Atlanta was his home. "If Atlanta succeeds," he said, "the South will succeed. If Atlanta fails, the South will fail, for Atlanta is the South in miniature."

IT SEEMED THAT HE HAD NO PRIVATE LIFE any more. He felt consumed by the movement, transformed into its most visible and sought-after public figure. He spoke in all directions for the NAACP, solicited contributions for CORE and served on its advisory board, and gave stemwinding SCLC speeches in churches and auditoriums from one coast to the other. He was the leading fund raiser for SCLC and the other major Negro organizations—"a helpful hand from you," wrote a thankful NAACP official, "is ten, twenty-five, one hundred times more productive than that of countless other friends."

But he had his critics, too. When he preached Negro self-help in Los Angeles, a black newspaper accused him of becoming the white man's lackey and selling Negroes a "dolled-up Uncle Tomism" reminiscent of Booker T. Washington. King expected flak from Negroes who disagreed with him—that went with being a big-time leader. But it still hurt him that anyone should think him an Uncle Tom.

Back in Montgomery, he tried to work on his book, but despaired of ever completing a first draft with all his other obligations. In desperation, he secured the services of a former Harper editor named Hermine Popper, who polished chapter drafts King sent her. She was not a ghostwriter; she functioned officially as his "editorial associate," tightening his prose, deleting repetitive material, and dividing excessively long chapters—corrections King himself would have made had he had the time. In whatever changes she made, though, she took pains to retain King's style and language. But it was still a marathon effort to get the manuscript completed, with Levison, Rustin, and others offering advice and criticism. On separate occasions, Marie Rodell and Popper even flew to Montgomery to expedite King's composition. "Dr. King has been under terrific pressure this year," his secretary noted in April. "The writing on his book which has an almost immediate date for press time, his heavy speaking schedule and the pressure from his own community have all taken their toll on him. His physician is urging him to slow down."

But he could not slow down. There was the Easter sermon to give at Dexter and SCLC meetings to attend on the Crusade for Citizenship. Meanwhile New York wanted revisions in his manuscript and more anecdotal and descriptive material to enliven the story. For his part, Harper editor Melvin Arnold was anxious about a passage in which King assessed the failures of both Communism and capitalism, for Arnold wanted nothing said in the book that could be construed as friendly to Communism. Accordingly, Arnold asked King to change "my response to Communism was negative" to "my response to Communism was and is negative." King made the change because that was exactly his sentiment. As for his remarks about capitalism (it failed to see "the truth in collective enterprise," failed to see that "life is social"), Arnold and Popper both thought him wrong. They urged him to distinguish between nineteenth-century European capitalism, which Marx assailed, and modern American capitalism, which in their view had developed a sense of social responsibility in order to survive. King refused to make that distinction outright; his "anti-capitalist feelings" would not permit him to do so. He settled for references only to the weaknesses of "traditional" or "nineteenth-century" capitalism, and in May sent off his final revisions to New York. *Stride Toward Freedom: The Montgomery Story* was done, and King was exhausted from the effort. His advance came to $3,500, out of which he paid Popper $2,000 for her editorial labors.

A slim and simply written book, *Stride Toward Freedom* was partly the story of the bus boycott, partly an autobiography, and partly an argument for nonviolence and racial change. King opened with a dramatic account of his return to the South in 1954 and what it was like to live in Montgomery as a Negro. Then he plunged into the story of the boycott itself, from Rosa Parks's momentous arrest down to "Desegregation at Last," with an interim chapter on his own "Pilgrimage to Nonviolence" at Crozer and Boston University. Throughout, King was careful not to overplay his own role in the protest. He was the central figure, to be sure. But the real hero was the new Negro in Dixie, who, in a time of world-wide revolutionary ferment, straightened his back and started battling for his own freedom. The spirit of the age was at work in Montgomery, moving in Rosa Parks, then in Nixon and the established leaders, then in King in his response to them. Then it ignited the people and propelled King himself to the forefront of the struggle. Though he did not say so in his book, he often thought that the Zeitgeist had been tracking him down all along, since he had come south in the same year as the Brown decision, at a time when the Negro masses were beginning to stir. As it turned out, the young preacher who had studied Gandhi and Christian activism in college was ideally prepared for the kind of moral leadership thrust on him in Montgomery. King became the voice and symbol of the nonviolent movement, a historical figure identified with the truth of his age.

The last chapter—"Where Do We Go from Here?"—brimmed with trenchant insights into America's historical crisis at midcentury. "The crisis developed," King wrote, "when the most sublime principles of American democracy—imperfectly realized for almost two centuries—began fulfilling themselves and met with the brutal resistance of forces seeking to contract and repress freedom's growth." Americans of King's generation then faced a crucial choice. "We can choose either to walk the high road of human brotherhood or to tread the low road of man's inhumanity to man." "History has thrust on our generation an indescribably important destiny—to complete a process of democratization which our nation has too long developed too slowly."

King went on to list the agencies—the federal government, labor unions, northern white liberals and southern white moderates, the church, and the Negro himself—that could produce meaningful change in American race relations. But King bristled at the hypocrisy of the church. "How often the church has had a high blood count of creeds and an anemia of deeds!" He quoted Dean Liston Pope of Yale Divinity School: "The church is the most segregated major institution in American society," one that lagged behind courts, schools, and even department stores when it came to desegregation. What an appalling irony it was "that the most segregated hour of Christian America is eleven o'clock on Sunday morning, the same hour when many are standing to sing, 'In Christ there is no East nor West.' "

Still, it was a great time for America's long-maligned Negro. "To become the instruments of a great idea is a privilege that history gives only occasionally. Arnold Toynbee says in *A Study of History* that it may be the Negro who will give the new spiritual dynamic to Western civilization that it so desperately needs to survive. I hope this is possible. The spiritual power that the Negro can radiate to the world comes from love, understanding, good will, and nonviolence. It may even be possible for the Negro, through adherence to nonviolence, so to challenge the nations of the world that they will seriously seek an alternative to war and destruction. In a day when Sputniks and Explorers dash through outer space and guided ballistic missiles are carving highways of death through the stratosphere, nobody can win a war. Today the choice is no longer between violence and nonviolence. It is either nonviolence or nonexistence. The Negro may be God's appeal to this age—an age drifting rapidly to its doom. The eternal appeal takes the form of a warning: 'All who take the sword will perish by the sword.' "

On the morning of June 23, 1958, King, Randolph, Wilkins, and Lester Granger of the National Urban League met with the President in a White House reception room. SCLC had persuaded Eisenhower to grant King an audience, and he and his associates had put together a six-page statement about what American Negroes wanted from their President. With Eisenhower standing at attention, Randolph read the statement in his melodious voice, urging that the President announce to the nation that he would uphold the Brown decision and the 1957 Civil Rights Act, press Congress to pass even more effective civil-rights legislation, safeguard the right of Negroes to vote and protect them from bombs and terrorism, and cut off federal funds to states that maintained segregated public facilities. The Negroes made it clear that they were unhappy with the administration's lackluster record in civil rights, and Eisenhower said he was surprised that they felt that way. King could scarcely believe what he heard. Did the President think them *happy* with his refusal to endorse school integration, *happy* with his lack of moral fervor and vigorous leadership in the crucial area of civil rights? Eisenhower spoke in generalities about how all citizens should have their rights, but he would not commit himself to a single point in the Negroes' statement. As the meeting broke up, he found King near him and sighed, "Reverend, there are so many problems . . . Lebanon, Algeria . . . "

King was disgusted with Eisenhower. Though King thought he seemed sincerely interested in the Negro, he had no idea how to translate that into public policy, or even to define civil rights as a domestic issue. "Moreover," King said, "President Eisenhower could not be committed to anything which involved a structural change in the architecture of American society. His conservatism was fixed and rigid, and any evil defacing the nation had to be extracted bit by bit with a tweezer because the surgeon's knife was an instrument too radical to touch this best of all possible societies."

In July King and Coretta escaped to Mexico for a vacation—their first real vacation since their marriage. King enjoyed the unhurried two weeks they spent in Mexico, but the poverty there made him "alternately rage and despair," Coretta said. Then it was home to his unrelenting schedule, including a conference with Harper & Brothers about the promotional campaign for his book; Harper planned a first printing of 30,000 copies. King himself sent inscribed advance copies to Eisenhower, Nixon, Truman, Arthur Schlesinger, Jr., and other notables. And he prevailed on influential figures (Ralph Bunche of the United Nations, Ralph McGill of the Atlanta *Constitution*) to write reviews.

King had scarcely returned to Montgomery when an ugly incident occurred. On September 3 the Kings accompanied Abernathy to the Montgomery County Courthouse, where Abernathy was involved in a case. At the courtroom door, a rude guard refused to let them enter the room. When King asked if they could speak with Abernathy's lawyer, the guard became enraged. "Boy," he yelled at King, "if you don't get the hell away from here, you will need a lawyer yourself." At that, two policemen rushed up to King. "Boy, you done done it; let's go." They twisted his arm behind him and dragged him outside and around the corner to the police station. Coretta ran after her husband. "Gal," one of the cops shouted over his shoulder, "you want to go, too? Just nod your head." "Don't say anything, darling," King warned her.

At the station, the desk sergeant growled, "Put him in the hole," and tossed the cops a key. Clearly they had no idea that this "sassy nigger" was Martin Luther King. Nor did they seem to notice that a photographer was taking pictures.

At a cell in the dim corridor, the two policemen made King raise his hands and frisked and kneed him. Then they grabbed him by the throat and choked him, spun him around, and kicked him into the cell. Minutes later King saw them returning and braced himself for another beating. But the cops were quiet, almost civilized, as they led him back to the front desk, where in a deferential atmosphere he was charged with insulting an officer and released on his own bond. Obviously some authority had discovered what a "colossal blunder" had been made and upbraided the two policemen for their imbecility.

To the embarrassment of the police department, news of the arrest hummed over the wires, and papers across the country published accounts and ran photographs of the two policemen twisting King's arm on the way to jail. Police Commissioner Sellers only made matters worse by telling the press that King's treatment was nothing unusual in his town. To avoid further embarrassment, Sellers could have apologized to King and dropped the charge against him. But for Sellers, a dedicated segregationist, apologizing to King was unthinkable. No, he was going to be tried like any other lawbreaker.

As his trial approached, King told Coretta and some friends that "the time has come when I should no longer accept bail. If I commit a crime in the name of civil rights, I will go to jail and serve the time." He brushed aside their objections. "You don't understand. You see, if anybody had told me a couple of years ago, when I accepted the presidency of the MIA, that I would be in this position, I would have avoided it with all my strength. This is not the life I expected to lead. But gradually you take some responsibility, then a little more, until finally you are not in control anymore. You have to give yourself entirely. Then, once you make up your mind that you *are* giving yourself, then you are prepared to do anything that serves the Cause and advances the Movement. I have reached that point. I have no option anymore about what I will do. I have given myself fully."

King stood trial on September 5, with the national press on hand to cover what had become front-page news. The judge could have dismissed the case and denied King any more publicity. But, no, that would mean that whites were giving in to "coloreds." So he found

King guilty of loitering and refusing to obey a police officer. The penalty was $10 and court costs or fourteen days in jail. King chose jail. Then he asked if he could read a statement, and the judge unwittingly agreed.

"Your Honor," King said in the hushed courtroom, "I could not in all good conscience pay a fine for an act that I did not commit and above all for brutal treatment that I did not deserve. . . . I also make this decision because of my deep concern for the injustices and indignities that my people continue to experience. Today, in many parts of the South, the brutality inflicted upon Negroes has become America's shame. Last month, in Mississippi, a sheriff, who was pointed out by four eye witnesses as the man who beat a Negro to death with a black jack, was freed in twenty-three minutes. At this very moment in this state James Wilson sits in the death house condemned to die for stealing less than two dollars. Can anyone at this court believe that a white man could be condemned to death in Alabama for stealing this small amount?"

Then he addressed the nation beyond. "I also make this decision because of my love for America and the sublime principles of liberty and equality upon which she is founded. I have come to see that America is in danger of losing her soul and can so easily drift into tragic Anarchy and crippling Fascism. Something must happen to awaken the dozing conscience of America before it is too late. The time has come when perhaps only the willing and nonviolent acts of suffering by the innocent can arouse this nation to wipe out the scourge of brutality and violence inflicted upon Negroes who seek only to walk with dignity before God and Man."

King handed his statement to the startled judge, and Abernathy distributed copies to the newsmen. It was brilliant theater, reminiscent of John Brown's legendary address to the Virginia court that sentenced him to hang for attacking Harpers Ferry and trying to free the slaves. Like Brown, King took advantage of the blindness of his adversaries to play on the moral conscience of his countrymen. And it worked, too, as sympathetic letters and telegrams poured into his office from all directions. Even whites in Montgomery were moved by the moral grandeur of his statement.

Though King was determined to serve his sentence, Commissioner Sellers paid King's fine himself, informing the press that he intended to foul up this "publicity stunt" and "save the taxpayers the expense of feeding King for fourteen days."

S*tride Toward Freedom* OFFICIALLY CAME OUT in September, with advance sales climbing to 18,000 copies. Ultimately the book would sell more than 60,000 hardback copies in the United States alone, would come out in a paperback edition from Ballantine Books, and would appear in at least twelve other countries, including Great Britain, Sweden, India, and Japan. The American reviews were almost all laudatory. "By any standards, North or South, Christian or secular, [King] has written a major tract for the times" enthused historian Perry Miller in the *Reporter*. The *New York Times* extolled King as "an original thinker as well as a man of generous spirit," and the *Christian Century* contended that "Dr. King and his people have unlocked the revolutionary resources of the gospel of Christ." Wrote southern novelist Lillian Smith in the *Saturday Review*. "Because their purpose was big, their philosophy firm, because the means they used were without hate, because all of it together cut through level after level of human experience, the account of a bus boycott in Montgomery will, I think, become a classic story—as has Gandhi's salt march—of man demanding justice and discovering that justice first begins in his own heart." In the South, though, the Chattanooga *News–Free Press* dismissed King's philosophy of love as "muddled thought sequences and 'non sequiturs.'" "It would appear, after many tedious pages, that this man envisions himself as a self-appointed arbiter to correct all ills, whether real or imaginary. Saner generations would have laughed him into scorn."

"Although we are facing some dark moments in the South now," King wrote one reviewer, "I am convinced that we stand in the glow of our nation's bright tomorrows. This is a daring faith, but I choose to invest my life in it." Meanwhile he was busily promoting his book, which was on display (and sold almost two hundred copies) at the National Baptist Convention in Detroit and which brought him even more fame. But his popularity caused a family friend a great deal of anxiety. You must beware, he wrote King after the convention. You must avoid even the appearance of evil, for you are "a marked man." All kinds of subtle attempts will be made to discredit you. Some Negroes in Montgomery would like to see you fail, as would most whites. Some might even try to lead you into error. But "one of the most daming influences is that of women. They themselves too often delight

in the satisfaction they get out of affairs with men of unusual prominence. Enemies are not above using them to a man's detriment. White
women can be lures. You must exercise more than care. You must be
vigilant indeed."

In mid-September, King was in New York for several days of radio
and television appearances, including the NBC *Today Show*. On a
dark Saturday afternoon, September 20, he turned up at Blumstein's
department store to autograph copies of his book. As he was inscribing
one at an improvised desk, a well-dressed Negro woman approached.
"Are you Martin Luther King?" she asked. "Yes," he said without
looking up. Suddenly he felt something beating at his chest. He heard
the woman cry, "Luther King, I've been after you for five years."
Then, as in a dream, she was running away, a man chasing after her.
King sat there in a daze, staring at an instrument stuck in his chest,
near his heart. The woman had stabbed him with a razor-sharp Japa-
nese letter opener. There was great commotion about him: voices, a
tattoo of footsteps. He knew he could be dying, yet was calm and felt
no pain. At one point he accidentally touched the blade and cut his
finger.

An ambulance bore him to Harlem Hospital, where orderlies
wheeled him to an operating table in an emergency room. As he lay
there, the police entered with the Negro woman so that King could
identify her. "Yah," she snarled, "that's him. I'm going to report him
to my lawyers." After they led her away, a black physician came in,
introduced himself as Aubré D. Maynard, and examined the blade in
King's chest. Assisted by an interracial surgical team, Dr. Maynard
had to remove one of King's ribs and part of his breastbone to get the
knife free. In a burst of inspiration, he made the incision over King's
heart in the shape of a cross. "Since the scar will be there permanently
and he is a minister, it seemed somehow appropriate," the doctor said.

After the operation, King lay in a private room with a tube in his
nose and throat to drain his chest. Though heavily sedated, he recognized Coretta when she arrived. Nurses said he'd been calling for her
through the night. She had flown up from Montgomery with Abernathy, fighting back her tears, telling herself that this could be fatal.
"If this is the way it's got to be," she kept thinking, "then this is the
way it's got to be." The doctor, however, assured her that King would
live.

By now, the news of King's stabbing had flashed across the nation, and radio and television stations broadcast hourly bulletins about his condition. New York Governor Averell Harriman, A. Philip Randolph, and other luminaries all rushed to his bedside, and Randolph helped raise more than $2,000 for King's hospital expenses. King was especially glad to see "Mr. Randolph," the "Dean of Negro leaders," whose life and dedication "served as a real inspiration to me." Coretta, for her part, screened his visitors as best she could, arranged all the fruit and flowers people sent him, tried to answer some of the thousands of telegrams and messages of sympathy he received.

For a time pneumonia hampered his recovery. But in a few days he felt strong enough to talk with Dr. Maynard, who disclosed how close he had come to dying. The tip of the letter opener had touched King's aorta, the main artery from the heart. "If you had sneezed during all those hours of waiting," the doctor said, "your aorta would have been punctured and you would have drowned in your own blood."

Four days after the operation, King was out of bed and moving about the room and the corridors in a wheelchair. He read through the messages of sympathy—telegrams from Eisenhower and Nixon, cards and letters from people all over the world. But one letter in particular caught his eye. He would never forget what it said.

Dear Dr. King,
I am a ninth grade student at the White Plains High School. While it shouldn't matter, I would like to mention that I'm a white girl. I read in the paper of your misfortune and of your suffering. And I read that if you had sneezed you would have died. I'm simply writing you to say that I'm so happy that you didn't sneeze.

That letter brought tears to his eyes. He told Coretta he was glad he hadn't sneezed too. "What makes you think you are the 'exclusive property' of the Negro race only?" a white woman wrote him. "You belong to us too, because we love you. Your voice is the only true voice of love today & we hear, we hear.... Please don't lose faith in us 'whites,' there are so many of us who are good & pray for your triumph."

After he left the hospital, King spent another three weeks recovering in the Brooklyn home of a friend. He talked with Coretta about his would-be killer, a demented woman named Izola (or Isola) Curry, age forty-two, "a rootless wanderer" who came from a broken home and failed in her marriage and almost everything else she tried. As she saw and heard King on television and read about him in the papers, her tormented mind became fixed on him as the author of all her woes. And so she tried to murder him. But King harbored no malice toward the woman. "Don't do anything to her," he counseled the authorities; "don't prosecute her; get her healed." Later he learned that she had been committed to an institution for the criminally insane.

As he convalesced, King had time to do what he had longed for all these months: he read books and meditated. And he talked a good deal about the trial he was going through. He decided that God was teaching him a lesson here, and that was personal redemption through suffering. It seemed to him that the stabbing had been for a purpose, that it was part of God's plan to prepare him for some larger work in the bastion of segregation that was the American South.

T HAT WINTER KING DECIDED to make his long-delayed trip to India. He thought it best to go now, instead of plunging back into "the seat of Southern segregation struggle." Besides, in this "very difficult period of my life," he was under doctor's orders to cut back drastically on his speaking engagements. And a trip to India would be good for his health. Through the efforts of Harris Wofford and Libby Holman Reynolds, the singer, King received a $5,000 grant from the Christopher Reynolds Foundation to defray expenses, and the American Friends Service Committee worked out his itinerary.

Not wanting to travel alone, King invited Coretta and L. D. Reddick to accompany him. Reddick had just completed a biography of King called *Crusader without Violence,* which Harper would publish that year, and he contended that King's ultimate test would come when Gandhi's disciples passed judgment on him and his work in Montgomery. Meanwhile Gandhi scholar Richard Gregg advised him on what to expect in India. "Beware of pick-pockets," Gregg wrote. "They are slick operators." And try to get out of the cities into the outlying villages. "To understand Gandhi's program you must see some of village life. You can't imagine the poverty; it must be seen to be comprehended and believed." With his plans solidified, King tried desperately to catch up on his work. Otherwise "my trip to India will be so frustrating that I won't gain the spiritual enrichment that that great country affords."

At last, on February 3, 1959, the Kings and Reddick flew out of New York, heading for India by way of Paris. Seven days later their plane broke out of the clouds over Bombay; it was nighttime, and a necklace of lights circled the harbor below. On the ground, riding in a bus through Bombay's narrow streets, King was shocked at all the destitution. Gregg was right—this had to be seen to be believed. Men everywhere wore grimy loincloths and people carried all their possessions in newspapers or rags. They scavenged garbage cans for food, huddled forlornly in doorways, slept in filthy blankets on the pavement—a homeless, miserable rabble of almost a million souls. King had never seen such suffering, not even in Nigeria. He blamed it all on British colonialism.

At the Taj Mahal Hotel, a man approached King with a starving child, gesturing at him and babbling in a tongue King could not understand. His sponsors had warned him not to give money to beggars, since the Indian government was trying to end the practice. But King soon ignored their advice. "What can you do when an old haggard woman or a little crippled urchin comes up and motions to you that she is hungry?" King asked.

The next day he flew to New Delhi, capital of India, to commence his visit in earnest. At the New Delhi Hotel, he told a crowd of reporters: "To other countries I may go as a tourist, but to India I come as a pilgrim." He visited the great shrine where Gandhi had been cremated, kneeling and placing a wreath there. He met President Rajendra Prasad in a home that was two blocks long and crowned with a golden dome, talked with Vice-President Sarvepalli Radhakrishnan, and dined with Prime Minister Nehru in a large, neo-classic brownstone house built by the British at the height of their empire. All three statesmen had been Gandhi's followers in the struggle for Indian independence, and meeting them, King said, was like seeing Washington, Jefferson, and Madison all in the same day.

In the days that followed, King toured New Delhi in a Gandhi cap, giving talks and asking questions about what the Mahatma had accomplished. Nehru told him a good deal about India's low-caste untouchables, so long maligned by high-caste Hindus. A lot of Indians were

still prejudiced against them, still thought it defiled a high-caste Indian to touch one. But it was no longer popular to admit to such prejudice, Nehru said. He explained that the Indian constitution prohibited
discrimination against untouchables, and that the Indian government
spent millions of rupees annually to improve their lot. Moreover, if an
untouchable and a high-caste Indian competed for college admission,
the school had to take the untouchable. "But isn't that discrimination?" Reddick asked. "Well, it may be," Nehru said. "But this is our
way of atoning for the centuries of injustices we have inflicted upon
these people."

King was impressed. In his view, India had made more progress
against caste untouchability than the U.S. had against racial oppression. True, both countries had laws against discrimination. But unlike
Americans, Indian leaders placed "their moral power behind the law."
From the Prime Minister down to the village councilman, "everybody
declares publicly that untouchability is wrong."

It was Gandhi, of course, who had brought this about. For Gandhi
not only denounced the caste system but acted against it. He called
untouchables "Harians," which meant "children of God," and even
adopted an untouchable as his daughter. He took untouchables by the
hand and led them into the temples that excluded them. "To equal
that," King said, "President Eisenhower would have to take a Negro
child by the hand and lead her into Central High School in Little
Rock."

From New Delhi, the Kings set out on a month-long tour of the
country. They rode clattering trains from one city to another and
bounced along in jeeps to the more remote villages. "Everywhere we
went," King recorded, "we saw crowded humanity—on the roads, in
the city streets and squares, even in the villages. The people have a
way of squatting, resting comfortably (it seemed) on their haunches."
Most men, if they had employment at all, toiled at seasonable agricul-
tural jobs. And nearly everyone was impoverished—the average personal income was less than $70 a year. And food shortages were epi-
demic. "They are poor, jammed together and half starved," King said
of Indians, "but they do not take it out on each other. . . . They do not
abuse each other—verbally or physically—as readily as we do. We saw
but one fist fight in India during our stay." In sharp contrast to the
poverty, King saw a lot of opulence, too, riding by great homes on vast
landed estates. "The bourgeoisie—white, black or brown—behaves

about the same the world over," he said.

As the Kings toured the sites of Gandhi's "War of Independence," they came one weekend to picturesque Cape Comorin, India's southernmost point, where the Indian Ocean, Arabian Sea, and Bay of Bengal all converged. He and Coretta sat on a large rock, "enthralled by the vastness of the ocean and its terrifying immensities." Waves unfolded in rhythmic succession and crashed like drums against the base of the rock. Off in the west, the sun was sinking into the ocean in a blaze of fire. When only the rim showed, a sliver of orange on the moving sea, Coretta touched him. "Look, Martin, isn't that beautiful?" He turned and saw the moon rising from the ocean in one direction as the sun was setting in another. When darkness fell, the moon shone like a silver beacon of hope. King thought how one often had some painful experience when the light of day seemed to vanish. And one drifted along in gloom and despair, bereft of any hope. Then one looked in the east—and there! another light was shining even in the darkness. Another light was always shining, if one had the faith to see it. King liked the imagery so much that he later included it in a sermon.

Soon after, the Kings headed back for New Delhi, having found the spirit of Gandhi very much alive in this sprawling land. On March 9 they left India with King in a pensive mood. He could not forget the contorted faces of all those hungry people he had seen in the towns and villages. He thought how America spent millions of dollars every day to store her surplus food, and he told himself: "I know where we can store that food free of charge—in the wrinkled stomachs of starving people in Asia and Africa." And he said so repeatedly on his return to America.

On their way home, the Kings stopped off in Jerusalem, where King inquired about the Arab-Israeli conflicts, "one of the most difficult problems in the world." Then he and Coretta rented a car and drove toward Jericho, following a treacherous road that wound up through remote and jagged country known in Jesus' day as "the bloody pass." "I can see why Jesus used this for the setting for his parable," King told Coretta. And he thought about what the Priest and the Levite said in the parable when they found the robbed man lying on the ground. "If I stop to help this man," they fretted, "what will happen to me? What if robbers are still around?" But the Good Samaritan, when he came along, asked a very different question. "If I do not stop to help this man, what will happen to him?" King loved that parable and tried to follow the example of the Good Samaritan. If more people did so, there would not be so many starving people in the world, or so much hatred, or so much war.

From Jerusalem, the Kings took off for Cairo and Athens, where King viewed the "towering acropolis" and ruminated on the days of Plato and Aristotle. Then it was home to Montgomery, on circuitous flights that left them exhausted. Still, King said his experiences in India were among the most rewarding in his life. It was "a marvelous thing" to see Indian and English people living in mutual friendship, based on "complete equality," within the Indian Commonwealth. He was convinced that nonviolence could produce a similar friendship between blacks and whites in the United States. Too, he was immensely impressed with what could be accomplished when a national government was determined to end discrimination. He stressed how much India had done to aid the untouchables, to help them "leap the gap from backwardness to competence," by granting them scholarships, financial aid, and employment opportunities. Why could America not do this for her own "victim of discrimination"—the Negro? From then on, King made special federal aid to blacks one of his cardinal demands.

In all, he came home with a deeper understanding of nonviolence and a deeper commitment as well. For him, nonviolence was no longer just a philosophy and a technique for social change; it was now a whole way of life. As Coretta said, he even tried to be more like Gandhi—more humble and spiritual than he had been before. Though he continued to live comfortably enough, he tried to be less concerned with material things now, insisting that "people who are doing something don't have time to be worried about all that." He trained himself to subsist on four hours of sleep a night, so as to devote more time to the struggle. And he vowed to set aside one day a week for meditation and fasting, in the spirit of the Mahatma. "My failure to reflect will do harm not only to me as a person, but to the total movement," he said.

But he could not keep his vow. Apart from limited successes in Shreveport and a few other places, the Crusade for Citizenship was foundering and SCLC itself operating in the red. King had scarcely unpacked his bags before he had to hit the fund-raising trail, to bring money into SCLC's empty coffers. As his work mounted, it became impossible for him to spend a day in meditation. He always found himself using that time to catch up on accumulated chores or to answer emergency phone calls. What an enemy the phone was to this American Gandhi. "I have felt terribly frustrated over my inability to retreat, concentrate, and reflect," he complained to a friend at Boston University. "My whole life seems to be centered around giving something out and only rarely taking something in."

THAT FALL, KING AND SCLC's BOARD OF DIRECTORS agreed to utilize every available resource to increase the number of Negro voters. In mapping out SCLC strategy for 1960, they resolved to file voter-registration complaints with the Civil Rights Commission, which was functioning increasingly as the government's conscience in civil rights and as an ally to King. He and SCLC strongly supported its recommendation that federal registrars be deployed in southern areas where blacks were systematically kept off the voting rolls and out of politics. If the South's 5 million eligible Negro voters could gain the ballot (at present only 1.3 million enjoyed this fundamental American right), King envisioned a solid bloc of 10 million Negro voters in the United States, who could wield "formidable political power" in the forthcoming presidential election.

At the same time, King wanted SCLC to mount a "full-scale assault" on all forms of segregation—an ambitious program for an organization whose staff consisted solely of Ella Baker. King and the SCLC board made plans to enlarge the staff, and also to establish an SCLC training program that would instruct youths and adult leaders in nonviolence and then send them into their communities to launch mass-action programs against segregated schools and eating and transportation facilities. King noted that the school situation was especially distressing. Five years after the Brown decision, Alabama did not have a single desegregated school. In fact, white officials had a mandate to close any school threatened with integration. King thought it time for SCLC to apply pressure on white officialdom—and the federal government itself—to obey the law of the land.

So that he could devote full time to SCLC, King now reached a decision he had contemplated for some time: he would move to Atlanta, so as to be close to SCLC headquarters and make maximum use of his time. To supplement his income, he would serve as co-pastor of his father's church. He also hoped to find time in Atlanta to meditate and "think through the total struggle ahead."

On November 29, King offered his resignation as Dexter's pastor. "For almost four years now," he told his congregation, "I have been trying to do as one man, what five or six people ought to be doing." He talked about "the strain of being known" and confessed that he had not served Dexter well, since the demands of the movement took him away from Montgomery for extended periods. "I have come to the conclusion that I can't stop now. History has thrust upon me a responsibility from which I cannot turn away. I have no choice but to free you now."

His parishioners stood and sang "Blest Be the Tie That Binds." King was crying, and so were many of them. They had gone through a great deal together, but he had to go now. History was calling him home to Atlanta, obliging him to abandon his role as a preacher with a concern for civil rights and become a militant movement leader with a private and abiding religious faith.

His resignation took effect on the last Sunday in January, 1960, at the dawn of a new decade. Among his final words to black Montgomery, he warned that freedom was never free. It was "always purchased with the high price of sacrifice and suffering." So let them protest "until every black boy and girl can walk the streets with dignity and honor."

PART FOUR

SEASONS
OF SORROW

So it was that King returned to Atlanta, moving his family into a rented two-story home on Johnson Avenue, near Ebenezer and SCLC headquarters on Auburn Avenue. He commented wryly that he was only co-pastor of the church—his Daddy remained the pastor. King still professed indifference to material things and still tried to be like Gandhi. He drove a dusty three-year-old Chevrolet, and his personal income was scarcely commensurate with his labors and prestige. He accepted only $1 a year as SCLC president, received an annual salary of $4,000 from Ebenezer and another $2,000 for "pastoral care," and kept only around $5,000 from his sizable royalties and honorariums (up to $230,000 in a good year, nearly all of which he donated to SCLC). Still, King was ambivalent about bourgeois values. He liked to stay in posh hotels and was always immaculately dressed in gray and black suits, white shirt, and tie. His work, of course, required that he be neat in appearance. Nobody, certainly no whites, would have attended his addresses or contributed to movement treasuries had he shown up in a Gandhian loincloth. Yet he had a fascination with men of affluence—a legacy from his father perhaps—and enjoyed the company of wealthy SCLC benefactors, especially in New York. He even served on the board of directors of the International Opportunity Life Insurance Company, advising people to invest in such a growing firm and even buying shares himself. What was more, he had more than fifty awards and honorary degrees arranged on the walls of his Atlanta home. Among them were honorary degrees from Morehouse, Howard University, Boston University, and the Chicago Theological Seminary, and the NAACP's coveted Spingarn medal, given to King in 1957 for the highest achievement in his field.

Because of his prominence, rumors flew about black Atlanta that

King was rich. "The first thing some people ask me," King said in bewilderment, "is, 'All right, Reverend, now where's the Cadillac?'" Many Negroes found it inconceivable that King had no flashy car, no personal fortune stashed away, no opulent mansion in a plush Negro neighborhood. But that was not the only problem he encountered in Atlanta. As it happened, many of the city's old guard Negro leaders viewed him as an aggrandizing upstart—and a sanctimonious one at that—and vehemently opposed his move to Atlanta. "Smug and affluent," they did not want King encroaching on their territory and stirring up the Negro masses. They had fashioned a "coalition of mutual self-interest" with white leaders like Police Chief Herbert Jenkins and Mayor William B. Hartsfield, the latter a spry seventy-year-old who expatiated on "my town" while pacing about his office. The established Negro leadership—which included Daddy King—had worked out a tacit understanding with white officials that desegregation should be gradual and nonviolent, in order to preserve the city's image. By now, the golf courses and city buses were desegregated, and a Negro even served on the Atlanta school board. The schools themselves were under a federal court order to start desegregating in September, 1961, when ten black students were to be assigned to white schools. Hartsfield and Jenkins and the Chamber of Commerce, too, all pledged to carry out the federal court order, which was a far cry from the mule-headed opposition of white officialdom back in Montgomery. "We're a city too busy to hate," Hartsfield declared. "Atlanta does not cling to the past. People who swear on the old Southern traditions don't know what the hell they are. I think of boll weevils and hookworms. Robert E. Lee wouldn't even spit on the rabble rousers we have today. Think of living through this changing South—what a dynamic story! And Atlanta is the leader."

These were enlightened words for a southern white mayor. But the sad truth was that Atlanta remained a largely segregated city. In fact, Hartsfield's own city hall maintained separate restrooms and drinking fountains for Negroes and a whites-only cafeteria. Across Atlanta, moreover, restaurants, theaters, lunch counters, and most of the parks were all closed to blacks. As Coretta said, a Negro who wanted a soda at a downtown drugstore still had to order it from a side door.

King was upset about all this and once even scolded his father for not doing more in these years to challenge Atlanta's segregated facilities. "I am different from my father," he said on one occasion. "I feel the need of being free now!" But King himself never undertook an SCLC campaign in the city, because of an understanding he reached with "the somewhat envious old guard," as an SCLC staffer put it. He could be a national leader, a regional leader, but not an Atlanta leader. He could use the city as his base and sanctuary, but he must not get involved in what was going on there. King agreed, said a close aide, because he knew that an SCLC action was doomed without the support of the local leadership.

King had barely settled in Atlanta when newspapers reported startling developments in Greensboro, North Carolina. On February 2, 1960, four Negro students from North Carolina A & T College marched into Woolworth's, sat down at its lunch counter, and refused to leave unless they were served. Electrified by their courage, hundreds of students, including some from white colleges in the area, assailed Woolworth's during the next week, and the celebrated student sit-ins were under way. CORE, of course, had pioneered the sit-in back in 1942, and NAACP youth groups had staged sit-ins in Kansas and Oklahoma in 1958. But the events in Greensboro, widely reported in newspapers and television, galvanized Negro college students across the South and ignited one sit-in movement after another. In Nashville, James Lawson, Jr., a tall, soft-voiced clergyman and a Ph.D. candidate at Vanderbilt, had started workshops on nonviolence, with plans to launch a nonviolent offensive against segregation. Several bright and articulate young Negroes gathered around Lawson—people like John Lewis, James Bevel, and C. T. Vivian, all of whom had been inspired by Montgomery and greatly admired Martin Luther King. On February 13, Lawson's group led the largest and most effective sit-in thus far, as five hundred students crowded white lunch counters in Nashville, singing "We Shall Overcome," an old labor-union song destined to become the hymn of the Negro movement. John Lewis told his followers to "Remember the teachings of Jesus, Gandhi, and Martin Luther King. God bless you all."

In Atlanta, King sensed that historic events were unfolding in North Carolina and Tennessee. At long last, Negro students were becoming involved in the struggle—students who had come of age since the Brown decision and had seen it flouted across Dixie. Now they were on the move, and he was proud of them. In point of fact, they were attempting to do what SCLC had on its own agenda for 1960: to desegregate eating facilities in southern cities. As the sit-ins spread, students from numerous campuses wrote King for help and advice, which he freely gave. He spoke to student groups in Durham, North Carolina, and corresponded with many others, imploring them to follow the "Montgomery way" and not strike back at whites who shoved and screamed at them. He also assured the sit-inners that this was *their* movement—he had no intention of usurping it—and that it was "one of the most significant developments in the civil-rights struggle."

But on another front developments were ominous. During the third week of February, a Montgomery grand jury indicted King on a charge of falsifying his state tax returns for 1956-1958, of deliberately lying about money he had received and spent as president of the MIA and SCLC. King was crushed by the news. "Many people will think I am guilty," he moaned to Coretta and his close friends. "You know my enemies have previously done everything against me but attack my character and integrity. Though I am not perfect, if I have any virtues, the one of which I am most proud is my honesty where money is concerned."

The more he agonized over the indictment, the more he considered it a vicious attempt to discredit him in the eyes of Negroes everywhere. No, it was worse than that. Montgomery officials were out to destroy the movement itself by besmirching him in public. How to fight such treachery? The only way to prove his innocence was to win in court. But no white court in Montgomery was going to exonerate him. He was certain to be found guilty and then "for the rest of my life," he groaned, "people will believe that I took money that didn't belong to me." He would never do that, would never betray his people. "But who will believe me?" He fell into a deep depression.

He canceled a speaking engagement in Chicago because he couldn't bear to face anybody. He shut himself in his study and paced and prayed. Finally he realized that he had no right to hide. Accused or not, he had to stand before those people in Chicago. He called the airport, made new reservations, and went. Had he not done so, as James Baldwin said, he would have lost even before he came to trial.

Because he needed a lot of money for legal fees, his New York friends—Harry Belafonte, Rustin, and Stanley Levison—formed an emergency fund-raising committee. But King didn't want them to help him alone. The students needed money, too, and so did SCLC for its voter-registration work. "In the long run of history," King argued, "it does not matter whether Martin Luther King spends ten years in jail, but it does matter whether the student movement continues and it does matter whether the Negro is able to get the ballot in the South." He wanted to make that "palpably clear." At his insistence, his friends promised to raise $200,000 for his defense and for the southern freedom movement.

"My personal trials have . . . taught me the value of unmerciful suffering," he wrote in the *Christian Century*. "If only to save myself from bitterness, I have attempted to see my personal ordeals as an opportunity to transcend myself and heal the people involved in the tragic situation that now obtains."

In that spirit, he turned back to the sit-ins. In early March, students at Alabama State College in Montgomery held a demonstration at the county courthouse. In retaliation, police invaded the campus with shotguns, rifles, and tear gas, and threatened to arrest the entire student body. Though facing trial in Montgomery, King went to Alabama State and gave the students a pep talk at a mass rally—"he endeared himself to that generation of students by being with us," recalled one young man. At the same time, King publicly condemned the "gestapolike tactics" of the Montgomery police and telegraphed Eisenhower "to take immediate action in your name to restore law and order" in the Alabama capital. But the President ignored him.

As March passed, sit-ins broke out in Atlanta and numerous other southern cities, and King tried to defend and interpret the student movement for the nation at large, contributing his observations to magazines like *U.S. News & World Report* and the *Progressive*. He corrected a popular misconception that he was the leader of the sit-ins—no, this was something the students had begun themselves. Historically, the sit-ins were a logical outgrowth of Negro discontent that had been building since World War II—a discontent with empty white promises, impotent committees, flatulent campaign oratory, hollow legislative enactments, and token integration. The students had grown up in an age of Negro activism, they themselves had fought on the front line of the school desegregation struggle. They also identified with nationalist movements in Africa and took inspiration from the fact that blacks in new African states could vote and run their own affairs. "But in state after state in the United States the Negro is ruled and governed without a fragment of participation in civic life. The contrast is a burning truth which has molded a deep determination to end this intolerable condition."

"A generation of young people," King wrote, "has come out of decades of shadows to face naked state power; it has lost its fears, and experienced the majestic dignity of a direct struggle for its own liberation. These young people have connected up with their own history— the slave revolts, the incomplete revolution of the Civil War, the brotherhood of colonial colored men in Africa and Asia. They are an integral part of the history which is reshaping the world, replacing a dying order with a modern democracy."

But to be truly effective the students must organize, must coordinate their activities and forge a South-wide strategy. At the recommendation of Ella Baker, King called a student conference, to meet at Shaw University in Raleigh, North Carolina, and SCLC contributed funds to help cover expenses. On the weekend of April 15–17, more than two hundred students from North and South alike gathered on the Shaw campus, holding workshops in humid classrooms or outside on shrub-scented lawns. Though pledging themselves to nonviolence, the students warned that "arrest will not deter us." "This is no fad. This is it." "We're trying to eradicate the whole system of being inferior."

King joined the conference on Saturday. There were speeches by James Lawson, known as "the young people's Martin Luther King," and Ella Baker, whom the students regarded as "our spiritual mother." But "the high point" of the conference occurred that evening, when they crowded into City Auditorium to hear King. He rehearsed his usual message about the goals of nonviolence, reminded the students that the American Negro was out to save the soul of America and create the beloved community. With an eye on reporters, who scribbled away in the press section, King refuted the accusation that the student movement was Communist inspired. "If a man is standing on my neck," King said, "I don't need Mr. Khrushchev to come over from Russia to remind me someone's standing on my neck."

Before and after his address, King talked to the students about the need to organize on a permanent basis. In fact, he invited them to become a youth wing of SCLC. But Ella Baker, on her way out as SCLC's temporary executive director, clashed with King over this. She urged the students to shun established organizations, so that they could develop their youthful zeal and idealism without adult interference. Ultimately the students agreed with her and voted not to affiliate with SCLC or any other Negro organization. In a spirit of exaltation and togetherness, the students all stood in a circle in a local church, hold-

ing hands and singing "We Shall Overcome." "We all believed," recalled a young southern white woman. "We thought all was going to
be okay."

In subsequent meetings in Atlanta, student leaders formed an independent organization called the Student Nonviolent Coordinating
Committee (SNCC), which was to orchestrate the sit-ins and mobilize
students across America to combat segregation through nonviolent protest. King, for his part, harbored no ill will toward the students for
refusing to align with SCLC. On the contrary, he served on SNCC's
Adult Advisory Committee, attended the students' organizational
meetings, raised money for them, and even provided SNCC with a
temporary office at SCLC's Atlanta headquarters. "The coordinating
committee owes its very existence to SCLC," SNCC leaders wrote him
later that year. "You have been an inspiration to us all."

In May, King met repeatedly with a battery of white and Negro
lawyers hired to represent him in his trial for tax fraud in Alabama.
He fretted over how much it cost to prepare his defense—$10,000
already spent for lawyers and accountants, who pored over his financial statements and the state examiner's review sheets. King complained that it was "immoral and impractical" to pay out so much
money on his case when the movement was in dire need of funds.
Besides, he was still convinced that he could not win in Montgomery.
Sure, his attorneys thought the state's case patently absurd, so ground-
less that not even a white jury would be able to find against him. But
King refused to be optimistic. "I have been in Alabama courts too
many times when the evidence was clearly in my favor, and yet I
ended up being convicted," he said. In his opinion, his only hope was
to win on appeal in a federal court. But he was glad about one thing:
the state of Alabama had failed to discredit his integrity among Negroes.

On Monday, May 23, King was back in Montgomery, standing trial
once again in the white man's court of law. Though his attorneys exposed the state's case as little more than a frame-up, forcing even the
prosecution's star witness to concede that King was honest, King had

little hope for a favorable decision. But on Saturday the jury returned a verdict of "not guilty," and King was astounded. It was hard to believe that a jury of twelve white men in the Deep South had let him off. What could he learn from so significant a victory? "I learned that truth and conviction in the hands of a skillful advocate could make what started out as a bigoted, prejudiced jury, choose the path of justice." He thought this boded well for the future of race relations in Dixie. It boded well for the movement, too, since Alabama's attack on him, which was really an attack on militant black leadership across the South, had been roundly defeated.

Still, the tax case left its mark on him. James Baldwin heard him preach in Atlanta after the trial, and King described the torment of white people who knowingly defended wrong. In Baldwin's judgment, "He made the trials of these white people far more vivid than anything he himself might have endured." King insisted that whites like them were ruled by terror, not by hate. If blacks and whites were ever going to live together as a community, they must not hate one another. "It was a terrible plea," Baldwin observed, "and it was a prayer." He surmised that King "had looked on evil a long, hard, lonely time" and had realized that it was probably here to stay. Perhaps he had discovered a new and more somber meaning in the command "Overcome evil with good," which was not to say that evil could be eradicated. Maybe evil could only be arrested, subdued, so that the forces of light could guide human destiny.

KING WAS WORRIED ABOUT SCLC. It was still desperately in need of money, its programs still largely unimplemented. On July 23, he installed Wyatt Tee Walker as permanent executive director, hoping that a man of Walker's talents could mold SCLC into a disciplined and effective outfit. A native of Massachusetts, with a B.S. in chemistry and a divinity degree from Virginia Union University, Tee had spent eight stormy years in Petersburg, Virginia, where he'd led Negro efforts to integrate public facilities. Blunt, aggressive, and egocentric, he was six feet tall and slender, with a mustache and eyes that blazed with intensity. He wore horn-rimmed glasses and was immensely sure of himself and proud of his candor. He called King "the leader" and referred to himself variously as "Dr. King's chief-of-staff," "attorney general," and "nuts-and-bolts man." He drove his subordinates as hard as he drove himself, demanding exactitude and close attention to detail. "Like Ray Charles said," he told his office people, "I'm not hard to get along with, darlings. I just have to have perfection." He set to work expanding SCLC's voter-registration efforts, refining direct-action techniques, and enlarging the organization's leadership training program, carried out in an SCLC facility in southeast Georgia. He launched an emergency fund-raising campaign and set up SCLC outposts in numerous northern cities (one was already functioning in New York), which served as a network to facilitate fund-raising operations. Henceforth Tee himself handled King's public appearances and always demanded top fees for his services. At the same time, Walker increased SCLC's staff, which now included Reverend Walter Fauntroy, who served as director of the organization's Washington bureau.

With Tee running the machinery of SCLC, King could devote more time to goals and strategy. In truth, he was the creative thinker of the organization, Walker the man who put ideas into action. "Our personalities sort of merged," Walker recalled. "People said that I was his alter ego. I think in many ways I was." Together, as a King friend and writer said, they honed SCLC "to a fine fighting edge," with an effective staff, affiliates across the South, and an annual operating budget by 1963 of around $900,000.

Inevitably, SCLC's growth brought about conflicts with the NAACP, as competitive staffers in both organizations took to demeaning one another. Certain SCLC people made no secret of their scorn for the NAACP, calling it a "black bourgeoisie club" that had outlived its usefulness. NAACP men replied in kind. Inordinately jealous of King's popularity, they accused him of laboring under a messiah complex.

King abhorred such sniping. When former baseball star Jackie Robinson wrote him about it, King replied that he had always stressed the need for cooperation between the two organizations, and had always made it clear that the NAACP was "our chief civil rights organization" and that it had done more for the Negro than any other. "I have constantly said that any Negro who fails to give the NAACP this backing is nothing but an ingrate." But "I have no Messiah complex, and I know that we need many leaders to do the job. . . . Please be assured that you can count on me to give my ultimate allegiance to the cause. Even if it means pushing myself into the background. I have been so concerned about unity and the final victory that I have refused to fight back or even answer some of the unkind statements that I have been informed that NAACP officials said about me and the Southern Christian Leadership Conference. Frankly, I hear these statements every day, and I have seen efforts on the part of NAACP officials to sabotage our humble efforts. But I have never said anything about it publicly or to the press." But let us not succumb to divisions and conflicts. "The job ahead is too great, and the days are too bright to be bickering in the darkness of jealousy, deadening competition, and internal ego struggles."

O N THE MORNING OF JUNE 22, 1960, King met privately with Senator John F. Kennedy of Massachusetts, and they talked for about an hour and a half over breakfast. Kennedy had won a series of dazzling primary victories in the presidential race of that year and was a front-running candidate for the Democratic nomination. Forty-three now, twelve years older than King, the senator was tanned and fit, with a shock of hair, a crisp Boston accent ("cah" for car), and a debonair style. The scion of a rich and famous Massachusetts family, Kennedy was a Harvard man, a war hero, a Pulitzer-prize historian, and a Catholic, which was a major obstacle to his presidential aspirations. In private, he described himself as an "idealist without illusions": a man who combined high purpose with a sense of irony and detached, dispassionate views toward social problems. His record on civil rights was unspectacular, and King at first was not very enthusiastic about his candidacy. But King changed his mind when he learned that two of his white liberal friends—Chester Bowles and Harris Wofford—were on Kennedy's campaign staff.

At breakfast with the senator, King talked about the urgent need for strong executive leadership in civil rights and doubtless specified what he wanted from a Democratic administration—federal registrars to oversee southern elections, endorsement of the sit-ins, legal reprisals against states that denied citizens the right to vote, and "a clear moral

stand against colonialism and racism in all its forms, East and West."
Perhaps Kennedy assured King (as he had prominent liberals) that he
favored congressional and executive action in support of voting rights
and the Supreme Court's desegregation decisions. The next day, King
wrote Bowles that the meeting with Kennedy was "very fruitful and
rewarding." The senator struck him as "forthright and honest" and
definitely concerned—if not deeply knowledgeable—about American
racial matters. King expected that he would do the right thing in civil
rights should he become President.

Still, King refused to endorse Kennedy, Adlai Stevenson, or any
other liberal candidate. As he repeatedly said, no white leader except
Lincoln had ever given enough support to the Negroes' struggle to
warrant their confidence. Moreover, "I feel that someone must remain
in the position of nonalignment, so that he can look objectively at both
parties and be the conscience of both—not the servant or master of
either."

When Kennedy won the Democratic nomination and squared off
against Richard Nixon, the Republican nominee, King followed the
campaign with a watchful eye. Whereas Nixon was appallingly silent
about civil rights, Kennedy promised vigorous presidential leadership
in that area. He denounced Eisenhower for not ending discrimination
in federal housing programs, which could be done "by a stroke of the
Presidential pen," Kennedy said. He also promised "innovative legislation" to integrate schools and strong measures to ensure the Negro's
right to vote and to fair employment in businesses connected with the
federal government.

Though King still declined to endorse Kennedy, he left little doubt
as to where he stood. He was "neutral against Nixon" and the Republican party. "I have always argued," he said, "that we would be further
along in the struggle for civil rights if the Republican party had risen
above its hypocrisy and reactionary tendencies." In particular, he
flayed right-wing Republicans for lining up with Dixiecrats to obstruct
new and creative civil-rights legislation.

But in September King seemed to cool toward the Democrats, too.
"The fact is that both major parties have been hypocritical on the
question of civil rights," he remarked in a speech in New York City.
"Each of them has been willing to follow the long pattern of using the
Negro as a political football." What was needed, he said, was a new
kind of white liberal, the kind "who not only rises up with righteous

indignation when a Negro is lynched in Mississippi, but will be equally incensed when a Negro is denied the right to live in his neighborhood, or join his professional association, or secure a top position in his business. This is no day to pay mere lip service to integration; we must pay life service to it."

On his way home to Atlanta, King stopped off in Georgetown to dine with Kennedy, whose forces were trying to woo the Negro vote and to secure King's help as America's most popular black leader. Frankly, Kennedy was worried about the attitude of black voters. The election was going to be close; what did King think he should do? "I don't know what it is, Senator, but you've got to do something dramatic," King said.

Home in Atlanta, King found himself caught in a bitter crossfire between SNCC and the established Negro leaders in town, including his own father. Last spring, the students had begun a sit-in movement in Atlanta, but it had dwindled when schools had closed for the summer. After the fall term began, however, student leaders planned an ambitious campaign against segregated facilities, to commence on October 19 and to include sit-ins and boycotts against Rich's and other downtown department stores with whites-only lunch counters.

But the old-guard Negro leadership objected to the projected campaign. They cringed at the idea of boycotts and sit-ins, fretted over how white Atlanta would react to such disruption. They wanted to fight segregation in the schools and at the voting polls, not in the streets. They worried, too, that the kids might march off with the Negro masses, thus undermining their hard-won status as spokesmen for Atlanta's black community. They would tell the students, "Don't you know you can't force Rich's to change? Rich's has millions of dollars. How are a bunch of little niggers going to do that? Some of you can't even buy a ten-cent handkerchief down there."

Repelled by such attitudes, the students prevailed on King for support. They regarded him as the symbol of the movement and pleaded with him to join their campaign. But King balked at doing so. For one thing, he had agreed to stay out of local affairs. For another, he hoped that there would be no new civil-rights disturbances until after the presidential election, which pollsters considered too close to call. In fact, King and Kennedy staffers were trying to work out a southern summit meeting between the two, perhaps to take place in Miami during the week the sit-ins were to start. King told the students he could not join them because he would likely be out of town.

At about this time a staff writer for *Life* magazine interviewed King about his role as symbol and leader of the movement. "At times I think I'm a pretty unprepared symbol," King said. "But people cannot devote themselves to a great cause without finding someone who becomes the personification of the cause. People cannot become devoted to Christianity until they find Christ, to democracy until they find Lincoln and Jefferson and Roosevelt, to Communism until they find Marx and Lenin. . . . I know that this is a righteous cause and that by being connected to it I am connected with a transcendent value of right."

During breaks in their discussions, the *Life* man talked with Coretta, too. "He is always calm and even-tempered," she said of her husband. "He sleeps at night. He is not a worrier. He knows that there are some things you can't do anything about." She added, "Still, it all takes a toll on the family. We like to read and listen to music, but we don't have time for it. We can't sit down to supper without somebody coming to the door. And the problems they bring Martin aren't always racial. Sometimes a man just wants to know how he can get his wife back." She paused to think. "The pressure of all this dulls you. Or perhaps you grow better prepared for anything. When some men came one night and burned a cross on the lawn, Martin was away and the children were asleep. But when I went outside and looked, I wasn't afraid. It just seemed like a piece of wood burning to me."

Later, in the quiet of his office, King spoke of the future. "We are dealing with a formidable opposition which is organized and using every method in the books to block our advance." He formed his hands in a pyramid before his face. "There is bound to be tension. I think we're creating the legal, moral and nonviolent tension. Socrates called himself the gadfly. Maybe that's what we are, the creative gadflies of society, bringing on the necessary tension." This was "the critical struggle of our time," he said, a struggle that would produce "the new Atlanta, the new Birmingham, the new Montgomery, the new South."

The students were back again: Lonnie King, Bernard Lee, and attractive coeds from Spelman College, all imploring him to go downtown and sit in with them. "You are the spiritual leader of the Movement," Lonnie King reminded him on the eve of the first demonstration, "and you were born in Atlanta, Georgia, and I think it might add tremendous impetus if you would go." By now he was beginning to waver. He felt morally obligated to join the protest, and anyway the Miami meeting with Kennedy had fallen through, mainly because King still opposed an official endorsement, and he no longer had a valid excuse for telling the students no. All right, he said, he would go to jail with them, in the spirit of Gandhi and Henry David Thoreau. But he made it clear to the public that he was not the leader of the protest, that it was student planned and student sustained.

On Wednesday morning, October 19, some seventy-five students launched what one journalist called "the Second Battle of Atlanta," setting up picket lines and conducting sit-ins at the major downtown stores. King joined a sit-in at Rich's snack bar, was arrested for trespassing and whisked off to jail in a paddy wagon. He refused to pay his $500 bond and promised to "stay in jail 10 years if necessary." As he'd told the *Life* reporter: "In order to serve as a redemptive agency for the nation, to arouse the conscience of the opponent, you go to jail and you stay. You don't pay the fine and you don't pay the bail. You are not to subvert or disrespect the law. You have broken a law which is out of line with the moral law and you are willing to suffer the consequences by serving the time."

He found himself in a cell with strapping Lonnie King, Bernard Lee, and several other male students. "Our prize was that Martin Luther King—our leader—was there with us," Lee recalled. He took a bunk next to theirs, and they spent the slow jail hours talking about segregation, nonviolence, Gandhi, Christianity, love, and the Montgomery bus boycott. "It was almost like a retreat for us," Lee said later. "We had our song fests. We had our meditation periods. We played games. I used to beat the dickens out of Dr. King playing checkers. He thought he could play and I'd just wear him out. He was very relaxed, in a way like a brother to us."

On Saturday Mayor Hartsfield announced that, on the personal recommendation of Senator Kennedy, he had reached an agreement with student leaders that called for the release of King and all other incarcerated Negroes.° In exchange for that, the students agreed to a temporary truce, during which the mayor was to negotiate with downtown merchants about desegregating their lunch counters. The protest

---

°Kennedy's staff denied that he had authorized Hartsfield's statement. A Kennedy aide, the staff said, had merely asked about King's constitutional rights.

ended for now, and the jailed students all went free.

King, however, remained imprisoned. When officials in contiguous DeKalb County learned that he was in Atlanta's Fulton County Jail, they asked that King be turned over to them, to stand trial for violating probation on a traffic fine he'd received months before. The incident had happened one night the previous spring, when the Kings had driven through DeKalb County with Lillian Smith, the eminent white novelist. A cop saw them and pulled King over because he had a white woman in the car with him. To his dismay, King had forgotten to secure a Georgia driver's license and his Alabama license had expired. The cop therefore cited him for driving with an invalid permit. In his trial in DeKalb County, Judge Oscar Mitchell had fined King $25 and placed him on a year's probation. King promptly paid the fine and gave no more thought to the probation, assuming that it related only to his driving privileges.

But now DeKalb County officials argued differently. According to them, his probation required that he stay out of trouble with the law for one year, and his arrest in Atlanta violated that probation. On Monday morning, DeKalb County sheriff deputies picked King up at the jail in Atlanta and sped him across the county line to face Judge Mitchell a second time. On October 25 the judge found him guilty and sentenced him to serve four months at hard labor in Georgia's public-works camp. He even denied King bail and informed his lawyers that they had better appeal in a hurry because he was going on a fishing trip.

King was stunned at the severity of his punishment, and so were his lawyers and supporters at the trial—among them, Roy Wilkins, who brought personal assurances from the NAACP. Coretta, for her part, openly wept in the courtroom, the first time she had cried in public since the movement began.

She and Daddy visited King briefly in jail, and she broke into tears again. DeKalb County was a haven for the Klan; Negroes had gone to jail here and never been seen again. What if she never saw Martin again? "Corrie, dear, you have to be strong," King said. "I've never seen you like this before. You have to be strong for me."

"You don't see me crying," Daddy King said; "I am ready to fight. When you see Daddy crying, Coretta, then you can start crying. I'm not taking this lying down."

But King said wearily, "I think we must prepare ourselves for the fact that I am going to have to serve this time." He asked Coretta to bring him some magazines, newspapers, and writing paper. She promised to do so in the morning, then left with Daddy, glancing back at her husband.

That night several men came to the cell where King lay sleeping with other prisoners. A flashlight shone in his eyes. "King! "King! Wake up!" The men hovered over him in the gloom, and he felt a pang of fear. For Negroes, midnight visits in jail could mean only one thing. They made him get dressed, clamped handcuffs on his wrists and chains on his legs, and dragged him out to a sheriff's car, which roared away into the night. The handcuffs were so tight that his wrists hurt. Where were they taking him? he asked the deputies, but they ignored him. They drove for hours along empty highways, the deputies silhouetted in the glare of the headlights. Every time they slowed the car, King tensed, his eyes wide in the dark.

At last they pulled up at the gates of a prison. A sign read "Reidsville Penitentiary." Reidsville! That meant they had driven him three hundred miles from Atlanta—for what purpose? What would they do to him now? In some dim and dismal room, officials outfitted him in a white prison uniform with green stripes down the pantlegs—all this the result of a minor traffic infraction. Guards marched him down an echoing corridor and pushed him into a cell reserved for hardened criminals. He was in real Klan country now, in a prison whose wardens were brutal and abusive, and he was alone. Well, it was going to be a long stay; he had better try to make the best of it. Somehow he secured some books to read—Dante's *The Divine Comedy*, Upton Sinclair's *The Cup of Fury*, John's Seldon Whale's *Victor and Victim*—and settled in with them.

But he couldn't keep his mind on the books. Cockroaches were crawling all over his narrow cell. And the food tasted awful—acidic black-eyed peas, beans, and greens. He pushed it away. Hungry, numb from the cold, worn down from tension and lack of sleep, he caught a terrible cold and lay shivering and hacking on his bunk.

But suddenly his fortunes changed. On October 28 the prison released him on a $2,000 bond, and SCLC sent a chartered plane to fetch him home. The plane landed at the suburban airport in DeKalb County, and King got off and fell into the arms of his worried wife. Atlanta journalist Pat Watters, who had never seen King until now, noted that he had "a look of vulnerability about him—not softness, not naivete, but somehow hurtable."

The Kings climbed into a large black sedan and rode away toward Atlanta. King had learned from reporters that the Kennedys had been instrumental in getting him out of Reidsville, and Coretta now filled him in on details. Senator Kennedy had phoned her and promised to do all he could to help her husband. And Robert Kennedy (who had initially opposed the senator's call, which was Wofford's idea) then phoned Judge Mitchell, who, in all the adverse publicity surrounding King's imprisonment, reversed his decision and ordered King released on bond.

Presently, the car came to the Fulton County line, where one hundred Negro students, veterans of the Atlanta sit-ins, waited in the dusk to welcome King home. The car stopped; the trailing cars did too; and King got out and waved to the students, silhouetted against a full moon. They broke into the lyrics of "We Shall Overcome," their voices, rising on a soft wind, young and unafraid. "Oh, deep in my heart I do believe, that we shall overcome some day. . . ."

The motorcade started up again and bore King to Ebenezer Church, where eight hundred people greeted him with songs and prayers. "I am deeply indebted to Senator Kennedy, who served as a great force in making my release possible," King had told reporters. "It took a lot of courage for Senator Kennedy to do this, especially in Georgia. For him to be that courageous shows that he is really acting upon principle and not expediency." He informed his people that "I never intend to reject a man running for President of the United States just because he is a Catholic"—a reference to his father, who opposed Kennedy strictly on religious grounds. Though King did not endorse Kennedy, the Atlanta *Journal* said "he did just about everything short of it." In fact, other papers reported that he had endorsed the senator, and millions of Negroes believed that he had. The story gained currency when Ralph Abernathy urged Negroes "to take off your Nixon buttons," and Daddy King himself announced that he was switching his vote to Kennedy, Catholic or no. With the election only a few days away, Kennedy forces distributed two million copies of a pamphlet called *"No Comment Nixon" versus a Candidate with a Heart, Senator Kennedy: The Case of Martin Luther King*, which recounted the Kennedy phone calls in King's behalf and stressed Nixon's silence.

According to many analysts, the entire episode won critical Negro votes for Kennedy and gave him the election in November. Official

returns assigned him 34,226,925 popular votes to Nixon's 34,108,662—
a margin of only 112,881. That Kennedy captured almost three-
fourths of the Negro ballots proved decisive in a contest in which Nixon had largely ignored the black electorate and gone after the white
South instead. For King, the election demonstrated what he had said
all along—that one of the most significant steps a Negro could take
was the short walk to the voting booth.

He rejoiced that Kennedy had won. Now, he believed, the country
had a chief executive who would use his powerful office to enforce
civil rights. But he insisted on correcting press reports that he had
endorsed the President-elect. "The price that one has to pay in public
life is that of being misquoted, misrepresented and misunderstood,"
King said. "I have tried to condition myself to this inevitable situation."

AFTER THE ELECTION, KING WAS SCHEDULED for a thirty-minute debate with James J. Kilpatrick, editor of the Richmond *News-Leader*,
on an NBC-TV show called "The Nation's Future." King said he suffered "a great deal of stress" before the debate, because his time in jail
and heavy schedule made it impossible for him to prepare adequately.
And he was up against a formidable opponent in Kilpatrick, one of
America's preeminent segregationists. They were going to debate a
complex issue—"Are Sit-in Strikes Justifiable?"—and King knew a
large national audience would be watching. What was more, his performance could affect events in Atlanta, where negotiations had broken down and the boycotts and sit-ins resumed. If Kilpatrick defeated
him, it might fuel white intransigence in Atlanta and everywhere else
in the South.

The debate took place on Saturday evening, November 26, in
NBC's New York studios. That day in Atlanta, Klansmen and Negro
students had demonstrated on opposite sides of the same street, and
Mayor Hartsfield was reported as saying that "Atlanta, Georgia, was
the only city in the country where Negroes and the Klan could picket
together to the tune of the Salvation Army." The NBC moderator introduced King first, and he stated his position calmly. The goals of the

sit-ins, he said, were scarcely debatable in a society founded on the principle of equality. Through nonviolence, student protesters were out to remove barriers between colors of men, which prevented America from realizing the ideal of brotherhood. Second, instead of showing disrespect for law (as many people charged), the students had so much respect for law that they wanted to see all laws conform to the moral law of the universe. They also hoped to square local laws with the federal constitution and "the just law of the land." Third, they drew from "the deep wells of democracy that were dug by the Founding Fathers of this nation," a nation that was created in protest (the Boston Tea Party, the Revolution itself). "And so, in sitting down, these students are in reality standing up for the highest and the best in the American tradition."

The cameras switched to Kilpatrick, who dismissed the sit-ins as insignificant. When seen in the overall context of race relations, he argued, "the question of who eats integrated hot dogs seems to me greatly exaggerated." Then he got down to the crux of his argument: the preservation of the white race. King, he maintained, wanted to stamp out segregation everywhere, and at the end of his argument lay "what has been termed the coffee-colored compromise, a society in which every distinction of race has been blotted out by this principle of togetherness." Like most southern whites, Kilpatrick took pride in his race, and he was puzzled—maybe King could comment on this— why Negroes "by and large seem to take so little pride in theirs." Southern whites, he went on, were out to save the predominant racial characteristics developed by white western civilization over the past two thousand years. Thus they fought against race mixing, especially in social areas where "intimate personal association" would foster an ethnic breakdown. As for the sit-ins, King was wrong in calling them nonviolent. On the contrary, they created "a great deal of tense pushing and shoving, in an atmosphere that is electric with restrained violence and hostility." But the essential question was one of property rights—the right of private store owners to serve whomever they please. If they did not want to serve Negroes, they had that right.

King listened to all this in considerable distress. These were complicated points—pretty much summing up white opposition to the sit-ins—and King had little time in which to refute them. He took off on the charge of violence, pointing out that the students hadn't pushed or shoved anybody; the white opposition had done that. The students had shown amazing discipline and dignity. As to property rights, the issue here went beyond exclusive private property. The sit-ins involved privately owned property that depended on the public for its support and livelihood.

But Kilpatrick interrrupted him. He wanted to return to King's recitation on law. "It is an interesting experience to be here tonight," Kilpatrick drawled, "and see Mr. King assert a right to obey those laws he chooses to obey and disobey those that he chooses not to obey and insist the whole time that he has what he terms the highest respect for the law, because he is abiding by the moral law of the universe. I would prefer here on earth that we tried to abide by the law of the land, by the statutes, by the court decisions, by the other acts that establish law here on earth."

But most of these local laws contradicted federal law, King said. Surely Mr. Kilpatrick would agree with that.

"I don't agree with that at all," Kilpatrick retorted.

All moral men, King went on, must agree with St. Augustine that "an unjust law is no law at all" and must be opposed. Local segregation laws were unjust, and that was why the students challenged them. For comparision, take the southern white resistance to the 1954 school decision.

"We thought we were resisting an unjust law, you see," Kilpatrick chuckled.

But you will have to agree, King insisted, that "there is a great distinction between the immoral, hateful, violent resistance of many white segregationists and the nonviolent, peaceful, loving civil resistance of the Negro students." The difference here was between *uncivil* and *civil* disobedience. Moreover—and this was the crucial point—an individual who in his conscience decides to disobey an unjust law must be willing to suffer the consequences and go to jail. "At that moment he is expressing the highest respect for the law," King contended.

Kilpatrick threw up his hands. "This is the most remarkable exposition of obedience to law that I ever remember taking part in. Everyone has the right to decide for himself on the basis of his conscience what laws he regards as just and what he regards as unjust." But he wanted to ask King about "the boycott business," which involved the right of Negroes not to buy. "Do you see any right comparable on the part of the store owners not to sell?"

King replied, "I would say that on the one hand those individuals who are in the common market with their stores should not deny individuals access to the common market. I think, on the other hand, we must see that the boycott method as used by the students is not a negative thing."

But time was up, and King left the studio feeling that he had not done very well. The issue of civil disobedience, he complained, was new to a lot of people and was almost impossible to explain in the brief time allotted to the debate by NBC.

In truth, lack of time was his greatest frustration. Already his schedule for 1961 was heavier than last year's, with an almost endless series of speeches, lectures, and other public appearances, and he feared that he was losing his freshness and creativity, feared that he was harming the southern struggle itself "by being away from the scene of action so often." But there were so many friends to oblige, so much money to raise, so much to be said about the movement, that he felt obligated to accept as many invitations as possible. Still, he longed for a few unhurried hours alone, so that he might write a systematic exposition of his philosophy. Months ago he had started a book of sermons which would elucidate his theological views. But his commitments were so great that he could not work on the book again until next summer.

Over the Christmas holidays, though, he found a few hours in which to prepare an article for *The Nation* called "Equality Now" and directed at John F. Kennedy, whose presidency would begin in the centennial year of Lincoln's first inauguration. The symbolism was not lost on King. He thought he had helped Kennedy get elected, and he intended to influence the new President in the matter of civil rights as Frederick Douglass had influenced Lincoln.

Toiling in his study, contending with an eternally ringing phone, King wrote that Kennedy's was the first administration in one hundred years with a chance to adopt "a radically new approach" in race relations and employ powerful and direct federal intervention to improve them. First, the President could "take the offensive" and fight for a far-reaching civil-rights bill that among other things would safeguard Negro voting rights. Second, he could use "moral persuasion," letting it be known "that he would not participate in any activity in which segregation exists" and thus setting "a clear example for Americans everywhere." Third, Kennedy could virtually abolish segregation through the executive order, one of the strongest weapons at his disposal. The Emancipation Proclamation was such an order, and so was Truman's directive which desegregated the armed forces. Through executive orders, Kennedy could eradicate discrimination in federal employment, in federally contracted business activity, and in federally financed housing and medical programs. In addition, he could deploy federal marshals in Dixie, remembering that in early American history "it was the federal marshal who restored law in frontier communities when local authority broke down." Finally, the President could appoint a Secretary of Integration to coordinate civil-rights activity, and he could urge the United States to provide the American Negro with the kind of special treatment that India accorded the untouchables.

The essay appeared in the February 4, 1961, issue of *The Nation*, and King and his aides distributed copies by the thousands. At the same time, he requested a hearing with Kennedy as soon as possible, so that he could press his suggestions.

Meanwhile King undertook a grueling public tour to raise funds for SCLC and SNCC, which was running the Atlanta boycotts and sit-ins. In Oakland, he set a crowd of 7,500 to "rattling the rafters" of the local auditorium—and collected some $10,000 in that single appearance. He tried to keep apprised of the situation in Atlanta, where the boycott against Rich's had proven almost 100 percent effective. At least his debate with Kilpatrick hadn't hurt the protest there.

When he returned home in mid-March, though, he found the black community ablaze with controversy. As it happened, the established Negro leaders—Daddy King among them—had negotiated an agreement with representatives of the all-white Chamber of Commerce and the fifty or so downtown stores. According to the terms, recorded and signed in the form of a contract, the stores would desegregate their lunch counters within thirty days after Atlanta schools began to accept Negroes in September. The boycott, however, would cease immediately, and students in jail would be released and charges against them dropped. Though at least two students had been present during the negotiations, Lonnie King and many others charged that they had been sold out—they wanted desegregation now, not in September—and black Atlanta rocked with recriminations. Once again King found himself in a bitter crossfire between the students and their elders.

The controversy reached a climax at a noisy mass meeting in one of the Negro churches. Young students and a prominent Negro dentist all inveighed against the agreement: the dentist claimed they had been railroaded; the students wanted to resume demonstrations. Daddy King rose and said he'd been working in this town for thirty years . . . "That's what's wrong," somebody shouted. And the malcontents booed and hooted him down. The established leaders could not control the meeting. It looked as though the agreement were doomed.

King was there that night and felt his father's humiliation. He had to do something to hold the community together. "He took to the pulpit," an observer recalled, "and stood before the crowd for a full minute, searching every face in the audience." Then he spoke extemporaneously in defense of his father and the older leadership, stressing their contribution to the cause. He lamented "the cancerous disease of disunity" that afflicted his people and exhorted them to march out of here stronger and more united than ever before. As for the agreement, he thought the students right in criticizing the date when desegregation was to start. Yet the agreement had much to recommend it, since it was the first written contract Atlanta Negroes had ever extracted from the white man. They had waited one hundred years for justice, so maybe they could wait another four or five months. "If this contract is broken," he concluded, "it will be a disaster and a disgrace. If anyone breaks this contract, let it be the white man."

He walked out of the church, leaving the crowd silent and subdued. Both students and adults agreed that it was a remarkable performance, one that dispelled "the lynch mood which was pervasive that night" and brought them all together. "I had heard him called 'Little Jesus' in the black community," said the president of the Chamber of Commerce, who was in the audience. "Now I understood why." In the end, black Atlanta rallied behind the accord and the boycotts and sit-ins all stopped. That fall, after the schools had accepted their first Negroes, the downtown stores and hotels quietly desegregated their lunch counters. "I am optimistic," King told a reporter, "and I base it on Atlanta itself. Here, we have all the forces on both sides, but the forces of defiance are not as strong as those who realize it's futile to stand on the beaches of history and try to hold back the tide."

SOMETIME THAT SPRING, King met privately with Kennedy in Washington. Harris Wofford, the President's civil-rights adviser, observed that there was always a strain between the two men, because King "came on with a moral tone that was not Kennedy's style and made him uncomfortable." To King's dismay, the President said he was not going to push for a new civil-rights bill as King wanted, mainly because it would alienate powerful southerners on Capitol Hill and imperil other necessary social legislation. "Nobody needs to convince me any longer that we have to solve the problem, not let it drift on gradualism," Kennedy said of racial injustice. "But how do you go about it? If we go into a long fight in Congress, it will bottleneck everything else and still get no [civil rights] bill." But if he would forgo legislation, the President would employ executive action against segregation, as King had urged him to do. Kennedy hoped that this and a strong presidential commitment to civil rights would be enough to mollify King and the other Negro leaders. "I never wanted—and I told him this—to be in the position that I couldn't criticize him if I thought he was wrong," King recalled. "And he said, 'It often helps me to be pushed.'" That was precisely what King intended to do.

King also met with Attorney General Robert Kennedy, thirty-five, slim and bushy-haired, known as "Ruthless Bobby" for his relentless prosecution of labor boss Jimmy Hoffa. Like his brother, Robert Kennedy was fiercely competitive and fiercely loyal to his family. But behind his combative, acerbic public image was a compassionate and sensitive individual who strongly identified with underdogs. As Arthur Schlesinger, Jr., remarked, Robert Kennedy possessed what T. S. Eliot termed "an experiencing nature." But at this juncture he had little experience with racial discrimination. John Seigenthaler, a Kennedy assistant, thought that King and the Attorney General liked one another well enough, but were never close in the sense of being friends, of calling one another Martin and Bobby.

King left Washington with the impression that the Kennedys did not fully understand the evils of segregation, did not regard it as the country's most glaring and most urgent social problem. But perhaps they would learn, if he pushed and goaded them enough. As he spoke around the Republic that spring. he closely monitored the administration's progress in civil rights, and in several areas he was not displeased. When it came to black officeholders, Kennedy altered the patterns of neglect and indifference that had characterized previous administrations and appointed more than forty Negroes to significant posts, naming Robert C. Weaver to run the Housing and Home Finance Agency and placing Thurgood Marshall, hailed as "Mr. Civil Rights" for his brilliant court work with the NAACP Legal Defense Fund, on the Second Court of Appeals in New York. The Kennedy Justice Department also opened negotiations with southern officials regarding school desegregation and initiated a strategy of legal action to gain southern Negroes the right to vote. "We are heartened," King wired Robert Kennedy," that your department is moving ahead with forthrightness and courage in a sincere attempt to solve many of the crises that face our Southland and nation." And he had nothing but praise for the Attorney General when he came south himself and gave a blunt and uncompromising speech on racial justice at the University of Georgia. No Eisenhower attorney general had ever done anything like that.

But King was incensed with the Kennedys over the Bay of Pigs fiasco in Cuba. With administration approval, a CIA-backed force of anti-Castro Cubans launched an invasion there in April, 1961, but Castro's forces threw them back amid a storm of anti-American indignation. "I think our country has done not only a disservice to its own citizens," King complained, "but to the whole of humanity in dealing with the Cuban situation. For some reason, we just don't understand the meaning of the revolution taking place in the world. There is a revolt all over the world against colonialism, reactionary dictatorship, and systems of exploitation. Unless we as a nation join the revolution and go back to the revolutionary spirit that characterized the birth of our nation, I am afraid that we will be relegated to a second-class power in the world with no real moral voice to speak to the conscience of humanity." He felt so strongly about the Bay of Pigs invasion that he signed a major newspaper advertisement denouncing it. "I did this," he said, "because I am as concerned about the international affairs as I am about the civil rights struggle."

He found some consolation in the fact that Kennedy rejected proposals that he hurl the marines into Cuba, and assumed full responsibility for the Bay of Pigs debacle. At least, King said, the President was "big enough to admit when he was wrong."

In EARLY MAY, 1961, James Farmer phoned King that CORE was launching Freedom Rides across the South to challenge segregated interstate bus facilities. In 1946, the U.S. Supreme Court had outlawed segregation on interstate buses and trains and in 1960 had extended the ban to terminals as well, but southern bus stations remained adamantly segregated, something CORE intended to dramatize. Under its auspices, interracial groups boarded two buses in Washington, D.C., and set out on a circuitous journey toward New Orleans, testing terminal facilities as they went. King had dinner with the Freedom Riders when they came through Atlanta, but elected not to accompany them. "CORE started the Freedom Ride," he told his staff, "and should get the credit. We will play a supportive role." Accordingly, SCLC bought the tickets that shuttled the riders off for Alabama, and SCLC affiliates stood ready to help in Birmingham and Montgomery.

In Alabama, the Freedom Rides turned into a nightmare. On Mother's Day, May 14, an armed mob surrounded the first bus just outside of Anniston and set the vehicle afire. The passengers narrowly escaped before the bus exploded in a shower of flames, a scene that newsmen captured in photographs that were widely publicized. The second bus managed to escape the Anniston mob and raced on to Birmingham. But as the Freedom Riders stepped off the bus there, a gang of Klansmen, promised fifteen minutes of immunity by the local police, beat them mercilessly with lead pipes, baseball bats, and bicycle chains.

Because of all the violence, the Freedom Rides got far more media publicity than the sit-ins and traumatized white officialdom from Montgomery to Washington, D.C. In Washington, Robert Kennedy worked behind the scenes to protect the riders and dispatched John Seigenthaler to meet with Alabama Governor John Patterson and see what could be done. Badly mauled, the CORE Freedom Riders canceled their bus trip and flew to New Orleans. But a group of intrepid student activists—many of them veterans of the sit-ins—gathered in Birmingham and vowed to continue the Freedom Rides on their own. By now, Governor Patterson was in a rage against "the namby-pamby" in Washington and the "mobsters" and "trained agitators" invading his sovereign state. "There's nobody in the whole country that's got the spine to stand up to the Goddamned nigger except me," he bellowed at Seigenthaler. "And I'll tell you I've got more mail in the drawers of that desk over there congratulating me on the stand that I've taken against what's going on in this country, the stand I've taken against Martin Luther King and those rabble-rousers." And Seigenthaler could tell this to the Attorney General: if the schools were integrated, by God, "blood's going to flow in the streets."

On Saturday, May 20, the Freedom Riders set off for Montgomery in a bus secured through the Attorney General's efforts. The Montgomery station was weirdly silent when the bus pulled in and the riders filed off. Not a single policeman was in sight. Suddenly a thousand armed whites materialized in the streets and screamed, "Git them niggers," "Kill the nigger-loving son-of-a-bitch," as they pummeled the riders with pipes and clubs.

In Atlanta, King saw the ugly scenes replayed on television and determined then and there to go to Montgomery and stand with the students. He phoned Abernathy and others that he was coming, and the word got out to Kennedy men on the scene in Montgomery. Robert Kennedy then called King and urged him not to go because whites there could not guarantee his safety. But King would not be dissuaded. He flew into Montgomery late Saturday night, and the next day five hundred federal marshals assembled at nearby Maxwell Air Force Base. Kennedy had sent them in because Governor Patterson would not call out the National Guard.

That evening, King spoke at a mass meeting in support of the Freedom Riders at Abernathy's church. A white mob had formed outside, though, and King could hear shouts and heckling. Presently, Fred Shuttlesworth of SCLC's Birmingham affiliate entered the sanctuary with CORE chief James Farmer, who had just arrived in Montgomery. Shuttlesworth had led him through the whites outside, crying, "Out of the way. Go on. Out of the way." And they were so astonished that they let him pass unmolested. Then the crowd went berserk, setting a car ablaze and then attacking the church itself, hurling rocks through its stained-glass windows. In the sanctuary, people huddled frantically together as glass rained down on them and tear-gas bombs bounced along the floor. A clear baritone voice began to sing "Leaning on His Everlasting Arms." In all the confusion, King made his way down to the basement and phoned Robert Kennedy in Washington that a mob was about to burn the church. Kennedy assured him that federal marshals were on their way at that very moment. Returning upstairs, King peered out the front door. As though by a miracle, the marshals had materialized in the gloom. King couldn't make out how many, but they were out there with armbands on, trying to shove the mob back.

As hand-to-hand fighting raged outside, King and the other ministers held a hurried war council. Maybe they ought to surrender, someone said. Wouldn't it be better to surrender than to be flushed out with tear gas and stoned to death as they attempted to escape? At that, King resolved to try and talk to the mob. He opened the door, and a gas bomb hurtled by just over his head. A preacher tossed it out the door; somebody else pulled King back, and he stayed with his people in the sanctuary, praying and singing as the racket of battle continued to punctuate the night.

Then suddenly it was quiet. The marshals, reinforced by a band of state police and a contingent of Alabama National Guardsmen, had finally broken the mob up. The blacks could go home now. National Guard trucks rumbled up to the church and hauled them away through the early-morning streets. The battle of Montgomery was over.

Afterward, Robert Kennedy tried to stop the Freedom Rides. His brother was away in Vienna, meeting with Khrushchev, and the rides were embarrassing him. "Doesn't the Attorney General know that we've been embarrassed all our lives?" said Ralph Abernathy. "I thought that people were going to be killed," Kennedy said later, "and they had made their point. What was the purpose of continuing with it?" When he called for a "cooling-off period," Farmer replied, "We have been cooling off for 100 years. If we got any cooler we'd be in a deep freeze." In a meeting at a minister's home in Montgomery, the Freedom Riders elected to continue their journey come what may and implored King to go with them. But King told them no. His advisers explained that he was on probation in Georgia and would be imprisoned again if he was arrested. "Look, I'm on probation too," a young rider said. And others chimed in, "So am I." "Me, too." "Me, too, and I'm going." But King would not risk going to jail at this critical hour, not when so many groups and incarcerated blacks depended on him to raise them money. And the riders would need him, too, if they ended up in some dreary Mississippi dungeon.

When King announced his decision at a press conference, several riders were bitterly disappointed. "I would rather have heard King say, 'I'm scared—that's why I'm not going,' " a young man complained. "I would have had greater respect for him if he had said that." Said a young woman: "He's a good man but as a symbol of this movement, he leaves a lot to be desired. He has been affected by a lot of middle-class standards. If he wanted to, he could really do something about the South. He could go to Jackson [with us] and tell those people why they should participate in and support the Freedom Rides."

And so King saw the riders off for Mississippi, a convoy of Alabama Guardsmen and a helicopter escorting them as far as the state line. The next King heard, they all had been arrested and locked up in Jackson. Over the summer, three hundred more Freedom Riders stormed into Jackson and got arrested, and more than one hundred others went to jail in additional southern cities. As civil-rights lawyers worked feverishly to get them freed, King plunged into a fund-raising campaign to help cover their legal expenses, soliciting contributions from various Jewish and Christian organizations and addressing rallies for the riders at St. Louis and other places. He also helped the Freedom Ride Coordinating Committee line up scholarships for student riders in need of financial assistance for the fall term.

Nor was that all. In an article published that fall in the *New York Times Magazine*, he tried to interpret the mission of the Freedom Rider for liberal whites. "He is carrying forward a revolutionary destiny of a whole people consciously and deliberately," King wrote. "Hence the extraordinary willingness to fill the jails as if they were honors classes." King pointed out that Negro collegians used to ape white students, dressing and acting like them and aspiring to a professional life cast in the image of their white middle-class counterparts. But this was no longer the case. Through the sit-ins and the Freedom Rides, Negro students were initiating change and liberating themselves from social and psychological servitude. And consider their achievements. To date, lunch counters had been desegregated in 150 southern cities. And Negro students were determined to stand in, sit in, kneel in, and ride in, until every facility in the United States supposedly open to the public admitted Negroes, Indians, Jews, or "what-have-you." It was time for all America, King asserted, to join the students in a campaign to "end Jim Crow Now."

As it turned out, the Freedom Rides dealt a death blow to Jim Crow bus facilities. At Robert Kennedy's request, the Interstate Commerce Commission that September issued regulations ending segregated facilities in interstate bus stations; the regulations were to take effect on November 1. King pronounced this "a remarkable victory" and attributed it to "the way in which the Freedom Riders dramatized the travel conditions in our nation for persons of color." But it would take two years of mopping-up activities before Kennedy could announce: "Systematic segregation of Negroes in interstate transportation has disappeared."

As he reflected on the Freedom Rides, King found another reason for their spectacular success. "Without the presence of the press, there might have been untold massacre in the South. The world seldom believes the horror stories of history until they are documented via mass media. Certainly, there would not have been sufficient pressure to warrant a ruling by the ICC had not this situation been so well-publicized." The lesson seemed unmistakable: to attain real success in civil rights, do something dramatic enough to command national media attention. As events were to prove, King learned that lesson better than any Negro leader of his generation.

ONE NIGHT IN LATE SEPTEMBER, the Kings were dining in a Nashville motel when Wyatt Walker introduced them to William and Lotte Kunstler. King was in town for an SCLC convention, and he had just given a speech on Negro voting rights that powerfully affected Kunstler, a Jewish lawyer deeply involved in civil-rights work. "I had expected someone with the guise of an Old-Testament prophet," Kunstler said. "Instead I found myself across the table from a pleasant-faced, youthful-looking Negro immaculately dressed in a well-tailored business suit. His most distinguishing features were a small, neatly trimmed moustache, high cheekbones, and slightly slanted eyes that gave his face a somewhat Mongolian cast." But the most memorable thing about King was his language. "I was convinced," Kunstler said, "that he was using the finest—and clearest—prose ever uttered."

What concerned King in Nashville was SCLC's sputtering voter-registration campaign. Thanks to increasing white resistance, thanks too to wide-scale Negro fear and apathy, only 29 percent of eligible southern Negroes were now registered to vote. In Alabama, the figure was about 13½ percent; in Mississippi, about 5 percent. These were scandalous conditions in a nation that claimed to be the freest in the world, and King was more than ever determined to rectify them. In his speech at the SCLC convention, King outlined a house-to-house voter-registration canvass that SCLC and allied organizations would undertake that winter. While the civil-rights movement must operate on many fronts, he said in a fund-raising letter, *"the central front . . . we feel is that of suffrage."*

Up in Washington, meanwhile, Robert Kennedy was arguing much the same thing. Legal action alone would never overcome Negro fear and passivity, he told civil-rights leaders. Neither would any more demonstrations like the Freedom Rides, which he was anxious to avoid. Convinced that the ballot was the key to racial justice in the South, that "from the vote, from participation in the elections, flow all other rights," Kennedy persuaded SNCC and CORE to concentrate on registering Negroes to vote in what became known as the Voter Education Project. Urged on by the Justice Department and financed by northern philanthropic organizations, SNCC workers dressed in overalls and boots—the uniform of the southern Negro poor—set up outposts in Dixie and organized registration drives similar to SCLC's.

In mid-October, meanwhile, King flew to Washington for another private talk with the President. King rehearsed the need for a civil-rights bill and for all Americans to enjoy equal opportunity. But his main point involved something new and "historic." It had been almost one hundred years since Lincoln had put forth his preliminary Emancipation Proclamation, King said, and he wanted Kennedy to issue a second Emancipation Proclamation in the form of an executive order eradicating all state segregation statutes. Later King made the same point at a White House dinner. As the Kennedys were showing him some renovations, King went into the room where Lincoln had signed the final decree. "Mr. President," King said, "I'd like for you to come back in this room one day and sit down at that desk and sign the second Emancipation Proclamation." At Kennedy's request, King later presented him with a formal document outlining an executive attack against all forms of segregation.

Kennedy was certainly more accessible to King than Eisenhower had ever been. Still, King was disappointed in Kennedy's civil-rights record for 1961. If his administration had sharply increased the number of Negroes in federal employment, it had also added southern segregationists to the federal bench—a set of rogues who cheerfully obstructed civil-rights litigation. The Kennedys had appointed them mainly to appease southern Democrats on Capitol Hill. For the same reason, the President had declined to sign a federal housing order, which he'd claimed in his campaign could be done "by a stroke of the pen." As a consequence, pens from civil-rights advocates were piling up in Kennedy's mail. King too was incensed that he had backed down on the housing order. "The President did more to undermine confidence in his intentions than could be offset by a series of smaller accomplishments," King wrote later in *The Nation*. True, "the vigorous young men of the Administration" had "reached out more creatively" than their predecessors and had "conceived and launched some imaginative and bold forays." But King deemed the overall record "essentially cautious and defensive" and aimed at "the limited goal of token integration."

In late October King was in London for an hour-long interview on BBC Television about racism in America and colonialism in Africa and Asia. In November he was back in Atlanta, helping the Georgia Council on Human Relations put on its first interracial dinner at the Progressive Country Club. "This, in itself," King said, "is an indication of how things are changing in Georgia." Atlantans themselves had recently elected a new mayor—a young businessman and racial moderate named Ivan Allen, Jr., who pledged to carry out the desegregation of the city. Not that Atlanta was now a mecca of interracial brotherhood. When the mayor-elect distributed a questionnaire about how Atlanta could best be improved, the typical white response was "run Martin Luther King back to Africa." With Atlanta slowly desegregating, with SCLC, SNCC, and CORE all trying to get Negroes on the voter rolls, the cries of a dying order rang across Dixie that fall and winter. At a Klan meeting, one William Hugh Morris declared that southern racial troubles would end if Martin Luther King were assassinated.

In his rare moments at home, King devoted himself to his children—six-year-old Yoki and four-year-old Marty. King worried that the movement robbed him of time with them, and he played with them intensely, trying to cram days and weeks into a few hours. He teased, tickled, and roughhoused them until they practically dismantled the house, Coretta said, looking on with feigned disapproval. Marty recalled that his father told them jokes, too, and was "really funny." As parents, he and Coretta tried to mix discipline with understanding, for King realized that much of what the children would become was being formed in these crucial years. Trying to learn from his father's mistakes, he insisted that what children needed was guidance, not suppression, so that they could learn to express their ideas and desires. A friend observed how relaxed King was with his children. As they talked in his study, the children would come in and ask him to arbitrate a dispute, and he would take care of them. "You know," he said, "we adults are always so busy, we have so many things on our minds, we're so preoccupied, that we don't listen to our children. We say to them, 'See, Daddy's busy.' We tend to forget that they are trying to survive in a world they have to create for themselves. We forget how much creativity and resourcefulness that takes."

Still, King insisted on proper manners. A New York couple who visited the Kings in Atlanta recalled how the children came well-dressed to the dinner table and how King corrected their grammar. Nor was he averse to spanking the children when he thought it necessary. "Whippings must not be so bad," he once remarked, "for I received them until I was fifteen."

As his parents had done, King tried to shield his children from racial prejudice. But inevitably they had to go through the same traumatic time as he: that first anguished recognition of what it meant to be "colored" in Dixie. For Yoki, it came when she begged her father to take her to Funtown, a segregated amusement park in Atlanta. King gave an evasive answer; he really didn't know how to tell her she couldn't go. One day she ran downstairs full of excitement. She had seen a television commercial inviting everyone to visit Funtown, and she wanted to go. At that, King and Coretta sat down with Yoki and for the first time tried to explain segregation to her. "I have won some applause as a speaker," King said later. "But my tongue twisted and my speech stammered seeking to explain to my six-year-old daughter why the public invitation on television didn't include her, and others like her. One of the most painful experiences I have ever faced was to see her tears when I told her that Funtown was *closed* to colored children, for I realized that at that moment the first dark cloud of inferiority had floated into her little mental sky, that at that moment her personality had begun to warp with that first unconscious bitterness toward white people."

But the Kings were determined that she would not become bitter. They taught her to be proud that she was a Negro and warned her that the term "white cracker" was as hateful as the word "nigger." And King assured her that there were plenty of good whites in the world. There were even some in Atlanta who wanted her to go to Funtown, and one day she would go. That was one of the major purposes of the movement—to ensure that children like her and Marty would grow up without the stigma of racial caste. When he spoke on the lecture circuit about the injuries of race, he often referred to Yoki and the Funtown episode. Yes, he wanted freedom *now*, not in some dim and distant future. He wanted it for his own children in this, the only lives they had.

As always, King believed it was mainly Coretta's responsibility to raise their children and care for their home. Of course, when he was there and needed to talk about some movement problem, she was "a great morale booster," said a friend and SCLC assistant. She listened patiently and offered indispensable encouragement and advice. In a way, she and the children were on the front line in their home as much as King was in the actual struggle. She spoke to Harold DeWolf of "the constant dangers they underwent, of the frequent warnings they had received from friends, and the many threatening letters." And though she wanted to play a more significant role in the movement (and later would do so), she idolized her husband and did what he said. Friends who dined with them recalled how she sat at the table quiet and subdued, content to let King hold forth about his work and his world.

Despite his crushing schedule, King tried to preach every other Sunday at his father's church and to do routine ministerial chores. But he spent most working days in Atlanta at SCLC headquarters, laboring on some upcoming speech or talking with Wyatt Walker or Ralph

Abernathy about some staff matter. "Ab," as some staffers referred to Abernathy, had recently moved to Atlanta, to assume the pastorship of West Hunter Baptist Church and be closer to King. King was happy to have him in Atlanta, for there was no man he loved and trusted more. "He trusted Ralph like he trusted Jesus," recalled one SCLC official. "Ralph gave him confidence, security, a strong soul to lean on." True, some of King's advisers thought Abernathy lacked "intellectual strength" and claimed that he sometimes fell asleep in meetings. Others complained about his "ego" and his insatiable need for recognition. But in King's eyes Abernathy was a clever, adoring friend who was always there when King needed him. "I want you to know how much I appreciate your loyalty," he once told Abernathy. "I get all the attention from the press, but you're just as important to the movement as I am. I couldn't do my work if you were not here with me. . . . People often forget that a leader is no stronger than his foundation, the often invisible people who give him support. I'll never forget that. The newspapermen, the cameramen, some of our own SCLC colleagues may forget it, but I want you to know that I *never, never* will forget it."

As several people described it, King and Abernathy had a friendship that was "spiritual," even "mystical." Abernathy is "Dr. King's spiritual brother in the movement and indispensable in that sense, because Dr. King is a man who needs companionship," Walker said. "Some people are loners; some people are like Damon and Pythias—the two fellows who are inseparable." Still, King found in Abernathy something more than spiritual companionship. An aide pointed out how effectively Abernathy arbitrated staff disputes and functioned as unofficial staff pastor, opening and closing meetings with a prayer. Then there was Abernathy's earthy language, which delighted King and never failed to arouse an audience. Negroes, Abernathy said in a recent speech, "will never give up the fight until we are as free to walk the streets of Montgomery as a jay bird is in whistling time."

Thanks to King's recruiting efforts, there were quite a few new faces around SCLC headquarters by late 1961. Two of the new aides, Bernard Lee and James Bevel, were the vanguard of several young Negroes who came to King from the ranks of the student movement. Lee was a stocky, easygoing Virginian who had served four years in the Air Force and then attended Alabama State, only to be expelled for participating in the sit-ins there. He had befriended King during the Atlanta sit-ins and had worked with SNCC before coming aboard SCLC, eventually functioning as King's assistant and constant traveling companion. James Bevel, twenty-four now, had grown up in a Mississippi farming community, become an ordained minister, helped establish SNCC, and joined SCLC in 1961 as head of direct action and a specialist in youth training programs. He usually wore overalls and a dungaree shirt, with a Jewish yarmulke pulled over his shaved head. "The Jewish prophets," he said, "have given more to the world in terms of truth than any others. I wear my yarmulke because I subscribe to the philosophy of the Jewish prophets completely." He was brooding and reckless. "You have to be reckless. That means going for broke. Jesus was reckless, and so was Moses." And he was haunted by a vision of the finality of human life. "I don't get hung up about a hereafter. I always tell drunks, 'Look, there is no heaven, so you might as well be a man while you're here.'" He liked to take young people to a cemetery and tell them, "In 40 years you're going to be here. Now, what are you going to do while you're alive?"

Then there was Andrew Young, twenty-nine that fall, a light-skinned Negro with thick, slanting eyebrows and an easy drawl. Born in New Orleans, where his father was a dentist, Young grew up in a poor neighborhood where drugs and junkies were commonplace. He fought constantly with whites—"If anybody calls you a nigger and you don't hit him," his grandmother admonished him, "don't come home unless you want a spanking." But his parents taught him that racism was a sickness and that there was nothing wrong with him, and he learned to negotiate his way out of difficulties. After high school, he attended Howard University in Washington, D.C., a training ground for black professionals, and competed on the swimming and track teams, offered his fraternity pin to a sorority girl, bragged about his sexual conquests, and prepared himself for life in the Negro middle class. But then he lost all sense of who he was and what he wanted to become. One day in the North Carolina mountains, he had a profound religious experience as he stood naked in a lashing rain. After that he enrolled in the Hartford Theological Seminary and became an ordained minister in the United Church of Christ. He studied Gandhi, married, preached in a south Georgia parish, listened to the music of Muddy Waters, Lightnin' Hopkins, Ray Charles, and Bessie Smith, and meanwhile wound up as an executive for the National Council of Churches in New York, where he specialized in youth work and learned the art of diplomacy in dealing with white preachers, especially in the South. Then came the sit-ins and Freedom Rides. "It really disturbed me that things were happening in the South and I wasn't there," Young recalled. Anxious to work with his people in Dixie, convinced of "the Toynbee prophecy that the Negro is the hope of America," he moved to Atlanta in September, 1961, to administer a voter-education program in close association with SCLC. "There is about him an almost hypnotic calm," two interviewers wrote later. "Nothing hurried, nothing worried." King soon appointed Andy as his special assistant, certain that his patience and experience with whites would make him an effective negotiator.

As December came on, King sought to strengthen SCLC's ties with organized labor, with which Negroes shared a "community of interests." Since SCLC's inception, King had actively solicited union support; and Randolph's Brotherhood of Sleeping Car Porters, the Packing House Workers of Chicago, and District 65 of the Distributive Workers of America, situated in New York, had all contributed generously to SCLC's coffers. King had visited and spoken so often before District 65 that it made him an honorary member. Now he prepared to address George Meany's AFL-CIO, the nation's most powerful labor organization, at its Fourth Constitutional Convention on December 11 in Bal Harbour, Florida, near Miami. This was an excellent forum for King to promote a Negro–big labor alliance, and also to help A. Philip Randolph in his troubles with Meany and the AFL-CIO Executive Council, of which Randolph was a member. Thanks largely to Randolph's influence, all unions in the AFL-CIO except one had dropped their constitutional clauses barring Negro members. Randolph had exhorted the AFL-CIO to expel the offending union and end all forms of discrimination in union ranks, and in 1960 he had become president of the Negro American Labor Council, which he viewed as a Negro-rights pressure group within organized labor. But Meany, a blunt and burly ex-plumber, denounced the NALC as a form of black separatism and Randolph himself as a renegade who refused to work with "the team" (there were militants in the NALC who envisioned it as independent of the AFL-CIO and wanted to fight Meany, but Randolph remained his loyal if critical ally). When Randolph, in a memorandum to the Executive Council, pointed out that several unions in the AFL-CIO either segregated Negroes into separate locals or excluded them by tacit agreement, and demanded that such practices be abolished within six months, Meany and his Executive Council overreacted: in October, 1961, they not only denied the charges but censured Randolph for making them. Negro and white leaders alike condemned the action—King called it "shocking and deplorable"—and rumors flew about that black unionists would picket the upcoming convention in Bal Harbour. According to Cleveland Robinson, an official of District 65 and an assistant to Randolph in the NALC, Meany invited King to address the convention as a peace offering to Randolph and his angry followers. On the prescribed day, standing before a massive gathering of unionists from all over America, King delivered a speech that implicitly defended Randolph—long his hero—and reminded all workers of their common bonds.

Well versed in labor history, he recalled how workers less than a century ago had led barren and exploited lives, enjoying few rights and little respect. He quoted Jack London's description of the twisted and stunted body of a child worker; he quoted Victor Hugo about how there was always more misery in the lower classes than humanity in the upper classes. But there came a time when the working man grew tired of his lot. Determined not to wait for "charitable impulses to grow in his employer," King said, the workingman organized in order to gain a fair share of the fruits of his toil. But he had to battle for years with those "who blindly believed their right to uncontrolled profits was a law of the universe." King pointed out that the most momentous labor struggles came in the 1930s, when legislation like the Wagner Labor Relations Act asserted labor rights but failed to deliver them. So labor itself had to implement the law by striking and demonstrating against a ruthless opposition. From all directions came warnings "to go slow, to be moderate, not to stir up strife." But labor ignored such entreaties and spread itself across the land, until "the day of economic democracy was born."

Negroes, King said, found that the history of labor "mirrors their own experience." Today, Negroes also confronted formidable forces that implored them to go slow and to rely on "the good will and understanding of those who profit by exploiting us." And Negro protest—boycotts and sit-ins—antagonized these forces as much as labor strikes had provoked anti-union people in the 1930s. What was more, Negroes had learned from labor the imperatives of sound organization and self-initiative. In truth "labor's historic tradition of moving forward to create vital people as consumers and citizens has become our own tradition," King said.

In his judgment, labor had done more for the Negro than any other agency in American life. Still, there were unions that were rife with racism. He repeated Randolph's charges that some unions not only barred Negroes from membership but erected "serious and vicious obstacles" to Negroes who sought jobs or improved conditions. This to King was intolerable, since labor and the Negro were natural allies. Negroes, after all, were almost entirely a working-class folk. Their needs were identical to labor's needs: decent wages and housing, fair working conditions, old-age pensions, and health and welfare programs. Moreover, labor and the Negro faced an array of common foes: fanatical right-wing organizations like the John Birch Society, the alliance between big industry and the military, and the coalition of southern Dixiecrats and northern reactionaries in Congress—all were anti-labor and anti-Negro. Organized labor must stamp out discrimination and bigotry within its ranks and join forces with America's twenty million Negroes. The Negro by himself could not eradicate the socio-economic problems that plagued him; he needed the help of organized labor. Labor, on the other hand, stood to gain enormous political strength should working-class Negroes in the South win the right to vote. Together, labor and the Negro could halt the march of automation, whose "humanlike machines," turning out "human scrap along with machine scrap," menaced black and white workers alike. Most important of all, labor and the Negro could reform the South and bring about a day when all workers could stand as one without distinction of color. Together, they could bring about the American dream— "a dream of equality of opportunity, of privilege and property widely distributed," "a dream of a nation where all our gifts and resources are held not for ourselves but as instruments of service for the rest of humanity. . . . That," King said, "is the dream."

Randolph, of course, had addressed his colleagues many a time about unionism and racial brotherhood. But as an orator King was unsurpassed in his ability to move people, to bring them together. "He made that great crowd of hardened unionists—most of them white— stand up and cheer and cheer," recalled Robinson. "I was so affected I found myself crying." Meany himself offered Randolph a conciliatory hand, remarking that those in the labor movement could understand the Negroes' struggle and maybe even their impatience. Before it adjourned, the convention unanimously approved a resolution summoning the AFL-CIO to reinforce its drive to secure equal rights for all Americans and the blessings of union membership to all workers regardless of race or creed. Maybe it could have been stronger, Randolph said, but it was "the best resolution on civil rights that the AFL-CIO has yet adopted"—and the first ever passed unanimously.

King's speech, published in the AFL-CIO *IUD Digest*, reached hundreds of thousands of additional workers and undoubtedly won converts to the civil-rights cause. As the movement intensified, King found an ardent and active friend in red-haired Walter P. Reuther, AFL-CIO vice-president and head of the United Automobile Workers. Within a couple of years, the AFL-CIO itself was functioning as a powerful lobby for civil-rights legislation. But to King's dismay the AFL-CIO failed to get up an uncompromising campaign against union discrimination, and labor's more conservative bosses frowned on Reuther's brand of civil-rights activism.

O N DECEMBER 14, four days after his Bal Harbour speech, King received an urgent phone call from William G. Anderson, a young Negro osteopath in Albany, Georgia. Anderson was president of the Albany Movement, an amalgam of Negro groups struggling to desegregate public facilities and register Negro voters in the city. The movement had begun earlier that year when SNCC workers arrived in Albany to start a voting-rights drive as part of SNCC's new southern strategy. Various local Negro groups had soon joined the students and clamored for an end to segregated public facilities as well as Negro disenfranchisement. A group of Negro students even invaded the bus and railway terminals, to test the ICC's integration order, which went into effect on November 1. But city officials ignored the order, rebuffed the Negro demands, and threw all demonstrators into jail. When local leaders called for mass protests, hundreds of aroused blacks streamed into Shiloh Baptist Church, clapped and sang freedom songs, and marched downtown to demonstrate at the Trailways Bus Terminal, the symbol of white resistance. But the police only arrested them, too. By mid-December hundreds of Negroes were languishing in jail, some in hellish conditions: fifty-four girls found themselves jammed into a cell designed for six people. Afraid that white intransigence was destroying the Albany Movement, Dr. Anderson called

King for help, overriding the strenuous objection of SNCC (they wanted to keep this a local people's movement, SNCC said; Dr. King would only attract a lot of outside attention and turn it into a leader's movement). But Anderson was convinced that King's presence would rally his people and maybe even scare the city into negotiations. "Please," he told King on the phone, "just speak for us one night."

King agreed to make an appearance—he had no intention of getting involved in Albany—and flew there the next evening with Walker and Abernathy. The plane swam through the winter night, until at last King could see the lights of the little Albany airport below. Situated in southwestern Georgia, Albany claimed a population of some 56,000 people, almost half of them Negroes, in what was now pecan, peanut, and corn country. Before the Civil War, though, Albany had been a slave-trading center in a region dotted with plantations. Perhaps King recalled what Du Bois had written about the area in *The Souls of Black Folk:* "For a radius of a hundred miles about Albany stretched a great fertile land, luxuriant with forests of pine, oak, ash, hickory, and poplar, hot with the sun and damp with the rich black swampland; and here the cornerstone of the Cotton Kingdom was laid."

Anderson met King and his companions at the airport and drove them through Albany's wide, flat streets to the Negro section. A nervous, excitable man, easily moved to tears, Anderson spoke with great feeling about the demonstrations and the large crowd awaiting King at Shiloh Baptist Church. Presently, they came to a red-brick, wide-gabled structure with three crosses on the roof, the middle cross lit up with neon. As King got out of the car, he could hear people singing inside:

> *Integration is on its way*
> *Singing glory hallelujah*
> *I'm so glad.*

Then they started shouting, "Aaa-men, Aaa-men, Aaaaaaaaa-men, Free-DOM, Free-DOM. Everybody say freedom. Everybody say freedom. Everbody say Freedom. Free-Dom, Free-DOM." King found the sanctuary so crowded that people were standing and sitting in the aisles. As he and Abernathy made their way to the platform, the people shouted louder still, "FREE-DOM, FREE-DOM, FREE-DOM, FREE-DOM! Martin Luther King says FREE-DOM." Their faces were transfixed with joy, white reporter Pat Watters noted, their voices chorusing spontaneously without a signal given or a beat missed. "I woke up this morning, With my mind, set on freedom, Hallelu . . . hallelu . . . hallelu. . . ." King could feel their excitement. There was something magical going on here, something electrifying. But suddenly the singing stopped, "the sudden quiet," Watters recorded, "as full of meaning as the great cry of the song." Abernathy, his "round face glistening," gave a preliminary speech to build the tension for King. Then amid a "pandemonium of applause," King walked smiling to the pulpit. He spoke slowly at first, almost falteringly. But then he moved into "the singsong cadence of his delivery," Watters said, and reached a fervor that matched the fervor of the crowd. "Go to jail without hating the white folks. . . . They can put you in a dungeon and transform you to glory; if they try to kill you, develop a willingness to die." As King sang on, an old black man punctuated each of his remarks with an explosive *"God Almighty!"*

"How long will we have to suffer injustice?" King asked.

"God Almighty!" the old man shouted.

"How long will justice be crucified and truth buried?"

"God Almighty!"

"Before the victory is won some must face physical death to free their children from a life of psychological handicaps. But we shall overcome." "Shall overcome," the crowd roared back. Then, with a current of emotion flowing back and forth between him and his audience, King cried, "Don't stop now. Keep moving. Walk together, children. Don't you get weary. There's a great camp meeting coming."

Abruptly he stopped. In the silence came the first notes of "We Shall Overcome." Then it rang out, verse after verse, until King felt the soul force of his people as he had never felt it before. Now young Anderson was on his feet, calling for a mass march tomorrow. "Be back in the morning at nine o'clock and bring your marchin' shoes, and Dr. King is gon' march with us. Dr. King will lead us, won't you, Dr. King?" And though he had vowed not to get involved here, King nodded his assent. Of course he would lead them tomorrow. He would go to jail with them tomorrow. Listen to that singing. He had never felt so close to his people.

The next morning, he and Anderson went to City Hall and tried to talk with the mayor and other city officials. Anderson had given them until noon that day to open negotiations; otherwise the Negroes would demonstrate en masse. But the mayor still refused to talk, and they returned to Shiloh Church, where black folk had been waiting to march since seven that morning. "Hundreds of our brothers and sisters, sons and daughters, are in jail," King told them. "We will not rest until they are released. I can't afford to stand idly by while hundreds of Negroes are being falsely arrested simply because they want to be free. We have a right to demonstrate. It is deeply imbedded in the Constitution—the right of assembly, freedom of speech.

"You hear it said some of us are agitators. I am here because there are twenty million Negroes in the United States and I love every one of them. I am concerned about every one of them. What happens to any one of them concerns all indirectly.

"I am here because I love the white man [cries of *yes, yes, well*]. Until the Negro gets free, white men will not be free. . . . I am here because I love America. I'm going to live right here in the United States and probably here in Georgia the rest of my life. I am not an outsider. Anybody who lives in the United States is not an outsider in the United States."

After King spoke, Anderson prayed with his fingertips on the pulpit and tears in his eyes. Then King led them all out of the church, 237 strong, with Anderson and Abernathy at his side. They turned left through the Negro business section, past Carver Junior High a block away, and then headed downtown, passing a building that housed a radio station (part of a chain called Johnny Reb) with an oversized Confederate flag drooping overhead. At last King halted the column at the bus station, where grim-faced policemen in yellow raincoats stood in line. Beyond them paddy wagons blocked the intersections. Police Chief Laurie Pritchett, a round-faced, impish-looking man with pink skin and light red hair, confronted King and Anderson, threatening to arrest them if they proceeded. With great dignity, King and his followers knelt to pray. Two little boys stood alone for a moment, smiling nervously, then got down on their knees as well. Then the marchers surged forward, and the police arrested and herded the lot of them to jail. As they lined up in an alley by the jail's booking office, Pat Watters noticed a Negro woman leaning against the building, her head back, eyes closed, mouth opened wide, singing in solitary exaltation, "We are not afraid, We are not afraid, We are not afraid, Today, Oh-oh-ooh deep in my heart, I know that I do believe, oh-ohh-oh, WE SHALL OVERCOME . . . Some day."

In the booking office, King, Abernathy, and the other demonstrators were charged with parading without a permit, disturbing the peace, and obstructing the sidewalk. King refused bond and surrendered himself to the jailer. "If convicted," he said, "I will refuse to pay the fine. I expect to spend Christmas in jail. I hope thousands will join me."

So here he was, locked up in Albany, the wire services flashing the news across the country. Would his imprisonment spur Washington to intervene? Force the city to negotiate? Word reached him of salutary developments on the outside. From what he could make out, the city had agreed to a truce with other local leaders. The demonstrations were over. King allowed his bond to be posted and left jail to celebrate the victory.

But there was no victory. As King now discovered, the Albany Movement was rent with factional bickerings, and his appearance in the city had made them worse. Jealous and resentful of him, fearful that he would grab all the headlines and usurp the movement, certain rival leaders had negotiated the settlement themselves. By its terms, the demonstrations stopped and the bus terminal desegregated, and the city promised to entertain a petition of Negro grievances in January. But the buses themselves, the parks, theaters, and lunch counters all remained segregated. The agreement was far short of the movement's original demands, and King was terribly embarrassed. "I'm sorry I was bailed out," he said later. "I didn't understand at the time what was happening. We thought that the victory had been won. When we got out, we discovered it was all a hoax."

City officials, of course, were ecstatic. They claimed a triumph over King and (with the mayor alone dissenting) refused to consider any Negro demands. Then the bus company simply shut down, leaving Albany Negroes without public transportation and the movement itself without a single gain. A black group did undertake a selective boycott of white businesses, but Pritchett's cops intimidated and arrested the pickets, and one officer killed a Negro man in what the police claimed was self-defense.

On February 27, 1962, the city's court found King and Abernathy guilty of all charges stemming from the march, but held their sentences in abeyance. Back in Atlanta, King pondered the situation in Albany. Should he risk getting any further engaged there? Could the factious Negro community be united, even under his leadership? He knew this for certain: more than seven hundred of his brothers and sisters were in jail and in desperate need of money for bail and legal fees. He had to help them.

He set out on another fund-raising tour, giving speeches and organizing benefit concerts. He turned up in New York for a luncheon and there met Harry Wachtel, a wealthy Jewish lawyer with powerful business and political connections. King found Harry immensely likable, with his affectionate grin and avuncular ways. Short and barrel-chested, he was a cultivated New Yorker with a mansion on Long Island and a thriving Manhattan law firm. There was something about Wachtel that made him easy to confide in, and he and King became fast friends. Because he wanted to help the civil-rights movement, King retained him as a free legal adviser (he refused any remuneration). In May, Wachtel and several of King's other friends established the Gandhi Society for Human Rights, a tax-exempt organization that raised funds for him.

On July 5, King was in Atlanta, speaking to the NAACP's annual convention in sweltering heat one delegate likened to a Turkish bath. With an eye on the Albany Movement, King warned Negroes that "we should not devour each other to the delight of onlookers who would have us corrupt and sully the noble quality of our crusade." Five days later, he and Abernathy were back in Albany for sentencing in the Recorders Court. After months of delay, the court now ordered them to pay a fine of $178 each or spend forty-five days in jail. In true Gandhi fashion, the friends elected to go to jail, and black Albany stirred again. Chief Pritchett, smiling, happy with himself, told reporters that the Negro leaders were on a cleaning detail. "They're good workers. We had no complaints from them." They prayed and fasted together, and King spent his spare time writing on his long-delayed book of sermons.

On July 13, however, Pritchett released them after an unidentified Negro man paid their fines. King protested bitterly: he wanted to remain in jail as a symbolic act of protest, one that would rally black Albany behind the movement. But Pritchett made them go. "I've been thrown out of lots of places in my day," Abernathy remarked at a mass meeting that night, "but never before have I been thrown out of a jail." King surmised that city officials or Pritchett himself had engineered their release, and he denounced such "subtle and conniving tactics." But a southern journalist later reported that the Negro who paid the fines was an Albany resident, sent by a coalition of white segregationists and conservative blacks who hoped to get rid of King and stop all the agitation.

King, though, resolved to stay and fight. He could not forget that night in Shiloh Church last December, could not forget the power he had sensed in the people. He now felt called to witness in Albany. Yes, God was summoning him here to do battle with injustice. Also, Negroes and whites alike were accusing him of negligent and lackluster leadership in Albany, insisting that nonviolent protest had failed here. If King did not produce a victory, nonviolence could suffer a serious reversal.

He brought his staff to town and announced that they would launch SCLC's first community-wide, nonviolent campaign here, seeking across-the-board desegregation of all public facilities in the city. But Walker and Andrew Young had reservations. "We couldn't see any handles to anything," Young said later. But Abernathy, speaking for King, argued that the spiritual strength of the people would ensure success. "When you are called on to witness," Abernathy said, "you can't always analyze what might happen. You just have to go."

And so they went in, a young and inexperienced SCLC team in its first real test of nonviolent battle. From SCLC field headquarters in the Negro section, King called on the mayor to open negotiations and consider Negro demands. When the mayor ignored him, King told a thousand cheering, shouting Negroes that they were going to "fill up the jails" and "turn Albany upside down." With the white establishment castigating him and his men as "interloping meddlers" and "social quacks," King sent wave after wave of black demonstrators through white Albany, seeking service at lunch counters, libraries, bowling alleys, parks, and movie theaters. Though he commuted in and out of the city, still giving speeches and raising money on the outside, King was in his glory in the mass meetings at Shiloh Church. Here he exhorted his flocks with fervent admonitions and sent them on their missions singing, "I'm walkin' tall, I'm walkin' strong, I'm America's *new* Black Joe."

But King's movement, for all its fervor, went nowhere. As fast as his nonviolent columns reached their targets, Chief Pritchett put them in paddy wagons and dispatched them to jails in other counties. Movement leaders could never muster enough recruits to fill all the jails at his disposal. Then, too, Pritchett treated the marchers with unruffled decorum; he had done his homework on King, studied his Gandhian speeches and methods, and planned to overcome nonviolent protest with nonviolent law enforcement. When demonstrators knelt in prayer, Pritchett bowed his head, then arrested them with a puckish smile. He never clubbed anybody, never called anybody names, and never let his men do so either. Consequently, reporters who covered the Albany campaign saw no brutality on the part of local police to photograph and report. "We killed them with kindness," chuckled one city official.

Pritchett also placed King under round-the-clock police protection, which irritated him and sent him complaining to the chief. But Pritchett was taking no chances. If King was attacked or killed, he said, "the fires would never cease." As the campaign progressed, King and Abernathy developed a grudging respect for him. Once King even canceled a demonstration so that Pritchett could spend the day with his wife. It was their wedding anniversary.

On July 20 the movement received a crippling blow when U.S. District Judge J. Robert Elliott, a Kennedy appointee and an avowed segregationist, handed down a temporary injunction against all forms of civil disobedience in Albany, specifically enjoining King, Abernathy, and other leaders from further civil-rights activities. At Dr. Anderson's home on unpaved Cedar Avenue, King and his lieutenants were in a quandary. Should they violate the injunction and go on marching? Yes, it was unjust and unconstitutional, King said. But he did not want to alienate the federal courts and the Justice Department. "The federal courts have given us our greatest victories," he said, "and I cannot, in good conscience, declare war on them." At a press conference in Anderson's backyard, King announced that he and the other leaders would obey the injunction and "work vigorously in higher courts to have it dissolved." Until then, those cited would lead no further demonstrations.

The next day a local minister himself conducted a march to city hall. "They can stop the leaders," King exulted, "but they can't stop the people." Still, his decision to obey the injunction cost him dearly. SNCC and many others in the black community were infuriated and questioned his credibility as a leader. Moreover, with King and his colleagues out of action, the movement simply lost its momentum.

On July 24, the Fifth Circuit Court of Appeals in Atlanta overruled Elliott's injunction, and King announced that he would lead a mass march on the morrow. But that night violence flared in the streets of Albany. A pregnant wife of a movement leader had taken food to demonstrators in a prison thirty-five miles from the city. There was a scene, and a sheriff's deputy knocked her unconscious and kicked her so viciously that she later miscarried. When city police arrested a protesting group at city hall, Albany blacks could no longer restrain their anger. By nightfall, July 24, some two thousand of them were on a rampage, fighting police with bottles and stones. "You see them nonviolent rocks?" Pritchett yelled at reporters. The governor offered 12,000 National Guardsmen to help restore order.

King was inconsolable. Now he and the movement would be blamed for inciting Negroes to riot. The next day he canceled his scheduled march, declared "A Day of Penance," and confined direct action for the rest of the week to small prayer vigils. He took the idea from Gandhi, who, after the Punjab disturbances of 1919, had suspended civil disobedience until nonviolent discipline could be restored. Then King toured the restaurants, dives, and pool halls in Albany's "Harlem" area, beseeching people to embrace nonviolence. "I hate to hold up your pool game," he told some fellows in one place. "I used to be a pool shark myself." Then he grew serious, his brows furrowed, his voice rising as though he were addressing a crowd. "We are in the midst of a great movement, and we are soliciting the support of all the citizens of Albany. We have had our demonstrations saying we will no longer accept segregation. One thing about the movement is that it is non-violent. As you know, there was some violence last night. Nothing could hurt our movement more. It's exactly what our opposition likes to see. In order that we can continue on a Christian basis with love and non-violence, I wanted to talk to you all and urge you to be non-violent, not to throw bottles. I know if you do this, we are destined to win." He said much the same at smoky beer halls, talking about "a sense of dignity within" to tough, sullen men in work clothes and soiled hats.

After the night of violence, King and his colleagues had a terrible time getting volunteers for jail duty, and the movement seemed on the verge of collapse. In desperation, King and Dr. Anderson turned to Washington for help, imploring the Kennedys to pressure Albany officials to negotiate with them. The Kennedys did urge negotiations, but otherwise refused to intervene. King and his people became incensed at the administration, and Young even claimed it "worked against us." In their view, the Kennedys seemed more concerned with quieting the

movement down than with removing the practices it opposed. A gubernatorial primary campaign was under way in Georgia, with arch-
segregationist Marvin Griffin running against Carl Sanders, who considered defiance of federal law bad for business. The adminstration
was worried that demonstrations might help Griffin and said so to
King. Young recalled that King got into "a pretty long argument" on
the phone with Robert Kennedy and Burke Marshall, Assistant Attorney General for Civil Rights. Sanders was a segregationist, too, and not
going to do much for Negroes, and King was not about to quiet down.
It was one of the few times Young saw him lose his temper. "You
know," King complained, "they do not understand what we are up
against."

Alas, King was up against more than white obstinance. Within the
movement itself, SNCC leaders were growing increasingly fretful. At a
backyard war council with King in the Negro section, they challenged
SCLC's right to monopolize the movement. King denied any such intent, but the students pressed on. They thought him too conservative,
error-prone, and aloof. Moreover, after the kicking of the Negro woman, they were no longer so dedicated to passive resistance, and they
regarded a day of penance as demeaning. Another movement leader
said that King showed amazing forbearance. He welcomed the students' criticism and admitted he had made mistakes. While the students respected his commitment, they left the parley far from reconciled. The rift between him and SNCC was deeper than he probably
realized.

Many local leaders were disillusioned, too. "There is a limit to the
number of people who feel the way to protest is to walk down Jackson
Street into jail," said one man. "Some of us think we can do the job
less wastefully"—that is, by fighting in the courts in the manner of the
NAACP. Moreover, those who expected King to bring freedom "here
and now" had dropped out of the movement when he failed to do so.
As a result, even the mass meetings had subsided in size and fervor. "It
took Gandhi 40 years to achieve independence," King said with a sigh.
"We can't expect miracles here in Albany."

He made a last, desperate attempt to hold the movement together.
On July 27, he and Abernathy led a small demonstration to city hall
and deliberately got arrested and imprisoned. Recalling how Gandhi
had shamed the British and aroused all India with his jailings and
fasts, King intended to remain in jail until the people were marching

again and the city agreed to negotiate.

Chief Pritchett was decent enough to the two prisoners. He had their cell cleaned up with disinfectant, and he let King have books and a radio. King wrote an article about Albany for New York's *Amsterdam News* and worked some more on his book of sermons, to be called *Strength to Love*. On August 5, Coretta turned up at the jail with the children, including a new baby, Dexter, who was born in January. The children had never visited King in jail, and he worried how they would react. So that they would not have to see him behind bars, the jailer let him come out to a shoeshine stand in a front corridor. There he enjoyed a fifteen-minute reunion with his family. Coretta looked very nice, dressed in a pleated dress and pearl earrings and a necklace. She told him how Yolanda had been crying for him, saying, "I want to see Daddy. I want him to come home." When Coretta explained that Daddy was in jail so that all people might go where they liked, Yoki said, "Good, tell him to stay in jail until I can go to Funtown."

After King returned to his cell, the older children frolicked in the foyer of City Hall while Coretta spoke to newsmen. "He looks well," she said of her husband. "I think he feels much better after seeing the children. It gave him a lift."

On August 8 he got another lift. The city was seeking a permanent injunction against the movement in Judge Elliott's court, but the Justice Department was disputing the move, on the grounds that the city had no right to an injunction because it maintained segregated public facilities. King considered this "no solution to the problems"—what was needed was strong federal action against all forms of segregation. Nevertheless, he was grateful for the "legal and moral support" of the Justice Department and claimed that its argument vindicated the movement's position.

Two days later King and Abernathy came to trial in the Recorders Court, and several associates, expecting them to be convicted and returned to jail, scheduled mass protest marches. But the city wanted to get rid of King and Abernathy and ax the movement once and for all. The court therefore suspended their sentences and ordered their release. They were free, thrown out of jail again.

By now, King had lost all control of the Albany Movement. In gloom, he suspended demonstrations and temporarily returned to Atlanta, in hopes that this would give negotiations a chance. On August 15 the City Commission did meet with local Negro leaders, but categorically rejected their demands. King himself returned to Albany several times and chastised city officials for their obstinacy, but it was no use. The Albany Movement was over. After months of Negro protest, the only public facility that was integrated was the library, but only after the chairs were removed to avoid interracial seating. The city shut down its parks and sold its swimming pool, and lunch counters and white schools all remained closed to Negroes. "Albany," chortled Chief Pritchett, "is as segregated as ever."

It was a staggering defeat for King, and he took a pummeling from his critics. Some pronounced themselves "appalled" at his lack of leadership; others accused him of grandstanding in jail and then fleeing town when the movement collapsed; still others declared that nonviolence itself was both impractical and moribund.

King suffered from such criticism. But he told Abernathy that "we must go on, anyhow." In a post-mortem analysis of the campaign, he and his staff conceded that they should not have obeyed the federal court injunction and that it had "broken our backs." King's inability to stay in jail had also hurt the movement, and so had Chief Pritchett's clever tactics. "We were naive enough to think we could fill up the jails," said one despondent aide. "Pritchett was hep to the fact that we couldn't. We ran out of people before he ran out of jails." Worse still, SCLC had charged into Albany without proper planning and preparation. "There wasn't any real strategy," Andrew Young recalled. "I remember being around and not knowing what to do. . . . We didn't know then how to mobilize people in masses." "Our protest was so vague," King confessed, "that we got nothing, and the people were left very depressed and in despair." Had they concentrated on a single target like the bus station or the lunch counters, they might have won a symbolic victory that would have "galvanized support and boosted morale." But given SNCC's hostility to SCLC and given the internal fighting and "tribal jealousies" within the movement, perhaps it had been doomed from the start.

King, Walker, and Abernathy pointed to something else, too. Albany had "too many Uncle Toms" who opposed the movement lest they lose their favored status and their connections with the white establishment. "There are Negroes who will never fight for freedom," King lamented. "There are Negroes who will seek profit for themselves from the struggle. There are even some Negroes who will cooperate with their oppressors. The hammer blows of discrimination, poverty and segregation must warp and corrupt some. No one can pretend that because a people may be oppressed, every individual member is virtuous and worthy."

Finally, there was the insensitivity of federal officials, from the Kennedys in Washington to FBI agents in Albany itself. King and his people could not forget that Robert Kennedy had congratulated the mayor for keeping "peace" in Albany. Nor could they forgive the Justice Department for its flagrant double standard after the movement ended. Though a local sheriff had caned a Negro man and seriously wounded another with pistol shots, the Justice Department refused to prosecute him, offering the lame excuse that FBI agents hadn't produced enough evidence to warrant federal action. But the truth was that they hadn't really tried. When Albany Negroes boycotted the store of a white juror, however, agents "were thick as hogs," complained a Negro leader, as eighty-six of them carried out a thorough and energetic investigation for the Justice Department, which then prosecuted Dr. Anderson and eight other Negro activists for "obstruction of justice." "They almost made an anarchist out of me," said an embittered Negro. "They played politics pure and simple." Said a Negro woman: "Son, I done found out that even the government is a white man."

As they reviewed the Albany campaign, King and his aides were convinced that the FBI was on the side of Albany segregationists. Throughout the movement, blacks time and again had filed complaints about violations of their civil rights, but FBI agents had done nothing about them, nothing at all. In a statement widely quoted in the press, King said, "One of the greatest problems we face with the FBI in the South is that the agents are white southerners who have been influenced by the mores of their community. To maintain their status, they have to be friendly with the local police and people who are promoting segregation. Every time I saw FBI men in Albany, they were with the local police force."

Although this was an accurate appraisal, FBI officials—particularly Director J. Edgar Hoover—became incensed when they read King's remarks in a newspaper. One of the most powerful men in government, an aloof, priggish martinet with an imperial ego, Hoover had built the FBI into his private empire and ruled it with an iron hand. He intimidated Presidents and legislators alike and brooked no criticism from anybody in or out of Washington. As it happened, Hoover was already convinced that King and the civil-rights movement were influenced by Communism, which he regarded as the number-one enemy of the Republic. Since January, in fact, he had bombarded Robert Kennedy with memos that King had Communist associates. His bureau, moreover, had placed King's name on "Section A of the Reserve Index," which listed dangerous people to be rounded up in case of a national emergency, and had launched a full security investigation of King and SCLC. But there was more involved here than the issue of Communism. Hoover detested King personally, blasting him as "no good" on the margin of one memo. Intolerant of Negroes anyway, the director had no stomach for a popular, aggressive, outspoken one like King who rocked the established order.

Urged on by his close deputies, Hoover directed that Assistant Director Cartha "Deke" DeLoach, head of the Crime Records Division, phone King and "correct" his impression of the FBI. But when King failed to return the call, DeLoach took it as a snub and became enraged, damning King as "a vicious liar" who "constantly associates with and takes instructions from [a] ... member of the Communist Party." These were Hoover's sentiments exactly. Attributing only the most sinister motives to King's criticism and seeming rebuff of his bureau, Hoover was determined to ferret out his "subversive" dealings if it was the last thing he and his men did.

PART FIVE

THE DREAMER COMETH

"I am not come to destroy, but to fulfill."

MATTHEW 5:17

In RETROSPECT, KING TRIED to convince himself that Albany had accomplished something, that at least "the Negro people there straightened up their bent backs." A local Negro agreed. "What did we win?" he asked. "We won our self-respect. It changed all my attitudes. This movement made me demand a semblance of first-class citizenship." Also, thanks to the voter-registration drive in Albany and similar efforts elsewhere in Georgia, which expanded the Negro electorate, Sanders defeated Griffin in the Democratic primary and went on to become governor. Since Sanders promised to enforce the law impartially, King supposed that he was preferable to a rabid segregationist like Griffin.

But King was wrong if he thought that much had changed in Georgia. Within a single week that September, 1962, the Klan dynamited four Negro churches in towns near Albany. When he saw those blasted sanctuaries, King gave in to bitterness. "Tears welled up in my heart and in my eyes," he wrote. "No matter what it is we seek, the Negro stands little chance, if any, of securing the approval, consent, or tolerance of the segregationist South."

He was steeped in anguish. So many of his own people seemed not to care about the struggle; so many whites were hostile or indifferent. The Kennedys showed no signs of making civil rights a major priority, which meant no new civil-rights legislation, no safeguards for Negro voting rights, no federal protection for blacks in Dixie, no second Emancipation Proclamation. Young later claimed that King was so disconsolate that he seriously thought about quitting the civil-rights movement. An offer came from Sol Hurok's agency to make him its chief lecturer around the world, with a guarantee of $100,000. Because the agency pressured him for an answer, King had to grapple with his doubts, Young recalled, and finally told them no. It was a decision, observed one writer, that "committed King irrevocably to the Movement."

With awakened resolution, he delivered a spirited address at SCLC's September convention in Birmingham, where Fred Shuttlesworth was directing a Negro boycott of white merchants. As King spoke, a two-hundred-pound white youth, a self-styled Nazi, leaped on stage and punched him in the mouth. Reeling under the boy's slashing fists, King made no effort to defend himself. At last the police and several SCLC delegates subdued his assailant, but King asked that he be allowed to sit back down. "This system that we live under creates people such as this youth," King remarked after the meeting. "I'm not interested in pressing charges. I'm interested in changing the kind of system that produces this kind of man."

Back home in Atlanta, King told Coretta about the incident, and she was horrified that he had wanted the boy to remain in the audience. "Suppose he had a knife or a gun?" she said. "Well, if he had, he would have used it before then," King replied.

That same month, King sat in horror before his television set, watching news clips of the James Meredith crisis at the University of Mississippi in Oxford. Armed with a federal court order, U.S. marshals tried to register Meredith, a Negro and an Air Force veteran. But Governor Ross Barnett and a cadre of state troopers turned them away from the administration building, while armies of white students waved Confederate flags and chanted "Glory, Glory, segregation," to the tune of "The Battle Hymn of the Republic." The Kennedy administration attempted to work out a deal with Barnett, but the governor railed against outside interference and vowed to preserve racial purity at Ole Miss. When federal marshals again sought to register Meredith there, whites opened fire and a terrible battle broke out in which two people were killed and 375 injured. Shocked that it should come to this, the Kennedys had no choice but to dispatch federal troops to quell the riot. At last Meredith registered at the university, but marshals had to escort him to his classes, where whites refused to sit anywhere near him.

"It has been difficult to believe what we have read in the newspapers and more difficult to believe what our television sets have hurled at our eyes," King wrote in *The Nation*. This was "Mississippi's most critical hour since secession," and he castigated the state's abysmal white leadership for allowing "Ole Miss to become a battleground for a cause that was lost a hundred years ago." And though the President had sent troops to Oxford, with southern whites howling that it was Reconstruction all over again, King was deeply disappointed in him. His behind-the-scenes maneuvering with Barnett "made Negroes feel like pawns in a white politician's game," King said. All Kennedy seemed concerned about was a token victory—one Negro enrolled in Mississippi—rather than a serious effort to integrate the nation's schools and improve the wretched lot of Negroes in this country. Where was Kennedy's moral passion anyway? And his vaunted sense of history? How could he fail to perceive that Oxford, Mississippi, had placed democracy on trial and that America more than ever needed "vigorous and firm exercise of the powers of the Presidency?"

The truth was that the President remained preoccupied with foreign affairs, particularly with crucial developments in the Cold War: not only an escalating arms race and ongoing troubles in southeast Asia, but the Cuban missile confrontation that October, which brought the United States and the Soviet Union to the very brink of nuclear war. In the end, Khrushchev backed down and withdrew Russia's missiles from Cuba; and Kennedy basked in what to him was a significant victory, one that compensated for the Bay of Pigs and that preserved American hegemony in this hemisphere. Compared to such Cold War events, from Kennedy's perspective, racial turbulence in the South seemed a succession of nagging, largely avoidable episodes.°

King, though, was more determined than ever to convince the President otherwise, to make him realize that the domestic race problem was a profound *historical* problem that menaced the very future of the Republic and that must be dealt with accordingly. During the late fall and early winter of 1962, in a procession of speeches and published articles, King mounted a personal crusade to make Kennedy act. January 1, 1963, he reminded the President, would be the centennial of Lincoln's Emancipation Proclamation. What better way to

---

*In point of fact, Kennedy was only now starting to comprehend the white South's rigidity and defensiveness on the race issue. Before Oxford, the President had subscribed to the old southern view of Reconstruction, which blamed Dixie's postwar suffering on the federal government, Yankee carpetbaggers, turncoat southern whites, and inept ex-slaves. After Oxford, the Mississippi legislature compiled a report that blamed the entire crisis there on the U.S. marshals. Once he read that, Kennedy told his brother that he could never again believe the old interpretation of Reconstruction. If southern whites could behave this way now, he said, they must have behaved the same way a hundred years ago.

commemorate that celebrated day, King asked, than for the President to promulgate a second Emancipation Proclamation, as King had been exhorting him to do? Doubtless Kennedy shrank from doing so because he believed that his margin of victory in 1960 had been too thin, that he had no mandate for so bold a thrust, and that he was afraid of offending the South and its northern allies. Lincoln's dilemma had been similar. Even though he thought slavery a monstrous moral wrong, Lincoln had shied away from an emancipation decree lest he alienate the loyal border states and provoke northern conservatives, too. But he no longer hesitated "when historic necessity charted but one course," King said. Castigated from all sides, assailed by all the winds of conflict and confusion, Lincoln searched his way through to his answer, embodied in his immortal words, "In giving freedom to the slave we assure freedom to the free, honorable alike in what we give and what we preserve." And so he put forth the Emancipation Proclamation, which broke the shackles of several million oppressed Americans and revived the principle of equality in the Declaration of Independence, of which Lincoln's decree was "the offspring." The proclamation placed "the North on the side of justice and civilization," as Frederick Douglass put it, and earned Lincoln a permanent place in history.

The centennial of Lincoln's proclamation, King instructed Kennedy, reminds us that "the forceful, extensive use of executive power is deeply rooted in our tradition." It reminds us that Lincoln's was the strongest measure ever to come from an American president, one that altered the economy, liberated an enslaved race, and helped shape a momentous social revolution. The Lincoln precedent should have inspired subsequent presidents to complete the process of emancipation, King said. But in the ensuing century not one possessed "the daring or the will" to do so.

Now Kennedy had the opportunity to do so and earn himself a place in history. On January 1, 1963, on the one hundredth anniversary of Lincoln's proclamation, Kennedy could "make its declaration of freedom real." The President could issue his own proclamation, one declaring that segregation—a modern form of slavery—was morally and legally indefensible, that it was henceforth abolished, and that the federal government would use all its power to enforce the Negro's constitutional rights. "The key to everything," King asserted, "is Federal commitment, full, unequivocal, and unremitting."

Years ago, King noted, Harvard's Arthur M. Schlesinger, Sr., had polled his fellow American historians and asked them to name the greatest Presidents. Lincoln led the list, not because of personal magnetism but because of his sense of history—his ability to identify himself with a historical turning point in his era. Now the Republic had reached a historical turning point in the sixty-second year of the twentieth century, King declared, and "the day has come for a modern Emancipation Proclamation," so that America at last could fulfill "the luminous promise of Democracy."

AFTER SCLC's CONVENTION IN SEPTEMBER, King had a series of pressing phone conversations with Fred Shuttlesworth, head of SCLC's Birmingham affiliate, the Alabama Christian Movement for Human Rights (ACMHR). For several years, Shuttlesworth and his people had struggled to desegregate Birmingham's buses, schools, parks, and lunch counters, only to meet brutal white opposition. Not only did Police Commissioner Eugene "Bull" Connor clap them into jail, but marauding whites bombed so many of their homes that one Negro section became known as Dynamite Hill.

King had followed events in Birmingham and had great admiration for Shuttlesworth, an absolutely fearless man who had made going to jail "a badge of honor." Alabama born and bred, he was a spare man with close-cropped hair and pastor of Bethel Baptist Church. Since 1956, when he had led an attack against the city's Jim Crow buses, Shuttlesworth had suffered unbelievable violence and abuse. On Christmas night, 1956, his home was bombed and Shuttlesworth himself almost killed. Announcing that God had saved him and that "I wasn't saved to run," he conducted another demonstration against the buses, and whites retaliated by blowing up his church. When he and his wife tried to enroll their children in a white school, a mob beat him with chains and brass knuckles and stabbed his wife in the hip. Because of his civil-rights militancy, he had gone to jail eight times, fought a $3 million lawsuit brought against him by city officials, and seen his car and personal property sold off in public auction. Yet he went on challenging segregation, because he knew it "wasn't just gon' die away."

In March, 1962, ACMHR and local Negro students launched a selective boycott of downtown stores; and Shuttlesworth urged SCLC to join them in a combined mass-action campaign in the city. In May, King and SCLC's Board of Directors seriously considered Shuttlesworth's proposal, but then King got involved in Albany. When SCLC chose Birmingham as the site of its fall convention, rumors flew about an impending SCLC invasion, and several merchants—already hurt by ACMHR's boycott—agreed to desegregate their lunch counters in a desperate effort to forestall demonstrations. In good faith, Shuttlesworth called off the boycott, but after the convention came and passed the merchants predictably reneged on their promise. And Shuttlesworth was mad. The only way this city was ever going to change, he told King, was for their two organizations to join forces and do battle with the "sin" and "darkness" here.

After Albany, King needed little persuasion. Here was a chance to make up for that debacle, to show all the country that SCLC could win a victory for the Negro and that nonviolence was not dead. Accordingly, he committed himself to a major direct-action campaign in Birmingham, and Shuttlesworth was euphoric. He was certain that with "SCLC's staff and know-how and dedication from Albany" and his own seven years of battle experience, they could "make a confrontation which would bring the nation . . . to recognize the injustice."

Still, King and his staff realized that it was going to be a tough campaign, a dangerous campaign. King himself called Birmingham "the most thoroughly segregated city in the country," an American Johannesburg that was ruled by fear and plagued by hate. Here Negroes not only lived with the constant threat of violence (recently Klansmen had castrated Negro and then left his mutilated body on a lonely road), but suffered from the full range of discrimination. Across the city, white moderates were intimidated and mute; nobody talked freely. Aroused whites had recently banned a book that featured black and white rabbits, and had launched a drive to prohibit "Negro music" from being played on white radio stations. Because of Birmingham's stringent segregation policies, the Metropolitan Opera no longer visited the city. And the Southern Association baseball team had also departed. Apart from bus and railway facilities, King said, about the only things whites and blacks shared were the streets and the water and sewage systems.

Yes, Birmingham was a mean and violent place. Yet as Walker said, "We felt that if we could crack that city, then we could crack

Martin Luther King, Sr., with Alberta (left), Grandmother Williams, A. D. (front left), Christine, and M. L. (*Martin Luther King, Jr.*)

King and Coretta (center), with Montgomery boycotters, after King's court conviction, March 22, 1956. (*UPI*)

Featured in *Time* magazine, February 1957. Seven years later, King was *Time*'s "Man of the Year." *(Walter Bennett, for Time, Inc.)*

With his mother and Coretta, King recuperates in Harlem Hospital after being stabbed. *(UPI)*

King's family in December, 1963, in Atlanta: Yolanda (Yoki), Coretta, Bernice (Bunny), Dexter, and Marty. *(Jay: Leviton - Atlanta)*

"Today, the choice is no longer tween violence and nonviolence. either nonviolence or nonexisten The Negro may be God's appeal to age." *(Henri Cartier-Bresson, Magnum)*

"Our capacity to deal creatively with shattered dreams is ultimately determined by our faith in God....However dismal and catastrophic may be the present circumstances, we know we are not alone." *(UPI)*

Albany, Georgia, in December, 1961. Police Chief Laurie Pritchett tells King and Dr. William G. Anderson that they are under arrest. *(UPI)*

King and Ralph Abernathy leading a march in Birmingham in direct violation of a court order. Bull Connor's police arrested and jailed them. *(UPI)*

In jail with Ralph Abernathy, St. Augustine, Florida, June, 1964. "Under a government which imprisons any unjustly," King had learned from Thoreau, "the true place for a just man is also a prison." *(UPI)*

Receiving the Nobel Peace Prize in Oslo, Norway, December 10, 1964. "There is still hope for a brighter tomorrow." *(UPI)*

"We're not on our knees begging for the ballot. *We are demanding the ballot!*" Leading the voting rights drive in Selma, Alabama, 1965. *(UPI)*

King commuted in and out of Chicago during the campaign there in 1966. Here he awaits his next plane with Andrew Young. *(Bob Fitch)*

In September, 1967, King was stu
against Lyndon Johnson and the Vi
War, as well as devising an all-ou
paign to help America's poor. (Mag

On the balcony of the Lorraine Motel in Memphis, Tennessee, April 3, 1968. From left: Hosea Williams, Jesse Jackson, King, and Abernathy. (Wide World)

any city." And "the results," said another King adviser, "would radiate across the South."

They had no intention, though, of dashing blindly into Birmingham as they had into Albany. At a three-day retreat, held at SCLC's training center in Dorchester, Georgia, King and his aides and advisers worked out a detailed plan called Project C, for Confrontation Birmingham. As in Albany, their goal was to activate the entire black community and force the desegregation of all public facilities in the city. But to bring that about, they would attack the business community rather than the city government, would treat with merchants rather than local politicians. As King explained, "You don't win against a political power structure where you don't have the votes. But you can win against an economic power structure when you have the economic power to make the difference between a merchant's profit and loss." Unlike Albany, where they had assailed all segregated accommodations and (in Walker's words) had "bit off more than we could chew," they would concentrate on a few downtown targets—Woolworth's, H. L. Green's, J. J. Newberry's—and harass them with boycotts and sit-ins. Once these were under way, King's forces would resort to mass marches and arrests to call attention to the plight of Birmingham's Negroes. They would escalate the marches, tighten up the boycotts, even fill up the jails, until they brought about a moment of "creative tension," when the evils of segregation would stand revealed and white merchants would be driven to the negotiating table.

On a more important level, the campaign was directed at the federal government itself. For even if they failed to break Birmingham, King and his men hoped to demonstrate "before the court of world opinion" the urgent need for change. They hoped to force the President and Congress to produce legislation that would desegregate public accommodations everywhere in Dixie.

All this reflected significant changes in King's thinking about nonviolent resistance. For Montgomery and Albany had both taught him that nonviolent persuasion by itself might not win over the oppressor. No, federal action seemed imperative to effect lasting change in southern race relations. Yet King understood that the federal government seldom responded without pressure. And he planned to generate that in the streets of Birmingham, where his legions would expose the violence inherent in segregation and so stab the national conscience that Washington would be obliged to intervene with corrective measures.

"Instead of submitting to surreptitious cruelty in thousands of dark jail cells and on countless shadowed street corners," King said, the nonviolent resister "would force his oppressor to commit his brutality openly— in the light of day—with the rest of the world looking on." In short, provocation was now a crucial aspect of King's nonviolent strategy.

In his view, Birmingham was an ideal target for aggressive nonviolence, for there was no Chief Pritchett here to deflate protests with well-publicized kindness. In fact, the City Commission only aggravated the racial tensions that gripped the city. City Commissioner Arthur Haynes warned whites that even to integrate the parks would eventuate in "a nigger mayor . . . or a nigger police chief." But the real scoundrel was Police Commissioner Connor, a white-haired, fleshy man of sixty-three, with a glass eye, jug ears, nagging sinuses, and a bullfrog voice. "An overgrown country boy," as one reporter described him, he had made himself famous in Birmingham by the cornpone way he used to announce baseball games. Ole Bull, as whites called him, hated "junkateering journalists" and snorted that "the trouble with America is Communism, socialism, and journalism," all of which were out to "inta-grate" America and destroy the white race. He cringed at the idea of blacks and whites mixing together. A newsman recalled him "running up and down the City Hall corridors exclaiming, 'Long as I'm po-leece commissioner in Birmingham, the niggers and white folks ain't gon' segregate together in this man's town.'" After the Brown decision, Ole Bull hurled epithets at the Supreme Court, offered to fight the Attorney General, and promised that "blood would run in the streets" before Birmingham would desegregate. If he remained in power, Bull Connor could probably be counted on to commit some dramatic blunder that would command national media attention.

That November, as it happened, Birmingham voted to replace its city commission form of government with a mayor-council system, the mayor to be chosen in a special election on March 5, 1963. As a consequence, a few white moderates broke their silence and urged Shuttlesworth to cease all civil-rights activities until a new government could be elected, after which meaningful change was bound to occur. But Shuttlesworth doubted that any white administration would alter Birmingham's apartheid practices on its own. In any case, Connor announced that he was going to run for mayor himself, and he stood a good chance of winning, given his popularity and Negro-hating ways. If so, he would remain King's chief adversary.

And beyond Connor loomed the specter of George Corley Wallace, who had recently won the Alabama governorship by the largest popular vote in Alabama gubernatorial history. An obstreperous, prancing little man, with a well-coiffed pompadour, he had attended the University of Alabama and had once been a racial moderate. But when a white supremacist trounced him in his first bid for governor, Wallace vowed never to be "out-niggered again." In the 1962 contest, he campaigned up and down the state with a hillbilly singer, deriding the U.S. Supreme Court and pledging to "stand in the schoolhouse door" to prevent desegregation. A writer for the *Saturday Evening Post* reported that he walked "with his back arched like a cavalry officer leading a charge against Yankee cannon at Shiloh." Once Project C were under way, this feisty, ill-tempered man might well send in the Alabama highway patrol, with their billy clubs and Confederate insignias, and attract still more national attention.

As King and his colleagues made their final preparations at Dorchester, they adopted code names to confuse the state and local police, who often tapped the phones of Birmingham's Negro leaders. Abernathy was "Dean Rusk," Shuttlesworth was "Bull," Walker was "RFK," and King was "JFK." Demonstrators were "baptismal candidates," and going to jail was "going to get baptized." There was a lot of merriment about the names and how they were certain to confound the police. But before the retreat ended, King gave his staff a solemn warning: "I want to make a point that I think everyone here should consider very carefully and decide if he wants to be with this campaign." He said, "There are less than a dozen people here assessing the type of enemy we're going to face. I have to tell you that in my judgment, some of the people sitting here today will not come back alive from this campaign. And I want you to think about it."

In January, 1963, King publicly announced that he was going to Birmingham and that he would lead demonstrations there until "Pharaoh lets God's people go." That same month, George Wallace was inaugurated as governor in Montgomery. He was standing, Wallace pointed out, on the same ground where Jefferson Davis had been inaugurated as president of the Confederacy. And now, Wallace cried, "from the cradle of the Confederacy, this very heart of the great Anglo-Saxon Southland, I draw the line in the dust and toss the gauntlet before the feet of tyranny. And I say, Segregation now! Segregation tomorrow! Segregation forever!"

Throughout January and February, King maintained a frenetic pace, speaking at fund-raising rallies in New York, California, and Texas, and working in another visit with President Kennedy. On the stump, he reminded his audiences—and the President—that the Birmingham campaign would commence in the centennial year of the Emancipation Proclamation, underscoring the dismal fact that a century later the Negro was still oppressed. "We have not seen the kind of action that the enormity of the situation demands," he complained of Kennedy. "Our churches are bombed and burned, people are shot, the vote denied." "Only a Negro understands the social leprosy that segregation inflicts upon him," he said in Chicago. "Like a nagging hound of hell, it follows his every activity, leaving him tormented by day and haunted by night. The suppressed fears and resentments and the expressed anxieties and sensitivities make each day of life a turmoil. Every confrontation with the restrictions is another emotional battle in a never ending war. He is shackled in his waking moments to tiptoe stance, never quite knowing what to expect next. Nothing can be more diabolical than a deliberate attempt to destroy in any man his will to be a man."

In February, King's constant proddings seemed to arouse Kennedy at last to act. While he spurned a second Emancipation Proclamation, the President did submit a new civil-rights bill to Congress, as King had adjured him to do. And Kennedy spoke of the wrong of segregation with a moral fervor that sounded like King himself. King very much admired the President's rhetoric, but found his bill a generally lusterless effort that ignored such critical problems as segregated schools and public accommodations. But no matter: the bill died in Congress anyway. "There wasn't any interest in it," said Robert Kennedy. "There was no public demand for it. There was no demand by the newspapers or radio or television. . . . Nobody paid any attention."

Maybe nobody cared now. But King intended to awaken the moral conscience of America in the streets of Birmingham.

Sometime that February, King arrived in Birmingham with his advance staff and installed SCLC's command post in Room 30 of the Gaston Motel, situated near Kelly Ingram Park in the Negro section. King's timetable called for the campaign to begin in the first week of March and then build to a peak of intensity at Eastertime, the second biggest buying season of the year. But in a secret meeting at the Gaston Motel, local Negro leaders objected to King's strategy, reminding him that Birmingham would elect its new mayor on March 5, with Connor and mild-mannered Albert Boutwell now leading the list of candidates. For the Negroes, Boutwell seemed the lesser of two evils, and they wanted nothing to happen that would help Bull Connor. To keep the campaign from becoming "a political football," King agreed to postpone demonstrations until two weeks after the election. Meanwhile Wyatt Walker, a skilled organizer, set about forming committees and enlisting recruits.

As luck would have it, the election produced no winner, forcing Boutwell and Connor into a run-off election, scheduled for April 2, and throwing King's entire timetable awry. By now, Walker had some 250 volunteers ready to go to jail. But under strong local pressure King delayed the campaign a second time, lest Connor use it to whip up racial fears and propel himself into city hall. At that, King pulled his staff out of Birmingham, with plans to return on the night of the run-off election and launch Project C the following day.

In the meantime he hastened to New York to consult with lawyers of the NAACP Legal Defense Fund about state-court injunctions and other legal barriers Birmingham's power structure might erect against him. In Harry Belafonte's "palatial" New York apartment, King explained the purpose of the campaign to seventy-five celebrities, activists, and politicos, who agreed to help raise funds for bail bonds. A committee under Belafonte was to maintain close contact with King's Birmingham headquarters and send him money as he needed it. By then, he had alerted SCLC affiliates, religious organizations, and labor friends across the land, and they too were busily getting up funds for the campaign.

Then King hurried home, where Coretta was nine months pregnant with their fourth child. On March 28 he was at the hospital when she gave birth to a daughter, whom they christened Bernice Albertine but called Bunny. Meanwhile Atlanta's Lovett School, which had Episcopalian connections, had rejected little Marty because of his race, and King was angry and eager for battle. At SCLC headquarters, he and his staff tended to final details of Confrontation Birmingham and by April 2 all was in readiness.

In Birmingham's mayoral election that day, Boutwell whipped Connor by almost 8,000 votes, prompting a local paper to headline, "NEW DAY DAWNS FOR BIRMINGHAM." But King and his colleagues regarded Boutwell as "just a dignified Bull Connor" and pointed out that as a state senator he had authored legislation that thwarted the Brown decision. That night King flew to Birmingham with his staff and flashed word out to Walker's volunteers that demonstrations would begin on the morrow. But because of all the delays, only sixty-five people responded to his call. "With this modest task force," King ruefully noted, "we launched the direct-action campaign in Birmingham."

It began in a vortex of confusion. On April 3 Connor and the other two commissioners, contending that they had been elected to serve until 1965, refused to vacate their offices and took legal action to prevent Boutwell from taking over the city. Until the courts decided the issue, Birmingham foundered under rival city governments, leaving Police Commissioner Connor with unchecked power to deal with "nigger troublemakers." That same day, King issued a "Birmingham Manifesto," which demanded that all lunch counters, restrooms, and drinking fountains in downtown department and variety stores be desegregated, that Negroes be hired in local business and industry, and that a biracial committee be established to work out a schedule for desegregation in other areas of city life. Directed at the economic power structure rather than either city government, the manifesto warned that demonstrations and boycotts would continue until these demands were met.

With that, "the battle for the soul of Birmingham" was on, as sixty-five Negroes staged sit-ins at five downtown department stores, and Connor's cops dragged twenty of them away to jail. At command center in the Gaston Motel, King orchestrated the sit-ins and made plans to go to jail himself, as a dramatic symbol of the Negro's plight in Birmingham. By now, a veritable army of national and foreign newsmen was in the city to cover King's campaign. "Go where the Mahatma goes," a prominent American newspaper instructed its southern correspondent. "He might get killed." Still, King was glad to see so many reporters. He wanted the drama of Birmingham to play on television sets and in the front pages of newspapers around the world.

On the first day, however, the campaign provoked a storm of adverse criticism. In Birmingham, Mayor-elect Boutwell blamed the sit-ins on outsiders "whose sole purpose is to stir strife and discord here," and he urged everyone, white and Negro alike, to ignore what was happening in his city. In Washington, Robert Kennedy bemoaned the campaign as "ill-timed" and pressured King to postpone it and give Boutwell a chance. Was it not ridiculous, King retorted, to speak of timing when "the Negro had already suffered one hundred years of delay"? But as he angrily noted, the Washington *Post* and most of the national press echoed Kennedy's argument, portraying King and his lieutenants as irresponsible hotspurs invading Birmingham just as it "was getting ready to change overnight into Paradise."

But in truth many local Negroes impugned the campaign, too, and insisted that "we ought to give Boutwell more of a chance." Some Negroes even voiced the "outsider" argument about King and SCLC. And some even opposed the campaign because they thought they truly were inferior and deserved their lot. King had encountered that attitude before, and it distressed and saddened him.

Because of the divisions in the Negro community (it was Albany all over again), King forgot about going to jail for now and consumed an entire week trying to rally local Negroes to his standard. While limited sit-ins and boycotts continued, he appealed to groups of business and professional people, reminded them that "Birmingham is the testing ground" and that Negroes must "stick together if we ever hope to change its ways." He pleaded with gatherings of Negro ministers to stop preaching "the glories of heaven" while ignoring conditions in Birmingham that caused men "an earthly hell." The ministers were the most independent and influential leaders in the black community. How could the Negro ever improve his station in life without their guidance, inspiration, and support? "The bell of man's inhumanity to man does not toll for one man," King said. "It tolls for you, for me, for all of us."

"I spoke from my heart," King wrote later, "and out of each meeting came firm endorsements and pledges of participation and support." With a new unity developing in the black community, King was certain that "the foundations of the old order were doomed."

Meanwhile, in nightly mass meetings at the Negro churches, he summoned volunteers "to serve in our nonviolent army" and make going to jail their badge of honor. "We did not hesitate to call our movements an army," King said. "But it was a special army, with no supplies but its sincerity, no uniform but its determination, no arsenal except its faith, no currency but its conscience. It was an army that would move but not maul. It was an army that would sing but not slay. It was an army to storm bastions of hatred, to lay siege to the fortress of segregation, to surround symbols of discrimination." And so "the peaceful warrior," as Abernathy styled King, called his people to nonviolent battle, to march against the Confederate flag of segregated Birmingham, the same flag that Lincoln's troops had fought against a hundred years before.

And they came forward, ten and twenty Negroes at a time, surrendering whatever weapons they had to King's stern-eyed staffers and attending workshops that trained them for nonviolent combat. Through socio-dramas that simulated real-life situations, the volunteers learned how to resist without rancor, how to be cursed and not reply, how to be beaten and not strike back. According to a Negro enlisted off the streets, King's message and methods controlled a great deal of pent-up rage in the black population. When he first called for recruits, some Negroes viewed this as "a chance to kill me a cracker." But King's aides would take such men to the mass meetings and get them to singing and clapping and amening to King's oratory, and that would quiet the angriest man in town, said one volunteer, because King "just had that thing about him." He had to have that thing about him; otherwise he feared that some of his brothers might try to fight the white man with guns and knives, which could ignite a race war in Birmingham in which the Negro minority would be exterminated.

By Wednesday, April 10, small columns of singing Negroes were parading before City Hall as well as picketing the downtown stores. Once the cops showed up with a police dog, which attacked one Negro bystander and snapped and snarled at others. As the campaign grew in intensity, the police had a hard time rounding up all the demonstrators in Connor's "jail 'em all" strategy. As fast as Connor would lock them up, movement leaders would bail the protesters out and send them back into the streets. Thus far some 300 Negroes had gone to jail—a modest number in comparison to the 738 imprisoned in the initial demonstrations in Albany. But at least SCLC had established a beach-head in the battle of Birmingham.

Iт was long after midnight, April 11, in Room 30 of the Gaston Motel, and King and his associates were talking intently over cups of coffee, the large room clouded with cigarette smoke. The sheriff had just served King with a state-court injunction, requested by city attorneys, which prohibited him, Abernathy, Walker, Shuttlesworth, and other movement leaders from conducting demonstrations. The injunction provoked a lively discussion in Room 30, with King reminding everyone how segregationists had vowed to block the Brown decision through a "century of litigation." Since then, the court injunction had become their major weapon against civil-rights operations, entangling them in litigation that sometimes consumed two or three years. The tactic had been "maliciously effective." King recalled how the injunction had been used to break up a student protest in Talladega, Alabama, and to cripple the Albany campaign beyond repair. Well, there was no question what King would do in this case. He would violate the injunction and get arrested. It was time for him and Abernathy to go to jail anyway and "present our bodies as personal witnesses in this crusade." This would also create a lot of sympathy for the movement, King said, and really "stir up the local Negro community behind us." They would break the injunction day after tomorrow, on Good Friday.

The next day, King held a press conference in the motel courtyard. Wearing faded denim overalls and an open-neck white shirt, he sat at a table crowded with microphones, facing a row of television cameras and some twenty reporters, with Negro supporters looking on from the motel balconies. He lashed the injunction as "raw tyranny under the guise of maintaining law and order" and said that "we cannot in all good conscience obey such an injunction." As he spoke, Shuttlesworth nodded at a policeman who scribbled notes on a pad. The reporters bombarded King with questions. Would the demonstrations continue? Yes, he said, through today, tomorrow, and through Easter and beyond. Would he lead a march on Good Friday? Yes, he would. "I am prepared to go to jail and stay as long as necessary," he said.

At a mass meeting that night, King brought people to their feet when he cried, "Injunction or no injunction, we're going to march. Here in Birmingham, we have reached the point of no return. Now they will know that an injunction can't stop us." For the first time, King would violate a state-court injunction and willingly go to jail for it. Maybe his example would put an end to that insidious legal obstruction.

But late Thursday night brought devastating news. King's bondsman had run out of bail money, and Belafonte's New York committee had no additional funds to send. In his motel room, King plunged into gloom. Scores of incarcerated volunteers were awaiting bail, and tomorrow fifty more would get arrested with him and Abernathy. Without bail money, his people would all have to stay in jail. There would not be enough recruits to continue the demonstrations and picket lines.

Early the next morning, King assembled twenty-four key lieutenants in Room 30 to discuss the crisis. After a while they fell silent, overcome by a feeling of hopelessness. Finally someone said, "Martin, this means you can't go to jail. We need money. We need a lot of money. You are the only one who has the contacts to get it. If you go to jail, we are lost. The battle of Birmingham is lost."

King was in agony. The man was right. Yet he had announced to Birmingham—to all the country—that he was going to get arrested today. How could he face his people if he broke his promise? What would his critics say—what would the country think—if he now refused to go to jail after urging hundred of Birmingham Negroes to make jail their badge of honor?

"I sat in the midst of the deepest quiet I have ever felt," King said later. Then he rose and went into a bedroom at the back of the suite. And he stood there in the middle of the room—and the center of "all that my life had brought me to be." There was no choice really. He had to make his witness, on the faith that God would not abandon him in this dismal hour. With that faith, he changed into his work clothes—blue jeans and a blue cotton shirt—and returned to the group in the next room. "I'm going to jail," he said. "I don't know what will happen. I don't know where the money will come from. But I have to make a faith act." Though there was muttering among his lieutenants, King had them join hands and sing "We Shall Overcome."

Then it was off to Zion Hill Church, where hundreds of people were waiting in the sanctuary and on the steps and walks outside, come this Good Friday to witness the march and arrest of Martin Luther King. At the pulpit, King declared that things were so bad in Birmingham that only "the redemptive influence of suffering" could change them. And he was heading to jail now, "a good servant of my Lord and Master, who was crucified on Good Friday." As he strode down the aisle, someone said, "There he goes. Just like Jesus."

He led his fifty volunteers downtown, past sunlit azaleas and yellow forsythia in full blossom, with hundreds of clapping Negroes surging in their wake. Police barricades cordoned off their line of march, and cops were everywhere, on foot, on rooftops, and in patrol and mobile communications centers. At last King came face to face with a shouting Bull Connor and knelt with Abernathy in prayer. At that detectives and motorcycle police grabbed them by the seats of their pants and threw them and all the other marchers into paddy wagons, which bore them to Birmingham city jail with sirens wailing.

And so for the thirteenth time King was arrested and jailed. This time he found himself in solitary confinement, locked away in a narrow, murky dungeon without a mattress or a pillow and blanket. Nobody, not even his attorneys, could get in to see him. He lay on a bedspring in a pool of darkness, a single shaft of light shining through a high window, casting a jail-bar illumination on the walls above. Time seemed to stand still. He worried constantly about the movement, whose entire future hung in the balance, depending on capricious events over which he had no control. How would his lawyers raise bail money? Would people continue to march and man picket lines? He worried about Abernathy and the other prisoners, for whom he felt personally responsible. He missed Abernathy; the loneliness was getting to him. How many hours had he been in here? "Those were the longest, most frustrating hours I have lived," he said. "I was in a nightmare of despair."

But the next day conditions mysteriously improved. A Negro lawyer was able to visit him briefly, to make sure he was all right. Across Birmingham, across America, people anxiously awaited word about his safety. Another day passed, another night. Then on Easter Sunday afternoon, the jailers let two of his lawyers see him. By now he was suffering from nervous exhaustion, so tired that his voice was strained. Beyond the jail, King's brother A. D., who pastored a church in Birmingham, was leading more than 1,500 Negroes on the largest protest march of the campaign. When his attorneys left, King felt isolated and depressed again. But on Monday another visitor materialized at his cell. It was Clarence Jones, a movement lawyer from New York. "Harry Belafonte has been able to raise fifty thousand dollars for bail bonds," Jones said. "It is available immediately. And he says that whatever else you need, he will raise it."

"I cannot express what I felt," King said later, "but I knew at that moment that God's presence had never left me, that He had been with me there in solitary."

After that his jailers were suspiciously courteous. They brought him a pillow and a mattress and allowed him out to exercise and shower. They even let him phone Coretta, who was immensely relieved to hear that he was all right. But he sounded so tired, so weak. Did he know that she had talked with the Kennedys? Worried sick about him, she had phoned Washington and finally gotten through to Robert Kennedy, who promised to find out why her husband was in solitary confinement. Then just fifteen minutes ago, she said, President Kennedy himself had phoned her and said that "we" had talked with Birmingham about King and that he would be calling her shortly. "So that's why everybody is suddenly being so polite," King said. "This is good to know." It meant that his imprisonment was causing anxiety in Washington, too. He told her, without mentioning names, to inform Wyatt Walker about her talk with Kennedy so that a statement could go to the press.

ON TUESDAY, APRIL 16, King's attorneys returned to his cell with a four-day-old copy of the Birmingham *News*, which carried two statements about the campaign. One was signed by more than sixty local Negro leaders and called for blacks to support King and for whites to commence negotiations. The other statement, however, rehearsed the standard objections to the protests (they were unwise and untimely and run in part by "outsiders"), praised the Birmingham police for their restraint, and urged local Negroes to shun the disturbances and press their case in the courts rather than the streets. It was signed by eight Christian and Jewish clergymen of Alabama, all of them white.

As King read over their statement, he had an inspiration. He was going to compose a rebuttal to those clergymen in the form of an open letter, a letter such as Paul might have sent them. He sensed a historic opportunity here, a chance not only to address the moral voice of the white South, but to produce a defense of the movement with profound symbolic import. Would not all America be stirred by a calm and reasonable disquisition on nonviolence, written by a Christian minister held in jail in the most segregated city in the country? With a pen smuggled in by his lawyers, King sat in the shadows of his cell and began writing on the margins of the Birmingham *News*—and continued on scraps of toilet and writing paper supplied by a friendly Negro trusty—this lyrical and furtive epistle.

"MY DEAR FELLOW CLERGYMEN:

While confined here in Birmingham jail, I came across your recent statement calling my present activities 'unwise and untimely.' . . . Since I feel that you are men of genuine good will and that your criticisms are sincerely set forth, I want to try to answer your statement in what I hope will be patient and reasonable terms."

Since the clergymen had been influenced by the argument about "outsiders coming in," King explained that he was in Birmingham because injustice was here and because he must respond like Paul to the Macedonian call for help. "Moreover, I am cognizant of the interrelatedness of all communities and states. I cannot sit idly by in Atlanta and not be concerned about what happens in Birmingham. Injustice anywhere is a threat to justice everywhere. We are caught in an inescapable network of mutuality, tied in a single garment of destiny. Whatever affects one directly, affects all indirectly. . . . Anyone who lives inside the United States can never be considered an outsider anywhere within its bounds."

The clergymen deplored the demonstrations in Birmingham but not, King was sorry to say, the conditions that made them necessary: all the unsolved bombings and the whole "ugly record of brutality" that made Negro life here so grossly unjust. The Negro had tried to negotiate with the city fathers (as the clergymen advised), but the city had refused to do so in good faith. Then the leaders of Birmingham's economic community agreed to remove those "humiliating racial signs" from their stores, only to break their promise. "As in so many past experiences," King wrote, "our hopes had been blasted, and the shadow of deep disappointment settled upon us. We had no alternative except to prepare for direct action, whereby we would present our very bodies as a means of laying our case before the conscience of the local and the national community."

The purpose of direct action, King said, was "to create such a crisis and foster such a tension that a community which has constantly refused to negotiate is forced to confront the issue. It seeks so to dramatize the issue that it can no longer be ignored." It was not a violent and destructive tension Negroes were after, but a "constructive, nonviolent tension" that led to growth. "Just as Socrates felt that it was necessary to create a tension in the mind so that individuals could rise from the bondage of myths and half-truths to the unfettered realm of creative analysis and objective appraisal, so we must see the need for nonviolent gadflies to create the kind of tension in society that will help men rise from the dark depths of prejudice and racism to the majestic heights of understanding and brotherhood."

Like many others, King wrote, the clergymen branded the Birmingham campaign as "untimely." But it was a fact of history, he contended, that privileged groups seldom surrendered their privileges on their own, and that groups (as Niebuhr stressed) "tend to be more immoral than individuals." The Negroes' own painful experience taught them that "freedom is never voluntarily given by the oppressor; it must be demanded by the oppressed. King reminded the clergymen that he had never engaged in a direct-action protest considered "well-timed" by those unscarred by segregation. For years the Negro had heard the word "Wait!" and "Wait" had nearly always meant "Never."

"We have waited for more than 340 years for our constitutional and God-given rights," King wrote. "The nations of Asia and Africa are moving with jetlike speed toward gaining political independence, but we still creep at horse-and-buggy pace toward gaining a cup of coffee at a lunch counter. Perhaps it is easy for those who have never felt the stinging darts of segregation to say, 'Wait.' But when you have seen vicious mobs lynch your mothers and fathers at will and drown your sisters and brothers at whim; when you have seen hate-filled policemen curse, kick and even kill your black brothers and sisters; when you see the vast majority of your twenty million Negro brothers smothering in an airtight cage of poverty in the midst of an affluent society; when you suddenly find your tongue twisted and your speech stammering as you seek to explain to your six-year-old daughter why she can't go to the public amusement park that has just been advertised on television; . . . when you have to concoct an answer for a five-year-old son who is asking: 'Daddy, why do white people treat colored people so mean?'; when you take a cross-country drive and find it necessary to sleep night after night in the uncomfortable corners of your automobile because no motel will accept you; when you are humiliated day in and day out by nagging signs reading 'white' and 'colored'; when your first name becomes 'nigger,' your middle name becomes 'boy' (however old you are) and your last name becomes 'John,' and your wife and mother are never given the respected title of 'Mrs.'; when you are harried by day and haunted by night by the fact that you are a Negro, living constantly at tiptoe stance, never quite knowing what to expect next, and are plagued with inner fears and outer resentments; when you are forever fighting a degenerating sense of 'nobodiness'—then you will understand why we find it difficult to wait. . . .

"You express a great deal of anxiety over our willingness to break laws," King went on. "This is certainly a legitimate concern. Since we so diligently urge people to obey the Supreme Court's decision of 1954 outlawing segregation in the public schools, at first glance it may seem rather paradoxical for us consciously to break laws. One may well ask: 'How can you advocate breaking some laws and obeying others?' The answer lies in the fact that there are two types of laws: just and unjust. I would be the first to advocate obeying just laws. One has not only a legal but a moral responsibility to obey just laws. Conversely, one has a moral responsibility to disobey unjust laws. I would agree with St. Augustine that 'an unjust law is no law at all.'

"Now, what is the difference between the two? How does one determine whether a law is just or unjust? A just law is a man-made code that squares with the moral law or the law of God. An unjust law is a code that is out of harmony with the moral law. To put it in the terms of St. Thomas Aquinas: An unjust law is a human law that is not rooted in eternal law and natural law. Any law that uplifts human personality is just. Any law that degrades human personality is unjust. All segregation statutes are unjust because segregation distorts the soul and damages the personality. It gives the segregator a false sense of superiority and the segregated a false sense of inferiority. Segregation, to use the terminology of the Jewish philosopher Martin Buber, substitutes an 'I-it' relationship for an 'I-thou' relationship and ends up relegating persons to the status of things. Hence segregation is not only politically, economically and sociologically unsound, it is morally wrong and sinful. Paul Tillich has said that sin is separation. Is not segregation an existential expression of man's tragic separation, his awful estrangement, his terrible sinfulness? Thus it is that I can urge men to obey the 1954 decision of the Supreme Court, for it is morally right; and I can urge them to disobey segregation ordinances, for they are morally wrong."

King wanted to make two honest confessions to his "Christian and Jewish brothers." First, King was deeply disappointed in the white moderate of the South. He was "the Negro's greatest stumbling block in his stride toward freedom," because the white moderate preferred order to justice and with his cries of "Wait" paternalistically set a timetable for another man's freedom. "Shallow understanding from people of good will is more frustrating than absolute misunderstanding from people of ill will," King said.

"I had hoped that the white moderate would understand that the present tension in the South is a necessary phase of the transition from an obnoxious negative peace, in which the Negro passively accepted his unjust plight, to a substantive and positive peace, in which all men will respect the dignity and worth of human personality. Actually, we who engage in nonviolent direct action are not the creators of tension. We merely bring to the surface the hidden tension that is already alive. We bring it out in the open, where it can be seen and dealt with. Like a boil that can never be cured so long as it is covered up but must be opened with all its ugliness to the natural medicines of air and light, injustice must be exposed, with all the tension its exposure creates, to the light of human conscience and the air of national opinion before it can be cured.

"In your statement you assert that our actions, even though peaceful, must be condemned because they precipitate violence. But is this a logical assertion? Isn't this like condemning a robbed man because his possession of money precipitated the evil act of robbery? Isn't this like condemning Socrates because his unswerving commitment to truth and his philosophical inquiries precipitated the act by the misguided populace in which they made him drink hemlock? Isn't this like condemning Jesus because his unique God-consciousness and never-ceasing devotion to God's will precipitated the evil act of crucifixion? We must come to see that, as the federal courts have consistently affirmed, it is wrong to urge an individual to cease his efforts to gain his basic constitutional rights because the quest may precipitate violence. Society must protect the robbed and punish the robber."

The clergymen spoke of King's activity in Birmingham as extreme. At first, he said, he was disappointed that fellow clerics should regard his nonviolent efforts as extreme. He pointed out that he stood between two opposing forces in the Negro community. On one side were the forces of complacency that had adjusted to segregation. On the other were the forces of hatred and bitterness, which found expression in black nationalist groups like Elijah Muhammad's Black Muslims, "who have lost faith in America, who have absolutely repudiated Christianity, and who have concluded that the white man is an incorrigible 'devil.'" Through nonviolence, King said, he had tried to offer an alternative to the "do-nothingism" of the complacent Negro and the hate and despair of the black nationalist. He had tried to channel the Negro's legitimate and healthy discontent into the "creative outlet" of nonviolence. But "if our white brothers dismiss as 'rabble-rousers' and 'outside agitators' those of us who employ nonviolent direct action, and if they refuse to support our nonviolent efforts, millions of Negroes will, out of frustration and despair, seek solace and security in black-nationalist ideologies—a development that would inevitably lead to a frightening racial nightmare. . . .

"Let me take note of my other major disappointment," King wrote. "I have been so greatly disappointed with the white church and its leadership. Of course, there are some notable exceptions. I am not unmindful of the fact that each of you has taken some significant stands on this issue. I commend you, Reverend Stallings, for your Christian stand on this past Sunday, in welcoming Negroes to your worship service on a nonsegregated basis. I commend the Catholic leaders of this state for integrating Spring Hill College several years ago.

"But despite these notable exceptions, I must honestly reiterate that I have been disappointed with the church. I do not say this as one of those negative critics who can always find something wrong with the church. I say this as a minister of the gospel, who loves the church; who was nurtured in its bosom; who has been sustained by its spiritual blessings and who will remain true to it as long as the cord of life shall lengthen.

"When I was suddenly catapulted into the leadership of the bus protest in Montgomery, Alabama, a few years ago, I felt we would be supported by the white church. I felt that the white ministers, priests and rabbis of the South would be among our strongest allies. Instead, some have been outright opponents, refusing to understand the freedom movement and misrepresenting its leaders; all too many others have been more cautious than courageous and have remained silent behind the anesthetizing security of stained-glass windows.

"In spite of my shattered dreams, I came to Birmingham with the hope that the white religious leadership of this community would see the justice of our cause and, with deep moral concern, would serve as the channel through which our just grievances could reach the power structure. I had hoped that each of you would understand. But again I have been disappointed."

King had not heard white ministers tell their flocks that integration was morally right and the Negro was their brother. Instead, "in the midst of blatant injustices inflicted upon the Negro," he had watched white churchmen stand on the sideline and "mouth pious irrelevancies and sanctimonious trivialities." At other times they had been arch defenders of the status quo. "I have traveled the length and breadth of Alabama, Mississippi and all the other southern states," King wrote. "On sweltering summer days and crisp autumn mornings I have looked at the South's beautiful churches with their lofty spires pointing heavenward. . . . Over and over I have found myself asking: 'What kind of people worship here? Who is their God? Where were their voices when the lips of Governor Barnett dripped with the words of interposition and nullification? Where were they when Governor Wallace gave a clarion call for defiance and hatred? Where were their voices of support when bruised and weary Negro men and women decided to rise from the dark dungeons of complacency to the bright hills of creative protest?'

" . . . In deep disappointment I have wept over the laxity of the church. But be assured that my tears have been tears of love. There can be no deep disappointment where there is not deep love. Yes, I love the church. How could I do otherwise? I am in the rather unique position of being the son, the grandson and the great-grandson of preachers. Yes, I see the church as the body of Christ. But, oh! How we have blemished and scarred that body through social neglect and through fear of being nonconformists." The judgment of God is on the church as never in history. "If today's church does not recapture the sacrificial spirit of the early church, it will lose its authenticity, forfeit the loyalty of millions, and be dismissed as an irrelevant social club with no meaning for the twentieth century."

But even if the white church ignores us, "we will reach the goal of freedom in Birmingham and all over the nation, because the goal of America is freedom. Abused and scorned though we may be, our destiny is tied up with America's destiny. Before the pilgrims landed at Plymouth, we were here. Before the pen of Jefferson etched the majestic words of the Declaration of Independence across the pages of history, we were here. For more than two centuries our forebearers labored in this country without wages. . . . If the inexpressible cruelties of slavery could not stop us, the oppression we now face will surely fail. We will win our freedom because the sacred heritage of our nation and the eternal will of God are embodied in our echoing demands."

King wanted to mention one other point in the clergymen's statement which troubled him profoundly. They warmly commended the Birmingham police for keeping "order" and "preventing violence." King did not share their praise for the police, not when they subjected Negroes here in the city jail to "ugly and inhumane treatment," cursed and pushed old Negro women and young girls, kicked and slapped old Negro men and young boys. Not when their purpose was "to preserve the evil system of segregation." King wished the clergymen had commended the Negro demonstrators of Birmingham for their courage, discipline, and willingness to suffer in the midst of provocation. One day the South would recognize its real heroes. They were the James Merediths, the old and battered women of the Montgomery bus boycott, the students and young ministers of the sit-ins who had struggled for the best in the American dream and the most sacred values of America's Judaeo-Christian heritage.

"Never before have I written so long a letter," King said. "I'm afraid it is much too long to take your precious time. I can assure you that it would have been much shorter if I had been writing from a comfortable desk, but what else can one do when he is alone in a narrow jail cell, other than write long letters, think long thoughts and pray long prayers?"

King wrote the last portion of his letter on a legal pad furnished by his attorneys. He begged the clergymen to forgive him if he had overstated the truth or been unreasonably impatient. He begged *God* to forgive him, though, if he had understated the truth or settled for anything less than brotherhood. "Let us all hope that the dark clouds of racial prejudice will soon pass away and the deep fog of misunderstanding will be lifted from our fear-drenched communities, and in some not too distant tomorrow the radiant stars of love and brotherhood will shine over our great nation with all their scintillating beauty." He signed his name and laid his pen aside, worn out by his effort.

The Birmingham police knew nothing about King's composition. His lawyers smuggled it out page by page, and Walker and others typed it in a fever of excitement at the Gaston Motel. "This is going to be one of the historic documents of this movement," Walker exclaimed. What should they entitle it? "Call it 'Letter from a Birmingham Jail,'" Walker said. First published in pamphlet form by the American Friends Service Committee, a Quaker group, "Letter from Birmingham Jail" also appeared in the *Christian Century, Liberation,* the *New Leader,* and many other periodicals, with almost a million copies circulating in the churches and other copies finding their way to Robert Kennedy, Burke Marshall, and others in Washington. The "Letter" became a classic in protest literature, the most eloquent and learned expression of the goals and philosophy of the nonviolent movement ever written. The eight Alabama clergymen never responded. "Letter from Birmingham Jail" was unanswerable.

O N SATURDAY, APRIL 20, King and Abernathy posted $300 cash bonds and walked out of Birmingham jail together, both sporting eight-day beards. Their contempt trial for violating the court injunction was scheduled for Monday, and King's attorneys, a high-powered team from the NAACP Legal Defense Fund, had persuaded him to post bail so that they could consult over the weekend. Because of all the publicity surrounding his arrest and imprisonment, King's lawyers wanted to convert the trial into a great court drama, to focus attention on the whole legal structure of segregation. But King rejected the idea. He thought it would confuse the issue and divert local and national attention away from the central goal of breaking the city's racial barriers. No, the main attack must remain in the streets.

To his dismay, though, the demonstrations had dwindled to mostly small-scale picket lines and sit-ins involving only a dozen volunteers a day. True, northern-based civil-rights groups were starting nationwide boycotts of chain stores with branches in Birmingham. Moreover, thanks to the enterprise of a brilliant young Negro minister named Vincent Harding, tentative negotiations had begun with representatives of Birmingham's business community, and ad hoc groups were now meeting in unofficial, semiprivate sessions in churches, homes, and deserted buildings. But it was clear to King's advisers that they must escalate the pressure before serious negotiations could begin. Something had to be done to stimulate recruiting, to get people marching again.

On Monday King and his colleagues climbed the steps of the Jefferson County courthouse, a nine-story building with a quotation from Thomas Jefferson engraved over the entrance: "Equal and exact justice to all men, of whatever state or persuasion." Inside, "WHITE" and "COLORED" signs marked restrooms and water fountains. Shuttlesworth liked to say that God had made water and that water was free, yet here the segregationists were, trying to separate something that was free. This illustrated what "a silly thing" segregation was and how it made "folks who are supposed to have a lot of sense act as if they never known what sense was." If the segregationists kept on, he guessed they would try to segregate the air after a while.

The contempt trial, a protracted legal battle lasting most of the week, took place in the courtroom of Judge William A. Jenkins, Jr., a husky Birmingham native. As it happened, city attorneys had charged King, Abernathy, Walker, and Shuttlesworth with both criminal and civil contempt—a potentially stupid move so far as King was concerned. Conviction for criminal contempt would send him to jail for only a few days. But if convicted for civil contempt, he would have to remain imprisoned until he apologized for his "offense," recanted his public statements about violating the court injunction, and promised the judge never to break it again. In short, he could stay incarcerated as long as he wanted.

But apparently the judge was smarter than the city lawyers. On Friday he dropped the civil contempt charge and found the defendants guilty of the lighter offense. The judge never gave the reason for his decision, but a couple of legal experts have pointed to a practical consideration: "None of the business leaders relished the idea of Martin Luther King languishing indefinitely in a Birmingham jail, while a

national campaign to free him created terrible publicity for the city."
In what was known as *The City of Birmingham* v. *Wyatt Tee Walker et al.*, or simply the Walker case, Judge Jenkins sentenced the four defendants to serve five days in jail, commencing May 16. King's lawyers appealed, and King himself announced that the mild sentence indicated that the bastions of segregation in Birmingham were crumbling.

But in truth it was the movement that was crumbling. By the end of the week, demonstrations had all but stopped, and Young and Walker said the situation was desperate. "We needed more troops," Walker recalled. "We had scraped the bottom of the barrel of adults who would go [to jail]. . . . We needed some new something." Out of spirited SCLC strategy sessions came a portentous decision. King's young lieutenants—Bevel, Lee, Dorothy Cotton, and others—had been out working in the city's Negro colleges and high schools spreading King's nonviolent message, and several college students had become involved in the campaign. Now, though, his staff would actively recruit high-school students to fill up their depleted ranks. King conceded that this would be controversial, but "we needed this dramatic new dimension."

What happened next made movement history. At the urging of King's young aides, hundreds of high-school students swarmed into SCLC workshops at the churches, all raring to march. But so did hundreds of their little brothers and sisters from the grade schools. "We had a terrible time trying to keep them out," Lee said. But the youngsters kept coming back, begging Bevel and Lee to let them march and go to jail with the big kids. Finally, Bevel went to King with an idea: why not launch a "D Day" when hundreds of school children of all ages would get arrested and imprisoned?

King gave this careful thought. Sending children into the streets was bound to provoke hostile criticism. Yet it might be the very thing he needed to revive the campaign and shock the city's business leaders to the bargaining table. Schoolchildren didn't hold jobs, so whites couldn't threaten them with economic reprisals as they did their elders. Thousands of demonstrating youngsters would tie up downtown Birmingham, and their arrests would cause a colossal overload of juvenile courts. With the children, King might literally be able to fill up the jails.

True, there were high risks involved. Some of the children might get hurt—or worse. But Negro children were maimed every day of their lives in the segregated South. If an incessant torture could be ended by a single climactic confrontation, he thought it worth the risk. Also, "our family life will be born anew if we fight together." And, too, the spectacle of schoolchildren marching for their freedom might awaken the entire country. "I hope to subpoena the conscience of the nation to the judgment seat of morality," he had said of his campaign. And here seemed a dramatic and symbolic way to do it.

And so he agreed to let the children march. In a staff meeting on May 1, he decided that the next day would be D Day—the start of a children's crusade to save the soul of Birmingham once and for all.

The next day more than 1,000 excited youngsters—some only six years old—thronged Sixteenth Street Baptist, King's "church command post," as *Time* called it. From here, adults and special march marshals led the children downtown two abreast, column after column, singing and clapping in holiday merriment. When Bull Connor saw all those "little niggers" demonstrating in his town, he charged about in a rage, commanding his men to lock them all up. As the police set about making arrests, the children delighted in confusing them: a decoy group would lead them astray while the main column would proceed to its downtown target. In one demonstration, a gruff cop confronted an eight-year-old walking with her mother. "What do you want?" the policeman asked. She looked him straight in the eye. "Fee-dom," she said.

In all, the police arrested more than 900 young people that day and had to bring in school buses to cart them all to jail. One police captain was deeply troubled by that sight. "Evans," he told another officer, "ten or fifteen years from now, we will look back on all this and we will say, 'How stupid can you be?'"

King and his lieutenants all rejoiced in the day's success. "Oh man," Walker exclaimed, "it's a great time to be alive." King himself had seen the encounter between the cop and the little girl. "It was beautiful!" He recalled what an old woman had said about her involvement in the Montgomery bus boycott: "I'm doing it for my children and for my grandchildren." Seven years later, King mused, "the children and grandchildren were doing it for themselves." As he expected, many newsmen deplored his "using" the children in this fashion. But he wanted to know where these writers had been "during the centuries when our segregated social system had been misusing and abusing Negro children."

Meanwhile his aides were drumming up an even larger children's march for the next day. "I want everybody to listen to me," Bevel told a rally of prospective young volunteers. "You get an education in jail, too. In the schools you've been going to, they haven't taught you to be proud of yourselves and they haven't taught you good history—they haven't taught you the price of freedom. . . . As long as one Negro kid is in jail, we all want to be in jail. If everybody in town would be arrested, everybody would be free, wouldn't they?"

That message worked like magic. The next day some 2,500 young-sters turned out to march, so revved up that King and his staff could scarcely restrain them. "Yesterday was D Day in Birmingham," King said happily. "Today will be Double D Day." He admonished his young followers, "Don't get tired. Don't get bitter. Are you tired?" "No!" they screamed back. Then off they went with their adult lead-ers, heading toward town with signs that read "FREEDOM."

As King and his men coordinated the marching columns, he could see the first one bearing down on a line of police and firemen, de-ployed by Bull Connor to block off the route downtown. A crowd of Negro bystanders had gathered under the tall elms in nearby Kelly Ingram Park, and they surged forward when the students reached Connor's barricade, shouting, "We want freedom!" It was a muggy afternoon, and the firemen stood sweating in dun-colored slickers, pointing high-powered firehoses at the marchers. And there was Bull Connor, a cigar in his mouth and a sweaty straw hat on his head, giving orders to his men. Several cops had German police dogs, which growled and strained at their leashes. When the demonstrators refused to return to the church, Connor bellowed, "Let 'em have it." With scores of reporters and TV cameramen recording what happened, the firemen turned on their hoses, which exploded with a noise like ma-chine-gun fire and sent columns of water crashing into children and adults alike, knocking them down, ripping their clothes, smashing them against the sides of buildings, sweeping them back into the street, driving them crying and bloodied into the park. When Negro bystanders hurled bricks and bottles in retaliation, Connor unleashed the dogs. They charged into the Negroes' ranks with fangs bared, lunging wildly at running children and biting three severely. In a ca-cophony of snarling dogs and screaming people, the march column disintegrated and children and adults all fled back to the church. "Look at those niggers run," Connor sneered. When the carnage end-ed at three that afternoon, a great many people had been injured and

250 arrested. "God bless America," said a reporter in disgust.

King too was revolted. If what had happened that day didn't rouse the moral conscience of the nation, then it had no moral conscience. With eyes blazing, he told a thousand followers that night that they were going on despite the dogs and fire hoses. They were going on because they had started a fire in Birmingham that water could not put out. They were going on because they loved America and loved democracy. And they were going to remain nonviolent. "Don't worry about your children who are in jail," he cried. "The eyes of the world are on Birmingham."

And they were indeed, as papers the next day carried front-page reports and photographs of Birmingham's day of infamy. Millions of readers in America—and millions overseas—stared at pictures of police dogs lunging at young marchers, of firemen raking them with jet streams, of club-wielding cops pinning a Negro woman to the ground. And television news brought similar macabre sights into millions of living rooms. Abroad, African and European journals universally condemned such police brutality. At home, a storm of indignation broke over the land, as newspapers and politicians and labor and religious leaders all excoriated Bull Connor and the city of Birmingham. In Washington, Senator Wayne Morse of Oregon declared that Birmingham "would disgrace the Union of South Africa." President Kennedy told an irate group of Americans for Democratic Action that what he saw in the papers made him "sick," but that there was nothing he could legally do to restrain Connor. Like his brother, the President regretted the timing of King's campaign. Yet he was not asking for patience. "I can well understand why the Negroes of Birmingham are tired of being asked to be patient." That same day, May 4, Burke Marshall, Robert Kennedy's Assistant Attorney General for Civil Rights, flew to Birmingham to seek a settlement.

With the nation and the world looking on, King escalated the pressure in the streets of Birmingham. Each day the demonstrations grew larger and more dramatic, as grade schoolers and high schoolers, parents and children, old and young together, marched and sang toward freedom's land. Again the firemen sprayed them with hoses, again Connor brought out his dogs and even added an armored car to his motorized forces. When someone in a building threw a little plaster on some officers, Director of Public Safety Al Lingo, itching to bring in his state troopers, ranted at a Birmingham cop, "I'd shoot them goddamn son-bitches, that's what I'd do."

And so it went in embattled Birmingham, as the police chased after elusive columns of children and the firemen pulled and grunted at their hoses. But the children baffled them, springing up first here, then there, then somewhere else, waving their signs "WE WANT FREEDOM." And when the police finally got them subdued and into the buses and paddy wagons, they shouted at the tops of their lungs on the way to jail, "WE WANT FREEDOM! WE WANT FREEDOM! WE WANT FREEDOM!" Then playfully, "*Every*body wants freedom! Bull Connor wants freedom! Our mayor wants freedom! The driver wants freedom!"

And over the noise of Birmingham, over the songs and the sirens, the cries and the clash of battle, sounded the haunting voice of Martin Luther King: "We must say to our white brothers all over the South who try to keep us down: We will match your capacity to inflict suffering with our capacity to endure suffering. We will meet your physical force with soul force. We will not hate you. And yet we cannot in all good conscience obey your evil laws. Do to us what you will. Threaten our children and we will still love you. . . . Say that we're too low, that we're too degraded, yet we will still love you. Bomb our homes and go by our churches early in the morning and bomb them if you please, and we will still love you. We will wear you down by our capacity to suffer. In winning the victory, we will not only win our freedom. We will so appeal to your heart and your conscience that we will win you in the process."

On Sunday, May 5, occurred the largest demonstration so far, as Reverend Charles Billups and other Birmingham ministers led more than 3,000 young people on a prayer pilgrimage to Birmingham jail, singing "I Want Jesus to Walk with Me" as they moved. King and his aides were in the streets that day, orchestrating operations with walkie-talkies, and King saw Billups's column approach the police barricade, the ministers and the children ready to pit their bodies against Connor's dogs, fire hoses, and armored car. King saw the column halt and then kneel in prayer, all the while Connor repeatedly ordered them to turn back. But the Negroes continued their prayer, calling up to God in rising exaltation, then singing, then praying again. Suddenly Billups stood and confronted the police. "We're not turning back. We haven't done anything wrong. All we want is our freedom. . . . How do

you feel doing these things? . . . Bring on your dogs. Beat us up. Turn
on your hoses. We're not going to retreat." Then he started forward,
followed by the other ministers and the children. Connor whirled
about and yelled, "Turn on the hoses." His men just stood there.
"Damnit! Turn on the hoses!" But as the blacks marched through their
ranks, the firemen and cops fell back "as though hypnotized." Some of
the firemen were crying. The Negroes continued their journey unim-
peded, prayed for their imprisoned comrades in front of the jail, then
headed back to the Negro section singing 'I Got Freedom Over My
Head."

"You would have to say that the hand of God moved in that demonstration," said one Negro. "For the people who went through the
line without being caned or kicked or beaten," said another, "well, it
did something to them. They had experienced nonviolence in its truest
form." King agreed. "It was one of the most fantastic events of the
Birmingham story. I saw there, I felt there, for the first time, the pride
and the *power* of nonviolence."

By Monday, May 6, more than 3,000 Negroes were in jail in Birmingham—the largest number ever imprisoned at one time in the history of the movement—and some 4,000 more were still parading and
picketing. In one demonstration, the police intercepted 500 youngsters
and simply dispersed them without arrests. There was no place to jail
them. "The activities which have taken place in Birmingham over the
last few days to my mind mark the nonviolent movement's coming of
age," said King. "This is the first time in the history of our struggle
that we have been able literally to fill the jails. In a real sense this is
the fulfillment of a dream, for I have always felt that if we could fill
the jails in our witness for freedom, it would be a magnificent expression of the determination of the Negro and a marvelous way to lay the
whole issue before the conscience of the local and national community. And I think in a real sense this Birmingham movement is one of
the most inspiring developments in the whole nonviolent struggle."

With the jails full, with Birmingham roundly condemned in the
court of world opinion and her economy hurting from the racial crisis,
business leaders agreed at last to start serious negotiations with King's
forces. Dave Dellinger, a notable pacifist who covered Birmingham
for *Liberation*, attributed the breakthrough to King's use of the children, because it forced white people to look at something they had

hidden from themselves: the impact of segregation and racism on Negro youngsters. Dellinger contended that the spectacle tortured the conscience of the white moderate—the South's "silent integrationist"—and that it got to hardened segregationists, too, that even they recoiled from the sight of a police dog lunging at a child. By exposing that kind of evil, King had indeed opened the boil of segregation to the medicine of air and light, as he had phrased it in "Letter from Birmingham jail." In that respect, the decision to enlist the children, as Abernathy said, "was an act of wisdom, divinely inspired."

IT WAS BURKE MARSHALL, a quiet, unobtrusive, patient man, who choreographed the start of direct negotiations. While the children marched in the streets, Marshall had gone back and forth between the two sides, trying desperately to get them to talk. But initially King was suspicious of him, given Robert Kennedy's criticism of the campaign. But Marshall assured him that Kennedy and others in the administration were doing all in their power to help produce a truce in Birmingham: the Attorney General himself was making hundreds of phone calls to influential southern officials and was prodding national businesses with subsidiaries in Birmingham to push for a settlement. At last Marshall won King's trust. And he earned the confidence of the business leaders, too, with his sincere and persistent ways. Thus, when the children's crusade reached a peak of intensity, Marshall spoke with distraught merchants and arranged for secret face-to-face meetings to commence between their representatives and King's.

But the merchants balked at accepting King's demands as set forth in the "Birmingham Manifesto." Though the demonstrations and boycotts were damaging their businesses, they were afraid of the public reaction if they attempted to desegregate their stores. So King attacked again. On May 7, as 125 of the city's most powerful business leaders met downtown, he mounted the largest demonstration of all to make them come to terms. As he and his staff monitored events by walkie-talkies, thousands of students filtered through Connor's police lines and flooded the downtown area, where the businessmen were gathered. The students tangled up traffic for several square blocks and disrupted store after store with sit-ins and stand-ins. When the businessmen broke for lunch and stepped outside, they faced a sea of marching, singing, clapping Negroes, with Connor once again calling for his dogs and fire hoses.

After the businessmen retreated inside their building, Connor's cops and fifty steel-helmeted sheriff's deputies cordoned off eight downtown blocks and drove many of the demonstrators back to Kelly Ingram Park, where hundreds of Negro bystanders jeered and taunted the police. Firemen roared up in trucks and trained jets of water on the Negroes, some of whom battled back with rocks. A blast of water knocked Fred Shuttlesworth unconscious against a building and he was carried away in an ambulance. Connor said it should have been a hearse. In all the mayhem, Birmingham seemed on the verge of complete social disorder.

At their meeting downtown, the businessmen were horrified at what was happening to their city. Real-estate executive Sid Smyer, who claimed he had recently met with President Kennedy, took the floor: "I'm a segregationist from bottom to top, but gentlemen you see what's happening." They all agreed that it was disastrous and that "we got to do something," got "to work something out." Whereupon they approved a plan to bypass city officials and reach a settlement with King on their own. A committee under Smyer would meet with him and his colleagues that night, in the downtown offices of a prominent insurance broker. Meanwhile Bull Connor pleaded with Governor Wallace for help, and by nightfall Al Lingo had 250 state troopers in Birmingham, with 575 more encamped on the outskirts of the city.

That night there began round-the-clock negotiations involving Smyer's committee, King and a committee of Negroes, Marshall, and a battery of bank presidents, insurance executives, white ministers, and lawyers. Vincent Harding thought how sad it was that it took a major crisis to bring them all together like this. For three smoke-filled days the negotiators went over the Negro demands, trying to fashion an agreement specific enough to satisfy the blacks and vague enough to protect individual merchants from white reprisals. As they worked together in those marathon sessions, the Negroes and whites came to have a genuine respect for one another. Once they agreed on the main issues, King and Shuttlesworth, the latter out of the hospital and reeling from hypos and pain, suspended demonstrations for twenty-four hours so that final details could be worked out.°

At last, on Friday, May 10, the two groups produced an accord that met every movement demand. Within ninety days, lunch counters, restrooms, fitting rooms, and drinking fountains in the downtown stores would be desegregated. Within sixty days, Negroes would be hired in clerk, sales, and other positions heretofore closed to them. Within two weeks, a biracial committee would be established to improve communications between black and white Birmingham. City officials, moreover, would be pressed to release all incarcerated Negroes on bond or their own recognizance. As it happened, Reuther's United Automobile Workers and other unions put up the huge sums of money needed for bail.†

When the terms became public, King's critics both black and white were quick to find fault. They pointed out that school desegregation had been ignored entirely and that he had settled for promises rather than immediate concessions. "I think the same thing about that agreement," sniffed one Negro, "as I do of the one that the white man made with the Indian." Moreover, both Mayor-elect Boutwell and the three city commissioners disavowed any responsibility for the accord. And Governor Wallace, too, announced that he would not be a party to a "compromise on the issue of segregation." When he said that, Al Lingo's state troopers were patrolling the streets of Birmingham with sawed-off shotguns.

Nevertheless, King and his movement colleagues were all proud of the agreement and confident that the merchants and their team of

---

* When Shuttlesworth got out of the hospital and first learned that King intended to cancel demonstrations, he blew up. "You and I promised that we would not stop demonstrating until we had the victory," he yelled at King. "Now, that's it. That's it." He reminded King of what his critics often said: "You go to a point and then you stop. You won't be stopping here." If King called off the marches, Shuttlesworth said, "I'm gon' lead the last demonstration with what last little ounce I have." But at last King and his lieutenants calmed him down and persuaded him to go along with them. "We had a terrible time with Fred," Walker recalled. "But Fred was under a great deal of strain himself. He was not well physically. He saw Birmingham as something which he built with spit and Scotch tape, and he did. We never could have been able to pull Birmingham off if it had not been for his Alabama Christian Movement for Human Rights. Some people said, 'Fred's a little crazy.' Well, you need to be a little crazy to be in Birmingham."

† The accord did not affect the Walker case and the five-day jail sentences Judge Jenkins had imposed on King, Walker, Abernathy, and Shuttlesworth. On May 15, 1963, the Alabama Supreme Court accepted their appeal and in December, 1965, sustained their convictions. The Walker appeal went on to the U.S. Supreme Court (see p. 446). Meanwhile King and the other defendants were free on bond pending final disposition of the case.

negotiators would abide by its terms. "The city of Birmingham has reached an accord with its conscience," King and Shuttlesworth told a packed press conference. "Birmingham may well offer for Twentieth Century America an example of progressive racial relations; and for all mankind a dawn of a new day."

On Saturday night, as exhausted as he had ever been, King left a small SCLC task force in Birmingham and flew home to his family. He wanted to preach at Ebenezer the next day and mingle with his friends and church members. The next day was Mother's Day.

LATE THAT SATURDAY NIGHT, King received a desperate phone call from Birmingham. It was his brother A. D., who lived and preached there and who had been active in the demonstrations. Vengeful whites—probably Klansmen—had bombed A. D.'s house and dynamited the Gaston Motel, too, in an obvious attempt to kill King and his lieutenants. Yes, A. D. and his family were safe, but several people had been injured at Gaston's. And Negroes were now rioting in retaliation. Over the phone, King could hear the pandemonium in the streets—shouts, the sound of breaking glass, the awful dogs again. Marauding blacks had already stabbed a cop and set a taxi and two stores ablaze. "Let the whole fucking city burn," some raged. "This'll show those white motherfuckers." With fires glowing against the night, Lingo's state troopers stormed into the Negro district and started beating people at random with billy clubs and gun butts. A. D. said that movement leaders were in the streets, too, trying to disperse the rioters before somebody got killed. Over the phone, King heard a chorus of voices rising above the din, and he got tears in his eyes. Led by SCLC's Dorothy Cotton, a group of Negroes were singing "We Shall Overcome."

The next day King rushed back to Birmingham and took to the streets himself to preach nonviolence and forestall further rioting. Clearly the bombs last night were the work of demonic men who wanted to destroy the accord and plunge the city into a bloodbath. And the Kennedys thought so too. On Sunday evening, the President announced to the nation that he would not let extremists imperil the pact in Birmingham. He ordered 3,000 federal troops into a position near the city and made plans to federalize the Alabama National Guard. That, King said later, put an abrupt end to the bombings.

King was deeply disappointed that violence had marred his long and arduous campaign. But he stood firmly behind the accord with Birmingham's business leaders. "This won't destroy the agreements," he and his associates declared; "this kind of thing didn't come from the men we were dealing with." "Whatever happens from here on, Birmingham will never be the same again."

And Birmingham never was the same again. Though recalcitrant city officials fought bitterly against the accord, the forces of reason won out in the end. On May 23, the Alabama Supreme Court ruled that Bull Connor and the other two city commissioners were out of office and that Boutwell's was the legal city government. One of the dethroned commissioners ranted about King—"This nigger has got the backing of the Attorney General and the White House"—and warned of the horrors of race mixing. But when Boutwell's government took over, it rescinded Birmingham's segregation ordinances and under strong Negro pressure eventually desegregated public facilities, including the library, municipal golf courses, public buildings, and finally even the schools themselves. Although initially interpreting the Birmingham accord as narrowly as possible, local merchants at last removed "WHITE" and "COLORED" signs on drinking fountains and restrooms, opened downtown lunch counters to Birmingham's long-suffering Negroes, and even hired some in hitherto whites-only positions. And if these were small breaches in the fortress of segregation, as some contended, King and most local Negroes thought them extraordinary achievements, given the power of the fortress.

But the greatest accomplishment of the campaign was its positive impact on local Negroes. As in Montgomery and Albany, they had learned for the first time that they could work together against the most determined opposition whites could muster. And this strengthened "the backbone of Negroes all down the line," said a local black, "whether he was middle class or no class." Indeed, as Dave Dellinger of *Liberation* pointed out, Birmingham was "a turning point in the civil-rights struggle" because of "the extent to which the whole community became involved." Not long after the campaign, Dellinger found Birmingham Negroes "so permeated by the sense of fulfillment and well-being . . . that there is practically no room left for fear and hate. They have learned that they can stand up to brutality without compromise."

For King himself, the Birmingham campaign was indisputable proof that nonviolent direct action could work, proof that he and his organization could mobilize people in masses and win a resounding victory for love and racial justice. In the eyes of his fellow Negroes, he now became the top black leader in the country. A *Newsweek* poll of Negro opinion indicated that 95 percent of black leaders and 88 percent of ordinary Negroes regarded King as their most successful spokesman, ranking him ahead of Jackie Robinson, James Meredith, Roy Wilkins, Thurgood Marshall, and Ralph Bunche. Though Atlanta student Julian Bond griped that King had "sold the concept that one man will come to your town and save you," most Negroes sampled praised him effusively for his willingness "to fight for his brother under any condition," as a black construction worker put it. "King's magic touch with the masses of Negroes remains," wrote a journalist in the *Saturday Evening Post*. "What they see is a powerful crusader for equality who does something instead of just talking, who sticks lighted matches to the status quo," and who "endows this American struggle with qualities of messianic mission."

After Birmingham, Negro Congressman Adam Clayton Powell proclaimed King "probably the greatest human being in the United States today." Glenn Smiley of the Fellowship of Reconciliation agreed. "In my book he's the best and freshest thing that ever happened in America, not just in Negro life, but in American life."

As JUNE CAME ON, King had his eye on Washington. Word was out that Birmingham had moved the Kennedys enormously and that the President was about to propose a new civil-rights bill to Congress. On a New York television show, King said he hoped that Kennedy would "do more than issue a call," because thus far his administration had substituted "an inadequate approach for a miserable one" in the matter of civil rights. If the President did not act, King warned, then civil-rights groups might stage "a march on Washington, even sit-ins in Congress." But Stanley Levison maintained that "the White House believes nothing has moved the nation and the world as Birmingham, and they are convinced the imprint will be long and lasting." Thanks to the tremendous outpouring of sympathy for King and his legions in Birmingham, the Kennedys decided that the time had come to make desegregation of public accommodations a matter of law.

But they did not reach that decision easily. In point of fact, a major debate raged within the administration over that point, and Robert Kennedy was the only cabinet member who urged his brother to send a civil-rights bill to the Hill. Thanks to "on the job sensitivity training," as one writer phrased it, Robert Kennedy had become the leading in-house advocate of civil-rights legislation. His training had begun with the Freedom Riders and continued with Ole Miss and the dogs and fire hoses in Birmingham. Then in June he and the President had to federalize the Alabama National Guard to get two Negroes enrolled at the University of Alabama, where Governor Wallace, in what King described as "a fatuous display of political pomposity," stood in the schoolhouse door before backing down under federal pressure. All this had finally gotten to Robert Kennedy. "The more he saw," said Burke Marshall, "the madder [he] became. You know he always talked about the hypocrisy. That was what got him." When asked to measure the rise of Kennedy's civil-rights consciousness, Marshall shot his right arm straight up.

And so it was Robert Kennedy who persuaded the President to throw the administration behind Martin Luther King and fight for the very thing he had advocated from the streets of Birmingham: a federal law that would open public accommodations across Dixie to Negroes. And though every other cabinet member opposed the move, Robert Kennedy prevailed.

On the night of June 11, the President gave a nationally televised address about civil rights, a response to Birmingham and the crisis at the University of Alabama and the moral issues at stake in this critical hour. Watching Kennedy on television, King was elated, because the President's argument was identical to what King had been saying in his own speeches and writings for two years now. This nation, Kennedy asserted, was founded "on the principle that all men are created equal, and that the rights of every man are diminished when the rights of one man are threatened," a paraphrase of King's own contention that a threat to justice anywhere is a threat to justice everywhere. Every American, the President went on, had the right to attend any

public institution, enjoy equal service in any public facility, and register and vote without having to take to the streets or call for federal
troops. "We are confronted primarily with a moral issue," Kennedy
told the nation. "It is as old as the Scriptures and as dear as the American Constitution. The heart of the question is whether all Americans
are to be afforded equal rights and equal opportunities; whether we
are going to treat our fellow Americans as we want to be treated." The
President identified passionately with the victimized Negro. "Who
among us would be content to have the color of his skin changed and
stand in his place? Who among us would then be content with the
counsels of patience and delay?" We say we are the land of the free.
We *are*, except for Negroes. The time has come for America to remove the blight of racial discrimination and fulfill her brilliant promise. Next week, Kennedy said, "I shall ask the Congress . . . to make a
commitment it has not fully made in this century to the proposition
that race has no place in American life or law."

So there it was at last: the President's long-delayed appeal to the
conscience of the nation. And if it was not the sweeping second Emancipation Proclamation King had wanted, he still acclaimed it "the
most earnest, human and profound appeal for understanding and justice that any President has uttered since the first days of the Republic." In his struggle of wills with the President, it seemed that King
was bringing him around now . . . that the James Merediths and the
Negroes of Birmingham were bringing him around.

That night came the news that Medgar Evers, an NAACP field
secretary, had been shot to death by a white man in front of his house
in Jackson, Mississippi. So this was the response of southern segregationists to Kennedy's appeal. A brave and gentle man was gone, another victim of the forces of hate in Dixie. "This reveals," King said, "that
we still have a long, long way to go in this nation before we achieve
the ideals of decency and brotherhood."

Himself "deeply disturbed" by all the racial violence in Dixie,
Kennedy submitted his new civil-rights bill to Congress on June 19. As
King happily noted, the measure not only outlawed segregation in in-
terstate public accommodations, but empowered the Attorney General
to initiate suits for school integration and shut off funds to all federal
programs in which discrimination occurred. With the Kennedys and
Vice-President Lyndon Johnson battling hard to get the bill through
Congress, King knew it was the start of a difficult journey for legisla-

tion "first written in the streets" of Birmingham.

In hopes of pressuring Congress to act, various civil-rights leaders laid plans for a mass march on Washington. They wanted it to be larger than that of 1957, larger even than the trek of 100,000 A. Philip Randolph had threatened to lead back in 1941. In recent years, Randolph and other civil-rights people had talked about staging a Washington demonstration to dramatize the need for Negro jobs. But in the heady aftermath of Birmingham, with major civil-rights legislation pending on the Hill, they elected to march for jobs and freedom legislation. The demonstration would end with a mass rally at the steps of the Capitol. King, for his part, was only peripherally involved in the planning of the march, which was largely the work of Randolph and Bayard Rustin. But he agreed to give a speech at the affair, which Randolph hoped would draw tens of thousands of people from all corners of the Republic.

On June 22 King went to the White House with Randolph, Farmer, Wilkins, and Whitney Young of the Urban League, to talk with Kennedy about the civil-rights bill and the projected march. Robert Kennedy, Johnson, and Walter Reuther were also present. The President described the situation on the Hill, where southerners were up in arms against his bill, and said he understood only too well why the Negro's patience was at an end. But "we want success in Congress," he said, "not just a big show at the Capitol. Some of these people are looking for an excuse to be against us. I don't want to give any of them a chance to say, 'Yes, I'm for the bill, but I'm damned if I will vote for it at the point of a gun.'" He conceded that demonstrations got results—the civil-rights bill was testimony to that—but insisted that they were in a legislative phase now and that Congress should be given "a fair chance to work its will."

Randolph and Farmer spoke up in defense of demonstrations, and so did King. "It is not a matter of either/or, but of both/and," King said to Kennedy. The march on Washington "could serve as a means through which people with legitimate discontents could channel their grievances under disciplined, non-violent leadership. It could also serve as a means of dramatizing the issue and mobilizing support in parts of the country which don't know the problems at first hand. I think it will serve a purpose. It may seem ill-timed. Frankly, I have never engaged in any direct action movement which did not seem ill-timed. Some people thought Birmingham ill-timed." The President broke in, "Including the Attorney General."

As they talked, the issue of police brutality came up. "I don't think you should all be totally harsh on Bull Connor," Kennedy said. There were gasps all around. "After all," the President explained with a smile, "he has done a good deal for civil-rights legislation this year."

Then Kennedy grew solemn. "This is a very serious fight. The Vice-President and I know what it will mean if we fail. I have just seen a new poll—national approval of the administration has fallen from 60 to 47 per cent. We're in this up to the neck. The worst trouble of all would be to lose the fight in Congress. . . . A good many programs I care about may go down the drain as a result of this—we may all go down the drain as a result of this—so we are putting a lot on the line. What is important is that we preserve confidence in the good faith of each other."

Kennedy said goodbye to the other Negroes, but asked King to wait. Then they left the Oval Office and walked into the Rose Garden, with its chirping birds and summer smells. Here the President related that he was getting a lot of flak from Senator Eastland of Mississippi to the effect that Communists had masterminded the entire Birmingham campaign and the upcoming march as well. Hoover's FBI was also concerned about Communist influences on King, the President said, and then added, "I assume you know you're under very close surveillance." In fact, Hoover thought King was consorting with known Communists and even had two on his staff. Kennedy specifically named Stanley Levison of New York, King's long-time adviser, and warned him not to discuss significant matters with Levison by telephone. The FBI had his phone tapped because Hoover believed him "a conscious agent of the Soviet conspiracy." Kennedy mentioned Jack O'Dell, too, a Negro associated with SCLC's New York office. "They're both Communists," the President said. "You've got to get rid of them." Otherwise civil-rights opponents like Eastland would try to discredit King with the Communist charge. "If they shoot *you* down, they'll shoot *us* down too—so we're asking you to be careful."

King thought he was careful enough. His organization had a "firm policy" against hiring Communists or Communist sympathizers. He was aware of the charges against O'Dell, who in his past had been a party organizer in New Orleans. In fact, when the FBI leaked to five newspapers a story that O'Dell was still affiliated with the American Communist party, King had asked for his resignation pending an

SCLC investigation.° But King was shocked that Kennedy should accuse Levison of being a Communist. "I know Stanley and I can't believe it," King said. "You will have to prove it." Kennedy promised
that Burke Marshall would show Andrew Young the evidence, then
excused himself. He had to get ready for a tour of Europe. In the
meantime they should keep in touch.

Later King recounted the Kennedy meeting to Young and other
aides. As far as the civil-rights bill was concerned, King said, "I liked
the way he talked about what *we* were getting. It wasn't something
that he was getting for you Negroes. You knew you had an ally." But
the talk in the Rose Garden was disconcerting. King pointed out that
the President had been afraid to say anything in his own office, and he
sort of laughed. "I guess Hoover is buggin' him, too."

Still, Kennedy was right that the cry of Communism could wreck
the civil-rights bill and imperil the movement. Thus King decided to
release O'Dell, who was not so close to him or so important to SCLC as
Stanley Levison. Although SCLC had failed "to discover any present
connections with the Communist Party on your part," King wrote
O'Dell, "the situation in our country is such . . . that any allusion to
the left brings forth an emotional response which would seem to indicate the SCLC and the Southern Freedom Movement are Communist-
inspired. In these critical times we cannot afford to risk any such im-
pressions. We therefore have decided in our Administrative
Committee, that we should request to make your resignation permanent."

That took care of the O'Dell problem. But Levison was another
matter. King had heard allegations before about his so-called affiliation with the American Communist party. Burke Marshall, John Seigenthaler, and Robert Kennedy himself had all warned King that the
FBI regarded Levison as "a secret party muckamuck," even "a high
official" of the CP, even a top Soviet spy. Although the bureau never
offered proof of its accusations, Robert Kennedy truly believed them
and was troubled when King refused to take them seriously. "Well,
he's just got some other side to him," Kennedy later complained of
King. "So he sort of laughs about a lot of these things, makes fun of

---

° O'Dell denied the story and continued to show up for work at SCLC's New York
office. Hoover and his men took due note of this, regarding it as further proof of King's
mendacity and deception.

[them]." But when Harris Wofford spoke with him, "King seemed dumbfounded and depressed," Wofford recalled, "and said he had far more reason to trust Levison than to trust Hoover."

He had known Levison since Montgomery days, when he'd become a loyal friend and shrewd counselor. He had helped King prepare his income taxes, write speeches, sign book contracts, produce *Stride Toward Freedom*, and raise funds for the movement and King's various court trials. And King often stayed with Levison and his wife when he was in New York. An attorney of independent means, he refused any remuneration and guarded King's interests with a singular distrust of people, particularly editors and businessmen. "My skills," he once wrote King, "were acquired not only in a cloistered academic environment, but also in the commercial jungle where more violence in varied forms occurs daily than is found on many a battlefront. Although our culture approves, and even honors, these practices, to me they were always abhorrent." King knew that the Senate Internal Security Subcommittee, acting on Hoover's imputations, had summoned Levison for interrogation in April, 1962. But he had taken the Fifth Amendment because he was reluctant, he claimed, "to rehash sensational and misleading charges which could only end up in unfairly smearing Dr. King's reputation." This was hardly a valid reason for pleading the Fifth Amendment, and Levison's performance did nothing to clear up Senator Eastland's question: "Isn't it true that you are a spy for the Communist apparatus in this country?" Levison confessed to King that he had known Communists in New York and had worked with some in Henry Wallace's 1948 presidential bid and in anti-McCarthy campaigns later on. Maybe this made him something of a fellow traveler in those days, but he claimed he had never been a card-carrying member of the Communist party. And anyway his Communist associations were all in the past. He was certainly no Communist now, not even a sympathizer. And King believed him.

While Levison had no ties with the American Communist party throughout his long affiliation with King, he wasn't telling the whole truth about his past. Through the reports of a key informant in the CP hierarchy, the FBI had amassed convincing evidence that Levison had been a secret benefactor of the CP between 1952 and 1955. After Levison severed his party connections in the latter year, the bureau lost interest in him until January, 1962, when it discovered that he was closely associated with King. Then Hoover and his men assumed that

Levison hadn't broken with the Communists after all, that he was really a cunning CP operator who had infiltrated King's inner circle and was influencing his and SCLC's activities. They became even more convinced of this when Levison, who had brought O'Dell to SCLC's New York office, recommended him as King's executive assistant. Intensive electronic surveillance of Levison, begun in March, 1962, turned up no evidence to support the bureau's supposition that he was a high CP official and a spy—indeed, the FBI learned that Levison had become "disenchanted" with the party, but refused to accept or to reveal that information. Hoover and his deputies were the kind of men who believed what they wanted to believe, especially about Communism and particularly about left-leaning whites in league with Negro activists out to change the old America. Thus the FBI kept a steady flow of memos to Robert Kennedy about the Levison-O'Dell-King connection.°

Anxious to know what proof the Kennedys thought they had about Levison, King dispatched Young to meet with Marshall in a federal courthouse in New Orleans. But Young did not return with much. "Burke never said anything about any evidence he had," Young recalled; "he always quoted what the Bureau said it had. I didn't feel this was conclusive. They were all scared to death of the Bureau; they really were."

King was sensitive to the Kennedys' plight, for anything that discredited him would be an administration disaster. At the same time, he was reluctant to break off with Levison. He went to see him about Hoover's charges and the worries of the President, then with considerable misgivings officially severed their ties. "I induced him to break," Levison reported later. "I said it would not be in the interests of the movement to hold on to me if the Kennedys had doubts. I said I was sure it would not last long." Still, King's decision troubled him deeply. Levison was a reliable, understanding friend, and King missed him.

But Levison was right—the break didn't last long. Soon King found himself contacting Levison indirectly to check facts for some speech or article he was writing. They used attorney Clarence Jones, now managing the Gandhi Society, as their go-between. As their communications became more frequent, even direct, Levison would ask King,

---

° The bureau refused to divulge its earlier evidence on Levison lest that endanger its source in the Communist Party.

"Aren't we drifting back together? Aren't we giving the opposition something to muck around with?" But King eventually restored him as an adviser. "I have decided I am going to work in the open," King said. "There's nothing to hide. And if anybody wants to make something of it, let them try."

KING HAD ANOTHER POWERFUL ADVERSARY that spring and summer besides the FBI and southern segregationists. If they branded him as a Communist and a rabble rouser, fiery Malcolm X of the Black Muslims, the voice of Negro rage and retaliation, was castigating King in magazine interviews and on radio and television as an Uncle Tom who had sold out to the white devil. What did Malcolm think of Birmingham? "An exercise in futility," he snapped. And the children's crusade? "Real men don't put their children on the firing line." And King's nonviolent philosophy? "There is no philosophy more befitting the white man's tactics for keeping his foot on the black man's neck." And King's vast popularity? "If you tell someone he resembles Hannibal or Gandhi long enough, he starts believing it—even begins to act like it. But there is a big difference in the passiveness of King and the passiveness of Gandhi. Gandhi was a big dark elephant sitting on a little white mouse. King is a little black mouse sitting on top of a big white elephant."

In a post-Birmingham television interview with Kenneth B. Clark, a prominent New York psychologist, Malcolm X stepped up his attack. Eyes flashing behind his horn-rimmed glasses, Malcolm asserted that the masses of black people did not support King. The *white* man did. "The white man pays Reverend Martin Luther King, subsidizes Reverend Martin Luther King, so that Reverend Martin Luther King can continue to teach the Negroes to be defenseless. That's what you mean by nonviolent, be defenseless. Be defenseless in the face of one of the most cruel beasts that has ever taken a people into captivity. That's the American white man." Yet King taught Negroes to love the white man, who turned dogs and fire hoses on them in Birmingham and had victimized black people for four hundred years. No, Birmingham was not a success. "What kind of success did they get in Birmingham? A

chance to sit at a lunch counter and drink some coffee with a cracker—that's success?" King was "just a twentieth century Uncle Tom"
out to lull blacks to sleep by urging them to eat in the same restaurant
with the white man.* As for King's supplications for federal help, Malcolm likened that to "asking the fox to protect you from the wolf,"
and he flayed President Kennedy as "a modern Pharaoh sitting in
Washington, D.C." What was the solution to the race problem? It
wasn't the turn-the-other-cheek philosophy of "ignorant Negro
preachers." It was the teachings of Elijah Muhammad, the leader of
the Black Muslims, who held that black people had the same right to
defend themselves as the white man, that Western society was sick
and disintegrating, that God was about to eliminate the white man
because he had never been a brother to anybody, and that blacks must
separate themselves entirely from his "sinking ship" and concentrate
on improving themselves.

King followed Malcolm's arguments that year, and they alarmed
and saddened him. In "Letter from Birmingham Jail" and other utterances, King had warned that the Negro masses, if their grievances
were not redressed, might seek solace and security in a black separatist
ideology like Malcolm's, which would lead to a racial nightmare. As
for the Muslims' philosophy, King grimaced at their "strange dream of
a black nation within the larger nation" and thought some of their
expressions bordered on a new race hate, black supremacy, and appeals to violence. Still, he regarded the Muslims as a challenge, for
they made him and SCLC work with renewed vigor to eradicate racial
discrimination and all other forms of exploitation that fed hate groups
like them.

As it happened, though, Kenneth Clark shared some of Malcolm's
unhappiness with nonviolence. A psychologist and a Negro, Clark argued that resentment and bitterness, not love, were "natural" human
reactions to humiliation and degradation. Moreover, white liberals
were apt to use King's doctrine to nurture the stereotype of the Negro
as meek and servile. Yes, King's goal of full equality was fine, his
tactics effective. But his philosophy of loving the oppressor, Clark said,

---

* Some of Malcolm's diatribes against King may have stemmed from jealousy. In
Newsweek's poll after Birmingham, American Negroes ranked Malcolm and the Muslims
last of all Negro groups in terms of popularity and effectiveness. Back in 1960, Malcolm
had called King "a spokesman and fellow leader of our people" and even invited him to
address a Muslim rally in New York.

was "unrealistic" and "psychologically burdensome" for the Negro.

King, of course, did not pretend to have all the answers. But he submitted that Birmingham proved dramatically that Negroes could triumph over police brutality without violent retaliation (which would only have gotten them killed) and that the philosophy of nonviolence could help dispirited blacks overcome the crippling disease of hate and make them strong and dignified and proud.

As for Malcolm X, King met him once in Washington and thought him very articulate, with a great concern for the problems Negroes faced as a race. But as he told *Playboy* later, he wished that Malcolm would talk less about violence, "because violence is not going to solve our problem. And in his litany of articulating the despair of the Negro without offering any positive, creative alternative, I feel that Malcolm has done himself and our people a great disservice. Fiery, demagogic oratory in the black ghettos, urging Negroes to arm themselves and prepare to engage in violence, as he has done, can reap nothing but grief."

IN LATE JUNE, KING EMBARKED on a triumphal speaking tour from California to New York. In Los Angeles, 25,000 people cheered his description of Birmingham and his quotation from an old Negro slave, "We ain't what we ought to be and we ain't what we want to be and we ain't what we're going to be. But thank God we ain't what we was." In Chicago, he brought 10,000 clapping people to their feet. In Detroit, he and labor friend Walter Reuther led 125,000 on a Freedom Walk down Woodward Avenue, and he thrilled a packed auditorium when he spoke of a dream of his, a dream rooted in the American dream, a dream of a day when all of God's children could sit together at the table of brotherhood. In New York's Harlem, he spoke to applauding crowds, too, with members of the press chasing after him. But amid all the cheers and popping cameras, some blacks—the "spiritual disciples" of Malcolm X—called him "a polished Uncle Tom" and pelted his car with rotten eggs.

King was shaken and hurt. He thought about all his suffering and sacrifices, and yet realized that some of his own people did not understand or appreciate his work and tried to destroy his image at every turn. But on reflection, he was able to get his mind off himself. "You know," he remarked later, "they've heard those things about my being soft, my talking about love, and they transfer their bitterness toward the white man toward me." He was confident that "all this talk about my being a polished Uncle Tom" would eventually die out and that nonviolence would triumph. That was the faith that kept him going, that helped him stand up against "sometimes unsurmountable odds."

He had reason to be optimistic, because nonviolence was sweeping most of black America with tidal force. That summer, the "miracle" of Birmingham ignited a veritable revolution across Dixie, as Negroes waged nonviolent, direct-action campaigns in some nine hundred cities, with an estimated one million Americans participating in solidarity demonstrations from New York to Los Angeles. To make white authorities consider their grievances, southern Negroes blocked construction sites, chained themselves to school doorways, sat in at state legislatures, hotels, banks, and restaurants, and tangled up traffic in tunnels and on bridges and highways. King himself led a demonstration in Danville, Virginia, the last capital of the Confederacy, despite a local injunction against civil disobedience. "I have so many injunctions," King said, "that I don't even look at them anymore. I was enjoined January 15, 1929, when I was born in the United States a Negro."

King rejoiced in the historical significance of what was taking place. "The summer of 1963," he explained, "was historic partly because it witnessed the first offensive in history launched by the Negroes along a broad front. The heroic but spasmodic slave revolts of the antebellum South had fused, more than a century later, into a simultaneous, massive assault against segregation." And the results were spectacular, as the Negroes' summer campaigns forced thousands of hotels, restaurants, schools, parks, and swimming pools to desegregate in 261 cities. "The invisible Man has now become plainly visible," reported *Time*, "in bars, restaurants, boards of education, city commissions, civic committees, theaters and mixed social activities." In "the summer of our discontent," King wrote, "the Negro became, in his own estimation, the equal of any man." Since Kennedy had shied away from a second emancipation decree, "the Negroes of America wrote an emancipation proclamation to themselves" and "shook off three hundred years of psychological slavery." "No period in American history, save the Civil War and the Reconstruction, records such breadth and depth to the Negro's drive to alter his life. No period records so many thaws in the frozen patterns of segregation." "It makes you feel this way," said a black organizational leader of the new Negro mood: "At last, by God, at last."

But despite the Negroes' hard-won gains, the fortress of segregation remained largely intact in Dixie, with most public facilities still closed to blacks, 1,888 schools still segregated, and obstacles to Negro voting still omnipresent. And *Time* was to use the word "backlash" to describe growing white resentment to the new Negro militancy, a resentment summed up in the idea that "the Negro is pushing too far, too fast."

That same argument reverberated through Congress that summer, as the parliamentary fight over Kennedy's civil-rights bill grew increasingly acrimonious. With the outcome of the measure greatly in doubt, Randolph, Rustin, and other civil-rights leaders worked out final details for the long-projected march on Washington, designed to unite in "one luminous action" all the forces at work on the long front of Negro protest that summer. March leaders predicted that 100,000 people from all over the country would participate. Final plans called for the affair to take place on August 28, with King and many other dignitaries each to give an eight-minute speech. But in deference to the President, march leaders agreed to hold the mass demonstration itself at the Lincoln Memorial rather than the Capitol. That would be more fitting anyway in this historic and symbolic year.

Predictably, controversy swirled up over the projected march, with prophets of doom warning that a horde of Negro "rowdies and uglies" would descend on the capital and plunge it into violence. On the floor of the Senate, Dixiecrat Strom Thurmond of South Carolina accused Bayard Rustin, the march's deputy director, of being a Communist and a draft dodger—a charge that Rustin vehemently denied in a press release. Civil-rights leaders—King among them—staunchly defended Rustin's integrity and promised that Negroes were coming to Washington, not to "stage violence or put on any stunts," but to show the government how strongly they felt about the need for federal help.

WHILE PLANNING FOR THE GREAT MARCH went apace, King tried to hide out that August to work on a quick book about Birmingham and the summer revolution, to be called *Why We Can't Wait* (in answer to whites who said the Negro should). New American Library contracted to publish the volume promptly in paperback and assigned King an August 31 deadline. These wretched deadlines! For three weeks he sequestered himself in a friend's house in Riverdale, New York, and worked mostly on the book. Alfred Duckett, a Negro journalist and public-relations man from New York, gave unstinting editorial and rewrite help as King labored on his manuscript. But he ran out of time and had to leave it, despairing of ever meeting his book deadlines.

On August 27, the day before the great march, King flew to Washington with Coretta and a retinue of aides and advisers, and set to work on his speech in a suite at the Willard Hotel. Because he had been allotted only eight minutes at the rostrum, King's lieutenants were upset. "There's no way in the world, Martin, that you can say what needs to be said in eight minutes," moaned Walter Fauntroy of SCLC's Washington office. "They can't limit you—the spokesman of the movement—to that."

"But they'll all be mad at me if I speak longer," King said. "I don't want Roy Wilkins saying I overstepped my bounds and everybody else was true to the time commitment but I had to show off." They went round and round about that, until finally King's aides threw up their hands. "Look, Martin, let the Lord lead you," Fauntroy said. "You go on and do what the Spirit say do."

King labored on his speech throughout the night, with Young, Walker, Abernathy, and Fauntroy hovering near, offering advice on theme and word choice. Despite the time limit, King wanted to say something meaningful, something Americans would not soon forget. He was to speak last, so his remarks would be the highlight and the benediction, not only for the crowd at the Lincoln Memorial, but for millions of people who would be watching on television or listening by radio. Two months ago, in Detroit, he had talked about his dream of a free and just America. But he doubted that he could elucidate that theme in only a few minutes. He elected instead to talk about how America had given the Negro a bad check and what that meant in light of the Emancipation Proclamation. "He intended to echo some of the Lincolnian language," Coretta said.

By morning, the speech was finished and proofed, and Walker hurried off to have it reproduced. When Coretta awoke, King was standing at the window of the suite watching the crowds outside. According to television reports, only about 25,000 people had turned out for the march, and King worried that it would fall short of expectations. But by midmorning it was clear that media reports were wrong. The word from march leaders was that some 90,000 people had already assembled on the lawns around the Presidential Mall and that thousands more were still streaming in. Among them were poor Negro sharecroppers from the southern black belt, brought up by SNCC workers to show them that they were not alone, that people in America did care about them. And whites were out there, too, thousands of clerics and teachers and students and professional and labor people like Walter Reuther, come to stand with their Negro brothers and sisters in a show of togetherness. There were movie stars like Charlton Heston, Harry Belafonte, Sidney Poitier, and Marlon Brando. There were gospel singers like the incomparable Mahalia Jackson and folk singers like Joan Baez, who had gone to Birmingham during the children's crusade and sung the youngsters her repertoire of ballads and protest songs, her voice as clear and brilliant as starlight.

Over in the White House, the Kennedys were monitoring the march closely, fearful that violence—vandalism, fights, something— might erupt and embarrass the administration. The President had officially approved of the march, and so had a number of distinguished senators—among them, Hubert Humphrey, Jacob Javits, and George Aiken. The only sour note, from the view of civil-rights forces, was that the AFL-CIO had refused to endorse the affair. King considered this "a blunder" that "served to strengthen the prevalent feeling that organized labor, not only on the national level but frequently on the local level as well, is lacking today in statesmanship, vigor and modernity." Though a number of international unions independently voiced their support, King was not mollified. "Negroes battling for their own recognition today have a right to expect more from their old allies," he said with an eye on the AFL-CIO.

When the Kings and SCLC aides left the hotel and reached the mall behind the White House, they were stunned by the size of the crowd. At least 250,000 people—the largest single demonstration in movement history—thronged the grassy, tree-shaded Ellipse behind the White House and the sloping park near the Washington Monument, and march marshals were moving them in steady lines past the rectangular reflecting pool that led to the Lincoln Memorial beyond. This was magnificent, King said, and certain to have a great impact on the country. For the first time, millions of Americans were getting a good look at Negroes engaged in a serious enterprise, and the old stereotype of the Negro was bound to suffer an irreversible blow. And "if the press had expected something akin to a minstrel show, or a brawl, or a comic display of odd clothes and bad manners, they were disappointed," King wrote later. Actually, he was impressed with the number of television crews and reporters covering the march. Usually Negro activities commanded press attention only when violence was likely to occur. This was the first organized Negro function, he believed, that received the "respect and coverage commensurate with its importance."

King now separated from Coretta and joined the other leaders on the mall. Since the march was already under way, they simply fell in line and surged along with the great mass of people, who sang old Negro spirituals and broke into the immortal refrain of "The Battle Hymn of the Republic," which Julia Ward Howe had written to the tune of "John Brown's Body" one sleepless night during the Civil War. Above the moving columns was a sea of placards and signs: "WE SEEK THE FREEDOM IN 1963 PROMISED IN 1863!" "NO U.S. DOUGH TO HELP JIM CROW!" "A CENTURY-OLD DEBT TO PAY."

Slowly the huge crowd encircled the Lincoln Memorial, and King and the other leaders took their assigned places before the monument, where the statue of Lincoln looked down "as if in meditation" at the multitude gathered before him. Because the lawn around the reflecting pool could not hold them all, hundreds of marchers spilled onto grassy places under elms and oaks. They lay down with their shoes off and unpacked picnic lunches while loudspeakers carried the platform program out to them. A reporter surveying the vast assemblage wrote that "tens of thousands of these petitioning Negroes had never been to Washington before, and probably would never come again. Now here they were. And this was their Washington, their very own Capital, and this was their lawn and that great marble memorial was their memorial to the man who had emancipated them."

At 1:30 Camilla Williams began the ceremonies with a rousing rendition of "The Star-Spangled Banner." There followed a seemingly endless parade of performers and speakers, their messages to America "clear, painfully clear, shamefully clear," a reporter said. By the time Roy Wilkins spoke, it was nearly three o'clock and people were getting restless and drifting away. Then Mahalia Jackson launched into "I've Been 'Buked and I've Been Scorned" and the restlessness stopped, because the man everybody had been waiting to hear was scheduled to speak next. When Randolph, "white-haired and statesmanlike," strode to the rostrum and introduced "the *moral* leader of the nation," the giant assembly broke into thunderous applause and chanted King's name.

He stood at the microphone in sweltering sunlight, the unofficial "President of the Negroes" and the trumpet of conscience for all his countrymen, thrilled to incandescence by the human spectacle spread out before him. Nobody, said a friend, got so "high on a crowd" as he. "Five score years ago," he began in a husky voice, "a great American, in whose symbolic shadow we stand, signed the Emancipation Proclamation. This momentous decree came as a great beacon light of hope to millions of Negro slaves who had been seared in the flames of withering injustice." He spoke louder now, repeating symbolic phrases with a rhetorical emphasis that brought cries from his audience. "But one hundred years later, we must face the tragic fact that the Negro is still not free. One hundred years later, the life of the Negro is still sadly crippled by the manacles of segregation and the chains of discrimination. One hundred years later, the Negro lives on a lonely island of poverty in the midst of a vast ocean of material prosperity. One hundred years later, the Negro is still languishing in the corners of American society and finds himself an exile in his own land. So we have come here today to dramatize an appalling condition.

"In a sense we have come to our nation's Capital to cash a check. When the architects of our republic wrote the magnificent words of the Constitution and the Declaration of Independence, they were signing a promissory note to which every American was to fall heir. This note was a promise that all men would be guaranteed the unalienable rights of life, liberty, and the pursuit of happiness.

"It is obvious today that America has defaulted on this promissory note insofar as her citizens of color are concerned. Instead of honoring this sacred obligation, America has given the Negro people a bad check; a check which has come back marked 'insufficient funds.' But we refuse to believe that the bank of justice is bankrupt. . . . So we have come to cash this check—a check that will give us upon demand the riches of freedom and the security of justice. We have also come to this hallowed spot to remind America of the fierce urgency of *now*. This is no time to engage in the luxury of cooling off or to take the tranquilizing drug of gradualism. *Now* is the time to make real the promises of Democracy. *Now* is the time to rise from the dark and desolate valley of segregation to the sunlit path of racial justice. *Now* is the time to open the doors of opportunity to all of God's children. *Now* is the time to lift our nation from the quicksand of racial injustice to the solid rock of brotherhood. . . .

"But there is something that I must say to my people who stand on the warm threshold which leads into the palace of justice. In the process of gaining our rightful place we must not be guilty of wrongful deeds. Let us not seek to satisfy our thirst for freedom by drinking from the cup of bitterness and hatred. We must forever conduct our struggle on the high plane of dignity and discipline. We must not allow our creative protest to degenerate into physical violence. Again and again we must rise to the majestic heights of meeting physical force with soul force. The marvelous new militancy which has engulfed the Negro community must not lead us to a distrust of all white people, for many of our white brothers, as evidenced by their presence here today, have come to realize that their destiny is tied up with our destiny. . . .

"There are those who are asking the devotees of civil rights, 'when will you be satisfied?' We can never be satisfied as long as the Negro is the victim of the unspeakable horrors of police brutality. We can never be satisfied as long as our bodies, heavy with the fatigue of travel, cannot gain lodging in the motels of the highways and the hotels of the cities. We cannot be satisfied as long as the Negro's basic mobility is from a smaller ghetto to a larger one. We can never be satisfied as long as a Negro in Mississippi cannot vote and a Negro in New York believes he has nothing to vote for."

As he spoke, thousands of people were clapping and shouting in cadence with him. And then on a surge of emotion, more inspired than he had ever been in his life, King abandoned his text and spoke from his heart, saying what he had truly wanted to say, his aides responding in delight, "Tell it, doctor!" "Awright!"

"I say to you today, my friends, that in spite of the difficulties and frustrations of the moment I still have a dream. It is a dream deeply rooted in the American dream. I have a dream that one day this nation will rise up and live out the true meaning of its creed: 'We hold these truths to be self-evident—that all men are created equal.' I have a dream that one day on the red hills of Georgia the sons of former slaves and the sons of former slaveowners will be able to sit down together at the table of brotherhood. I have a dream that one day even the state of Mississippi, a desert state sweltering with the heat of injustice and oppression, will be transformed into an oasis of freedom and justice. I have a dream that my four little children will one day live in a nation where they will not be judged by the color of their skin but by the content of their character.

"I have a dream today.

"I have a dream that one day the state of Alabama, whose governor's lips are presently dripping with the words of interposition and nullification, will be transformed into a situation where little black boys and black girls will be able to join hands with little white boys and white girls and walk together as sisters and brothers.

"I have a *dream* today." Below him, people had joined hands and were swaying back and forth, crying out to him, "Dream some more."

"I have a dream that one day every valley shall be exalted, every hill and mountain shall be made low, the rough places will be made plains, and the crooked places will be made straight, and the glory of the Lord shall be revealed, and all flesh shall see it together.

"This is our hope. This is the faith I shall return to the South with. With this faith we will be able to hew out of the mountain of despair a stone of hope. With this faith we will be able to transform the jangling discords of our nation into a beautiful symphony of brotherhood. With this faith we will be able to work together, pray together, struggle together, go to jail together, stand up for freedom together, knowing that we will be free one day.

"This will be the day when all of God's children will be able to sing with new meaning 'My country 'tis of thee, sweet land of liberty, of thee I sing. Land where my fathers died, land of the pilgrim's pride, from every mountainside let freedom ring.' And if America is to be a great nation this must become true. So let freedom ring from the prodigious hilltops of New Hampshire. Let freedom ring from the mighty mountains of New York. Let freedom ring from the heightening Alleghenies of Pennsylvania. . . . But not only that; let freedom ring from Stone Mountain of Georgia. Let freedom ring from Lookout Mountain of Tennessee. Let freedom ring from every hill and mole hill of Mississippi. From every mountaintop, let freedom ring.

"When we let freedom ring, when we let it ring from every village and every hamlet, from every state and every city, we will be able to speed up that day when all of God's children, black men and white men, Jews and Gentiles, Protestants and Catholics, will be able to join hands and sing in the words of the old Negro spiritual, 'Free at last! Free at last! Thank God almighty, we are free at last!'"

In a crescendo of shouts and applause, King stepped down from the podium numb with emotion. Abernathy embraced him and said that the Holy Spirit had taken hold of him in that speech. And Walker congratulated him, too, going on about how he "just went on into that thing." With the crowd still roaring, march marshals formed a circle around him to keep him from being mobbed. Now Coretta was at his side, slipping her arm into his, as they made their way through an ocean of people. A British journalist managed to speak to him in all the din. He thought King's speech "the most moving and magnificent public address I have ever heard."

And if there were voices of dissent that day (Malcolm X dismissed the whole scene as "the Farce on Washington"), James Baldwin captured the overwhelming sentiment: "That day, for a moment, it almost seemed that we stood on a height, and could see our inheritance; perhaps we could make the kingdom real, perhaps the beloved community would not forever remain that dream one dreamed in agony."

There was a reception in the White House afterward. "The President was bubbling over with the success of the event," Wilkins recalled, and was relieved that nothing untoward had happened. "All smiles," he shook King's hand vigorously and said, "*I* have a dream." When he learned that the Negro leaders had not had lunch, the President ordered sandwiches and beverages brought up from the White House kitchen, and they all sat around eating and chatting amiably in the afterglow of an unforgettable day.

Back at the Willard that evening, King was "totally outside of himself with elation," Rustin remembered, "but not about himself." He was happy because Mr. Randolph had finally gotten his mass march, the march he had dreamed of leading back in 1941 and again in 1947. For King, it was not *his* hour; it was Mr. Randolph's hour. He sought out the grand old man and congratulated him warmly for getting his march "after all these years."

Later, King relaxed in his suite with Coretta and members of his staff, who teased him for exceeding his allotted time at the rostrum and warned him to "watch out for Roy now." They talked for hours about the day's events, and King finally allowed himself a little personal contentment. Millions of whites had heard his message for the first time, heard what he'd been trying to say since Montgomery. More than that, he had spoken that day as a modern Lincoln, taking his theme from the Gettysburg Address of one hundred years before. At Gettysburg, Lincoln had called for a national rededication to the proposition that all men were created equal, a determination to fight for a new birth of freedom so that government by and for *all* the people might endure. Now King had stood at Lincoln's statue, reminding Americans in 1963 that they too had a commitment to a new birth of freedom.

At a small interracial breakfast the next morning, King was still in high spirits. "Now I want y'all to have a good southern breakfast," he told his companions. "What's a good southern breakfast?" one of them asked. "Well," King said, "we're gonna have steak and eggs and home fried potatoes and grits and cornbread. I've already ordered it." A waitress entered the room to find out how they wanted their steaks cooked. As she went around the room, the Negroes ordered theirs medium or well done, but the whites all wanted theirs rare. King turned to Rustin with a grin. "You see, Bayard, now I know why these white folks are so vicious. They eats too much rare meat."

That day newspapers at home and abroad carried reports of the Washington march and excerpts from King's speech, and editorial notices outside the South were almost all favorable. Journalist David Halberstam caught the art in King's performance and later said that the affair reminded him of "a great televised morality play." But along with accounts of the march came news that W. E. B. Du Bois, the celebrated Negro intellectual, co-founder of the NAACP and long-time editor of *Crisis*, historian and author among many other books of the inimitable *Souls of Black Folk* and *Black Reconstruction*, was dead in Ghana at ninety-five. King had exchanged correspondence with him during the Montgomery bus boycott, and Du Bois had praised King as "honest, straight-forward, well-trained, and knowing the limits." But Du Bois had given up on America, so embittered in his later years that he had become a Communist and an expatriate, brooding on the tragedy of the age: "not that men are poor—all men know something of poverty; not that men are wicked—who is good? Not that men are ignorant—what is truth? Nay, but that men know so little of men."

Sometime after the march, King entertained friends of both sexes in his suite at the Willard; Coretta was no longer with him. King had always been a passionate man, and his feelings were still running high from his oratory and the response of the crowd. What he did not know was that a hidden microphone, installed by somebody in authority (Robert Kennedy and two of his associates later pointed to the Washington Police Department), was recording the party—and what happened afterward.

A tape of the recording found its way into the hands of J. Edgar Hoover and his deputies at FBI headquarters. The Justice Department later acknowledged that the tape indicated "sexual activity" in King's room. This, of course, was more than Hoover could bear. He already abhorred King, convinced as he was that this increasingly influential Negro was concealing Communist affiliations. True, the FBI's security investigation had turned up no evidence of Communist influences on King or the civil-rights movement, and William Sullivan, head of the bureau's Domestic Intelligence Division, had recently filed a report and a memo to that effect.[*] Hoover was furious. "This memo reminds me vividly of those I received when Castro took over Cuba," he berated Sullivan. "You contended then that Castro and his cohorts were not Communists and not influenced by Communists. Time alone proved you wrong." Sullivan knew better than to question his imperious boss. "The Director is correct," Sullivan reported after the march on Washington. "We were completely wrong about believing the evidence was not sufficient to determine some years ago that Fidel Castro was not a Communist." As for King, "I believe in the light of King's powerful demagogic speech yesterday he stands head and shoulders over all oth-

---

[*] Investigations by a U.S. House Select Committee in 1978 found no such evidence on King either.

er Negro leaders put together when it comes to influencing great masses of Negroes. We must mark him now, if we have not done so before, as the most dangerous Negro of the future in this Nation from the standpoint of Communism, the Negro, and national security."

That was exactly what the director wanted to hear. And now here was the Willard Hotel tape, proving to Hoover's satisfaction that King was a philanderer who copulated with white as well as black women. Doubtless he had already heard rumors and allegations to that effect (Governor Wallace had recently warned the President himself that King was a "faker" who slept with "nigger women, and white and red women too," and local police officials, bugging King's hotel rooms, may have taped evenings similar to that at the Willard). A confirmed bachelor who dined alone with his cherished lieutenant, Clyde Tolson, Hoover was obsessed with the sexual behavior of those in public life. For him, extramarital sex was vile enough. But interracial sex was "moral degeneracy." In Hoover's eyes, in the eyes of his hand-picked deputies, King was a frightening specter, a reprobate and a subversive who masqueraded as a moral leader of the nation and who won over a lot of white people—including the President and the Attorney General—with his hypocritical cant about love and nonviolence. Now more than ever this menace had to be stopped. In righteous indignation, the director stepped up the bureau's flow of anti-King memos to Robert Kennedy. At the same time, Hoover discovered that King had resumed his association with Stanley Levison and "joyously" informed Kennedy so. On October 7, at the director's instigation, the bureau officially requested permission to tap King's phones.

All this created a dilemma for the Attorney General. He was certain that the FBI was right, that Levison was a secret official of the Communisty party, and that King's connections with Levison damaged the civil-rights movement, and "also damaged us." Like the President, Kennedy genuinely admired King's leadership and had no doubts about his own patriotism. But he was irked by King's indifference to the FBI's accusations and his carelessness about associating with men Kennedy thought were Communists. If Hoover wanted to, he had enormous power to hurt King, the Kennedys, and the civil-rights bill, which was in enough trouble as it was. "To protect ourselves," Kennedy said, he now took a fateful step. On October 10, 1963, he authorized the FBI to put a wiretap on King's home phone in Atlanta, and subsequently approved taps on SCLC's phones as well.

But Kennedy made it clear that the taps were to be conducted strictly on a thirty-day trial basis, after which they would be evaluated and the question of continued surveillance decided.

How could the Attorney General justify such blatant invasion of King's privacy? If the taps indicated Communist activity in King's circle, Kennedy could confront him with the evidence and force King to sever all ties with Levison and any other Communist friends, thus protecting King's and the Kennedys' reputations. If the taps proved King innocent of Communist associations, then the FBI would have to leave him and Kennedy both alone.

Hoover now went to work on King with a vengeance, ordering his men to establish a wiretap command post in Atlanta and send bureau headquarters tapes of all they overheard. Acting on a recommendation by Sullivan, Hoover even had an eleven-page monograph compiled which not only stressed King's Levison connection, but indicted him as "an unprincipled man" in his personal life, apparently citing details from the Willard Hotel party. Though one of his own lieutenants warned that this could be construed as "a personal attack" on King, Hoover replied, "We must do our duty." Out went copies to the Attorney General, the White House, the secretaries of State and Defense, the CIA, and the military.

For his part, Robert Kennedy was truly shocked by the FBI's revelations. But he did not think King's private life affected his integrity as a public figure and regarded the monograph as a *"very, very unfair"* picture of King. Unhappy with the FBI for circulating it, he phoned Hoover and told him to retrieve all copies of the document. Bitterly the director did as he was told. But he hated the Attorney General for trying to control his bureau (Kennedy had even had the audacity to say that he should hire more Negroes). Well, Hoover wasn't going to sit idly by while that loathsome preacher ran amuck with women and Communists. That winter, the FBI devised a secret plan to expose King as "a fraud, demagogue, and scoundrel," as Agent Sullivan put it, "to take him off his pedestal and to reduce him completely in influence."

At this juncture, King and his men knew nothing about Hoover's hatred of him personally or about the FBI's ghoulish campaign to pry into his personal affairs. But apparently somebody in the government did alert them to the wiretaps authorized by the Attorney General. "We knew they were ... bugging our phones," Andrew Young said later; "but that was never really a problem for us. . . . When you were anxious about your life, civil liberties seemed a tertiary consideration. In our conduct of a nonviolent movement there was nothing that we did not want them to know anyway." What was more, neither King nor his lieutenants held the wiretaps against Robert Kennedy. The McCarthy period hadn't been over very long, as Levison said, and they understood that the administration was frightened of "a terrible political scandal."

On Sunday morning, September 15, King preached at Ebenezer Church, still glowing from the triumph of the Washington march. Then came devastating news from Birmingham. While King was at his pulpit in Atlanta, a bomb made of dynamite exploded in Birmingham's Sixteenth Street Baptist Church—a center for rallies and marches during the recent campaign—and four Negro girls were dead. In despair, King rushed to Birmingham and wandered about in the church wreckage talking with people. From what he could gather, four hundred Negroes were gathered here for Sunday worship, and the girls—Denise McNair, age eleven, and Cynthia Wesley, Carol Robertson, and Addie Mae Collins, all fourteen—were at the back of the church, putting on their choir robes, when the dynamite went off and blasted them into eternity. The explosion blew a hole in the side of the church, too, and sent people screaming into the streets. Out of the hole stumbled a twelve-year-old girl, her hands covering her blinded eyes. A woman stood in a glass-littered street and wept, "My God, we're not even safe in church!" Negroes searching in the rubble found a blood-stained copy of a kindergarten leaflet containing the day's prayer: "Dear God, we are sorry for the times we were so unkind."

King was overwhelmed with grief and bitterness. Not since the days of the Christians in the catacombs had God's church, in a Christian country, suffered such naked violence as Negro churches were in America. He noticed that the bomb had blown away Christ's face from a stained-glass window, and he was certain that this symbolized "how sin and evil had blotted out the life of Christ." He shook his head, unable to believe or to bear what had happened here. "If men were this bestial," he thought, "was it all worth it? Was there any hope? Was there any way out?"

There seemed no end to the hate that melancholy Sunday, as Birmingham police killed a Negro youth in the streets and white toughs murdered another who came riding by on a bicycle. Authorities did investigate the church bombing and even arrested a suspect, a local Klansman named Robert Edward Chambliss, but eventually let him go.° With another unsolved bombing added to the long list, angry Negroes dubbed the city "Bombingham."

What was more, Birmingham whites seemed not to care. King called it "the poverty of conscience of the white majority." Only a few dared break the white silence about the atrocity—among them a young attorney, Charles Morgan, Jr., who had gone to the University of Alabama and had his eye on a political career in the state, maybe even the governorship. But he threw all that away on the Monday after the bombing, when he stood before the all-white Young Men's Business Club and told them who was really responsible: "Every little individual who talks about the 'niggers' and spreads the seed of his hate to his neighbor and his son. The jokester, the crude oaf whose racial jokes rock the party with laughter. . . . every governor who ever shouted for lawlessness and became a law violator. . . . Each citizen who has not consciously attempted to bring about peaceful compliance with the decisions of the Supreme Court; every citizen who has ever said, 'They ought to kill that nigger.' Every person in this community who has in any way contributed to the popularity of hatred is at least as guilty, or more so, as the demented fool who threw that bomb."

King gave the eulogy at a joint funeral service for three of the girls, still shaken that any man could degenerate to such a tragic level of inhumanity and evil as to murder children in church. Before the funeral, Negro novelist John Killens announced that the bombing marked the end of nonviolence and that "Negroes must be prepared to protect themselves with guns." But Christopher McNair, grieving for his daughter, replied, "I'm not for that. What good would Denise have done with a machine gun in her hand?" In his eulogy, King called the girls "heroines of a holy crusade for freedom and human dignity," whose deaths tell us to work "passionately and unceasingly to make

---

° In November, 1977, Chambliss was tried for the bombing and convicted of first-degree murder in a local trial that made national headlines. His attorney was Art Haynes, the former city commissioner.

the American dream a reality." Then he spoke to himself as much as to the tear-filled church: "They did not die in vain. God still has a way of wringing good out of evil. History has proved again and again that unearned suffering is redemptive. The innocent blood of these little girls may well serve as the redemptive force that will bring new light to this dark city." But he observed that not a single city official attended the funeral. Save for a few brave ministers, no white people came at all.

I N LATE SEPTEMBER, KING PUBLISHED in the *New York Times Magazine* a fiery manifesto to white America called "In a Word—*Now*." Negroes, he asserted, wanted *everything* in Kennedy's civil-rights bill, *immediate* and effective federal protection against police brutality, the right to walk unafraid and unopposed to the ballot box, and an end to unemployment, "a form of brutality." In early October he and his aides were back in Birmingham, back at that battlefront, threatening to resume demonstrations if Negro policemen were not hired and conditions that spawned the bombing not rectified. This disproved the accusation of SNCC and other civil-rights rivals that King always left a city after a direct-action campaign and never returned to follow up his initial success. But others in the movement opposed renewed demonstrations, and King yielded to them because "the fullest unity was indispensable," he wrote later, against "the formidable adversaries we faced."

On October 23, King was in New York for the thirtieth anniversary of District 65 of the Distributive Workers of America, held in Madison Square Garden. King praised this small union for giving broader and more consistent support to the movement than any other in America. When all trade unions followed its example, "the brotherhood of which men have dreamed will begin to live in the real world around us." But, alas, that dream was nowhere near in 1963, as "Negroes, north and south, still live in segregation, eat in segregation, pray in segregation and die in segregation."

When he was back in Atlanta, which was not often, King tried to work on his book about Birmingham, which was proceeding at glacial speed even with the help of his New York agents and another editorial and rewrite assistant named Nat Lamar. With endless interruptions and New York pestering him to hurry, King was as harried as he had ever been while writing *Stride Toward Freedom*.

Early in the afternoon of November 22, King was upstairs in his Atlanta home, making preparations for a Los Angeles fund-raising appearance and vaguely listening to a television program in the background. Suddenly, an announcer interrupted with a special bulletin: President Kennedy had been shot in Dallas, just after landing there during a political trip to Texas. At first the news was fragmentary. On CBS TV, a distressed Walter Cronkite relayed a UPI report that three shots had been fired on the presidential motorcade in downtown Dallas. "The first reports say that the President was 'seriously wounded,'" Cronkite added. By 1:45 the three networks were all on the air with the news, and reports and special announcements crowded the television screen. Coretta and Bernard Lee came up from downstairs, and the three of them huddled in silent vigil before the television set. Shortly after 2:30 came the dreaded bulletin: John Fitzgerald Kennedy, thirty-fifth President of the United States, was dead of a sniper's bullet in Dallas's Parkland Memorial Hospital. King listened to the news with a quiet intensity. Then he said, "I don't think I'm going to live to reach forty."

"Oh, don't say that, Martin," Coretta pleaded.

But King persisted. "This is what is going to happen to me also. I keep telling you, this is a sick nation. And I don't think I can survive either." There was a painful silence, Coretta and Lee unable to answer.

The children gathered around, and six-year-old Marty asked, "Daddy, President Kennedy was your best friend, wasn't he, Daddy?"

Yes, in a political sense he was, and now he was gone, cut down in the prime of his life, and King grieved for him and for his country. The phone rang constantly that day, with the wire services and other media wanting a statement from King about what the assassination meant to civil rights, to America, to him personally. What could one say at such times? "I am shocked and griefstricken," King's statement read. "He was a great and dedicated President. His death is a great loss to America and the world. . . ."

The country was traumatized. For three eternal days and nights the television networks stayed on the air, uninterrupted by commercials, reporting the aftermath in a blur of images, with Cronkite, Chet Huntley and David Brinkley, and other newsmen trying to comment on something beyond understanding. "The events of those days don't fit, you can't place them anywhere," Brinkley said. "It was too big, too sudden, too overwhelming, and it meant too much." Those who sat before their television sets would never forget the picture of a distraught Lyndon Johnson taking the oath of office on *Air Force One* with Jacqueline Kennedy, in shock, still dressed in bloodstained clothes, standing beside him . . . would never forget the sight of her flying back to Washington with her husband's coffin . . . would never forget the spectacle of Jack Ruby, Dallas strip-joint operator, shooting alleged assassin Lee Harvey Oswald just two days after Kennedy's murder—and doing so in a crowded tunnel under the Dallas police station, in front of a national television audience . . . would never forget the heartbreaking grandeur of Kennedy's funeral in Washington— the drums that shattered the sunlit day, the riderless horse, the farewell salute John, Jr., gave his father's passing coffin, the eternal flame wavering at the grave in Arlington National Cemetery.

As the nation entered a period of soul searching, King jotted down his own reflections on Kennedy, some of which appeared in his Birmingham book, others in speeches and articles, including one for *Look* entitled "It's a Difficult Thing to Teach a President." Nineteen sixty-three, King observed, was a year of assassinations: a white postal worker from Baltimore slain on a "freedom walk" in Alabama, Medgar Evers gunned down in Mississippi, six Negro children murdered in Birmingham, and "who could doubt that these too were political assassinations?" And so the contagion spread until it got "the most eminent American," and "we mourned a man who had become the pride of the nation, but we grieved as well for ourselves because we knew we were sick."

There was so much he remembered about Kennedy. How to assess him for posterity? Like Lincoln, he had a tremendous capacity for growth. And in two areas that concerned King the most—civil rights and world peace—Kennedy was growing up to the very day he was killed. In the international theater, King wrote, the young President had abandoned his old view of the Cold War as a "conflict of ultimate destinies" and sought to make the world a safer and more peaceful place to live. He had, for example, forged a successful nuclear test-ban treaty in 1963 that prohibited atomic explosions in the atmosphere.

Kennedy would be remembered, King thought, not because he was a conqueror who built an empire or brought home the spoils of war, but because he presided over the world's mightiest nation with intelligence and restraint. "His memory will persist because he understood something a clergyman of the Civil War era declared, 'Greatness lies not in being strong, but in the right use of strength.'"

In domestic affairs, he would be remembered for his remarkable growth in civil rights. Timid and ineffectual in his first two years, Kennedy emerged in 1963 as "a strong figure" with a deepening commitment to end racial discrimination. "Always willing to listen" and respond to creative pressure, he had the courage and vision to see the problem in all its dimensions. "History will record that he vacillated like Lincoln, but he lifted the cause far above the political level" to the moral level. He recognized, too, that the Negro's struggle was part of a global movement against oppression, and that he lived in an era in which human rights were the central world issue. "No other American President had written with such compassion and resolution to make clear that our nation's destiny was unfulfilled so long as the scar of racial prejudice disfigured it." Had Kennedy lived, King said he would have broken his policy about political endorsements and supported him for re-election in 1964.

A *Look* writer, assessing King's comments, contended that it was his own unrelenting pressure that had made Kennedy grow in civil rights. The black Baptist preacher and the white Catholic President, the writer said, had engaged in a three-year-long struggle of wills. They agreed on principle but not on tactics or urgency. "The black man won. Near the end, he shaped events so that the white man had to use every resource, his audacity and skill, to avoid national disaster, and to earn his most likely claim on history."

So now Lyndon Baines Johnson of Texas was President. What kind of friend would he be to the movement? King had talked with him a number of times while he was Vice-President and had been impressed with his "emotional and intellectual involvement" in the quest for racial justice. Still, the new President was a tempestuous and mercurial man who merited careful scrutiny if King was to trust him as an ally. King, of course, had heard stories about Johnson's monumental ego and hunger for power, and the stories would proliferate in the days ahead. In the Senate, he had proven himself a legislative genius and a consummate manipulator of men, using honey-coated flattery, chest-punching intimidation, two-hour monologues, or shrewd bargaining skill to get measures passed. But his self-esteem was inordinate. Once he gave the Pope a huge plastic bust of himself. At his ranch in south-central Texas, he flew his own flag with his initials on it. He spiced his language with boisterous profanity and scatological references, and took obscene delight in drawing certain advisers into the bathroom with him and dictating orders while he sat in noisy flatulence on the commode. He relished smutty stories about political rivals, once slapping his thighs in delight when he learned that a Republican senator frequented a Chicago bordello and had "some kinky sexual preferences." He drove his staff without mercy and demanded absolute loyalty. "I heard Johnson say one time," recalled Congressman Emanuel Celler of Brooklyn, "that he wanted men around him who were loyal enough to kiss his ass in Macy's window and say it smelled like a rose." And he could be astonishingly mendacious, even to the point of claiming that he had a relative at the Alamo (he did not) and depicting his childhood as far more deprived than it was. Schooled in the tangles of Texas politics and the shifting alliances of the U.S. Senate, he came to believe that politics contained no accidents, only conspiracies, and he saw conspiracies against him everywhere. "I don't trust anybody but Lady Bird," he once said, in reference to his wife, "and sometimes not even her." He always insisted that Kennedy had been murdered by a Communist plot, in retaliation for a supposed Kennedy attempt to have Castro assassinated.

And yet there was another side to this pungent and suspicious man, a strain of idealism and sensitivity to Negroes and other minorities that made King hopeful. In his early congressional years, Johnson had voted against six different civil-rights measures. Yet he did not regard himself as a southerner. As he pointed out, there were no "darkies" or plantations in the harsh Texas hill country where he grew up. He had never been a son of the Lost Cause, had never sat on the knees of a Civil War grandpappy and heard romantic tales about the old Confederacy. No, that was not his tradition. In Stonewall and Johnson City in the Pedernales country, he had been raised among ranchers and listened to stories about his great trail-driving grandpa and Indian fights and cowboy life on the Chisholm Trail. The closest big city for him was San Antonio, with its Spanish missions and legacy. As a schoolteacher in dusty Cotulla, where Mexican-Americans comprised 75 percent of the population, he felt deep compassion for his Mexican-American pupils, who were poor and hungry; he could see "the pain of injustice" in their eyes, and he yearned to help them.

Yet when he entered politics and went to Washington, his compassion did not extend to Negroes, not right away. He was a prideful Texan, and his state had a historical connection with Dixie in the Civil War, and he would flare up defensively when some Yankee would describe the South "as a blot on our national conscience." As a consequence, he found himself voting with southerners to defeat civil-rights legislation, arguing that this wasn't the answer to the problem. But by 1957, when he was serving as Senate majority leader, civil rights had become a major national issue that could no longer be shelved without endangering his party and his own leadership. Johnson was no white supremacist anyway. He understood the discrepancy between segregation and the American dream. He reminded himself that he was a Roosevelt Democrat with a deep well of sympathy for poor people— and that must include Negro people. He concluded that "the Senate simply had to act, the Democratic Party simply had to act, and I simply had to act; the issue could wait no longer." On the Senate floor, this tall, jug-eared man, speaking in his south-Texas drawl, threw his enormous parliamentary talents behind the 1957 civil-rights bill and got it enacted. Later, as Vice-President, he chaired Kennedy's Committee on Equal Opportunity, trying to stop discrimination by corporations with federal contracts.

And now, as President, Johnson swore to use "every ounce of strength I [possess] to gain justice for the black American." On November 27, in his first presidential address to Congress, he declared: "No memorial oration or eulogy could more eloquently honor President Kennedy's memory than the earliest possible passage of the civil rights bill for which he fought so long." Then he summoned black leaders one after another to the White House, to reassure them that "John Kennedy's dream of equality had not died with him."

King met with Johnson on December 3, after the President had importuned congressional leaders to "give it the old college try" in getting the civil-rights bill through. "He means business," King said after his session with the President. "I think we can expect even more from him than we have had up to now. I have implicit confidence in the man, and unless he betrays his past actions, we will proceed on the basis that we have in the White House a man who is deeply committed to help us." But King confided in his staff that one thing about Johnson troubled him. When you went to see Kennedy, King said, he listened to *you* for an hour and asked questions. "When you went to see Lyndon Johnson, *he* talked for an hour."

I N MID-DECEMBER, KING WAS HOME in Atlanta, surveying the pace of desegregation in this so-called citadel of southern racial enlightenment. Negotiations were currently under way between white and Negro leaders to desegregate other areas of Atlanta life, but King found them so outrageously slow that he lashed out at the city for the first time in a long while, venting the hurt and frustration he felt from a whole autumn of sorrow. "While boasting of its progress and virtue," he told 2,500 Negroes shivering in an icy wind in a downtown park, "Atlanta has allowed itself to fall behind almost every other Southern city in progress toward desegregation." King was not out "to embarrass our city, but to call Atlanta back to something noble and plead with her to rise from dark yesterdays of racial injustice to bright tomorrows of justice for all. We must honestly say to Atlanta that time is running out. If some concrete changes for good are not made soon, Negro leaders of Atlanta will find it impossible to convince the masses of Negroes of the good faith of the negotiations presently taking place."

The city council got the hint. The next day, noting that the courts had outlawed local segregation statutes one after another, the council rescinded "all ordinances which require the separation of persons because of race, color or creed." Out went measures that prohibited bars from serving Negroes and whites in the same room, Negro barbers from cutting white women's hair, white and Negro baseball teams from playing within two blocks of one another, and blacks from visiting whites-only parks.

So it was that Atlanta, "the city too busy to hate," joined the list of southern municipalities that made strides toward freedom that year of the Negro revolution in Dixie. Even Funtown—the segregated amusement park that had upset Yoki so—had quietly opened its doors to Negroes. King took his daughter there for a day of cotton candy and whirling rides, and clouds of uninhibited delight now replaced clouds of inferiority in her little mental skies. Whites came up to him and asked, "Aren't you Dr. King, and isn't that your daughter?" King nodded, and Yoki heard them say "how glad they were to see us there."

PART SIX

LIFE'S

RESTLESS SEA

INSIDE THE JETLINER, which raced from Atlanta toward Los Angeles, King sat against a white pillow, looking out the window at the shadowy outlines of the Appalachians below. Suddenly the plane shuddered in severe turbulence. King turned to a reporter sitting beside him and said with a wry smile, "I guess that's Birmingham down below."

The reminder of the campaign there set King to discussing the events of 1963, "when the civil rights issue," he said, "was impressed on the nation in a way that nothing else before had been able to do. It was the most decisive year in the Negro's fight for equality. Never before had there been such a coalition of conscience on this issue."

And never before had an American Negro attained such fame as King had in 1963. Among scores of other honors, he was *Time*'s "Man of the Year"—the first American Negro to win that distinction—and his portrait graced the cover of *Time*'s January 3, 1964, issue. In 1963, he had worked twenty hours a day, traveled some 275,000 miles, and given more than 350 speeches, though it was his "I Have a Dream" speech at the Lincoln Memorial that had borne him to glory.

When he reached California, it seemed that everywhere he went friends wanted him to appear here and say a few words there, and he was "running all over the place," a woman friend recalled. Going up a hotel escalator, King said wearily, "It's not going to be the movement that will kill me. It's going to be my friends." It distressed him that he had to give the same address over and over, with no time to revise or even polish his utterances. "I have lost freshness and creativity," he complained. "I cannot write speeches each time I talk, and it is a great frustration to have to rehash old stuff again and again."

But people idolized him all the same, whites because he appealed to the best in America and did not rant at them, Negroes because he articulated their longing, hurts, and aspirations with what *Time* called an "indescribable capacity for empathy." The adoration of the Negro masses really did make him their Gandhi. But his popularity could be a terrible hindrance. Wherever he found himself in public, in hotels, restaurants, and airports, swarms of people hounded him for his autograph. Harry Wachtel claimed that even on a rare vacation, say to the Bahamas, King virtually had to hide out in his hotel room to escape the crowds. And all the attention embarrassed him, his intimates said, because King was an extremely humble man. "Martin did not have any of this pompous arrogance that characterize so many people who have high education and also get into a position of leadership and power," recalled a friend. "I never met a man in my life," said Wyatt Walker, "who has been so completely unaffected by the attention that has come to him in the world. He's always just Martin around anybody. . . . There isn't any swagger to his psyche at all."

He worried that people viewed him as a saint, an angel with a halo, a messiah. "I'm no messiah," he kept saying, "and I don't have a messiah complex." Behind his public image, aides and friends were quick to point out, "Martin was very, very human." Sure, he could be unrelentingly serious in public, seemingly devoid of a sense of humor (as *Time* said). But away from the crowds, away from the reporters and television cameras, he could relax with close companions and laugh and tell his preacher jokes. "Doc thought he was a great joke teller," said Hosea Williams, a newcomer to SCLC's staff. "His jokes weren't very funny to me sometimes. But *he* thought they were." He loved to banter with his young aides. It was a way to let off steam, especially during a campaign, and "keep us from being so uptight all the time," Lee said. In mock derision, they would call him "Liver Lip King"—a favorite segregationist nickname—and giggle that he couldn't be recognized if he kept a hand over his mouth. Gleefully, King would razz them back, twitting Young as "a Tom" and ribbing Lee mercilessly about how his eyes crossed in a moment of danger. "He could tease you harder than anybody I know," Lee remembered. "I mean, he could really get on your case." When something struck him as hilarious, "he would practically fall out of the chair, he'd laugh so hard."

There was a droll, ironic side to him, too. He could make white liberals squirm with mirth when he recounted, in a heavy southern accent, how one of his Montgomery followers had responded to his plea for nonviolence: "Aw right, Reverend, if you says so. But Ah still thinks we oughta kill off a few of 'em." He grinned with delight when Wyatt Walker told the story of "this big Negro guy" who stood up to an insulting bus driver, saying, "I want you to know two things. One, I ain't no boy. And two, I ain't one of those Martin Luther King nonviolent Negroes." Once, when he and some white associates were riding an elevator up to Wachtel's Manhattan law offices, a white woman got on and said to him, "Six, please." Despite his business suit and tie, she thought him the operator. "And Martin just pushed the button," Wachtel said, "and when she got off he laughed as hard as everyone else."

Thanks to all the sedentary traveling, the endless breakfasts and luncheons, King was now "a heavy-chested 173 lbs.," as *Time* reported. To keep his weight down, he used a sugar substitute and tried to diet, though that was difficult given his love for good food. At a table with friends and staff members, he had a habit of sampling their salads and entrées, eating joyfully from everyone's plate. He fancied chicken wings and frequented a fast-food place in Washington, D.C., which served them up with a zesty sauce.

Though in public he could be remarkably self-assured, unflappable in interviews and at the rostrum, he was deeply sensitive and easily hurt. Severe criticism depressed him. And depression often brought on the hiccups, which would last for hours. Once, Lee recalled, King had an attack before he was to give a speech, a sure sign that he was dejected. Amazingly, the hiccups stopped when he went to the podium, and he spoke with his usual lucidity for an hour and fifteen minutes. After he said "Thank you" and sat down, he started hiccuping again.

By his own admission, King had "a troubled soul"—troubled not only by the misery and inequity he saw everywhere, but by his own inner conflicts. "Martin could be described as an intensely guilt-ridden man," said his friend Stanley Levison, because "he didn't feel he deserved all the tribute he got." Raised in material comfort and given a superior education, he had never suffered like the Negro masses who loved him so. He felt he had not earned the leadership they thrust on him. So he would think of ways to justify his renown—would talk about taking a vow of poverty and giving up possessions like his house, so that "he could at least feel that nothing material came to him from his efforts." But, of course, he never took such a vow. How could he provide for his family if he did? In any case, he still enjoyed the amenities of life—a nice hotel suite, a good meal with wine—and was still impressed with multi-millionaire Jewish benefactors in New York.

But there were other reasons for King's troubled soul. He felt a great deal of anger in him for the evils he had witnessed in Dixie— particularly the murder of those four Birmingham girls—and relied more than ever on "creative nonviolence" to funnel his fury into constructive channels. He was talking about his own feelings when he argued that a man must have the courage to resist an evil system nonviolently; otherwise he ran the risk of a self-destructive explosion. He never told Negroes not to be angry, as many of his black critics charged. On the contrary, "Martin always felt that anger was a very important commodity," recalled his close friend Harry Belafonte, "a necessary part of the black movement in this country." It was anger, after all, that fueled Negro resistance, anger that helped black people overcome lifetime habits of shame and servility and start fighting for their rights. But theirs must not be a hateful anger, for that was debilitating and ruinous; it must be a disciplined, nonviolent anger—what King called a "creative dissatisfaction." "It is still my basic article of faith," he told *Playboy* in 1964, "that social justice can be achieved and democracy advanced only to the degree that there is firm adherence to *nonviolent* action and resistance in the pursuit of social justice." But he stated with equal emphasis: "As much as I deplore violence, there is one evil that is worse than violence, and that's cowardice."

When King spoke of "the deep longing for the bread of love" in the world, he was not just talking philosophically. True, he still believed in Gandhi's Satyagraha as the salvation of the human race—as the great moral force that would bring on the brave new order he had long prophesied. Yet he also needed love personally, needed companionship, acceptance and approval. To be sure, he cared deeply for his wife and could be tender to her when they were together, extremely tender. By his own estimation, though, he spent only about 10 percent of his time at home, and his long absences took their toll. Lonely and troubled, gone from home so much of the time, he surrendered himself to his passionate nature and sought intimacy and reassurance in the arms of other women, sometimes casually, sometimes with "a very real feeling," as he told a confidant. He needed desperately not just to be free as a man, but to be cherished and loved as a man. "My life," he complained constantly, "is one of always giving out and never stopping to take in." At night, away from the crowds and the cameras, he found a way to take in.

His close associates were aware that he strayed and did not judge him for it. "I didn't see Martin as a saint, a god, no way, shape, or form," recalled one staff member, echoing what others said. "I saw him as a man." Some white friends argued that King had an unconscious need to demonstrate that he was as virile as his father. Certain black friends, on the other hand, cited "the historic obligations of evangelical preachers in the South to the women of their congregations." As one Negro put it, "Martin really believed in the gospel of love." And there were plenty of women who wanted him, who were attracted by his impassioned voice, his gentleness, his air of vulnerability. Wherever he went, females of both races, old and young, married and single, sought him out. "I can't tell you the number of women that would proposition me in hopes of getting to Martin," recalled Bernard Lee, his special assistant and traveling companion. "If I were a dishonest person . . . and greedy, I could have gotten rich."

Still, with his enormous conscience, King felt guilty about his sexual transgressions. In *Strength to Love*, his book of sermons, he betrayed something of his suffering when he wrote of how every man had good and evil warring inside and how we see evil expressed in "tragic lust and inordinate selfishness." He bemoaned "the evils of sensuality" and warned that "when we yield to the temptation of a world rife with sexual promiscuity and gone wild with a philosophy of self-expression, Jesus tells us that 'whosoever looketh on a woman to lust after her hath committed adultery with her already in his heart.'" But in moments of loneliness, beset with temptation, he would succumb again to his own human frailties. Perhaps those were weighing on him when he asserted in a speech that segregation was "the adultery of an illicit intercourse between injustice and immorality" and could not "be cured by the Vaseline of gradualism."

King confided to friends that "I am conscious of two Martin Luther Kings" and that "the Martin Luther King that the people talk about seems to be somebody foreign to me." "Each of us is two selves," he remarked in a later sermon. "And the great burden of life is to always try to keep that higher self in command. Don't let the lower self take over." But he confessed that "every now and then you'll be unfaithful to those that you should be faithful to. It's a mixture in human nature."

In early 1964, King was still not aware that the FBI knew about his "lower self" and was snooping into his private life. In fact, in January and February, Hoover's agents launched counterintelligence, "dirty tricks" operations against him, planting unauthorized and illegal microphones in his hotel rooms from Washington out to Honolulu and forwarding tapes of the recordings to Hoover and his deputies, who then had national political and religious leaders secretly briefed about his personal conduct as well as his alleged Communist associations. In January, a bug in King's room in the Willard Hotel recorded a party that involved King, some SCLC colleagues, and two Negro women employed at the Philadelphia Naval Yard. When he heard highlights of the tapes, Hoover exulted that this would "destroy the burrhead"— his favorite nickname for King—and had a transcript sent to the White House. In February, at the Los Angeles Hyatt House Motel, King and his companions delighted in some lascivious repartee, and King himself told a joke about the supposed sexual practices of John F. Kennedy, unaware of course that an FBI bug was recording it all. "This is excellent data," beamed a bureau official, "indicting King as one of the most reprehensible . . . individuals on the American scene today."

That individual, so celebrated in public, was paying a heavy price indeed for his fame and his cause. He suffered from stomach aches and insomnia—symptoms of the guilt he felt and the stress he was under—and took sleeping pills a New York physician and friend gave to him. Yet "suffering is part of the process of life," he once said. "Ultimately the question is not whether or not we will suffer, but whether or not we will have the inner calm to face the trials and tribulations of life." To face the tribulations of his life, he subjected himself to painful self-analysis and attempts at self-purification. "I can't afford to make a mistake," he would tell Coretta or a friend. And he would ask himself: Am I making the correct decision? Maintaining my sense of purpose? Holding fast to my ideals? Guiding "the people" in the right direction? Confronting my own shortcomings and doubts?

"But whatever my doubts, however heavy the burden," he said to *Playboy*, "I feel that I must accept the task of helping to make the nation and the world a better place to live in—for *all* men, black and white alike." Whatever his flaws as a man, he found comfort—a sense of security—in the knowledge that the struggle itself was right, "because it is a thrust forward . . . that will save the whole of mankind, and when I have come to see these things I always felt a sense of cosmic companionship. So that the loneliness and the fear have faded away because of a greater feeling of security, because of commitment to a moral ideal." In his efforts to "do God's will," he could lose himself and prepare to lay down his life. "The quality, not the longevity, of one's life is what is important," he assured *Time*, in reference to the mounting threats to murder him. "If you are cut down in a movement that is designed to save the soul of a nation, then no other death could be more redemptive."

Armed with that conviction, King demonstrated extraordinary physical courage in the face of danger. Observers who saw him in action were struck by "the feeling of power" he projected "while physically remaining so calm." His gentle manner, wrote a *New York Times* journalist, cloaked "a core of steel." "He was the truest militant I ever met," said Hosea Williams. "He not only talked that talk; he walked that walk." Williams was with him on occasions when "I had so much fear the flesh trembled on my bones." During one southern campaign, Williams saw King walk right through a mob of white toughs gathered across the street from a courthouse. As he pushed forward, smiling, saying, "Excuse me, please," they were stupefied and made way for him without raising a hand or saying a word.

He had the strength, too, to be tender with people, listening patiently to their troubles, commiserating with them. In need of love himself, he could give love to others with enormous sensitivity. He was especially affectionate toward members of his executive staff, whom he treated as an extended family that belonged to him. "He was able to find that common bond of love and worth in each of us that would make us produce our best," said Andrew Young. "We were strong-willed," Williams remembered, "and it took a terrible amount of love to handle us. I would lose my temper, and Dr. King would caution, 'Hosea.' Just like that. Where others would get angry with me around the table, he had the capacity to love me instead."

When it came to SCLC, various observers disparaged King as a poor administrator, a man "more at home with a conception than he is with the details of its application," a man with "small talent for organizing outside or inside his own group." Even Bayard Rustin asserted that leaders like King were "great dreamers," not effective administrators. But Wyatt Walker emphatically demurred. "When you say it like that, you sound like that's an indictment. He's Martin Luther King! What else does he need to be? He's a symbol that there needs to be a moral voice in America talking about the injustice and inequity. . . . That's his job. That's his function. And that's all he needs to be. He doesn't need to know how to answer a telephone or write a sentence straight. It is his honor and glory that he's also an author, that he's a profound religious thinker who has had an impact on modern-day theology, and that he's one of the great orators of the nation, maybe of the world."

Although King himself said that "I can do a much better job in the spiritual than in the administrative area," he was a superior administrator in many ways, not the least of which was his mastery of the art and technique of fund raising. As one staff member said, money dictated the movement's priorities, and King had no equal when it came to drumming up funds for its treasuries. What was more, he brought to SCLC a group of talented and dynamic assistants who had been leaders themselves. "He surrounded himself with what I feel is one of the most competent staffs in the whole area of civil rights," said one associate, "and he respected hell out of all of us."

Always alert to new talent, King had several newcomers on his staff in 1964. Among them was C. T. Vivian, a tall, angular, high-strung young man with small features and a neatly trimmed mustache. When he spoke, there was drama and a touch of mysticism in his language. He had an ironic sense of humor that bordered on the sardonic, and a spirited, tut-tutting laugh that punctuated his conversation with thespian artistry. When he discoursed on some human folly, he would close one eye as though sighting a distant target. In high school in Illinois, he came under the spell of a creative English teacher who "gave us that understanding of how great writing fits with the whole integrity of man." He went on to Western Illinois University, got married, divorced, married again, found himself at American Theological Seminary in Nashville, and wound up as an editor on the Sunday School Publishing Board there. Across his desk came the speeches of the young minister who was heading the Montgomery bus protest. In 1957 Vivian heard King give a talk on nonviolence in a packed Nashville church, and he was spellbound. He had studied Gandhian techniques, but until now had never understood the philosophy behind them. Determined to preserve King's utterances, Vivian prepared an article that featured his speeches and writings. "It frightened me," he wrote King in 1958, "to think that you might die and your speeches be lost. I did what I could with my funds and talent. I hope to continue to put your words and thoughts into the hearts and minds of any person I contact." Quoting King himself, Vivian became involved in the Nashville sit-ins and the next year went on the Freedom Ride to Mississippi, where he was brutally beaten on a prison farm. After that he pastored a church in Chattanooga, Tennessee, and participated in demonstrations there. Impressed with this philosophical, energetic, laughing man, King invited him to join SCLC as director of affiliates.

Another new aide, Hosea Williams, was a tempestuous, self-styled "workaholic" with a rasping voice and a brawling style. He was born in poverty in rural southwest Georgia, "reared up with no father," he recalled; "I'm a bastard child—my mother was never married to my father—reared up on a white man's plantation." He had suffered his share of racial violence in his youth. Once whites accused him of messing around with a "po" white girl and tried to lynch him. During World War II, he was wounded in action in Europe and returned to Georgia on crutches. On his way through Americus, he limped into a bus station to get a drink of water at a white fountain, only to be drubbed mercilessly by berserk whites. "I was violent by nature," he said of those bitter early years. Yet he had enough pride and sense of direction to educate himself and become upward bound: he secured a position as a chemist with the U.S. Department of Agriculture in Savannah, bought a new house and a new car, married and started a family. Later, after his sons were refused service at Savannah lunch counters, he joined the NAACP and plunged into the civil-rights movement. But his pugnacity offended the local NAACP brass, and he quit the organization in disgust. Inspired by the work and message of Dr. King, he accepted nonviolence and went to work with SCLC's affiliate in Savannah, where he launched a direct-action campaign and caught King's eye with his aggressive style, which was to hit the streets and "keep on pressin', pressin'." In early 1964, King appointed him to his Atlanta staff as director of voter registration. Something of a maverick among the other executive staffers, who were seminary-trained ministers, Williams was a superb grass-roots organizer, with a special touch among the masses of poor folk because he had suffered privation, too. "Martin had a lot of confidence in my ability to mobilize and move people," Williams claimed. "He saw me and said, 'That's my crazy man. That's my wild man. That's my Castro.' " "Doc understood Hosea's ability to create tension," Vivian said with a sly chuckle. "When Hosea can't have his way, he creates a lot of tension."

By 1964, King had assembled a cadre of bright and brash young lieutenants who were fiercely loyal to him and supremely confident in themselves. "Who could tell us anything?" Vivian said. "We were the movement." Not every Negro leader was secure enough to have strong subordinates, he pointed out, but "Doc" had six or seven "horses in their own right" who battled one another at SCLC's often stormy staff sessions. "Phew," said a visitor to SCLC, "that kinda meeting would tear up any organization I ever belonged to. It's interesting that you guys are still together." It was King, of course, who "kept all those wild horses together." Impartial, never taking sides in staff skull sessions, he would ask questions and let his assistants debate and argue— Walker tangling with Bevel, Williams with Young—all the while he would sit there thinking and scratching at his painful whiskers. He would continue raising questions until they had worked through a problem collectively and reached a conclusion. "When he no longer had anything to ask." Vivian said, "we had it together."

"We were very young, very strong, very articulate," Williams declared, "and it was amazing how he could orchestrate us." "Martin is such a soft, easygoing fellow," Walker said, and "so absolutely moral in his leadership that there never has been any vying for his spot. It's just out of the question. Everybody gives him allegiance." "He had greater commitment than any of us," Vivian remembered. "He could walk us out into the deep water." But not only that. "Doc outthought everybody, too. No one programmed him. Doc was the *head* of all of us. That's why he was our leader." In awe of him, they competed with one another for his ear and his favor. "It was like children in the family," said one staffer, "in the sense that everybody wanted the father's attention."

To be sure, King had administrative drawbacks. As one young aide recalled, he tended to function "by the spirit" in ways that were amazing, exasperating, and infuriating by turns. Anybody who dealt with King found that he and his staff ran by what they jocularly called "CPT"—Colored People's Time—and kept appointments with cheerful disregard for punctuality. In addition, King was indifferent to staff discipline. "If one of them got absolutely obstreperous," Rustin said of King's assistants, "Dr. King would come in and tell him to calm down. But in terms of assigning jobs, people just pretty much ran off and did what they wanted." Abernathy complained that King made him "do what I called his dirty work" and tend to disciplinary problems, because King was reluctant to hurt anybody. He was unwilling to fire people, too, even if they were dishonest. Once the staff released an office worker for stealing SCLC funds, but the person persuaded King to take him back. "What do you do to a devil?" King asked his aides. "Do you take a devil and throw him out in the world? Or do you try to bring him closer to you, convert him, redeem him? We're supposed to be the church. So do you throw a man out of the church? Or do you try to keep him in the church and right his wrongs?"

His assistants did not dispute him. "He was a preacher," Young explained. "And whenever we argued, he'd get to preaching. You never won an argument because he would take off on flights of oratory, and you'd forget your point trying to listen to him."

His preaching, though, was the touchstone of his leadership. He always made decisions on moral grounds, as Walker said, and he excited audiences of all colors and conditions with his unique mixture of southern Negro evangelism and theological erudition. If he could make Negroes in a country church say amen to a quotation from St. Thomas Aquinas, he could make university professors and students applaud a quotation from an unlettered slave. "Doc really communicated on other levels than just the intellectual," said Vivian, the student of his words and a minister himself who understood the hallmark of great preaching. "He communicated on the emotional level, too, so that you really didn't have to understand his words to understand what he meant. That's why the No D.'s and the Ph.D.'s could be moved by the same speech. Besides, Doc conveyed the sense that he cared. He wasn't some disinterested conveyor of crafted sentences. He believed that the right word, emotionally and intellectually charged, could reach the whole person and change the relationships of men."

That wasn't the only quality that set King apart. His sense of history enabled him to perceive the broad historical canvas on which the civil-rights movement was taking place. It convinced him that the progress of America was forward, not backward; that he was better off in 1964 than his forebears; that thousands of people in the past had struggled to enlarge his own freedom. King's historical perspective made him an optimist; it contributed to the calm under fire that became his trademark. And it strengthened his belief that the mission of the American Negro (as Gandhi and others had contended) was to introduce a new moral standard into the United States and the world.

Like Gandhi, King was both an activist and a theoretician, a protagonist at the center of a great historical struggle and a philosopher concerned with ultimate questions about God and man. Like Gandhi, he identified downward with the poor, the forgotten, and the disinherited. He walked among the black masses, philosophizing as he went, and he furnished them something no other American Negro leader had been able to give them: "a tool," as a black scholar phrased it, "for removing the invisible shades of segregation."

Ved Mehta, a distinguished student of India, discerned something else about King, something David Halbertstam also glimpsed. In 1961, in an article in the *New York Times Magazine*, Mehta contended that both King and Gandhi had a flair for arranging demonstrations as though they were theatrical performances. It was art, not economics or politics or theology, that was the essence of the movements they led. By century's end, Mehta predicted, both apostles of nonviolence would be remembered because "they were imaginative artists who knew how to use world politics as their stage."

I N MID-JANUARY, 1964, King led his staff away to Black Mountain, in the foothills of North Carolina, for a retreat at the site of a defunct experimental community in art, education, and lifestyle. King loved staff retreats. They afforded him the opportunity to stroll in the forest and meditate in solitude, as he longed so much to do in the maelstrom that was his life. At retreats, he and his aides would pray and sing, eat, and play pingpong and basketball together. "Cat could really play basketball," staffer Willie Bolden said of King. He would dart and glide down court and push off shots high in the air, only to beg his exhausted young lieutenants once the game was over, "Aw fellas, come on, let's play another ten points." When they all gathered for the evening discussions, which might continue in King's room until well past midnight, he would go around introducing everyone, narrating their biographies with a phenomenal memory for detail.

At the Black Mountain retreat, King introduced a procession of topics for discussion—among them, the hostility of SNCC, of Hoover and the FBI— and gave sermonlike recitations on them. "In some ways," said Harry Wachtel, who was at Black Mountain, "he was still the Bapist minister talking to his congregation." They also reviewed SCLC's leadership training program at Dorchester, Georgia, which was turning out "the noncommissioned officers of the civil rights movement," as King phrased it. People from small towns and rural areas came there to learn how to conduct voter-registration drives, combat illiteracy, and secure government benefits, and then returned to their communities to implement what they had learned. By 1963, some six hundred Negroes had graduated from the SCLC program and were spreading the movement far and wide in Dixie.

Because SCLC was now the most popular civil-rights organization among American Negroes, as reported in *Newsweek's* poll of July, 1963, King explored at Black Mountain the possibility of converting SCLC from a southern coalition of affiliates into a national membership organization that would attack segregation throughout the country. Many of King's followers argued that this would enable him to reach a level of prestige and power unsurpassed by any Negro in American history. "I will have to face the decision soon on whether I should be limiting myself to the South," King had told a writer for the *Saturday Evening Post*. "In the North there are brothers and sisters who are suffering discrimination that is even more agonizing, in a sense, than in the South. . . . In the South, at least the Negro can see progress, whereas in the North all he sees is retrogression." But the idea of a national membership organization never got beyond the talking stage. According to Wachtel and others, King realized that such an organization would threaten the NAACP and Roy Wilkins—not to mention the leaders of CORE and the National Urban League—and likely wreck the fragile alliance then existing among the various civil-rights groups. To keep peace, King decided that SCLC should remain a regional organization of affiliates, but one with national interests.

One outgrowth of the Black Mountain retreat was the creation of a Research Committee, a kind of brain trust that would advise King on a structured basis. The committee consisted of Young, Fauntroy, and Abernathy from the SCLC staff; historian L. D. Reddick, now teaching at Coppin State College in Baltimore; Rustin, Wachtel, Levison,

Clarence Jones, Negro labor leader Cleveland Robinson, and others from New York and Chicago. The group held late-night conference phone calls and tried to meet three or four times a year, generally in Wachtel's New York law offices, to "kick around ideas and give reactions," Young said. King found the meetings stimulating and refreshing; they gave him a chance to get away from the southern front and debate ideas with a coterie of articulate northerners, in the manner of the old Philosophy Club back at Boston University. The Research Committee functioned strictly as an advisory group, though, and King never took a vote. After their meetings, Wachtel recalled, King "did whatever he damn well wanted."

As King and his advisers surveyed the various civil-rights battlefronts in early 1964, they found little to cheer about. Kennedy's civil-rights bill had passed in the House, but faced a crippling southern filibuster in the Senate. Though President Johnson was using all the power and persuasion of his office to get the measure approved, King was certain that additional civil-rights campaigns would be necessary to pressure the Senate to act.

In "The Hammer of Civil Rights," which he wrote for *The Nation*, King pointed out how successful southerners had been in using the filibuster to block civil-rights legislation over the years, and he enjoined the Senate to put an end to it as a fitting tribute to the Negro girls assassinated in Birmingham. At the same time, he demanded federal police protection for Negroes in Dixie, where local officials had fielded an awesome force. In Mississippi, for example, the mayor of Jackson openly bragged about the armor he had amassed for a projected summer campaign on the part of SNCC to register Negro voters. In addition to an armed contingent of five hundred men and a reserve of state troopers, deputies, civil employees, and neighborhood citizens' patrols, the mayor commanded a "Thompson Tank," two searchlight tanks, an armored battlewagon that carried twelve men equipped with shotguns and machine guns, three troop lorries, and three huge trailer trucks. Thus a veritable mechanized division awaited nonviolent demonstrators with "undisguised hostility and the familiar trigger happy eagerness for confrontation."

Across the South, King wrote, nonviolent Negroes found themselves at war. Yet "the most powerful federal government in the world" had left them "almost solely to their own resources to face a massively equipped army." This "cries out for resolution." Though the country had a national power beyond description, "it cannot enforce elementary law even in a remote southern village."

According to a Negro dentist named Robert B. Hayling, elementary law had ceased to exist for the Negroes of St. Augustine, a small tourist town on Florida's northern Atlantic coast. Sometime in late February or early March, Hayling visited King in Atlanta and told him what was going on in St. Augustine, where the dentist lived and practiced. A haven for the Klan and other extremist groups, St. Augustine was the oldest permanent European community in North America and one of its most viciously racist. Here Sheriff L. O. Davis, "a buffoonish, burly, thuggish man," employed an auxiliary force of one hundred deputies, many of them prominent Klansmen, to "keep the niggers in line." Here barrel-chested Holsted "Hoss" Manucy, dressed in cowboy paraphernalia, led a bunch of Klan-style bullyboys who called themselves the Ancient City Gun Club. They patrolled the county in radio cars with Confederate flags on their antennas, harassing Negroes at will. Manucy boasted that he had no vices, that he didn't smoke, drink, or chase women. All he did was "beat and kill niggers."

In 1963, inspired by King's Birmingham campaign, Hayling, an Air Force veteran, set out to end the atmosphere of terror in St. Augustine. He wrote President Kennedy and Vice-President Johnson about the racial violence that plagued the city and even got up a local movement to desegregate public accommodations and gain uninhibited Negro voter registration. But the police beat and jailed the demonstrators with ruthless precision, and stood idly by while the Klan bombed and strafed Negro homes and fired shotguns into Negro nightclubs. In September, Klansmen abducted Hayling and three other blacks, hauled them out to an open field where a crowd was waiting, and beat them unconscious with brass knuckles and ax handles. As the crowd roared and a woman screamed, "Kill 'em! Castrate 'em!" Klansmen prepared to douse the four Negroes with kerosene. "Did you ever smell a nigger burn?" one asked. "It's a mighty sweet smell." Only the timely arrival of the sheriff prevented them from being incinerated.

Nor was that all. In February, 1964, whites blasted Hayling's home with shotguns, almost killing his pregnant wife and two children, and burned the homes of two Negro families whose children had been admitted into an all-white school. Meanwhile the Klan threatened violent retaliation against white businesses that voluntarily desegregated. And Washington not only ignored Hayling's calls for aid, but pledged $350,000 to help white leaders celebrate St. Augustine's four hundredth birthday, come 1965.

The situation was so grim, Hayling told King, that the St. Augustine movement was finished unless he and SCLC moved in and took over. Only King could gain national attention for St. Augustine's battered Negroes. Only he could get them to march and demonstrate again. Would he come and lead them?

King was profoundly upset by Hayling's tale of woe. He could not understand why Johnson and the Justice Department had failed to send federal marshals to St. Augustine. Equally distressing was the fact that Washington intended to use taxpayers' money—including that of Negro taxpayers—to subsidize segregated birthday festivities in that unhappy town. On March 6, during an SCLC rally in Orlando, King met again with Hayling and assured him of SCLC's support. Though a small SCLC task force was away in Selma, Alabama, working on voter registration, King and his staff had decided to convert St. Augustine into a major "nonviolent battlefield." They intended to expose Klan savagery to the eyes of the nation and the world; then maybe Washington would provide police protection for Negroes and civil-rights workers in Dixie. By dramatizing the segregated conditions of America's "Ancient City," they aimed to win federal guarantees that Negroes, too, could participate in St. Augustine's quadricentennial celebrations and eat and sleep in public accommodations of their choice. "The Negro takes pride in this nation and his contributions to its greatness," King wrote Senator Hubert H. Humphrey, "but these continued denials to our citizenship place a heavy burden on our confidence in the American dream." Once the Senate realized that voluntary desegregation was impossible in southern communities like St. Augustine, maybe it would break the filibuster and enact the civil-rights bill at last.

King sent Vivian, Williams, and Lee ahead to prepare St. Augustine for nonviolent combat, with plans to join them once they had the Negro community mobilized. Through March and April, King spoke around the country, with FBI field agents single-mindedly bugging his hotel rooms. Meanwhile he somehow finished his Birmingham book, *Why We Can't Wait*, and mailed the last revisions off to New York. Because of the pace of events (the assassination of Kennedy, the rise of

Johnson, the onset of a presidential election year), King had dropped
the idea of a "quickie" about Birmingham and instead had produced a
serious work that included a blueprint for racial justice. He hoped it
"would answer many questions for many people for some time to
come." Hermine Popper, who had helped with *Stride Toward Freedom,* had finally taken over the editorial labors and had done such a
"constructive and important" job in polishing the text while preserving
King's style that he accorded her a special acknowledgment in the
book. Harper & Row, which had published *Strength to Love* the year
before, would bring out a hardcover edition of *Why We Can't Wait*
in June, with New American Library to follow with a paperback edition in August.

Meanwhile King kept in constant contact with his lieutenants in St.
Augustine. Ready to start pressing, Hosea Williams secured King's permission to conduct night marches to the old Slave Market in St. Augustine's public square. The Slave Market was to be the symbol and rallying point for all demonstrations. King realized that night marches
were dangerous, that something drastic could happen. But "he saw
this as the creative tension that would make the whole nation see what
was happening in St. Augustine," Vivian said.

On the night of May 28, while King was in Los Angeles, a riot
broke out in St. Augustine. When Andrew Young led a Negro column
around the Slave Market, lights from television and newspaper cameras suddenly flashed in the darkness, whereupon Klansmen poured
out of the market and fell on the demonstrators with bicycle chains
and iron pipes, the police looking on indifferently. A white thug
knocked Young unconscious and others kicked and beat him while he
lay in the street. Finally the cops stopped the violence, and the marchers streamed bleeding and crying back to St. Paul's church in the Negro district, located southeast of the plaza. That same night, white
marauders shot up an empty beach cottage SCLC had rented as King's
headquarters.

The next day, King wired the White House that "all semblance of
law and order has broken down in St. Augustine, Florida," and that
the President must provide federal protection for Negroes there. But
the administration felt that state and local authorities could handle the
city, though it assured King that the FBI would "stay on top of the
situation."

That must have struck King as a cruel joke. On Sunday, May 31, he arrived in St. Augustine to take command, only to learn that Sheriff Davis had secured a local court injunction that banned night marches. That very evening, in fact, he and his deputies broke up a demonstration with force. In a press conference later, his bulletin board crowded with letters from all over America praising his handling of Negro "troublemakers," Davis announced that the FBI was in town to protect Martin Luther King so that he would not become a martyr. He added with smug satisfaction, "The FBI insists Dr. King is a communist."

On Monday, King and a retinue of lawyers and aides took their complaints to the U.S. District Court in Jacksonville, asking Judge Bryan Simpson, a native southerner, to overrule the local court injunction and permit the night marches to continue without police interference. At hearings called by the judge, Young and other witnesses described the mob attack at the old Slave Market. Sheriff Davis took the stand, too, and admitted that he had "special" deputies beyond his regular and auxiliary forces. Simpson demanded a list of names. When he came to Hoss Manucy, the judge exclaimed, "Why that man's a convicted felon in this court!" Vivian rejoiced that Davis was "on the hot seat" now. Sensing victory, King's attorneys put Dr. Hayling on the stand, and the judge listened, visibly moved, as Hayling recounted how the Klan had beaten and almost cremated him and three comrades.

The judge wanted to study the case, and King and Hayling agreed to suspend demonstrations until he reached a decision. Back in St. Augustine, King evangelized a mass meeting in a hot Negro church, beads of sweat glistening on his brow. The cries and amens punctuating King's oratory recalled the fervor that had rocked Shiloh Church at the height of the Albany Movement. "I want to commend you for the beauty and dignity and the courage with which you carried out demonstrations last week," King said. "I know what you faced. And I understand that as you marched silently and with a deep commitment to nonviolence, you confronted the brutality of the Klan. But amid all of this you stood up."

He went on: "You know they threaten us occasionally with more than beatings here and there. They threaten us with actual physical death. They think that this will stop the movement. I got word way out in California that a plan was under way to take my life in St. Augustine, Florida." He continued amid volleys of applause, "We have long since learned to sing anew with our foreparents of old that

> Before I'll be a slave [*yes, all right, well?*]
> I'll be buried in my grave [*amen, amen*]
> And go home to my Father [*amen*]
> And be saved. . . .

At King's behest, Harold DeWolf and four Boston University colleagues came down to St. Augustine to help open negotiations with the local white leadership. SCLC guards escorted them through elaborate safety procedures to a Negro home where King had his command post. To DeWolf's surprise, little Marty ran out—"Uncle Harold!" he cried, and gave DeWolf a hug.

"Marty, what on earth are you doing here?" DeWolf asked.

"Oh, I'm with Daddy."

Shaking the hand of his old teacher, King explained that it was impossible to shield the children from danger, that he had so little time to spend with his family and thought his boys especially needed more fatherly companionship. So he had brought Marty with him.

King gave DeWolf a list of demands—public accommodations in this city must be desegregated, Negroes hired as policemen and firemen, a biracial committee established to work out harmonious race relations—and DeWolf conveyed them to local white leaders. "They could have been on opposite sides of the world," he lamented, "so far as communication was concerned." As expected, the whites categorically rejected King's demands.

There was excellent news from Jacksonville, though. On June 9 Judge Simpson enjoined Sheriff Davis and the city of St. Augustine from interfering with night marches and prohibited the sheriff from subjecting his prisoners to any further "cruel and unusual punishment." In his court order, the judge cited instances in which Davis and his henchmen had crammed ten demonstrators into a small concrete sweatbox and herded twenty-one women into a circular padded cell ten feet in diameter and left them there for an hour and eighteen minutes; one of the women was a polio victim on crutches "and unable to stand without them."

King was overjoyed that a southern judge had found in favor of the movement. At a mass meeting that day, he exhorted his cohorts to "march tonight as you've never marched before." And he decided that it was time for him and Abernathy to generate "creative tension" by

going to jail. They marched to Monson Motor Lodge, which overlooked Matanzas Bay, and demanded service in the restaurant, refusing to leave until the police came and arrested them.

That night, while King was in jail, a screaming white mob overran
a police cordon and assaulted four hundred Negroes as they trekked
through the plaza. At last state police dispersed the rowdies with tear
gas, one of them sobbing, "Niggers have more freedom than we do!"
From jail King telegraphed President Johnson that St. Augustine had
just experienced the "most complete breakdown of law and order
since Oxford, Mississippi" and that he must send federal marshals before somebody got killed.

The next day, in Washington, administration forces won a vote of
cloture in the Senate, thanks to the conversion of minority leader Ev-
erett Dirksen of Illinois, who proclaimed in King's favorite words that
the civil-rights bill was "an idea whose time has come." While King
was locked up in Florida, the hated southern filibuster went down to
defeat, all but assuring the passage of Kennedy's year-old civil-rights
measure.

The following day, June 11, King bailed out of jail looking haggard
and frightened. Hayling claimed that he had been in solitary confinement and didn't like to discuss what had happened. Perhaps that experience and the good news from Washington explained his abrupt departure from jail. In any event, he flew off to collect an honorary
degree at Yale University, and his detractors howled in disgust, deriding his brief imprisonment as just another "publicity stunt."

While he was gone, his aides kept up the demonstrations, including
"swim-ins" at all-white beaches. On Friday, J. B. Stoner, a rotund Atlanta attorney and vice-presidential candidate of the National States'
Rights party, came to town and harangued a white crowd at the Slave
Market. "Tonight," Stoner cried, "we're going to find out whether
white people have any rights. The coons have been parading around
St. Augustine for a long time!" Now whites were going to march, and
neither "Martin Luther Coon," a "long-time associate of Communists," nor the "Jew-stacked Communist-loving Supreme Court" could
stop them. Escorted by the police, he and 170 other whites headed
through a mostly darkened Negro section, dogs barking and snarling
as they tramped down the dusty street sporting Confederate flags and
signs that read "KILL THE CIVIL RIGHTS BILL."

Throughout the next week, tension mounted in St. Augustine, as

Stoner ranted at milling crowds in the plaza and King's battalions continued their swim-ins and nightly marches to the Slave Market. Back from New Haven, King was almost mobbed one night when he rode by a Stoner rally with Lee and Abernathy. As they waited at a traffic light, someone screamed, 'There's Martin Luther Coon!" Whites surged around the car, started rocking it, and might have turned it over had not Lee stomped on the accelerator and run the red light in a successful getaway.

On the beaches, meanwhile, roving gangs whipped Negro bathers with chains and almost drowned C. T. Vivian. When black and white demonstrators jumped into the swimming pool at Monson Motor Court, the manager flung muriatic acid into the water to flush them out. King himself led a small column to the motor court, only to encounter a swarm of hecklers. Hosea Williams, who couldn't swim, was certain they were going to throw him into the water, and he wanted to "get the hell out of here." But King restrained him. "I'm not going to run, Hosea." With the ruffians encircling them and shouting, "Hey, coons," King led his party quietly back to their cars. "I was scared they were going to jump us," recalled a young white staffer. "But King was so calm. His eyes—I don't know how to describe eyes like that. You could just look at them and think, well, if he can do it, somehow nothing will happen to me."

Though nothing happened that day, Stoner and Hoss Manucy were determined to foment a Negro massacre in the streets of St. Augustine. When news came that the Senate had passed the civil-rights bill, they raged that it would "bring on a race war" and whipped a thousand whites into a frenzy of anti-Negro hatred. On the night of June 25, eight hundred club-wielding Klansmen moiled out of the Slave Market and slashed into a silent Negro column marching through the square. A white journalist reported that "the mob emitted an eerie cry as it crossed and recrossed the plaza," clubbing Negroes to the pavement, ripping the clothes off a thirteen-year-old girl, and then mauling a *Newsweek* reporter when he intervened and helped her escape.

King and Abernathy were standing on the corner at Dr. Hayling's office when two young marchers ran by in near hysteria, crying that it was "a mob scene up there, people lying in the street all over the place." The two leaders raced to the Negro church where the beaten demonstrators and other blacks were gathering. "People felt so badly and so hurt over what had happened," recalled SCLC staffer Dana

Swann. "Everybody was angry. Some were ready to go to war." But King and Abernathy calmed and soothed them: "You know the risk. . . . If you go back there, if you retaliate, somebody will get killed. . . .There have to be some sacrifices made." Then Hosea Williams led them in singing "Nobody Knows the Trouble I've Seen." Said Dr. Hayling: "To see the wounds and the split skulls and the broken noses and broken arms . . . It required tremendous control to see these and not get motivated at some point to want to set up some type of reprisal or to fight back."

For King and his followers, St. Augustine had become a nightmare. The Johnson administration still refused to send federal marshals there, and Florida governor Farris Bryant, instead of curtailing the Klan, ignored Judge Simpson's injunction and banned any more night marches in the city. With the state government blatantly supporting St. Augustine's segregationists and his people terrorized by unchecked white gangs, King's campaign was stalemated.

Fearing another Albany, he conferred with his Research Committee about how to bail himself out of St. Augustine with dignity. The civil-rights bill only needed Johnson's signature to become law, and SCLC had other projects and strategies for the 1964 election that demanded King's attention. To make matters worse, he had lost the services of one of his most valuable subordinates. Wyatt Walker had resigned as SCLC's "chief of staff" to take a position with Education Heritage, which was planning a multivolume series on Negro history and culture. In private, Walker confessed that he had "had it emotionally" and that he could not survive on the $10,000 annual salary SCLC paid him. "I'm reluctant to let him go," King said, "but the development of the Negro Heritage Library is so critical to the long-range goals of the Negro community that he goes with my blessings." Eventually King named Andrew Young to replace Walker as SCLC's executive director.

As it turned out, events in St. Augustine allowed King a graceful exit. Prodded by Judge Simpson, Governor Bryant established an emergency biracial committee to open negotiations between white and Negro leaders in St. Augustine and try to reach a settlement. King pronounced this "a significant first step" toward "reconciliation and the creation of the beloved community." To "demonstrate our good faith" and give negotiations a chance, he called off the campaign and on June 30 left for Atlanta with his executive staff.

Had the campaign accomplished anything? Hayling thought it had dramatized to the nation the fact that the oldest European community in America was a bastion of segregation. Undoubtedly the "raw and rampant" violence exposed there had helped administration forces get the civil-rights bill through the Senate. And King's presence had created the pressure that got city officials to talking with Hayling and his people, although it remained to be seen whether St. Augustine would comply with a federal law desegregating public accommodations.

"St. Augustine," said an SCLC official, "was the toughest nut I have seen in all my days of working in cities in direct-action campaigns." And King, too, branded it the "most lawless" community he and SCLC had ever worked in. They were lucky no Negroes had been slain. Still, veterans of the campaign had nothing but praise for King, who had gone there to help his people regardless of the consequences. "Once he recognized the need and symbolism in that need," said a Negro associate, "he was willing to go all the way and give all."

O N JULY 2 KING AND OTHER NEGRO LEADERS were on hand when the President signed the civil-rights bill into law in the East Ballroom of the White House. The cabinet and J. Edgar Hoover were also present. Addressing national radio and television, Johnson asserted that "those who are equal before God shall now be equal in the polling booths, in the classrooms, in the factories, and in hotels, restaurants, movie theaters, and other places that provide service to the public." The "WHITES ONLY" signs that had hurt and angered King since boyhood would now come down everywhere in Dixie, thanks to the moral and political force exerted by him and his marching legions. "Let us close the springs of racial poison," Johnson said in his conclusion. "Let us lay aside irrelevant differences and make our Nation whole. . . ."

Afterward, in an informal meeting with civil-rights leaders in the Cabinet Room, Johnson argued that the need for direct-action protest was over. He actually believed that the Civil Rights Act eliminated "the last vestiges of injustice in our beloved America" and that further demonstrations were therefore unnecessary and "possibly even self-defeating."

Though the 1964 Civil Rights Act was the strongest ever produced in America, King was under no illusions that it was a panacea that ended all racial injustice there. True, it opened public accommodations to Negroes, who on cross-country drives would no longer have to sleep in their automobiles because no motel would accept them. In addition, the measure prohibited racial discrimination in large business and labor unions and established a federal commission to ensure equal employment opportunity. Yet as it finally emerged the act had glaring deficiencies. For one thing, there was no powerful, unambiguous section on Negro voting rights. "You will never have a true democracy until you can eliminate all restrictions," King said. What the country needed was a universal method of voter registration, literally "one man, one vote," and in fact SCLC had on the drawing boards a southern campaign designed to bring that about. For another thing, the Civil Rights Act ignored the whole problem of fair housing and Negro poverty. Nor did it do anything to stop the civil war raging in the South from St. Augustine to Jackson, Mississippi. When would Washington realize that federal protection was imperative if Negroes were ever to be safe in war-torn Dixie?

After the passage of the Civil Rights Act, King heard the same question over and over: "What more will the Negro want? What will it take to make these demonstrations end?" This was the prevailing sentiment in white America, and it vexed him. "Why," he snapped, "do white people seem to find it so difficult to understand that the Negro is sick and tired of having reluctantly parceled out to him those rights and privileges which all others receive upon birth or entry in America? I never cease to wonder at the amazing presumption of much of white society, assuming that they have the right to bargain with the Negro for his freedom. This continued arrogant ladling out of pieces of the rights of citizenship has begun to generate a *fury* in the Negro."

In *Why We Can't Wait*, which came out during the St. Augustine campaign, King answered the white cry "What more does the Negro want?" "The Negro wants absolute freedom and equality, not in Africa or in some imaginary state, but right here in this land today." The Negro was no longer interested in compromises over his fate. American history, King pointed out, was full of compromises over slavery—the compromise that deleted the slave-trade reference in the Declaration of Independence, the Missouri Compromise that allowed slavery to spread into the southern half of the Louisiana Purchase Territory, the Hayes-Tilden Compromise that ended Reconstruction by withdrawing federal troops from Dixie and leaving Negroes there to the mercy of their former masters, and the "Supreme Court Compromise" in *Plessy* v. *Ferguson* which upheld the doctrine of separate-but-equal. "These measures compromised not only the liberty of the Negro but the integrity of America," which was why the Negro today regarded the word compromise as "profane and pernicious." Freedom and equality were his birthrights, too, and he wanted them fully and he wanted them now.

Then King got down to specific suggestions. He recalled what a nightclub comic said about the Greensboro sit-ins: if the young demonstrators had been served at the lunch counters, some could not have paid for the meal. Alas, there was painful truth in his observation. Even if statutory discrimination ended tomorrow, King wrote, the impoverished condition of black people—the institutionalized and historical consequences of color—would remain. As he had pointed out elsewhere, citing historian Henrietta Buckmaster, Negroes at the time of emancipation owned nothing but the skin on their backs. The federal government failed to grant them economic security, instead leaving them bound over to their former masters in Dixie as a largely landless class. During all his years in servitude, the Negro had been "robbed of the wages of his toil," and he had continued to be exploited ever since, thanks to practices that confined him to unskilled or semiskilled jobs. King believed it time to correct this profound historical problem. "Negroes must not only have the right to go into any establishment open to the public," he contended, "but they must also be absorbed into our economic system in such a manner that they can afford to exercise that right."

What he proposed was a Bill of Rights for the Disadvantaged, named after the GI Bill of Rights, which would provide massive federal aid to the poor. Of course, no amount of money could ever compensate for "the exploitation and humiliation of the Negro in America down through the centuries." But a Bill of Rights for the Disadvantaged, "our veterans of the long siege of denial," would certainly help the Negro catch up to whites in a race in which he had started three hundred years behind. King had in mind a sort of Marshall Plan for America's poor—not only the black poor, but the "large stratum of forgotten white poor." He admitted that the program would cost billions of dollars, but argued that its benefits would be worth the price.

Like *Stride Toward Freedom*, King's book was a blend of argument, philosophy, and narrative history. He recounted the story of Birmingham in vivid detail, from "Bull Connor's Birmingham" on the eve of demonstrations down to "the new day" the campaign brought about. He included "Letter from Birmingham Jail," described the Negro revolution that swept the country that summer and culminated in the great march on Washington, and placed the events of 1963 in historical perspective, relating the Negro's own long search for freedom since the Emancipation Proclamation. Again his hero was the mass of Negroes who resolved to stand up and make their freedom real through the technique of nonviolent protest. King's was the symbolic story of the boy who stood in Harlem and the girl who rose in Birmingham. "Across the miles they joined hands, and took a firm, forward step. It was a step that rocked the richest, most powerful nation to its foundations." In relating the historical background and significance of Birmingham, King proved that he was not only the movement's preeminent leader, but one of its ablest contemporary historians.

The book enjoyed a respectable sales in the United States, with 24,000 hardback and 150,000 paperback copies in print by November, 1964, and it appeared in translation in France, Germany, Italy, Poland, Denmark, Holland, Sweden, Spain, Japan, and in the Oriya language in India. American reviews were generally enthusiastic, although Robert Penn Warren, writing in the *New York Review of Books*, disparaged King's "debt" theory as "fraught with mischief." The volume enjoyed a warm reception in England, where the *Spectator* thought it a "brilliantly re-created" story and urged Britons to read it; and the *Guardian*, praising King's demands as correct, asserted that "American politics would gain immeasurably from the kind of idealism, self-sacrifice and sense of public service which has characterised responsible Negro leadership," of which King was an outstanding example.

There was trouble again in St. Augustine. At first city officials promised to abide by the 1964 Civil Rights Act. But when white businesses refused to do so and thugs attacked Negroes who entered restaurants and other public places, the city resegregated. Back came King, warning that this kind of action would become a pattern in Dixie unless it was blocked here and now. Again movement lawyers filed a grievance with Judge Simpson, who then ordered St. Augustine businessmen and city officials to comply with the law or face contempt charges. This gave them the excuse of external coercion to take down the "WHITES ONLY" signs—"what else can we do?"—and desegregation came at last to strife-torn St. Augustine. Judge Simpson also issued a restraining order against the likes of Sheriff Davis and Hoss Manucy, which ended their reign of terror and moved Abernathy to quip that the movement changed Manucy "from a Hoss to a mule."

In mid-July violence erupted with volcanic fury in the long-smoldering ghettoes of Newark and Harlem. Time and again, King had warned that ghetto Negroes would resort to violence if their grievances were not redressed. And now, in grisly scenes carried on television and in the press, Negroes were rioting in the streets of the urban North, looting and setting stores ablaze.

At once the President summoned King and other Negro leaders to the White House. Johnson intended to be the Democratic candidate in this year's election and feared that riots and other civil disturbances would help the Republicans—who were certain to offer up conservative Barry Goldwater on a strong law-and-order platform—and would also impede the implementation of the Civil Rights Act. He persuaded King, Wilkins, and Whitney Young of the Urban League to stand with him against the forces of disorder and reaction. Out of the meeting emerged a statement in which the various civil-rights leaders asserted that "the present situation" required a "temporary alteration in strategy" and that "the greatest need now is for political action." Accordingly, "we call on our members voluntarily to observe a broad curtailment if not total moratorium on all mass marches, picketing and demonstrations until after Election day, November 3." For now, they and the man in the White House were united by a common purpose.

King meanwhile had gone to New York City, where Mayor Robert Wagner conferred with him about cooling Harlem down. The trip was a disaster. While King toured the riot sites, embittered Harlemites booed him and spouted anti-Semitic vitriol that made him grimace. At the same time, local Negro leaders fumed that no "outsider" imported by the mayor had the right to invade their territory and tell them what to do.

King was greatly troubled. He warned Harlem Negroes that violence would only exacerbate their problems and beseeched them to follow his course of nonviolent resistance. With an eye on the New York police commissioner, who was "utterly unresponsive" to the needs of Negroes, King also warned against "shallow rhetoric condemning lawlessness." What was needed, he said, was "an honest soul-searching analysis and evaluation of the environmental causes which have spawned the riots." As for black anti-Semitism, "I solemnly pledge to do my utmost to uphold the fair name of Jews. Not only because we need their friendship, and surely we do, but mainly because bigotry in any form is an affront to us all."

On July 20 King and his staff launched a People-to-People tour of Mississippi, to help SNCC and CORE in a Freedom Summer campaign to educate and register disenfranchised Negroes. Largely at SNCC's invitation, scores of white college students from the North were toiling side-by-side with SNCC and CORE field workers, holding freedom schools and voter workshops in the Mississippi backcountry. King and his people admired the students' zeal and idealism but feared they were in for a rude awakening if they thought atavistic Mississippi could be transformed in a summer. "We tried to warn SNCC," Young said. "We were all Southerners and we knew the depth of the depravity of Southern racism. We knew better than to try to take on Mississippi. We saw Birmingham as having realistic possibilities, as the reality." In cities like Birmingham, SCLC's nonviolent forces could capture international media attention and expose southern racism to a world audience. But that was all but impossible in a rural state like Mississippi, where the Klan and other rowdies could attack students on lonely byroads away from media cameramen.

The casualties of SNCC's Mississippi campaign were climbing steadily, as white Mississippians beat and murdered people at will and burned one Negro church after another. There were reports that King himself would be assassinated by a Mississippi guerrilla contingent under a retired army major, and King's staff, always fretful about his safety, begged him to cancel the tour. "I have a job to do," King retorted. "If I were constantly worried about death, I couldn't function." Besides, he felt his cause was "so right, so moral, that if I should lose my life, in some way it would aid the cause."

In five days, King visited several towns and rural communities in Mississippi, and "I have carried with me ever since," he told a *Playboy* interviewer later that year, "a visual image of the penniless and the unlettered, and of the expressions on their faces—of deep and courageous determination to cast off the imprint of the past and become free people." In one town, the only restaurant was white-owned and refused to serve King and his staff. So they drove out to a Negro country store and feasted on pig skins and pickled pigs' feet. Said Abernathy: "Our staff in that little crowded black man's country store had a fellowship, a *kononia*, together. We had a purpose and we had a universal sense of love that they did not have downtown."

When King's party reached Philadelphia in dangerous Neshoba County, a massive federal search was under way for three young CORE workers—James Chaney, a Mississippi Negro, and Andrew Goodman and Michael Schwerner, Jews from New York—who had last been seen in Philadelphia looking for Negroes brave enough to try to register. FBI agents and 210 Navy men dragged rivers and creeks, with helicopters and a photo-reconnaissance jet flying overhead. Mississippi whites claimed that it was all a publicity stunt and that the three were in Cuba, swilling beer and joking about the hunt for them. Sheriff Lawrence Rainey, a wad of tobacco in his mouth, fulminated against all the outside meddling in his county and even complained to Hoover when FBI agents guarded King during his stay in town.

In Philadelphia, as in Meridian, Vicksburg, and other places, King galvanized local Negroes when he outlined his Bill of Rights for the Disadvantaged and said he planned to introduce it at the Democratic convention. Here was one famous brother who really did care about them. Still, everywhere King went there was "a strong undertow of disaffection," as one writer phrased it. Members of Jackson's black middle class, loyal to the NAACP, clapped politely after he addressed them, then drove home in expensive automobiles. SNCC workers grumbled about how "de Lawd"—SNCC's nickname for King—came in, gave a few speeches, and then took off with an escort of police and FBI men, leaving them behind to do the field work. It was typical of "de Lawd," SNCC liked to say, that he thought charisma alone could sustain a movement.

King could not understand SNCC's hostility toward him. "Why do they call me de Lawd?" he would ask his aides and friends. Was it just envy because he commanded the spotlight? "I do draw more attention," he said. "But I can't help that." Then petulantly: "Look, I helped organize SNCC. No one ever talks about what we did to put SNCC in business." His staff and friends agreed. "They think they started the movement," Walker said. "The SNCC people have a thing about it. They don't even mention Montgomery. All they talk about are the student sit-ins. They think they started the revolution. They give no credit to the NAACP." Walker added, "I think Dr. King showed a great deal of restraint and patience [in dealing with them], more than I ever could have shown."

In fact, King had a lot of respect for SNCC. Maybe the students were arrogant and their assault of Mississippi unrealistic, but their concern for the rural Negro deserved nothing but praise. And he was impressed with the formation of the Mississippi Freedom Democratic party, an interracial organization that grew out of SNCC's voter-registration campaign and that intended to unseat the all-white regular Democratic delegation at the Democratic convention in August.

August brought grim news from Neshoba County. At a construction site five miles southwest of Philadelphia, federal authorities found the bullet-riddled bodies of Chaney, Goodman, and Schwerner buried under an earthen dam. Months later the FBI arrested twenty-one local whites—most of them Klansmen—including Sheriff Rainey himself and Deputy Sheriff Cecil Ray Price. A murder conviction was impossible in this bastion of white supremacy; the governor and state attorney general announced that they would not prefer charges. Eventually the Justice Department took the case to a federal grand jury in Meridian, Mississippi, which indicted eighteen of the suspects on charges of conspiring to deprive the victims of their civil rights. But U.S. District Judge W. Harold Cox, a Kennedy appointee and an avowed segregationist who compared Negro voter applicants to chimpanzees, dismissed or reduced the charges to misdemeanors. The U.S. Supreme

Court did overrule Cox and ordered the accused to stand trial on the conspiracy charges; but most civil-rights people thought the case doomed since no white jury in Mississippi had ever convicted white defendants in a civil-rights case. Free on bond, Rainey and the others became heroes in white Mississippi, and Confederate flags sprang up around the federal building in a symbolic taunting of national authority.°

As it turned out, the violence SNCC encountered in Mississippi's "magnolia jungles" broke its staff mentally and physically. "People were bitter, frustrated, torn-apart, battle-fatigued, and everything else," said SNCC chairman John Lewis. The casualties in SNCC's Freedom Summer were staggering: six people had been killed, eighty beaten, two wounded by gunfire, more than a thousand arrested, and thirty-seven Negro churches and thirty-one Negro homes burned or dynamited in a civil war over racial tensions and national destiny that was still going on.

King too was distressed about the violence in Mississippi, and he wondered what it required to convince Washington of the desperate need for preventive police protection in Dixie. True, President Johnson had made Hoover himself go to Jackson, "the spiritual capital of white supremacy," and open an FBI office there. But King had little faith in the FBI's southern agents, and he continued to say so.

I T WAS A LONG HOT SUMMER, not only in Mississippi but in the ghettoes of Chicago, Philadelphia, and Jersey City, which also exploded in riots. In comparison to Roy Wilkins, who drew up in "stuffy indignation" over the disturbances, King pleaded with white America to understand what caused them. "America will be faced with the ever-present threat of violence, rioting and senseless crime as long as Negroes by the hundreds of thousands are packed into malodorous, rat-plagued ghettoes; as long as Negroes remain smothered by poverty in the midst of an affluent society; as long as Negroes are made to feel

°More than three years after the murders, thanks to new testimony, a white federal jury found Price and six of the other defendants guilty, and Cox sentenced them to three-to ten-year jail sentences. Rainey and seven others, however, were acquitted.

like exiles in their own land; as long as Negroes continue to be dehumanized; as long as Negroes see their freedom endlessly delayed and diminished by the head winds of tokenism and small handouts from the white power structure. No nation can suffer any greater tragedy than to cause millions of its citizens to feel that they have no stake in their own society." But when he said this to politicians like Mayor Wagner, most had little idea what he was talking about. "I have found that these men seriously—and dangerously—underestimate the explosive mood of the Negro and the gravity of the crisis," King said.

During the third week of August, King appeared before the Democratic convention in Atlantic City and implored party bosses to understand the crisis and include his Bill of Rights for the Disadvantaged in their platform. True, thanks to the President, Congress had recently enacted a $1 billion antipoverty program, but King thought this merely a ploy to buy time, rather than a serious attack against the causes of urban blight. That would cost at least $50 billion in federal antipoverty measures, King maintained, which was still less than the country spent annually on defense. The Democratic party, however, politely rejected his plan.

Meanwhile King worked hard to get the delegates of the Mississippi Freedom Democratic party seated at the convention. But President Johnson, manipulating its proceedings from Washington, offered a compromise to keep party unity, and the credentials committee overwhelmingly endorsed it. The party accepted the regular Mississippi Democrats, but offered MFDP two at-large seats and outlawed segregated delegations at future conventions. King and Bayard Rustin, who was at the convention, realized that this was the best they were going to get. But the MFDP delegates were up in arms. At a stormy meeting in an Atlantic City church, King asked them to face political reality. Yes, he said, there was a lot wrong with the country, they had paid "a heavy price," and they had "a long road to travel." But they could not travel it alone. This was the only party that had helped the struggle, and although it had segregationists in it, it was the best they had and they "must work to make it better." He went on: "I'm not going to counsel you to accept or to reject. That is your decision. But I want you to know that I have talked to Hubert Humphrey. He promised me there would be a new day in Mississippi if you accept this proposal." He regarded it as "an entering wedge" that would lead to a MFDP triumph in 1968 and an end to lily-white delegations.

As King spoke, SNCC Executive Director James Forman, a burly, ironic man, a year King's senior, was aghast at his "naïveté." But after Forman spoke against the Johnson compromise, Rustin asserted that it was Forman and SNCC who were naïve about American politics. In the end, the MFDP rejected the proposal. "We didn't come all the way for no two votes!" exclaimed Fannie Lou Hamer, irrepressible heroine of the Mississippi campaigns.

After the convention, which nominated Johnson and Humphrey as the Democratic standard bearers, King took to the hustings against Republican candidate Barry Goldwater of Arizona. Though he never officially endorsed Johnson, King's speeches amounted to the same thing. "I'm not going to tell you who to vote for," he said to American Negroes, "but I will tell you who I'm *not* going to vote for." Across the country, King damned Goldwater as the voice of the white backlash, a reactionary who sneered at the Negro and "fawned on the segregationists." In the Senate, King noted, Goldwater had voted against the civil-rights bill, implied that Negro poverty derived from the Negro's own laziness, derided social security and welfare as un-American, and advocated "a trigger-happy" policy toward Communist countries that could plunge the world into annihilation. Johnson, by contrast, ran as a peace and social-reform candidate under the banner of the only party that Negroes could trust. If Goldwater whipped the President, it would mean the destruction of America "as we know it." Before the campaign ended, said Andrew Young, King and SCLC had gone to every major American city to mobilize the Negro community against Goldwater. On election day in November, the vast majority of black voters went for Johnson, who buried Goldwater in a record-breaking landslide, winning more than 61 percent of the popular vote.

Still, as British journalist James Cameron observed, it was an anxious and difficult time for King himself, as he caught increasing flak from both sides: from "those who assail him for moving too fast and those who denounce him for moving too slowly." "It cannot possibly be easy," Cameron said. "Dr. King is a brave man; he has somehow created from the ingredients of intolerance and injustice a mutation of rational determination and courage, and he will overcome one day."

IN MID-OCTOBER, KING HAD CHECKED into Atlanta's St. Joseph Infirmary for a rest. Coretta said he was "simply exhausted" and needed a few days away from his crushing burdens. That night he took a sleeping pill and enjoyed his first sound sleep in weeks.

The next morning Coretta phoned him bursting with excitement. The Associated Press had just reported that he had won the Nobel Peace Prize. Of course, they had known he was being considered. Newspaper stories had even claimed that he was high on the list. But King had told Harry Wachtel that he didn't think he would win. "If I do," King said, "I'll carry your bags." Wachtel called him from New York. "Are you ready to carry my bags?"

King was ecstatic. Nothing could mean more to him than to be recognized as a world leader for peace. At thirty-five, he was the youngest recipient in Nobel history. Only two other Negroes had ever won the Peace Prize—Ralph Bunche and Chief Albert Luthuli of South Africa, whom King greatly admired.

When he put the award in perspective, King said later, "it made me feel very humble indeed." At a press conference in his hospital room, he read a prepared statement: "I do not consider this merely an honor to me personally, but a tribute to the discipline, wise restraint and majestic courage of the millions of gallant Negroes and white persons of good will who have followed a nonviolent course in seeking to establish a reign of justice and rule of love across this nation of ours." Later he said he would donate most of the $54,600 prize money to SCLC, the rest to SNCC, CORE, the NAACP, the National Council of Negro Women, and the American Foundation for Peace.

Not everybody in the country was impressed. Aside from Atlanta's Mayor Allen, no southern political figure complimented King, even though the award made him the South's most celebrated citizen. The Nobel Prize committee was inundated with letters from the United States protesting his selection. Novelist John O'Hara said he didn't deserve it. "They're scraping the bottom of the barrel," snorted Bull Connor. A Los Angeles segregationist argued that it "only shows the Communist influence." And J. Edgar Hoover was fuming. "He was the last person in the world who should ever have received it."

Still, King had plenty of defenders. Archbishop Paul Hallinan of

Atlanta congratulated him personally at the hospital, pronounced a blessing, then startled King by kneeling and asking for *his* blessing. The *Christian Century* observed: "Some would-be Negro leaders are quite willing to pull the house down on everyone, destroying the Negro in the process. King has not only won more battles for the Negro than any other individual of our times; he has done so in a spirit and wisdom which provide the ground for new and even more extensive Negro victories." Ralph McGill, sage columnist for the Atlanta *Constitution* and voice of the southern white moderate, thought the prize indicated that Europeans had a clearer view of King than Americans. Like Asians and Africans, they saw in him "manifestations of the American promise" and an eloquent champion of what that held for the world. "The South one day will be grateful when it realizes what the alternative would have been had Dr. King, with his capacity to stir and inspire, come preaching violence, hate and aggression," McGill wrote. "This Nobel reminds us that the sooner Southern people get down to some simple things like getting along together with dignity and equality before the law, the sooner they will realize their potential."

November found King back on his feet and hard at work again, planning a major voting-rights campaign to commence early next year in Selma, Alabama. He was to receive his Nobel award in Norway early in December and asked Bayard Rustin to handle his public relations and itinerary. He took time off to grant *Playboy* a long interview, part of which occurred during one of his rare evenings with his family, his four children affectionately chiding him for "not being home enough." After dinner, King talked about the movement, the Nobel Prize, and the future. "I dream of the day when the demands presently cast upon me will be greatly diminished." He did not foresee much let-up in the next five years, in the North or the South. But after that perhaps he could realize one of his oldest dreams—that of teaching theology in some university. Still, he said, "I welcome the opportunity to be a part of this great drama, for it is a drama that will determine America's destiny. If the problem is not solved, America will be on the road to its self-destruction. But if it is solved, America will just as surely be on the high road to the fulfillment of the founding fathers' dream, when they wrote: 'We hold these truths to be self-evident. . . .' "

Still rundown from overwork, King escaped to Bimini off the Florida coast for a brief rest. Up in Washington, meanwhile, J. Edgar Hoo-

ver had become so exercised over King's Nobel award that he seemed
to have lost his senses. On November 18, in an interview with a group
of newswomen, the director castigated King for his repeated criticism
of the FBI and called him "the most notorious liar in the country."
This was sensational copy, and the press and major news magazines
quoted the director under screaming headlines. On Bimini, King was
shocked at the news. He had his Atlanta office telegraph Hoover: "I
was appalled and surprised at your reported statement maligning my
integrity. What motivated such an irresponsible accusation is a mys-
tery to me." King issued a press statement that Hoover "has apparently faltered under the awesome burdens, complexities and responsibilities of his office," and he complained in phone conversations (with
Hoover's men listening in) that the director "is old and getting senile"
and must be "hit from all sides." In response, Hoover "carried on
wildly" in a speech out in Chicago, raving about "zealots of pressure
groups" who resorted to "carping, lying and exaggerating" and were
spearheaded by "Communists and moral degenerates."

It was clear to King's camp that something evil was afoot. Then
came a phone call from CORE's James Farmer, who wanted to see
King as soon as possible. On his way through New York City, King
met with Farmer in an airport lounge and learned to his horror that
the FBI was spreading "this story" that he had engaged in group sex
and that Hoover was "determined to get him" on three counts: personal misconduct, financial irregularity, and Communist associations.
King vigorously denied all the charges, especially that about group sex.

"I'll forget it," Farmer said about the sex story.

"Don't forget it," King rejoined. "No, let's do what we can to stop
it. If something like this comes out, even if it isn't true, it will damage
all of us in the whole movement."

It was depressing—and scary. How widely had Hoover circulated
the story? Did the director really have something on him? Then somebody else high in the movement—Wachtel claimed it was Roy Wilkins—relayed word to King that Hoover was going after him "on the
unholy trilogy of sex, Communism, and finances." King had his lieutenants probe news sources to find out what Hoover was saying, and
the rumors alone were enough to make them pause.

As it happened, Hoover's "liar" charge was the climax of an intense FBI crusade to depose and denigrate King under the excuse of
protecting national security. In addition to using vast electronic sur-

veillance and counterespionage activities, which treated King as though he were a Russian agent, Hoover and his men expanded their scurrilous monograph on King compiled the year before. The revised edition not only belabored the old Communist charge, but accused King of directing SCLC funds into private bank accounts in Switzerland. Worse, it contained lurid information culled from the bugs FBI agents had planted in King's hotel rooms that year. Carl Rowan, head of the U.S. Information Agency, had access to the bureau's "dirt" on King and claimed that "90 percent of it is barnyard gossip." He did not comment on the other ten percent. The truth was that the bureau's ever-widening electronic dragnet had snared King in some compromising situations.

Under Hoover's orders, Assistant Director Deke DeLoach and his men in the crime records division showed the dissertation to various bureaucrats, senators, and congressmen and even played them tapes from the hotel microphones. "I was shocked," said Acting Attorney General Nicholas Katzenbach when he found out about the FBI's dossier on King, and he took the matter directly to the President. But Johnson made no effort to rein Hoover in. He could ill afford to alienate the powerful director, said he would rather have him "inside the tent pissing out than outside pissing in," and liked him in any case. In fact, Johnson not only read Hoover's monograph, which an aide compared to "an erotic book," but listened to the tapes, apparently delighting in the squeak of the bedsprings.

Meanwhile Agent DeLoach was busily peddling his salacious materials from one newspaper to another. Chicago *News* columnist Mike Royko dismissed them as "gossip" and asserted that King's personal affairs had nothing to do with national security or his probity as a civil-rights leader. Though he got a similar reception at the Washington *Post* and the *New York Times*, DeLoach was nothing if not persistent. He had the King dossier offered to Eugene Patterson of the Atlanta *Constitution*, but Patterson rejected it, contending that his was no "peephole journal." The FBI also approached segregationist editors in the South, but not one of them would touch the sex stories. "Hell," one told Patterson, "I wouldn't print that stuff. That's beyond the pale."

Though never given the FBI monograph, syndicated columnist Jack Anderson did see some of the FBI evidence on King and published a quotation that involved an incident with a woman. Anderson claimed that he interviewed her before going into print with the story. Actually, he believed the FBI surveillance of King revealed less about him than about Hoover. In fact, Anderson reported that the director had collected data on the sexual conduct of many other prominent Americans—among them, Jane Fonda, Paul Newman, Muhammad Ali, Zero Mostel, and Joe Namath. "Indeed, from the quantity and detail of information," Anderson wrote, "we suspect there was as much voyeurism as sleuthing involved in the investigations."

Still, it was King's sexual conduct that obsessed Hoover, tormented him. Ramsey Clark of the Justice Department said that "you couldn't talk very long with Mr. Hoover without him bitterly criticising Dr. King as being an immoral person, a bad person." In late November, Hoover and Sullivan concocted a scheme to remove this "moral degenerate" once and for all, a scheme that they hoped would frighten him so badly that he would remove himself from public life, even commit suicide. Ignoring the fact that the bureau's hateful vendetta against King was flagrantly illegal and unconstitutional, the director authorized Sullivan to prepare a special tape—a composite of occurrences recorded at the Willard Hotel in Washington and other places—and send it to King in care of SCLC's Atlanta headquarters.

K ING KNEW NOTHING about Hoover's latest tape. But what he knew about the others was profoundly disquieting. He conferred with a group of trusted advisers in a hotel room in New York City, and he and some of them feared it was "the end of the game." Was there any truth to the FBI's charges? Wachtel asked. "I know all about the Communist part. I'm assuming there is something around on sex. But I know nothing about the financial. You know, Martin, the most damaging thing would be finances. If they can show you lining your pockets, that would be the most potent attack on you in the black community."

"We're all right on money," King said. "There's no problem on that." But he confessed that "there could be embarrassment" so far as his private life was concerned. What did Harry and the others think he should do?

Kenneth Clark and Clarence Jones urged defiance. "Let Hoover reveal his damned tapes"—they would hurt him more than King. But Wachtel feared the tapes would damage King among his white supporters and argued in favor of a peace offer. It seemed clear to Wachtel that Hoover was trying to prevent King from accepting the Nobel Prize. But he thought the director had gone too far and would retreat if given a chance. "Show him you respect his office," Wachtel counseled. "Make an historical record that you called on him, talked all this out, came to a better understanding of one another. It saves him and it saves us."

On reflection, King agreed with Wachtel. "I'm going to extend the hand of peace," he said.

"Damn it," Clark exploded, "you may be Christ-like, but you're not Christ." King and the others laughed.

What became known as "the summit meeting" took place in Hoover's office on the afternoon of December 1. Deke DeLoach of Georgia sat with a scowling Hoover; Young, Abernathy, and Fauntroy with King. First, King said, he wanted to clear up his criticism of the FBI. His main concern was that special agents, assigned to investigate Negro complaints of police brutality, had been seen consorting with local police, especially in Albany. King had meant no personal slur against Hoover; he was only articulating southern Negro grievances. Second, he was no Communist and could never be, because Communism was "a crippling totalitarian disease" and because he was a Christian.

But Hoover butted in and monopolized the rest of the discussion. He lectured King on how Communists thrived on trouble and chaos, how they cared nothing for Negroes, how King "of all people" should know that. He boasted about the FBI's record in the South, telling how it had put "the fear of God" into the Klan, especially in Mississippi, and referring to "watermoccasins, rattlesnakes and redneck sheriffs" in the Magnolia State. Then he gave King some advice. He and other Negro leaders ought to urge their people to vote. That was the best thing they could do for themselves. They should also get educated so that they could compete "in the open market." He even mentioned some professions in which Negroes could easily gain the necessary skills. In essence he told King to wait, contending that "in due time" attitudes and practices in the South would change.

Unperturbed, King pointed out that SCLC was planning voter-registration work in Selma, Alabama, to begin "in the near future." Hoover broke in and cited five cases in which the FBI had been involved there. Would agents be in Selma when SCLC got there? King asked. Hoover promised that they would be and that they would record and report any violations of civil rights.

The session ended with both men agreeing that they should "stay more in touch." In Hoover's reception room afterward, King told reporters that the session had been "friendly" and that he and Hoover had found "new levels of understanding." He added: "I sincerely hope we can forget the confusions of the past and get on with the job."

Though the public feud now abated, King and Hoover continued to detest one another. King complained of the summit meeting that "the old man talks too much," and Hoover said he held King "in complete contempt." For their part, King's aides were unhappy because none of the problems had been resolved. Nothing had been said about the FBI bugs and tapes, SCLC's finances, or King's personal conduct. Worse, they learned that the bureau continued to spread its stories about that. In fact, while King was meeting with Hoover, an FBI official showed a Chicago journalist waiting in the reception room a photograph of King and a woman leaving a motel.

ON DECEMBER 4, KING SET OUT for Norway and the Nobel Prize ceremonies. His traveling entourage—the largest in Nobel history— numbered twenty-six people, including his parents, Coretta and A. D. King, the Abernathys, the Wachtels (the only whites in the group), and Bayard Rustin, who had arranged King's schedule. Rustin was disgusted with the large and happy bunch. "It was a circus," he recalled. "Just a circus."

On the plane, King sat alone with a confidant and unburdened his feelings about the FBI tapes. He indicated that there had been some things in the past, but that was over now. He realized how difficult and touchy the problem was; now that the Nobel award had placed him on a world stage as a moral leader, he had to live more carefully. Even if it deprived him of something he needed, he was going to be "spartan" in his conduct.

On December 6 King and his companions stopped in London for three days of speeches and appearances before going on to Oslo. The

English treated the Nobel laureate as though he were visiting royalty. When he left his Hilton Hotel suite, a Princess limousine driven by a personal chauffeur conveyed him from one conference to another. At the Palace of Westminster he met with the Lord Chancellor of Britain and members of Parliament and called for economic sanctions against South Africa. Rustin had arranged for him to speak at historic St. Paul's Cathedral, but the Kings were late in getting started, and in the ride there he and Rustin exchanged heated words over his going by "Colored People's Time" in England. King momentarily lost his temper and suggested that Rustin call Canon John Collins and tell him to get another preacher.

But at the pulpit of St. Paul's, the only non-Anglican to stand there in the church's 291-year history, King was the picture of self-control as he addressed a congregation of 4,000. He preached on "The Three Dimensions of a Complete Life," the sermon he had given in his trial visit to Dexter Church a decade ago. After a reception at the canon's home, the Kings took off on a sightseeing tour, visiting Westminster Abbey and the Tower of London and then driving down Whitehall past rows of government buildings. There stood the Admiralty and the Foreign Office—edifices of Britain's former imperial glory. Anger stirred in King again. Those buildings reminded him that the grandeur of London "was built by exploitation of Africans and Indians and other oppressed peoples."

On December 8 King's party flew to Oslo over a stormy sea, touching down at Gardernoen Airport early in the afternoon. A group of enthusiastic Nobel officials greeted King in heavy fog and rain. His schedule called for him to receive his award in Oslo on Thursday, then fly to Stockholm for a reception in honor of all the Nobel Prize winners. In the hotel lounge that night, the Kings threw a huge birthday party for a friend. As the champagne was about to be popped, Daddy King stepped forward. "Wait a minute before you start all your toasts to each other. We better not forget to toast the man who brought us here, and here's a toast to God." Then in a quavering voice, he told what his son's prize meant to him. "I always wanted to make a contribution, and all you got to do if you want to contribute, you got to ask the Lord, and let Him know, and the Lord heard me and in some special kind of way I don't even know He came down through Georgia and He laid His hand on me and my wife and He gave us Martin Luther King and our prayers were answered and when my head is cold and my bones are bleached the King family will go down not only in American history but in world history as well because Martin King is a Nobel Prize-winner."

King was moved. So were all the others. "The champagne just stayed there," recalled a King friend, "and they made the toast to God and the champagne just stayed there afterwards. No one drank any, not even Bayard Rustin."

The next day, King held a press conference and charmed the Norwegian press corps by introducing Ralph Abernathy as his "perennial jailmate." Abernathy himself reveled in all the attention, could not get enough of it. He had such need for recognition as King's "alter ego" and first vice-president that he would elbow people out of the way so that he could be photographed beside King.

As the conference progressed, the Norwegians pressed King for his opinions on international issues. For them, he was no longer just an American civil-rights leader; he was a Nobel laureate whose views on global matters were of great interest to Europeans. For several years, the United States had given financial and military assistance to a United Nations police force in the Congo, a former Belgian colony racked by civil war. Would he comment on American action there in connection with Belgian paratroopers? Would he demand that his government withdraw? "No, I haven't gone that far," King said. "But the Congo civil war will not be resolved until all foreign elements are withdrawn."

There were rounds of meetings and visitations. Then on December 10 came the grand event: the presentation of King's award in the auditorium of Oslo University, with King Olav V and other Norwegian royalty in attendance. "We had quite a time getting him ready," Coretta said of her husband. He put on striped trousers and a gray tailcoat and then fussed as Coretta and others worked on the ascot, a broad-ended necktie, swearing that he would never wear one of these things again. When the ceremony began in the auditorium, King sat stiffly in front of the stage, glancing at Coretta, nervously clasping and unclasping his hands, while a procession of speakers lauded his achievements and the Norwegian Broadcasting Orchestra played Gershwin and Mozart. When the chairman of the Norwegian Parliament introduced him as "an undaunted champion of peace . . . the first person in the Western world to have shown us that a struggle can be waged without violence," King wiped his eyes and swallowed repeatedly. Then trumpets blared. Somebody nudged him, and in a burst of applause he climbed the stage to get his prize. Gazing across the overflow crowd into the glare of television lights, King said he considered this award "profound recognition that nonviolence is the answer to the crucial political and moral questions of our time—the need for man to overcome oppression and violence without resorting to violence and oppression." And he accepted the award with "an abiding faith" in his country and the future of mankind. "I refuse to accept the idea that man is mere flotsam and jetsam in the river of life which surrounds him. I refuse to accept the view that mankind is so tragically bound to the starless midnight of racism and war that the bright daylight of peace and brotherhood can never become a reality. I believe that even amid today's mortar bursts and whining bullets, there is still hope for a brighter tomorrow."

He spoke of "the tortuous road which has led from Montgomery, Alabama, to Oslo" and said that the Nobel Prize was really for the millions of Negroes on whose behalf he stood here today. Their names would never make *Who's Who.* "Yet when the years have rolled past and when the blazing light of truth is focused on this marvelous age in which we live—men and women will know and children will be taught that we have a finer land, a better people, a more noble civilization—because these humble children of God were willing to suffer for righteousness' sake."

Outside the auditorium, hundreds of torch-carrying students stood around a giant Christmas tree in the university square. When King and Coretta came out and a black limousine bore them away, the students chanted "Freedom now!" "We Shall Overcome!" The songs and slogans of the movement had become part of a universal vocabulary—proof that King and his black followers had injected a new meaning and dignity into the veins of civilization as he had prophesied they would do in his first boycott speech in 1955.

W HEN KING AND HIS ENTOURAGE returned to New York after the reception in Stockholm, fireboats saluted him in the East River, the city awarded him a medallion of honor, and 10,000 people cheered him lustily on "Martin Luther King Night" in the Harlem Armory. "For the past several days I have been on the mountaintop," he told a packed Negro church, in reference to the Biblical story about how Jesus took his disciples to the mount of the Transfiguration to see God's glory, then led them back into the valley to do God's work. "I really wish I could just stay on the mountain," King said, "but I must go back to the valley." Cries and clapping drowned him out; he waited for the crowd to quiet. "I must go back, because my brothers and sisters down in Mississippi and Alabama can't register and vote. I've got to go back to the valley. . . . There are those who need hope. There are those who need to find a way out. . . . Oh, I say to you tonight, my friends, I'm not speaking as one who's never seen the burdens of life. I've had to stand so often amid the chilly winds of adversity, staggered by the jostling winds of persecution. I've had to stand so often amid the surging murmur of life's restless sea. But I go back with a faith. . . . And I *still* have a dream."

On his way back to Atlanta, he stopped off in Washington for a visit with President Johnson. King urged him to push a voting-rights bill without delay, but Johnson was not encouraging. Although his administration was actually planning some sort of action against Negro disfranchisement (either legislation or a constitutional amendment), the President told King that he could not get a voting bill out of Congress in 1965, not when it had just passed the Civil Rights Act. All right, King told himself, then we will write a voting bill ourselves, down in the streets of Selma, Alabama.

PART SEVEN

AIN'T GONNA LET

NOBODY

TURN ME AROUND

Bᴙ Cʜʀɪsᴛᴍᴀs ᴛɪᴍᴇ, 1964, Kɪɴɢ ᴀɴᴅ ʜɪs sᴛᴀFF had completed final plans for Project Alabama, the direct-action campaign in Selma designed to win southern Negroes the unobstructed right to vote. Since 1957, Negro enfranchisement had been one of King's central concerns, and over the years his organization had mounted a number of voter-registration drives in Dixie. But these had foundered in a welter of legal obstacles, violent white resistance, and Negro fear and apathy. SCLC's only recourse had been to file suits with the Justice Department, but eight years of case-by-case litigation in the federal courts had convinced King of the ineffectiveness of that approach. While the South's large cities and border states had witnessed a marked increase in Negro voters in the early 1960s, there had been no significant gain in the deep southern states of Louisiana, Mississippi, and Alabama, where a combination of state laws and ruthless local practices kept the mass of Negroes off the rolls.° In Alabama, 80.7 percent of the eligible Negro voters were still not registered. In Dallas County, of which Selma was the county seat, a mere 333 out of 15,000 voting-age blacks could exercise their basic American right and cast ballots in an election. Yet it had been here, said a Justice Department official, that litigation had been tried the hardest. "Our experience has been that it takes years to undo in the courts what segregationists do in a day in the legislative halls of the South," King remarked. The only way to ensure Negro voting rights, he contended, was through a strong and

---

°There had been gains in Georgia and South Carolina, although more than half the eligible Negroes there still couldn't vote. An average of 72 percent of the voting-age blacks remained disfranchised in the five deep southern states; 57 percent in the South as a whole. The overall increase in the number of registered voting-age Negroes in Dixie was only 14 percent between 1960 and 1964. For King and other civil-rights leaders, this was unacceptable.

strictly enforced national law, one that sent federal registrars to Dixie.

But only a direct-action campaign was likely to get such a law out of Congress. "Demonstrations, experience has shown, are part of the process of stimulating legislation and law enforcement," King said. "The federal government reacts to events more quickly when a situation cries out for its intervention." And he and his staff intended to create that situation in Selma, by applying all the skill and experience they had acquired in the battles of Albany, Birmingham, and St. Augustine. As demonstrations in Birmingham had created a national mood in favor of desegregated public accommodations, demonstrations in Selma, King hoped, would so arouse the national conscience that Washington would be forced to wipe out obstacles to Negro voting. He could count on help, too, from the Leadership Conference on Civil Rights, a coalition of SCLC and some 120 other organizations now lobbying for civil-rights legislation on Capitol Hill. If a voting-rights act could be produced in 1965, two million Negroes could theoretically be added to southern voting rolls. It fired King's imagination to think what political muscle that eventuality would give his people. They could form powerful alliances with labor, progressive Democrats, and even the white poor, alliances that might vote segregationists out of office, annihilate discriminatory practices, and take America a long step closer to realizing her dream of equality for all.

There was good reason why King circled Selma for his newest and most ambitious campaign. The town seemed to have all the ingredients necessary for a direct-action victory. Consisting of some 29,000 people, more than half of them black, Selma was an old black-belt community situated on the banks of the murky Alabama River some fifty miles west of Montgomery. It was the birthplace of Bull Connor and Alabama's first White Citizens' Council, and it maintained a rigid racial caste system that was typical of the South's small towns and rural areas. The system relegated blacks to an impoverished and unpaved "nigger" section and ten years after the Brown decision still restricted their children to "colored" schools. Except for schoolteachers and a few professional and business people, black Selmans eked out a hard-scrabble existence, mostly as menials and maids for white employers. Whites here expected "niggers" to "know their place," argued that they were happy with segregation, and viewed the Brown decision, the Civil Rights Act, and the movement itself as part of a sinister outside conspiracy to destroy the southern way of life.

The movement had come to Selma back in 1963, when SNCC sent in several young workers as part of its own grassroots voting-rights effort. A local judge, noting that the students were racially mixed, wore blue overalls, and came mostly from outside Alabama, branded them as "Communist agitators" in the employ of Moscow, Peking, and Havana. At once the students began stirring up trouble. They canvassed Negro homes, talked about the constitutional right of every Negro citizen to vote, and pointed out villainies on the part of the Dallas County Board of Registrars which whites did not want to hear about. The reason so few Negroes were registered was that the Board met only two days a month and cheerfully rejected black applicants for any reason whatever, such as failing to cross a "t" on the registration form. The students also stirred up trouble by leading small, tentative protest marches to the courthouse in downtown Selma. At the same time, a dental hygienist named Marie Foster, a proud, forthright Negro who served as secretary of a black organization called the Dallas County Voters' League, conducted nighttime citizenship classes for her black neighbors. These in turn led to weekly mass meetings at the Negro churches on Sylvan Street, where blacks discussed the humiliation of being called "nigger" and the importance of gaining the ballot. Meanwhile SCLC's James and Dianne Bevel arrived in town and started trying to register Negroes under King's auspices.

As the movement gained momentum, the white community sharply disagreed over what should be done. Hefty Wilson Baker, new director of the city police, a professional lawman who had taught at the University of Alabama, was determined to avoid the kind of racial explosions that had shaken other southern cities. With the support of Mayor Joe T. Smitherman and Selma's old and affluent families, Baker intended to overcome the protestors with nonviolent law enforcement, deal quietly with federal officials, and get around national civil-rights laws with minimal compliance. But the diehard segregationists—particularly the rural folk of Dallas County—vowed to protect the old ways come what may. They argued that "agitators" should be shot and slapped emblems on their bumpers that showed a tattered Confederate soldier crying, "Hell No, I Aint' Forgettin!"

Their spokesman was Sheriff Jim Clark, a burly, blusterous fellow who hailed from rural Coffee County, where populism and Negrophobia both ran deep. Clark's crude language, military swagger, and tough-guy approach to civil rights repelled Baker and Selma's old families, who never approved of him. But Clark was undaunted. He was out "to preserve our way of life," he told his wife, and "not let the niggers take over the whole state of Alabama." And, "by God," nobody was going to get in his way.

In July, 1964, with King and his staff monitoring events in Selma, a state judge banned all marches and Negro meetings there, and Sheriff Clark enforced the injunction with a vengeance. He and his deputized possemen—many of them Klan members—beat the SNCC marchers into inactivity and suppressed all Negro gatherings on Sylvan Street. By November, the movement was paralyzed. In desperation, local Negro leaders asked the Bevels if Dr. King could be induced to come in and take charge. He was their only hope. Without him, the movement was dead.

Evidently James Bevel took their request to King and sold him on Selma as the ideal city in which to launch his long-contemplated Alabama voting-rights crusade. Not only did the local leadership want him to come, but Sheriff Clark seemed the perfect villain for the drama King intended to stage for the country. "Wherever you had a Jim Clark or an Al Lingo," Bernard Lee asserted, "that was the place you needed to be." For King and his lieutenants, Selma was "a theater for an act that had to be played," a theater where Clark could be counted on to commit some brutal outrage that would rally the nation to SCLC's banners. And so King instructed Bevel: "Go tell the people down there that I will be there on the first of January, and we are going to have a mass rally. We're going to have a march. We're going to launch a voter registration campaign." But he made it clear that he wanted an official invitation from Selma's local Negro leaders, to off-set the static he was bound to get from SNCC that he was transgressing on their territory. As he left for Oslo in December, Bevel and Vivian headed for Selma to start organizing the Negro community.

In late December, with King back in Atlanta, a Committee of Fifteen, representing all factions in black Selma, officially invited him to take command of the movement there. After Christmas, SCLC got out a six-page order of battle which stressed that "arrests should continue over the months to create interest in the freedom registration and freedom vote." At the right time, King himself would go to jail and pen a message to America like his "Letter from Birmingham Jail."

On January 2, 1965, King and Abernathy were on their way to Selma by car, heading along Highway 80—popularly known as the

Jefferson Davis Highway—that led from Montgomery. As they passed through undulating farm country, with its squalid Negro shanties and wintry fields, King talked about the violence they would likely encounter here in the black belt, that fertile crescent across central Alabama and Mississippi where cotton plantations had flourished and slavery had been the cruelest before the Civil War. "Ralph," King said, "I thought I would have been assassinated in Mississippi, but it did not happen. So it will probably come to me over here in Selma, so I want to fix it so that you will automatically become my successor without having to have a board meeting or anything." But Abernathy protested that he didn't want the SCLC presidency. Besides, anybody who shot King would get him, too, since they were almost always together. Actually, he didn't think they were going to be assassinated. He agreed with Andy Young that the rough days were behind them now and that nothing like that was going to happen. But King feared there would be some killing before this campaign was over.

It was late in the afternoon when they drove across the Edmund Pettis Bridge into Selma. There was "an unreal air about it," wrote scholar and activist Howard Zinn when he visited Selma in 1964. "It is as if a movie producer had reconstructed a pre-Civil War Southern town—the decaying buildings, the muddy streets, the little cafes, and the huge red brick Hotel Albert, modelled after a medieval Venetian palace" and built by slave labor. Selma had been a slave market before the Civil War—one three-story house, still standing, had held four to five hundred Negroes at a time to be auctioned off—and a military depot during the Confederacy. Wagons loaded with cotton and drawn by mules still clattered through the streets, though cotton production had fallen off considerably by the 1960s.

King and Abernathy swung down Sylvan Street past a parked police car. They were in the Negro section now, and the unpaved red sand road divided identical rows of dreary brick dwellings known as the George Washington Carver Development. In a moment they pulled up at Brown Chapel, a quaint red-brick building with twin steeples, where a mass meeting of local Negroes was already under way. They had been awaiting King much of the afternoon, transported with excitement that a man of his renown should come to lead them personally. When he entered the church and mounted the speaker's platform, the crowd broke into such a tumultuous ovation that the entire church seemed to tremble.

Dressed in a black suit, his eyes glistening, King reviewed the impediments to Negro voting in Dallas County and then fired his audience with a declaration of purpose: "Today marks the beginning of a determined, organized, mobilized campaign to get the right to vote everywhere in Alabama. If we are refused, we will appeal to Governor George Wallace. If he refuses to listen, we will appeal to the legislature. If *they* don't listen, we will appeal to the conscience of the Congress. . . ." He noticed one of Al Lingo's state troopers and two impassive deputies sitting in the back, taking notes. He was all manly defiance now. "Our cry to the state of Alabama is a simple one: *Give us the ballot!*"

"Give us the ballot!" the crowd roared back.

"We're not on our knees begging for the ballot. *We are demanding the ballot!*"

At that his people were on their feet, shouting and clapping in the most fired-up meeting ever seen in Brown Chapel. Then they broke into "We Shall Overcome," and King spotted the lawmen slipping out of the sanctuary to avoid having to hold hands and sing with Negroes. Before he left, King promised to return to Selma again and again until they reached the Promised Land.

After the meeting, King held a two-hour strategy session in the home of Mrs. Amelia Boynton, a Negro businesswoman and civil-rights activist. As it happened, SNCC chairman John Lewis was also working in Selma and was prepared to march with King in a show of civil-rights solidarity. The son of an Alabama tenant farmer, a small, quiet young man with a fierce inner intensity, Lewis had personally idolized King since the Montgomery bus boycott, and he did not agree with most of his SNCC colleagues, who griped that King was "piggybacking" on them in Selma. King was immensely pleased that Lewis was with him, for he wanted above all to avoid the family squabbles that so often hindered the movement.

King put Bevel in charge of Selma as project director and instructed fiery Hosea Williams to start drumming up grassroots support. King would return to lead the first march, scheduled for January 18, the next registration day. Then he climbed into a car with other aides and headed back for Montgomery, followed by cars filled with police, sheriff's deputies, and FBI agents.

Trouble awaited him at home. On January 5, while sorting and cataloging tapes of King's speeches, Coretta came across an anonymous package mailed from Miami, Florida. Apparently it had arrived at SCLC headquarters before they left for Oslo and had been placed in a pile of similar boxes of tapes for shipment to the King residence, where Coretta collected them. When she opened the package, she found a note and a recording, listened to some of it, and called her husband.

"King," the note read, "look into your heart. You know you are a complete fraud and a great liability to all of us Negroes. White people in this country have enough frauds of their own but I am sure they don't have one at this time that is anywhere near your equal. You are no clergyman and you know it. I repeat you are a colossal fraud and an evil, vicious one at that. You could not believe in God. . . . Clearly you don't believe in any personal moral principles.

"King, like all frauds your end is approaching. You could have been our greatest leader. You, even at an early age have turned out to be not a leader but a dissolute, abnormal moral imbecile. We will now have to depend on our older leaders like Wilkins a man of character and thank God we have others like him. But you are done. Your honorary degrees, your Nobel Prize (what a grim farce) and other awards will not save you. . . .

"King, there is only one thing left for you to do. You know what it is. You have just 34 days in which to do (this exact number has been selected for a specific reason, it has definite practical significant). You are done. There is but one way out for you. You better take it before your filthy, abnormal fraudulent self is bared to the nation."

The tape was the composite recording that Hoover had authorized Sullivan to compile and send to King back in November, 1964. On Sullivan's orders, an agent had mailed it from Miami on November 21, exactly thirty-four days before Christmas. The tape was to indicate that the FBI could back up the threats in the note by exposing defamatory personal information about him. It contained highlights of various recordings, including that of the Willard Hotel party in January, 1964, and possibly of the episode there after the 1963 Washington march. King bravely played the tape before Coretta, Young, Abernathy, and Reverend Joseph Lowery, and they knew right away that only J. Edgar Hoover would do something like this. "What does he think I am?" King stormed. That Hoover should peddle his tapes to politicians and editors was evil enough, but to send this thing to King and brazenly hint that he should kill himself—that was unbelievably vicious.

Whether or not the tape actually incriminated King may never be known. Years later Coretta told the *New York Times*, "We found much of it unintelligible. We concluded that there was nothing in the tape to discredit him." Young subsequently conceded in published interviews that the tape contained a recording of "a bunch of guys sitting around together who are very good friends and who are kidding each other very intimately." "Toward the end there was a recording of somebody moanin' and groanin' as though they were in the act of sexual intercourse, but it didn't sound like anybody I knew, and certainly not Martin."

It is likely that Young and Coretta were trying to protect King in remarks intended for public consumption. Perhaps the voice could not be positively identified as King's. But the fact remains that the activities illegally recorded on the tape had occurred in his hotel rooms; and he had succumbed to the temptations of the flesh during his long and arduous trips.

Moreover, King himself was distressed and frightened. Obviously Hoover would claim that it was King on all his tapes, and those who heard them would probably take Hoover's word for it. According to Wachtel and Young himself, King realized that this was the most serious kind of intimidation he had ever faced. "They are out to break me," he groaned to a friend. "They are out to get me, harass me, break my spirit," he told another. "What I do is only between me and my God." Still, he or his lieutenants had to see Hoover or DeLoach at once; King couldn't stand this lack of privacy. As it turned out, Hoover was not available, but Young secured an appointment with DeLoach for Monday, January 11. Over the weekend, in a New York City hotel room, King, Young, and Lee talked over what Young should say to DeLoach. King was distraught. He felt that the tape was "a warning from God" that he "had not been living up to his responsibilities in relation to the role in which history had cast him."

On Monday, Young and Abernathy went to Washington and in Young's words confronted DeLoach about "the whole mess," particularly the stories that "there was some kind of wild sexual activity going on around Dr. King personally." DeLoach, of course, denied that the FBI was saying anything at all about King. Afterward, Young was convinced that they were dealing with "a kind of fascist mentality" at the Federal Bureau of Investigation.

In sum, there was to be no truce with Hoover, no end to the FBI vendetta. King now had the choice of steeling himself for the worst or getting out of the movement. At this point, as Wachtel has pointed out, a lesser man than King might have quit in shame, leaving Hoover and his deputies to gloat in righteous triumph. But King's determination to go on "in spite of" was a fierce countervailing force; anguished and guilt-stricken though he was, he resolved not to be bullied into cringing inaction. If he kept brooding about what Hoover had on him and what he was doing, he would indeed be paralyzed, his leadership finished. He must believe that God did not judge him by his mistakes but by "the total bent" of his life. With God's help (and forgiveness), he must keep on keeping on.

Still, he was more careful in his private matters now, and he and his staff did take precautions. They had their own spies in the Justice Department and elsewhere in government—Negroes loyal to King and the movement—who alerted him to the FBI surveillances. To foil Hoover's men, King and his aides would rent a hotel room under the name of a trusted local friend and hold confidential meetings there. Or, once they checked into a hotel, they would immediately rent another room down the hall for conferences or private purposes, thus avoiding the FBI bugs.

Even so, it was dispiriting to know that FBI agents were constantly on their trail. They were everywhere, Abernathy said: on airplanes, in pursuing cars, at rallies and meetings, in hotel lounges and restaurants. Young said they always knew when the FBI was at some hotel: it was hard to miss those plain green Plymouths with two-way radios parked in the lot. Once Young walked around a motel and passed a room with its curtain partly drawn; he peered inside and saw a man with earphones on, listening on a tape recorder.

Assuming that the FBI was bugging almost every place they went, King and his people relied on humor to ease the strain. Since "all life is a recording studio for us," they would joke about who would become a member of "the FBI Golden Record Club." When someone made a fresh or flippant remark, King would chuckle, "Ol' Hoover's

gonna have you in the Golden Record Club if you're not careful."
When Abernathy found a bug or a transmitter, he would call it a
"*doo*hickey" and start talking in to it, "Mr. President," "Mr. Hoover,"
"Whoever you are," while King and his young aides whooped in delight. On the phone, they would ask one another, "How are you doing?" and then add merrily, "Well, J. Edgar, how are *you* doing?" As
for those ubiquitous agents, King liked to leave a meeting by another
door, sneak up on them, and suddenly introduce himself, "Hello, I'm
Martin Luther King. I want to thank you for your 'protection.' "

And so it went in hotels and public meetings across America, as
Hoover's men stalked, bugged, and smeared King relentlessly. By now,
the bureau had even hired an SCLC informant—a young Negro
named Jim Harrison, who worked in SCLC's accounting office. The
bureau had given King a code name, "Zorro," after the masked television character, and approached anybody who would listen about Zorro's "filthy, fraudulent" behavior.° But as an Atlanta agent admitted,
the bureau was naïve in assuming that its dossier on King would repel
his followers and destroy him within the black community. "As far as
Dr. King's private life is concerned," Rustin said, "most people in our
community would say that's his own business. We're not even interested." As a consequence, SCLC officials told the Atlanta agent that
"they couldn't care less" what the FBI said about Doc.

O N MONDAY, JANUARY 18, KING WAS BACK in Selma for the opening
of the campaign. While black teams successfully "tested" seven Selma
restaurants, making certain they were abiding by the Civil Rights Act,
King and John Lewis led four hundred Negroes off to the courthouse,
Sheriff Clark's green-marbled lair. Bespectacled Wilson Baker, however, stopped them en route and made them break up into small groups.

° The bureau continued to bug King's hotel rooms until January, 1966, when a threatened congressional investigation impelled it to terminate the electronic surveillance of King.
On April 30, 1965, King moved to a new home in Atlanta, but the FBI for some reason did
not tap his new phone. The telephone taps on SCLC's Atlanta headquarters ended in June,
1966, when Attorney General Nicholas Katzenbach ordered them discontinued. Thereafter,
informant Harrison was the FBI's chief Atlanta source for information about King and
SCLC.

Otherwise he would have to arrest them for parading without a permit, and Baker wanted no arrests and no incidents. He had studied King's Albany operation, noting how Chief Pritchett had killed the movement with kindness. Like him, Baker intended to defuse King's campaign by depriving it of the publicity it needed to succeed.

At the courthouse, though, King and his marchers passed into Sheriff Clark's jurisdiction. And the sheriff stood there now, wearing his military-style uniform and braided-trimmed hat, clenching his teeth and gripping his billy club, as King recited the grievances of local Negroes and in his most dignified manner—with an eye on nearby reporters—asked that the Negroes be registered to vote. Going along with Baker for now, Clark managed to restrain himself and simply ushered King and his people into a back alley and left them there. Among the leering whites around the courthouse, King spotted corpulent J. B. Stoner and American Nazi party chairman George Lincoln Rockwell.

Turned away from the courthouse, King and his aides went to the Hotel Albert, a symbol of Selma white supremacy, and registered without incident, the first Negroes ever admitted into the hotel as guests. But as King crossed the lobby, a member of the National States Rights party walked up and punched him, while a white woman stood on a chair screaming, "Get him! Get him!" Baker subdued King's assailant before he could land another blow and dragged him off to jail. Unruffled, King told a humming church rally that thousands of Negroes would march and fill up the jails "to arouse the federal government" if Alabama refused to register them.

Back in the Hotel Albert, King and his staff were up most of the night planning their next move. They were frankly disappointed that Clark had behaved himself that day. They would try another march tomorrow: if nothing happened, they would move the campaign to Camden in contiguous Wilcox County, where no Negroes at all were registered.

Then King's intelligence reported heartening news. In a conference with Baker and Smitherman that same night, Clark had started raving about all those "niggers" surging around his courthouse and had sworn to arrest "every goddamn one of them" if they came back.

To test Clark's threat, King dispatched fifty volunteers to the courthouse the next day. With a gaggle of reporters looking on, Clark not only arrested the lot of them, but seized businesswoman Amelia

Boynton by the collar and shoved her viciously down the block to his car. At a mass meeting that night, Abernathy suggested that the Dallas County Voters' League make Clark an honorary member, for his service in dramatizing the plight of Selma's black people. At a strategy session afterward, King elected to keep the campaign centered in Selma. Something about Clark's manic reaction that day convinced him that in Clark they had another Bull Connor. King's impression was ratified when his intelligence reported that Baker and Smitherman thought Clark "out of control."

Over the next two days, King's forces escalated the battle, as wave after wave of Negroes besieged Clark's courthouse. To King's delight, even the Negro teachers staged a protest march—a spectacle that astonished whites and blacks alike, since educators tended to be the most conservative Negro group in the matter of race relations. With the campaign attracting blacks of all ages and occupations, King's young lieutenants told one another happily, "Brother, we got a *move*ment goin' on in Selma."

King meanwhile was in and out of town. He left for a brief speaking tour, turned up in Atlanta to preach at Ebenezer, then hurried back to Selma for the demonstrations on Monday, January 25. As he directed operations, a column bore down on Clark's courthouse singing "Ain't Gonna Let Nobody Turn Me Around." Now they were protected by a federal court order, handed down in Mobile over the weekend, that overruled Clark's injunction and forbade city and county officials to impede the "orderly process" of voter registration. But Clark and the registrars created various obstructions to frustrate the Negroes and keep them off the rolls. In response to their demands, Clark now wore a lapel button that read "NEVER" and strode angrily down the line, shoving people around. When Mrs. Annie Lee Cooper, a huge woman, remarked that "There ain't nobody scared around here," Clark pushed her so hard that she lost her balance. Enraged, she punched the sheriff to his knees and then slugged him again. A deputy grabbed her from behind, but she stomped his foot and elbowed him in the stomach and then knocked Clark down a second time. At last three deputies subdued Mrs. Cooper and held her fast as Clark beat her methodically with his billy club, ignoring the reporters who trained their cameras on him.

Several black men started to interfere, but King stopped them. "Don't do it, men. I know how you feel because I know how I feel. But hold your peace." In truth, King was as furious as they were. But he was determined that Selma Negroes adhere to his philosophy and tactics of nonviolence, something he and his staff had been drilling into them since the movement had begun. As James Bevel told them, any man who had the urge to hit white officers was a fool. "That is just what they want you to do. Then they can call you a mob and beat you to death." In any case, they were exposing the viciousness inherent in segregation now, one of the goals of direct action. A photograph of the beating of Mrs. Cooper was soon circulating widely across the country.

That Monday night, with passions running high over Mrs. Cooper, local blacks crowded into Brown Chapel to hear Ralph Abernathy. King asked him to give the main talk because he excelled at soothing people through droll wit and defiance. In Brown Chapel that night, he treated his people to a memorable show. He pointed to a radio antenna attached to the pulpit and said the police had installed that "doohickey" and had warned him to watch what he said. "But they forgot something when they said that," Abernathy exclaimed with his jowly face set in a frown. "They forgot that Ralph Abernathy isn't afraid of any white man, or any white man's doohickey either. In fact, I'm not afraid to talk to it *man to man.*" He held the antenna up and cried, "Doohickey, hear me well!" and shouts and waves of laughter rolled over the sanctuary. "We don't have to spread out when we go down to that courthouse, doohickey. And the next time we go we're going to walk *together,* we're not going to go two together twenty feet apart. We're not going to have a parade, we're just going to walk down to the courthouse. When we want a *parade,* doohickey, we'll get the R. B. Hudson High School Band and take over the town!"

The next day King left his staff to run the campaign and returned to Atlanta for an interracial banquet in his honor. As a Nobel laureate, he was Atlanta's most famous resident, and Benjamin Mays, Ralph McGill, Mayor Allen, and other prominent Atlantans had organized the affair to give King the recognition he was due in his home town. The banquet, however, had whipped up a tempest of controversy, with many white businessmen in hot opposition. "We ain't gonna have no dinner for no nigger," raged a top bank executive in town. The FBI, of course, tried to sabotage the affair by making "covert contacts with community leaders with charges about King's personal life," recalled an Atlanta agent. At one point things were so acrimonious that King said he didn't care whether there was a banquet or not. But at last the voices of good will prevailed. Former Mayor Hartsfield be-seeched opposition businessmen, "Let's keep our good reputation and be known as an adult town." In honoring King, Rabbi Jacob Rothchild pointed out, "we honor not him alone, but ourselves and our city as well." At the same time, a *New York Times* story about the dispute scandalized image-conscious Atlanta and helped gain King's sponsors the business support they needed to proceed. The first of its kind in Atlanta history, the banquet took place on the night of January 27 in the old Dinkler Hotel in the center of downtown.

King arrived late with Coretta and their three oldest children. The police were out in force—there had been a raft of bomb threats—and Klansmen in full regalia were picketing on the sidewalks. When he reached the banquet room, King found more than 1,500 people await-ing him, including many Negroes and almost every major white busi-ness leader in the city. At the head table, he leaned over and apolo-gized to Mayor Allen for being late. "I forgot what time we were on."

"How's that?" Allen said.

"Eastern Standard Time, CST or CPT," King said.

"CPT?"

"Colored People's Time," King said with a grin. "It always takes us longer to get where we're going."

With his children scampering about under the table, King sur-veyed the room and was deeply moved. Four years before, he had been jailed in Atlanta for trying to eat a sandwich at a downtown lunch counter. Tonight he was the honored guest at a downtown din-ner in which Negroes and whites, yardmen and bankers, maids and social matrons, sat and ate together. Here in microcosm was his dream fulfilled, a dream that one day in Dixie the sons of former slaves and the sons of former slaveowners might sit down together at the table of brotherhood.

At the rostrum now, prepared to say a few words of thanks, King had tears in his eyes. "This is a very significant evening, for me and for the South," he said. "I must confess I've enjoyed being on this mountaintop, and I'm tempted to stay here and retreat to a more quiet and serene life. But I must return to the valley." Mayor Allen gave him a proclamation bound in a lavender velvet portfolio, reflecting that the Nobel laureate had "every reason in the world to be some-what bitter and pompous toward people who had spent much of their past lives fighting what he had dedicated his life to do. But he was a big man, a great man." At the end of the ceremonies, everybody in the room—black people and white—joined hands and sang "We Shall Overcome."

ON SUNDAY, JANUARY 31, KING WAS BACK in Selma, staying with Dr. Sullivan Jackson, a friend and local dentist whose home now served as King's staff headquarters. Mrs. Jackson, an articulate, animated schoolteacher, recalled that King was so busy, so much on the move, that he would often arrive at the Jackson home without a change of clothes and would have to borrow her husband's suits, socks, and pajamas. He frequented Mrs. Jackson's kitchen, smelling and sampling her stews, blackeyed peas, and whatever else she was cooking for his staff. When she said she felt like "the movement's cook" because she had to prepare meals for so many people, King would smile and say expansively, "Lady, you will go down in history as being one of the greatest cooks."

At a staff meeting, King and his aides worked out battle plans for the week. Colonel Al Lingo and a squad of state troopers were in Selma now, rumbling around town in their menacing two-tone Fords, with the stars and bars of the Confederacy emblazoned on their front bumpers, and hankering to break the heads of some "outside agitators." After Abernathy's "doohickey" speech, Mayor Smitherman had called Lingo in, fearing that Negroes were about to riot and that the city needed reinforcements. With Lingo here, King sensed that the moment of "creative tension" was fast approaching. Now was the time for mass marches and mass arrests and for King himself to go to jail.

That night, King sat behind the pulpit in Brown Chapel, his hands clasped in front of his chin and a pensive expression on his face, as his assistants exhorted a mass rally. This was becoming the pattern in the campaign. With Brown Chapel serving as the movement's command post, there would be a mass meeting at night followed by another the next morning, after which marchers would set out for Clark's courthouse. Now it was King's turn to speak, and Hosea Williams marveled at how he could "let loose, really get down," with these black-belt folk, many of them in from the countryside. A slim, bright-eyed third-grader named Sheyann Webb, introduced to King as "his youngest freedom fighter," never forgot him in these mass meetings. He would seek her out and sometimes hold her in his lap behind the pulpit, the two of them joining the crowd in singing "Ain't Gonna Let Nobody Turn Me Around," the anthem of the Selma movement. And when King spoke, "it just really put something through me," Sheyann said later, "it just do something to me. . . . I just enjoyed looking at him, besides listening to him." When he finished he would turn to her and say, "Sheyann, what do you want?" And she would say, "Freedom."

The next morning, King told hundreds of marchers gathered around Brown Chapel why they were going to jail this day. "If Negroes could vote, there would be no Jim Clarks, there would be no oppressive poverty directed against Negroes, our children would not be crippled by segregated schools, and the whole community might live together in harmony. Whatever it takes to get the right to vote in this state we're going to follow that course. . . . If it takes filling up the jails . . . if it takes marching on the state capital en masse and standing before the governor to demand our rights."

Then he led some 250 marchers en masse down Selma's streets, forcing a disheartened Wilson Baker to arrest them for parading without a permit. He shepherded them off to the county jail—the city jail was too small to hold them all—and left King and Abernathy and other singing Negroes in the dayroom there. It was a bleak place, with steel-gray walls and rancid mattresses lying helter-skelter on the floor. Across a catwalk from the dayroom was a row of cells filled with county prisoners, who subsisted on the prison fare of one cup of black-eyed peas and a square of cornbread twice a day. One Negro told King that he had been behind bars for twenty-seven months, after lawmen had arrested and beaten him one Saturday night. He didn't know for certain what they had charged him with, but heard it was for raping a white woman. Another Negro said he had been locked up for two years without bond privileges and was still awaiting trial. King thought this grim evidence of black-belt justice for Negroes.

As was their custom in jail, King and Abernathy fasted for two days, prayed and meditated, sang hymns and exercised, and held conferences with SCLC aides and lawyers, who reported that hundreds of marchers—including several hundred school children—had been arrested on Tuesday and that a sheriff's deputy was reported to have shocked Hosea Williams with a cattle prod. On Thursday, February 4, Coretta visited King in jail and told him that Malcolm X had been in

Selma that day and had spoken at Brown Chapel, where several hundred Negroes were awaiting marching orders. King was astonished that Malcolm would invade "my own territory down here," but not surprised that it was SNCC that had invited him. Coretta had talked with Malcolm, though, and he had given her a message for King. "Will you tell Dr. King that I had planned to visit with him in jail? I won't get a chance now because I've got to leave to get to New York in time to catch a plane for London. . . . I want Dr. King to know that I didn't come to Selma to make his job difficult. I really did come thinking that I could make it easier. If the white people realize what the alternative is, perhaps they will be more willing to hear Dr. King."

King appreciated Malcolm's sincerity. In fact, he was aware that Malcolm had broken with Elijah Muhammad and the Muslims, made a pilgrimage to Mecca and converted to orthodox Islam, and moderated his views on the inherent evil of the white man—if not the basic racism of American society. For Malcolm, the days of unrelenting hatred for the "white devil" were behind him now. "The sickness and madness of those days," he told a black journalist, "I'm glad to be free of them. It's a time for martyrs now. And if I'm to be one, it will be in the cause of brotherhood. That's the only thing that can save this country. I've learned it the hard way—but I've learned it." King thought it a propitious sign that this proud and brilliant man seemed to be moving away from racism. (In two and a half weeks, though, Malcolm X would be dead, shot down by Negro assassins in New York City, and King would reflect that Malcolm was a victim of the violence in America that had spawned him.)

From his jail cell, King continued to direct the Selma movement, jotting on Waldorf-Astoria stationary detailed battle instructions to his executive director, Andrew Young. First, King wrote, Young should call LeRoy Collins, former governor of Florida and head of the Federal Community Relations Service, and implore him to come to Selma and talk with city and county officials about expediting voter registration. Young should urge President Johnson to send an emissary, too, and appeal to Selma's white leaders in a White House press conference. Above all, Young should work on getting a congressional delegation to come down and investigate conditions in Dallas County. The local newspaper editor, speaking for county and city officials, had already telegraphed Johnson to dispatch such a delegation, and King insisted that "we should join in calling for this. By all means don't let them get the offensive. They are trying to give the impression that they are an orderly and good community because they integrated public accommodations. We must insist that voting is the issue and here Selma has dirty hands." Meanwhile Young should keep the pressure on in the streets. Get the teachers to march again. Keep some activity going every day this week. Even consider a night march to the courthouse "to let Clark show [his] true colors."

As Young and other movement people contacted Washington, the mass marches continued until Dallas County jails were bursting with more than 3,000 Negroes. When King's field lieutenants failed one day to mount a demonstration, King scolded Young in a note: "please don't be soft. We have the offensive. It was a mistake not to march today. In a crisis we must have a sense of drama."

By now, King's imprisonment had made national headlines and brought reporters and television newsmen streaming into Selma from across the country. In response to a flurry of telegrams in King's name, a congressional delegation was coming to Selma on Friday, February 5, to see for themselves what was going on. And President Johnson, in a White House press conference, promised to secure the right to vote for "all our citizens."

So far everything was going precisely as King had hoped. Assured of a national audience, he penned "Letter from a Selma Jail."

Dear Friends,

When the King of Norway participated in awarding the Nobel Peace Prize to me he surely did not think that in less than sixty days I would be in jail. He, and almost all world opinion will be shocked because they are little aware of the unfinished business in the South.

By jailing hundreds of Negroes, the city of Selma, Alabama, has revealed the persisting ugliness of segregation to the nation and the world. . . . Why are we in jail? Have you ever been required to answer 100 questions on government, some abstruse even to a political-science specialist, merely to vote? Have you ever stood in line with over a hundred others and after waiting an entire day seen less than ten given the qualifying test?

THIS IS SELMA, ALABAMA. THERE ARE MORE NE-GROES IN JAIL WITH ME THAN THERE ARE ON THE VOTING ROLLS.

But apart from voting rights, merely to be a person in Selma is not easy. When reporters asked Sheriff Clark if a woman defendant was married, he replied "She's a nigger woman and she hasn't got a Miss or Mrs. in front of her name."

This is the U.S.A. in 1965. We are in jail simply because we cannot tolerate these conditions for ourselves or our nation.

"We need the help of all decent Americans. . . .

Martin Luther King, Jr.

The "Letter" appeared as an advertisement in the February 5 issue of the *New York Times*. That same Friday, King bailed out of jail and held a news conference about his next move: he would personally ask the President to sponsor a voting-rights bill for southern Negroes, stressing in particular the need for federal registrars in the South. Then he lunched with the congressional task force at Dr. Jackson's home and rehearsed the horrors that black people endured here in the black belt. In some demonstrations, whites had even thrown snakes on Negroes seeking to register. Repelled by what they found in Selma, the congressmen returned to Washington and promoted their own voting-rights legislation on Capitol Hill. With the Leadership Conference on Civil Rights also hard at work, King's hopes were soaring.

On February 9 he flew off to Washington for a round of talks with administration officials. But it required some remarkable operatics before he could see the President. After King had announced his visit in Selma, Harry Wachtel had called the White House and tried to arrange a meeting. But Johnson was distinctly cool to the idea. His response was that "nobody—not even a Nobel Prize winner—had the right to invite himself to the White House." Sure, the President hoped to push for a voting-rights bill. But he didn't want the country to think that King was making him do it. Finally Wachtel and a Johnson aide named Lee White worked out a staged meeting that avoided the impression that King could come to the White House whenever he wanted. According to the script, King conferred with Attorney General Katzenbach and Vice-President Humphrey, who, for his part, expressed doubts that Congress would pass additional civil-rights legislation so soon after the 1964 measure, but added that it might "if the pressure was unrelenting." Then, on cue, Johnson phoned the Vice-President and asked him to bring the German ambassador by for a scheduled visit. Since King was in his office, Humphrey, following the script, nonchalantly invited him to come along and say hello to the President. So it was that King got his hearing with Johnson, who then assured him that he would send a voting-rights message to Congress "very soon."

Though appalled at Johnson's vanity, King thought the session worthwhile, because it publicly linked the Selma campaign to the President's general commitment to some form of voting legislation. Even so, his talks in Washington reinforced his conviction that only by increasing the pressure from Selma could a meaningful voting bill ever be enacted.

Back in Selma, King found that Clark was doing his part to keep things stirred up. During King's absence, the marches had actually begun to dwindle, and Baker's own hopes had risen: if Clark could be restrained, maybe King's crusade could yet be derailed. But Clark could not be restrained. On February 10, he and his possemen attacked a column of young student marchers and drove them out of town at a run, hitting and shocking them with cattle prods. "You wanted to march, didn't you?" the possemen yelled. *"Now march!"* They chased the youngsters a mile or so, until they stumbled vomiting and crying into ditches.

In protest, King led 2,800 furious Negroes on the biggest march of the campaign, promising them and all the nation beyond that they were going to bring a voting-rights law into being in the streets of Selma. At the courthouse, Clark responded by jabbing C. T. Vivian in the stomach with a billy club. When Vivian wrested it away, a deputy smashed him in the mouth with his billy club. All this occurred right in front of scribbling reporters and television cameramen. As *Time* reported, Clark was the movement's energizing force: every time it faltered, the sheriff and his deputies revived it with some new outrage. And *The Nation* proclaimed King himself "the finest tactician the South has produced since Robert E. Lee." Like Lee, *The Nation* observed, King got a lot of help from the stupidity of his opponents.

Clark, in the meantime, had checked into Vaughan Memorial Hospital complaining of chest pains. "The niggers are givin' me a heart attack," he wailed. And he would curse and castigate them for trying to gain "black supremacy" in Dallas County. The sheriff collected shirts—had eighty-eight of them now—and used to give the old ones to Negroes who kept their place. But not any more. "No, sir," said his wife, "he's not giving any more of his good shirts to those niggers after what they've put him through down here." While he convalesced, though, two hundred young demonstrators stood in the rain in front of the courthouse, praying for his recovery—in mind as well as body.

By now King had escalated the campaign again, expanding it into adjacent Perry and Wilcox Counties and calling for night marches there as well as in Selma to heighten pressure on local white authorities. As he and his staff drove through rural Wilcox County, King was horrified at the racial oppression he found there. On one plantation, blacks had never seen U.S. currency; they used octagonal tin coins parceled out by the white owners, and shopped at the plantation commissary like slaves. On the courthouse lawn in Camden, King confronted Sheriff P. C. "Lummy" Jenkins in a futile effort to get Negroes registered. King learned that Jenkins had such a reputation for ferocity that a Negro wanted for some "crime" would come in voluntarily and surrender. "This is intimidation and degradation reminiscent only of chattel slavery," King said. "This is white supremacist arrogance and Negro servility possible only in an atmosphere where the Negro feels himself so isolated, so hopeless, that he is stripped of all dignity." Conditions were almost as bad in Perry County, where SCLC staffers were organizing. In the county seat of Marion, where King and Coretta had been married eleven years before, Negroes crowded around King in a desperate effort to see and touch him. Later King learned that some whites had planned to assassinate him, but couldn't get a clear shot because of the crush of Negroes around him and his staff.

Aroused by his visit, a group of Marion Negroes attempted a night march on February 18, but Lingo's state troopers ambushed the luckless blacks and clubbed them screaming through the streets. When Jimmie Lee Jackson, a young pulpwood cutter, tried to defend his mother and grandfather, a trooper shot him in the stomach with a revolver. An ambulance rushed him to the Negro hospital in Selma, where doctors did all they could to save his life. As he hovered near death, Colonel Lingo served Jackson for assault and battery with intent to kill a police officer.

King fell ill with a fever and had to spend the weekend in bed. On Monday, though, he called on Jackson in the hospital and could only shake his head at the madness of what had happened. Only twenty-five, darkly handsome and muscular, Jimmie just this last year had been elected the youngest deacon in the history of his home-town church. Angry, in despair, King headed for Brown Chapel to lead a night protest march, in defiance of a ban issued on Saturday by Governor Wallace. But King's aides begged him to call it off. The Justice Department and the FBI had both warned them of a plot to assassinate King if he marched that night. The plot called for a diversionary group to attack the middle of the column and draw off the police, then a death squad to shoot him in the front. King protested that he couldn't give in to such threats, but his frightened staff finally persuaded him to stay off the streets that night.

Two days later Jimmie Lee Jackson died, and King and all his colleagues and hundreds of area Negroes heralded him as a martyr and escorted his hearse on a rain-streaked pilgrimage back to Marion. Here, in Jimmie's church, a plain wooden building with wooden floors, King gave the eulogy before four hundred mourners. In the front row, Jimmie's mother wept and his eighty-two year-old grandfather, Cager Lee, a small and brittle man, stared at King with eyes of ineffable sorrow. Who killed Jimmie Lee Jackson? King asked rhetorically. He was killed by every lawless sheriff, every racist politician from governors down, every indifferent white minister, every passive Negro who "stands on the sidelines in the struggle for justice." Yet "Jimmie Lee Jackson's death says to us that we must work passionately and unrelentingly to make the American dream a reality." Under weeping skies, King and hundreds of others buried Jimmie in a hillside cemetery, where pine trees stood dark and still, laying him to final rest beside his father, killed in a car wreck several years before.

After the funeral, King and his staff escalated the campaign again. In a press conference, wearing his overalls and skull cap, a brooding James Bevel announced that King would lead a mass march to the Alabama capitol in Montgomery. It was to begin in Selma the next Sunday, March 7. Pressed by reporters, King confirmed what Bevel said: they were going to petition George Wallace to end police brutality and grant Alabama Negroes the elective franchise. "I can't promise you that it won't get you killed," King told a hushed crowd in Brown Chapel. "But we must stand up for what is right."

The announcement stunned Alabama officials, for the image of hundreds of flag-waving Negroes descending on the state capitol was more than they could bear. Governor Wallace banned the march and instructed Lingo to enforce his order "with whatever means are available." Wallace aides, though, assured Mayor Smitherman that there would be no violence, and Smitherman in turn promised the full cooperation of the city police. But all this infuriated Wilson Baker. Smitherman and Wallace were both crazy, he said, if they believed that Lingo and Clark would not molest the marchers, and Baker threatened to resign before he would let his men participate in a bloodbath. At last Smitherman relented and allowed the city police to stay out of the matter. Once the marchers crossed Edmund Pettis Bridge and left Selma, they would be in the hands of Lingo and Clark.

On Friday, March 5, King was in Washington for a long talk with Johnson and then returned to Atlanta on Saturday. He now decided to postpone the march until the following Monday. On a conference call with his aides in Selma, he explained that he had neglected his congregation for two straight Sundays and that he really needed to preach in Ebenezer the next day. He would return to Selma on Monday and lead the march then. All of his staff agreed to the postponement except rambunctious Hosea Williams. "Hosea," King warned, "You need to pray. You're not with me. You need to get with me."

On Sunday morning, though, King's aides reported that more than five hundred pilgrims were gathered at Brown Chapel, and that Williams wanted permission to march that day. In his church office, King thought it over and relayed word to Brown Chapel that his people could start without him. Since the march had been banned, he was certain that they would get arrested at the bridge and that he would simply join them in jail. He expected no mayhem on Highway 80, since even the conservative Alabama press had excoriated Lingo's troopers for their savagery in Marion.

He did not know what happened on Highway 80—the Jefferson Davis Highway—until his excited aides phoned him later in the afternoon from the Brown Chapel parsonage. Five hundred and twenty-five people, led by Williams and SNCC's John Lewis, had left Brown Chapel and crossed the bridge toting bedrolls and blankets, only to confront a chilling sight: "Wallace's storm troopers," as civil-rights workers called the highway patrol, stood three deep across all four lanes of Highway 80, wearing gas masks beneath their sky-blue hard hats and armed with billy clubs. State trooper cars, with the Confederate stars and bars on their bumpers, were parked everywhere along the roadside. As the blacks approached the wall of troopers, an officer raised a bullhorn and shouted, "Turn around and go back to your church! You will not be allowed to march any further! You've got two minutes to disperse!" One minute later, King's men told him, the officer ordered a charge, and the troopers waded into the Negroes with clubs flailing. They shoved the front ranks back like dominoes, fractured Lewis's skull, hammered women and men alike to the ground. Then the troopers regrouped and attacked again, this time firing canisters of tear gas. The marchers fell back in clouds of smoke, choking and crying in pain.

As white onlookers cheered wildly, Clark's mounted posse now rode out between some buildings along the highway, and Clark shrieked, "Get those goddamn niggers!" With a rebel yell, the possemen charged into the Negroes, lashing them with bullwhips and rubber tubing wrapped in barbed wire. "Please, no!" cried a Negro. "God, we're being killed." Reeling under the blows, the blacks retreated pell mell back to Brown Chapel, the road behind them littered with bedrolls, shoes, and purses. At the chapel, some Negroes hurled bricks and bottles at the possemen, while Williams and Lewis, his head covered with blood, guided their stricken people inside. The air reeked of tear gas as they huddled in the sanctuary, some groaning and weeping, others in shock.

Outside, Wilson Baker tried to assume jurisdiction in the area, but the sheriff shoved past him. "I've already waited a month too damned long about moving in," Clark bellowed. Whereupon his possemen rioted in the Negro section, beating people and storming into the First Baptist Church, where they seized a Negro youth and flung him through a stained-glass window depicting Christ as the Good Shepherd. Before it was over, seventy Negroes had been hospitalized and seventy others treated for injuries.

In Atlanta, King was stricken with grief. "I shall never forget my agony of conscience for not being there when I heard of the dastardly acts perpetrated against nonviolent demonstrators that Sunday," he said later. But then he got an inspiration. He had long complained that clergymen had "too often been the taillight rather than the headlight" of the civil-rights movement, and here was a tremendous opportunity to enlist them actively in the struggle. Accordingly he sent out a flurry of telegrams, summoning religious leaders across the nation to join him in Selma for "a ministers' march to Montgomery" on Tuesday, March 9. "In the vicious maltreatment of defenseless citizens of Selma, where old women and young children were gassed and clubbed at random, we have witnessed an eruption of the disease of racism which seeks to destroy all America," King said in his call. "The people of Selma will struggle on for the soul of America, but it is fitting that all Americans help to bear the burden."

As King's telegrams flashed across the Republic, ABC Television interrupted its Sunday-night movie, *Judgment at Nuremberg*, to show a vivid film clip of Selma's "bloody Sunday." And stories and photographs about it ran in all the major newspapers and news magazines. The news shook the country as had no other event in the civil-rights struggle—not even the dogs and fire hoses in Birmingham. In Washington, President Johnson deplored such brutality, and 1,000 people marched in protest. In Detroit, the Democratic mayor and the Republican governor led 10,000 people in a sympathy march for Selma's battered Negroes. A thousand people demonstrated in Union, New Jersey, 2,000 in Toronto, Canada, and thousands more in cities from New England to the West Coast.

Meanwhile the response to King's telegrams was sensational, as clergymen in one city after another dropped whatever they were doing and headed for the nearest air terminal. In Boston, Reverend James Reeb, a soft-spoken white Unitarian and director of a low-income housing project for Negroes, told a colleague that it was time for those who really cared for human freedom "to make a direct witness." He left his wife and four children and set out for Selma by plane and bus. So did former Kennedy assistant Harris Wofford, back from two years in Africa, who said that King's was "a call I couldn't refuse." Overnight, some four hundred ministers, rabbis, priests, nuns, students, and lay leaders—black and white alike—rushed to stand in Selma's streets with Martin Luther King and face Alabama officials in the name of human dignity. State authorities, of course, branded them agitators one and all. "Why not?" retorted one cleric. "An agitator is the part of the washing machine that gets the dirt out."

King spent most of Monday in Atlanta, talking on the phone with Washington, Selma, and Montgomery. Because of the recent threats on his life, King's aides were greatly concerned about his safety, but King was going back to Selma that evening come what may. For him, it was "a matter of conscience." In Montgomery, meanwhile, his attorneys filed into Judge Frank M. Johnson's U.S. District Court and asked that he enjoin Alabama officials from blocking Tuesday's march. King expected a favorable ruling since Johnson had the best civil-rights record of any judge in the Deep South. A native Alabamian, Johnson had attended the University of Alabama with Wallace and had once been his friend. But they had fallen out over civil rights, so much so that Wallace referred to the judge as "a low-down, carpetbaggin', scalawaggin', race-mixin' liar."

But Judge Johnson refused to hand down an injunction that Monday. Instead he asked King's forces to postpone the march until after a court hearing on Tuesday. At first King agreed. But when he reached Selma on Monday evening and found all those clergymen prepared to stand with him, he resolved to march as planned. "We've gone too far to turn back now," he exhorted a mass meeting in Brown Chapel. "We must let them know that nothing can stop us—not even death itself. We must be ready for a season of suffering." There were plenty who were ready, too, especially among local Negroes. Enraged and emboldened by Sunday's beatings, they were eager indeed for a show of defiance. "I had the flu yesterday and wasn't able to march," an old man told James Bevel, "but I'm going to be out there tomorrow." "We're going, and nothing can stop us," declared a youngster at a youth meeting, and the children chanted back, "Nothing. Nothing. Nothing."

That night, in Dr. Jackson's home, King and other movement leaders debated for three intense hours about what kind of march should be undertaken. Should they attempt to reach Montgomery or settle for a token demonstration here in Selma? Clearly the troopers and possemen would be massed out on Highway 80 the next day, itching for bloodshed. Under considerable duress, King argued that it was not the nonviolent way to try to break through an armed wall, and he sold his colleagues on a compromise. They would march to the site of Sunday's beatings and confront the police line, making it clear to all the world that Alabama planned to stop them with violence. Then they would turn back, in hopes that the spectacle would have a salutary impact on Washington.

Tuesday morning brought an unexpected blow: Judge Johnson officially banned the march that day, and King and his lieutenants groaned in despair. For the most part, the federal judiciary had been a powerful ally of the movement, helping it time and again with favorable decisions. Now King would have to proceed in defiance of a federal court order, and some advisers pressed him to cancel the march lest he alienate the very Washington politicians on whom he depended for voting-rights legislation. Yes, King was upset about the decision, felt "it was like condemning the robbed man for being robbed," said it created an awful dilemma for him. Yet he would not cancel the march, could not cancel it. He remembered only too well the lesson of Albany, where he had honored a federal injunction and it had broken his momentum. If he waited until after protracted court hearings, all the clergymen in Selma might leave, public interest evaporate, and a decisive moment in the struggle be irretrievably lost. And there was still another consideration: if he did nothing today, pent-up emotions might explode into "an uncontrollable situation." He had to provide his people with "an outlet." He had to march at least to the police barrier.

Meanwhile Attorney General Katzenbach phoned and asked King not to march. "Mr. Attorney General," King said, "you have not been a black man in America for three hundred years." Then an administrative task force under LeRoy Collins, head of the Federal Community Relations Service, arrived at the Jackson home and beseeched King in the name of President Johnson to call off the demonstration. But King still refused. A while later, Collins returned with the news that he had met with Lingo and Clark in the back room of an auto agency and persuaded them to restrain their men so long as King turned back. Some said King's only response was a smile. Clark and Lingo had broken promises before, and whites who knew them thought a lot of people would be dead by nightfall.

At Brown Chapel that afternoon, some 1,500 marchers listened quietly as King spoke of his "painful and difficult decision" to defy the court injunction. "I do not know what lies ahead of us. There may be beatings, jailings, and tear gas. But I would rather die on the highways of Alabama than make a butchery of my conscience. There is nothing more tragic in all this world than to know right and not do it. I cannot stand in the midst of all these glaring evils and not take a stand."

He led them through town two abreast, stopping at the Pettis Bridge to hear a U.S. marshal read the court's restraining order. Then he walked them out to the Jefferson Davis Highway, where columns of state troopers, brandishing billy clubs at waist level, again barred their way.

"You are ordered to stop and stand where you are," Major Cloud boomed through his bullhorn. "This march will not continue."

"We have a right to march," King shot back. "There is also a right to march on Montgomery."

When Cloud repeated his order, King asked him to let them pray. "You can have your prayer," Cloud replied, "and then you must return to your church." Behind him, the troopers stood sullen and still. One leered at King from under his hard hat, the stub of a cigar stuck in the corner of his mouth. As hundreds of marchers knelt in the crisp sunlight, King motioned to Abernathy. "We come to present our bodies as a living sacrifice," Abernathy intoned. "We don't have much to offer, but we do have our bodies, and we lay them on the altar today." In another prayer, a Methodist bishop from Washington, D.C., compared this to the exodus out of Egypt and asked God to part the Red Sea and let them through. As he finished, Cloud turned to his men and shouted, "Clear the road completely—move out!" At that the troopers stood aside, leaving the way to Montgomery clear. The Methodist bishop was awe-struck, certain that God had answered his prayer.

King eyed the troopers suspiciously. What were they up to now? One Negro thought this an attempt to embarrass him by exposing his "lack of militancy." But King sensed a trap. "Let's return to church," he said, "and complete our fight in the courts." And the marchers, some singing "Ain't Gonna Let Nobody Turn Me Around," headed unmolested back into town. Confronted by scores of white ministers and King himself, all in full view of national television cameras, the state troopers this time had restrained themselves.

Back at Brown Chapel, King called the march a victory and promised that he and his people would get to Montgomery one day. Immensely relieved that they had not been beaten or killed, most of his followers were content with the abbreviated march, even regarded it as a kind of triumph, too. "We really weren't disappointed," said Marie Foster. "We didn't have knapsacks and gear and didn't really expect to march all the way that day."

The Methodist bishop, however, felt betrayed. And James Forman and other SNCC people were furious. They had wanted to storm on to Montgomery that day, even if it meant crashing through Lingo's troopers. The students were already mad at King, since SNCC had begun the Selma movement (as it had that in Albany) and yet once again King and "Slick" got all the publicity and the glory. Now they censored him bitterly for turning around at the police barrier, fumed too about all the white people he had brought into the movement, denounced his admonitions to love those who pummeled and oppressed them, vowed not to "take any more shit." The students wanted to retaliate against white America, hold militant sit-ins and demonstrations in Washington as well as Alabama. "If we can't sit at the table of democracy," raged Forman, "we'll knock the fucking legs off." Soon SNCC was in virtual rebellion against "de Lawd" and officially withdrew from his projected Montgomery trek, although members could still participate as individuals if they so desired. John Lewis was one of the few who did.

King lamented SNCC's defection and tried to talk with Forman and his student colleagues, tried to ease the friction between them. He fretted that they would jeopardize the entire Selma campaign if they carried out their threats to picket the White House and hold sit-ins in the Justice Department. Journalist Pat Watters was convinced that what SNCC really wanted was to wrest away King's "symbolic leadership."

The departure of SNCC was not the only casualty of Tuesday's demonstration. That night, James Reeb and several other white Unitarians dined at a Negro café whose specialty was soul food—fried chicken and collard greens, cornbread and sweet-potato pie. Afterward, on their way to SCLC headquarters, Reeb and two other clergymen walked by the Silver Moon Café, a notorious den for whites. "Hey, you niggers!" a voice rang out. Four white toughs emerged from the shadows and fell on the ministers with clubs, one tough smacking Reeb in the head as though he were swinging a baseball bat. Reeb lapsed into a coma, and an ambulance sped him to a hospital in Birmingham.

All the next day, King "stayed in seclusion" in the rear of Brown Chapel. But he could hear the commotion out in front, where Wilson Baker tied a rope across Sylvan Street to enforce the city ban on further demonstrations. Civil-rights people dubbed Baker's rope "the Berlin wall" and started a round-the-clock, sit-down prayer vigil in front of the chapel. King could hear them singing throughout the day:

> We've got a rope that's a Berlin Wall
> We're gonna stand here till it falls
> Hate is the thing that built that wall
> Love is the thing that'll make it fall

Thursday, March 11, found King in Judge Johnson's court in Montgomery, where hearings began on the projected march from Selma and on King's own defiance of Johnson's injunction. When King explained why he'd led the abbreviated march, testifying that he hadn't intended to go on to Montgomery that day, the judge dropped contempt charges against him. On Thursday evening, King learned that Reeb had just died in Birmingham, his wife at his side. "A morally inclement climate" killed that brave man, King said, the same "atmosphere of inhumanity in Alabama" that had spawned bloody Sunday and the murder of Jimmie Lee Jackson.

Reeb's murder provoked a storm of public indignation. The American Jewish Committee condemned this "shameful exhibition of brutality." The AFL-CIO was "appalled," and the United Steelworkers laid the blame on Wallace and his "storm troopers." As King pointed out, there had been no such public outcry over Jimmie Lee Jackson's death, because white America was accustomed to the killing of Negroes in Dixie. But a white minister was another matter, and telephones and telegraphs into Washington blazed with demands that federal troops be sent to Selma. In the White House, Johnson conceded that he was "concerned, perturbed, and frustrated." He and Mrs. Johnson both phoned their condolences to Mrs. Reeb, and the President sent flowers and then dispatched *Air Force One* to fly her home.

Deeply affected by Reeb's death, the President announced that he intended to appear before Congress the following Monday night, March 15, and personally submit a strict new voting-rights bill before national television. As King had hoped, events in Selma—and the wide-scale outrage they had ignited—had convinced Johnson that he should draft a stronger voting bill than his administration had been contemplating, and had aroused moderate and progressive members of both parties in Congress, thus assuring Johnson of the support he needed to get the measure enacted. "The real hero of this struggle is the American Negro," Johnson said himself. "Who among us can say that we could have made the same progress" without the Negro's protests, which were "designed to call attention to injustice, designed to provoke change, designed to stir reform?" The President even asked King to be his special guest in the Senate gallery, a symbolic tribute to the success of his campaign.

But King was in Selma that Monday, conducting a memorial service for Reeb at the courthouse. That night he and his assistants settled into the Jackson living room, to watch Johnson's congressional appearance on television, the first time a President had personally given a special message on domestic legislation in nineteen years. "It is wrong—deadly wrong—to deny any of your fellow Americans the right to vote," Johnson said in his slow Texas drawl, and he reviewed all the obstacles to Negro voting in the South, impediments his bill proposed to abolish through federal overseers who would supervise registration in segregated countries—exactly what King had been demanding. "We have already waited 100 years and more," the President went on, paraphrasing King's own language, "and the time for waiting is gone." On the issue of the Negro's right to vote, "there must be no delay, or no hesitation, or no compromise." With Congress interrupting him repeatedly with applause, Johnson pointed out that "at times history and fate meet at a single time in a single place to shape a turning point in man's unending search for freedom. So it was at Lexington and Concord. So it was a century ago at Appomattox. So it was last week in Selma, Alabama." But, "even if we pass this bill, the battle will not be over. What happened in Selma is part of a far larger movement . . . the effort of American Negroes to secure for themselves the full blessings of American life." In closing, he spoke out of his south Texas past and his own brush with poverty and racism as a young Texas schoolteacher. "Their cause must be our cause too. Because it's not just Negroes, but really it's all of us who must overcome the crippling legacy of bigotry and injustice." He added slowly and deliberately, "And we *shall* overcome!"

Congress exploded in a standing ovation, the second of the evening. As television cameras swept the cheering hall, Mrs. Jackson glanced at King in her living room. He was crying. "President Johnson," he said later in a statement, "made one of the most eloquent, unequivocal and passionate pleas for human rights ever made by the President of the United States."

Two days later, in Montgomery, Judge Johnson handed the movement still another victory. After almost a week of hearings, the judge now approved the Selma-to-Montgomery march and ordered Alabama officials not to interfere. The plan Johnson endorsed, devised with military precision by SCLC, called for the pilgrimage to commence on March 21 and culminate in Montgomery three days later. Only three hundred select people were to cover the entire distance, with a giant rally at the Alabama capitol to climax the historic journey. "The extent of the right to assemble, demonstrate and march should be commensurate with the wrongs that are being protested and petitioned against," Judge Johnson ruled. "In this case, the wrongs are enormous."

King and his followers were jubilant. But Johnson's decision threw Wallace into a tirade. On state-wide television, he told a stomping, cheering legislature that Judge Johnson was a hypocrite who presided over a mock court and that the marchers were "Communist-trained anarchists" goaded on by "a collectivist press." Such venom turned King's stomach. He thought Wallace "a demagog with a capital D," who symbolized in America "many of the evils that were alive in Hitler's Germany. He is a merchant of racism, peddling hate under the guise of States' rights." King wasn't sure Wallace believed all the poison he preached, but he was artful enough "to convince others that he does."

After his television speech, Wallace telegraphed President Johnson that Alabama could not protect the marchers because it would cost too much. Scolding the governor for refusing to maintain law and order in his state ("I thought you cared strongly about this"), the President federalized 1,863 Alabama National Guardsmen and dispatched a large contingent of military police, U.S. marshals, and other federal officials to Selma. At last King had the kind of national protection he had long called for.

In Selma, King and his staff plunged into feverish preparations for the march. Field Director Hosea Williams rounded up latrine trucks and other support vehicles, organized a "loaves and fishes" committee responsible for food, and sent teams scouring the countryside along Highway 80 in search of campsites. King himself promised that the journey would be a "gigantic witness to the fulfillment of democracy" and invited movie stars, entertainers, social and political celebrities— "all our friends of goodwill"—to join the marchers for a grand finale in Montgomery on Thursday.

And so on Sunday morning, March 21, a cast of 3,200 zealous people gathered under the sunlit chinaberry trees around Brown Chapel, ready to participate in act one of King's unprecedented drama. Wearing sunglasses, Abernathy scanned the vast crowd and said, "Wallace, it's all over now." Then King stood at the microphone, a Hawaiian lei around his neck, Coretta beaming nearby. "You will be the people that will light a new chapter in the history books of our nation," he sang out in the crisp spring air. "Those of us who are Negroes don't have much. We have known the long night of poverty. Because of the system, we don't have much education and some of us don't know how to make our nouns and verbs agree. But thank God we have our bodies, our feet, and our souls."

Then he and Abernathy set out for Montgomery, flanked by Ralph Bunche of the United Nations and Rabbi Abraham Heschel of the Jewish Theological Seminary of America, a remarkable-looking man with his flowing white beard and wind-tossed hair. Behind the leaders came a motley force of maids and movie stars, coeds and clergymen, nuns and barefoot college boys, civil-rights veterans and couples pushing baby carriages. In downtown Selma, Clark's deputies directed traffic and the sheriff himself, still wearing his NEVER button, stood scarcely noticed on a street corner. As two state-trooper cars escorted the marchers across the bridge, a record-store loudspeaker blared out "Bye-bye Blackbird."

King led his huge procession out the Jefferson Davis Highway now, helicopters clattering overhead and armed troops standing at intervals along the route. Several hundred whites lined the roadside, too, and a car painted with racial slurs ("cheap ammo here," "open season on niggers") cruised by in the opposite lane. Confederate flags bristled among the bystanders, some of whom heckled the column, gesturing obscenely and holding up signs that read "Nigger lover," "Martin Luther Kink," "Nigger King go home!" King tried to ignore them, but some incidents could not be ignored. With two children looking up at her, a woman in her early thirties screamed, "You all got your birth-control pills? You all got your birth-control pills?" Several small children chanted "white nigger!" and waved popguns and toy rifles as the column passed. But only a young white man lost control of himself. He started screaming and lunged at the marchers, but friends grabbed him and held on as he raged hysterically, his arms thrashing the air. On the whole, though, the spectators were subdued, looking on in silence as King and his fellow blacks, United States flags swirling overhead, trampled forever the old stereotype of the southern Negro as a submissive Uncle Tom.

At the first encampment some seven miles out, most people headed back to Selma by car and bus; and King and the rest bedded down for the night in well-guarded hospital tents, the men in one and the women in another. Throughout the night, King could peer outside his tent and see the silhouettes of soldiers around glowing campfires. "Most of us were too tired to talk," recalled Harris Wofford, but a group of Dallas County students sang on and on:

> Many good men have lived and died,
> So we could be marching side by side.

The next morning, wrote a New York Times reporter, "the encampment resembled a cross between a 'Grapes of Wrath' migrant labor camp and the Continental Army bivouac at Valley Forge," as the marchers huddled in blankets around their campfires downing coffee and dry oatmeal. At eight King led them out under a cloudless sky, the marchers chanting in unison:

> Old Wallace, never can jail us all.
> Old Wallace, segregation's bound to fall.
>
> Pick 'em up and put 'em down
> All the way Montgom'ry town.

As they tramped through the rolling countryside, carloads of federal authorities guarded their front and flanks, and a convoy of army vehicles, utility trucks, and ambulances followed in their wake. Far ahead, King could make out army patrols checking every bridge and searching the fields and forests along the highway. Presently a sputtering little plane circled over the marchers and showered them with racist leaflets. They came from "The Confederate Air Force."

At the Lowndes County line, where the highway narrowed to two lanes, the column trimmed down to the three hundred Alabama Freedom Marchers chosen to go the entire distance. Most of them were local Negroes and veterans of the campaign, the rest assorted clerics and civil-rights people from across the land. There was Sister Mary Leoline of Kansas City, a gentle, bespectacled nun whom roadside whites taunted mercilessly, suggesting what she really wanted from the Negro. There was one-legged James Letherer of Michigan, who hobbled along on crutches and complained that his real handicap was that "I can't do more to help these people." There was Cager Lee, Jimmie Lee Jackson's aged grandfather, who could march only a few miles a day, but would always come back the next, saying, "Just got to tramp some more." There was seventeen-year-old Joe Boone, a Negro who'd been arrested seven times in the Selma demonstrations. "My mother and father never thought this day would come," he said. "But it's here and I want to do my part." There was vivacious Marie Foster, who'd helped pioneer the voting-rights drive because "I had taken enough and decided to do something about it," marching now in her finest clothes, her hair in a fetching permanent. There was Andy Young, running up and down the line tending the sick and the sunburned. Above all there was King himself, clad in a blue shirt and a green cap with earmuffs, reading newspapers and strolling with Coretta and John Lewis at the front of his potluck army. Walking alongside was rumpled and rangy John Doar, Assistant Attorney General for Civil Rights, a four-year veteran of the southern campaigns and a hero of the southern Negro (Marie Foster and Amelia Boynton wanted to run him for President), making certain that Judge Johnson's restraining order was obeyed. Ahead of the column rolled a large open truck, brimming with cameramen and reporters who (in the words of an *Ebony* journalist) recorded "every twist of the mouth and wrinkle of the forehead of leader King." From time to time, Abernathy would introduce King to wayside Negroes as another Moses sent by God to lead his people out of the wilderness.

They were inside Lowndes County now, a remote region of dense forests and snake-filled swamps. Winding past trees festooned with Spanish moss, the column approached a large two-story house, where several whites and a Negro servant were standing in the front yard. The whites, gesturing at the marchers, whispered something and broke out laughing. The Negro woman also laughed. Behind King, a young black couple embraced and sang happily as they swung by the whites: "Ain't Gonna Let Nobody Turn Me Around." Eying the Negro woman, they shouted an improvised line: "Ain't Gonna Let Aunt Jemima Turn Me Around."

Further down, King pointed to a weather-beaten pine shack (one of many they would pass that day), a shipwreck Negro home, smoke curling from its chimney, that epitomized the rural black poverty in Lowndes County. In the yard, nine ragged Negroes watched the remarkable parade without a word or even a smile.

Presently the column came to a dusty little Negro community called Trickem Crossroads. Walking next to King, Young pointed at an old church and called back to the others: "Look at that church with the shingles off the roof and the broken windows! Look at that! That's why we're marching!" Across from the church was a dilapidated Negro school propped up on red bricks, a three-room shanty with asphalt shingles covering the holes in its sides. King spotted a group of old folk and children standing under two oak trees in front of the school, squinting at him in the sunlight. When he halted the procession, an old woman ran from under the trees, kissed him breathlessly, and ran back crying, "I done kissed him! I done kissed him!" "Who?" another asked. "The Martin Luther King!" she exclaimed. "I done kissed the Martin Luther King!"

Another woman kissed him, too, and said, "God will keep His arms around you." "Yes," King replied. "Trust in Him." Oh, she could not believe it was him. She had first heard his name when whites had bombed his home in Montgomery, and she had loved to hear his name and look at his picture ever since. "I trust in God," she sighed, "and I'll hug the Martin Luther King anytime I see him. They can't bother me 'bout huggin' the Martin Luther King."

Young asked the old folk, "Now are you people gonna register to vote? We're not just marchin' here for fun."

"Yes, sir," they said, nodding at him and King. "Yes, sir." (And they did too: inspired by the Martin Luther King, fifty people from Trickem went to Hayneville, to the old jail there that housed the registrar's office, and sought their voting rights.)

On the move again, King saw an old black man limping with a cane across a field, heading this way. When he got to the highway, he reached for a hand among the marchers. "Did you ever see Dr. Martin Luther King?" asked one. "No, sir," said the old man. "Well, you're shaking hands with him now," the marcher said. "Oh, Lordy!" cried the old man. "I just wanted to walk one mile with y'all," he told King. He ended up walking all the way to the next campsite. "I been called a little boy long enough, don't you think?"

In camp, King rubbed a sore foot and spoke to reporters about the old Communist charge. On the line of march, the column had passed a large billboard with a picture purportedly showing King at a "Communist training school." Actually it was a photograph of King at the Highlander Folk School at Monteagle, Tennessee, originally a training center for union organizers and later a meeting ground for interracial civil-rights groups. Rosa Parks had visited the school and left with renewed hopes for the future of integration; Harris Wofford had once taken an Indian leader there; and King, Eleanor Roosevelt, and others had spoken at the school on the occasion of its twenty-fifth anniversary. An undercover agent for Georgia segregationists had taken the

photograph, and the Klan and White Citizens' Councils had distributed copies across the South, claiming that they showed him associating
with "known Communists." Segregationists branded Highlander as a
"Communist training school," and the state of Tennessee eventually
closed and confiscated it. King told the reporters about his single appearance at the school and laughed about the billboard: "If I was
trained there, it was mighty short training." He scoffed at accusations
that the march was infested with Reds. "There are as many Communists in the Civil Rights movement," he said, "as there are Eskimos in
Florida."

After a doctor treated his foot, King headed back to Selma with
Coretta and Lee, ignoring a report of yet another plot to assassinate
him. The next day, he flew off for an important speaking engagement
in Cleveland; he would rejoin the marchers outside of Montgomery.
Inevitably, some people chastised him for taking off like that. But
Hosea Williams stoutly defended him. "It isn't the President's job to
be in the sun and the mud all the time. His job was to lead us out of
Selma—that was the most dangerous part. Then he's gone, trying to
raise our budget around the country. He is telling our story. That's the
job of the President."

While King was away, the Alabama legislature charged by a unan-
imous vote that the marchers were conducting wild interracial sex or-
gies at their camps, were everywhere exposing themselves, kissing, and
copulating. "All these segregationists can think of is fornication," said
one black marcher, "and that is why there are so many shades of
Negroes." Said another: "These white folks must think we are super-
men, to be able to march all day in that weather [it had rained hard on
Tuesday], eat a little pork and beans, make whoopee all night, and
then get up the next morning and march all day again."

On Wednesday, as the weary marchers neared the outskirts of
Montgomery, the Kings, Abernathys, and hundreds of others joined
them for a triumphal entry into the Alabama capital. "We have a new
song to sing tomorrow," King told them. "We *have* overcome." James
Letherer hobbled in the lead now, his underarms rubbed raw and his
face etched in pain. Flanking him were two flag bearers—one black
and one white—and a young Negro man from New York who played
"Yankee Doodle" on a fife. Suddenly it began to rain in torrents. Marie Foster could see King striding ahead, the rain soaking him and
spattering two feet off the pavement. But the storm ended and the sun

reappeared, flooding the marchers with a burst of light. As they swept past a service station, a crewcut white man leaped from his car, raised his fist and started to shout something, only to stand speechless as the procession of clapping, singing, flag-waving people seemed to go on forever.

And so they were in Montgomery at last, come to petition George Wallace and remonstrate against racial oppression in Alabama. That night, in a muddy ballpark at St. Jude's Catholic complex, the movement put on a grand show to celebrate the occasion. Ten thousand people clapped and cheered as Harry Belafonte, Joan Baez, James Baldwin, Leonard Bernstein, and other celebrities put in appearances, and joined Peter, Paul, and Mary in singing Bob Dylan's "Blowin' in the Wind." Then King stood on the flood-lit platform with his pant-legs rolled up over knee-length hiking boots, and he led them in the movement's ritual chant.

"What do you want?" King cried.

"Freedom!"

"When do you want it?"

"*Now!*"

The next day, March 25, he led some 25,000 people on a climactic march through Montgomery, first capital and much-trumpeted cradle of the Confederacy. Protected by 800 federal troops, the procession moved by the Jefferson Davis Hotel, with a huge Rebel flag draped across its front, and Confederate Square where Negroes had been auctioned off in slavery days. King had passed these places many times while he lived in Montgomery. But the symbolism today was striking. At Confederate Square, the throng halted and sang:

> *Deep in my heart, I do believe*
> *We have overcome—today.*

Moving up Dexter Avenue now, King could make out his old church, as serene and dignified as always, and it conjured up a lot of memories. The march from Selma had brought the Negro protest movement full circle, since it had all begun with the Montgomery bus boycott a decade before.

Behind King tramped a horde of nonviolent warriors—the largest civil-rights demonstration in southern history. There were the three hundred Freedom Marchers in front, all clad in orange vests to distinguish them. There were hundreds of Negroes from the Montgomery area, one crying as she walked beside Wofford, "This is the day! This is the day!" There was a plump, bespectacled white woman who carried a basket in one arm and a sign in the other: "Here is one native Selman for freedom and justice." There were cavalcades of notables and groups of civil-rights people from as far away as Canada, all waving signs and banners overhead. Like a conquering army, they surged up Dexter Avenue to the white capitol building, with Confederate and Alabama flags snapping over its dome. The spectacle was as ironic as it was unprecedented, for it was up Dexter Avenue that Jefferson Davis's inaugural parade had moved, and it was in the portico of the capitol that Davis had taken his oath of office as President of the slave-based Confederacy. Now, more than a century later, Alabama Negroes— most of them descendants of slaves—stood massed at the same statehouse, singing "We Have Overcome," with state troopers and the statue of Davis himself looking on.

Wallace refused to come out of the capitol and receive the Negroes' petition, which demanded the right to vote and an end to police brutality. But they could see the governor peering out the blinds of his office. After Abernathy gave him an extravagant introduction, saying he was "conceived by God," King stood on the flatbed of a trailer, television cameras focusing in on his round, intense face. Behind him, the sun was setting on the capitol. "They told us we wouldn't get here," he cried over the loudspeaker. "Tell it, doctor!" Bernard Lee responded. "And there were those who said that we would get here only over their dead bodies, but all the world today knows that we are here and that we are standing before the forces of power in the state of Alabama saying, 'we ain't goin' let nobody turn us around.' " For ten years now, those forces have tried to nurture and defend evil, "but evil is choking to death in the dusty roads and streets of this state. So I stand before you today with the conviction that segregation is on its death bed, and the only thing uncertain about it is how costly the segregationists and Wallace will make the funeral."

Not since his "I Have a Dream" speech had King been so inspired as he was this day. His audience listened transfixed as his words rolled over the loudspeaker in rhythmic, hypnotic cadences, older Negroes shouting, "Speak! Speak!" "Yessir! Yessir!" "We are on the move now. Yes, we are on the move and no wave of racism can stop us." The burning of our churches, the bombing of our homes, the clubbing and killing of our clergymen and young people will not deter us. "Let us march on to the realization of the American dream." Let us march on the ballot boxes, march on poverty, march on segregated schools and segregated housing, march on until racism is annihilated and "the Wallaces of our nation tremble away in silence."

"My people, my people, listen! The battle is in our hands. . . . I must admit to you there are still some difficult days ahead. We are still in for a season for suffering." But we must struggle on with faith in the power of nonviolence. "Our aim must never be to defeat or humiliate the white man but to win his friendship and understanding. We must come to see that the end we seek is a society at peace with itself, a society that can live with its conscience. That will be a day not of the white man, not of the black man. That will be the day of man as man."

How long will it take? "I come to say to you this afternoon however difficult the moment, however frustrating the hour, it will not be long, because truth pressed to earth will rise again. How long? Not long, because no lie can live forever. How long? Not long, because you will reap what you sow. How long? Not long, because the arm of the moral universe is long but it bends toward justice. How long? Not long, cause mine eyes have seen the glory of the coming of the Lord, trampling out the vintage where the grapes of wrath are stored. He has loosed the fateful lightning of his terrible swift sword. His truth is marching on. . . . Oh, be swift, my soul, to answer Him. Be jubilant, my feet. Our God is marching on.

> *Glory, glory hallelujah!*
> *Glory, glory hallelujah!*
> *Glory, glory hallelujah!"*

AND SO THE GREAT MARCH was over. Even if Wallace had refused their petition, Alabama Negroes had exercised the right of all Americans to protest their grievances, demonstrating to Congress and all the country their determination to gain the ballot.° But alas, like so many others in the campaign, the great march itself ended in violence. That night, in a high-speed car chase on Highway 80, Klansmen shot and killed civil-rights volunteer Viola Liuzzo; and the movement had another martyr and the nation another convulsion of moral indignation. . Yet as *Ebony* correspondent Simeon Booker put it, the great march really ended with two deaths that Thursday—Mrs. Liuzzo's and Jim Crow's.

In truth, the Selma campaign was the movement's finest hour, was King's finest hour. Congress was well on the way toward enacting the voting-rights bill, which King expected to occur early in the summer. As Robert C. Maynard of the Washington *Post* said, King had proven himself "a master organizer of demonstrations" and had exposed "the plight of the Negro in the South as had never been done before. As television journalism zeroes in, Dr. King brought . . . Alabama dramatically into the homes of Americans. He made racism in the South come alive."

In early April, Stanley Levison wrote King about other significances of Selma. For the first time in the struggle, Levison pointed out, King had brought whites and Negroes from all over the land on an actual pilgrimage to the Deep South. Birmingham had been a milestone because hundreds of thousands of Americans had moved "from paper resolutions of support to sympathy meetings and marches in their own communities and in Washington. Selma brought them to the battleground itself." And the pilgrims were not merely the long-committed liberals who had come south before. "They were new forces from all faiths and classes," Levison observed. Moreover, King himself was "one of the exceptional figures who attained the heights of popular confidence and trust without having obligations to any political party or other dominant interests. Seldom has anyone in American history come up by this path." As a consequence, King had emerged as "the great moral force in the country today," an independent leader utterly devoid of the taint of power and political ambition.

For King, the overriding question now was "What do we do next?" As he often said, the movement had grown like ever-widening circles,

° Five days later, Wallace finally met with a biracial committee and promised to consider the Negroes' petition. Later an interracial group placed ten black-draped coffins on the marble walk outside the capitol; the coffins equaled the number of civil-rights murders in Alabama during the previous two years.

from attacks on segregated transportation and public facilities in single cities (as in Montgomery and Albany) to direct-action campaigns aimed at segregated public accommodations and Negro disfranchisement across the entire South (as in Birmingham, St. Augustine, and Selma). What, then, to do for an encore to Selma?

For six weeks, King and his staff debated that question, with James Bevel, adamant and animated, calling for more black-belt demonstrations and a national boycott of Alabama to fight racial oppression there. Hosea Williams, on the other hand, sponsored what became known as SCOPE—the Summer Community Organization and Political Education Project—which would utilize scores of northern college students in a mass voter-registration effort in the South, designed to implement the voting-rights measure once it became law. At first, King approved both projects. But when he proposed Bevel's boycott idea on NBC's *Meet the Press*, it provoked such widespread criticism from liberal sources that he quietly dropped it. Further demonstrations in the black belt seemed impossible, too, since Negroes there were too emotionally and physically drained to take to the streets again. And to what end? Finally King settled for SCOPE, and Williams went about assiduously recruiting more than 300 student volunteers to register southern Negroes and dramatize the need for federal registrars, thus maintaining pressure on Congress.

But King's heart was really not in any southern project. As the spring of 1965 passed, he had his eye increasingly on the teeming ghettoes of the North. In an SCLC board meeting in Baltimore, he talked about circuit riding into troublesome northern cities where riots had flamed up last summer. As yet he had no specific plan of action. But he told a fund-raising rally, "You can expect us in New York and in Philadelphia and Chicago and Detroit and Los Angeles. Selma, Alabama, isn't right but Baltimore isn't right either, and New York City isn't right."

At SCLC's board meeting, King solemnly advised the directors that Ralph Abernathy was to succeed him as president in the event of his death. "I can think of no man who is closer to me or who could better carry on than my longtime friend and associate," King said. A hush fell over the room. Privately, a lot of people were appalled at his choice, but nobody dared challenge him. Should King die, and that was a distinct possibility given the rash of assassination threats recently, many SCLC officials thought it would mean the end of the organization. Abernathy may have shared their fears. Put on the spot, he said quietly, "I do not look forward to filling the shoes of Martin Luther King. I don't think anybody can fill them."

With heightening concern over the ghettos, King visited New York and then set out for Boston, where the mayor proclaimed April 23 as "Martin Luther King Day," despite FBI attempts to block it. After touring the slums of Roxbury, King remarked that "some of the same things wrong with Alabama are wrong with Boston, Massachusetts." With a bitter fight raging there over racial busing, reporters solicited his opinion. "Busing would be an inconvenience," King replied. "But I think our white brothers should be willing to suffer a little inconvenience to rectify a social situation far greater than an inconvenience." In short, the real problem was not busing. It was the monstrous network of discriminatory practices that had created Negro slums and unequal Negro schools in the first place.

King's trip to Boston and other northern cities convinced him that his next stop must be the North. In a June retreat at Airlee House in Virginia, he assembled his staff and advisers and announced that the time had come to make theirs a truly national crusade for Negro freedom. While SCOPE would continue voter registration in the South, he and the rest of his staff would launch a People-to-People tour of various northern cities, looking for a target city—a northern Birmingham—in which to launch a direct-action campaign against slums.

King's decision to move north was not impulsive. He had worried for years about the miseries of the ghetto Negro—miseries which the elective franchise alone could not alleviate (northern Negroes already had the vote). Like other civil-rights leaders, though, King had believed that the North would benefit derivatively from the gains of the southern movement. But this, he confessed, was a miscalculation. "We forgot what we knew daily in the South—freedom is not given, it is won by struggle." While the southern Negro learned a new dignity and won his right to eat in restaurants, attend desegregated schools, and vote, Negro slum life continued unabated. Blacks who streamed into northern cities found themselves walled into ghettoes by racist real-estate practices and the federal housing authority itself, which encouraged neighborhoods of "the same social and racial classes." Within the ghettoes themselves, "avaricious and unprincipled" landlords exploited Negro tenants ruthlessly, charging them exorbitant rents but refusing to maintain minimum health and housing standards. Restricted to the ghettoes, Negroes had no choice but to attend squalid, overcrowded slum schools and suffered from an epidemic shortage of jobs. Trapped in a bewildering nightmare from which there was no escape, the ghetto Negro was seething with unarticulated fury and frustration. With summer at hand, King feared that the ghettoes were going to erupt in more riots, worse even than last year, unless he and SCLC could channel Negro unrest into nonviolent, well-orchestrated protests that would dramatize ghetto conditions and force indifferent city officials to pay attention. He recalled how many northern mayors had welcomed him to their cities and extolled the heroism of the southern Negro. But when he confronted them about the squalor of their own slums, they politely but firmly dropped the subject. All his experience insisted that voluntary reform was chimerical. "There was blindness, obtuseness, and rigidity that would only be altered by a dynamic movement," he contended.

Though Rustin, Wachtel, and other advisers had serious reservations about a northern campaign, King would not be dissuaded. He was no longer a spokesman and a combatant solely for the southern Negro. He was a national leader—an international leader—whose moral vision encompassed the entire country.

As King prepared his People-to-People tour of the North, he received several urgent communications from Al Raby of Chicago's Coordinating Council of Community Organizations, a coalition of thirty-four civil-rights, religious, and civic groups. As Raby explained it, CCCO was currently involved in a fierce struggle against de facto school segregation in Chicago and was trying desperately to oust Superintendent Benjamin C. Willis, whose policies had worsened school conditions in Chicago's slums. In June, CCCO had launched school boycotts and mass demonstrations to get rid of Willis. But the protest had begun to dwindle, and Raby, CCCO's "convener" and a teacher himself, wanted King to help revive it. "We came South to help you in Selma," Raby said, "now we need you here."

King came on July 23 and huddled with Raby, a lean, nervous man with a heavy mustache and balding head. Then King embarked on a whirlwind two-day tour of Chicago's ghettoes, speaking at one street corner after another in support of CCCO's battle with Willis. A reporter observed that he styled his message to suit his audience, "playing the role of a fourth generation Southern Baptist preacher at one street corner and alternating as a smooth, articulate national leader of the civil rights movement to the next group." The highlight of his visit came on July 26, when he led 30,000 people on a march to City Hall at the peak of rush-hour traffic. It was twenty times larger than the biggest demonstration thus far in Chicago, and Negro leaders there were euphoric. "Chicago will never be the same now that the people here see what he brought," said William C. Berry of the Chicago Urban League. Even Mayor Richard Daley, whose powerful political machine controlled the city, called the march a "tribute" to King and unctuously declared that "all right thinking Americans" shared his position on poverty and segregation.

Though suffering from bronchitis and extreme fatigue, King was happy with his trip, regarding it as "one of the most successful experiences" of his career. The giant march to City Hall seemed proof of his drawing power in the North, proof that he could get up a "dynamic movement" there to rival that in Selma and Birmingham. Before leaving for other northern cities, King told Raby that if the fight against Willis didn't go as planned, he would return to Chicago and "stay as long as possible to lend aid."

D URING HIS NORTHERN TRAVELS, King kept in close contact with civil-rights forces in Washington, which were lobbying to get the strongest possible voting bill enacted. The major dispute involved a poll-tax ban in state and local elections, which the administration ruled out of the bill on grounds that it would probably be declared unconstitutional. With bipartisan support, the measure passed in the Senate on May 26, in the House on July 9. At Howard University's commencement exercises, a triumphant Lyndon Johnson announced that the "next and more profound" goal in the civil-rights struggle was "not just legal equity but human equity—not just equality as a right and a theory but equality as a fact and a result." King loved that "magnificent" speech and sent Johnson a telegram saying so. At this time, their public friendship had never been warmer: they exchanged copies of their addresses, and King had access to the President by telephone.

There was only one thing about Johnson that troubled King: the administration was escalating American involvement in an embattled little Asian country named Vietnam.

In early August, Congress approved the final version of the voting-rights bill, and King flew to Washington for the presidential signing. The day before that celebrated event, he met with Johnson in the White House, and they talked about the remarkable achievements of 1965, not only the voting bill, but other measures in Johnson's heralded Great Society program—Medicare, federal aid to education, relief for preschool children from poor families, a large additional anti-poverty program—which were now on the books and which Johnson thought would improve the lives of all Americans, particularly Negroes. King believed that Johnson possessed "amazing sensitivity to the difficult problems that Negro Americans face in the stride toward freedom." In fact, the voting-rights bill marked the high point of the Johnson consensus on civil rights, with Rustin, Wilkins, Randolph, and other Negro leaders all acclaiming him the greatest President the American Negro ever had. And that, said Randolph, included Abraham Lincoln.

The next day, August 6, King and his colleagues gathered in the Rotunda of the Capitol for the voting-bill ceremonies. The President stood directly in front of a statue of Lincoln, facing radio microphones and television cameras. "Today is a triumph for freedom as huge as any victory that's ever been won on any battlefield," Johnson said. He recalled how the slaves had come here "in darkness and chains" three hundred years ago and asserted that "today we strike away the last major shackle of those fierce and ancient bonds." Then he strolled into the President's Room and signed the voting bill into law. It was the same room in which Lincoln had endorsed the first Confiscation Act in 1861, which had seized all slaves employed in the Confederate war effort. In the Cabinet Room afterward, Johnson met with King, Wilkins, Randolph, and Clarence Mitchell of the Leadership Conference on Civil Rights, which had lobbied for the bill on Capitol Hill. "There was a religiosity about the meeting," recalled a Johnson aide, "which was warm with emotion—a final celebration of an act so long desired and so long in achieving."

The act meant business. It outlawed all literacy tests and similar voting restrictions, empowered the Attorney General to supervise federal elections in seven southern states by appointing examiners to register those kept off the rolls, and instructed him "forthwith" to challenge the constitutionality of poll taxes in state and local elections in the four states where they were still law (the 24th Amendment had already prohibited the poll tax in federal elections). At the time, political analysts almost unanimously attributed the voting act to King's Selma campaign. Without the pressure from there, it would have taken years to extract such legislation from Congress. Now, thanks to his own political sagacity, his understanding of how nonviolent, direct-action protest could stimulate corrective federal legislation, King's long crusade to gain southern Negroes the right to vote, which had begun with the formation of SCLC in 1957, was about to be realized.

That summer, Washington moved swiftly and forcefully to implement the new law, filing suits against all southern poll-tax statutes and dispatching federal registrars to counties in Alabama, Louisiana, and Mississippi with the stiffest barriers to Negro voting. Once federal examiners were supervising voter registration in all troublesome areas in Dixie, Negroes were able to get on the rolls and vote by the hundreds of thousands, forever altering the pattern of southern politics. In Alabama, where the number of registered Negroes rose by 150 percent in three years, there were incredible spectacles: George Wallace himself courting the Negro vote. . . . Al Lingo, in an unsuccessful bid for Jefferson County sheriff, allowing himself to be photographed as he contributed money to an SCLC collection plate. . . . Sheriff Jim Clark, his NEVER button gone now, throwing a barbecue for Selma's Negro voters in a bitter re-election campaign, only to lose to Wilson Baker, who enjoyed solid black support. As King had predicted, Alabama Negroes, once they gained the ballot, voted the Lingos and Clarks right out of office.

In truth, the impact of King's campaign was nowhere more evident than in Selma, the old black-belt town where it had started. Within a few years the city's racial caste system was dead—the obstacles to Negro voting gone, the city council and the police force both racially mixed, the schools and public accommodations all desegregated. While racial prejudice continued to infect the white community ("we still need a few more funerals," Mrs. Jackson said), some upper-class whites considered it stylish to invite prominent Negroes to their social gatherings. And Negroes and white moderates could now befriend one another without fear of reprisals. In time, Mrs. Jackson found that she and a white team teacher, a Mississippi woman, could

tease and talk to each other without worrying about a color barrier—
something that would have been impossible before 1965.

Selma Negroes rejoiced at the tremendous changes the movement
had brought about. They spoke with unabashed reverence for "Dr.
King," never forgetting the pensive way he had looked at them, his
hands clasped before his face, during those wondrous mass meetings in
Brown Chapel. "I just love that man," Marie Foster would say, her
voice trailing off as she searched for words to describe all he meant to
her. When out-of-town visitors would call, she would bring out a box
and exhibit a pair of shoes. Across the box she had written: "Shoes that
carried me through 50 mile trek from Selma to Montgomery, Ala.
1965. We walked for freedom, that we might have the right to vote."

For her and the others who participated, the movement of 1965
became the central event of their lives, a time of self-liberation when
they stood and marched to glory with Martin Luther King. Yes, they
were surprised at themselves, proud of the strength they had displayed
in confronting the state of Alabama, happy indeed, as Marie Foster
said, to be "a new Negro in a new South—a Negro who is no longer
afraid."

And that perhaps was King's greatest gift to his long-suffering people in Dixie: he taught them how to confront those who oppressed
them, how to take pride in their race and their history, how to demand and win their constitutional rights as American citizens. He
helped them "destroy barriers of fear and insecurity that had been
hundreds of years in the making," said a young Negro leader. "He
made it possible for them to believe they *could* overcome." And the
powerful civil-rights legislation generated by his tramping soldiers
eventually ended statutory racism in the South, enabling Negroes
there to realize at least the political and social promise of Lincoln's
Emancipation Proclamation.

King, though, had no illusion that legislation alone would end racism itself, convert his country into a "symphony of brotherhood," and
restore the beloved community he still dreamed of. But he had learned
that legislation was indispensable in making that community possible.
"It may be true that you cannot legislate integration," he had said in
Boston, "but you can legislate desegregation. It may be true that you
cannot legislate morality, but behavior can be regulated. It may be
true that the law cannot make a man love me, but it can restrain him
from lynching me." Because legislation and court orders could pro-

scribe a man from killing, excluding, and oppressing him with impunity, they were "of inestimable value" in bringing about a desegregated society. But as he said on another occasion, "desegregation is only a partial, though necessary, step toward the final goal which we seek to realize, genuine inter-group and interpersonal living." And here laws and vigorous law enforcement were not much help. While they could alter the habits of men, King believed, they could not eliminate "fears, prejudice, pride, and irrationality, which are barriers to a truly integrated society. These dark and demonic responses will be removed only as men are possesed by the invisible, inner law which etches on their hearts the conviction that all men are brothers and that love is mankind's most potent weapon for personal and social transformation. True integration will be achieved by true neighbors who are willingly obedient to unenforceable obligations."

A T THE TIME JOHNSON SIGNED the voting-rights bill, King was increasingly apprehensive about administration policies in Vietnam. For more than twenty years, war had racked that distant Asian land, as Communist forces under Ho Chi Minh battled to liberate their country, first from the French, then from the United States. After France withdrew in 1955, the U.S. moved in, ignored an international agreement in Geneva which called for free elections, and installed a repressive, anti-Communist regime in South Vietnam, supplying it with money, weapons, and military advisers. From the outset, American policy makers viewed Ho Chi Minh's government in North Vietnam as part of a world Communist conspiracy directed by Moscow and Peking: if Communism was not halted in Vietnam, they feared, then all Asia would ultimately succumb. American intervention, of course, aroused Ho Chi Minh, who rushed help to nationalist guerrillas in South Vietnam and set out to unite all of Vietnam under his leadership. With civil war raging across South Vietnam, the United States stepped up its flow of military aid to Saigon. Under Kennedy, the number of American advisers rose to 23,000, but Kennedy became disillusioned with American involvement in Vietnam and actually devised a disengagement plan before he was assassinated. Johnson, however, nullified the plan and continued American assistance to South Vietnam, though he scarcely mentioned the war in his first State of the Union message. In the Gulf of Tonkin Resolution in August, 1964, Congress did empower the President to use armed force against "Communist aggression" in Vietnam, but Johnson repeatedly vowed, "We are not going to send American boys nine or ten thousand miles away from home to do what Asian boys ought to be doing for themselves."

But over the winter all that changed. In November and December, South Vietnamese guerrillas of the National Liberation Front (or Vietcong) killed seven U.S. advisers and wounded more than a hundred others in mortar and bomb attacks, and Johnson got mad. He wasn't going to let them shoot our boys out there, fire on our flag. He talked obsessively about Communist "aggression" in Vietnam, about Munich and the lesson of appeasement, about how his enemies would call him "a coward," "an unmanly man," a "Weakling!" if he let Ho Chi Minh run through the streets of Saigon. He couldn't depend on the United Nations to act—"It couldn't pour piss out of a boot if the instructions were printed on the heel." In February, 1965, with the Vietcong pounding American outposts at Pleiku and Quinhon, the administration became convinced that the coup-plagued Saigon government was about to collapse and that the United States had to do something drastic or South Vietnam would be lost and American international prestige and and influence severely damaged. Accordingly, Johnson moved to Americanize the war and sent waves of U.S. warplanes roaring over North Vietnam in a sustained bombing attack called Operation Rolling Thunder. In March he ordered the first American combat troops into South Vietnam, and 3,200 marines waded ashore near Da Nang.

The next month Johnson's propensity for deviousness and concealment began to show. He announced that the United States was ready for "unconditional discussions" with an eye toward a negotiated peace, but then added a condition—the hated Vietcong could not participate, which guaranteed that Hanoi would spurn his offer. The truth was that Johnson and his planners were now sold on a military solution: American firepower would blast the Vietnamese to the peace table and save the South (or what was left of it) for freedom.

The Americanization of the war took place with such stealth that people at home were hardly aware of the change. As David Halberstam later wrote, U.S. decision makers "inched across the Rubicon without even admitting it," and the task of their press secretaries was "to misinform the public." The biggest misinformers were Johnson and his spokesmen, who lied about costs (which were staggering), casualties, victories, and buildups. By June, more than 75,000 American soldiers were in Vietnam, and combat troops were fighting Vietcong and North Vietnamese regulars in an Asian land war Johnson had sworn to avoid. When the U.S. commander in Vietnam clamored for 200,000 men, the President resolved to "meet his demands." By August, troops were pouring in, and the war reeled out of control as each American escalation stiffened Vietcong and North Vietnamese resistance, which in turn led to more American escalation. In the eyes of the administration and the Pentagon, it was unthinkable that America's awesome military power could fail to crush tiny North Vietnam and the pajama-clad Vietcong.

The events in Vietnam haunted King through the summer. He could not bear to see his country muscling its way into the internal affairs of another nation, bombing and shooting people—and brown-skinned people at that—under the deluded excuse of stopping Communism. When was America ever going to understand the nationalistic fervor sweeping the colored people of the world, including the Vietnamese? When was she ever going to get on the right side of the revolutionary spirit of the age? He hated war anyway, had denounced "the madness of militarism" since Montgomery days, and had long hoped that once he and SCLC had broken down Dixie's racial barriers, they could apply creative nonviolence to the world theater. And now that moment had arrived. "I'm not going to sit by and see the war escalate without saying something about it," he told his SCLC followers. "It is worthless to talk about integrating if there is no world to integrate in. The war in Vietnam must be stopped."

His aides and advisers were deeply divided over his speaking out. Even pacifist Bayard Rustin urged caution. King and Johnson were on the best of terms now, and criticism of the war might alienate the President and Congress, too. The country was extremely hawkish over the war—Congress rushed through huge supplementary military appropriations with scarcely a dissent—and Levison feared that SCLC would lose its donors and slide into bankruptcy. The northern crusade against slums and poverty would have to be abandoned.

But King would not be restrained. Racial injustice, poverty, and the Vietnam War were all "inextricably bound together," he asserted, and in August he made his stand. On the platform, in press conferences, and on a CBS television show, he urged the United States to stop bombing North Vietnam and "make an unequivocal and unambiguous statement" that she was willing to negotiate with Hanoi and the National Liberation Front. He warned that if the United States continued to escalate the war, it could imperil "the whole of mankind." He even offered to mediate himself—was he not a Nobel laureate for peace?—and try to bring the United States, Russia, China, and the Vietnamese to the conference table.

Reactions were swift and hostile. "Is he casting about for a role in Vietnam because the civil rights struggle is no longer adequate to his own estimate of his talents?" chided columnist Max Freedman. Roy Wilkins and Whitney Young, courting the President's favor, begged King to be quiet about Vietnam lest he wreck the Johnson consensus on civil rights. And the President himself was furious—who in the hell did King think he was?—and moved behind the scenes to shut him up. "They told me I wasn't an expert in foreign affairs," King recalled of the warnings he received from the administration, "and they were all experts. I knew only civil rights and should stick to that."

That attitude rankled King. He had thought that Johnson respected him and welcomed his views even if they challenged administration policy. Clearly that was not the case. Given all that he had done for the Negro, the President expected King to agree with his war policy and regarded him as an ingrate when he did not. King was only now beginning to understand Johnson's "ego thing."

During the second week of August, as King was taking his stand on Vietnam, Al Raby met with him in Birmingham and implored him to return to Chicago and conduct demonstrations against segregated housing as well as segregated schools. Since King's visit, the Chicago movement had flagged so badly that Raby was down to leading "nine people and a dog." He reminded King of his promise to come back and "lend a hand."

King was still looking for a target city for a northern direct-action campaign, and he agreed to give Raby's request careful and prayerful consideration. Then he flew to Puerto Rico for a religious convention and a little rest. While he was there, the Watts ghetto of Los Angeles exploded in the worst race riot in American history. Negroes there burned and looted stores for six days before police and California guardsmen could quell the disturbances. Thirty-four people had been killed, 900 injured, some 3,500 arrested, $46 million worth of property destroyed, and incalculable harm done to the civil-rights movement. White America recoiled in revulsion, contending that ghetto Negroes were too lawless to merit help or sympathy. "Everything seemed to collapse," Ramsey Clark moaned of the white backlash. "The days of 'We Shall Overcome' were over."

King was devastated by the news. He had warned America that something like Watts was going to happen, that time bombs were ticking away in her neglected cities. He flew to Los Angeles with Rustin and Bernard Lee and walked the streets of Watts, pleading with residents to understand that violence and rioting were not the answer to their miseries. All around him were fire-gutted stores and smoldering shops, shabby bars and pool halls, boarded-up doors and windows and garbage-strewn alleys. People he spoke to were skeptical and angry; some even heckled him. When a group of youngsters announced that "we won," King was stunned. "How can you say you won when thirty-four Negroes are dead, your community is destroyed, and whites are using the riots as an excuse for inaction?" "We won," explained an unemployed young man, "because we made the whole world pay attention to us."

It was a painful lesson for King. He called rioting "the language of the unheard," a desperate and suicidal cry of one "who is so fed up with the powerlessness of his cave existence that he asserts that he would rather be dead than ignored." It was no accident, he and Rustin noted, that the rioting moved in almost a direct path toward City Hall. It was significant, too, that the rioters had assaulted stores notorious for high prices and hostile attitudes; they had spared Negro-owned establishments, white stores that gave credit to Negroes, and nearly all public facilities like schools and libraries. In looting pawn shops, groceries, liquor and department stores, the rioters took things that "all the dinning affluence of Los Angeles had never given them," Rustin observed.

Which was what he and King tried to tell Mayor Sam Yorty and

Police Chief William Parker. The riot broke out, they explained, because Watts was four times as congested as the rest of Los Angeles, because 30 percent of Watts's working-age Negroes had no jobs, because the police treated every Negro as a criminal merely because he was a Negro, because California voters only last year had rescinded the state's fair-housing law, which convinced Watts's Negroes that their own city and state were reinforcing racial barriers against them ... because nobody in city hall seemed to care ... because over Watts hung a miasma of rage and despair. . . .

But Yorty and Parker were not impressed. Los Angeles had no racial prejudice, they said. As for the housing-law vote, "That's no indication of prejudice. That's personal choice." When Rustin asked the police chief why he had referred to rioters as "monkeys" and "the criminal element," Parker huffed that this was the only language that Negroes understood.

King left Los Angeles certain of Parker's "blind intransigence and ignorance of the social forces involved." All those rioters had not been criminals: more than a third of those taken into custody had never been arrested before and most of the others had only minor police records. King complained that this city, this "luminous symbol of luxurious living for whites," was inviting a holocaust if it did not wake up to the wretched conditions that had produced the rioting. But Los Angeles did not wake up. An official report on Watts—the McCone Report—devoted not a single word to the social and economic ills that plagued Watts, instead accepting Parker's contention that "criminals" were behind the outbreak and citing him for exemplary service to "this entire community." At the same time, President Johnson also denounced urban violence like that in Watts, and powerful voices on Capitol Hill chorused that rioting was the Negroes' answer to all that Congress had done for them.

All this convinced King that he must get on with his northern crusade without delay. He must make the country tend to its smoldering cities before they all went up in flames. Negroes in Los Angeles had invited him to come there, but King knew where he was going now. Back in Atlanta, he informed his staff they they were heading for Chicago. Here they would mount their northern direct-action campaign. Here they would spotlight the myriad slum conditions—substandard housing and unequal job opportunities, racist real-estate practices, police brutality, de facto school segregation—that fomented riots. Of all the cities he had considered, only Chicago had a strong Negro leadership structure already functioning and a local movement already under way. He had "great faith" in Raby and CCCO and thought an effective campaign could be built around them. Moreover, he considered Chicago the closest northern equivalent to Birmingham. It was the most "ghettoized" city in America, the symbol and capital of segregation in the North. If he and SCLC could solve northern problems here, King felt, they could solve them anywhere.

He intended to give Chicago itself a last chance—an alternative to Watts. The city was due for a major eruption; yet if he could produce a nonviolent movement in Chicago, he sincerely believed that he could reduce the possibilities of riots by 80 percent.

But several of his aides and advisers raised objections. Hosea Williams, trying to salvage SCOPE, insisted that SCLC ought to stay home in the South and register Negroes under the new voting law. "We need to clean up at home," argued Williams and his SCOPE staff. "Chicago is not our turf."

Bayard Rustin agreed. He was a New Yorker; he knew what King would be up against in a big northern city like Chicago: a complex, interlocking chain of realtor interests, City Hall, banks, and other businesses that was far different from Selma and Birmingham. Worse, he would be taking on Mayor Daley, whose sophisticated machine had inroads in the black community itself. Was King prepared to fight Daley himself? Was he ready to battle Daley's Negroes? "You won't beat Daley on his home ground," Rustin warned, "and you'll come away with nothing meaningful for all your efforts."

King realized that Chicago would be tough—the toughest challenge he had ever faced. But he was not going to stay away because the odds were against him. He was not going to surrender to "the paralysis of analysis." No, he felt that he had "divine guidance," felt that God was calling him to work in the valleys of Chicago. The poor needed him there; he had to go. God wanted him to go.

King's other staffers were spellbound. "Well, Bayard," said Andrew Young, "Martin's been called by God to go to Chicago and therefore he should go." With planning and effort, Young thought SCLC could raise a nonviolent army of 100,000 people in Chicago, whose black population, numbering almost a million, was larger than that in some individual southern states. Think what an army of 100,000 could accomplish if it conducted a week-long vigil in the

"Spaghetti Bowl" interchange of Chicago's expressway system. For Young, it boggled the imagination.

But Rustin was still skeptical. When King acted on inspiration, as he had in Albany, he was usually wrong. Rustin feared "a fiasco."

King had made up his mind, though, and that was that. In early September, he called Raby to Atlanta to discuss the goals of the campaign. When Raby reported back to Chicago, the CCCO people were ecstatic—they thought the messiah was coming. King meanwhile dispatched an advance team under James Bevel to lay the groundwork for battle, to hold workshops on nonviolence and the causes of slums. King planned to scale down SCOPE and eventually augment his forces in Chicago to two hundred field workers—the largest of any previous campaign. In announcing the Chicago project, which he hoped would be operational by the spring or early summer of 1966, King contended that poverty was the fundamental problem of Negroes in this country. "The nonviolent movement must be as much directed against the violence of poverty, which destroys the souls of people, as against the violence of segregation." He pronounced Chicago "an experiment in faith" and "the test case for the SCLC and for the freedom movement in the North." He was going there with "some fear and trembling," because the difficulties were vastly more complex and his enemies craftier than any he had faced in Selma or Birmingham. "In the North we will not be aided as much by the brutality of our opponents," he added. "Egypt still exists in Chicago but the Pharaohs are more sophisticated and subtle."

In EARLY SEPTEMBER, THE PRESIDENT asked King to talk with United Nations Ambassador Arthur Goldberg about the situation in Vietnam. On September 10, in the company of Rustin, Wachtel, and Young, King conferred with Goldberg in New York and maintained his position that there must be a negotiated settlement that included the Vietcong. Goldberg looked at Wachtel with a pained expression, as if to say, "Can't you do something with this man?" The ambassador assured King that the United States was committed to peace in Vietnam and that he could expect a resolution of the war in the near future.

But King was far from convinced. "We weren't sure that Goldberg even believed what he was saying," Young recalled.

In a press conference afterward, King took another controversial stance: he asserted that the United States must "seriously consider" reversing its policy toward the People's Republic of China. He meant that Communist China should not only be admitted into the United Nations—something the United States bitterly opposed—but be included in any peace negotiations. The leading power in Asia and the largest country in the world, Communist China was crucial to any lasting solution in Vietnam. King's remarks, Young said, started "the holocaust," as Democratic and labor bosses howled in protest. In the fall of 1965, King's stand on Vietnam was unpopular enough; his views on Communist China were heresy. Wachtel claimed that several New York businessmen who had pledged large sums of money to King and SCLC canceled them in a furor. And the pressure from the White House and the conservative Negro leadership was unrelenting for him to stay "in his own depth" and stick to civil rights.

But King had his defenders too. Coretta had been active in the Women's International League for Peace and Freedom and had even addressed an antiwar rally that year in California, and she urged her husband to hold his ground on the war, as did Harold DeWolf and pacifist A. J. Muste, whom King had criticized back in Crozer days. Dr. Benjamin Spock, a popular pediatrician and a spokesman for an incipient antiwar movement, met King on an airplane that autumn and urged him to make a world tour for peace and then return to unite the antiwar forces in a national crusade. Spock regarded King as "the most important symbol for peace in this country" and the one personality around whom people would rally.

King shared Spock's feelings about the war. But he couldn't do everything. He couldn't go on a world tour and lead a national peace movement at the same time that he was organizing the Chicago operation and battling the slums of the North. Still, Vietnam continued to torment him. By the end of 1965, some 185,000 American soldiers—a disproportionate number of them Negroes—were fighting in that fire-scarred land; and the administration was soon talking about escalating U.S. forces to 450,000 men. Despite Goldberg's claims, peace was obviously not close at hand. And the rising civilian casualties were intolerable. "Now in the confrontation of the big powers occurring in our country," a Vietnamese Buddhist monk wrote King, "hundreds and perhaps thousands of Vietnamese peasants and children lose their lives every day, and our land is unmercifully and tragically torn by a war which is already twenty years old. I am sure that since you have been engaged in one of the hardest struggles for equality and human rights, you are among those who understand fully, and who share with all their hearts, the indescribable suffering of the Vietnamese people. The world's greatest humanists would not remain silent. You yourself cannot remain silent. . . . Recently a young Buddhist monk named Thich Giac Thanh burned himself to call the attention of the world to the suffering endured by the Vietnamese, the suffering caused by this unnecessary war—and you know that war is never necessary. . . . Nobody here wants the war. What is the war for, then? And whose is the war?"

One day in early 1966, King sat in a parked car with Harold DeWolf, several blocks from SCLC headquarters in Atlanta. King was going through spiritual turmoil about how strongly he should oppose the war. He had answered his pro-war critics in a recent column for the Chicago *Defender*, a Negro newspaper: "The Negro must not allow himself to become a victim of the self-serving philosophy of those who manufacture war that the survival of the world is the white man's business alone." But how far could he go at this time in making the war a major issue? According to Young, he finally elected to restrict his antiwar criticism to carefully chosen thrusts, trying to find some middle ground between the majority of civil-rights leaders who supported Johnson and the out-and-out antiwar advocates, some of whom Young viewed as "kooks." But one of King's former staffers, a young white named Charles Fager who had served with him in Selma, lamented King's perilous and tortuous middle course on Vietnam. In an article published in the *Christian Century*, which was put out in Chicago, Fager contended that "Vietnam is perhaps the gravest challenge of Dr. King's career." "When he accepted the Nobel peace prize he baptized all races into his congregation and confirmed the world as the battleground for his gospel of nonviolence and reconciliation. He is no longer—and probably never can be—a spokesman for just an American Negro minority." In his struggle with himself over Vietnam, Fager contended, King must answer not only to all races in the world, but to history. If in his agony he failed to lead, would history forgive him?

IT WAS A DISPIRITING WINTER for King. The Chicago campaign was running behind schedule, and he planned to move there in mid-January to take personal charge of operations. Coretta would remain in Atlanta, where Yoki and Marty were now enrolled in a desegregated public school—one of the best in Atlanta; Coretta had seen to that. Just before he left for Chicago, the Kings attended a school program on "Music That Made America Great." The children—Yoki and Marty included—sang melodies of various immigrant groups, and the Kings looked on with approving smiles, certain that the chorus would conclude with a Negro spiritual, the most original of all American music. Instead, the children ended with "Dixie," the hymn to the Old South. As the Kings rose to go, they looked at one another in amazement and indignation that not a single Negro song had been on the program. "I wept within that night," King wrote later. "I wept for my children, who, through daily miseducation, are taught that the Negro is an irrelevant entity in American society; I wept for all the white parents and teachers who are forced to overlook the fact that the wealth of cultural and technological progress in America is a result of the commonwealth of inpouring contributions."

PART EIGHT

THE ROAD
TO JERICHO

In January, 1966, a newsman observed, King "hit Chicago in a swirl of jet smoke and under a screen of secrecy." He met in strategy sessions with CCCO and SCLC—now combined into the Chicago Freedom Movement—and emerged after two days to sound the trumpets of battle. "Our primary objective will be to bring about the unconditional surrender of forces dedicated to the creation and maintenance of slums," he told reporters—and Chicago's city leaders beyond. The Chicago movement would press the political power structure to "find imaginative programs to overcome the problem." King's order of operations, to unfold in stages, called for block-by-block canvassing of black neighborhoods to generate grassroots support (which was already under way), followed by the formation of a "Slum Union" to bargain with absentee slumlords and organize strikes and boycotts if necessary to improve conditions. Around May 1, the campaign would build into mass direct action in the form of southern-style street demonstrations, designed to expose and protest "the slow, stifling death of a kind of concentration camp life" in the ghetto. In the process, the movement would demonstrate to slum dwellers that all was not hopeless, that they could "do something about their problems." The aim of the movement, King went on, was to secure the blessings of America for Negroes, in housing and educational and social opportunities. But its overall goal was "to create the beloved community," which required a qualitative change in our souls and a quantitative change in our lives. "It will be done by rejecting the racism, materialism and violence that has characterized Western civilization and especially by working toward a world of brotherhood, cooperation and peace."

King's entry into Chicago generated tremendous media interest— and plenty of skepticism too. "Can the trumpet tactics of the South work in the North?" more than one reporter wondered. "The white walls of the North may be trumpet-proof." Mayor Daley pointed out that Chicago already had a slum-clearance program and invited King to join in if he wanted to help. But members of Daley's staff were furious. "What the hell is he doing here anyway?" they asked. "Does he think we don't care about slums? Why Chicago, instead of Atlanta or Harlem? King has no knowledge of Chicago."

On January 26 King inspired Chicago Negroes by moving into a flat on the West side, where he planned to stay for the duration of the campaign, commuting back to Atlanta once a week or so. The flat was on the third floor of a faded brick building on South Hamlin Street in North Lawndale, a dismal Negro section known as "Slumdale." Some two hundred slum dwellers cheered when King arrived at the tenement with Coretta, who had come up from Atlanta to help him get settled. On the sidewalk, SCLC staffers played guitars and serenaded King with freedom songs, which earned him a new nickname, "The Pied Piper of Hamlin Avenue." "You can't really get close to the poor without living and being here with them," King explained to a bevy of reporters and photographers clambering into the tenement after him. The front door was unlocked and open, and "the smell of urine was overpowering," Coretta said, since drunks came in from the street and relieved themselves in the hallway. The group climbed three flights of stairs and entered what Coretta described as "a railroad flat," with a dingy front sitting room and two bedrooms, a kitchen, and a bath all joined like cars on a train. King learned that his white absentee landlords, when they found out who their new tenant was, had dispatched an eight-man crew to scrub and repair the place. This convinced the Chicago *Sun-Times* that King could end the slums by moving to successive tenements around the city and forcing embarrassed landlords to clean them up. But Coretta was not impressed with the renovations in her husband's flat. Checking around, she found that the rickety refrigerator was broken down and that the heaters hardly worked either. It was bitter cold outside—and winter inside, too. For this cramped, unfurnished place, King paid $90 a month, not counting utilities. Later he found out that this was the usual rent for a four-room ghetto apartment. He also discovered that in the all-white suburbs of Gage Park, South Deering, and Belmont-Cragin, renters paid an average of less than $80 a month for five-and-a-half-room modern apartments.

That night, King held a "hearing" in a local church, and five hundred Slumdale residents crowded into the sanctuary to recite the harsh facts of their lives. King stood at the pulpit, eyes shining, as a large woman in a black sweater said to him: "I get down and scrub all day. I'm tired of giving people my money. Just filled to the brim. Tired of being walked over. Tired of being mistreated. Thank God you came here, Rev. King. My house, just now the kitchen is falling in. I'm not going to pay no rent where there are rats and nobody going to throw me out." Her remark elicited a wave of bitter laughter from the others.

King addressed them with great emotion. "Many things you said tonight I heard in the same kind of session out in Watts right after the riots." He looked at the reporters jotting down his words. "I say to the power structure in Chicago that the same problems that existed, and still exist, in Watts, exist in Chicago today, and if something isn't done in a hurry, we can see a darker night of social disruption." He announced a special all-day workshop on how to fight slums. "We're going to organize," he said, "to make Chicago a model city. Remember, living in a slum is robbery. It's robbery of dignity, and the right to participate creatively in the political process. It's wrong to live with rats."

The next day, King toured Lawndale with several aides and six members of a youth gang who had offered to show him around. The temperature hovered around zero, and their conversation produced puffs of vapor as they walked along the sidewalk, past grimy buildings with "END SLUMS" scrawled on their walls in white chalk and endless rows of tenements, gray and prisonlike in the cold. "This is truly an island of poverty in the midst of an ocean of plenty," King would say. Chicago had one of the highest per-capita incomes of any city in the world, but you would never know it from walking through Lawndale. Everywhere children were playing in the streets. "Hey, are you Dr. King?" they would ask—and grin happily when he took the time to talk with them. King was distressed at how skimpily they were dressed in the bitter Chicago wind. The mucus in the corners of their eyes reminded him that flu shots and vitamins cost too much for them. He ruminated on how the "runny noses" of Slumdale were graphic symbols of the medical neglect in this, the richest nation in the world.

In the days that followed, King observed the ebb and flow of daily slum life. And he wrote and spoke caustically about the conditions he witnessed: "I am appalled that some people feel that the civil rights struggle is over because we have a 1964 civil rights bill with ten titles and a voting rights bill. Over and over again people ask, What else do you want? They feel that everything is all right. Well, let them look around at our big cities." Let them look around Chicago, where a system of "internal colonialism" flourished in the slums "not unlike the exploitation of the Congo by Belgium." The system imprisoned 97 percent of Chicago's 837,000 Negroes in neighborhoods so segregated that some schoolchildren thought Negroes the majority race in America. The system not only charged Negroes inflated rents for substandard housing, King said, but conspired to maintain inferior schools that prepared blacks only for unskilled jobs and thus perpetuated Negro inferiority. Though Chicago's 2.3 percent unemployment rate was one of the lowest in America, the ghettoes were suffering "a major depression," as King put it, with 13 percent of the work force out of jobs. If the entire country were afflicted with such an unemployment rate, white leaders would call it an economic catastrophe. In ghetto stores, moreover, consumer goods ran from 10 to 20 percent higher than in suburban white stores, even though they often belonged to the same chain. The Chicago Urban League dubbed this a "color tax"— the price Negroes had to pay for living in the slums. How could such discrimination be sustained? King asked. Because many ghetto residents had no cars and couldn't get out to shop anywhere else. It became a vicious circle. First, you couldn't get a job because you had a poor education. So you had to go on welfare, which in Chicago meant that you couldn't own property, not even a car. So you were condemned to buy at neighborhood stores, whose owners exploited you mercilessly on the assumption that you were inferior anyway because you didn't work and were on welfare. If the Negro ever made it through this maze of handicaps and set foot outside the jungle of poverty and exploitation, realtors would not sell him a house in white neighborhoods even if he had the money. And he had no recourse in the courts, which only enforced the entire system of exploitation.

As for the cops, King found that the most grievous complaint against them was not police brutality, which was real enough, but their indifference to ghetto crime. Organized crime thrived in slum sanctuaries, operating numbers, narcotics, and prostitution rackets with little or no police interference. Because crime and poverty were omnipresent, with glittering white opulence only a few steps away, many ghetto dwellers surrendered to self-destructiveness, turning to alcohol, drugs, gang warfare, and the cynical nihilism of black separatist ideologies.

Oh, King was mad at what he saw in Chicago. He was going to bring about the unconditional surrender of the slum system if it was the last thing he did. He was going to organize slum dwellers and mount demonstrations "on a scale so vast that they would dwarf some of the biggest demonstrations we have seen in the history of the movement." He set about wooing influential white religious leaders like Archbishop John P. Cody of Chicago, who seemed to King in substantial agreement with his goals. (The FBI, however, briefed Cody about King and reported that the archbishop was "not impressed" with him, thought he had "a glib tongue," and said he intended to be "most circumspect" in his dealings with the Negro leader.) King hurried about Negro neighborhoods enlisting nearly all the city's Negro clergy in his crusade and urging people to join his Slum Union because "together we can do much more than we can divided and unorganized." The idea behind the union was to build a permanent structure that would remain in Chicago once SCLC moved on. This "organizational undergirding," King believed, would enable Chicago Negroes "to demonstrate from a position of power. When people are organized, they become a greater political force."

So he told church audiences, too, sounding like the evangelizing King of Albany, of Birmingham and Selma.

"*What* is our problem?" King would ask.

"Tell us!" the people would cry.

"It is that we are powerless—how do we get power?"

"Tell us, Martin!"

"By organizing ourselves. By getting together."

"That's right!"

"We are *somebody* because we are *God's* children."

"That's right!"

"You don't need to hate anybody. You don't need any Molotov cocktails. A riot can always be stopped by superior force. But they can't stop thousands of feet marching nonviolently!" He waited for the applause to subside. "We're going to change the whole Jericho road!"

To change one slum building in his own neighborhood, King simply took the place over and used rent money collected by his lieutenants to pay for badly needed repairs. A court order finally halted what

King called his "supra-legal trusteeship." But his action got results, since the court also ordered the absentee landlord to clean up the tenement in accordance with the city building code or face imprisonment.

When King wasn't pushing his union or soliciting help and money for the cause, he was talking with members of Chicago's youth gangs—violent, mysterious outfits with names like the Vice Lords, Cobras, and Blackstone Rangers. Bevel, James Orange, and other SCLC staffers were working closely with gang members, and they would bring them by King's flat to meet "the Leader" and share sandwiches with him. One exclaimed incredulously, "Is that really you? Is that really Martin Luther King?"

"This is me," King said. "I'm Martin Luther King."

"You mean to tell me I'm sitting here with the cat who's been up there talking to Presidents!" the young man said. "He's been up there eating filet mignon steaks, and now he's sitting here eating barbecue just like me."

King would visit with the youths late into the night, listening intently as they recounted their hassles with the police and related how Communists and Muslims sought to recruit them and mobsters to use them as dope pushers. But they didn't mess with narcotics, or rape or prostitution either. Sure, they stole things—no denying that—and they fought. They took pride in their street battles with one another, pride in their toughness and military code of honor. Yes, they would "kill you as soon as look at you." Why shouldn't they be violent? This whole country was violent, man. Look at the movies and TV. Look at Vietnam. If the country could use guns in Vietnam, why couldn't they use guns in Chicago?

Gently, with great sincerity, King would explain the nature and purpose of nonviolence, asking them to try it as an experiment and put away their guns and knives. If they did, he wanted them to serve as marshals once the marches began. The demonstrations would show them the power of nonviolent confrontation. "Power in Chicago," he told them, "means getting the largest political machine in the nation to say yes when it wants to say no." He and his aides held nonviolence workshops for the gangs, and Bevel even showed them a film of Watts, contending that thirty Negroes had died there and only five whites and that the same cops were still in power. In Selma, though, Negroes organized under the flag of nonviolence and now Jim Clark was looking for a job. "That's the difference between a riot and thinking," Bevel said.

In time, some two hundred gang members agreed to give nonviolence a chance and turn out for the demonstrations "as soon as Brother Martin gives the word." They respected him enormously. "The only person we have faith in is Dr. King," said one gang leader. "I think Martin Luther King is a very heavy stud," said another. "Maybe we will get a better deal now."

By mid-March, though, King's campaign was in trouble, with money running short, most Negroes apathetic about his union, and many CCCO people grumbling about his emphasis on the slums—they wanted to stress educational improvement, the original goal of the Chicago movement. Worse still, King and his staff seemed unable to devise a coherent strategy to combat ghetto evils. "Is this something to read about," complained one welfare mother, "or is it something to help us?" "We haven't gotten things under control," Young conceded. "The strategy hasn't emerged yet, but we know what we are dealing with and eventually we'll come up with answers." "We are not perfect," King told a gathering of Chicago journalists, "we will make mistakes, we are not omniscient or omnipotent . . . and we need a great deal of support."

King's biggest problem was Mayor Daley, who was out to short-circuit the campaign with a flurry of antislum activity. He boasted that Chicago's own programs would end the slums by the end of 1967; he contrived a much-publicized investigation of building-code violations in Negro sections where King was operating and bombarded ministers and other potential King allies with fact sheets about what Chicago had done for Negroes without "outsiders telling us what to do." According to the fact sheets, the city had sprayed 29,000 apartments for rats and insects within the last year, maintained Head Start kindergartens for thousands of ghetto youngsters, constructed 31,000 public-housing units in the last twenty years and would build 3,000 more in the next four. With much fanfare, Daley held a meeting with King and forty-five leading ministers—among them Archbishop Cody—and recited what his administration was doing against the slums. King engaged the jowly mayor in a twenty-minute dialogue about riots, stressing the "collective guilt" of all for the plight of Chicago's Negroes. But Daley, rotund and gesticulating, argued that Chicago hadn't created Negro poverty—that came from "a thousand miles away in Mississippi, Georgia, and Alabama," where most Chicago blacks had originated. The King-Daley confrontation generated rumors that King would oppose the Mayor's re-election the next year.

But King scotched the stories. "I'm not campaigning against Mayor Daley," he said. "I'm campaigning against slums." Still, Daley was taking no chances. He solicited Negro votes, making a great fuss about how benefits from Johnson's Great Society program would reach Chicago blacks through his antipoverty administration. By April, Daley had neutralized King politically, had the mass of Negro voters "hogtied and hornswoggled" through his own antipoverty projects and promises, and had used the patronage to enlarge his potent outposts in the black community. He felt strong enough to suggest that King go home to Georgia, and seven Negro ward committeemen seconded him.

Back in SCLC headquarters, in a rotting old church in Lawndale, King talked with his staff about what a shrewd politician Daley was, smarter even than he had expected. It would require all their well-honed skills to make him admit that his antipoverty program was mostly cosmetic, that it failed to address the fundamental causes of slums and riots. And neither for all their promise did the President's Great Society benefits, which Daley was trumpeting in his own behalf. True, Johnson had recently unveiled a Model Cities plan in Washington, which called for a federal outlay of $2.3 billion to transform America's decaying cities into "the masterpieces of civilization." King thought this an "imaginative" plan that correctly defined racial discrimination as "a central issue." But as he'd said before, it would take "billions and billions" of dollars to reconstruct the ghettoes. He pointed out, too, that most of the Great Society's social legislation remained unimplemented. What was missing was not legislation but "the will to make it operative." "The Negro in 1966," King said, "now challenges society to make law real on the neighborhood level, down to the ghetto streets where he lives, works and seeks opportunity."

On May 18, King was in Hollywood, Florida, speaking before the Unitarian-Universalist Association. "We should be proud of the steps we've made to rid our nation of this great evil of racial segregation and discrimination," he said. "On the other hand, we must realize that the plant of freedom is only a bud and not yet a flower. The Negro is freer in 1966, but he is not yet free." He made reference to Vietnam again. "The alternative to disarmament under a strong U.N., the alternative to a suspension of nuclear tests, the alternative to a negotiated settlement in Vietnam, and the point of coming to that condition of not bombing the north, the alternative to admitting China may well be a civilization plunged into the abyss of annihilation. And our earthly habitat can be transformed into an inferno that even the mind of Dante could not imagine."

Two weeks later he was in New York City for a "White House Conference on Civil Rights," which Johnson had rigged to demonstrate Negro support for his policies. Pro-administration Negroes praised his accomplishments in civil rights and stated that the Negro cared less about Vietnam than about "the rat at night and the job in the morning." King was not asked to talk or play any role whatever in the highly staged proceedings. The White House had even opposed inviting him until those preparing the conference warned that it would not take place without Martin Luther King.

So this was the price he paid for speaking out on Vietnam. The President had simply written him off and was no longer speaking to him. King's aides were so incensed that they urged him to withdraw from the conference after the first day. But King refused to let Johnson's snubbing drive him away: he stayed on to lobby for A. Philip Randolph's Freedom Budget for All Americans, which advocated a ten-year federal expenditure of $180 billion to abolish poverty.

ON JUNE 6, KING WAS IN A STAFF MEETING in Atlanta when word came that James Meredith had been shot. The day before, Meredith had left Memphis on a one-man march down to Jackson, to demonstrate that Negroes were not afraid of whites in Mississippi and to encourage blacks there to register. Just inside the Mississippi line on Highway 51, an unemployed white man rose from the bushes and blasted Meredith with a shotgun. Alarmed, King phoned Memphis and found that Meredith was alive in hospital there, his back peppered with buckshot. Though King hoped to launch demonstrations in Chicago later that month, he sensed an opportunity here to heal the rifts in the civil-rights movement caused by Vietnam; he could bring the various organizations together in a co-sponsored march that would take up where Meredith had fallen. Together, they could expose the "ugly racism" that infected Mississippi, still the most lawless and backward state in the Deep South.

The next day, King flew to Memphis and huddled in Meredith's hospital room with Floyd McKissick, new national director of CORE, and Stokely Carmichael, new chairman of SNCC. Both men reflected an increasingly militant and independent mood spreading among Negro civil-rights workers. McKissick, "a down-home lawyer" from North Carolina, argued that Negroes must acquire political and economic power on their own now. But it was Carmichael even more than McKissick who personified the new Negro militancy. A tall, lanky twenty-four-year-old with sparkling eyes and an infectious smile, he had come from Trinidad, spent his formative years in Harlem, the East Bronx, and Howard University, and joined the movement in 1961, when he went on the Freedom Rides and became a SNCC field organizer known for his cocky brilliance and adaptability. A black journalist reported that one week Carmichael was in the southern backcountry, wearing bib overalls and coaxing Negroes to vote "in a southern-honey drawl." The next week found him in Harlem, dressed in Italian boots and a tight suit, talking to "cats" about the cause in the cool hip of the ghetto. A fortnight later he was addressing a student audience at a university, quoting Camus, Sartre, and Thoreau with a finger pointed at the floor. He was so highstrung, so intense and sensitive, that he had an ulcer by twenty-two. He brooded about the violence in Dixie and went to pieces when he saw a group of Negroes clubbed and beaten in a SNCC demonstration in Montgomery during King's Selma campaign. "I started screaming and I didn't stop until they got me to the airport," he said later. "That day I knew I could never be hit again without hitting back." After Selma, he formed the all-black Lowndes County Freedom Organization in Alabama—its symbol a snarling black panther—and electrified a new generation of Negro youth with his appeals to black pride and black consciousness.

Despite SNCC's organizational feud with King and SCLC, Carmichael admired King and told him so. As they conferred in Meredith's hospital room, Carmichael and McKissick voiced their approval of a co-sponsored march through Mississippi under SCLC, SNCC, and CORE flags. But what about Meredith? King knew what an unpredictable loner he was and feared that he might object to a group's continuing his work. But Meredith gave the project his blessing, and the three leaders left the room assuring him that they would continue the march "in his spirit." They would seek as never before to instill "a new sense of dignity and manhood" in the mass of Mississippi Negroes, who were too poor to eat in desegregated restaurants and too frightened of white reprisals to vote.

With a group of aides and field workers, the three drove out to the desolate spot on Highway 51 where Meredith had been shot and took off for Jackson on "The James Meredith March Against Fear." As they trekked along in scorching summer heat, escorted by the Mississippi state police, King overheard some young Negroes from SNCC and CORE talking in the ranks. "I'm not for that nonviolence stuff any more," one said. "If one of these damn white Mississippi crackers touches me, I'm gonna knock the hell out of him." Then the issue of white participation came up. "This should be an all-black march. We don't need any more white phonies and liberals invading our movement. This is our march." Once King halted the column to sing "We Shall Overcome." But when they reached the stanza "black and white together," a few marchers stopped singing. Later King asked them why. "This is a new day," they replied, "we don't sing those words any more. In fact, the whole song should be discarded. Not 'We Shall Overcome,' but 'We Shall Overrun.'"

"The words fell on my ears like strange music from a foreign land," King wrote later. "My hearing was not attuned to the sound of such bitterness." But he told himself he should not be surprised. After all, these young people were affected by an atmosphere of unfulfilled white promises and continued white violence. He should expect them to question nonviolence. He reminded himself that disappointment breeds despair, despair breeds bitterness, and "the one thing certain about bitterness is its blindness. Bitterness has not the capacity to make the distinction between some and *all*."

The marchers returned to Memphis for the night, checked into a Negro motel, and there plunged into a heated debate over the nature of their journey. Roy Wilkins and Whitney Young were present. And so were several Negroes armed with snub-nosed .38s and semi-automatic rifles—members of the Louisiana-based Deacons for Defense, a paramilitary black organization invited up by SNCC. King pleaded with his brothers, including his Deacon brothers, to remain true to nonviolence. But the Deacons didn't "believe in that naked shit no way," and SNCC and CORE seconded them because they were tired of seeing Negroes hit and shot without armed protection. But King pressed on. He was *not* arguing that Negroes shouldn't protect themselves and their homes when attacked. Yet self-defense was not the point here. The point was whether they should carry guns in an organized demonstration. To do so would only confuse and obscure the moral issues, and it would not expose Mississippi injustice. If Negroes came marching through the state brandishing .38s and rifles, they were bound to precipitate a calamitous confrontation. Whites from the governor down would use it as an excuse to start shooting Negroes at random.

But Carmichael and McKissick disagreed. McKissick asserted that nonviolence had outlived its usefulness in this racist country and that Negroes ought to break the legs off the Statue of Liberty "and throw her into the Mississippi." Carmichael argued shrilly that blacks should seize power in areas where they outnumbered whites—"I'm not going to beg the white man for anything I deserve. I'm going to take it." As far as white participation was concerned, he and McKissick were adamant that this was a *black* march.

As Carmichael tangled with Wilkins and Young about this, King thought back over the glory years when they had worked together across the South and joyously welcomed white allies. What had caused Carmichael to change? King surmised that it had been all the articulate, well-educated, idealistic white students who had poured into Mississippi in the Freedom Summer of 1964 and simply overwhelmed SNCC's poor black workers. Perhaps Carmichael thought this had increased their feelings of inadequacy. As Carmichael argued on, King reminded him and McKissick that racial understanding came from contact, from the ability of Negroes and whites to work together. King insisted that the march be interracial. They were out to enlist consciences, not just racial groups. Remember that many dedicated whites had bled and died on civil-rights battlefronts. To reject whites now would be "a shameful repudiation" of all they had sacrificed for.

King pleaded for unity, too, but that seemed impossible as Carmichael and McKissick wouldn't let up on Wilkins and Young. Finally they had had enough. They refused to support the march and left for New York. King threatened to withdraw, too, unless Carmichael and McKissick agreed to a nonviolent, interracial march. To prevent King from defecting, they accepted his terms. "If you got any notions that Negroes can solve our problems by ourselves," Abernathy said when the march resumed, "you got another thought coming. We welcome white people."

As a gesture of solidarity, King signed a joint manifesto issued to the press: "This march will be a massive public indictment and protest of the failure of American society, the Government of the United States, and the state of Mississippi to 'fulfill these rights,'" in reference to the slogan of the recent White House conference in New York. The manifesto summoned Washington to endorse Randolph's 'Freedom Budget' for all Americans and require states and counties to employ Negroes as lawmen and jurors in direct ratio to their population.

As the column headed for Greenwood, controversy continued to plague it. Why were they marching anyway? asked mercurial Charles Evers, brother of the slain civil-rights leader and director of the Mississippi NAACP. "I don't see how walking up and down a lot of highways helps: I'm for walking house to house and fence to fence to register Negro voters." Despite the voting-rights act, Mississippi still lagged behind the rest of the South, with only 30 percent of its eligible Negroes on the voting rolls. King and the other leaders talked it over and decided that Evers was right. Henceforth their main objective would be to register Negro voters. In Grenada, 1,300 Negroes followed King to the courthouse, where specially appointed black registrars worked through light and darkness to put five hundred of them on the county voting rolls. In one memorable scene in Grenada, SCLC's Robert Green planted a U.S. flag between the arms of Jefferson Davis's statue. "The South you led will never stand again," Green told the statue. "Mississippi must become part of the Union."

As the marchers headed south for Greenwood, thousands of black people from all over the countryside flocked to the highway for a glimpse of King. They would stand along the roadside as Negroes had done in Alabama, waiting in the boiling sun, looking for him from under the brims of their bonnets and soiled straw hats. When the column appeared, someone would shout, "There he is! Martin Luther King!" And they would rush toward him in such numbers that his aides would have to join hands and cordon him off, to prevent him from being crushed. On such occasions King always seemed surprised and bewildered. He would smile a little and nod his head in gratitude and touch as many groping hands as he could.

When the marchers encamped for the night, King would speak to local Negroes in some ramshackle church, "getting down" with the country folk and preaching "from the heart" as in Selma days. A white reporter was astounded at the impact he had on those rural Negroes. In one church he spoke so eloquently that a five-year-old girl started sobbing and saying over and over, "I want to go with him."

As the procession moved deeper into Mississippi, white bystanders grew ugly. In "a grotesque parody of small-town America," as one journalist put it, they congregated at gas stations and grocery stores, shouting obscenities, waving Confederate flags, and throwing things as the marchers passed. At the same time, Carmichael and his people became more belligerent, singing a ditty that made King grimace: "Jingle bells, shotgun shells, Freedom all the way, Oh what fun it is to blast, A trooper man away."

It was a harrowing experience for King. To make matters worse, he had to shuttle back and forth to Chicago, where things were threatening to get out of hand, too. On June 12, a riot had flared in the Puerto Rican section, with police and civilians exchanging gunfire. King feared that it was going to be a long hot summer there despite all his efforts.

When he rejoined the Mississippi march in Greenwood, his staff was in a state of high tension. Carmichael had been arrested for trying to erect some tents on a Negro schoolground, only to find 3,000 people awaiting him at a SNCC rally when he got out of jail. "This is the twenty-seventh time I have been arrested," he yelled from a flatbed truck, "and I ain't going to jail no more!" The crowd broke into cheers. "The only way we gonna stop them white men from whuppin' us is to take over. We been saying freedom for six years and we ain't got nothin'. What we gonna start saying now is Black Power!" The crowd roared in unison, "BLACK POWER!" Then SNCC's Willie Ricks, called "Reverend" because of his fiery evangelical style, jumped up beside Carmichael and shouted in a parody of SCLC's chant:

"What do you want?"

"BLACK POWER!"

"What do you want?"

"BLACK POWER!"

"What do you want? Say it again!"

"BLACK POWER!! BLACK POWER!!! BLACK POWER!!!!"

King's aides were horrified. Though Negroes like Paul Robeson and Adam Clayton Powell had used the term before, "Black Power" created a sensation on the Mississippi march, as the media seized on it and warned of an impending race war. Worse still, Carmichael had instructed his staff that Black Power was to be SNCC's war cry for the rest of the march. King's staff believed that he was trying to capture headlines and usurp the movement.

As the march started up again, King mulled over SNCC's new slogan and thought it "unfortunate," because it gave the impression of black supremacy, which he considered just as evil as white supremacy. To his dismay, a bitter rivalry broke out between those who trumpeted "Black Power" and those who cried "Freedom Now," SCLC's slogan. At roadside rallies, SNCC and SCLC speakers vied with one another in stirring up crowds with their respective chants. At one rally, SCLC even got a local band to drown out Carmichael when he launched into his Black Power theatrics. By the time the column reached Yazoo City, some Black Power advocates were crying for white blood and inciting young Negroes to shout, "Hey! Hey! Whattaya know! White people must go—must go!"

King had heard enough of this. "Some people," he exclaimed at Yazoo City, "are telling us to be like our oppressor, who has a history of using Molotov cocktails, who has a history of dropping the atomic bomb, who has a history of lynching Negroes. Now people are telling me to stoop down to that level. I'm sick and tired of violence! I'm tired of the war in Vietnam! I'm not going to use violence, no matter who says so!"

He said the same thing to Carmichael, McKissick, and their aides in a five-hour parley at a small Catholic parish house. "I pleaded with the group to abandon the Black Power slogan," King recalled. "A leader has to be concerned with semantics. Each word has a denotative meaning . . . and a connotative meaning. . . . Black Power carried the wrong connotations." The press, he pointed out, had already stressed the implication of violence in the term, and the rash and bellicose statements of some SNCC marchers had only added to this impression.

Carmichael said: Violence versus nonviolence is irrelevant. The real question is the crying need for black people to organize themselves and consolidate economic and political resources to gain power. "Power is the only thing respected in this world, and we must get it at any cost." Then, looking King in the eye: "Martin, you know as well as I do that practically every other ethnic group in America has done just this. The Jews, the Irish and the Italians did it, why can't we?"

King: "That is just the point. No one has ever heard the Jews publicly chant a slogan of Jewish power, but they have power. Through group identity, determination and creative endeavor, they have gained it. The same thing is true of the Irish and Italians. Neither group has used a slogan of Irish or Italian power, but they have worked hard to achieve it. This is exactly what we must do. We must use every constructive means to amass economic and political power" and "to build racial pride and refute the notion that black is evil and ugly. But this must come through a program, not merely through a slogan."

Carmichael and McKissick: "How can you arouse people to unite around a program without a slogan as a rallying cry? Didn't the labor movement have slogans? Haven't we had slogans all along in the freedom movement? What we need is a new slogan with 'black' in it."

King: Yes, we need slogans. But not ones that will confuse our allies, isolate us, and give whites who might be ashamed of their bigotry an excuse to justify it. "Why not use the slogan 'black consciousness' or 'black equality'? These phrases would be less vulnerable and would more accurately describe what we are about. The words 'black' and 'power' together give the impression that we are talking about black domination rather than black equality."

But Carmichael and McKissick didn't think King's suggestions carried the emotional force of "Black Power." They were determined to make it the slogan for both their organizations and project it across the land. The two sides were at an impasse. To save the march, King recommended that both "Black Power" and "Freedom Now" be dropped for the remainder of the trek to Jackson. Out of respect for him, Carmichael and McKissick agreed. But Carmichael added, "Martin, I deliberately decided to raise the issue on the march to give it a national forum, and force you to take a stand for Black Power."

"I have been used before," King said. "One more time won't hurt."

A few days later, the column came to Neshoba County where Chaney, Schwerner, and Goodman had been murdered two years before. In Philadelphia, King conducted a memorial service for them on Main Street. A crowd of whites encircled the marchers and responded to King's every phrase with a taunt. "Sometimes," said a journalist, "they listened and screamed so carefully that Dr. King appeared to be leading them in a responsive reading." Then they charged forward, clubbing the marchers with hoes and ax handles while the police looked the other way. Only when the Negroes started fighting back did the police intervene and drive the whites away. That night, violence broke out again as white marauders and armed marchers shot at one another. Trying desperately to maintain nonviolence, King announced a return march to this hateful town—but warned that only those committed to nonviolence could participate. Carmichael and McKissick backed him up "100 per cent." King also wired the President to send federal marshals lest civil war break out in Mississippi. But the White House did not respond.

On June 23 the column reached Canton in a driving rainstorm and tried to set up camp in a soaked Negro schoolyard. With sinister precision, a wall of state and local police closed in on the schoolyard, ordering the marchers—2,000 of them now—to pitch their tents somewhere else. But King and the other leaders refused: their people were wet and weary, and anyway this was a Negro school. With explosive force, the police laid down a barrage of tear gas and then crashed into the marchers with whips, sticks, and gun butts. With Negroes falling all around him, Carmichael became hysterical. "Don't make your stand here," he sobbed, "I just can't stand to see any more people get shot." A local Negro woman, her eyes red from tear gas, picked herself up from the mud and shouted, "We are not going to stay ignorant, and backward, and scared." Andrew Young toppled off a truck, vomiting from tear gas, thinking, "If I had a machine gun, I'd *show* these motherfuckers!" John Doar of the Justice Department clamped a handkerchief over his nose and waded into the melee in a useless attempt to restrain the police. Somehow King and McKissick got the marchers away to a nearby Negro church, where they tended their wounds in bitter despair. Veterans of Selma's bloody Sunday claimed this was worse. King himself had never witnessed anything so vicious. Only in Mississippi would the police assault unarmed Negroes under his personal leadership. Again he telegraphed Washington to send U.S. marshals down here before somebody was killed. Again Washington ignored him, and King ascribed its cynical attitude to his stand on Vietnam. Federal presence on the march was confined to Doar, a man from the Federal Community Relations Service, and a few indifferent FBI agents.

Understandably, SNCC and CORE were furious. To hell with Johnson, McKissick raged. "I'm committed to non-violence, but I say what we need is to get us some black power." When King rejected a proposal that they go back and put the tents up anyway, the SNCC and CORE leaders deserted him. "What we do from now on will be on our own," one said. Over King's objections, they carried a vote that excluded the NAACP from a final rally at the statehouse in Jackson. "It's all right," said Charles Evers. "I'll be here when they're all gone."

King was perplexed, angry, and deeply apprehensive about what was unfolding in Mississippi. But his courage did not desert him. On June 24, with motorists speeding within inches of them, King led 300 nonviolent volunteers back to Philadelphia, to show its white citizens that "we can stand before you without fear after we were beaten and brutalized the other day." As he and Abernathy approached the courthouse to pray, Sheriff Lawrence Rainey intercepted them. "You can't go up these steps," he drawled menacingly. "Oh yes," King said, "you're the one who had Schwerner and the other fellows in jail." Rainey was proud to say he had done that all right. King looked behind him at a white crowd gathering around the courthouse, and he thought for sure he was going to die. As he and Abernathy knelt to pray, King said under his breath, in reference to the slain civil-rights workers, "I believe the murderers are somewhere around me at this moment." "You damn right," Rainey said, "they're right behind you." King and Abernathy rose, walked away from Rainey and the mob at the courthouse, and somehow got their people out of Philadelphia without mishap. With aides later, King recounted the scene at the courthouse steps, with Rainey and all those whites behind him. "And *brother*," King said, "I sure did not want to close my eyes when we prayed." He grinned. "Ralph said he prayed with his open."

In searing heat, King and his cohorts headed into Jackson for the climactic rally. Coretta and the older children—Yoki and Marty— joined him for the procession to the statehouse, a band playing "When the Saints Go Marching In." At the capitol grounds, 11,000 to 15,000 people applauded as King, Carmichael, and McKissick all gave speeches in blazing sunlight. But civil-rights veterans noticed that whites who had marched with King in other demonstrations were not in Jackson. Afterward, as the marchers prepared to leave, Carmichael approached a white SCLC staffer and shot him between the eyes with a water pistol.

Had the march accomplished anything? "Oh, I think so," King told a reporter. "It's just unfortunate that we weren't able to get across the incredible conditions, the degradation Negroes live under in Mississippi, because of all the dissension within." Although the march had left voter-registration teams everywhere in its wake, it was the cry of

"Black Power" that alerted the country and thrust Carmichael to national prominence as the new Malcolm X. "We've learned a lesson from this march," Bernard Lee told *The Reporter*. "We can't work with SNCC, or for that matter with CORE either. This time it was unavoidable. We had to pick up the march once Meredith was shot. And SNCC was here when we arrived. But we've learned. From now on we'll keep Stokely off Dr. King's coattails. Did you notice that every time the cameras were running, there was Stokely right next to Dr. King?"

For King, the Meredith March Against Fear was a terrible blunder. He had undertaken it to unify the civil-rights movement and confront white Mississippi under the banners of nonviolence. Instead, the march had unleashed a combustible slogan that embarrassed and bewildered him and that fragmented the movement, perhaps irreparably. As Carmichael and McKissick stormed across the country, crying "Black Power" and giving it various definitions, Roy Wilkins had no doubt what it connoted. "No matter how endlessly they try to explain it, the term black power means anti-white power. It has to mean 'going it alone.' It has to mean separatism. . . . We of the NAACP will have none of this." For Wilkins, the slogan was "the father of hate and the mother of violence." Rustin too declared it "positively harmful." Vice-President Humphrey called it reverse racism. And journalist Pat Watters thought it signaled that SNCC and CORE had given up appealing to the best in their people and were now appealing to the worst. "No Negro who is fighting for civil rights," said Randolph, "can support black power, which is opposed to civil rights and integration." "This is no time for romantic illusion and empty philosophical debates about freedom," King said wearily. "What is needed is a strategy for change, a tactical program that will bring the Negro into the mainstream of American life as quickly as possible."

KING FLEW BACK TO CHICAGO determined to find an answer to Black Power. If he could extract from Daley a real commitment to fair housing and equal jobs, perhaps he could nullify Black Power by demonstrating to the Negro masses that they could share the blessings of

America through integration, not separation. He was "almost desperately determined" to gain economic advancement for black people within the system. "We have got to deliver results—nonviolent results in a Northern city—to protect the nonviolent movement," Young said.

With SNCC and CORE promoting Black Power right here in Chicago, King announced that it was time for mass civil disobedience, to force the Daley machine to make Chicago "a just and open city." SCLC would kick off demonstrations with a mass rally and a march to City Hall on July 10, "Freedom Sunday." And if there were those who thought King naïve in taking on Chicago's "enlightened bossism," King felt that he had no other choice. For him, the future of integration—of the movement, the country, and maybe humankind itself—was increasingly on the line in this perilous hour. It was the great mission of America to prove that people of all racial, ethnic, and national backgrounds could live together in love and equality as children of God. If America could demonstrate that, then God's Kingdom could begin here. But if America failed in her mission, if human beings could not get along here as brothers and sisters, then no doubt they could not do so in the world at large.

As he hurried about Chicago, urging Negroes to turn out for Freedom Sunday, trying to convey an idea of the issues at stake, he was booed in one meeting by members of the Black Power movement. He recalled how he had spoken countless times around the country, even before hostile whites, but until now nobody in an audience had booed him. "I went home that night with an ugly feeling," he said later. "Selfishly I thought of my sufferings and sacrifices over the last twelve years. Why would they boo one so close to them? But as I lay awake thinking, I finally came to myself, and I could not for the life of me have less than patience and understanding for those young people. For twelve years I, and others like me, had held out radiant promises of progress. I had preached to them about my dream. I had lectured to them about the not too distant day when they would have freedom, 'all, here and now.' Their hopes had soared. They were now booing because they felt that we were unable to deliver on our promises."

Still, the boos rang in his ears. Sometimes he felt too discouraged to go on. But he reminded himself that "there is a balm in Gilead that makes the wounded whole. There is a balm in Gilead that heals the sin-sick soul." In the frenetic countdown to Freedom Sunday, he reflected on the story of Martin Luther, his namesake, the German monk who had ignited the Protestant Reformation in the sixteenth century. It all began when the Catholic Church, which controlled Europe then, raised the levies, or indulgences, it imposed on its vast flock. The church's system of collection had become a form of "high spiritual finance," crass, commercial, and hypocritical. In 1517, Martin Luther challenged the system in a symbolic act that shook the medieval world: he nailed the ninety-five theses against indulgences on the door of the Castle Church at Wittenberg. This led to a showdown with the Pope that aroused all Germany and set in motion a religious revolution that helped open the way for the very concepts King was struggling for in Chicago—equality, representation, and self-determination, not for the pleasure of some, but for the liberty and dignity of all. The episode at Wittenberg inspired King to do something equally symbolic. On Freedom Sunday he would nail his own ninety-five theses on the door of City Hall.

Freedom Sunday came in with a heat wave. By the time of the rally, the temperature stood at 98 degrees, and more than a half million Chicagoans swamped the beaches of Lake Michigan. Only 30,000 people—movement leaders had hoped for 100,000—gathered in Soldiers Field to hear King give the keynote address of the campaign. Speaking under a black parasol that shielded him from the sun, he called on Chicago blacks to withdraw their money from all banks and finance houses that discriminated against them, and to boycott any company that refused to employ an adequate number of Negroes, Puerto Ricans, and other ethnic minorities in better-paying jobs. They must say to Mayor Daley: if you do not respond to our demands, our votes will decide the next mayor of Chicago. We will fill up the jails here in order to end the slums.

Then with thousands in pursuit, he set out for City Hall with his own version of the ninety-five theses—a set of demands that called for an end to police brutality and discriminatory real-estate practices, increased Negro employment, and a civilian review board for the police department like that in New York City. But the oppressive heat got to him; already worn down from the tension and exertion of the Mississippi march, he had to ride part of the way in an air-conditioned car. At City Hall, with some 36,000 followers looking on, King strode to the LaSalle Street entrance and stuck his theses on the metal door with adhesive tape. Then he faced the cheering multitude, hoping that this day marked the symbolic beginning of an American reformation.

The next day, King returned to City Hall and presented his demands to Daley himself. But the mayor, his face red with anger, rejected them on the grounds that Chicago already had a "massive" anti-slum program. For Daley and his men, King was becoming an intolerable nuisance. They found it incomprehensible that he couldn't be bought off. Here he stood, solemn and obdurate, warning Daley that he was inviting "social disaster" if his administration did not do something bold, something meaningful, to rectify the "seething desperation" in the ghettoes. To expose racial oppression in Chicago and force a recalcitrant Daley to act, King promised to launch sit-ins, camp-ins, boycotts, and mass demonstrations in the streets.

BACK IN HIS LAWNDALE FLAT, King was learning firsthand what a pressure cooker ghetto life was in the summer. After the Mississippi march, Coretta and the children had moved into the apartment with King, intending to stay until the fall. Right away, the children started whining. There was nothing to do except play outside in patches of black dirt. Even the pitiful playground was black dirt. The streets were too congested and dangerous for them to release their stored-up energy there. Because the ghettoes had no swimming pools or parks, there was no place for them to escape the torrid heat. Confined too often to King's small, suffocating flat, the children fought and screamed at one another and even reverted to infantile behavior. "I realized that the crowded flat we lived in," King said, "was about to produce an emotional explosion in my own family."

On July 12, the day after King's face-off with Daley, the West Side exploded in a riot that left nine people injured and twenty-four in jail. To cool off in the 100-degree temperature, youths on the West Side had turned on water hydrants and frolicked in the spray. But the police came in their flashing cars to shut the hydrants off; a crowd gathered, and a fight broke out between a cop and one youth that set off a powder keg. Two hundred and fifty Negroes—most of them gang members—took to the streets, breaking windows and hurling Molotov cocktails at police cars, setting one ablaze.

With the whole ghetto threatening to blow, King and his aides called slum residents to a mass meeting in a Negro church and urged them to speak from the floor "to relieve the tension." Six gang members King had gotten out of jail claimed that the police had beaten them, and their comrades in the audience swore retaliation. When a man rose and said he had lived in Chicago all his life and couldn't understand why anybody would want to tear up the neighborhood, the gang members walked out in a huff, scoffing at King's entreaties. Through the night insurgent gangs roamed the streets and shattered windows.

So it had come to this—what King had warned and feared would happen since the start of the campaign. All the next day he held emergency staff sessions, searching for ways to prevent another eruption. He blamed last night's disorders on police brutality—and Daley's stubborn refusal to make concessions. "He can do much more to stop riots than I can," King told the press. And he reiterated his demand for a civilian review board to oversee the police and importuned City Hall to install swimming pools and parks on the West Side.

That night rioting broke out anew after another clash over the fire hydrants. Four hundred police swept West side streets in wedge formations, and hundreds of Negroes in housing projects hurled bricks and Molotov cocktails down on them. In King's own neighborhood, across from his flat, Negro boys smashed shop windows, cried "Black Power," and ran off. As lightning splintered the sky and rain lashed Chicago, King and his aides toured the riot-torn area, preaching nonviolence and pleading with people to stay inside. But it was no use. The next day, July 14, war flamed up on the West Side as hundreds of police shot it out with Negro snipers in a high-rise apartment building, and youth gangs fire-bombed white-owned stores. King and his men were in the streets until 4 A.M., King speeding by car from one battle site to another in a desperate attempt to stop the fighting. By dawn, 2 people had been killed, 56 injured, and 282 thrown in jail. One of the dead was a girl, fourteen and pregnant. The next day, Governor Otto Kerner ordered 4,000 National Guardsmen to Chicago, and by dusk soldiers with carbines and bayonets were patrolling the riot area in jeeps and troop trucks. The West Side looked like Vietnam.

Chicago rocked with recriminations. Pro-Daley Negroes blamed the disturbances on "outside interference," and the mayor himself pointed a finger at anarchists, Communists, and then at King's own staff, which he accused of instructing Negroes "how to conduct vio-

lence" by showing them films of Watts. But in a ninety-minute confrontation at City Hall, King persuaded the mayor to make concessions
lest the rioting and killing continue. The city rushed in ten portable
swimming pools for the West Side and affixed sprinklers to water hydrants there for the children to use in summer weather. Later Daley
even established a citizens' committee to make a study of the police
department. No, King admitted, these measures scarcely dealt with
the "basic needs" of the ghetto, but they were something "concrete to
offer people."

After his meeting with Daley, King contacted fifteen top leaders of
the Cobras, Vice Lords, and Roman Saints, whose members had been
at the forefront of the disorders, and assembled them in his flat for a
dialogue. For hours, he let them pour out their grievances against the
police, the Daley machine, and its Negro "pawns." Then he beseeched
them to renew the commitment they had made to nonviolence, reminded them what he had said before—that demonstrations were far
more "sensible and effective" than aimless rioting. Civil disobedience
was about to commence, and he asked them again to serve as march
marshals. At last, Richard "Peanut" Tidwell, leader of the Roman
Saints, pledged himself to King and went around the room, persuading
each of the other leaders to do the same. Then they left to subdue
their followers and prevent any further trouble. When peace returned
to Chicago, the New York Times correspondent attributed it not so
much to the show of military force as to King's influence with the
Negro gangs.

Before the riots, King had been scheduled to leave Chicago and
address the World Conference on Church and Society in Geneva,
Switzerland. But the difficulties in Chicago made it impossible for him
to go. So he recorded "A Knock at Midnight," a sermon that reflected
his mood, and sent the tape to Geneva. On Sunday, July 17, at St.
Peter's Cathedral, four hundred delegates sat in rapt attention as King's
disembodied voice boomed from a tape recorder at the empty pulpit:
"It is . . . midnight in our world, and the darkness is so deep that we
can hardly see which way to turn. . . . On the international horizon
nations are engaged in a colossal and bitter contest for supremacy.
Two world wars have been fought within a generation, and the clouds
of another war are dangerously low. . . . In the terrible midnight of
war, men have knocked on the door of the church to ask for the bread
of peace, but the Church often disappointed them. . . . Those who

have gone to the Church to seek the bread of economic justice have been left in the frustrating midnight of economic deprivation. . . . The Church today is challenged to proclaim God's son, Jesus Christ, to be the hope of men in all of their complex personal and social problems."

O<small>N</small> J<small>ULY</small> 30, <small>IN</small> N<small>EW</small> F<small>RIENDSHIP</small> B<small>APTIST</small> C<small>HURCH</small>, King told his followers that the time for "creative tension" had arrived in Chicago. They were going to march against segregated housing in all-white neighborhoods that ringed the ghettoes, starting with those around Gage and Marquette parks on the Southwest Side. Realtors there had refused to show their listings to black civil-rights teams, in violation of Chicago's own ill-enforced fair-housing ordinance, and King intended to expose such practices to national opinion and dramatize how the walls of this city sealed Negroes off into enclaves of "poverty and human misery." He realized, of course, that he couldn't lead his indigent followers overnight into "the promised land of suburbia," as one writer put it. Negroes whose yearly income averaged only $4,700 could scarcely afford the $15,000 to $30,000 homes in white communities. But by leading slum blacks into those segregated neighborhoods, King hoped to throw a fright into City Hall—and the state and national capitals beyond—and coerce them into guaranteeing open housing to Negroes, so that they would not feel permanently and psychologically chained to the ghetto. When critics wailed that violence was bound to occur, King replied as he had in Selma and Birmingham: "We do not seek to precipitate violence. However, we are aware that the existence of injustice in society is the existence of violence, latent violence. We feel we must constantly expose this evil, even if it brings violence upon us." If we bring the evil out in the open, then "this community will be forced to deal with it."

King was away on a speaking engagement when Young, Raby, and other movement leaders took the first column of interracial demonstrators into an Irish and Lithuanian working-class neighborhood abutting Marquette Park. When King returned, his staffers related that whites out there had jeered and heckled them viciously and even shoved two of their cars into a muddy lagoon. Sensing the dramatic possibilities here, King exhorted his followers: "We aren't gonna march with any molotov cocktails. That isn't our movement. We aren't gonna march with any weapons. That isn't our movement. We aren't gonna march with bricks and bottles. We're gonna march with something much more powerful than all of that. We're gonna march with the force of our souls. . . . We're gonna move out with the weapons of courage. We're gonna put on the breastplate of righteousness and the whole armor of God. And we're gonna *march*."

On August 5, he led 600 Negroes and whites out to Marquette Park for a second trek through an all-white section, this one consisting mostly of second-generation Poles, Lithuanians, Italians, and Germans. A special force of 900 police was on hand to escort the procession and maintain order. As the marchers assembled in the park, a thousand whites stood on a knoll nearby, waving Confederate flags, unfurling Nazi insignias, and shouting "Nigger go home!" "We hate niggers!" "We want Martin Luther Coon!" "Wallace for president!" "Kill the niggers!" Suddenly they let fly with a barrage of rocks, bottles, and bricks. One brick struck King just above his right ear, causing him to stumble to the ground. Reporters surrounded him as he shook off the blow. "Oh, I've been hit so many times I'm immune to it," he said. Then the march would go on? "Oh, yes, very definitely. We can't stop the march."

Behind a flying wedge of police, King marched his followers eight abreast through a residential area, with cadres of Vice Lords, Cobras, and Saints protecting their flanks, moving between the column and whites who lined the sidewalks. "Again there was that terrible noise of people shouting at us," Al Raby said. "Women are among the most vicious, screaming 'you monkeys' at the blacks and 'you white trash' at the others. They called all of us *apes* or told the blacks to go back to Africa." The procession was heading down a narrow street now, and whites were everywhere—on porches and lawns and up in the trees— screaming insults, chanting "White Power," and throwing so many rocks that even the police were ducking and getting hit. In one salvo, it seemed that hundreds of cops went down, and King felt an eerie sensation of "the inevitability of death"—the same sensation he'd felt in Philadelphia during the Mississippi march. When the police battered a path to a realtor's office in a cluster of shops, King and his people knelt in prayer, while hundreds of bystanders shrieked, "Hate! Hate! Hate!" In all the bedlam, a white threw a knife at King, but it missed and stuck in the shoulder of a white onlooker.

Somehow the police got the marchers safely back to Marquette Park. It was dusk now, and the crowd there had swelled to some 2,500 people—among them well-dressed women and businessmen. As buses and cars filled with demonstrators pulled away, whites chased after them, smashing windows and raging at the cops: "You nigger-loving sons of bitches!" A crazed old woman stood in the tumult sobbing, "God, I hate niggers and nigger-lovers." An old man railed at a group of marchers, "I worked all my life for a house out here, and no nigger is going to get it!"

The police were stunned. Many of them were second-generation Poles, Italians, and Germans themselves; these were *their* people stoning and calling them "nigger lovers," *their* people sporting Rebel flags and banners of the American Nazi party and battling them in the streets long after the marchers were gone, *their* poeple who were rioting now.

"I've never seen anything like it," King said of the march that day. "I've been in many demonstrations all across the south, but I can say that I have never seen—even in Mississippi and Alabama—mobs as hostile and as hate-filled as I've seen in Chicago." And yet he felt a surge of joy at the conduct of the young gang members who had marched with him. He had seen their noses bloodied and broken, but not one of them had retaliated. Surely this demonstrated that "even very violent temperaments can be channeled through nonviolent discipline."

Chicago, though, could not face the hate King had exposed here. Across the city, white editors, politicians, religious leaders, conservative Negroes, and even some CCCO people, all vilified King, accusing him of creating the racial tensions in Chicago and insisting that he stop the marches.

"You want us to stop marching, make justice a reality," King retorted in a Negro mass meeting. "I don't mind saying to Chicago—or to anybody—I'm tired of marching. I'm tired of marching for something that should've been mine at birth. If you want a moratorium on demonstrations, put a moratorium on injustice. If you want us to end our moves into communities, open these communities. . . . I don't mind saying to you, I'm tired of living every day under the threat of death. I have no martyr complex. I want to live as long as anybody in this building. And sometimes I begin to doubt whether I'm going to make it through. . . . So I'll tell anybody, I'm willing to stop marching. I don't march because I like it. I march because I must, and because I'm a man, and because I'm a child of God."

Over the next week, his lieutenants led one march after another into white neighborhoods, stirring up more hate, shouts of white power, dancing swastikas and Rebel flags. King himself, back from SCLC's annual convention in Jackson, Mississippi, and a speaking engagement on the West Coast, promised to lead an even larger demonstration on the forthcoming Sunday. But Mayor Daley moved to derail King's escalating campaign. On August 19, he secured from Cook County Circuit Court a temporary injunction curtailing King's operation to one march of 500 people a day. Undaunted, King countered with an announcement that panicked officials from Chicago to Springfield. On Sunday he would lead a huge interracial march into all-white Cicero, a suburb outside Cook County that wasn't covered by the injunction. Cicero was perhaps the most virulently anti-Negro community in the Chicago area. When a Negro family had tried to move there in 1951, whites had gone on such a rampage that Governor Adlai Stevenson had been obliged to send 4,000 National Guardsmen there to restore order. Recently, white toughs had murdered a Negro youth who went to Cicero looking for work. Now King threatened to take a column of blacks and whites into Cicero, marching arm in arm. The sheriff of Cook County said it was suicidal. Governor Kerner put the state police and National Guard on alert. City Hall, Archbishop Cody, and other progressive whites begged King to call the march off. But King vowed that "no one is going to turn me around at this point" and that the demonstration would be "the biggest ever." "Not only are we going to walk to Cicero, we're going to work in Cicero, we're going to live in Cicero."

As the fateful day approached, Chicago girded itself for the worst. The Negro couple who had tried to move to Cicero in 1951 appeared on CBS Television, recalled the frenzy of the mob they had faced, and the man said, "I'm scared to death. I don't know what will happen." Ironically, though, King's projected march captured the imagination of the young militants in local CORE and SNCC chapters, who hungered for a showdown with Cicero whites and swore to be out there with King on Sunday.

The real showdown, however, was between King and Daley. And it was the mayor who backed away. Horrified by King's threatened march and by the ugliness exposed in his city, Daley agreed to meet with King and try to work something out. This was tantamount to admitting that Chicago's housing and slum policies did need serious improvement—something Daley had steadfastly denied—and King, Raby, and other movement leaders regarded it as a tremendous breakthrough. Now maybe they could wangle some major concessions out of City Hall.

On August 26, at the Palmer House, they sat down for two and a half hours with Daley and powerful municipal, labor, and business leaders, and reached what became known as the "Summit Agreement." According to its terms, Chicago's Commission on Human Rights would require real-estate brokers to post a summary of the city's open-housing policy, and the city itself would redouble efforts to enforce it and to encourage state housing legislation; the Chicago Real Estate Board, which had been lobbying against such a bill, would no longer do so (though it refused to drop a legal battle it was waging against Chicago's own fair-housing ordinance); Chicago's savings and bankers' associations agreed to lend money to qualified families regardless of race, thus meeting one of King's cardinal demands; the Chicago Chamber of Commerce and an impressive array of other business, labor, and municipal organizations all pledged themselves to work in behalf of fair housing. The agreement also set up the Leadership Council for Metropolitan Open Housing, comprising the major leadership associations in the city, to implement the entire accord.

King, Raby, and other members of the Chicago Freedom Movement all accepted the accord because they thought it the best they could get. If the agreement mentioned no specific timetable, it was still the most comprehensive of any of King's previous accords, including that in Birmingham. King himself hailed the Summit Agreement as "the most significant program ever conceived to make open housing a reality in the metropolitan area," and he "deferred" the Cicero march indefinitely. "But if these agreements aren't carried out," he warned, "Chicago hasn't *seen* a demonstration."

What had the accord actually accomplished? Journalist Paul Good and various Negro leaders believed it demonstrated that King's forces could move machine politics in a test of strength, and they praised him for driving Daley to the conference table, which set a valuable precedent for future negotiations. But Chester Robinson of the local West Side Organization called it "a sell out" and promised to march on Cicero "come hell or high water." "This agreement is a lot of words that give us nothing specific we can understand," Robinson complained. "We want it to say: apartments should be painted once a year. Community people should have jobs in their community. . . . This situation is just pathetic. We're sick and tired of middle-class people telling us what we want. And we're gonna march in Cicero on Sunday." And CORE, SNCC, and other Black Power dissidents backed him solidly. Even some of King's white friends in CCCO were upset. "We told King that we haven't won anything in this agreement," recalled Meyer Weinberg, a Chicago teacher. "Hell, Daley and his guys are all crooks. You can't believe anything they say." Weinberg surmised that the accord gave King an excuse to bail out of Chicago, and others also judged it "a hydra-headed face saver."

After the meeting, King appeared at a CCCO-sponsored "victory rally" at a Baptist church on the embattled West Side. On Roosevelt Avenue two blocks away, dozens of storefronts were boarded up and glass from broken windows glittered on the sidewalks. From a crowded lounge blared the lyrics of a jukebox hit, "Let's Go Get Stoned." In the Baptist church down the way, Negroes sang, "This Little Light of Mine, I'm Gonna Let It Shine." Then King stood at the pulpit, looking imperturbable. "Some people tried to frighten me," he told his followers. "They said nonviolence couldn't work in the North. They said you can't fight city hall; you better go back down South. But if you look at what happened here it tells you, nonviolence can work." He mentioned Robinson and the local CORE and SNCC people who planned to march on Cicero without him and said fine, they went with his prayers and hopes. Still, there was a strained and plaintive tone in his conclusions, as he confessed something he had long realized: "Let's face the fact: Most of us are going to be living in the ghetto five, ten years from now. But we've got to get some things straightened out right away. I'm not going to wait a month to get the rats and roaches out of my house. . . . Morally, we ought to have what we say in the slogan, Freedom Now. But it all doesn't come now. That's a sad fact of life you have to live with."

As IT TURNED OUT, ROBINSON CANCELED his plans to demonstrate in Cicero. But not CORE and SNCC. On September 4, they staged an anticlimactic march of some 200 people there, with local and state police and 2,000 rifle-toting National Guardsmen holding maddened crowds at bay. King meanwhile announced that jobs were now the main priority in Chicago and that Operation Breadbasket, a program SCLC had tried with considerable success in Atlanta, would be responsible for gaining breakthroughs in hiring for the disadvantaged. Chicago's Jesse Jackson, a flamboyant young Negro who'd joined SCLC's staff, was in charge of the operation, which utilized a network of Negro preachers and churches to conduct negotiations and selective buying campaigns. Under Jackson's watchful eye, Negro preachers investigated the hiring practices of white establishments with a heavy Negro trade. If they did not employ blacks in appreciable numbers and in higher positions, the preachers urged their congregations to boycott the guilty stores. King claimed that within eight months Jackson's operation produced nine hundred new jobs for Negroes and increased Negro community income by an estimated $6 million.

With Operation Breadbasket under way, King closed down his Chicago campaign and returned to Atlanta with his executive staff. In the fall, he did send a voter-registration team back to Chicago, but a snowstorm immobilized a "D Day" drive to register 3,000 new Negro voters for the upcoming mayoral election. Daley's machine and Negro apathy brought the voter-registration attempts to a standstill, too. "Jesus Christ could have come to Chicago and not been able to make an effort," sighed one gloomy SCLC staffer.

Excepting Operation Breadbasket, almost everybody involved in the Chicago Freedom Movement wrote it off as a failure. Many of King's aides viewed it as a northern Albany: the best that could be said of Chicago was that Doc would learn from his mistakes. Others argued that King had postulated the problem on too narrow an issue—open housing—which was irrelevant for the mass of destitute slum dwellers. And Wachtel claimed that King often said that, too. Al Raby, who quit CCCO and returned to college for graduate work, pointed out that too many Chicago Negroes looked to King as a messiah who could accomplish anything. Well, he wasn't a messiah. "It frustrates me," Raby said, "that people keep looking for instant miracles." He conceded that the campaign had gained "very little" and that the slum system went on, bad as ever. The major problem, he contended, was that their goal—the unconditional surrender of the forces that maintained the ghettoes—was unrealistic to begin with. "I don't think that Martin or any of us realized what a tough town this is and how strong the Democratic organization is. For us, it had to be a learning process in understanding the power structure." What had they learned? "That we are in for a much larger and longer fight than any of us thought it was ever going to be." And what distressed him was that *there may never be an answer!*"

King, too, was besieged with doubts. Despite all his efforts, Negroes had rioted not only in Chicago, but in Cleveland, Milwaukee, Atlanta, and thirty-nine other cities that spring and summer, and whites still refused to understand why. Moreover, the depth of hatred he had found in Chicago appalled him. He could not shake the image of all those maniacal faces, taunting and screaming at him on the march from Marquette Park. He believed that the people of Mississippi ought to visit Chicago "to learn how to hate." Nor could he forget the obstinacy and blindness of Chicago's white leaders, the indifference of the federal government, and the silence of white liberal opinion across the land. Truly, in the era of Vietnam, of ghetto riots and the white backlash, King's old "coalition of conscience" was over. As he told David Halberstam later, Chicago convinced him that most whites did not really want integration, did not really want the Negro as a brother. Up to now he had thought they did. Up to now he had thought he was reaching the best in white America. After Chicago, though, he decided that only a small minority of whites—mostly college students—were committed to the cause of racial equality. His feelings seemed confirmed by polls that year which indicated that 85 percent of white Americans believed that Negroes were demanding too much, going too far, and that 50 percent objected to Negroes living next door to them and 88 percent to interracial dating. King contended that the majority of American whites were not ready for equality because they had made no genuine effort to educate themselves out of their racial ignorance.

Not that he was going to give up on white America and stoop to some black nationalist or Black Power argument that all whites were devils. He had to remind himself that when the brick struck him in Marquette Park a white man was marching at his side. He had to remind himself that "We've got some black devils too." He had met some in the slums of Chicago—"street corner preachers" who exhorted Negroes to burn America down, and other blacks so caught up in frustration and irrational rage that they mouthed racist epithets against Jews, blaming them for all their woes. For King, black anti-Semitism in the ghettoes was "a freakish phenomenon" and deeply troubling. He understood that many slumlords and ghetto shop owners were Jews, and that ghetto Negroes, surrendering to racial stereotypes, generalized about a group of people on the basis of a few. They seemed impervious to the fact that Jews had been heavily involved in the civil-rights movement from the outset. In Chicago, King had taken a strong stand against black anti-Semitism "because it's wrong, it's unjust, and it's evil." It still left him depressed. The whole Chicago experience left him depressed. He didn't know where he was going from here.

I T WAS AN UNHAPPY AUTUMN. In Vietnam, American planes were turning the land to rack and ruin, blasting it with bombs, searing it with napalm, wasting it with chemical defoliation. More than 350,000 American troops were fighting there now, and Johnson saw the Alamo in every U.S. outpost, Davy Crockett in every U.S. soldier. In late October, in Cam Ranh Bay, the President urged American troops to "come home with that coonskin on the wall."

At home, Stokely Carmichael was criss-crossing the country, calling Johnson a "liar," a "hunky," and a "buffoon" and denouncing Vietnam as a white racist war, black soldiers there as the white man's mercenaries. At the same time, he damned integration as "a subterfuge for the maintenance of white supremacy" and summoned "Afro-Americans"—the term "Negro" was out now—to sever all ties with white Americans, something that SNCC had already done. "If we are to proceed toward true liberation," argued a SNCC document written largely by Carmichael, "we must form our own institutions, credit unions, co-ops, political parties, write our own histories," and "construct an American reality defined by Afro-Americans."

Soon Carmichael was telling black audiences that "if we don't get justice we're going to tear the country apart" and urging them to "fight for liberation by any means necessary." As he said later, he was grateful to King for teaching blacks how to confront and for taking a moral stand against racism. But King was not political enough; he was not helping to fashion a revolutionary ideology—the purpose of Black Power—for the awakening black masses. "We refuse to be the therapy for white society any longer," Carmichael told a Berkeley crowd in October. "I look at Dr. King on television every single day, and I say to myself: 'Now there is a man who's desperately needed in this country. There is a man full of love. There is a man full of mercy. There is a man full of compassion.' But every time I see Lyndon on television, I say, 'Martin, baby, you got a long way to go.' "

Carmichael's rhetoric resounded in Atlanta, too, right in King's own home. He was living in a new place now, one he'd bought the year before on Sunset Avenue. Here, as in his flat in Chicago, young Black Power advocates argued with him over cups of coffee late into the night. Their hero was Frantz Fanon, a black psychiatrist from Martinique and author of *The Wretched of the Earth.* Quoting Fanon passionately, King's young friends asserted that violence for oppressed people was psychologically healthy and tactically sound, that only violence could bring about black liberation. Don't sing us any songs about nonviolence and progress, they said, for nonviolence and progress belong to middle-class Negroes and whites, "and we are not interested in you."

King tried to reason with them. "The courageous efforts of our own insurrectionist brothers, such as Denmark Vesey and Nat Turner, should be eloquent reminders to us that violent rebellion is doomed from the start," he said. Negroes in this country today are outnumbered ten to one. What were the chances and potential casualties of a minority rebellion against a rich and heavily armed majority with a fanatical right wing "that would delight in exterminating thousands of black men, women and children"? Anyway, history amply demonstrated that violent revolution could only succeed if the government had already lost the allegiance of the military and most of the people. "Anyone in his right mind knows that this will not happen in the United States." Moreover, violence only multiplied hate, intensifying the brutality of the oppressor and the bitterness of the oppressed. "Darkness cannot drive out darkness," King said: "only light can do that. Hate cannot drive out hate: only love can do that."

In *The Wretched of the Earth,* Fanon maintained that blacks must shun Europe and create new institutions, new nations, and finally a new man. King was glad that his young brothers were quoting these words. But Fanon's argument contained a fatal contradiction: he wanted to create a new man on the basis of old concepts of violence. Humanity, King insisted, was waiting for more than a blind imitation of the past. The new man must be a man of love, a man of power imbued with a sense of justice and humanity. "A dark, desperate, confused and sin-sick world waits for this new man and this new kind of power."

But King won few converts among his Black Power brothers. In truth, as William Manchester observed, the torch seemed to be passing to a new generation of black leaders, and it was a real torch. Wherever King went, people asked him: "Since violence is the new cry, isn't there a danger that you will lose touch with the people in the ghetto and be out of step with the times if you don't change your views on nonviolence?" King told them, "I refuse to determine what is right by taking a Gallup poll of trends of the time." A true leader "is not a searcher for consensus but a molder of consensus." "If every Negro in the United States turns to violence, I will choose to be that one lone voice preaching that this is the wrong way."

To combat Black Power, Randolph, Rustin, Wilkins, and Whitney Young signed a statement in October, 1966, which repudiated violence and demagoguery and welcomed—urged—"the full cooperation of whites," and King wrote in *Ebony* that the talk of violence in the Negro community was that of "fearful men." He assured his staff that SCLC wasn't going to reject whites, because "we have come too far down the path now to turn back. There have been too many hymns of hope, too many anthems of expectation, too many deaths, too many dark days of standing over graves of those who fought for integration for us to turn back now. We must still sing 'Black and White Together, We Shall Overcome.'" He reminded them, too, that it was a fact of history that no revolution ever progressed in a straight line, that there were always lulls, dips and curves and meandering points, that somehow they would get through this traumatic time and on "to the city of fulfillment."

Still, he couldn't help but worry about the fractures in the movement. To make matters worse, the white backlash had claimed another victim, as Congress rejected open-housing legislation sponsored by the administration, and the media started playing taps for civil rights.

"After more than a decade of the Civil Rights Movement," asserted *Ramparts* magazine, "the black American in Harlem, Haynesville, Baltimore and Bogalusa is worse off today than he was ten years ago. . . . The Movement's leaders know it and it is the cause of their despair. . . . The Movement is in despair because it has been forced to recognize the Negro revolution as a myth."

King had to do something to refute such outrageous inaccuracies, stem the drift toward violence in the black community, win back the movement's traditional allies, clarify his own ideas about directions and programs, get the Negro revolution back on line. In Atlanta, he announced that he was going on a two-month sabbatical to write a book about the movement called *Where Do We Go from Here?* In early January, 1967, he repaired to Jamaica and secluded himself in a phoneless cliffside villa that afforded a sweeping view of the Caribbean and the Green Mountains with their puffs of clouds. Here, surrounded by tropical vegetation, clad in pajamas, slippers, and a bathrobe, King toiled twelve to fourteen hours a day in a marathon effort to meet a February 15 deadline imposed by Harper & Row.

Apart from a descriptive passage on the march through Mississippi, King had no time for dramatic narration in his new work, no time for the stories of Selma and Chicago. In a style that alternated between historical analysis and exhortation, he rehearsed the enormous gains of a decade of struggle—Negro voter registration up by 300 percent in Virginia and 600 percent in Alabama, the Negro's own hard-won sense of pride and dignity—which proved the efficacy of nonviolent protest. He pointed out that fewer people had fallen in ten years of nonviolent campaigning in Dixie than had died in three nights of rioting in Watts.

Up to now, though, reforms had come at bargain rates. It hadn't cost white America anything to let Negroes vote and share libraries, schools, parks, restaurants, and hotels. But the struggle was in a new phase now, in which Negroes sought an end to economic exploitation and racism itself. And this phase was going to cost white America a great deal—up to $1 trillion, according to the Office of Economic Opportunity—to wipe out slums and poverty. And "stiffening white resistance," King wrote, "is a recognition of that fact."

In 1966, the term "white backlash" inhabited newspapers across America. But King noted that this was nothing new. It was merely the surfacing of ancient prejudices, ambivalences, and rationalizations that had characterized white racial attitudes since the colonial era. In modern times, those attitudes thrived in American history books, which almost totally ignored Negro achievements and contributions and thus intensified the Negro's sense of "nobodyness." Those attitudes even infected the English language, as one found out if one consulted *Roget's Thesaurus.* There one found 120 synonyms for "blackness" and 60 were offensive words like "blot," "soot," "grime," "foul," and "devil." By contrast, there were 134 synonyms for white and all connoted purity, cleanliness, innocence, and chastity. Maybe Ossie Davis was right, King wrote: maybe the English language should be reconstructed so that black children would no longer be taught 60 ways to hate themselves and white children 120 ways to feel superior.

Today, King went on, Negroes were bombarded with a persistent argument: "Other immigrant groups such as the Irish, the Jews and the Italians started out with similar handicaps, and yet they made it. Why haven't the Negroes done the same?" Whites who asked that seemed unable to understand that the black experience in America had been vastly different from theirs, vastly more cruel and complex. No other ethnic group had been forcibly brought here as slaves. No other had come with the stigma of color and been systematically victimized by laws and attitudes that not only treated them as inferior but too often made them feel inferior. The emotional damage inflicted by "the color shock" was incalculably worse than anything white groups had had to bear. To illustrate, King related how a colleague gave his three-year-old daughter a test for color sensitivity in young children. The test required her to use the appropriate crayon on a tree, an apple, and a child. The little girl applied a green crayon to a tree, a red one to the apple. But when she came to the child, she gripped a purple crayon in her fist and slashed the figure with violent thrusts.

Out of the whirlpool of Negro anger and despair came the cry of "Black Power" now sounding in the Negro community. Because it was the first public challenge to the philosophy of nonviolence, King took great pains to explain why the new slogan existed at all and to assess its positive and negative sides. Unlike his conservative colleagues, he did not dismiss the slogan out of hand. No, there were positive things about it. Black Power rightly emphasized strength through unity, rightly summoned the Negro to assert his manhood, take pride in his blackness and his African past, rid himself of his old fear and awe of the white man. But Black Power was too nihilistic to become the basic strategy of the civil-rights movement. True, revolutions often derived from despair. But it required hope to sustain a revolution, and Black Power advocates were bereft of hope because they were convinced that Negroes could not win in America. And so they championed black separatism, even an independent black state. King thought this absurd. "There is no salvation of the Negro through isolation"—the whole notion was chimerical. In a multiracial society, no group could make it alone. The Irish, Jews, Italians, and other ethnic minorities did not acquire power through separatism. They stuck together, yes, but they also formed alliances with trade unions and political machines. And so must the Negro have allies. "In the final analysis the weakness of Black Power is its failure to see that the black man needs the white man and the white man needs the black man." Worse, too many Black Power exponents called for violence and thus trapped themselves in a woeful contradiction. They talked incessantly about not imitating white society, and yet in urging violence they copied "the most brutal and the most uncivilized value of American life."

"Where do we go from here?" King asked. After 338 years of oppression, the Negro was expected to be as resourceful, responsible, and productive as whites who had known no such history. Yes, King conceded, it seemed an impossible task. Yet there were times when you had to attempt the impossible, go on anyway, "keep on keeping on." The Negroes of America must proudly and cheerfully assert who they were. "We are descendants of slaves," King wrote. Say it without shame. "We are heirs of a great and exploited continent known as Africa. We are the heirs of a past of rope, fire and murder. I for one am not ashamed of this past. My shame is for those who became so inhuman that they could inflict this torture upon us." And yet we are Americans too, King said. We are Afro-Americans, "a true hybrid, a combination of two cultures." Scorned and abused though we are, our destiny is still America's destiny; it is not in some nebulous black nation within a nation. Remember Cicero's injunction, "Freedom is participation in power." That is what we want, King said.

Where do we go from here? We must say to ourselves and the world, "I am somebody. I am a person. I am a man with dignity and honor." We must tell our children that "black people are very beautiful" and that they must stand tall and walk with their heads held high. We must convince ourselves and our white brothers that "life's piano can only produce the melodies of brotherhood when it is recognized that the black keys are as basic, necessary and beautiful as the white keys." Then maybe whites will one day understand that integration is not an obstacle, King wrote, "but an opportunity to participate in the beauty of diversity."

We must remember that we have "a rich and noble history, however painful and exploited that history has been," King said. We must reverse "the cultural homicide" committed against us in American histories and remind ourselves and our country of our contributions to American life. All too many whites and Negroes are oblivious to the fact that it was a Negro physician named Daniel Hale Williams who performed the first heart operation in America; that it was another Negro physician, Charles Drew, who largely developed a method of separating blood plasma and storing it in large quantities, a process that saved countless thousands of lives in World War II; that it was a Negro named Norbert Rillieux who invented an evaporating pan that revolutionized sugar refining; that it was another Negro, Granville T. Woods, an electric motors expert, whose patents accelerated the growth and development of railroads at the start of this century. We must remember how our forebears struggled to save their families from the shattering blows of slavery: how mothers on the African coast fought fiercely against slavers to protect their children . . . how parents on plantation after plantation stole and fought and sacrificed and died for their families . . . how one family trudged after Sherman's army in a desperate march to freedom, the father holding one child and the mother another, and eight other toiling children tied to her by a rope . . . how mothers after the Civil War wandered across roadless states in search of children sold off before the conflict . . . and how in the last decade parents and their children have marched hand in hand against guns, clubs, cattle prods, and mobs. We must remember that "the Negro was crushed, battered and brutalized, but he never gave up. He proves again that life is stronger than death. The Negro family is scarred; it is submerged; but it struggles to survive."

Where do we go from here? "We must make full and constructive use of the freedom we already possess," King wrote. We must not wait for full equality before we set out to make our collective and individual contributions to our national life. We must recall the inspiring examples of Negroes "who with determination have broken through the shackles of circumstance." Booker T. Washington rose from a slave cabin in Virginia's hills to become "one of America's great leaders."

From "the oppressive hills" of Gordon County, Georgia, Roland Hayes emerged as a famous singer who entertained kings and queens. From an impoverished background in Philadelphia, Marian Anderson became a celebrated contralto, so honored that Toscanini claimed that a voice like hers happened only once in a century. From "the racial bastion of Laurel, Mississippi," Leontyne Price rose to prominence in the Metropolitan Opera as a soprano and actress. We must remember the example of James Weldon Johnson and Langston Hughes, who reached up and touched "a star in the poetic sky." We must remember the examples of Harry Belafonte, Mahalia Jackson, Ray Charles, Duke Ellington, and Sidney Poitier, of W. E. B. Du Bois, Richard Wright, Ralph Ellison, and James Baldwin; of Joe Louis, Jack Johnson, Muhammad Ali, Jackie Robinson, Roy Campanella, Willie Mays, Henry Aaron, Bill Russell, Wilt Chamberlain, Jesse Owens, Althea Gibson, and Arthur Ashe—all of whom have shown us that, despite our lack of complete freedom, we can make contributions here and now.

Where do we go from here? We must continue nonviolent demonstrations in the North, organize units of power that bring the haves and have-nots together in solidarity, boycott banks and all other businesses that discriminate against us, and continue to demand special treatment from Washington, on the grounds that "a society that has done something special *against* the Negro for hundreds of years must now do something special *for* him, in order to equip him to compete on a just and equal basis." Finally, King wrote, we must broaden our movement and form allies with Mexican Americans, Puerto Ricans, Indians, and Appalachian whites—the poor and forgotten of all races and ethnic groups—and enlist them in our war on poverty. "Let us be those creative dissenters who will call our beloved nation to a higher destiny, to a new plateau of compassion, to a more noble expression of humaneness." If we do, perhaps we can yet inject "new meaning into the veins of American life."

IN LATE FEBRUARY, KING SENT his final revisions off to New York, where freelance editor Hermine Popper and Stanley Levison helped prepare the manuscript for publication. King's editors at Harper &

Row were ecstatic. "I have seldom been as moved, inspired and enlightened all at once," said one. "It is a distinguished work in every sense—in its breadth of vision, compassion, freshness and felicity of style." Cass Canfield also thought it "superb" and a privilege to publish, which Harper planned to do in the summer with the first run of 25,000 copies. Serial rights went to the *New York Times Magazine* and the *Progressive*, and foreign rights to publishers in England and five other European countries.

But King was already preoccupied with something else. While he was in Jamaica, James Bevel left his post as SCLC project director and became Executive Director of the Spring Mobilization Committee to End the War in Vietnam, which intended to organize a national antiwar crusade. A. J. Muste, Dave Dellinger, and other Committee leaders secured Bevel in hopes of getting King, and Bevel was pressuring King to join forces with them, arguing that the war was so heinous that it took precedence over everything, even civil rights.

In Jamaica, King brooded over the war during breaks in his writing. Bevel was a passionate and brilliant lieutenant, and it troubled King that he would leave SCLC for the Spring Mobilization Committee. It was symptomatic of what the war was doing to America—draining off manpower and money that were urgently needed in the domestic war against poverty. King noted that by 1967 relatively twice as many black soldiers as white were fighting and dying in Vietnam, and that the American government was spending approximately $332,000 for every enemy killed there, as compared to $53 per person in its antipoverty programs. It challenged his imagination to think "what lives we could transform if we were to cease the killing," as he wrote in *Where Do We Go from Here?*

One day King was sitting on the porch of his Jamaican villa reading *Ramparts* magazine. He froze when he came to a section on Vietnam, with color photographs of a mother and her baby killed by American firepower. How could he keep quiet about such things? Stokely Carmichael wasn't doing so. He was still getting into the papers with his denunciations of the war ("Hell, no, we won't go!" "Ain't no Vietcong ever called me nigger." "If I'm going to do any fighting it's gonna be right here at home."), which made King's current silence sharply noticeable. Back in the United States, he sat before his television set, watching news clips from Vietnam. He saw rice fields and entire villages in flames. He saw mothers run from blazing huts with children clutched to their chests. He saw American and Vietnamese soldiers with their limbs and faces blasted away. He saw the burned and disfigured bodies of Vietnamese children. A war that incinerated children was a war that mutilated his conscience.

He remembered Dante's warning: *the hottest places in hell are reserved for those who in a moment of moral crisis seek to maintain their neutrality.* "I can't be silent," King told his aides and friends. "Never again will I be silent." He had to make the war one of his major concerns, before it destroyed his movement and his country. No more guarded criticisms in speeches on civil rights. He was going to devote entire addresses to Vietnam, and he was going to make America listen. In February, he conferred with his Research Committee and sent Rustin in search of facts to document his points. He even phoned the President—never mind his hostility—and made it clear that he would be taking a more forthright stand against the war. But "I am not centering this on President Johnson," he said. There was "collective guilt" in this misadventure, stemming from America's arrogant belief that she had some divine mission to police the world, without letting young nations like Vietnam go through the same growing pains, turbulence, and revolution that had characterized American history. It was a painful irony that a country that had initiated much of the revolutionary spirit of the modern world should behave like an arch anti-revolutionary. Ultimately "a great nation is a compassionate nation," and he meant to make his country set its house in order.

PART NINE

THE HOUR OF
RECKONING

On February 25, 1967, at the *Nation* Institute in Los Angeles' Beverly-Hilton Hotel, King gave his first speech devoted entirely to Vietnam, "one of history's most cruel and senseless wars." Throughout his address, he referred to "our" tragedy and "our" guilt in Vietnam, "our paranoid anti-Communism, our failure to feel the ache and anguish of the have nots." Unlike Carmichael, who had given up on America, King was still a patriot—America was still his country—and he could not abide the destruction she was wreaking in Vietnam and here at home, where the promises of the Great Society were being shot down, too, and "an ugly repressive sentiment to silence peace-seekers" was loose in the land, vilifying them as "quasi-traitors, fools, and venal enemies of our soldiers and our institutions." Yes, "the bombs in Viet Nam explode at home: they destroy the hopes and possibilities for a decent America." And so "I speak out against it not in anger but with anxiety and sorrow in my heart, and above all with a passionate desire to see our beloved country stand as the moral example of the world. . . . We must combine the *fervor* of the civil rights movement with the peace movement. We must demonstrate, teach and preach, until *the very foundations of our nation are shaken.*"

Thus King entered the small but growing ranks of war protesters—the most prominent American at this point to do so. He was now marching in step with Coretta (who had continued her peace activities while he was involved in Chicago) and a farrago of antiwar groups, most of them centered at Berkeley and on other college and university campuses. In Congress, a handful of doves—Senator William Fulbright of Arkansas chief among them—made objections to Johnson's Vietnam policy as they voted him appropriations to continue it. And on March 2, Robert Kennedy—now a U.S. Senator—joined the doves in a speech that Johnson had tried to stop "in the interest of national security." Standing in the Senate, Kennedy decried "the ever-widening war," spoke of its atrocities, and called as King did for a halt to the bombing and a negotiated settlement. King had had little contact with Kennedy since he had resigned as Attorney General in 1964 and become U.S. Senator from New York. Even now he avoided any direct association with Kennedy, both men content with a "distant" comradeship as they traveled parallel paths of opposition to the war, poverty, and racism.

Their respective speeches infuriated American hawks, particularly Lyndon Johnson. At a private dinner party he argued that the American people would not tolerate "a dishonorable settlement disguised as a bargain for popularity purposes." By now, both the White House and the FBI were closely monitoring King's antiwar course, which the FBI suggested to "friendly" news sources was remarkably similar to Communist efforts.

Through March, King rode the antiwar trail, denouncing Vietnam in Chicago, Louisville, and Atlanta, with a posse of FBI agents in pursuit. His stand on Vietnam put him on a collision course with pro-administration Negroes like Whitney Young of the Urban League. After a fund-raising affair on Long Island, Young argued that he was fighting the other war in the ghetto and that King's speeches would cost the movement dearly when it came to White House support.

"Whitney," King flared, "what you're saying may get you a foundation grant, but it won't get you into the kingdom of heaven."

They stood face to face now, Young accusing King of not caring about the ghettoes, of eating and dressing well despite his high and mighty words, King angrily retorting that he opposed the war because it was hurting the ghettoes. Finally, Wachtel broke up the argument and took King to his home in Great Neck. By then King's anger had turned to regret and self-recrimination. "I never saw Martin so disgusted at himself," Wachtel said. He complained about his failure to control his temper and handle his quarrels. It was irrelevant, he moaned, that Young had assailed him first; King had no excuse for being "so cruel" to him. Later he phoned Young and did his best to make amends, but the episode was one more example of how the war was tearing Americans apart.

The *New York Times* and other news sources pressed King for interviews and statements about why he was becoming so outspoken on Vietnam. Anxious for a public forum where he could make his position clear, King and his advisers arranged for him to deliver a major address in New York's Riverside Church, under the auspices of Clergy and Laymen Concerned About Vietnam, on the evening of April 4.

King warmed up in a news conference at the Overseas Press Club, where he called on Negroes and "all white people of goodwill" to boycott the war by becoming conscientious objectors to military service. That evening, a clear, crisp night in New York City, 3,000 people filed into Riverside Church for a star-studded antiwar program. King was to give the main address, followed by comments from historian Henry Steele Commager of Amherst College, Rabbi Abraham Heschel who had marched with King in Selma, and Dr. John C. Bennett, president of Union Theological Seminary. Outside the cathedral, some thirty-five pickets—a few of them black nationalists—marched and chanted in protest.

When King rose to speak, the throng in the cavernous sanctuary gave him a standing ovation. He came here tonight, King said, not to address Hanoi or the National Liberation Front of South Vietnam, but to make "a passionate plea to my beloved country," which bore with him the responsibility for ending this tragic war. "Over the past two years, as I have moved to break the betrayal of my own silences and to speak from the burnings of my own heart, as I have called for radical departures from the destruction of Vietnam, many persons have questioned me about the wisdom of my path. . . . Why are *you* speaking about the war, Dr. King? Why are *you* joining the voices of dissent? Peace and civil rights don't mix, they say. Aren't you hurting the cause of your people, they ask? And when I hear them, though I often understand the sources of their concern, I am nevertheless greatly saddened, for such questions mean that the inquirers have not really known me, my commitment or my calling. Indeed, their questions suggest that they do not know the world in which they live. . . .

"Since I am a preacher by trade, I suppose it is not surprising that I have several reasons for bringing Vietnam into the field of my moral vision. There is at the outset a very obvious and almost facile connection between the war in Vietnam and the struggle I, and others, have been waging in America. A few years ago there was a shining moment in that struggle. It seemed as if there was a real promise of hope for the poor—both black and white—through the Poverty Program.

There were experiments, hopes, new beginnings. Then came the build-up in Vietnam and I watched the program broken and eviscerated as if it were some idle political plaything of a society gone mad on war, and I knew that America would never invest the necessary funds or energies in rehabilitation of its poor so long as adventures like Vietnam continued to draw men and skills and money like some demoniacal destructive suction tube."

But the war was doing more than devastating the hopes of the poor at home. "It was sending their sons and their brothers and their husbands to fight and die in extraordinarily high proportions relative to the rest of the population. We were taking the black young men who had been crippled by our society and sending them 8,000 miles away to guarantee liberties in Southeast Asia which they had not found in Southwest Georgia and East Harlem. So we have been repeatedly faced with the cruel irony of watching Negro and white boys on TV screens as they kill and die together for a nation that has been unable to seat them together in the same schools. So we watch them in brutal solidarity burning the huts of a poor village but we realize that they would never live on the same block in Detroit. I could not be silent in the face of such cruel manipulation of the poor."

He opposed the war for other reasons too. He could not condemn violence in American ghettoes without speaking against "the greatest purveyor of violence in the world today—my own government." He opposed the war because his Nobel Peace Prize took him beyond national allegiances. He opposed the war because he was a Christian minister, a reason that was so obvious that he often marveled at those who questioned why he was speaking out. He opposed the war, finally, because he could not tolerate what it was doing to the Vietnamese people. And he felt called this night to speak for them—for the weak, the voiceless, the victims of the United States and those it called its enemies—for they too were his brothers.

"And as I ponder the madness of Vietnam and search within myself for ways to understand and respond in compassion my mind goes constantly to the people of that peninsula. I speak now not of the soldiers of each side, not of the junta in Saigon, but simply of the people who have been living under the curse of war for almost three continuous decades now. I think of them too because it is clear to me that there will be no meaningful solution there until some attempt is made to hear their broken cries.

"They must see Americans as strange liberators," King said. After World War II, we rejected Ho Chi Minh's revolutionary government on the grounds that the Vietnamese people were not "ready" for independence. For nine long years we supported the French in their efforts to recolonize Vietnam. And when they moved out, we took their place, refusing to let Ho Chi Minh unify his own country, refusing to let the Vietnamese people hold general elections as prescribed by the 1954 Geneva Agreement. Instead we converted a civil war over national unification into an American war over world Communism. The peasants watched as we supported a ruthless dictatorship in South Vietnam which aligned itself with extortionist landlords and executed its political opponents. The peasants watched as we poisoned their water, bombed and machine-gunned their huts, annihilated their crops, and sent them wandering into the towns, where thousands of homeless children roamed the streets like animals, begging for food and selling their mothers and sisters to American soldiers. What do the peasants think as we test our latest weapons on them, as the Germans tested new medicine and tortures in Europe's concentration camps? "Where are the roots of the independent Vietnam we claim to be building? Is it among these voiceless ones?" We have destroyed two of their most cherished institutions: the village and the family. We have inflicted twenty times as many casualties on them as have the Vietcong. We have destroyed their land and crushed their only non-Communist revolutionary political force—the Unified Buddhist Church. "We have corrupted their women and children and killed their men. What liberators!"

And what of the National Liberation Front and North Vietnam? What must they think when we accuse them of aggression and violence, and yet support the cruelty and repression of the Saigon regime and rain thousands of bombs down on "a poor weak nation" more than 8,000 miles away from our shores?

"Somehow this madness must cease," King said. "We must stop now. I speak as a child of God and brother to the suffering poor of Vietnam. I speak for those whose land is being laid waste, whose homes are being destroyed, whose culture is being subverted. I speak for the poor of America who are paying the double price of smashed hopes at home and death and corruption in Vietnam. I speak as a citizen of the world, for the world as it stands aghast at the path we have taken. I speak as an American to the leaders of my own nation.

The great initiative in this war is ours. The initiative to stop must be ours."

He outlined several concrete steps the United States should take immediately to start extricating itself from "this nightmarish conflict." It should halt the bombing and declare a unilateral ceasefire in hopes that this would create an atmosphere for negotiation. It should include the National Liberation Front not only in the peace talks but in any future Vietnamese government. And it should set a date for the removal of all foreign troops from Vietnam in accordance with the Geneva Agreement.

"We must move past indecision to action," King said. "We must find new ways to speak for peace in Vietnam and justice throughout the developing world—a world that borders on our doors. If we do not act we shall surely be dragged down the long dark and shameful corridors of time reserved for those who possess power without compassion, might without morality, and strength without sight.

"Now let us begin. Now let us re-dedicate ourselves to the long and bitter—but beautiful—struggle for a new world. . . . The choice is ours, and though we might prefer it otherwise we *must* choose in this crucial moment of human history."

Commager, Bennett, and Heschel also condemned the war that night, but it was King's haunting eloquence that dominated the meeting. "There is no one who can speak to the conscience of the American people as powerfully as Martin Luther King," Bennett said in his own remarks. "I hope that he will make us see the monstrous evil of what we are doing in Vietnam." King's speech, in fact, was not only accurate in its historical detail; it was the most unequivocal denunciation of the war to come from so eminent and influential an American. More than any other, it marked his emergence as a global leader who applied his incomparable oratory and philosophy of redemptive love to the international theater. Young Charles Fager had been right in his essay the year before in the *Christian Century:* King could never again be just a spokesman for American Negroes. As Daddy King said after the Riverside speech, "He did not belong to us, he belonged to the world." And his vision mesmerized those close to him. "I'm not a mystic," Wyatt Walker said. "But I am absolutely convinced that God is doing something with Martin Luther King that He is not doing with anyone else in this country."

 Bᴜᴛ ɪɴ Aᴘʀɪʟ, 1967, ᴍᴏsᴛ ᴏғ Kɪɴɢ's ᴄᴏᴜɴᴛʀʏ supported the Vietnam War, and his address provoked a fusillade of abuse from all sides.
The Jewish War Veterans of America blasted it as "an extremist tirade" that belabored an "ugly parallel" with the Germans, revealed
"an ignorance of the facts," pandered to Ho Chi Minh, and insulted
"the intelligence of all Americans." The FBI claimed that Stanley
Levison had shaped if not written the Riverside speech, and bureau
documents denigrated King as "a traitor to his country and to his
race." Taking his cue from the FBI, a Johnson aide remarked that
King's argument was "right down the Commie line," and Congressman Joe D. Waggonner, in communication with the White House and
the bureau, charged on Capitol Hill that King's "earlier training at
such gatherings as the Communist Highlander Folk School has called
him on to another Communist end, mobilizing support for Peking and
Hanoi in their war against South Vietnam."

   In media circles, *Newsweek* accused King of plunging in "over his
head" and mixing evangelical passion with "simplistic political judgment," which indicated that he had abandoned his dream of an integrated America in favor of a country "in which a race conscious minority dictated foreign policy." *Life* wailed that he advocated "abject
surrender in Vietnam" and sounded like Radio Hanoi, and the Washington *Post* maintained that King had "diminished his usefulness to his
cause, to his country, and to his people." The *New York Times*, in an
editorial called "Dr. King's Error," decreed that Vietnam and the
cause of Negro equality were "distinct and separate" problems and
belittled King for his "facile" fusing of the two, which did "a disservice to both" and led "not to solutions but to deeper confusion." The
editorial condemned his German analogy as reckless slander, reproved
King for "whitewashing Hanoi," and suggested that the place for his
leadership was the battleground of the ghettoes, not Vietnam.

   King's black colleagues opened up on him, too. Carl Rowan, encouraged by Johnson's White House, complained publicly that King
had "delivered a one-sided broadside about a matter on which he obviously has an abundance of indignation and a shortage of information," and that he had made himself "persona non grata to Lyndon
Johnson." "I am convinced he is making a very serious tactical error

which will do much harm to the civil rights movement," asserted Ralph Bunche of the United Nations. King "should realize that his anti-U.S. Vietnam crusade is bound to alienate many friends and supporters." Whitney Young, Roy Wilkins, Jackie Robinson, and Senator Edward Brooke of Massachusetts all disagreed with King in public. And on April 12 the NAACP's sixty-member board unanimously opposed any effort to fuse the civil-rights and antiwar movements.

At first, King was crushed by the public clamor against him. Of all the salvos, the *New York Times* editorial wounded him the deepest. The *Times* was the most prestigious paper in America and King had great respect for it, had given it an interview about Vietnam two days before his Riverside address, and was totally unprepared for its hostile reaction. What could he do to defend himself? He didn't think a letter-to-the-editor would do any good. He was so distraught and hurt, his advisers said, that he sat down and cried.

Behind all the uproar, King and his advisers glimpsed the specter of Lyndon Johnson. It appeared to them that this crafty and vindictive man was orchestrating the critical bombardment against King and ready to go all out to punish him for turning against the President. Six days after Riverside, in fact, the President received an expanded edition of the FBI's dissertation on King and permitted Hoover to circulate it in and out of Washington.

When he realized the extent of the fight he was in, King regained his composure and lashed back at his critics in a series of statements, press conferences, and speeches. Maybe his views on the war were not safe or politic or expedient, maybe they did offend and alienate former allies, but "I will not stand idly by when I see an unjust war taking place and fail to take a stand against it." No, he was not whitewashing Hanoi. The truth was that "we initiated the buildup of this war on land, on sea and in the air and we must take the initiative to end the war." No, he hadn't spoken too strongly about U.S. violence. The U.S. "at this moment" was practicing more violence than any other nation. No, he had not compared "the war in Vietnam to Hitler and what he did to the Jews." He "merely said" that the use of new weapons and testing in Vietnam were " 'reminiscent' of World War II actions." (In fact, he had compared American weapons' testing to what the Germans did in the concentration camps.) Though he had repeatedly said that "we must combine the fervor of the civil rights movement with the peace movement," he now steadfastly denied that he desired to merge the two. This was "a myth" perpetuated by the NAACP. While he would personally continue in both movements, SCLC would concentrate on civil rights. Nevertheless, King believed that "no one can pretend that the existence of the war is not profoundly affecting the destiny of civil rights," and "I challenge the NAACP and other critics of my position to take a forthright stand on the rightness or wrongness of the war, rather than going off creating a nonexistent issue."

As for those who claimed that he should stick to civil rights: "I've fought too long and too hard now against segregated accommodations to end up segregating my moral concerns." If other civil-rights leaders wanted to go along with the administration, that was *their* business. "But *I* know that justice is indivisible. Injustice *any*where is a threat to justice everywhere."

Though his opponents continued to attack him, King was not without supporters. Carmichael defended his theories about the interrelatedness of the war and civil rights; McKissick, who like Carmichael was outspoken against the conflict, said that "Dr. King has come around and I'm glad to have him with us"; and Bayard Rustin, Benjamin Mays, Reinhold Niebuhr, Murray Kempton of the New York *Post*, and John David Maguire of *Christianity and Crisis* all insisted that he was entitled to express his convictions. Mays added that history would decide whether his stand on Vietnam was right or wrong. Murray Kempton, who happened to agree with King about the war, was especially incensed at the *New York Times*. "Are Nobel Peace laureates to be instructed by the *New York Times* as to when it is proper or improper for them to state their views on peace?" Rustin feared that the attacks against King indicated that "America really does not believe that Negroes, as citizens, have yet come of age. Like children, we should be seen but not heard." Reinhold Niebuhr, in a foreword to a pamphlet edition of King's *Nation* Institute and Riverside speeches, pointed out that too many people confused King's position on nonviolent resistance with absolute pacifism. Niebuhr had once confused the two positions himself, as King had observed in *Stride Toward Freedom*, in a chapter on his pilgrimage to nonviolence at Crozer and Boston University. But now Niebuhr had learned from King. "I think, as a rather dedicated antipacifist, that Dr. King's conception of the nonviolent resistance to evil is a real contribution to our civil, moral and political life." And he hoped that King's speeches would enjoy a wide reading.

On April 15, King returned to New York for a giant antiwar rally at the United Nations building, an affair sponsored by Bevel's Spring Mobilization Committee. Bevel had asked King to participate because his eminence would give the demonstration tremendous prestige, and King had agreed to do so against the advice of Rustin and others on his Research Committee. The UN rally would draw people from across the entire antiwar spectrum, from respectable pacifists like Dr. Spock to radical Vietcong flag wavers. "Too many of these people are kooks," Rustin warned King. "They'll wave Vietcong flags in your face and you'll be horribly embarrassed. Besides, you'll be breaking from your real coalition, which is the clergy." But King had made up his mind to ally with Bevel's people, and there was no shaking him.

More than 100,000 people marched with King, Bevel, Spock, Belafonte, folk singer Pete Seeger, Carmichael, and McKissick that day, in the largest demonstration against Vietnam the city had seen. Out in San Francisco, Coretta addressed 50,000 protesters in Kezar Stadium, and Lyndon Johnson, from his Texas ranch, let it be known that the FBI was watching all this antiwar activity. As the New York marchers made their way down Manhattan to the UN building, etched against a somber sky, younger demonstrators chanted, "Hey, hey, LBJ. How many kids did you kill today?" King felt ill-at-ease with such people— seventy of them had burned their draft cards and somebody had set an American flag on fire. In his remarks at the UN building, King sounded "as if he were reading someone else's speech," noted journalist David Halberstam. He just read it, without extemporizing. When he finished, a black embraced him, and he left as soon as he could. He even refused to sign a manifesto of the Spring Mobilization campaign, because he thought its reference to American "genocide" too extreme.

Even so, his was now the most popular voice in the antiwar movement, and students at Berkeley clamored for him to attend their own Spring Mobilization rally. King called for 10,000 student volunteers to participate in a "Vietnam Summer," educating and organizing communities against the war. Then he headed for California with a retinue of aides and David Halberstam, who was doing a piece on him for *Harper's Magazine*. They stopped off in Cleveland so that King could meet with a group of harried Negro ministers. The year before, four people had died in riots there, and the word was out that disorders were going to be worse this summer, and the preachers wanted King to come in and help avert the storm. King was edgy about Cleveland, because the Negro community was badly divided and he feared another Chicago. Still, the city had definite possibilities for a successful civil-rights campaign: it was smaller than Chicago, and there was no Daley machine with roots deep in the black community. At a three-hour session with the ministers, King agreed to bring SCLC to Cleveland and start a summer voting-rights drive. All hoped that this would ward off another summer of violence.

Afterward, King dined at a Negro café with several preachers, some of them old friends. "The middle-class Negroes are our problem," one said. "They've all gone to Shaker Heights and don't give a damn about being Negro any more." Alas, King said, it was the same everywhere in the North. They ate in a jovial atmosphere, though, and fell to joking. One dark minister pointed at another and remarked how much darker *he* was. King was almost reproachful. "It's a new age, a new time," he warned them. "Black is beautiful."

On the plane again, heading west for Berkeley, King admitted that he was becoming a more radical critic of America, of its "domestic colonialism" in the North and its violence in Vietnam. Halberstam said he sounded like a nonviolent Malcolm X, but King disagreed. No, he could never endorse black separatism. "We are all on this particular land together at the same time, and we have to work it out together." Later, though, he commented on how tragic it was that Malcolm had been assassinated. "He was really coming around, moving away from racism," King said. "He had such a sweet spirit."

Halberstam reflected that King was closer to Malcolm now than anybody would ever have anticipated five years before—and much farther from such traditional allies as Wilkins and Whitney Young. In private, King and his staff were sharply critical of both men: they tried to secure things for Negroes through the white establishment, an approach that forced them to tolerate attitudes they privately disdained. Their argument was that the white man owned 90 percent of the country and that the only course was to work through him. This was fine up to a point, King said. But the problem was that the white establishment had become corrupt, and Negroes who tried to model themselves after it, to work with and through it, inevitably picked up the same corruptions. This was what had happened to Wilkins and Young on Vietnam.

But there were fundamental differences here, deeper than Vietnam. "For years," King told Halberstam, "I labored with the idea of reforming the existing institutions of the South, a little change here, a little change there. Now I feel quite differently. I think you've got to have a reconstruction of the entire society, a revolution of values." Though King did not say so, SNCC and CORE had reached a similar conclusion after the violence and frustration of the Mississippi Freedom Summer. But as they subsequently turned to black separatism and independence, King searched for solutions that would hold the races together. Reconstructing American society, he said, might require the nationalization of vital industries, as well as a guaranteed income for impoverished Americans and an end to the slums. It would certainly necessitate a spiritual change in white Americans, to rid them of the racism that infected virtually all levels of white society and that contaminated many Negroes, too.

Halberstam thought no Negro a tougher critic of America. Yet King assumed a radical stance without writing the country off, screaming at whites, or waving a Vietcong flag.

King's plane landed at San Francisco on a sunlit day, and a young black dean and several students fetched him across the bay to the University of California campus, currently the nerve center of antiwar protest and "the conscience of academia," as King put it. At the rally, there were signs promoting a "King-Spock" presidential ticket, and the students and an impressive gallery of the world press responded enthusiastically as he gave a stemwinding talk against the war. "We have flown the air like birds, and swum the sea like fishes," King said, "but we have not learned the simple act of walking the earth like brothers." Afterward he answered questions and said that, no, he would not run for President, though the students' support touched him deeply.

As he left the rally, a white graduate student suddenly blocked his path. "Dr. King, I understand your reservations about running for President, but you're a world figure, you're the most important man we've got, you're the only one who can head a third-party ticket. And so when you make your decision, remember that there are many of us who are going to have to go to jail for many years, give up our citizenship, perhaps. This is a very serious thing."

King was stunned. The student pressed on: "This is the most serious thing in our lives. Politically you're the only meaningful person. Spock isn't enough. So please weigh our jail sentences in the balance when you make your decision."

It was the first time Halberstam had seen anyone get to King. He stood there, waiting for the student to say more, then realized that there was nothing more to say. "Well," King said, "you make a very moving and persuasive statement."

On the way back to San Francisco, King was still shaken by the encounter, and he talked about the alienation of the young. In a meeting with "Afro-American" students, one had told him that America was fighting in Vietnam solely to perfect weapons for the extermination of the Negro. Another had advocated violence, another black separatism. "What's your program?" King asked. "What are you offering?" "We don't need to talk mean, we need to act mean." In the car, King said it was good that young people were identifying with the ghettoes more than students had ten years ago, but there was danger now of paranoia.

As King headed back across the country, his tour seemed very much like a presidential campaign, with its frenetic schedule and plethora of news conferences, speeches, and meetings. King had traveled 3,000 miles in a few days, always somber and confident, always dressed in his dark, interchangeable suits and ties. "The people, the faces, the audiences, the speeches were already blending into each other," Halberstam wrote. "Only the terrible constancy of the pressures remained. One sensed him struggling to speak to and for the alienated while still speaking to the mass of America, of trying to remain true to his own, while not becoming a known, identified, predictable, push-button radical, forgotten because he was no longer in the mainstream."

As KING BARNSTORMED THE COUNTRY that May and June, calling for "teach-ins" and "preach-ins" against the war, Johnson kept escalating the bombing and sending more and more troops into Vietnam. By 1967, the Untied States was spending $20 billion a year on the conflict, and some 485,000 American soldiers were fighting there. With no end to the war in sight, King elected to go all out to defeat Johnson in the Presidential election of 1968, to make Vietnam so unpopular that no contender could support it. He announced that SCLC would depart from past practices and endorse candidates on all levels who opposed

the war. Was he going to run for President? reporters asked. "I understand the stirrings across the country for a candidate who will take a
firm, principled stand on the question of the war in Vietnam," King
replied. "But I must also add that I have no interest in being that
candidate."

But the White House did not believe him. Though a recent Harris
poll claimed that 75 percent of the American people as a whole, and
48 percent of American Negroes, disagreed with King's position on the
war, a Johnson aide warned him that King was a potentially strong
third-party candidate who could draw off "a substantial number of
Negro voters" and a million or so whites. Even if he did not run, he
was capable of throwing half of all Negro voters behind any candidate
he endorsed in 1968—which was clearly not going to be Johnson. Already alarmed by an incipient "dump Johnson" movement within the
Democratic party, the President fulminated against King's antiwar
stance—"Goddamnit," he raged at an assistant, "if only you could
hear what that hypocritical preacher does sexually"—and let the FBI
step up its vendetta against him. The bureau lumped SCLC in with
other "Black Nationalist–Hate Groups" and initiated COINTELPRO
activities against them, which entailed the kind of tough counterintelligence action used against Russia. The FBI kept Johnson apprised of
the intelligence it amassed on King and other antiwar dissidents, and
the President became convinced that the Soviets were building up
congressional opposition to Vietnam and that Red China was financing
the peace demonstrations. This in turn only made him more aloof,
more obsessed with winning the war through massive bombing of
North Vietnam. "How can I hit them in the nuts?" he badgered one
cabinet member. "Tell me how I can hit them in the nuts." With
Johnson growing more belligerent and irrational about the war, Robert
Kennedy groaned, "How can we possibly survive five more years of
Lyndon Johnson? Five more years of a crazy man?"

As the war intensified, the tensions in the ghettoes threatened to
blow America's cities apart. As planned, King's staff started a summer
voter-registration drive in Cleveland, and King himself commuted in
and out of the city during breaks in his antiwar activities. Week after
week, he and his staff walked the streets of Cleveland's ghetto, where
50 percent of the Negro men were either unemployed or earning incomes below poverty level. Nevertheless, SCLC and its local allies got
an impressive number of Negroes out to vote, which helped make Carl

Stokes the first black mayor of a major American city. Thanks to King's presence and SCLC's campaign, Cleveland had no race riot that year.

But a hundred other cities did in the longest, hottest summer ever. In June, street fighting broke out in Boston's Roxbury district, parts of downtown Cincinnati went up in flames during five awful days and nights of shooting and Molotov cocktails, and Newark convulsed in six days of the worst rioting since Watts. In July came the biggest explosion of all, as Detroit blazed in a four-day holocaust that consumed 43 lives and $50 million in property. On July 24, Johnson sent tanks and paratroopers into Detroit, explaining his decision over nationwide television without a single reference to the human misery that had helped ignite the Detroit inferno.

King "labored with heavy heart" through the news of Detroit, moaning that the administration had "created the bizarre spectacle of armed forces of the United States fighting in ghetto streets while they are fighting in the jungles of Asias." On July 25 he fired off a telegram to Johnson: "The chaos and destruction which now spreads through our cities is a blind revolt against the revolting conditions which you so courageously set out to remedy as you entered office in 1964. The conditions have not changed." What happened in Detroit was "the externalization of the Negro's inner torment and rage," which congressional ignorance and inactivity only exacerbated. In recent months, Congress had killed a rent-supplement bill, drastically cut the Model Cities proposal, and thrown out "a simple bill" to protect cities from rats! "The suicidal and irrational acts which plague our streets daily are being sowed and watered by the irrational, irrelevant and equally suicidal debate and delay in Congress. This is an example of moral degradation. This hypocrisy and confusion seeping through the fabric of society can ultimately destroy from within the very positive values of our nation which no enemy could destroy from without."

What could be done? "Let us do one simple direct thing—Let us end unemployment totally and immediately." Let America create something like Roosevelt's old Works Progress Administration, a national agency that would provide a job to every person who needed employment—white or black, old or young. Unless Congress acts at once, "this tragic destruction of life and property" will spread. "Mr. President, this is an emergency state." The life of our nation is literally at stake at home. "I urge you to use the power of your office to establish justice in our land by enacting and implementing legislation of reason and vision in the Congress."

But Johnson ignored him. Instead of condemning the causes of the riots and working swiftly and constructively to remove them, the President rebuked the rioters and lectured Negroes to obey the law. "How," King asked, "can the administration with quivering anger denounce the violence of ghetto Negroes when it has given an example of violence in Asia that shocks the world?. . . Only those who are fighting for peace have the moral authority to lecture on nonviolence." When a government has as much wealth as America, and offers no more than it does to curb the riots, "it is worse than blind," King said, "It is provocative."

But many whites thought it was *King* who was provocative, *King* who had caused the riots with his marches and demonstrations. Commentator Lionel Lokos asserted that the "criminal disobedience" in Newark and Detroit was the inevitable consequence of King's "civil disobedience." By flouting laws he considered unjust, King invited ghetto blacks to do the same. "He has been outstripped by his times," Andrew Kopkind wrote in the *New York Review of Books*, "overtaken by the events which he may have obliquely helped to produce but would not predict."[*]

Even the U.S. Supreme Court had succumbed to the current mood. On June 5, with several northern cities ablaze with riots, the court handed down a decision on *Walker* v. *Birmingham*, which had come up on appeal from the Alabama Supreme Court. During the Birmingham campaign, King and seven colleagues had been convicted for violating an Alabama state court injunction against demonstrations and sentenced to five days in jail. Now, at a time when whites equated demonstrations with riots, the Supreme Court justices voted in a split decision to uphold the conviction and ordered King and his associates to commence their jail terms in the fall. "No man can be judge in his own case, however exalted his station, however righteous his motives, and irrespective of his race, color, politics, or religion," Potter Stewart wrote in the majority decision. "One may sympathize with the petitioners' impatient commitment to their cause. But respect for judicial

---

[*] This was in a harsh review of *Where Do We Go from Here?*, which came out that embattled summer and which Kopkind dismissed as a middle-class tome. Historian Martin Duberman, on the other hand, found the book a justifiably severe indictment of white America. Other reviewers praised King in particular for his analysis of Black Power.

process is a small price to pay for the civilizing hand of law."

The ruling left King terribly sad. "The Supreme Court," he said, "has placed a weapon for repression—an injunction against legitimate protest—in the very hands of those who have fostered today's malignant disorder of poverty, racism, and war." He told Wyatt Walker, "We used to have the Supreme Court as an ally; now even they have turned against us." "This is it, the turning point of the 1960s," moaned a veteran of Birmingham. "We knew that if the justices ruled against King, then no other black leader could expect much when he ran afoul of racist justice."

Never in the history of the movement had whites and Negroes seemed so polarized. On one side, backlashing whites argued that the flames of Detroit had "cremated" nonviolence and that white people had better arm themselves against Negro rioters. On the other side, Carmichael called on Negroes to "kill the Honkies," and H. Rap Brown, who had replaced Carmichael as SNCC chairman, exhorted Negroes to "get your guns" and "burn this town down." After Brown said that in Cambridge, Maryland, and Dayton, Ohio, blacks set sections of both cities afire. SNCC's Chicago chapter announced that "we must fill ourselves with hate for all white things. We have to hate and disrupt and destroy and blackmail and lie and steal and become blood-brothers like the Mau-Mau." SNCC dropped "nonviolent" from its name and lobbied against civil-rights legislation, and Carmichael himself joined the paramilitary Black Panthers, founded in Oakland in 1966. In an article in *Harper's Magazine*, historian C. Vann Woodward pronounced the civil-rights movement moribund and pointed to "disturbing parallels" with the end of Reconstruction.

All around King, the country was coming apart in a cacophony of hate and reaction. "I seriously question the will and moral power of the nation to save itself," he fretted. There was such rage in the ghetto and such bigotry among whites that he feared a race war was about to break out. If that happened, there was likely to be a right-wing takeover of the country. In King's view, time was running out for America, for nonviolence, for the new moral order he had struggled so long and so hard to build here for his fellow man. He felt he had to do something to pull America back from the brink. He told his staff that they had to mount a new campaign that would halt the drift to violence in the black world and combat stiffened white resistance, a nonviolent action that would "transmute the deep rage of the ghetto into a constructive and creative force."

But he doubted that another Chicago movement was the answer. In fact, the failures of Chicago had convinced him that the southern tactics of street marches and demonstrations were unsound in the northern ghetto. As he pointed out, a march down a street in Selma, Alabama, was a revolutionary step, but a march through the northern ghetto was scarcely even distracting because the turbulence of city life absorbed the march "as mere transitory drama." In the South, the street march had caused a social earthquake. In the North, it was only "a faint, brief exclamation of protest." Something else had to be found "within the arsenal of nonviolence," a new approach that would salvage nonviolence as a tactic, as well as dramatize the need for jobs and economic advancement for the poor.

Out of King's deliberations sprang a plan, one so bold and so daring that it surprised some of his aides when he revealed it to them in mid-August. Elaborating on a suggestion by Marian Wright Edelman, who had worked with poor blacks in Mississippi and Washington, D.C., King told his staff and advisers that nonviolence must mature to a new level to meet the crisis they faced in this country. And that new level was mass civil disobedience in the national capital itself. Marian had once participated in a small poor people's "tent-in" in Lafayette Park across from the White House. On her advice, King wanted to try something like this on a vaster scale—a campaign that would bring thousands of unemployed Negroes to Washington, to camp out in front of government buildings for an extended period, like the Bonus Marchers of 1932. Yes, the time had come to confront the federal government itself, for it was that government which had become the reactionary force in American life, that government which was killing poor people in Asia and condemning them to death in America's riot-torn ghettoes, that government which was persecuting King because he dared to challenge its evil policies. King hadn't worked out details yet, but their goal, he told his followers, was "to cripple the operations of an oppressive society" until it listened at last to the cries of its poor.

To RAISE MONEY FOR THE PROJECTED CAMPAIGN, King set out on a nation-wide tour that fall of 1967, with the FBI dogging him as always, disseminating to "friendly" news sources a Negro newpaper editorial that castigated him as a "misguided Moses" and "a traitor to his country." In late October he broke off his tour and flew into Birmingham with Walker, Abernathy, and his other convicted colleagues, to begin their five-day jail terms. It was King's nineteenth time behind bars, and he had never felt so disconsolate about what was happening "in this dark hour" in America. With a steady rain falling outside, he tried to study John Kenneth Galbraith's *The New Industrial State*, to clarify his ideas about the upcoming campaign. But he was so run-down that he contracted a virus and had to see a prison doctor. On the fourth day of his sentence, an Alabama circuit judge ordered him released because "we don't want to work a hardship on anyone. He's served enough time."

A few days later, he felt well enough to give a strong antiwar speech before a Chicago labor conference for peace. But it was a terrible time for King, the lowest ebb in his civil-rights career. It seemed that everybody was attacking him—young black militants for his stubborn adherence to nonviolence, moderate and conservative blacks, labor leaders, liberal white politicians, the White House, and the FBI for his stand on Vietnam. It had been two years since he'd produced a nonviolent victory, and contributions to SCLC had fallen off sharply. Adam Clayton Powell, who had once called him the greatest Negro in America, now derided him as Martin Loser King. And the incessant attacks were getting to him, creating such anxiety and depression that his friends worried about his emotional health.

Desperate for a victory that would silence his critics and save his shattered movement and his country, King called a series of staff meetings and a retreat that November and forged an even bolder plan of operations. What he had in mind now, he told his aides and advisers, was a genuine class movement that would mobilize poor people across racial lines and get them marching on Washington. "Gentlemen," he said, "we're going to take this movement and we're going to reach out to the poor people in all directions in this country. We're going into the Southwest after the Indians, into the West after the

Chicanos, into Appalachia after the poor whites, and into the ghettoes after Negroes and Puerto Ricans. And we're going to bring them together and enlarge this campaign into something bigger than just a civil-rights movement for Negroes." He intended, he said, to launch a broad attack against class-based economic and social discrimination, of which Negroes were the worst victims, but not the only victims. The poor of all races and ethnic backgrounds suffered from a system that deliberately exploited them, deliberately kept them impoverished, and he planned to expose and dramatize that ugly truth by bringing a veritable poor people's army to Washington. He spoke of causing "major massive dislocations" at government buildings and installations, of tying up hospitals with waves of sick youngsters—all to call attention to the plight of America's thirty-five million poor, who were being murdered psychologically for want of jobs.

He had given this a lot of grave and painful thought. Since his college days, he had brooded over the cruel exploitation of the poor in capitalist countries, especially the black poor in America. As early as 1964, he had raised the possibility of a poor people's alliance and had actually advocated that in *Where Do We Go from Here?* Now King was ready to put his words into action—ready to launch a movement that would confront the class and racial basis of economic discrimination.

Several staffers were alarmed by King's plan, certain that SCLC lacked the resources to bring off so monumental a campaign. They recalled, too, how the government had brought out the army to disperse the Bonus Marchers and feared that this would be their fate as well. But it was James Bevel who objected the hardest. Back with SCLC now, still wearing jeans and a yarmulke, he pointed out that the peace movement had grown steadily that year, thanks in no small part to King's influence. Some 20,000 young people had participated in the Vietnam Summer, thousands of others had held anti-draft protests that fall, and in late October (while King was facing imprisonment) some 50,000 demonstrators had marched on the Pentagon, against a sizable police and military force called up to protect it. Bevel was adamant that SCLC's major thrust must be against the war. The issue of peace was far more critical to the survival of mankind than a movement aimed at domestic economic issues. As he argued, he revealed the extent of his own alienation from whites. "You cannot solve the problem of the dilemma of this world until you emphatically tell the truth about who the American white people are," something he thought an all-out peace crusade would do. "They are the most savage, bestial, corrupt, murderous people on earth; and they engage in war games, killing, tricking all the time. They can't help that. It's not because they are mean. It's because they are mentally ill."

King was not about to subscribe to such an extreme view of whites, and it hurt him that one of his own lieutenants should do so. He was critical of whites too—thought most of them "unconscious racists"— but Bevel seemed to overlook the fact that whites predominated in the very movement he championed. And in any case King disagreed that the war overrode everything else. He personally supported an all-out peace offensive, but felt that the time had come to gain a national hearing on fundamental economic questions, and anyway the war was part of the whole problem of economic exploitation. "He kept talking about racism, militarism, and the kind of capitalism that exploited people," assistants recalled, and about how his projected campaign would bring all that out. He vowed that federal authorities "aren't going to run me out of Washington" and that he would "stay in jail six months" if necessary. As King talked on, referring to the Washington project as his "last, greatest dream," Bernard Lee felt a terrible urgency in King"s voice and realized with a start that "we are going for broke this time."

On December 4, King revealed his new campaign to a crowded press conference at Ebenezer Church in Atlanta. "America is at a crossroads of history," he said, "and it is critically important for us, as a nation and a society, to choose a new path and move upon it with resolution and courage. It is impossible to underestimate the crisis we face in America. The stability of a civilization, the potential of free government, and the simple honor of men are at stake." Beginning in early April of next year, SCLC would undertake a "strong, dramatic, and attention-getting campaign" of mass civil disobedience in Washington, D.C., to force the federal government to guarantee jobs or incomes for all Americans, and to start tearing down the slums once and for all. SCLC was planning, he said, to recruit 3,000 poor people from five rural areas and ten major cities, train them for three months in the techniques of nonviolence, and then bring them to Washington to disrupt transportation and government operations until America responded to the needs of her poor.

"The Negro leader's mood seemed deeply pessimistic," noted the *New York Times* reporter. "He said the confrontation in Washington vas a 'last desperate demand' by Negroes, an attempt to avoid 'the worst chaos, hatred and violence any nation has ever encountered.'" Yes, the ugly mood of ghetto Negroes made the campaign a "risky" one, King said, but "not to act represents moral irresponsibility." He thought—he hoped—that "angry and bitter" people would respond to nonviolence "if it's militant enough, if it's really doing something." He reminded the press that the government "does not move to correct the problems involving race until it is confronted directly and dramatically." He added, "These tactics have done it before, and this is all we have to go on." One thing he felt for certain: continued inaction on the part of the national government would bring down "the curtain of doom" on America.

But there was more to it than that. As he explained in a series of lectures for the Canadian Broadcasting Corporation that autumn and winter, the crisis in America was "inseparable from an international emergency which involves the poor, the dispossessed, and the exploited of the whole world." The crisis was between the haves and have-nots, the exploiters and exploited, the economic and political imperialists and their luckless victims in the ghettoes, reservations, and Appalachian wastelands of America and in the Third World. In a "Christian Sermon on Peace," aired over the Canadian Broadcasting Corporation on Christmas Eve and delivered in person at Ebenezer Church, King called for a total reconstruction of society for the benefit of white and colored peoples the world over. Human life, he warned, could not survive unless human beings went beyond class, tribe, race, and nation and developed a world perspective. It all came down to something he had long believed—that "all life is interrelated," that "we are all caught in an inescapable network of mutuality." In this interdependent world, no nation, race, or individual could possibly survive alone. Today, Americans couldn't leave for their jobs in the morning without relying on most of the world to get them started. In the shower, you bathed with a sponge from a Pacific Islander and soap from a Frenchman. In the kitchen, you drank coffee provided by a South American, or tea by a Chinese, or cocoa by a West African, and you buttered toast from an English-speaking farmer. "And before you finish eating breakfast in the morning, you've depended on more than half of the world. This is the way our universe is structured, this is its interrelated quality. We aren't going to have peace on earth until we recognize this basic fact of the interrelated structure of all reality."

Aᴌᴌ ᴏꜰ Kɪɴɢ'ꜱ ᴘʀᴇᴠɪᴏᴜꜱ ᴄᴀᴍᴘᴀɪɢɴꜱ had suffered adverse criticism, but none of that rivaled the nearly universal hostility his Washington project was generating. Predictably, most of the Negro leadership, the press, and the white liberal community complained about how unwise and untimely this was and fretted that King's poor people's army would incite a riot, plunging Washington into flames. Roy Wilkins accused King of "bowing to the trend" of the militants and giving peaceful demonstrations an "alarming twist." A Negro named George Schuyler asserted in a column in the St. Louis *Globe-Democrat* that King and his "peripatetic parsons" were plotting a "new racial war" with shock tactics reminiscent of the Vietcong. And mail opposing the projected march flooded into the White House. "You had better lock up Martin Luther King," wrote one enraged citizen, "or we will have a social revolution."

Johnson himself was furious that King was bringing a Negro army to protest against *him,* to disrupt and dislocate *his* government. What man had ever done more for the Negroes than he? Johnson thundered. Why didn't the Negroes appreciate him? It was bad enough that King should mouth those lies about him and Vietnam, but an invasion of Washington was intolerable. When was King coming? Johnson badgered his aides. One replied that Deke DeLoach of the FBI would let them know once King set a date. In fact, DeLoach passed on to the White House secret SCLC documents, obtained through the FBI's paid informant on King's staff, that pertained to the organization of the campaign. Convinced that subversive hordes would soon be battering at the gates of Washington, Johnson appealed directly to King to call the operation off. When King refused, a presidential assistant lumped him with Carmichael and H. Rap Brown and accused him of plotting "criminal disobedience" against the government. And Johnson himself publicly warned that he would not permit lawlessness "in whatever form and in whatever guise." The President, wrote George Schuyler in the St. Louis *Globe-Democrat,* did not plan "to preside over the liquidation of the American nation or sit fiddling in the White House while Washington burns." He could easily mobilize 25,000 troops to repel a militant invasion of the capital, and "Dr. King better believe that."

The FBI too was certain that King's campaign would precipitate a "massive bloodbath in the nation's capital," and it set out to sabotage the campaign by stirring up public indignation against it. The bureau for the first time specifically targeted King in its COINTELPRO activities against "black nationalist hate groups" and used forty-four field officers to spread pernicious news stories about him. The stories charged King with violent and revolutionary intentions in Washington, with forming "an apparent alliance" with Elijah Muhammad and the Black Muslims, with aspiring to become "a 'Messiah' who could unify and electrify the militant Black nationalist movement." At the same time, the bureau got out still another edition of the King monograph, with still more stories about sex, Communism, and embezzlement, and not only fed it to the entire intelligence community, Secretary of State, Joint Chiefs of Staff, and various army and naval commanders, but "briefed" outstanding religious leaders about its contents.

King himself was aware of the FBI's escalating campaign against him, and he and his advisers were convinced that Johnson was behind it, convinced that the President himself was now collaborating with Hoover to thwart the Washington campaign and turn the country so completely against King that he would be driven scorned and hated from public life. It depressed King that his relationship with Johnson had degenerated to such a hostile state. What new stories about his faults—his "sins," as he called them—were Johnson and Hoover whispering into the ears of America? (The bureau was now claiming that King had "a Mistress"—the wife of a California dentist—whom he met in motel rooms.) In this difficult time, the FBI's intensifying vendetta heightened King's guilt over "the things" in his personal life. He later acknowledged that there was "a Mr. Hyde and a Dr. Jekyll in us" and that he was no saint, no, "I am a sinner like all of God's children." Yet he wanted so to be "a good man"—wanted so to hear a voice say to him one day, "I take you in and I bless you because you tried." He was trying now, as hard as he had ever tried in his life. He would not give up. Despite Johnson and Hoover, despite wide-scale public disfavor, despite his own "sins," he was going to Washington because he felt that God was calling him there.

Still, he had deep forebodings. By 1968, the FBI had logged fifty assassination threats against him, and the Klan and other hate groups had him targeted for violence. With the announcement of the poor people's campaign, right-leaning businessmen across the land viewed him as a fiendish black devil out to wreck capitalism and establish a Communist social order that would ring the bells of doom for "free enterprise," white supremacy, and their own personal wealth. Such people hated King, cursed his cause, and wished him dead. In the St. Louis area, a couple of aging right-wingers, both active in Wallace's American Independent party and supporters of Wallace for President, plotted to have King murdered. John Kauffmann, a motel operator with a criminal record, had a standing offer of $20,000 to $30,000 for anybody who would kill "the big nigger." His friend John Sutherland, a St. Louis patent attorney given to wearing a Confederate colonel's hat and decorating his study with Confederate flags, had put up $50,000 for King's head.

King knew nothing about any specific contracts against his life, but he realized that the Washington project made him more visible, increasing his chances of getting killed. He and many of his assistants had a feeling that he was being stalked now and that the end could come at any time: a knife thrust out of a crowd, a gunshot. . . . His staff worried constantly about his safety, but what could he do? he asked. He certainly couldn't go to the FBI or the police. And he was not going to carry a gun or let anyone around him do so either. That would violate everything he preached, everything he stood for. Anyway, what good would a gun do? Anybody who wanted to could shoot him at any time. Look how easily Oswald had killed Kennedy.

He tried to joke about the danger he felt, about the possibility that he or one of his young aides might be gunned down. He would say, "If it's you, Andy, I sure will preach you a great eulogy," and then he would preach it to the amusement of everyone around. At other times, he would philosophize as always. "You know, I cannot worry about my safety; I cannot live in fear. I have to function. If there is any one fear I have conquered, it is the fear of death." And he would quote, "If a man has not found something worth giving his life for, he is not fit to live."

But he remained apprehensive all the same. One staffer, remembering his talk about the likelihood of death, thought "the strain of wondering when it was coming was almost overpowering." Only when King was someplace where he couldn't be shot—such as in a room without windows—could he relax with his aides and be "the Martin Luther King of the early days." In public, there was "almost a learned response to let his eyes wander and gaze," the staffer said. "It was an unconscious response. He was looking, cautious, uncomfortable."

By 1968, King was working at a frenzied pace, telling his followers—telling Coretta herself—that "if anything happens to me, you must be prepared to continue." Unable to sleep, he would stay up all night thrashing out ideas or testing speeches on his weary staff. Andrew Young was worried about him. "You oughta go have a good physical exam," Young advised. "Start takin' a little better care of yourself . . . slack off on the pace." King was just thirty-nine; he had a lot of years left. But King would not slow down. It was as if he were cramming a lifetime into each day. Yet even his frantic pace could not assuage the despair he felt, a deepening depression that left him morose, distracted. His friends and aides did not know what to make of it or to do for him. One confidant recommended that he consult a psychiatrist. But King was personally hostile to psychoanalysis—had been since Boston University days—and rejected the advice. He drove himself harder than ever, plunging into the planning and organization of the poor people's campaign like a man possessed.

In January, he called an SCLC meeting in Miami, Florida, and secured official SCLC approval for what he now called the Washington Spring Project. But King was running into stiffening resistance among his own advisers, chief among them Bayard Rustin. "Given the mood in Congress," Rustin warned King, "given the increasing backlash across the nation, given the fact that this is an election year, and given the high visibility of a protest movement in the national capital, I feel that in this atmosphere any effort to disrupt transportation, govt. buildings, etc., can only lead to further backlash and repression." Too, the campaign would attract "elements that can't be controlled," as had the Meredith March in Mississippi. As for an alliance of the poor, "You are attempting the impossible. There is no way for Martin Luther King to bring white poor, Puerto Rican poor, black poor, Irish poor together in any meaningful way." George Meany, boss of the AFL-CIO, had spent millions each year trying to organize such people into unions, and "he falls flat on his face year after year." How could King accomplish what Meany had failed to do? Finally, if King undertook civil disobedience against government installations in Washington, "there is likely to be a swift and vigorous effort by the government to close the project down." King "might lose face" in the movement if he canceled the operation, but he would lose a lot more face if he conducted the demonstrations and failed. Then what would become of

King? of SCLC? of nonviolence itself?

After a series of meetings with King and his advisers and staff, Rustin announced that King had rejected his advice. "But Dr. King is sincere in believing there is a terrible urgency and that if Congress does not act, the Nation will be faced with more riots. And he believes he can succeed in making them act. I respect him for his sincerity and still regard him as the leader of the civil rights movement."

In mid-January, King dispatched forty veteran SCLC field workers to selected rural areas in the South and to Baltimore, Philadelphia, Newark, New York, Boston, Cleveland, Detroit, and other riot-plagued cities, to start recruiting destitute volunteers for King's poor people's army. King named young Bernard Lafayette, Jr., a former SNCC field secretary and a new SCLC officer, to direct the campaign. Then he launched a promotional tour out to the West Coast, telling crowds in churches and auditoriums along the way what he hoped to do in Washington. At a fund-raising affair in Hollywood, he spoke with James Baldwin, who thought him "five years wearier and five years sadder" than he'd been during the great Washington march of 1963. King was still petitioning Washington, Baldwin mused, "but the impetus was gone, because the people no longer believed in their petitions, no longer believed in their government." Now, five years after King's "I Have a Dream" speech, it seemed that "we had merely postponed, and not at all to our advantage, the hour of dreadful reckoning."

In truth, King himself was experiencing "deep apprehensions" about how the Washington project was going to turn out. It would attract new forces, less disciplined forces, far more excited and angry than any he had ever led. What if he could not control them? What if they turned Washington into another Detroit, as many of his critics were predicting? And what if he couldn't form an alliance with the Indians, Chicanos, and white poor? Moreover, what new treacheries were Johnson and the FBI plotting against him? And there were money problems too. Rustin estimated that it would cost $400,000 to sustain a poor people's "tent" city in Washington. With so many of his financial sources gone because of his opposition to Vietnam, where would he get that kind of money? And so many of his friends were against the campaign, warning him that he could never pull it off, telling him over and over that he was failing. Yes, failing.

By early February, he was beginning to lose faith himself. "We're in terrible shape with this poor people's campaign," Williams heard him complain. "It just isn't working. People aren't responding." There seemed to be a spiritual death settling across America that threatened all his work, all his teachings. Abernathy, returning from an extended trip abroad, was shocked at how melancholy King had become. "He was just a different person," Abernathy remembered. "He was sad and depressed. And I did everything I could to help him but I couldn't do much."

On Sunday, February 4, King delivered a poignant personal message to the Negro people of Ebenezer, his one undivided community in this season of doom. "Every now and then I think about my own death, and I think about my own funeral. I don't think about it in a morbid sense. Every now and then I ask myself, 'What is it that I would want said?' And I leave the word to you this morning. If any of you are around when I have to meet my day, I don't want a long funeral. And if you get somebody to deliver the eulogy, tell them not to talk too long." His congregation responded with sympathetic "amens" as his voice rose, sweeping the sanctuary in an ecstasy of grief and consecration. "Tell them not to mention that I have a Nobel Peace Prize. That isn't important. Tell them not to mention that I have three or four hundred other awards. That's not important. Tell them not to mention where I went to school. I'd like somebody to mention that day, that *Martin Luther King, Jr.*, tried to give his life serving others. I'd like for somebody to say that day that Martin Luther King, Jr., tried to love somebody. I want you to say that day I tried to be right on the war question. I want you to be able to say that day that I *did try* to feed the hungry. I want you to be able to say that day that I *did try* in my life to clothe those who were naked. . . . I want you to say that I tried to *love* and *serve* humanity. Yes, if you want to say that I was a drum major, *say* that I was a *drum major* for justice. Say that I was a drum major for peace. That I was a drum major for righteousness. And all of the other shallow things will not matter. I won't have any money to leave behind. I won't have the *fine* and *luxurious* things of life to leave behind. But I just want to *leave* a committed life behind. And that's all I want to say. . . ."

Depressed though he was, King somehow found the inner strength to go on. Two days after his sermon, he flew to Washington for rounds of talks with local black people. He met with Carmichael and SNCC chairman H. Rap Brown in a highly secret session in a Washington motel, explaining the poor people's campaign to them as he had to other groups. Some wondered why King would bother to talk with SNCC at all. Racked by internal dissent and defections (John Lewis and others had quit because of its violent, antiwhite policies), SNCC had fewer than ten field offices in full operation and had ceased to function as an effective civil-rights organization. Carmichael himself had recently toured several Communist countries, where he had championed black revolution, and was now in Washington with a small black staff, working for Negro unity. Because he and Brown had a following among ghetto youths there, King approached them as part of his own efforts to unify Washington Negroes behind his project; he didn't want Carmichael and Brown to undermine it by preaching violence against "honkies." In fact, he hoped to neutralize the two by letting them vent their anger on him and then persuading them to "give us a chance."

After the meeting, King would only say that "there were areas of agreement and disagreement." But he later deplored SNCC's antiwhite stance. "We have not given up on integration," he said. "We still believe in black and white together." That is why "we need this movement. We need it to bring about a new kind of togetherness between blacks and whites. We need it to bring allies together and to bring the coalition of conscience together."

Over the next two days, King and his staff rehearsed a constant theme in dealing with Washington blacks, from garbage collectors to ministers and businessmen: "We are here to deal with a serious problem in a sick society. We would like to have your support and understanding." Newspapers reported some intense confrontations with black nationalists, though, as King made it emphatically clear that this was to be a nonviolent, integrated, dignified protest and that he wanted no rabid elements involved in it.

He said the same thing to Negroes and Puerto Ricans in other cities. And he talked and negotiated with poor whites, Indians, and

Chicanos in the South, Southwest, and Far West. He hoped they would march to Washington with him, because power for poor people meant developing "the ability, togetherness, the assertiveness, and the aggressiveness to make the power structure respond."

By February 12, meanwhile, he and his staff had completed the master plan for the Washington campaign. In phase one, to commence in late April, several thousand poor people—the initial force now being recruited in the cities and the South—would march on Washington and encamp in a plainly visible shantytown. King even thought of a mule train traveling from Mississippi to Washington to help dramatize the pilgrimage. "We hope that the sound and sight of a growing mass of poor people walking slowly toward Washington will have a positive, dramatic effect on Congress," King said later. Once assembled in Washington, the poor would undertake brief, exploratory demonstrations and then hold a giant rally like that at the Lincoln Memorial in 1963, a rally that would draw hundreds of thousands of people for a show of togetherness that might last several days. King hoped it would be the largest march ever to occur in the national capital.

In phase two, the poor-people's army would start disrupting government operations with nonviolent sit-ins and demonstrations and get themselves arrested. As they went off to jail, hundreds of thousands of reinforcements, recruited from college campuses and the Washington ghetto, would continue demonstrations, dislocating the Labor Department and other federal agencies, until Washington jails were packed to capacity with singing, disciplined, nonviolent warriors. What they were organizing, King explained in a *Look* magazine article, was a "Selma-like, Birmingham-like" effort to arouse "a moribund, insensitive Congress to life" and force it to grant poor people "an Economic Bill of Rights," including guaranteed jobs to all people who could work and a guaranteed income for those too old, too young, or too disabled to do so.

The projected campaign was not without precedent. A. Philip Randolph had long dreamed of a Washington march for jobs and income, and that had been the original purpose of the great 1963 demonstration at the Lincoln Memorial. SNCC, too, had once envisioned militant sit-ins and demonstrations in the national capital. What King was planning, though, was a full-scale war on poverty, to last three months or longer, putting relentless pressure on Congress and spotlighting for the entire nation the paradox of "poverty amid plenty" and the miserable realities of America's poor. He intended, he said, "to dramatize the gulf between promise and fulfillment, to call attention to the gap between the dream and the realities, to make the invisible visible. All too often in the rush of everyday life there is a tendency to forget the poor, to overlook the poor, to allow the poor to become invisible, and that is why we are calling our campaign a poor people's campaign." He would expose, too, how Congress was playing "Russian roulette" with riots, ignoring the social maladies that ignited them while squandering America's ample resources on the accursed war in Vietnam.

He realized, though, that Congress might not respond. "It is a harsh indictment, but it is an inescapable conclusion, that Congress is horrified not at the conditions of Negro life but at the product of these conditions—the Negro himself." If Congress did not act, King would launch phase three of the campaign: he and his legions would undertake nationwide boycotts of selected industries and shopping centers in big cities targeted for action. These would be supported by continued demonstrations and arrests in Washington and allied marches in other parts of the country. The boycotts, accompanied perhaps by sit-ins at factories, would force business leaders to press Congress to meet King's demands, and Congress, he hoped, would be unable to resist that kind of persuasion.

It was going to be "a mammoth job," King admitted. "Before we have mobilized one city at a time, now we are mobilizing a nation." Apart from an alliance of the poor, the most novel feature of the campaign was the idea of national boycotts, which grew out of the Alabama boycott he had contemplated in 1965 and the local boycotts SCLC had conducted in its previous campaigns and was still employing in its Operation Breadbaskets. Recalling how SCLC had forced Birmingham merchants to meet movement demands, King and his lieutenants intended in phase three to take the problems of the poor beyond the state to the very center of the economic system.

As Rustin said, King was getting up a class movement against the national economic power structure, which included not just Washington, but the powerful corporations and business moguls of capitalism itself. There were similarities here to the Populist crusade of 1892 and the organized labor movement of the 1930s, both of which had sought major economic reforms for the victims of industrial consolidation and had tried with varying success to bridge the cleavages between races and classes. Though much thinking and planning remained, "there was an awareness," recalled King's advisers, "that we were going to confront the economic foundations of the system and demand reforms"—in short, said Bernard Lee, "what the powers of the country will kill you for." "White America must recognize," King wrote in an article published in *Playboy*, "that justice for black people cannot be changed without radical changes in the structure of our society," changes that would redistribute economic and political power and that would end poverty, racism, and war.

This was reminiscent, of course, of Rauschenbusch's Social Gospel. In truth, the poor people's campaign was King's "last, greatest dream" because it sought ultimately to make capitalism reform itself, presumably with the power of redemptive love to win over economic oppressors, too, and heal antagonisms. Certainly the projected campaign reflected King's unhappiness with capitalism, an unhappiness that had begun in his youth, even before he had studied Rauschenbusch's impassioned denunciations of it. This hardly made King a Marxist. He meant it when he told his staff that Marx "got messed up" when he failed to "see the spiritual undergirding of reality" and embraced an odious "ethical relativism" which led him to believe that the ends justified the means. And King continued to preach against the evils of Russia's dictatorial Communist state. No, somehow a better social order than Communism or capitalism had to be constructed, one that creatively blended the need for community and the need for individuality. Perhaps in this, his most imaginative, desperate, and far-reaching scheme, he could take his country a step closer to the realization of an old dream: the forging of a Christian commonwealth that was neither capitalist nor Communist, but a synthesis of the best features of collective and individual enterprise, a commonwealth that cared for its weak and handicapped even as it encouraged its strong and gifted.

The stakes and risks involved were enormous, and King himself expected massive resistance from both the public and private sectors. But he was convinced that anything less than the poor people's campaign was not enough. It was either that or more devastating riots and possibly guerrilla warfare in the cities. This was "the showdown for nonviolence," King warned his countrymen, "a 'last chance' project to arouse the American conscience toward constructive democratic change."

PART TEN

FREE
AT LAST

Whenever you set out to build a temple, you must
face the fact that there is a tension at the heart
of the universe between good and evil.

MARTIN LUTHER KING, JR., *1968*

In his public appearances, King seemed confident and composed. But among his intimates, away from the crowds and cameras, he showed the prodigious strain he was under. Abernathy thought him more troubled than ever; "he was nervous and very, very jittery." In mid-February, 1968, he got away for a few days before the final drive on Washington. He went to Jamaica with Coretta and Young and then to Acapulco with Abernathy. On the plane to Acapulco, King acted strange. He preached his sermons to Abernathy and even repeated his self-eulogy, "A Drum Major for Justice," which he'd given at Eben- ezer. One night in Acapulco, the two friends went out to eat and then came home to bed. Around three in the morning, Abernathy awoke with a start. King's bed was empty. "I was terribly frightened," Aber- nathy said, "and I went out in the living area looking for him." But King wasn't there, and Abernathy didn't know what to do. Should he call hotel security? Then he saw King standing on the balcony in his pajamas, gazing in the gloom at the Pacific. Abernathy went to him. "Martin," he said, "what are you doing out here this time of night? What is bothering you?"

King kept staring at the ocean, listening to the roar of the waves. "You see that rock out there?" he said.

"Oh, sure, I see it," Abernathy said.

"How long do you think it's been there?" King asked.

"I don't know," Abernathy said. "I guess centuries and centuries. I guess God put it there."

"Well, what am I thinking about?" King asked him.

Abernathy was perplexed. He didn't know what King was think- ing, what was troubling his friend.

"You can't tell what I'm thinking?" King asked again.

"No," Abernathy said.

Then King started singing, "Rock of Ages, cleft for me; let me hide myself in thee. . . ."

Abernathy was deeply concerned. King seemed so distraught, so frightened. On the plane home, he kept repeating his sermons and telling Abernathy what he wanted him to do with SCLC.

But in a few days he seemed to pull himself together. On February 23 he appeared in Carnegie Hall for a tribute to W. E. B. Du Bois. "He confronted the establishment as a model of militant manhood and integrity," King said of Du Bois. "He defied them and though they heaped venom and scorn on him, his powerful voice was never still."

King's own voice was never still. Despite his moods, his recurring depression and sense of doom, he took to the road again, visiting his field staff in the cities and the South and trying to muster support for the Washington project. In his public utterances, he insisted that he was still an optimist. No matter how desperate things were, no matter how grave the crisis, no matter how much his dreams had been shattered, he refused to become a hard, grim, bitter man. He might well falter and fail, he wrote in a magazine article, but he would remain secure in his knowledge that "God loves us: He has not worked out a design for our failure. Man has the capacity to do right as well as wrong, and his history is a path upward, not downward. The past is strewn with the ruins of the empires of tyranny, and each is a monument not merely to man's blunders but to his capacity to overcome them. While it is a bitter fact that in America in 1968, I am denied equality solely because I am black, yet I am not a chattel slave. Millions of people have fought thousands of battles to enlarge my freedom. Restricted as it still is, progress has been made. This is why I remain an optimist, though I am also a realist about the barriers before us."

In late February, he read a summary of the report of the Kerner Commission, appointed by Johnson to investigate the origins of race riots. The report warned that the United States was "moving toward two separate societies, one black, one white—separate and unequal"—and concluded with what King had been saying since 1964: that brutalizing discrimination had spawned the riots and that the nation must strike at the roots of urban disorder by allocating massive funds to improve education, unemployment, and housing opportunities for Negroes. King declared this "a physician's warning of approaching death with a prescription to life. The duty of every American is to administer the remedy without regard for the cost and without delay."

But Johnson didn't see it that way. The President announced that it would cost $30 billion to implement the Kerner proposals and that the United States could not afford them. "This means he's not going to do anything about the war and he's not going to do anything about the cities either," cried Robert Kennedy. To deal with urban disorders, in fact, the administration was mobilizing an awesome military force. The Justice Department, functioning as the nation's command post for riots, was watching pressure points and working up "response capacities," and the army was stockpiling military equipment and opening liaisons with the National Guard and state and local police for maximum response should violence erupt in any of 124 "hot" cities. It was as though the administration were preparing for civil war.

Meanwhile the war in Vietnam ground on without end. Though Johnson had boasted that "the enemy has been defeated in battle after battle" and that America was winning the war, the Vietcong on the last day of January launched a massive Tet offensive in South Vietnam, attacking thirty-six of forty-four provincial capitals, sixty-four district towns and countless villages, twelve U.S. bases, and even the American Embassy in Saigon. Here was undeniable proof that Johnson's military solution was a failure and that the claims of the President and his generals could not be believed. The Tet offensive proved that the Vietcong were a power to be reckoned with and that the South Vietnamese people were not loyal to the Saigon government. Yet American reinforcements continued to be shipped in, and King grumbled that Johnson "seemed amazingly devoid of statesmanship," incapable of admitting an error and caught in an irreversible spiral of "irrational militarism." But at least the Tet offensive inflamed public opinion against the administration and gave new life to the "Dump Johnson" movement within the Democratic party. On March 12, dovish Eugene McCarthy, U.S. Senator from Minnesota, almost whipped Johnson in the New Hampshire primary, which stunned the President and astonished political analysts. Four days later, Robert Kennedy announced that he too would run against Johnson for the Democratic Presidential nomination.

Wherever King went, people asked which peace candidate he intended to support—McCarthy or Kennedy? He hedged in public, saying that he thought highly of both men and that both their candidacies offered excellent alternatives to Lyndon Johnson. But in private he was leaning toward Kennedy. He had never been close to McCarthy, whose campaign was white-oriented and who had given little credit to King's antiwar activity, which had helped make his campaign possible. Kennedy, on the other hand, was an old battle-tested ally. Not only was Kennedy's office cooperating with SCLC representatives in organizing the Washington project; he was also speaking out in behalf of the poor and the powerless. He had taken up the cause of itinerant farm workers in California, visited Indian reservations, toured the Mississippi delta to see for himself what black poverty was like, and become increasingly absorbed in the problems of the northern ghettoes. His compassion made him immensely popular among American Negroes, especially in the slums. Asked what he would do if he were President, Kennedy replied that he would have the major television networks show in prime time a two-hour documentary about ghetto life—maybe that would shock white Americans out of their apathy. And he would push for recovery within the ghettoes, so that black people could develop a sense of pride and cultural identity before moving out into white communities. A Negro minister thought no white leader more welcome in the slums than Kennedy, because he "had this fantastic ability to communicate hope to some pretty rejected people." "Kennedy *is* on our side," said a ghetto youth. "We know it. He doesn't have to say a word."

That wasn't the only thing King appreciated about Kennedy. In international matters, the senator sounded like King in criticizing America for failing to identify herself with the nationalist movements in the Third World and for siding much too often with repressive, anti-Communist regimes there. Moreover, Kennedy also enjoyed the unmitigated hatred of the man in the White House, who called him that "little fart" and viewed him as "the enemy." Though King made no official endorsement of Kennedy at this juncture, taking pains not to divide the inchoate anti-Johnson forces, he knew they were allies in a common struggle.

But in King's view the salvation of America did not rest with Kennedy or any other white leader. What she needed was Negro political leaders who would adopt an integrated foreign policy and teach the country how to get along with the colored majority in the world. United States involvement in Vietnam, King wrote in an article for *Playboy*, was the result of "racist decision making" from "men of the white west" who had grown up in "a racist culture" and couldn't respect anybody who was not white. There could be no peace on earth without mutual respect, and those who had suffered racial discrimination themselves would make better policy decisions and conduct better negotiations with underprivileged and emerging nations. White men, he admitted, had no monopoly on sin and greed and warfare. But Negroes had a collective experience, "a kind of shared misery," that made them generally more sensitive to the misery of others. Because the American Negro had roots in both the white and the black worlds, he had the capacity to bridge them both. Instead of being inferior "drones," as white society had characterized them since slavery days, black Americans could be the nation's best leaders, providing "a new soul force for all Americans, a new expression of the American dream that need not be realized at the expense of other men around the world, but a dream of opportunity and life that can be shared with the rest of the world."

THERE WAS TROUBLE IN MEMPHIS, trouble in the valley in Tennessee. James Lawson, an old friend and pastor of the Centenary Methodist Church in Memphis, contacted King and briefed him on the situation there. Memphis's sanitation workers—nearly all of them black—had established a local chapter of the American Federation of State, County, and Municipal Employees and had asked the city to recognize the union and grant them a contract that improved wages and working conditions. But the city adamantly refused, and on February 12 most of Memphis's 1,300 Negro sanitation employees went on strike, vowing to stay away until their demands were met and holding protest marches with signs reading, "I AM A MAN." When the police broke them up with mace and night sticks, an aroused black community closed ranks behind the sanitation workers, organized a strike-support group called the Community on the Move for Equality (COME), and staged daily marches from Mason Temple to city hall. But Mayor Henry Loeb refused to negotiate and threatened to fire the strikers if they did not return to their jobs; and the city secured a local court injunction against further marches. At that, Lawson and other COME members voted to bring in King and other national leaders to give speeches and rally local support for the strike. "We wanted to escalate the whole effort," said one Negro. "We were still at the point in this city where Martin Luther King could pull out a lot of people."

Lawson pleaded with King to come and address at least one mass meeting. The sanitation workers and the black community needed him. Besides, Memphis wasn't Harlem or Chicago. Memphis was in the South, King's home, where hundreds of thousands of Negroes still looked to him as their Moses. Even if he could make only one appearance, it would help the movement immeasurably.

King thought it over. The strike seemed a prototype of the kind of campaign he was planning for Washington. Here were poor black garbage collectors, asking a racist city government for decent pay and seeking a place in the union movement, a movement that had improved the lot of millions of whites. Here were Negro strikers, enjoined from exercising their constitutional right of assembly by a local court injunction—the very weapon the U.S. Supreme Court had endorsed in the Walker decision. For King, it was unthinkable to ignore the sanitation workers in their struggle. "These are poor folks," he told his staff. "If we don't stop for them, then we don't need to go to Washington. These are part of the people we're going there for."

In mid-March, he embarked on a People-to-People tour to recruit volunteers for the march to Washington, a tour that was to take him through Mississippi—one of the rural target areas—and on up to cities in the East. Since he was going to be in Mississippi, he elected to make an exploratory trip to Memphis; he rearranged his crowded schedule and on March 18 flew there with his staff, taking rooms at the Lorraine Motel—a Negro motor lodge in the waterfront area—where he usually stayed while he was in town. He conferred with Lawson and other local leaders and then hurried to Mason Temple, where 17,000 people gave him a rousing welcome.

The clapping, the songs, the upturned faces—all were reminiscent of the movement's glory days—and King spoke to them with the fervor of old. "You have assembled for more than thirty days now, to say, 'We are tired. We are tired of being at the bottom. . . . We are tired of having to live in dilapidated, substandard housing. We are tired of working our hands off and laboring every day and not even making a wage adequate with the daily basic necessities of life. We are tired of our men being emasculated, so that our wives and our daughters have to go out and work in the white ladies' kitchens.'" The crowd responded again and again with applause and cries of *yessir! awright!* "And so I say we're not gonna let any dogs or water hoses turn us around. We aren't gonna let any injunction turn us around [cries and shouts]. We've gotta march again, in order to put the issue where it is supposed to be, force everybody to see that thirteen hundred of God's children are suffering, sometimes going hungry " Over the stamping and shouting, he called for a massive downtown march on Friday, March 22, and urged all Negro employees to boycott their jobs and all Negro students to stay away from school that day. "Try it," King cried, "and they will hear you."

His people in Mason Temple certainly heard him (and so did two FBI agents among them). Glory, look at that crowd! Thrilled by what he felt here, King decided to come back to Memphis and lead the huge march himself, and he told Lawson and his colleagues so. He believed they had a good movement going here, with plenty of local enthusiasm and competent leadership. For the first time, a black community was solidly behind a labor organization drive, and the parallels with the Washington project were striking indeed. If local Negroes could make Memphis deal with poor garbage workers, maybe King could force Washington to deal with all of America's poor.

But there were difficulties in Memphis nobody told him about. A group of Black Power youths were determined to challenge the established Negro leadership and its nonviolent approach. In fact, thirty to forty of them had recently interrupted a meeting in Clayborn Temple and distributed pamphlets that contained mimeographed drawings of how to fashion a Molotov cocktail, along with a quotation from Rap Brown that Negroes "must move from resistance to aggression, from revolt to revolution." At another meeting, an angry young voice had sounded from the floor: "When you talk about fighting a city with as many cops as this city's got, you better have some guns! You're gonna need 'em before it's over."

King knew nothing about such youths, nothing about any generational feuds and disaffection within Memphis's black community. All he knew was that 17,000 people in Mason Temple were pouring out their love to him and that Lawson and his colleagues were overjoyed that he was returning. Memphis seemed so safe that King didn't bother to leave any staff members to help organize Friday's march.

He headed back to Mississippi and resumed his People-to-People tour, employing a tenant farmer's shanty as the symbol of his campaign. In a town called Marx, he came face-to-face with what his current struggle was all about. He saw scores of Negro children walking barefoot in the streets, their stomachs protruding from hunger. Their mothers and fathers were trying to get funds from Washington, but nothing had come through yet. They raised a little money here and there trying to feed their children, trying to teach them something. Some parents were unemployed and had no sources of income—no pensions, no welfare checks, nothing. "How do you live?" King asked, incredulous. "Well," they said, "we go around—go around to the neighbors and ask them for a little something. When the berry season comes, we pick berries; when the rabbit season comes, we hunt and catch a few rabbits, and that's about it." Sometimes, though, it was really bad. Sometimes they couldn't get any food at all, not even for the children.

When King heard that, he broke down and cried. He vowed to bring them all—every Negro in Marx, Mississippi—to Washington for Congress and the President to see. Maybe that would wake them up to what he was trying to end in America.

On March 21, he was back in Memphis, holding a strategy session for tomorrow's march. There had been a threat on his life that day: a man with a foreign accent had phoned radio station WHBQ in Memphis and warned that King would be shot if he returned there. Rumors were abroad in the black community that Carmichael and Rap Brown were coming to town and that militant youths had invaded Negro schools, threatening any teacher and student who showed up for classes the next day. At a meeting with local ministers, one young man had scoffed at marching. What good would that do? "If you want honkies to get the message," he said, "you got to break some windows."

The next day a blizzard struck Memphis, paralyzing the city with sixteen inches of snow and forcing King and Lawson's group to cancel the march. They rescheduled it for Thursday, March 28, and King flew off to New York for meetings with his Research Committee. By now, the depression was on him again, worse than ever. In New York, Lee, the Wachtels, and Rustin all noticed that something was wrong with him. "Bayard," King said when they were alone, "I sometimes wonder where I can go from here. I've accomplished so much. What can I do now?" Rustin told Wachtel, "You know, Harry, Martin really disturbs me." Both thought something was happening to him, a kind of psychological deterioration that was hard to describe. "It got scary," Rustin recalled. "It was a very strange thing. When you would sit and talk philosophy with him or anything, it was the same old Martin. His judgments were not affected. But he was terribly preoccupied with death. And this flaw of 'will I continue to develop, will I continue to do things?'" Of course, given the tension and danger he was under, Rustin conceded that "he had some very good reasons to feel anguished." But Lee thought it was more than the pressure and lack of sleep. "It was deeper than that." His friends couldn't quite fathom what it was.

On March 25 King was scheduled to appear before the annual convention of the Rabbinical Assembly, held in the Catskill Mountains, to solicit support for the poor people's campaign. He rode out to a New York airport with Wachtel and Young, only to become very agitated when he saw a single-engine plane waiting on the runway. He never rode in single-engine planes; even his secretary knew that. How could Young and Wachtel let him risk his life in a plane like that? Wachtel apologized, said they had no other choice, finally got him calmed down and on board the aircraft for the short flight to the Catskills.

At the convention, the rabbis gave King a special greeting: they sang "We Shall Overcome" in Hebrew. Then his old friend and ally, Rabbi Heschel, introduced him to the assembly: "Martin Luther King is a voice, a vision and a way. I call upon every Jew to harken to his voice, to share his vision, to follow in his way. The whole future of America will depend upon the impact and influence of Dr. King."

King thanked the rabbis for the special rendition of "We Shall Overcome." He'd never heard it sung in Hebrew, and "it was a beautiful experience for me." He was not going to make a speech (he was too tired for that) and proceeded directly to their questions, speaking so lucidly that nobody could have guessed him depressed.

What was King's view of Negroes who preferred segregation and separation to integration?

King gave his standard reply that all races in America were tied together and that separate white or black paths would lead to "social disaster." But then he clarified what he thought true integration would entail. True integration did not mean some romantic mixing of colors. In the past, he said, it had been discussed too much that way and it had "ended up as merely adding color to a still predominantly white

power structure." True integration meant that Negroes would have a
real share of power and responsibility in America. In fact, "there are
points at which I see the necessity for temporary separation as a temporary way-station to a truly integrated society." He cited some cases
he'd seen in the south, where schools and teachers' associations had
been integrated. "Often when they merge, the Negro is integrated
without power. The two or three positions of power which he did have
in the separate situation passed away altogether, so that he lost his
bargaining position, he lost his power, and he lost his posture where he
could be relatively militant and really grapple with the problems. We
don't want to be integrated *out* of power; we want to be integrated
into power."

How would he get rid of the ghettoes?

King had thought a great deal about this since Chicago. "We must
seek to enrich the ghetto immediately in the sense of improving the
housing conditions, improving the schools in the ghetto, improving the
economic conditions. At the same time, we must be working to open
the housing market so there will be one housing market only. We must
work on two levels. We should gradually move to disperse the ghetto,
and immediately move to improve conditions within the ghetto, which
in the final analysis will make it possible to disperse it at a greater rate
a few years from now."

Then came the question he had been expecting—one that Wachtel
had warned him was on all the rabbis' minds. Would King comment on
"the vicious anti-Semitism" and anti-Israel sentiments of the H. Rap
Browns and Stokely Carmichaels?

King knew what they were referring to. After the Six Day War in
the Middle East the year before, SNCC had blamed "the Palestine
problem" on "Zionist imperialists," denounced U.S. aid to Israel, and
ranted against Zionism itself. King explained what he had said before—that black anti-Semitism, "virtually nonexistent in the South,"
was an ugly product of the northern ghetto. "We have made it clear
that we cannot be the victims of the notion that you deal with one evil
in society by substituting another evil," King said. "You cannot substitute one tyranny for another, and for the black man to be struggling
for justice and then turn around and be anti-Semitic is not only a very
irrational course but it is a very immoral course, and wherever we
have seen anti-Semitism we have condemned it with all our might."

Thus far, King's answers reflected his maturest ideas to date on some of the critical racial problems besetting the country. Then he attempted to answer a difficult and wordy question about what he would say to those Negroes who supported the Arabs against Israel solely because of color. King ascribed that view to some "so-called young militants" who did not represent the vast majority of American Negroes. "There are some who are color-consumed and they see a kind of mystique in being colored," King said, "and anything non-colored is condemned. We do not follow that course in the Southern Christian Leadership Conference." He went on to offer an opinion about the Middle East crisis itself. What the Middle East needed, obviously, was peace. But that meant one thing for Israel, another for the Arab states. "Peace for Israel means security, and we must stand with all of our might to protect its right to exist, its territorial integrity. I see Israel, and never mind saying it, as one of the great outposts of democracy in the world and a marvelous example of what can be done, how desert land almost can be transformed into an oasis of brotherhood and democracy."

On the other hand, peace for the Arabs meant security on another level. It meant economic security. This was how those in the Southern Christian Leadership Conference tried to see the problem. "These nations, as you know, are part of that third world of hunger, of disease, of illiteracy," and these conditions caused tensions and led to "an endless quest to find scapegoats. So there is a need for a Marshall Plan for the Middle East, where we lift those who are at the bottom of the economic ladder and bring them into the mainstream of economic security."

Of course, economic problems alone scarcely accounted for the Arab view of Israel or for the manifold internal troubles of many Arab states. Though King was speaking extemporaneously and was probably getting tired, his remarks about the Arabs did betray a shallowness of thought, indicating that he had yet to refine his ideas about the complex and troublesome Middle East.

There were final questions about the poor people's campaign and what the rabbis could do to help "our colored brethren." Since the press "has gone out of its way in many instances to misinterpret what we will be doing in Washington," King explained in detail the goals and initial stages of the project there, which was to culminate in a massive demonstration on June 15. He hoped that the rabbis would encourage their congregations to participate in that march and support the demands of America's poor.

After the meeting, they seemed ready and eager to back the Washington campaign, and King left for New York in high spirits. "He went back practically flying without the plane," Wachtel said. But something happened back in New York that made him despondent again. Before returning to Memphis, he and Lee visited with Marion and Dr. Arthur Logan, a couple King had known for years. Marion was a top fund raiser for SCLC, but like Rustin she opposed the poor people's campaign because she questioned its political value and feared it would end in violence. She had even said so in a memo to SCLC's Board of Directors—which only convinced King that she and Rustin were ganging up on him. Now, in the Logans' brownstone on the Upper West Side, he sat on a sofa, coat and shoes off, feet propped up on a coffee table, talking nonstop about the Washington project in a desperate effort to win Marion over. There had always been people who warned him against his campaigns. "If I'd have listened to them, there wouldn't have *been* a Birmingham, there wouldn't have *been* a Selma-Montgomery, if I'd have listened to *them*, we'd not have *anything*! We'd never have *had* a *movement*, Marion. Of *all* people, I never thought I'd have to *explain* this to you." He talked almost until dawn, lounging, sitting up, standing, swilling orange juice and vodka—the Logans had never seen him drink so much—and going through mood swings, now agitated, now gentle and measured, now apparently relaxed, his right fist clenched and his thumb rubbing ceaselessly against his fingers.

But the Logans would not be persuaded; Marion opposed the campaign and that was final. "It really did get to Martin," Lee remembered. These were his friends, and it hurt him that they did not understand what he was trying to do. He concluded that they had never understood him, not even in the beginning. After he left the Logans, King told Lee that he felt "a great sense of loss and remorse." But he had to go on. He was trying to brace himself for what lay ahead, to be ready for it. He couldn't escape the feeling, he said, "that Washington, D.C., might be the place he would be clubbed to death, where he could possibly get assassinated."

On Thursday morning, March 28, King and Lee returned to Memphis for the big march. Abernathy met them at the airport and took them to Clayborn Temple downtown, where 6,000 people were milling about, waiting for King. It was now 11 A.M.—about two hours after the march was supposed to begin. The crowd was tense and restless, and march marshals went about cautioning people. Maxine Smith of the Memphis NAACP looked down the line and saw some "very unsavory characters" removing heavy sticks from picket signs. She had never seen picket signs that large—they looked more like clubs. She thought, "We're going to have trouble today."

At last the column surged forward, heading chaotically toward Main Street. As King and Abernathy marched at the front of the procession, young Negroes came up and patted King and said how great it was to have him here. Suddenly there was a crash—the sound of shattering glass. At the back of the line, black teenagers were smashing windows and looting stores. Signs appeared on the sidewalks: "Damn Loeb—Black Power is here." Ahead, police in full riot gear were cordoning off Main Street and advancing this way. King signaled to Lawson, who came over with a bullhorn. "I will never lead a violent march," King said, "so, please, call it off." While Lawson yelled in his bullhorn for everybody to return to the church, King and Abernathy climbed into a car commandeered by Lee, and a motorcycle cop led them away through a police barricade. King wanted to go to the Lorraine Motel, but the policeman said that fighting had broken out and that the route there was blocked. So he escorted them to the Rivermont Holiday Inn on the banks of the Mississippi, where they checked into a two-room suite and switched on the television set.

Downtown everything was pandemonium. When the police encountered Negro youths with rocks and picket signs, they fired tear gas and clubbed looters, marchers, bystanders—anybody with a black face—and then raked the street with gunfire. By the time the battle ended 155 stores had been damaged, 60 people injured, and a sixteen-year-old Negro boy killed by police gunfire. Mayor Loeb imposed a curfew at once, and the governor of Tennessee sent in 3,500 National Guardsmen to patrol the city.

In his Rivermont suite, King was horrified, unable to believe that somebody had been killed, that violence had broken out on a march he had led. It was the first time that this had ever happened. When reports blamed the disorders on a militant youth group called the Invaders, King was even more upset. Why hadn't Lawson and the others told him about the Invaders? Told him that there were people in Memphis who preached violence? "We should have had some intelligence work done before we came here," Lee groaned. "We walked right into this thing."

This was a disaster. King did not know what to do. Now what would the press and his legion of critics say about him? That he couldn't lead a nonviolent demonstration? That this was a harbinger of what would happen in Washington? That Martin Luther King was finished? There was a report that Roy Wilkins said he should forget the entire Washington project because mass street marches would only lead to violence. A mass meeting scheduled for that night, to feature King, had to be canceled. King was inconsolable. He kept thinking about that boy shot down by the police, about the rioting youths. He couldn't sleep, wouldn't sleep. Abernathy could not get him to sleep that night. In the depths of despair, he told Abernathy that "it may be that those of us who adhere to nonviolence should just step aside and let the violent forces run their course, which will be very temporary and very brief, because you can't conduct a violent campaign in this country."

But he could not step aside. His guilt would be intolerable if violence engulfed the land. He had to hang on. He had to come back to Memphis and lead another march. Before, the city had been a minor detour, the kind of "itinerant aid" he had often supplied local movements. But now he was trapped here. He would never get the Washington campaign under way unless he proved that he could conduct a peaceful march through the streets of Memphis, Tennessee. "Yes," he said, "we must come back. Nonviolence as a concept is now on trial." He would say so in a press conference already scheduled for that morning. Then he lay down for a few minutes of rest.

Abernathy woke him, scowling. Three Invaders were here and wanted to talk to him. "Well, Ralph, you can take care of it," King said. He had to shave for the press conference. In the bathroom, he could hear Abernathy arguing with the young men in the other room. At that, King went out and "there was a complete change in the atmosphere," one Invader recalled, as King greeted the youths cordially and calmed everyone down. They spoke in whispers, King asking for their side of the story, the young men admitting their role in inciting the violence but insisting that they only wanted to play a significant part in the strike. They had tried to meet with the established leadership, only to be snubbed and left out of the action. They felt "rejected" and angry, and one of the reasons violence had broken out yesterday was because the strike leaders had ignored them. King said he wanted to see the Invaders when he returned to Memphis, but warned that he would not condone any group that advocated violence.

Then he left for the press conference, followed by Lee and Abernathy. He marched into the room and took charge, not even waiting for Lee to introduce him, as was his custom. Ladies and gentlemen, he said, he was coming back to Memphis as early as April 3 and no later than April 5, and he was going to lead "a massive nonviolent demonstration" here. He admitted that he had come to Memphis without adequate preparation—his staff had not been involved in planning the march yesterday and his intelligence had been nonexistent. He did not know that there were blacks in Memphis who were talking about violence. Had he known that, he would have sought them out and made them parade marshals, as he had done with Negro gangs in demonstrations in other cities, with great success. No, he had not left yesterday's march "in a hurry," as the media reported. He had departed because he would not be associated with a violent demonstration, but he had "walked" to the car, "agonizing over what had happened." As far as the Washington project was concerned, the disorders yesterday in no way affected his plans to start the campaign on April 22.

Back in the suite afterward, Abernathy hugged him. "I had never seen the lion in him come forth like that," Abernathy said later. "He was just—he was so beautiful." But King"s mood had changed again. "Ralph," he murmured, "I want to get out of Memphis. Get me out of Memphis as soon as possible. You've got to get me out of Memphis."

They flew back to Atlanta that Friday afternoon.

As KING FEARED, THE PRESS from the *New York Times* to papers in Memphis linked the disrupted march to the poor people's campaign, reinforcing what a good part of America already believed: that King and rioting were equated. An editorial in the Memphis *Commercial Appeal* was representative: "Dr. King's pose as a leader of a non-violent movement has been shattered. He now has the entire nation doubting his word when he insists that his April project . . . can be peaceful. In short, Dr. King is suffering from one of those awesome credibility gaps. Furthermore, he wrecked his reputation as a leader as he took off at high speed when violence occurred, instead of trying to use his persuasive prestige to stop it."

The ever-vigilant FBI issued a blind news story about Memphis, which the St. Louis *Globe-Democrat* printed almost verbatim in a derogatory editorial. What happened in Memphis, the paper asserted, "could be only the prelude to civil strife in our Nation's Capitol" and proved that King was more dangerous than Stokely Carmichael because he "continues to talk non-violence even as it erupts all about him." "This is the real Martin Luther King," the paper warned, "a man who stoops to using anti-Democratic and dictatorial means to try to force his will on the highest legislative body in the United States, a man who hides behind a façade of 'non-violence' as he provokes violence." To illustrate, the paper ran a cartoon showing a haloed, thick-lipped King shooting up "trouble," "violence," and "looting" with a pistol. "I'm not firing it," the caption read, "I'm only pulling the trigger."

The FBI and papers like the *Globe-Democrat* only contributed to a growing climate of hatred against King and his projected marches in Memphis as well as Washington. In fact, one man who read the *Globe-Democrat* editorial was John Ray, a St. Louis tavern owner and brother of escaped convict James Earl Ray. Both Ray brothers were active in the American Independent party in the St. Louis area, where Kauffmann and Sutherland had their $20,000 and $50,000 offers for King's life.

On Saturday morning, March 30, King assembled his executive staff at Ebenezer Church in Atlanta and told them about Memphis. It was a stormy session, with much of the staff against his returning there. But Walter Fauntroy defended King's decision. "We've got to go all the way with Martin because he's Martin. I don't care what your reservations are. He's our leader. Let's do what he wants." A black union organizer, attending the meeting, said that the press had done a vicious job on King in accusing him of running out on Thursday's march, and he thought that impression had to be challenged. As the debate raged on, Bevel and Jesse Jackson raised objections to the poor people's campaign itself. Yes, Bevel was still fighting it. "I don't even know how to preach people into the Poor People's campaign," he said. Abernathy looked at King. "He was very depressed," Abernathy said. "He was back in his shell." Around noon, he simply walked out of the room, leaving his aides dumbfounded.

Abernathy ran after him. "Martin, what is wrong with you? Tell me."

"I can't take it any more," he said. "I'm going to the country to stay with one of my members. I need to go to the farm, and I'm going down there."

"Well, tell me what is bugging you," Abernathy persisted.

"All I'll say is, Ralph, I'll—I'll snap out of it. Didn't I snap out of it yesterday? You said I did yesterday at the press conference. I'll pull through it."

That afternoon, Abernathy contacted King and said the staff wanted him to come back to the church. Around three, he walked into the room where they awaited him, worried and chastened. He was right, they chorused: they had to return to Memphis in order to save the poor people's campaign and King's own credibility as a nonviolent leader. The Washington project might have to be postponed for a couple of weeks until they resolved the problem in Memphis. King was glad they were with him, but still seemed "really demoralized," Fauntroy thought, "really in the dumps on this thing." As they left the church, Jackson called out insistently, "Doc," as though to continue the argument. King whirled around on the steps. "Jesse, don't bother me. It may be that you want to carve your own niche in society. Go ahead and carve it. But for God's sake don't bother me." His aides had never heard him speak so harshly to young Jackson, the head of SCLC's Operation Breadbasket in Chicago.

To avoid the debacle of the first march, SCLC planned the next one in minute detail: Rustin, Jackson, and other lieutenants set about recruiting labor leaders, public officials, churchmen, and entertainers

to join King in Memphis. On Sunday, Bevel, Williams, and other staffers went there to hold workshops on nonviolence and lay the groundwork for the march, now scheduled for Friday, April 5. Young and
other staff members soon followed.

King was in Washington that Sunday, preaching to a mostly white
audience in the Washington Episcopal Cathedral. That evening, he
watched Lyndon Johnson give a nationally televised speech. The President faced almost certain defeat at the hands of McCarthy in the
forthcoming Wisconsin primary; Johnson's organization, in fact, was
coming unraveled. Kennedy wasn't entered in Wisconsin, but his
strength was growing daily. Discredited by his own Vietnam policy,
assailed by both McCarthy and Kennedy, Johnson announced on television that he had ordered a reduction of the bombing in Vietnam,
dwelled on all the ugly strife that plagued America, said the country
needed unity. Then he raised his right arm—a signal that he wanted
to add a postscript. "I have concluded that I should not permit the
Presidency to become involved in the partisan divisions that are developing in this political year," he said. "Accordingly, I shall not seek,
and I will not accept, the nomination of my party for another term as
your President."

King was astounded. Did he dare believe what he had just heard?
He spoke to Wachtel on the phone, and Wachtel offered his congratu-
lations. "What are you congratulating me for?" King asked. "For getting rid of Johnson," Wachtel said. "You really did it. In my opinion,
you're one of the strongest people who set the groundwork for his
quitting." King took heart from this auspicious turn of events. With
Johnson out of the way, maybe the civil-rights and peace forces could
elect a compassionate President who would end the Vietnam nightmare, save the cities, and put America back on the high road toward
the fulfillment of her destiny. Now the poor people's campaign assumed an even greater urgency, and he returned to Atlanta and prepared for the Memphis trip with awakened resolution.

King was in good spirits when he, Lee, Abernathy, and several
others left for the Atlanta airport on the morning of April 3. But there
had been a bomb threat and the Memphis flight was delayed. When
they finally boarded the jet, the pilot announced over the intercom:
"We're sorry for the delay. But we have Dr. Martin Luther King on
the plane. And to be sure that all the bags were checked and to be sure
that nothing would be wrong in the plane, we had to check out every-

thing carefully. We've had the plane protected and guarded all night."

King laughed, thought this "ridiculous," and fell to talking about the other threats on his life. On the flight to Memphis, King continued to act "very, very well," Abernathy thought.

At the Memphis airport, Lawson and several other local Negroes greeted King's party at the gate. There was the usual bevy of reporters and cameramen and a security detail of four detectives from the Memphis police department. King did not want a security detail—the police were not his friends, and the detectives made him jumpy. "We don't want no police around him," a Negro yelled at one detective. "Get the hell out of here."

King's escort whisked him away to the Lorraine Motel and checked him and Abernathy into Room 306, which overlooked a courtyard parking lot and a covered swimming pool. Police cars pulled up at the Lorraine, too, and two detectives set up a surveillance post in a nearby fire station, noting that SCLC staffers and several Invaders kept going in and out of the motel's conference room. Because King and his hosts were hostile to the security detail, the police subsequently called it off despite the threats to King's life. But the two detectives in the fire station continued to observe the Lorraine from behind a papered-up window. King's activities generated media interest, too, and at least one radio station announced that he was staying at the Lorraine and even gave his room number.

It was a busy afternoon for King, filled with meetings and conferences about Friday's march. Word reached him that a U.S. district court judge in Memphis had issued a temporary restraining order against the demonstration. SCLC's legal counsel Chauncey Eskridge intended to challenge the injunction in the federal courthouse the next day, but King promised to lead the march regardless of the outcome. "We are not going to be stopped by Mace or injunctions," he told reporters.

By late afternoon, King was unsettled again. Tornado warnings were out for Memphis, and the weather fit his mood: dark, menacing skies, cracks of thunder. By nightfall, a heavy rain lashed the city. King was supposed to address a rally at Mason Temple, but he didn't want to go. He feared that only a few people would turn out in this storm and that the press would point to a small crowd as evidence of his failing appeal. And anyway he was too exhausted to go out tonight.

So he sent Abernathy to speak in his place, changed into his pajamas, and tried to relax.

Around 8:30 the phone rang. It was Abernathy, telling King that he had to come down to the temple. Two thousand very enthusiastic people were there, along with a large press and television cameras. When Abernathy had entered the temple, the people had gone wild because they thought King was with him. They were extremely disappointed, Abernathy said. They all wanted to hear King, "the most peaceful warrior of the 20th century."

King still didn't want to go. "Come on, Ralph. Can't you talk to them? Won't they listen to you?"

"I really think you should come down," Abernathy persisted. "The people want to hear you, not me. This is your crowd."

Finally King gave in. He trusted Abernathy's judgment: if the people were coming out and really wanted him, then he would speak tonight. He didn't want to—he was tired, in low spirits—but he would do it for the people. He dressed and went out into a driving rain.

When he mounted the speaking platform and looked at the blur of faces and blaze of lights in the temple, King appeared nervous. After Abernathy introduced him, King told the crowd, "Ralph Abernathy is the best friend that I have in the world." He went on without reference to a script, his voice filled with sadness. As he spoke, thunder rumbled outside, and rain beat desperately against the roof.

Something was happening in Memphis, he said. Something was happening in the world. If he were standing at the beginning of time and God asked, "Martin Luther King, which age would you like to live in?" he would take his "mental flight" by Egypt to see Moses leading his people across the Red Sea toward the Promised Land; by Mount Olympus to see Plato and Aristotle and Euripides and Aristophanes as they discussed "the great and eternal issues of reality"; by Europe during the Renaissance and then by Germany to see Martin Luther tack his ninety-five theses on the door of the church at Wittenberg; by 1863 to see a vacillating President sign the Emancipation Proclamation; by the early 1930s to view a leader grappling with the bankruptcy of a nation. But King would not stop at any of these times. "Strangely enough," he said, "I would turn to the Almighty and say if you allow me to live just a few years in the second half of the twentieth century, I will be happy.

"Now that's a strange statement to make, because the world is all messed up. The nation is sick. Trouble is in the land, confusion all around." But "only when it's dark enough can you see the stars." And King saw God working in this period in a way that men were responding to. The masses of them were rising up in South Africa, in Kenya and Ghana, in New York City, Atlanta, Jackson, and Memphis, and everywhere their cry was the same: "We want to be free."

Today, King said, men were forced to grapple with problems that had troubled humankind throughout history—war and peace and human rights. But the issues were far more urgent today, because man's very survival was at stake and King's generation had to do something about them. If something were not done—and done in a hurry—to bring the world's colored people out of their long years of poverty, hurt, and neglect, the whole world was doomed. Now King was just happy that God had allowed him to live in this period, to see what was unfolding. And King was happy that God had allowed him to be in Memphis.

He was in Memphis to help the sanitation workers for the same reason that the Good Samaritan stopped to help the man in need. The question, King said, was not what would happen to him if he stopped to help those men. "The question is, if I do *not* stop to help the sanitation workers, what will happen to them. *That's* the question." The crowd roared with applause.

He recalled being stabbed in New York City almost ten years before, telling how the blade had been so close to his aorta that if he'd sneezed, the doctor said, he would have died. He remembered the high school girl who had written him how glad she was that he hadn't sneezed. He wanted to say tonight that he too was happy he hadn't sneezed. Because if he had sneezed, he wouldn't have been around to see the student sit-ins and Freedom Rides. He wouldn't have seen the Negroes of Albany straighten their backs and the Negroes of Birmingham arouse the conscience of a nation and bring the civil-rights act into being. He wouldn't have stood at the Lincoln Memorial and told America about a dream he had. He wouldn't have seen the great movement in Selma or been in Memphis to see a community rallying behind its suffering brothers and sisters. Yes, he was so happy he hadn't sneezed.

"Now," he said, "it doesn't matter [*go ahead! go ahead!* sounding from the audience]. It really doesn't matter what happens now." He described the bomb threat on his plane that morning and told how some began to talk about the threats that were out, about what would happen to him "from some of our sick white brothers. Well," he said, "I don't know what will happen now. We've got some difficult days ahead [*yeah! oh yes!*]. But it really doesn't matter with me now [*oh yes!*]. Because I've been to the mountaintop [cries and applause]. Like anybody I would like to live a long life. Longevity has its place. But I'm not concerned about that now. I just want to do God's will. And He's allowed me to go up to the mountain [*go ahead*]. And I've looked over [*yes, doctor*]. And I've *seen* the Promised Land [*go ahead, doctor*]. And I may not get there with you [*yes sir, go ahead*]. But I want you to know tonight that we as a people *will* get to the Promised Land [applause, cries, *go ahead, go ahead*]. So I'm happy tonight. I'm not worried about *any*thing. I'm not fearing *any* man. Mine eyes have seen the glory of the coming of the Lord [cries, applause]. I have a dream this afternoon that the brotherhood of man will become a reality. With this faith, *I* will go out and carve a tunnel of hope from a mountain of despair. . . . With this faith, *we* will be able to achieve this new day, when all of God's children—black men and white men, Jews and Gentiles, Protestants and Catholics—will be able to join hands and sing with the Negroes in the spiritual of old, 'Free at last! Free at least! Thank God almighty we are free at last.'"

Many who heard the "Mountaintop" speech were convinced that King had had a premonition of death. Young thought it "almost morbid," and others also worried about its tone of resignation and impending doom. Certainly death weighed heavily on him that night, because of the bomb scare on the plane and the other threats against his life. Yet what his friends missed was how much the address summed up and reaffirmed King's life: his intellectual odyssey through history during his college days; his awareness that something was happening in his time, that the Zeitgeist was tracking him down to lead the masses who were on the move in America as they were across the globe; his life of struggle, plagued with the constant threat of death, especially in these difficult days; his vision from the mountaintop where he saw God's glory—that world of brotherhood, love, and solidarity which Rauschenbusch had prophesied and which King had labored in the valleys to build; his lyrical repetition of "I have a dream" as though he were back in 1963 at his moment of greatest glory. The speech was truly an affirmation of life—"I want to *live*," he kept saying. Yet he took consolation from the fact that history would go on if he died; the forward progress of history would yet carry mankind to the Promised Land.

One thing was for certain: the speech and the warmth of the audience proved therapeutic for King. The anxiety that had bothered him before the address was gone now. "He had broken the cycle again," said Lee, "had broken the despair." Back at the Lorraine that night, he was relaxed and happy as he worked on a sermon for the following Sunday. After midnight, his brother A. D. arrived from Louisville, and King visited with him so late that it was after 4 A.M., April 4, before he got to bed.

AROUND MIDMORNING, Abernathy woke him gently. "Come on now," he said, nudging King, "it's time to get up." King said "yes" in a voice heavy from sleep but didn't move. "It's time to get up now," Abernathy said. "You know we can't win this nonviolent revolution in bed." King was awake now, bantering with Abernathy, telling him he was still a farmer for arousing him at this hour. "I'm never going to get the farmer out of you," King said, chuckling. Alert, jovial, he was eager to get to work. As he showered and shaved, he had Abernathy make critical phone calls and take notes concerning the day's business.

Then King met with his executive staff, going over plans to bring in the celebrities and keep the march nonviolent. So that all the legal and logistical problems could be worked out, they elected to postpone the march until the following Monday, April 8, and Young carried the news down to the federal courthouse where Eskridge was battling city attorneys in an effort to get the injunction lifted. The owner of the motel recalled that King, usually so business like, was playful that morning, "teasing and cutting up."

In a motel conference room, King and his staff sat down with fifteen or sixteen Invaders and members of the Black Organizing Project, a militant student coalition of which the Invaders were a part. King explored the possibility of employing the young men as march marshals and sending them into the schools to preach nonviolence. Abernathy thought them clean-cut and intelligent looking—not like the bearded malcontents SCLC had skirmished with in Washington and other cities—but they came on in an aggressive, almost belligerent style. Sure, they said, they could go talk to the kids, but they couldn't guarantee that they would be nonviolent. One young man thought it absurd to ask them to maintain peace when not even the cops could do that. But should they agree to cooperate, they wanted things from SCLC—such as four or five cars to get around in and help in securing funds for a "community unification program" of theirs. By now, several SCLC staffers were openly hostile—"they felt we were trying to rip them off," an Invader recalled—and King too was completely put off. He refused their demands and sent them away. Afterward, he was incensed to discover that one of his assistants—Williams or Bevel—had put three or four Invaders on SCLC's staff and payroll. He would not, he told his aides, tolerate advocates of violence on his staff. Chastened, they conveyed the message to the youths, who subsequently checked out of the motel.

Back in room 306, King and Abernathy ordered a lunch of catfish and salads brought up from the dining room. Alas, the waitress arrived with the catfish all on one plate. Irritated, Abernathy started to send her back for another plate, but King intervened. "It doesn't matter," he told Abernathy. "You and me can eat from the same plate." The catfish was delicious—one of their favorite dishes. As they shared the platter, King sampled both bowls of salad, eating out of Abernathy's too.

After lunch, Abernathy lay down for a nap and King visited A. D. in his room. The brothers called their mother in Atlanta, and she was glad her sons were together this day. Around four, King phoned Abernathy, waking him up, and asked him down to A. D.'s room to share their fellowship. He told Abernathy about the call to his mother. "You know," King said, "she's always so happy when A. D is with me."

In A. D.'s room, the conversation turned to their evening plans— King and his staff were all going out to Reverend Samuel Kyles's home for dinner. Since he was not a man who liked a lot of cauliflower, broccoli, and asparagus, he asked Abernathy to phone Mrs. Kyles and find out what she was serving. On the phone, Abernathy repeated the fare as she ran through it: prime rib roast and lots of soul food— chitterlings, greens, blackeyed peas, and pigs' feet. King was delighted.

Presently, Young and Eskridge burst into the room. They had been in court most of the day, challenging the city's contention that another march would trigger violence "worse than Watts or Detroit." Eskridge had put Young and Lawson on the stand, and they had given "a magnificent philosophical presentation" about how a nonviolent march would unify the black community and ward off explosions of rage like that in Detroit. Impressed with their argument, the judge ruled to let the march take place on Monday, so long as King's people moved six abreast with marshals at every four ranks. "We're home free!" Eskridge exclaimed. Though King had been prepared to march anyway, he was so tickled at the news that he grabbed Young and wrestled him to the bed, everybody joking and laughing in all the horseplay.

Around five, King and Abernathy returned to their room and dressed for dinner. King shaved again, applying the pungent, sulfurous depilatory powder he always used to remove his heavy beard. Then he splashed on Aramis aftershave lotion to cover up the awful smell. As they talked, Abernathy confessed that he couldn't attend the initial march to Washington because he had to conduct a revival in his church in Atlanta at that time. But King wouldn't even consider going to Washington without Abernathy. "You will have to go to West Hunter and tell them that you have a greater revival, a revival to revive the soul of this nation and cause America to feed the hungry, to have concern for those who are downtrodden, and disinherited, and they'll understand." Abernathy agreed. "We have been together so far," he said, "and there is no need for us to separate now."

Around 5:30, Reverend Kyles arrived. "OK, Doc," he said, "it's time to go." King's chauffeur, Solomon Jones, was waiting in the parking lot below, ready to drive them to Kyles's place in a limousine on loan from a Negro funeral home.

Finished dressing, King asked Kyles if his tie matched his suit. Still in a good mood, he teased Kyles about dinner, recalling how he'd once gone to a preacher's house and had ham and Kool-Aid, and the ham was cold to boot. He jested, "I don't want to go to your house for cold food," and then said to Abernathy, "Are you ready?" They put on their coats. "Wait just a minute," Abernathy said. "Let me put on some aftershave lotion." "OK," King said. "I'll be standing out here on the balcony."

He and Kyles stepped outside and stood at the iron railing along the balcony. In the parking lot below, King's aides were standing around, waiting to leave for dinner. Young was talking to Lee and Williams, and Bevel and big James Orange were wrestling playfully. "Don't let him hurt you," King called down to Bevel. It was chilly after last night's storm, and Solomon Jones encouraged King to bring his topcoat. "Solomon," King said, "you really know how to take good care of me," and he asked Abernathy to fetch his topcoat. Then he spotted Jesse Jackson, modishly clad in brown slacks and brown turtle-neck, standing in the lot with Ben Branch, leader of Jackson's Bread-basket Band.

"Ben," King said, "make sure you play 'Precious Lord, Take My Hand' at the meeting tonight. Sing it *real* pretty."

"OK, Doc, I will," Branch said.

"Jesse," King said, "I want you to go to dinner with us this eve-ning." He spoke affectionately, no longer angry at Jackson as he had been in Atlanta. "And you be sure to dress up a little tonight, OK, Jesse? No blue jeans, all right?"

It was six now and time to go. As Kyles headed down to the park-ing lot, King stood at the iron railing by himself, facing a row of rundown buildings in some trees beyond Mulberry Street. At that sec-ond, there was a report of a highpowered rifle, and a bullet tore into the right side of King's face with such force that it drove him violently backward. He grasped for his throat, crumpling to the balcony floor with his feet protruding through the bottom rail. Below, King's assis-tants shouted, "Take cover!" and fell to the pavement or hid behind a car. Abernathy, who'd heard a "pop" like a firecracker, ran out onto the balcony and saw King lying diagonally there, his hands rigid at his throat. "Oh my God," Abernathy cried "Martin's been shot." A wom-an screamed. Abernathy stepped over King and bent down, relieving a man (an undercover policeman, it turned out) who was trying to stem the flow of blood from King's face with a towel. The bullet had torn away the right side of his jaw and neck, and his head lay in a spread-ing pool of blood. Abernathy thought he seemed conscious and terribly frightened, and he started caressing the left side of King's jaw, saying, "Martin, this is me, this is Ralph, this is Ralph. Don't be afraid." King's mouth quivered once, as though he were trying to speak. Then he looked at Abernathy, "and I got a message from his eyes," Aber-nathy said. People were running up the balcony steps now, yelling and ducking down in case there were more shots. Kyles found himself in Room 306, screaming into the telephone in a futile attempt to get the operator, banging his head again and again against the wall. Outside, Young had reached King and was groping for his pulse, sobbing, "Oh my God, my God, it's all over." "No, it's *not* over," Abernathy raged in tears. "Don't you *ever* say that."

A young man crawled over with a pillow, and Abernathy put it under King's head, trying frantically to stop the bleeding. By now Lee, Williams, Jackson, and a young woman were on the balcony, too. A photographer snapped a picture of Young and several others pointing in the direction of the gunshot—toward the old buildings on Mulberry Street. In all the commotion, Lee glanced up and saw some of King's flesh on the ceiling of the balcony. "He's dead," Lee thought with a stab of anguish. "He's really dead."

Within a few minutes, the courtyard was brimming with policemen. An ambulance had arrived, and stretcher bearers came and carried King away. Abernathy climbed into the ambulance with him, refusing to leave "my buddy." As the ambulance raced for St. Joseph's Hospital, Abernathy helped the attendant check King's fading pulse and give him oxygen.

At the hospital, Abernathy helped roll King down to a brilliantly lit emergency room and lay him on the table there. Bernard Lee was beside him now, numb from shock. A nurse ordered them to leave, but they refused to budge, trying to explain who they were. When she still told them to go, Lee snapped, "Don't worry about us. Just take care of Dr. King."

As they stood vigil against the wall, hands clasped before them, a team of doctors worked feverishly on King under a bright fluorescent light, machines flickering with dials and screens nearby. There was no time to disrobe him, so they cut away his coat and shirt, tucking them under his back, and started massaging his heart and tending his wounds. The bullet, a metal-jacketed .30-06, had smashed through his neck, severing vital arteries and fracturing his spine in several places. Abernathy abandoned hope when he saw the full damage—there was a hole in King's body, he thought, large enough to put both his fists in. Lee kept watching a pulse monitor above the operating table: it barely registered a signal. A small neurosurgeon came in to examine King and concluded that he had suffered irreparable brain damage from lack of oxygen. He laid his instruments down and walked out shaking his head. As the doctors kept working on King, one came over to Abernathy. "I'm afraid it's over," he said, "and it will be an act of God if it is, because if he lives, he will be a vegetable for the rest of his life, for he will be paralyzed from the neck down."

In a few minutes, the doctors stepped back from the table. "I'm sorry," the head physician told Abernathy and Lee, "but we've lost him. It's all over." The physician recorded the time: 7:05 P.M., April 4,

1968. While the nurses did something at the machines with their dials and screens, King lay unattended at the table, face straight up. Had he been able to see, he would have gazed on a little silver figure of Jesus on the cross, directly on the wall above, looking down at him.

Abernathy took King's personal effects from his coat—a checkbook and some papers—and Lee gathered what there was in his left trouser pocket. Then Lee took a last look at him, thinking back over all the years they had been together, all the thousands of miles they had traveled in the rush and tumble of his life. "We were always tired," Lee thought. "I know he was tired. Now maybe he'll get some rest."

He and Abernathy walked into a small anteroom where Andrew Young waited with his head buried in his hands. SCLC's attorney Chauncey Eskridge came in from an adjoining room, and Abernathy said, "Now Martin is gone from us. Now we are alone."

"Ralph," Eskridge said, "you have to become our leader. You now are our leader. The television people are waiting outside. We know Coretta is on her way here. We are going to take you in front of the TV cameras and you say your say, and then we'll go to the airport and wait for Coretta."

Without a word, Abernathy reached out with his arms, and the three men came to him; they hugged one another and wept with their faces together. Then Abernathy said a prayer for King, and Eskridge and Young each took him by the arm and helped him out the door to face the din of reporters and television cameramen. He said what had to be said, then climbed into a waiting car with the other three men and headed for the airport.

There they found out that Coretta had canceled her flight; she wasn't coming to Memphis until tomorrow. In a daze, Abernathy and Young wound up at the John Gaston Hospital—the Memphis morgue—where the medical examiner wanted permission to do a thorough autopsy on King's body, which had been brought there from St. Joseph's Hospital. He and the other authorities were anxious to avoid all the confusion and unanswered questions that had marked Kennedy's assassination in Dallas. Abernathy put him in touch with Coretta by phone, and she gave him permission to proceed. Then he asked Abernathy to perform one other duty. "I must have witnesses," he said. "You must attest that it is Dr. King in the next room."

Abernathy entered the morgue, pulled back the piece of brown paper that covered the body of "my friend and my buddy," and touched him gently on the cheek. The man who had been their leader, inspiration, and spokesman couldn't speak any more—that marvelous voice stilled now. How could they get him and not Abernathy too? He had always assumed they would be killed together, but God in His wisdom intended otherwise. Somehow Abernathy had to go on without King, somehow had to continue his work. He felt an overpowering loneliness, weighed down by the sheer impossibility of taking King's place. No one could ever take his place. There was no one else like him. Still, his words would never die. Even now, television and radio stations across America and other lands were playing highlights of his most famous speeches. Like the words of Jesus, Abernathy believed, "they will live in our minds and our hearts and in the souls of black men and white men, brown men and yellow men as long as time shall last."

"Yes, that's him," Abernathy told the medical examiner, and left the hospital.

IN ATLANTA, Coretta had learned about the shooting from a friend and had set out for the airport with Mayor Allen and his wife, only to find out there that King had died. In shock, unable yet to accept what she had prepared herself for all these years, she elected to go home to her children. In this shattering hour, she said her place was with them. Over in Ebenezer Church, Daddy and Momma King heard the news over the radio, and they sat there, unable to say anything, weeping silently together. "Suddenly, in a few seconds of radio time, it was all over," Daddy King remembered. "My first son, whose birth had brought me such joy that I jumped up in the hall outside the room where he was born and touched the ceiling—the child, the scholar, the preacher . . . all of it was gone."

That night and the next day, King's stricken country convulsed in grief, contrition, and rage. Only four and a half years after Kennedy's assassination, another national leader had been gunned down in his prime, and Americans in all corners of the Union worried about the stability of their country. "Dr. King's murder is a national disaster," editorialized the New York Times, "depriving Negroes and whites alike of a leader of integrity, vision and restraint." "When white America killed Dr. King," cried Stokely Carmichael, "she declared war on us." "Get your gun," he told blacks. And a lot of them did, as riots flared up in 110 cities, and 39 people were killed, most of them Negroes. More than 75,000 federal troops and National Guardsmen patrolled America's streets. The hardest hit was Washington, D.C., where 711 fires blazed against the sky and 10 people died, among them a white man dragged from his car and stabbed. From the air, Washington looked as though it had been bombed; smoke even obscured the Capitol. That King's death should trigger the worst outburst of looting, arson, and theft thus far was a cruel and final irony. In Atlanta, an FBI agent yelled with joy, "They finally got the s.o.b.!" In Arlington, Texas, a milkman argued that he got what he preached, and white students in the dormitory of the University of Texas at Arlington cheered when they heard the news. Meanwhile, a massive federal manhunt was under way for the suspected sniper, a white man in a white Mustang, seen racing away from the murder area where police had found a .30-06 rifle in a bundle tossed in a doorway. Authorities would later identify him as escaped convict James Earl Ray.

With sections of Washington and many other cities still ablaze, President Johnson proclaimed Sunday, April 7, as a day of national mourning, and flags around the country flew at half mast and countless thousands of Americans, blacks and whites together, marched and prayed and sang freedom songs in King's honor. On Monday, Abernathy, Coretta, and her three older children led 19,000 people in a silent memorial march through the streets of Memphis, proving to all the nation that a nonviolent demonstration could be conducted in King's spirit. The strike ended eight days later when the city recognized the sanitation workers' union and agreed to wage increases and other benefits. King's death had seen to that.

The *New York Times* had called it a disaster to the nation; the London *Times* said it was also a great loss to the world. Not since the assassination of Kennedy had an American death caused such grief and consternation abroad. Everywhere news of the shooting dominated the press, television, and radio. Pope Paul VI, who had granted King a private audience in 1964, poured out his "profound sadness" in a cablegram to the entire American Catholic hierarchy, sent to his Apostolic Delegate in Washington. In Japan, Foreign Minister Takeo

Miki reported that his country was "gravely concerned." In South Africa, newspapers printed special editions about King and blacks lined up on street corners to get them. In Lagos, Nigeria, officials bemoaned "this sad and inhumane killing," and the U.S. Embassy hung a portrait of King draped in black crepe outside its front door. In France and Britain, the press made much of the violence and racism that cursed America, and both parties in the English House of Commons introduced resolutions expressing horror at what had happened. In West Germany, both houses of parliament stood in silent tribute, and Mayor Klaus Schutz led a march of 1,000 Germans and Americans through West Berlin to John F. Kennedy Square. In Tanzania, Reverend Trevor Huddleston, expelled from South Africa for standing against apartheid, contended that King's death was the greatest single tragedy since the assassination of Gandhi in India and that it challenged the complacency of the Christian Church the world over.

Meanwhile, with tributes and condolences flowing in from all corners of the globe, Coretta and A. D. brought King home in an Electra jet chartered by Robert Kennedy. He lay in state in the chapel of Spelman College, where weeping mourners of all races and religions filed by his open casket at the rate of 1,200 an hour, women touching and kissing him. Daddy King brought Alberta, Coretta, and the four children to pay final respects, to look one last time at the father, the husband, and the son. Overcome with grief, Daddy King reached into the casket. "M. L.!" he cried. "Answer me, M. L." Then he collapsed, sobbing, "He never hated anybody, he never hated anybody."

On April 9, a hot and humid day in Atlanta, Abernathy officiated over King's funeral service in Ebenezer Church, where almost 800 people were packed in the sanctuary. From 60,000 to 100,000 surrounded the church outside, listening to the proceedings over loudspeakers, and thousands more waited at Morehouse College, where a public service was scheduled. Inside Ebenezer, Negro comedian and civil-rights activist Dick Gregory observed dozens of Negro celebrities in attendance, many of whom had marched with King on various civil-rights battlefronts. There were Harry Belafonte and his wife, Sammy Davis, Jr., Floyd Patterson, Thurgood Marshall, Mahalia Jackson, Diana Ross, Lena Horne, and many others, come to pay homage to a man who had extolled the strength of black people and endowed them with the noblest mission of any Negro leader before. There was King's special family of staffers and former aides—Young and Lee, Williams,

Fauntroy, and Vivian, Bevel, Jackson, Orange, and others—who felt lost without him, suffering a sorrow so deep that for some it would never heal. Here and there in the crowded sanctuary were King's fellow civil-rights leaders—Wilkins and Whitney Young, Carmichael, McKissick, Forman, and John Lewis—who had quarreled so often with him or one another this past year and a half, brought together by his death. Carmichael had appeared at the church with six bodyguards, causing a brief disturbance because there were no seats for the guards. There were scores of white friends and dignitaries too: the Wachtels and Levisons, Attorney General Ramsey Clark, labor and religious potentates, a regiment of mayors and governors, numerous congressmen, and all the major presidential contenders that year save George Wallace. There were Robert Kennedy with his wife Ethel, Eugene McCarthy, and Richard Nixon, the front-running Republican, whose presence evoked cries of "politicking" and complaints of "crocodile tears" among some Negroes. But it was the arrival of Jacqueline Kennedy, dressed like Coretta in a black silk mourning suit, that created the greatest sensation outside the church. The crowds surged around her with such force that she had to be pulled and pushed inside the door, her face looking frightened for a moment. Just before the services began, Vice-President Hubert H. Humphrey entered through a side door, greeted the family, and found his seat; he was standing in for Lyndon Johnson. No, the President did not attend the funeral of one of the first citizens of the world, as the World Council of Churches referred to King. (Neither did Georgia Governor Lester Maddox, a white supremacist who refused to close the schools and even protested against lowering the flag to half mast.) In the front row, facing the African mahogany coffin with its cross of flowers, was King's grieving widow, children, and parents.

With the organ groaning in the background, Abernathy intoned, "We gather here this morning in one of the darkest hours in the history of the black people of this nation, in one of the darkest hours in the history of all mankind." The choir sang some of King's favorite hymns—"When I Survey the Wondrous Cross" and "In Christ There Is No East Nor West"—and Harold DeWolf gave the tribute. At Coretta's request, Abernathy had a tape played of King's own eulogy, "A Drum Major for Justice," given at Ebenezer the past February. Once again that mellifluous voice swept through the church, the church he had joined on another spring day thirty-four years before, the church in which he had been baptized and ordained to spread the gospel of his Christ. "But I just wanted to leave a committed life behind," his voice cried in the hushed sanctuary. "Then my living will not be in vain."

The pallbearers carried him out to a special hearse—a farm cart drawn by two mules, which symbolized his poor people's campaign, his own last and greatest dream. Then with bells shattering the humid day and 120 million Americans watching on television, the cart started forward to the clop, clop of the mules, carrying Martin Luther King on his last freedom march, with Abernathy and his young aides— many of them dressed in the poor people's uniform of faded jeans and overall jackets—moving beside and behind their fallen leader. Some 50,000 people toiled along behind the cart, suffering from the muggy heat as they passed thousands of muted onlookers, most of them black. The line of march led past the domed Georgia capitol, where Lester Maddox was sitting in his office under a heavy guard. At last the great cortege reached the tree-shaded campus of Morehouse College, where King had discovered Thoreau and found his calling under the guidance and inspiration of Benjamin Mays. Now, at the portico of Harkness Hall, Mays gave the eulogy to King, to a man who had come preaching love and compassion and brotherhood rather than cynicism and violence; a man who, as a Negro, had had every reason to hate America but who had loved her passionately instead and had sung of her glory and promise more eloquently than anyone of his generation, maybe of any generation.

"We have assembled here from every section of this great nation and from other parts of the world to give thanks to God that He gave to America, at this moment in history, Martin Luther King, Jr.," Mays said. "Truly God is no respecter of persons. How strange! God called the grandson of a slave on his father's side, and said to him: Martin Luther, speak to America about war and peace; about social justice and racial discrimination; about its obligation to the poor; and about nonviolence as a way of perfecting social change in a world of brutality and war."

But that world was behind him now, life's restless sea was over. His anguished staff gathered round the coffin and prayed together for guidance and strength, their hearts breaking in this, their final farewell. Then his family, friends, and followers escorted him to South View Cemetery, blooming with dogwood and fresh green boughs of spring, and buried him near his grandparents, near his Grandmother Williams whom he had loved so as a boy. On his crypt, hewn into the marble, were the words of the old slave spiritual he had quoted so often:

FREE AT LAST, FREE AT LAST
THANK GOD ALMIGHTY
I'M FREE AT LAST

ACKNOWLEDGMENTS

I could never have written this book without the support of others. A Senior Summer Fellowship from the National Endowment for the Humanities facilitated my research forays into the South in 1978, and I thank the Endowment for its financial aid. I am also grateful to the Lyndon B. Johnson Library in Austin, Texas, for a Moody grant which helped defray my expenses there, and to Tina Lawson, Nancy Smith, and Linda Hanson of the Library's staff for their prompt and cheerful assistance. William Johnson, Henry J. Gwiazda, and Deborah Green of the John F. Kennedy Library in Boston made my stay there both comfortable and rewarding, and I am in their debt. Meyer Weinberg, Director of the Horace Mann Bond Center for Equal Education at the University of Massachusetts, Amherst, introduced me to the Center's collection on the Chicago campaign and regaled me with graphic stories about his role in it. I am much obliged to him. I want to express my gratitude to Dr. Howard Gotlieb, Director of the Special Collections of Boston University's Mugar Memorial Library, and his entire staff for their help, and to Joan Daves, Agent of the Martin Luther King, Jr., Estate, for permission to quote from documents in the Library's King papers. Joan Daves also opened her private papers to me and stood by my work from the very outset. My thanks, too, to D. Louise Cook, Director of the Library and Archives of the Martin Luther King, Jr., Center for Nonviolent Social Change in Atlanta, for her professional and enthusiastic service during my labors there. She has made the Center's one of the most efficiently organized archives I have ever had the pleasure of working through. Coretta Scott King, President of the Center, proved sympathetic and understanding in a long discussion we had about my book and the quartet of which it is a part. Though this is not an official, authorized life of King (I am a fiercely independent biographer who writes his own books), I am indebted to Mrs. King for making the Center's holdings available to me without restrictions. Because of her and her energetic staff, the King Center is now the foremost library in the United States for the study of Martin Luther King, Jr., and the civil-rights movement.

When it comes to thanking friends and colleagues, I scarcely know where to begin. Ruth Byrne, Peter Eddy, Jonathan Hensleigh, Sandra Katz, Elizabeth Lloyd-Kimbrel, Ann Meeropol, and Will Ryan of the Amherst Creative Biography Group heard sections of the book during our Friday night readings, and I deeply appreciate their constructive remarks. I can never repay Ruth Byrne for all the additional help she provided. She not only listened with alacrity and patience as I read the manuscript to her, but proofed and criticized it and offered invaluable moral support. Charles C. Alexander and Alonzo Hamby of Ohio University examined the manuscript in its entirety and furnished incisive critiques that made it a better book than it otherwise would have been. John Hicks of *The Massachusetts Review* made many cogent suggestions about King's college years, and Paul Mariani, a poet and a fellow biographer, perused the entire manuscript and gave me encouragement when I needed it the most. Harry Wachtel perceived the value of my work in its initial stages, and I very much appreciate his constant support. He gave generously of his time in protracted interviews, sent me manuscript materials when I needed them, answered questions when I found myself in trouble, and with his wife Lucy assisted me in countless other ways. No expression of thanks to them could ever suffice.

I am grateful, too, to Sally Ives for typing the final draft of the manuscript, to Michael Kirkby for proofreading it with a careful eye, to N. J. Demerath and David Garrow for their courtesies, and to Hugh Carter Donahue, G. Barbara Einfurer, Fred and Elise Turner, Betty Mitchell, Mark Gerstein, and O. C. Bobby Daniels for their kindness and friendship during the past five years. Finally, I owe a special debt to the University of Massachusetts, Amherst, which helped more than any other institution to make this book a reality. The University not only provided me with funds for supplies, research, and typing, but granted me a remunerative Graduate Faculty Fellowship that released me from teaching duties for a year so that I could complete the biography. Though often misunderstood and maligned in the state it represents, the University has excellent students, a talented, nationally acclaimed faculty, and a firm commitment to creative scholarship.

REFERENCES

The sources listed below are abbreviated in the reference notes according to the key on the left. All other sources are identified in the notes. For a full index of King's own published writings, consult Daniel T. Williams, "Martin Luther King, Jr., 1929–1968: *A Bibliography*," typescript copy in MLK(BU), which see below.

AOC—"Attack on the Conscience," *Time* (Feb. 18, 1957), 17–20.

Autobiography—Martin Luther King, Jr., "Autobiography of Religious Development," MLK(BU). Written for a graduate course at Boston University, this is a remarkably revealing account of King's early experiences and sentiments.

Bennett—Lerone Bennett, Jr., *What Manner of Man: A Biography of Martin Luther King, Jr.* (4th rev. ed., Chicago, 1976). Written by a friend of King's and a fellow Morehouse man, this biography, first published in 1964, carries the story down to 1965, with a brief epilogue.

BOHC—Ralph J. Bunche Oral History Collection, Moorland-Spingarn Research Center, Howard University, Washington, D.C. The collection is a rich storehouse of interviews, conducted in 1967–68, with Ella Baker, James Bevel, Harold L. DeWolf, John Lewis, Rosa Parks, Glenn E. Smiley, Fred Shuttlesworth, John Seigenthaler, C. T. Vivian, Wyatt Walker, and many others involved in the civil-rights movement.

Coretta King—Coretta Scott King. *My Life with Martin Luther King, Jr.* (New York, 1969).

Daddy King—Martin Luther King, Sr. (with Clayton Riley), *Daddy King: An Autobiography* (New York, 1980).

DTTP—Martin Luther King, Jr., "It's a Difficult Thing to Teach a President," *Look* (November, 1964), 61, 64.

FAR—*The Final Assassinations Report: Report of the Select Committee on Assassinations, U.S. House of Representatives* (New York, 1979).

Friends—CBS TV News Special, "Some Friends of Martin Luther King," hosted by Charles Kuralt, April 7, 1968, transcript, BOHC. Reminiscences of King by Harry Belafonte, Ralph McGill, Hosea Williams, Reverend Sam Williams, and Andrew Young.

HMB—The Horace Mann Bond Center for Equal Education, University of Massachusetts library, Amherst. The center has a valuable file of newspapers, clippings, and other matter relating to King's Chicago campaign and the school fight there against Superintendent Benjamin C. Willis.

Howell—Leon Howell, "An Interview with Andrew Young," *Christianity and Crisis* (Feb. 16, 1976), 14–20.

HSCAH—U.S. House of Representatives, *Investigation of the Assassination of Martin Luther King, Jr.: Hearings Before the Select Committee on Assassinations of the U.S. House of Representatives*, 95th Cong., 2d sess., 1978, vols. I, IV, VI, and VII.

JD—Joan Daves Papers, New York City. Daves, one of King's literary agents, currently represents King's literary estate. Her papers include some speeches and valuable correspondence and other documents relating to his published writings.

JFK—John F. Kennedy Library, Boston. Several collections housed here contain materials germane to King and the civil-rights movement. Among them are the papers of Robert F. Kennedy, Burke Marshall, and Harris Wofford, as well as interviews with the three men, Clarence Mitchell of the NAACP, and many others.

Kunstler—William M. Kunstler, *Deep in My Heart* (New York, 1966).

LBJ—Lyndon B. Johnson Library, Austin, Texas. The library has extensive holdings that bear on King and civil rights. They can be found in the White House Central File, the Confidential File, the White House Diary and Diary Backup, and various Aides' Files. There are also transcripts of interviews with Chester Bowles, Ramsey Clark, James Farmer, Nicholas Katzenbach, Burke Marshall, Clarence Mitchell, A. Philip Randolph, Bayard Rustin, Roy Wilkins, Andrew Young, and a great many others. Unfortunately for the King student, many "sensitive" documents involving King remain classified.

Lincoln—C. Eric Lincoln (ed.), *Martin Luther King, Jr., A Profile* (New York, 1970). This is an anthology of contemporary writings about King by James Baldwin, Reese Cleghorn, August Meier, Vincent Harding, David Halberstam, Carl T. Rowan, Ralph Abernathy, and others.

MLK(BU)—Martin Luther King, Jr., Collection, Mugar Memorial Library, Boston University. An indispensable archive for the serious King student, the collection contains some 83,000 documents that pertain to the King story down to around 1964. Among them are King's papers, examinations, notebooks, and other matter accumulated during his studies at Boston University; his "Autobiography of Religious Development," listed above; his private correspondence and official correspondence as MIA and SCLC president; voluminous incoming correspondence from friends, colleagues, agents and editors, religious and political leaders both in the United States and abroad, and love and hate mail from the public; typescripts of King's speeches and drafts of his books, articles, and sermons; telegrams, press releases, itineraries, newspaper clippings, magazine articles about King, and miscellany; and MIA and SCLC records, too, such as reports, minutes of meetings, press releases, and fund-raising letters.

MLK(CSC)—Martin Luther King, Jr., Papers, Martin Luther King, Jr., Center for

Nonviolent Social Change, Atlanta, Georgia. This rich repository comprises King's private and official correspondence chiefly from 1962 to 1968; his vast mail from the public; transcripts of many of his unpublished speeches and sermons; memoranda, press releases, and other public utterances from around 1955 to 1968; valuable documents pertaining to the Albany, Birmingham, St. Augustine, Selma, Chicago, and poor people's campaigns; transcripts of oral history interviews with those who knew and worked with King; and thousands of other items.

MOY—"Man of the Year: Never Again Where He Was," *Time* (Jan. 3, 1964), 13–16, 25–27.

NYT—*New York Times*.

PI—Martin Luther King, Jr., "Interview," *Playboy* (January, 1965), 65–74, 76–78.

PN—Martin Luther King, Jr., "Pilgrimage to Nonviolence," *Christian Century* (Apr. 3, 1964), 439–441.

Poston—Ted Poston, "Martin Luther King, Jr.," *New York Post Magazine* (May 13, 1968).

Raines—Howell Raines (ed.), *My Soul Is Rested: Movement Days in the Deep South Remembered* (New York, 1977). This is a superb compendium of interviews with such civil-rights veterans as James Farmer, E. D. Nixon, Bayard Rustin, John Lewis, Fred Shuttlesworth, Andrew Young, Randolph Blackwell, Ralph Abernathy, Benjamin Mays, and Martin Luther King, Sr., as well as with lawyers, lawmen, and members of the white opposition.

Reddick—L. D. Reddick, *Crusader Without Violence: A Biography of Martin Luther King, Jr.* (New York, 1959).

SCLC—Southern Christian Leadership Conference, Records, Martin Luther King, Jr., Center for Nonviolent Social Change, Atlanta, Georgia. This collection covers the years from 1957 to 1968 and is arranged by offices. For the King student, the most helpful are the records of the President, which include many of King's speeches and a fair amount of his correspondence as head of SCLC; the records of the Executive Director, which are filed under the names of those who held the post (John Tilley, Ella Baker, Wyatt Walker, and Andrew Young); and the records of the Program Director, which contain material on the Chicago and poor people's campaigns.

Selby—Earl and Miriam Selby (eds.), *Odyssey: Journey Through Black America* (New York, 1971).

SL—Martin Luther King, Jr., *Strength to Love* (reprint of 1963 ed., Cleveland, Ohio, [n.d.]).

SSCFR—U.S. Senate, Senate Select Committee to Study Government Operations with Respect to Intelligence Activities, *Final Report: Book III, Supplementary Detailed Staff Reports on Intelligence Activities and the Rights of Americans*, 94th Cong., 2d sess., 1976.

SSCH—U.S. Senate, Senate Select Committee to Study Government Operations with Respect to Intelligence Activities, *Hearings: Federal Bureau of Investigation*, 94th Cong., 1st sess., 1976, vol. VI.

STF—Martin Luther King, Jr., *Stride Toward Freedom: the Montgomery Story* (New York, 1958).

Tallmer—Jerry Tallmer, "Martin Luther King, Jr., His Life and Times," New York *Post* (Apr. 8, 1968).

Testament—Martin Luther King, Jr., "A Testament of Hope," *Playboy* (January, 1969), n.p., 194, 231–34, 236.

TC—Martin Luther King, Jr., *The Trumpet of Conscience* (New York, 1968).

Watters—Pat Watters, *Down to Now: Recollections of the Civil Rights Movement* (New York, 1971). A passionate and deeply insightful personal account of the movement by a southern white journalist who covered it.

W and M—Alan F. Westin and Barry Mahoney, *The Trial of Martin Luther King* (New York, 1974).

Walton—Norman W. Walton, "The Walking City: A History of the Montgomery Boycott," *Negro History Bulletin*, pt. I (October, 1956), 17–20; pt. II (November, 1956), 27–33; pt. III (February, 1957), 102–105; pt. IV (April, 1957), 147–48, 150, 152, 166.

WCW—Martin Luther King, Jr., *Why We Can't Wait* (paperback ed., New York, 1964).

WGH—Martin Luther King, Jr., *Where Do We Go from Here: Chaos or Community?* (paperback ed., New York, 1968).

Wofford—Harris Wofford, *Of Kennedys and Kings: Making Sense of the Sixties* (New York, 1980).

Yeakey—Lamont H. Yeakey, "The Montgomery, Alabama, Bus Boycott, 1955–56" (unpublished Ph.D. dissertation, Columbia University, 1979).

YPI—Andrew Young, "Interview," *Playboy* (July, 1977), 61–62, 78, 80, 82–83.

page　　　　　　　　　　PRELUDE

xii "perpetuate a man": Paul Murray Kendall, *The Art of Biography* (New York, 1965), ix.

xii "human portrayal": Leon Edel, "The Figure Under the Carpet," in Marc Pachter (ed.), *Telling Lives* (Washington, D.C., 1979), 20.

xiii "literature of actuality": Barbara W. Tuchman, *Practicing History: Selected Essays* (New York, 1981), 51.

xiii "fashions a man": Edel, 20.

xiii "psychologically coherent": Justin Kaplan, "The Real Life," *Harvard English Studies 8* (Cambridge, Mass., 1978), 2. For a discussion of how the first three volumes of my quartet fit together, see Stephen B. Oates, *Our Fiery Trial* (Amherst, Mass., 1979), 121–29.

PART ONE: ODYSSEY

3 "Get ahead" to "moment": Autobiography.

4 "along with people" and "perfect child": *ibid.*

5 "very dear," "saintly grandmother," "very intimately," "my father": *ibid.*

5 "motherly cares" and "noble": *ibid.*

5 "*smell* like a mule": Reddick, 44; Coretta King, 77; Daddy King, 38.

page

5   "have things": Reddick, 45; Raines, 461.

6   "Some day": Coretta King, 77; Daddy King, 109.

6   "sulfurous evangelism": David L. Lewis, *King, A Critical Biography* (2nd ed., Urbana, Ill., 1978), 4; Esther A. Smith, "A History of Ebenezer Baptist Church, Atlanta, Ga.," MLK(BU). A reissue of the 1970 edition with only the postscript revised, Lewis's *King, A Critical Biography* is based almost entirely on printed materials up to 1969 and makes no effort to bring King alive; it is marred, moreover, by Lewis's often condescending and gratuitous criticisms of his subject, to whom he refers throughout as "Martin."

8   "stoic impassivity": William Robert Miller, *Martin Luther King, Jr.: His Life, Martyrdom and Meaning for the World* (New York, 1968), 9.

8   "peculiar child": Bennett, 24; Lincoln, 101.

9   suicide attempt: Reddick, 60; Miller, *King*, 7; Bennett, 18; AOC, 14.

9   "wait and see": Tallmer; Autobiography.

9   "before he could read": Coretta King, 80.

9   "talkative chap": Tallmer.

10 "puffed up": Coretta King, 80.

10 white playmate and "never feel": Autobiography; King's remarks in Hugh Bennett (ed.), *Face to Face* (New York, 1965), 78. Other versions claim there were two playmates.

10 "hate every white person": Autobiography.

12 "less than": King in Bennett, *Face to Face*, 78.

12 "little nigger": Reddick, 59–60.

12 "How can I love": Autobiography. See also *STF*, 90, and King in Bennett, *Face to Face*, 78.

12 "straightening out": Reddick, 57.

12 "show me your license": Coretta King, 83; Reddick, 57.

12 "when I stand" to "with the system": Coretta King, 82–83; Bennett, 20; Ralph McGill in Friends.

12 "real father" and "extreme": Autobiography.

13 second suicide attempt: This is my interpretation of King's motivation inferred from *ibid.*, with facts from Reddick, 61, and AOC, 14.

13 "don't blame": Daddy King, 109; see also Autobiography.

13 "major force": Bennett, 20.

14 "precocious type": Autobiography.

14 "shocked Sunday School class" and "doubts": *ibid.*

14 "didn't understand" and "emotionally satisfying": MOY, 14; AOC, 18; also Autobiography, Daddy King, and Bayard Rustin interview with Oates, Dec. 12, 1979.

15 "fullback": Tallmer.

15 "middle-class combat" and "to the grass": Bennett, 21, 24; Tallmer. It is a myth that King was nonviolent even in his youth.

15 "outwrestle" and "hellion": Tallmer.

15 "can't spell a lick": Reddick, 11.

page

16 "chick to chick": Tallmer.

16 "greatest talent": Bennett, 17–18.

16 "black son-of-a-bitch" and "angriest": PI, 66.

17 "sense of freedom": Coretta King, 85.

17 "selfhood": *ibid.*; Bennett, 25.

17 "at that point": Bennett, 25–26.

18 "fallacy of statistics": Lewis, *King*, 19.

18 "root of evil": Miller, *King*, 12.

18 Chandler: Morehouse College, *The Alumnus* (fall, 1965), 2–5; *Jet* (Oct. 7, 1965), 23; King to Mrs. G. Lewis Chandler, Sept. 28 [1965], and Frederic L. Ellis to Mrs. Chandler, Sept. 27, 1965, in possession of Beth Chandler Warren, Peaks Island, Me.

19 "behind the legends" and "fundamentalism": Autobiography; also King's statement in Maude L. Ballou to Joan Thatcher, Aug. 7, 1959, MLK(BU).

19 Mays: Lerone Bennett, Jr., "The Last of the Great Schoolmasters," *Ebony* (Dec., 1977), 74, 77–78; Benjamin E. Mays, *Born to Rebel* (New York, 1971), 89–90, 174, 241.

20 "a real minister": Bennett, "Schoolmasters," *Ebony*, 74; also King's handwritten statement about Mays's retirement [1967], MLK(CSC), and Mays, *Born*, 265.

20 "God had placed" and "personal immortality": Autobiography. King acknowledged that his father's powerful example also influenced his decision to become a minister.

20 "no little trepidation" and "just seventeen": Bennett, 27–28.

21 "learn their plight": Coretta King, 84–85; also *STF*, 90; PN, 440; Reddick, 74.

21 "more of white people": AOC, 18; Autobiography.

21 "positive quest": Bennett, "Schoolmasters," *Ebony,* 74.

21 "race problem": AOC, 18.

22 "obnoxious negative peace": King said this many times, but see "A Realistic Look at the Question of Progress in the Area of Race Relations," May 17, 1956, typescript, MLK(BU).

23 "perceived immediately": Bennett, 27; also Mays, *Born*, 265.

23–24 "mighty young" and "fine girl": Coretta King, 87, 60. Daddy King paid his son's expenses at Crozer (see Autobiography).

24–25 "minute late to class" and "bright young man": Reddick, 86, 78; see also Kenneth L. Smith to King, Sept. 30, 1959, MLK(BU), and Walter McCall interview with Herbert Holmes, MLK(CSC).

25 "from Plato": *STF*, 92.

26 "moribund religion": PN, 440; *STF*, 91–92.

26–28 Communism and capitalism: Autobiography; PN, 440; *STF*, 92–95; King's "The Challenge of Communism to Christianity," cited in Melvin Watson to King, Aug. 14, 1952, MLK(BU), was an early version of his sermon "How Should a Christian View Communism?" in *SL*, 96–

page

105; see also *ibid.*, 19, 28, 67–75, 140; Coretta King, 58–59; Reddick, 22; Ernest Dunbar, "A Negro Leader Talks about the Struggle Ahead," *Look* (Feb. 12, 1963), 95; *TC*, 69, 70; and King, "Facing the Challenge of a New Age," Dec. 3, 1956, MLK(BU) for the "togetherness" theme, which he repeatedly stressed.

29   "yourself at home": Reddick, 83.

29   "eat more": Lewis, *King*, 28. See also McCall interview, MLK(CSC).

29–30   Maple Shade and white student incidents: Reddick, 81–83; McCall interview (CSC); Miller, *King*, 21.

31   Nietzsche: *STF*, 95–96; PN, 440.

31–33   Gandhi: PN, 440; *STF*, 96–97; King to Lawrence M. Byrd, Apr. 25, 1957, MLK(BU); Reddick, 18–20, 80–81; Coretta King, 58–59; King, "Love, Law, and Civil Disobedience," *New South* (Dec., 1961), 5.

33   "absolutely convinced": PN, 439; Autobiography.

33–34   the young white woman: Poston; Lewis, 33.

34–35   Niebuhr: *STF*, 97–99; PN, 439; Smith to King, Sept. 30, 1959, MLK(BU).

36   "uniformly courteous" and "so much": Warren Carberg, "The Story Behind the Victory," *Bostonia* (spring, 1957), 7.

37   "self contained," "humor," and "liked": L. Harold DeWolf interview with John H. Britton, Apr. 23, 1968, BOHC.

38   "real to me": Autobiography; see also King's essay reviews of Winifred V. Richmond's *Personality: Its Study and Hygiene* and Ruth Davis Perry's *Children Need Adults* and King's papers and examinations in MLK(BU). Niebuhr, of course, may have had some influence on King's views of psychology.

38   "anxiety and conflict": PN, 439–40.

38–39   Hegel: *STF*, 95, 100–101; *SL*, 9; AOC, 18.

39   Niebuhr resolved: King, "Religious Answer to the Problem of Evil," "Reinhold Niebuhr's Ethical Dualism," "How Modern Christians Should Think of Man," and lecture notebooks and examinations, MLK(BU); *STF*, 100–124; Pilgrimage, 439.

40   personalism: King, "A Comparison and Evaluation of the Philosophical Views Set Forth in J. M. E. McTaggart's *Some Dogmas of Religion*, and William E. Hocking's with Those Set Forth in Edgar S. Brightman's Course on 'Philosophy of Religion,' " "The Personalism of J. M. E. McTaggart UNDER CRITICISM," "A Conception and Impression of Religion Drawn From Dr. Brightman's Book entitled *A Philosophy of Religion*," and examinations on personalism and on the history of Christian thought and doctrine, MLK(BU); *STF*, 100; Pilgrimage, 441; *SL*, 128–37.

41   "ambivert": Reddick, 6; Bennett, 18.

41   "antitheses strongly marked": *SL*, 9.

41   "these girls": Whitaker to King, Oct. 31, 1952, MLK(BU).

41   "gallivanting around": W. T. Handy, Jr., to King, Nov. 18, 1952, *ibid.*

page

42–45 Coretta Scott and marriage: Coretta King, 51–74, is the major source; see also Lincoln, 103; Reddick, 104–6; Bennett, 46–47; DeWolf interview, BOHC; King to Mr. Henry Kelley [n.d.], MLK(BU).

46 "real man" and "shared relationship": Coretta King, 91.

46 "Nodoze": expenses notebook, MLK(BU).

46 thesis: correspondence and materials about in *ibid.*; DeWolf interview, BOHC.

47 "scholar's scholar" to "prominent scholarship": DeWolf interview, BOHC.

47–50 Dexter Church: *STF*, 15–22; B. J. Simms interview with Oates, Sept. 17, 1978; Rev. J. C. Parker to King, Mar. 10, 1954, and Dexter Pulpit Committee to King, same date, MLK(BU); Coretta King, 97; Reddick, 109.

50 "elated," "decree," and "sublime": W and M, 24; *SL*, 81; King's speech, Washington Prayer Pilgrimage, May 17, 1957, MLK(BU).

51 "what you want": Coretta King, 100.

PART TWO: ON THE STAGE OF HISTORY

56 "soul beauty" and "court": Reddick, 5–6.

56 "break in marriage": King to V. L. Harris, Jan. 10, 1959, MLK(BU).

56 "feel so helpless" to "amount of love": King to Miss Myrtle Beavers, June 23, 1958, and to Walter R. Chivers, Nov. 5, 1960, *ibid.*; King's "Advice for Living" columns in *Ebony*, Sept., 1957 to Dec., 1958.

56–57 King's preaching: King's note in folder on preaching, MLK(BU); *STF*, 26–27, 36; Coretta King, 59. See also among other studies E. Franklin Frazier, *The Negro Church in America* (New York, 1963), 46; Benjamin E. Mays and Joseph W. Nicholson, *The Negro's Church* (New York, 1933, 1969), 281; Charles V. Hamilton, *The Black Preacher* (New York, 1972), 12, 14, 19–28.

57 "suave . . . persuasive": James Pierce quoted in Yeakey, 148; Simms interview with Oates.

57 "that little boy" and "my own son": Coretta King, 100, 184; Reddick, 131.

57 "a good preacher" and "have a son": J. Raymond Henderson to King, May 12, 1955, and to Martin Luther King, Sr., same date, MLK(BU).

57 "every way I turn": Daddy King to "My Dear M. L.," Dec. 2, 1954, *ibid.*

58–59 "vital liaison," "corroding sense," and "lack of unity": AOC, 18; *STF*, 34, 37.

59–60 Abernathy: Abernathy to Oates, Aug. 16, 1978; Harris Wofford, "Birthday Party for a Bus Boycott," typescript, MLK(BU); Charles Fager, *Uncertain Reconstruction: the Poor People's Washington Campaign* (Grand Rapids, Mich., 1969), 28; Reddick, 117.

60 "graceful jab": Reddick, 118.

page

60 "on stage": Mrs. Sullivan Jackson interview with Oates, July 8, 1977; Abernathy interview with Oates, Aug. 16, 1978; Rev. Howard Creecy interview with Oates, Aug. 2, 1978.

60 "searching study": DeWolf interview, BOHC.

61 "called them by name": Louisa R. Alger to Oates, May 4, 1979, letter in author's possession.

61 "compromise": Coretta King, 106.

62 "full of niggers": Dan Wakefield, *Revolt in the South* (New York, 1960), 32–33.

64 "militant man": Rosa Parks interview with John H. Britton, Sept. 28, 1967, BOHC; also Nixon interview with Oates, Aug. 17, 1979; Raines, 38–39; *STF*, 138–42; Yeakey, 33–34, 111–30.

64–65 Rosa Parks: Selby, 54, 57–59; Parks interview, BOHC; Nixon interview with Oates; Raines, 43–44.

65 "have took": *STF*, 44–45; Selby, 59.

66 "clock on the wall": *STF*, 48; also Yeakey, 290–91.

66 "external expression": *STF*, 51–52.

67 "come quickly": *ibid.*, 53.

67 "My Gawd": Nixon interview with Oates; Selby, 60.

67–68 "Mr. Chairman": *STF*, 56. Yeakey, 324, 324n, indicates that the meeting established a permanent organization.

68 "much time": Nixon interview with Oates; Raines, 49.

68 "has to do it": Coretta King, 116.

68 choice of King: Nixon interview with Oates; S. S. Seay interview with Judy Barton, Jan. 25, 1972, and Rufus Lewis interview with Barton, Jan. 24, 1972, MLK(CSC); Selby, 61; Yeakey, 324–25; Simms interview with Oates; *Ebony* (Dec., 1964) 126.

68 "what the hell": Raines, 49; also Nixon interview with Oates; *STF*, 57; Reddick, 124; Selby, 61–62.

69 "whatever you do" to "eternal edicts": *STF*, 59–60.

70–72 King's speech: Donald H. Smith, "Martin Luther King, Jr.: In the Beginning at Montgomery," *Southern Speech Journal* (fall, 1968), 12–16; Yeakey, 334–40; *STF*, 60–64; Simms interview with Oates; text of speech in the Harry Wachtel Papers, New York City.

72 "has been moved": *I have a Dream: Highlight. from the Speeches of Martin Luther King, Jr.* (Center for Cassette Studies, Hollywood, Calif., [n.d.]).

72–73 "my heart" to "open your mouth": *STF*, 64–70.

74 "Caleb": Lincoln, 224.

74–75 meeting with city commissioners: *STF*, 108–13; Montgomery *Advertiser*, Dec. 9, 1955; Atlanta *Journal*, Dec. 8–9, 1955; Yeakey, 430–37.

75 "rainy day": Walton, pt. I, 17–20.

76 "talked shop": Simms interview with Oates.

76 "not walking for myself": *STF*, 77–78.

page

77 "soul is rested": Raines, 61; *SL*, 125.
77 "Pooh!": George Barrett, "Montgomery: Testing Ground," *NYT Mag.* (Dec. 16, 1956), 50.
77 "boycott terrible": *STF*, 79.
77 "believe": Simms interview with Oates; also Barrett, "Montgomery," *NYT Mag.*, 50.
77 "race pride": Carl T. Rowan, *Go South to Sorrow* (New York, 1957), 127.
77 "Negroes of Montgomery": Montgomery *Advertiser*, Dec. 12, 1955. Because of her letter, segregationists subjected Juliette Morgan to a steady barrage of abuse by letter and telephone. A fragile and sensitive young woman, she could not bear the persecution she received: in 1957, she killed herself with an overdose of sleeping pills.
78 "little illustrative gestures": quoted in Reddick, 12.
78–80 King's teachings: These paragraphs are a composite of King's remarks at the mass meetings. They draw from *STF*, 85–87; *I Have a Dream* (cassette); Reddick, 12–13; Chester Bowles, "What Negroes Can Learn from Gandhi," *Saturday Evening Post* (Mar. 1, 1958), 93.
80 "that boy talkin' about": Abernathy interview with Oates; also Simms interview with Oates.
80 "hears Dr. King": Wofford, "Birthday Party," MLK(BU); Reddick, 131; Tallmer.
80 "only language": *STF*, 88.
80–82 second meeting: *STF*, 113–18; Montgomery *Advertiser*, Dec. 18, 1955; Yeakey, 445–54.
82 "firmly he believed": *STF*, 119.
82 Graetz: AOC, 20; Walton, pt. II, 19; Reddick, 123–24.
82 "folded their hands" to "mistake": PI, 66–67; *STF*, 209.
83 mayor's committee meeting: *STF*, 119–21; Yeakey, 454–59.
83 "outside agitators" to "love campaign": Rowan, *Sorrow*, 122, 125, 133; Montgomery *Advertiser*, Dec. 13, 1955.
84 "disturbers of the peace": PI, 68.
84 "communist infiltration": King to Homer Greene, July 10, 1956, MLK(BU); Abernathy interview with Oates. See also King's remarks about fear, Mar. 23, 1956, MLK(CSC).
84 "all these years": King, "Civil Disobedience," *New South*, 9; *STF*, 39–40.
84 boycott song: Walton, pt. I, 18–19.
85 rivalries and King's resignation offer: *STF*, 122–23; Yeakey, 482; Coretta King, 122.
85 "about the boycott": Walton, pt. I, 19; also Montgomery *Advertiser*, Jan. 22, 1956.
86 "pussy-footing": *STF*, 126; Walton, pt. I, 20.
86 King's arrest: *STF*, 127–31; Montgomery *Advertiser*, Jan. 29, 1956.

page

87 hate letters and phone calls: "A Good white citizen of Montgomery" to King [n.d.], MLK(BU); *STF*, 132–33; AOC, 19.

87–88 King's fears: Walton, pt. I, 152; DeWolf interview, BOHC; Martin Luther King, "Reflections," Chicago speech, 1966, in *Dr. Martin Luther King, Jr.: Speeches and Sermons* (tape); *STF*, 133; *SL*, 125–26.

88–89 voice in kitchen: King, "Reflections"; *SL*, 113; *STF*, 133–34; AOC, 19; Montgomery *Advertiser*, Jan. 27, 1957.

89–90 bombing: Coretta King, 128–30; *STF*, 137–38; Walton, pt. I, 20; AOC, 19; Montgomery *Advertiser*, Jan. 31, 1956.

90 "not bad men": *STF*, 138–39.

91 "totally nonviolent": Bayard Rustin interview with Oates, Dec. 12, 1979; Rustin interview with T. H. Baker, June 17 and 30, 1969, LBJ.

91 "sense of manhood": Testament, 233; *STF*, 140–44; Abernathy interview with Oates.

91 "course of human events": Bayard Rustin, "Montgomery Diary," *Liberation* (Apr., 1956), 9–10; Montgomery *Advertiser*, Feb. 11, 1956.

92 "Autherine," "like war," and "bomb us": Martin Luther King, Jr., "Our Struggle," *Liberation* (Apr., 1965), 5; Rustin, "Diary," *ibid.*, 7.

92–93 stands up to Daddy King: *STF*, 143–46; Raines, 64–65, 353–54; Mays, *Born*, 267–68; Yeakey, 520.

94 "holiday atmosphere": *STF*, 146; Montgomery *Advertiser*, Feb. 24, 1956.

94 "wonderful talk": Coretta King, 138.

94–95 Rustin: Rustin interview with Oates; Rustin interview, LBJ; Bayard Rustin, *Down the Line* (Chicago, 1971), 109–10; Raines, 54; Selby, 245–61.

95 "make the challenge": Raines, 55.

95 Daddy King's prayer: *ibid.*, 57; Rustin interview with Oates.

95–97 King's trial: *New Republic* (Apr. 2, 1956), 5; *Newsweek* (Apr. 2, 1956); Montgomery *Advertiser*, March 20 and 21, 1956; *STF*, 146–50; Yeakey, 521–27; Reddick, 142–45; Walton, pt. II, 27–28; Roy Wilkins to King, Mar. 18 and May 8, 1956, and King to Wilkins, May 1, 1956, MLK(BU).

97 "international stamping grounds": Simms interview with Oates; clippings in B. J. Simms scrapbook.

97 "thumbnail sketch": Glenn Smiley interview with Katherine M. Shannon, Sept. 12, 1967, BOHC.

97 "electronic perception": Watters, 45.

98 "THANK YOU": "Chris" to King, Feb. 27, 1956, MLK(BU).

98 "statesmanlike leadership": H. C. Diehl to King, Nov. 26, 1956, *ibid.*

98 "personal direction": Friends. The love and hate mail to King was voluminous (see MLK[BU]).

98 "must confess": King to H. Bulacher, Sept. 20, 1956, and to Wilbert J. Johnson, Sept. 24, 1956, *ibid.*, are two examples.

page

98 "worry about him": Reddick, 177.

98 "so involved": King to Rustin, July 10, 1956, MLK(BU).

99 "extremely vulnerable": King to Dr. William L. Bentley, Nov. 1, 1956, *ibid;* Reddick, 7; see also the many letters containing contributions, in MLK(BU). Dominic J. Capeci, Jr., "From Harlem to Montgomery: The Bus Boycotts and Leadership of Adam Clayton Powell, Jr., and Martin Luther King, Jr.," *Historian* (Aug., 1979), 732–33, documents Powell's contributions to the Montgomery protest. At the height of the protest, MIA's weekly expenses ran around $5,000, mostly for the transportation system and the office (see King to Rustin, Sept. 20, 1956, MLK[BU]).

99 "tragic sabotage": *STF*, 151. See Yeakey, 500ff, for the complicated legal maneuvers.

99–101 King's world view: These paragraphs are a composite of King's speeches and public utterances that year. These include "The Death of Evil upon the Seashore," in the Cathedral of St. John the Divine, New York City, May 17, 1956, typescript copy in MLK(BU), published in *SL*, 76–85; "A Realistic Look at the Question of Progress in the Area of Race Relations," given before the NAACP Legal Defense Fund, New York City, May 17, 1956, MLK(BU); speech given before the NAACP national convention, San Francisco, Calif., June 27, 1956, typescript in *ibid.*, published version in *U.S. News & World Report* (Aug. 3, 1956), 82, 87–89; "The Most Durable Power," *Christian Century* (Nov., 1957), 708; "Facing the Challenge of a New Age," given at the First Annual Institute on Nonviolence, Montgomery, Ala., Dec. 3, 1956, typescript in MLK(BU), published in *Phylon* (Apr., 1957), 25–34.

101 "without eating": King to S. S. Robinson, Oct. 3, 1956, and King affidavit, Dec. 10, 1956, MLK(BU).

101 "spiritual renewal": DeWolf to King, Nov. 9, 1956, *ibid.;* DeWolf interview, BOHC.

101 "powerful address": Nov. 27, 1956, MLK(BU).

102 "If the city officials": Coretta King, 141.

102 "backed us up" and "these months": PI, 66; *STF*, 158–59; *SL*, 65.

102 "clock said": Charles E. Fager, *Selma, 1965* (New York, 1974), 132–35.

102–103 "United States Supreme Court" and "God Almighty": *STF*, 160; Nixon interview with Oates.

103 "Any attempt," "allow niggers," "circus parade": Martin Luther King, Jr., "We Are Still Walking," *Liberation* (Dec., 1956), 6; *STF*, 162, 167; *Afro-American*, Dec. 1, 1956.

103–104 meeting at Holt Street Baptist Church: Walton, pt. III, 104; *STF*, 160–62; Montgomery *Advertiser*, Nov. 15, 1956; King, "Still Walking," *Liberation*, 7.

104 "a Messiah": AOC, 20.

104 "May God" and "Your fight": William Holmes Borders to King, Dec. 19, 1956, and anonymous letter to King, Dec. 31, 1956, MLK(BU).

page
104   "City Commission": *STF*, 170.
105   "spiritual force": *ibid.*, 169; King to Sellers and others, Dec. 19, 1956, MLK(BU); Smiley interview, BOHC.
105–106   King's speech: typescript in MLK(BU), published in *Phylon* (Apr., 1957), 25–34.
107   "rather die," "Reverend King asked," "sit in front": *STF*, 172–74; Wofford, "Birthday Party," MLK(BU).
107   "pains me": Rowan, *Sorrow*, 129. For the cost of the boycott, see Walton, pt. III, 103, and AOC, 19.
107   "Almost every week": King's Annual Report to Dexter Avenue Baptist Church, 1956–57, 3–4, MLK(BU).
108   "Dr. King's charisma": Rustin interview, LBJ; Rustin interview with Oates; see also Ella Baker's interview with John H. Britton, June 19 and July 19, 1969, BOHC.
108   leaflets: Walton, pt. IV, 148–49.
108–109   southern conference call: copy, Jan. 7, 1957, MLK(BU); King to Sidney Kaufman, Nov. 7, 1960, *ibid.*; Rustin, *Line*, 160; Baker interview, BOHC.
109   "When they bomb": Walton, pt. IV, 150.
109   SCLC manifesto: MLK(BU); Reddick, 184–85.
109   "wish I could": Rustin, *Line*, 103.
110   "have to die": *STF*, 177–78; *Ebony* (May, 1968), 142.
111   "We decided": Reddick, 210.
111   "things in Montgomery," "those Negroes," "anyone fool you": *STF*, 181, 184; Abel Plenn, "Report on Montgomery a Year After," *NYT Mag.* (Dec. 29, 1957), 11, 36, 38; also Barrett, "Montgomery," *ibid.*, 50, and Simms and Nixon interviews with Oates. On the other hand, Wakefield, *Revolt*, 91–93, found little change in white attitudes after the boycott.
112   "race-mixing": *STF*, 185.
112   "unarmed, unorganized": *WCW*, 34.
112   "tremendous facility": Raines, 56; Yeakey, vii.
112   "our heads up": Plenn, "Report," *NYT Mag.*, 36.
112   "great transforming power": King to Rev. J. O. A. Stevens, Dec. 22, 1959, MLK(BU).
112   "new heights": Joseph R. Washington, Jr., *Black Religion: the Negro and Christianity in the United States* (Boston, 1964), 25, in an otherwise muddled critique of King's love as "the regulating ideal."
112   "really disturbed": Coretta King, 149–50; Lincoln, 119.

PART THREE: FREEDOM IS NEVER FREE

115   "idea out of my mind": Jan. 4, 1957, MLK(BU).
116   "white South": PI, 72; Reddick, 22–23.
116–117   Ghana trip: Reddick, 181–82; King's speech as quoted in the Charleston *Gazette*, Jan. 25, 1960; King's sermon, Nov. 15, 1964, MLK(CSC);

page

Homer A. Jack, "Conversation in Ghana," *Christian Century* (Apr. 10, 1957), 446–47.

117 "talked angrily": Coretta King, 157.

118 "land of my father's fathers" and "rebirth": Reddick, 21–22, 183.

118 King's African concerns: King to Chief Luthuli, Dec. 8, 1959, and to Editorial Committee of *Dissent*, June 1, 1959, MLK(BU); King's typescript introduction to an American Committee on Africa pamphlet, Oct., 1959, and scores of other documents and correspondence relating to Africa in *ibid.* and in MLK(CSC).

118 "return to Africa": King to Edward H. Page, June 12, 1957, MLK(BU).

120 "French Revolution" and "never separated": "The Most Dangerous Negro," *Time* (May 28, 1979), 18; also Jervis Anderson, *A. Philip Randolph: A Biographical Portrait* (New York, 1973).

120 "spiritual undergirding": Thomas Kilgore, Jr., and others to James Hicks, June 4, 1957, MLK(BU); Rustin interview with Oates; Reddick, 186–90.

120–121 King's speech: typescript, MLK(BU).

121 "from Prayer Pilgrimage": New York *Amsterdam News*, June 1, 1957.

121 "After living": King to Congressman Charles E. Chamberlain, May 1, 1957, MLK(BU).

122 "His travels": King to Mazo, Sept. 2, 1958, *ibid.*

122 "lethargy": Arthur M. Schlesinger, Jr., *Robert Kennedy and His Times* (Boston, 1958), 287; also Steven F. Lawson, *Black Ballots: Voting Rights in the South, 1944–1969* (New York, 1976), 140–202.

123 "right to vote": King letters to Benjamin Mays and to many others, Dec. 12–17, 1957, and SCLC news releases, memoranda, and other items relating to SCLC's formation and the Crusade for Citizenship, MLK(BU); King to Thor Andersen, Jan. 31, 1962, MLK(CSC). See also August Meier and Elliott Rudwick, *CORE: A Study in the Civil Rights Movement* (paperback ed., Urbana, Ill., 1975), 72–79. Rustin maintains that King added "Christian" to the SCLC's initial name of the Southern Leadership Conference (Rustin interview with Oates).

124 Ella Baker: Baker interview, BOHC. While Baker was deeply committed to the movement and a leading spirit behind the formation of SCLC, she had sharp ideological differences with King that subsequently embittered her memories of him and the SCLC ministers with whom she worked. In May, 1958, John L. Tilley, a Baltimore pastor and educator, became permanent executive director, with Baker functioning as associate director. But in April, 1959, King relieved Tilley because he was "not producing" (King to Theodore E. Brown, Oct. 19, 1959, MLK[BU]). Baker then served as executive director until Wyatt Walker assumed the post in 1960.

124 "spiritual strategy": King to Byrd, Apr. 25, 1957, MLK(BU).

125 "a tragic revelation": King to Joseph Tusiani, August 8, 1959, *ibid.*

125–128 King's speech and conversation afterward: King, "Some Things We

page

Must Do," MLK(CSC), and Wofford, "Birthday Party," *ibid;* Paul Simon to Oates, Aug. 14, 1978; Chester Bowles, "What Negroes Can Learn from Gandhi," *Saturday Evening Post* (Mar. 1, 1958), 89; Wofford, 12.

128 "We have been growing": Dec. 13, 1957, MLK(BU).

128 "immediately and tremendously winning": Lincoln, 90–94.

129 "great pity": Jan. 3, 1958, MLK(BU).

129 "We feel": King's remarks on voting, Nov. 6, 1957, MLK(CSC), and King to Jesse Hill, Jr., Jan. 28, 1959, MLK(BU).

129 King's speech: MLK(BU).

130 "joy" and "Atlanta succeeds": King to Hill, Jan. 28, 1959, *ibid.*

130 "helpful hand": Arthur L. Johnson to King, Mar. 6, 1958, *ibid.*

130 "dolled-up Uncle Tomism": Los Angeles *Herald-Dispatch*, Feb. 27 and Mar. 6, 1958.

131 "writing on his book": Hilda S. Proctor to Mark Starr, Apr. 22, 1958, MLK(BU). The extensive correspondence surrounding the preparation of *STF* is in *ibid.* Stanley Levison warned King not to make it seem as though everything in the protest "depended on you" and was especially critical of King's final chapter, offering some revisions that were used in the text. A few days later, though, he wrote King that he hadn't praised the chapter enough and that it contained "a wealth of striking ideas of high leadership caliber." (Levison to King, Apr. 1 and 7, 1958, *ibid.*) King asserted later that "the Montgomery story was never a drama with only one actor. More precisely it was always a drama with many actors, each playing his part exceedingly well." (King's MIA speech, Dec. 3, 1959, SCLC.)

131 Arnold's and Popper's objections: Arnold to King, May 5, 1958, and Popper to King, [n.d.], *ibid.;* also *STF*, 93.

134 "so many problems," "President Eisenhower," and "rage and despair": Reddick, 223; *WCW*, 143; and Coretta King, 162.

134–136 King's arrest and trial: Reddick, 225–29; Coretta King, 162–65; King's statement to Judge Eugene Loe, Sept. 5, 1958, MLK(BU).

137 reviews: clippings and copies of, as well as correspondence on sales and foreign-language editions, in *ibid.*

137 "dark moments": King to Harry S. Ashmore, Jan. 22, 1959, *ibid.*

137 "a marked man": J. Raymond Henderson to King, Sept. 17, 1958, *ibid.*

138–139 King's stabbing: King's recollections in "I've Been to the Mountaintop," Apr. 3, 1968, Memphis, Tenn., MLK(CSC); "The Woman Behind Martin Luther King," *Ebony* (Jan., 1959), 33; *WCW*, 17; King to Randolph, Nov. 8, 1959, MLK(BU); Mrs. L. Zinberg to King, 1958, *ibid.;* Coretta King, 168–72; Reddick, 229–31. Ultimately, Randolph and New York City citizens raised $2,287.50 for King's hospital expenses (see Randolph to King, Dec. 18, 1958, MLK [BU]).

140 "Southern segregation struggle," "difficult period, "pick-pockets," and "so frustrating": King, "My Trip to India," 2, typescript, MLK(BU);

page

King to Hilda S. Proctor, Dec. 22, 1958, and Gregg to King, Jan. 23, 1959, *ibid.*

140–143   India trip: King, "My Trip," 2–11, published as "My Trip to the Land of Gandhi," *Ebony* (July, 1959), 84–86, 88–90, 92; newspaper clippings, Feb. 13, Mar. 3 and 13, 1959, MLK(BU); *WCW*, 134–35; *SL*, 84–85; *TC*, 69; Coretta King, 173–77.

143   "difficult problems": King to James Bristol, Mar. 30, 1959, MLK(BU).

143   Good Samaritan: King, "Mountaintop," Apr. 3, 1968, MLK(CSC).

144   "marvelous thing" to "victim of discrimination": PN, 441; King, "Hammer on Civil Rights," *Nation* (Mar. 9, 1964), 95; King's statement, Mar. 18, 1959, MLK(BU).

144   "doing something": Lincoln, 103; King to Corrine Johnson, Mar. 23, 1959, MLK(BU); Coretta King, 178–79.

144–145   "My failure" and "terribly frustrated": King to Allan Knight Chalmers, Apr. 18, 1960, MLK(BU).

145   SCLC strategy: *Southern School News* (Jan., 1960), 9; Coretta King, 183; King's recommendations at the SCLC Board meeting, fall and Dec., 1959, SCLC press releases and reports of the executive director, fall, 1959, MLK(BU); King's MIA Speech, Dec. 3, 1959, SCLC.

146   "total struggle": King to Chalmers, Apr. 18, 1960, and press releases, Dec. 1 and 8, 1958, *ibid.*; *Southern School News* (Jan., 1960), 9; King's MIA speech, Dec. 3, 1959, SCLC.

146   "trying": Coretta King, 181–83.

146   "black boy and girl": *Southern School News* (Jan., 1960), 9; statement, Feb. 1, 1960, MLK(BU); Washington, *Black Religion*, 13.

PART FOUR: SEASONS OF SORROW

149   King's finances and ambivalent attitudes: PI, 77; documents on royalties and honorariums in MLK(BU); Lincoln, 119; Harry Wachtel interview with Oates, Sept. 20 and Oct. 18, 1978; King to Ruth Cunningham, Aug. 5, 1979, MLK(BU). Halberstam, in Lincoln, 203, reported that King in later years became so unconcerned about money that his friend Harry Belafonte set up an educational trust for each of his children.

150   "first thing": Loudon Wainwright, "Martyr of the Sit-ins," *Look* (Nov. 7, 1960), 132.

150   "coalition" and "too busy to hate": John D. Hutcheson, Jr., *Racial Attitudes in Atlanta* (Atlanta, Ga., 1973), 5; Leonard, "Martyr," *Look*, 35; also Harold H. Martin, *William Berry Hartsfield, Mayor of Atlanta* (Athens, Ga., 1978); Melvin W. Ecke, *From Ivy Street to Kennedy Center: Centennial History of the Atlanta Public School System* (Atlanta, Ga., 1972), 345–56.

150–151   scolded his father and tacit agreement: Carl Holman interview with John H. Britton, Oct. 3, 1967, BOHC; Edwin Guthman, *We Band of*

page

Brothers (New York, 1971), 154–55; Wyatt Walker interview with John H. Britton, Oct. 11, 1967, BOHC; Lincoln, 106–11. Mays, *Born*, 273, reported that it was a long time before he and others could get King appointed to the Morehouse Board of Trustees, thanks to Negroes who "bitterly opposed his election."

151 "the teachings": Raines, 99; John Lewis interview with Katherine M. Shannon, Aug. 22, 1967, BOHC. See also William H. Chafe, *Civilities and Civil Rights: Greensboro, North Carolina, and the Black Struggle for Freedom* (New York, 1980); and Milton Viorst, *Fire in the Streets: America in the 1960s* (New York, 1979), 93–117.

152 "significant developments": Watters, 78–80; newspaper clippings and King to Ruby Nell Burrows, Apr. 13, MLK(BU).

152 "Many people" and "rest of my life": Coretta King, 185.

152–153 "run of history," "personal trials," "endeared himself," and "gestapo-like tactics": King to Jackie Robinson, June 19, 1960, MLK(BU); King, "Suffering and Faith," *Christian Century* (Apr. 27, 1960), 510; Bernard Lee quoted in Watters, 87; King to Eisenhower, Mar. 9, 1960, and SCLC press release, Mar. 11, 1960, MLK(BU).

153–154 defense of sit-ins: *Newsweek* (Feb. 29, 1960), 25; *U.S. News & World Report* (Mar. 21, 1960), 77; King, "The Burning Truth in the South," *Progressive* (May, 1960), 8–10; Nashville *Banner*, Apr. 21, 1960. King elaborated on his arguments in his speech, "Love, Law, and Civil Disobedience," *New South* (Dec., 1961), 3–11.

154 "no fad": Wakefield, *Revolt*, 126–27; see also the documents pertaining to the Youth Leadership Meeting in Raleigh, MLK(BU).

154 "young people's Martin Luther King" and "spiritual mother": Cleveland Sellers and Robert Terrell, *The River of No Return: the Autobiography of a Black Militant and the Life and Death of SNCC* (New York, 1973), 35; Lewis interview, BOHC.

154 King's speech: newspaper clipping, Apr. 23, 1959, MLK(BU).

155 "all believed": Watters, 129, 132. Baker interview, BOHC, Sellers, *River*, 36–37, Bernard Lee interview with Oates, Aug. 29, 1978, and James Forman, *The Making of Black Revolutionaries* (New York, 1972), 216–17, give different versions of King's offer of affiliation. Forman, for his part, all but accuses King of attempting to take over the student movement. Student leaders at the time certainly didn't feel that he was, as evidenced by their correspondence with King that year (see the next note). Throughout the spring, in fact, King emphatically denied news stories that he was the leader and initiator of the sit-in movement.

155 "its very existence" and "inspiration": Marion S. Barry, Jr., and Jane Stembridge to King, July 13 and 25, 1960, and Lonnie C. King, Jr., to King, Feb., 1961, MLK(BU).

155 "immoral and impractical": King to Benjamin F. Mays, Apr. 1, 1960, *ibid*. Legal correspondence regarding the case is in *ibid*.

155–156 "Alabama courts," "truth and conviction," "these white people": King

page

to Robert E. Hughes, Apr. 23, 1960, *ibid.*; Kunstler, xxiii–xxiv; Lincoln, 104–5.

156–157 Wyatt Tee Walker: Walker interview, BOHC; Selby, 282–87; Walter Fauntroy interview with Oates, Aug. 28, 1978. James Wood, an NAACP and labor organizer, became King's administrative assistant, Dorothy Cotton his administrative secretary, and Dora McDonald his personal secretary. At this time, Bayard Rustin was serving as King's special assistant, but soon departed, in part because of conflict with Adam Clayton Powell. See Rustin interview, LBJ, and his letter to *Harper's Magazine*, Feb. 6, 1961, MLK(BU). David J. Garrow, *The FBI and Martin Luther King: from "Solo" to Memphis* (New York, 1981), 69–70, maintains that Rustin's "widely known homosexuality" also played a role in his leaving.

157 "black bourgeoisie club": Claude Sitton, "King, Symbol of the Segregation Struggle," *NYT Mag.* (Jan 22, 1961), 10; Walker interview, BOHC.

157 "chief civil rights organization": King to Robinson, June 19, 1960, Robinson to King, May 5, 1960, and Benjamin F. Mays to Robinson, MLK(BU).

158–159 Kennedy meeting: Martin Luther King, Jr., interview for JFK Library with Berl I. Bernhard, MLK(CSC); King to Bowles, June 24, 1960, *ibid.*; DTTP, 61.

159 "nonalignment": *Nation* (Sept. 23, 1961), 180; *WCW*, 147.

159 "neutral against Nixon," "always argued," and "both major parties": Wofford, 12; King to I. G. Whitchurch, Aug. 6, 1959, MLK(BU); Cleveland Robinson interview with Oates, Feb. 27, 1980; King, "The Rising Tide of Racial Consciousness," Sept. 6, 1960, MLK(BU).

160 "what it is, Senator": DTTP, 61; King interview for JFK, MLK(CSC).

160 "can't force Rich's": John Gibson interview with John Britton, Apr. 26, 1968, BOHC; Holman interview, *ibid.*; also Daddy King, 164–65.

161 interview: Wainwright, "Martyr," *Life*, 126, 128–29, 132, 134.

161 "spiritual leader": Raines, 88–90; Lee interview with Oates, Aug. 29, 1978; Wofford, 12–13.

162 "Second Battle": George B. Leonard, Jr., "The Second Battle of Atlanta," *Look* (Apr. 25, 1961), 31–40.

162 King's arrest and "Our prize": Atlanta *Journal*, Oct. 19, 1960; Atlanta *Constitution*, Oct. 20, 1960; Wainwright, "Martyr," *Life*, 129; Lee interview with Oates.

163 King's trial: Atlanta *Constitution*, Oct. 26, 1960; Atlanta *World*, Oct. 26, 1960.

163–164 "Corrie, dear," "this time," and Reidsville: Coretta King, 194–95; King interview for JFK, MLK(CSC); *Jet* (Nov. 10, 1960), 4.

164–165 "vulnerability" and "We Shall Overcome": Watters, 53–54.

165 King on Kennedy: Wofford, 22–23; King to Mrs. Frank Skeller, Jan. 30,

page

1961, MLK(BU); DTTP, 61; King's statement, Nov. 1, 1960, MLK(CSC). *Afro-American*, Nov. 12, 1960.

165 *"No Comment Nixon"*: Carl M. Brauer, *John F. Kennedy and the Second Reconstruction* (New York, 1977), 49–50.

166 "price": King to Mrs. Skeller, Jan. 30, 1961, MLK(BU).

166–169 "stress" and Kilpatrick debate: King to John H. Harriford, Mar. 31, 1961, transcript of the debate in *ibid*.

169 "scene of action": King to A. J. Muste, Mar. 22, 1961, *ibid*.

170 "rafters": press releases from Frank Clarke [n.d.], *ibid*.

170–171 Atlanta agreement and King's speech in church: Accounts vary as to details. I've put the story together from King to Upper Manhattan Committee, Apr. 21, 1961, *ibid*.; Raines, 91–93; Holman interview, BOHC; Ivan Allen, Jr. (with Paul Hemphill), *Mayor: Notes on the Sixties* (New York, 1971), 40–42, 44; Leonard, "Atlanta," *Look*, 32, 34.

171 "optimistic": Leonard, "Atlanta," *Look*, 34.

172 "moral tone": Wofford, 128; also Wofford interview with Berl Bernhard, Nov. 29, 1965, JFK; King to John F. Kennedy, Mar. 16, 1961, MLK(BU).

172 "convince me" and "never wanted": DTTP, 61; Arthur M. Schlesinger, Jr., *A Thousand Days: John F. Kennedy in the White House* (Boston, 1965), 930–31.

172 "experiencing nature" and Martin and Bobby: Arthur M. Schlesinger, Jr., *Robert Kennedy and His Times* (Boston, 1978), xi; Seigenthaler interview with Robert F. Campbell, July 10, 1968, BOHC.

173 "We are heartened" and "our country": King to Robert Kennedy, Apr. 28 [1961], and King to Barbara Lindsay, May 3, 1961, MLK(BU).

173 "big enough to admit": Testament, 234.

174 "CORE started": Walker interview, BOHC; Lee interview with Oates; Selby, 75; also Viorst, *Fire in the Streets*, 133–43, and Meier and Rudwick, *CORE*, 135–37.

174 "whole country": Seigenthaler interview, BOHC; also Selby, 75.

175–176 mob at Abernathy's church: Raines, 122–23; John Lewis and Walker interviews, BOHC; Robert F. Kennedy interview with Anthony Lewis, Dec. 4, 1964, V, 556–59, JFK; Burke Marshall interview with Louis Oberdorfer, May 29, 1964, 51, *ibid*.; Lucretia Collins's account in Forman, *Revolutionaries*, 155–56; Viorst, *Fire in the Streets*, 154–55.

176 "Attorney General know": Schlesinger, *Robert Kennedy*, 299.

176–177 "on probation too" and "heard King say": Raines, 123–24; Lewis interview, BOHC; Lee interview with Oates; Forman, *Black Revolutionaries*, 147–48.

177 King's work for the Freedom Riders: see, for example, King to Dr. Harold Fey, June 4, 1961, to Robert Cobb, June 12, 1961, to Theodore Kheel, Aug. 9, 1961, and E. B. Joyner to King, June 26, 1961; and Walker to George W. Lee, Aug. 5, 1961, MLK(BU). Walker and seven

page

others went on their own freedom ride out to Mississippi and back, and Walker filed a report about it with Robert Kennedy, July 3, 1961, in *ibid.*

177   "He is carrying": King, "The Time for Freedom Has Come!" *NYT Mag.* (Sept. 10, 1961), 25, 118–19.

178   "remarkable victory" and "Systematic segregation": King to Russell Buckner, Oct. 25, 1961, MLK(BU); Schlesinger, *Robert Kennedy*, 300.

178   "presence of the press": King to Harold Courlander, Oct. 30, 1961, MLK(BU).

178   "prophet": Kunstler, 75–76, 78–79.

179   *"central front"* and "from the vote": Schlesinger, *Robert Kennedy*, 302; Kunstler, 77; SCLC news releases, MLK(BU); Robert F. Kennedy interview with Lewis, V, 22–23, JFK.

179   "historic" and "Mr. President": King to Harry Wachtel, Nov. 7, 1961; SCLC news release, Oct. 18, 1961, MLK(BU); DTTP, 61.

180   "President did more": King, "Fumbling on the New Frontier," *Nation* (Mar. 3, 1962), 190–93.

180   "This, in itself" and "run King": King to Sidney Poitier, Sept., 1961, MLK(BU); Allen, *Mayor*, 82–93.

180   Klansman Morris: *FAR*, 502.

181   "really funny," "You know," and "Whippings": Atlanta *Constitution*, Jan. 14, 1978; Alfred Duckett interview with Oates, Sept. 19, 1978; Reddick, 5; Coretta King, 215–16; Harry and Lucy Wachtel interview with Oates, Sept. 20, 1978.

181–182   "won some applause": PI, 66. Coretta King, 213–14, gives a somewhat different version.

182   "morale booster" and "constant dangers": Lee interview with Oates; DeWolf interview, BOHC.

183   "trusted Ralph" and "want you to know": Hosea Williams quoted in Fager, *Resurrection*, 25–26; Abernathy quoted in Mark Lane and Dick Gregory, *Code Name "Zorro": The Murder of Martin Luther King, Jr.* (Englewood Cliffs, N.J., 1977), 120; and Abernathy interview with Oates.

183   "King's spiritual brother": Walker Interview, BOHC; C. T. Vivian interview with Oates, Aug. 16, 1978.

183   "give up the fight": newspaper clipping (spring, 1961), MLK(BU). Reddick, 129, contrasted the opposite styles of the two friends in their description of the new Negro. King: "The new Negro has replaced self-pity with self-respect; self-deprecation with dignity." Abernathy: "The Negro no longer grins when he isn't tickled nor scratches when he isn't itching."

183–184   Bevel: newspaper clippings dated Aug. 23 and Sept. 12, 1965, HMB; Bevel interview with Katherine Shannon, July 6, 1968, BOHC.

184–185   Young: YPI, 61–62, 72, 74; Selby, 82–85; Young, "Desegregation/Integration: Still Live Issues in America," *NEA Advocate* (Apr./May,

page

1980), 2; Young to King, Mar. 24, Aug. 8, and Sept. 11, 1961, MLK(BU). When Young first wrote King in March, asking questions about his career as though they knew one another, King was dumbfounded. "I cannot for the world of me place Andrew Young!" he wrote Miles Horton, director of Highlander Folk School in Tennessee. King was all the more astonished because he had a remarkable memory for names and people. Still, he liked what Young had to say and asked Stanley Levison to find out more about him, to see whether he was "the kind of man who could work with me at SCLC." (King to Horton, Apr. 25, 1961, and to Levison, same date, *ibid.*). Evidently Levison gave King a favorable report.

185   "community of interests": King to David Dubinsky, Dec. 31, 1958, *ibid.*

186   "shocking": Anderson, *Randolph*, 308; Cleveland Robinson interview with Oates, Feb. 27, 1980; Rustin, *Line*, 227.

186–187   King's speech: typescript, MLK(BU), published as "We Shall Overcome," *IUD Digest* (spring, 1962), 19–27; *NYT*, Dec. 12, 1961. The FBI, on the basis of hearsay, reported that Levison had written King's speech. Perhaps Levison helped him draft it (Rustin may have as well), but the language, style, and sense of history are King's.

187–188   "great crowd" and "best resolution": Robinson interview with Oates; Anderson, *Randolph*, 309.

189   "just speak": Raines, 425; also Forman, *Black Revolutionaries*, 255, for SNCC's objections. For SNCC's role in Albany, see Clayborn Carson, *In Struggle: SNCC and the Black Awakening of the 1960s* (Cambridge, Mass., 1981), 56–65.

189–190   King's speech: Watters, 13–16, 11–15; Raines, 425; Lincoln, 124.

191   "our brothers": Watters, 365–66.

192   "refuse to pay" and "bailed out": MOY, 15; Walker interview, BOHC.

193   Wachtel and Gandhi Society: Wachtel interview with Oates, Sept. 20, 1978; King's speech at the formation of the Society, May 17, 1962, MLK(BU); Kunstler, 91–92. Wachtel conceived of the Gandhi Society and New York attorney Theodore Kheel became its president. But Wachtel and New York lawyer Clarence Jones actually managed it. See the documents bearing on the Society in MLK(CSC).

193   King's speech: MLK(BU).

193   "good workers," "thrown out," "subtle and conniving": King's statement, July 13, 1962, MLK (CSC); clippings from Atlanta *World* dated July 11, 13, and 14, 1962, *ibid.;* Kunstler, 98–99; Raines, 362–63. Raines is the source for the Negro bondsman.

194   "any handles" and "called": Watters, 175; see also King's statement, July 12, 1962, MLK(CSC).

194   "upside down" and "walkin' tall": Atlanta *Constitution* and Atlanta *Journal* clippings, dated July 17, 1962, MLK(BU); PI, 68.

194–195   Pritchett and "never cease": *NYT*, July 23, 1962; Raines, 365; Atlanta

page

World clipping, dated July 17, 1962, MLK(BU); Abernathy interview with Oates.

195 "federal courts" and "work vigorously": Kunstler, 101–6; W and M, 45–46.

196 "nonviolent rocks" and "pool game": Watters, 210–16; *Time* (Aug. 3, 1962), 12.

196–197 "against us," "long argument," and "up against": Andrew Young interview with Thomas H. Baker, June 18, 1970, LBJ; DTTP, 64; Coretta King, 206.

197 "a limit" to "here in Albany": *Time* (Aug. 3, 1962), 12–13.

197–198 King in jail: *NYT*, Aug. 6, 1962; Coretta King, 205; Ernest Dunbar, "A Negro Leader Talks About the Struggle Ahead," *Look* (Feb. 12, 1963), 93; King's jail diary in yellow spiral notebook, MLK(BU).

198–199 "no solution" and "segregated as ever": *NYT*, Aug. 9, 1962; Atlanta *Constitution*, Aug. 9, 1962; Bauer, *Kennedy*, 175; Lincoln, 124.

199 "appalled," "go on, anyhow," "broken our backs," "naive enough," "being around," and "so vague": Lincoln, 124–25, 225; W and M, 59; Watters, 146–47, 233; MOY, 15; PI, 66. See also Howard Zinn, "Albany: A Study in National Responsibility" (Atlanta: Southern Regional Council, 1962).

199 "never fight": *WCW*, 44–45; Abernathy to Oates, Aug. 16, 1978; Walker interview, BOHC.

200 "thick as hogs," "an anarchist," and "done found": Victor S. Navasky, *Kennedy Justice* (New York, 1977), 121–22; Watters, 149, 220.

200 "greatest problems": Atlanta *Constitution*, Nov. 19, 1962, and *NYT*, same date. King made his remarks to a *NYT* reporter, who asked if King agreed with Howard Zinn's criticism of the FBI's role in Albany which appeared in a Southern Regional Council report. Arthur L. Murtagh, a southern FBI agent during that time, later testified that King's own assessment was "absolutely" valid (HSCAH, V, 96). Other government officials agreed. See Ovid Demaris, *The Director: An Oral Biography of J. Edgar Hoover* (New York, 1975), 208–9, 211, and Burke Marshall interview, LBJ.

200–201 Hoover and the FBI: *FAR*, 535, 568–71; HSCAH, VI, 64, 91–96, 98, 131–36, VII, 41, 141; SSCFR, 82, 87–91; SSCH, VI, 198, 209; Hoover to Robert F. Kennedy, Sept. 30, 1963, Civil Rights Policy File, JFK; Demaris, *Director*, 12–96, 128, 197, 201, 233; William C. Sullivan (with Bill Brown), *The Bureau: My Thirty Years in Hoover's FBI* (New York, 1979), 135–36. Garrow, *FBI*, 26–56, 78–85, demonstrates that the FBI's "pronounced interest" in King began before his criticism of the FBI in Albany (Hoover and his men "honestly" believed that Stanley Levison, King's friend and adviser, was a Communist influence on him); Schlesinger, *Robert Kennedy*, 353, also notes that the FBI scrutiny of King began before his Albany remarks.

page

PART FIVE: THE DREAMER COMETH

205 "Negro people," "we win," and "Tears": PI, 66; quoted in Watters, 158; quoted in Lewis, *King*, 168–69. See also King's unpublished article on Albany, MLK(CSC).

205 Sol Hurok's offer: Raines, 427.

206 "This system" and "had a knife": Dunbar, "Negro Leader," *Look*, 95–96.

206–207 "difficult," "made Negroes feel," and "vigorous and firm": King, "Who Is Their God?" *Nation* (Oct. 13, 1962), 209–10; DTTP, 64; King, "Bold Design for a New South," *Nation* (Mar. 30, 1963), 259–62. See also King's statement on Ole Miss, Sept., 1962, MLK(CSC).

208–209 second Emancipation Proclamation: King, "The Luminous Promise," *Progressive* (Dec., 1962), 34–37; King, "Emancipation Proclamation," New York *Amsterdam News*, Nov. 10, 1962; King's speech before the Interfaith Conference on Civil Rights, Chicago, Jan. 15, 1963, MLK(CSC); King, "Bold Design," *Nation*, 262. See also King's speech before District 65, DWA, New York City, Oct. 23, 1963, recorded on *Dr. Martin Luther King, Jr., Speaks to District 65 DWA* (New York, [n.d.]). King had also discoursed on a second Emancipation Proclamation in May, 1962, when he had presented Kennedy with a bound draft of such a document (see King's speech of May 17, 1962, in MLK[BU]).

209 "badge of honor": King telegram to Shuttlesworth, Apr. 4, 1960, MLK(BU).

209–210 Shuttlesworth: Raines, 154–55; Fred Shuttlesworth interview with Mosby, Sept., 1968, BOHC; newspaper clippings in Fred Shuttlesworth Papers, MLK(CSC); *WCW*, 51–53.

210 "know-how": Shuttlesworth interview, BOHC.

210 "segregated city": Los Angeles newspaper clipping, dated Jan. 8, 1960, MLK(BU).

210–211 "crack that city" and "radiate": Walker interview, BOHC; Stanley Levison in Jean Stein and George Plimpton (eds.), *American Journey: The Times of Robert Kennedy* (New York, 1970), 114.

211 "don't win" and "we could chew": MOY, 15; Walker interview, BOHC; *WCW*, 43, 54–55. Garrow, *FBI*, 58, drawing on bureau documents opened to him, indicates that the retreat occurred on Jan. 10 and 11, 1963. King and other participants said it was a three-day retreat.

211–212 "world opinion" and "Instead of submitting": *TC*, 54; *WCW*, 37; also King's speech in Nashville, Tenn., Dec. 27, 1962, MLK(BU); Lee interview with Oates; Levison in Stein and Plimpton, *American Journey*, 114–15; Shuttlesworth in Raines, 155. David J. Garrow, *Protest at Selma: Martin Luther King, Jr., and the Voting Rights Act of 1965* (New Haven and London, 1978), 221–25, also argues this point, although he downplays the moral, idealistic side of Project C. Andrew Young, in his interview in LBJ, denied that provocation ever became

page

part of SCLC's strategy, but the weight of evidence proves him wrong.

212 "nigger mayor" and Bull Connor: Joe David Brown, "Birmingham, Alabama: A City in Fear," *Saturday Evening Post* (Mar. 2, 1963), 16–17; American Heritage Foundation, Freedom Train Records, Box 219, National Archives; *Newsweek* (Apr. 22, 1963), 28–29, and (Dec. 8, 1969), 79.

213 Wallace: Brown, "Birmingham," *Saturday Evening Post*, 14; Marshall Frady, *Wallace* (Cleveland, Ohio, 1968), 131–35.

213 code names, "make a point," "cradle of the Confederacy": MOY, 16; Walker interview, BOHC; Levison in Stein and Plimpton, *American Journey*, 115; Brown, "Birmingham," *Saturday Evening Post*, 14; Frady, *Wallace*, 142.

214 "kind of action" and "Only a Negro": Dunbar, "Negro Leader," *Look*, 96; *Integrated Education* (Mar. 1963), 18–19.

214 "any interest": Schlesinger, *Robert Kennedy*, 328.

215 "political football" and planning: WCW, 53–58; Walker interview, BOHC; Lee interview with Oates; W and M, 51–56.

216 "dignified Bull Connor" and "task force": WCW, 58, 59.

216–217 "soul of Birmingham, "Mahatma goes," "sole purpose," and "ready to change": *ibid.*, 62, 66; Watters, 265; W and M, 64.

217–218 unifying the Negro community: WCW, 65–68; PI, 67; Walker interview, Shuttlesworth interview, and Emory Jackson interview with Stanley Smith, Feb., 1968, BOHC; Raines, 143; Kunstler, 183–84.

218 "did not hesitate" and "a cracker": WCW, 62; Raines, 148–49; Vincent Harding, "A Beginning in Birmingham," *Reporter* (June 6, 1963), 16.

219 "personal witnesses": WCW, 71; Raines, 143–44; Walker interview, BOHC.

219 "raw tyranny" to "can't stop us": statement in MLK(CSC).

220 meeting in Room 30: WCW, 71–74; Abernathy interview with Oates.

221 "redemptive influence of suffering" and "like Jesus": Coretta King, 223.

221–222 "most frustrating hours" and "cannot express": WCW, 74–75; PI, 78; Stanley Levison to Joan Daves, [1963], JD.

222 "so polite": Coretta King, 227.

222–223 how King wrote the "Letter": Levison to Daves, [1963], JD; Coretta King, 228; Kunstler, 187. Walker, in his BOHC interview, denied that any portion of the "Letter" was written on toilet paper. But in his interview in Selby, 285, he contradicted himself, asserting that parts of the document were "written on toilet paper and newspaper."

223–229 "Letter": WCW, 76–95. For a textual analysis, see Haig Bosmajian's essay in Lincoln, 128–43.

230 "historic documents" and "Call it": Walker interview, BOHC; also Selby, 285. John W. Macy, Jr., chairman of the U.S. Civil Service Commission, read the "Letter" and sent a copy to Robert Kennedy. "I have

page

found the reading of this document a very enlightening experience," he wrote in an accompanying missive. "Although the views are expressed passionately they have an intellectual and spiritual value which demonstrates the strength of King's leadership." (Macy to Kennedy, June 6, 1963, Burke Marshall Papers, JFK.) The *New York Times* chose not to publish the "Letter" because it was to appear in other periodicals. (See Lewis Bergman to King, May 17, 1963, MLK[CSC].)

231   "silly thing": Watters, 237.

231–232   "business leaders" and "more troops": W and M, 141; Walker interview, BOHC; also YPI; Kunstler, 188–89.

232   "new dimension" and "terrible time": *WCW*, 96; Lee interview with Oates.

233   "family life": *WGH*, 128; *WCW*, 96; Lee interview with Oates; Abernathy interview with Oates; Walker interview, BOHC; Kunstler, 189; Coretta King, 231.

233   "you want": *WCW*, 98; PI, 78; Dave Dellinger, "The Negroes of Birmingham," *Liberation* (summer, 1963), 21.

233   "fifteen years from now": Raines, 171.

233   "Oh man," "beautiful," "for my children," and "during the centuries": Walker interview, BOHC; PI, 78; *WCW*, 97, 99.

234   "everybody to listen" and "Double D Day": Barbara Deming, "Notes After Birmingham," *Liberation* (summer, 1963), 15; Coretta King, 229.

234   dogs and fire hoses: *NYT*, May 4, 1963; Deming, "After Birmingham," *Liberation*, 14; Lincoln, 113–14; Raines, 146; *Time* (May 10, 1963), 19.

235   "your children": *Time* (May 10, 1963), 19; King's remarks to the mass meeting, May 3, 1963, MLK(CSC); W and M, 145.

235   "disgrace" and "well understand": *FAR*, 348; U.S. Information Agency, Survey of World-wide Response to Birmingham, May 9 and 11, 1963, Robert F. Kennedy Papers (Attorney General Correspondence), JFK; Schlesinger, *Thousand Days*, 959.

235–236   "them goddamn son-bitches" and "WE WANT FREEDOM": Raines, 177; Deming, "After Birmingham," *Liberation*, 15; Walker interview, BOHC.

236   "our white brothers": King's universal message on Negro nonviolence since the Montgomery bus boycott, recorded on *I Have a Dream* (cassette).

236–237   Billups march: Dellinger, "Birmingham," *Liberation*, 19; *WCW*, 101; PI, 67.

237   "activities which have taken place": King's statement, May 7, 1963, MLK(CSC).

237–238   children's impact: Dellinger, "Birmingham," *Liberation*, 21; Abernathy interview with Oates.

239–240   negotiations: Harding, "Beginning," *Reporter*, 13–19; Burke Marshall interview with T. H. Baker, Oct. 28, 1968, LBJ; *WCW*, 102–06;

page

Raines, 145, 163–65; Walker interview, BOHC; Young in Stein and Plimpton, *American Journey*, 116–117; Wachtel interview with Oates; Schlesinger, *Robert Kennedy*, 329.

240 Shuttlesworth: Shuttlesworth interview and Walker interview, BOHC; Raines, 157–60.

240–241 "same thing" and "city of Birmingham": W and M, 149.

241 "whole fucking city": Wyatt Walker quoted in Lewis, 202; also *WCW*, 107; PI, 67; King, "What a Mother Should Tell Her Child," May 12, 1963, MLK(CSC); Deming, "After Birmingham," *Liberation*, 13; Walker interview, BOHC; Birmingham *News*, May 12, 1963.

242 "won't destroy," "Whatever happens," and "This nigger": Harding, "Beginning," *Reporter*, 13, 18; Michael Dorman, *We Shall Overcome* (paperback ed., New York, 1965), 197.

242 campaign accomplishments: Kenneth C. Royall and Earl H. Blaik, Report, Dec. 16, 1963, Marshall Papers, JFK; *Newsweek* (Dec. 8, 1969), 79; *WCW*, 113–14; W and M, 195–96.

242 "backbone of Negroes": Jackson interview, BOHC.

242 "turning point": Dellinger, "Birmingham," *Liberation*, 18, 21; "Seeds of Liberation: Integration Leaders Examine Lessons of Birmingham," *ibid.* (June, 1964), 4; Shuttlesworth interview, BOHC.

243 poll: *Newsweek* (July 29, 1963), 30–32.

243 "magic touch," "greatest human being," and "my book": Lincoln, 116–17; *U.S. News & World Report* (June 13, 1963), 21; Smiley interview, BOHC.

243–244 "issue a call" and "White House believes": Atlanta *Constitution*, June 10, 1963; Levison to Joan Daves, [1963], JD.

244 "sensitivity training": Navasky, *Kennedy Justice*, 96.

244 "fatuous display": King, "The Negro Vote," May, 1966, JD.

244 "more he saw": Navasky, *Kennedy Justice*, 97, 99, 441; also Schlesinger, *Robert Kennedy*, 343, 346–47; John Doar and Burke Marshall in Stein and Plimptom, *American Journey*, 122–23.

244–245 Kennedy's speech: Schlesinger, *Thousand Days*, 964–65.

245 "most earnest": *WCW*, 144; copy in MLK(CSC).

245 "This reveals": King's statement, June 12, 1963, MLK(CSC).

246 "first written": King, "Let Justice Roll Down," *Nation* (Mar. 15, 1965), 271–72; King, "Comments on John F. Kennedy," JD.

246–247 meeting with Kennedy: Schlesinger, *Thousand Days*, 968–71; *WCW*, 132; A. Philip Randolph interview with Thomas H. Baker, Oct. 29, 1968, LBJ.

247 Rose Garden: Howell, 17; Raines, 430–31; Demaris, *Director*, 210; SSCFR, 97; DTTP, 64; Navasky, 143; Schlesinger, *Robert Kennedy*, 357–58; Garrow, *FBI*, 40–44, 57–61.

248 "present connections": King to O'Dell, July 3, 1963, copy in Marshall Papers, JFK; also in Navasky, *Kennedy Justice*, 143–44.

page

248–249   "some other side" and "dumbfounded": Kennedy and Marshall interview with Lewis, VI, 674–81; Wofford, 216.

249   "My skills," "misleading charges," and "a spy": Levison to King, Dec. 15, 1959, MLK(BU); Navasky, *Kennedy Justice*, 148; transcript of the Levison hearing, Apr. 30, 1962, in the Robert Kennedy Papers, JFK; Schlesinger, *Robert Kennedy*, 354.

249–250   Levison's Communist background: Garrow, *FBI*, 26–57, 85.

250   "Burke never said": Howell, 17.

250–251   "induced him to break," "drifting back," and "I have decided": Schlesinger, *Robert Kennedy*, 358; Navasky, *Kennedy Justice*, 144, 146, 148. Navasky suggests that King and Levison openly resumed their association in the fall of 1963. King asked Wachtel to meet with Levison and hear his story; Wachtel did so and "cleared him" for King, who then restored Levison as an adviser. Wachtel thought this occurred in 1965 (Wachtel to Oates, Feb. 26, 1980). In early 1964, however, Levison contributed $100 to SCLC, and King wrote him a letter of thanks (Feb. 7, 1964). See the correspondence in MLK(CSC).

251   "exercise in futility" to "tell someone": *NYT*, May 11, 1963; Gordon Parks, *Born Black* (New York, 1971), 44.

251–252   TV interview: Malcolm X in "The Negro and the American Promise," hosted by Kenneth B. Clark and produced for National Educational Television by WGBH-TV, Boston, film copy in the Audio-Visual Department, National Archives. Clark also interviewed King and James Baldwin in the series and published all three interviews in Clark (ed.), *The Negro Protest* (Boston, 1963). Since Malcolm X's language was considerably toned down in the published version, I have drawn quotations from the original televised interview.

252   "strange dream": King to Kivie Kaplan, Mar. 6, 1961, MLK(BU).

252n   "fellow leader": Malcolm X to King, July 21, 1960, *ibid.*

252–253   Clark's criticisms: M. H. Ahmann (ed.), *The New Negro* (Notre Dame, Ind., 1961), 36, 37; Clark's comments in "The Negro and the American Promise," National Archives.

253   "because violence": PI, 74; see also King's interview with Robert Penn Warren, Mar. 18, 1964, and King to Mrs. Malcolm X, Feb. 26, 1965, MLK(CSC).

253   "ain't what we ought to be": MOY, 27.

253   "they've heard those things": King's interview with Warren, Mar. 18, 1964, MLK(CSC); also King to Henry Hitt Crane, July 24, 1964, *ibid.*

254   "so many injunctions": Kunstler, 228.

254   "summer of 1963" to "at last": *WCW*, 15–26, 111–12, 116–17; MOY, 25–26.

255   planning the march: Rustin interview, LBJ; Bayard Rustin, "The Washington March—a 10-Year Perspective," *The Crisis* (Aug.–Sept., 1973), 224–27; Rustin, *Line*, 109; NBC, *Meet the Press: Guests—Mr.*

page

Roy Wilkins ... and Dr. Martin Luther King ... August 25, 1963 (Washington, D.C., 1963); *WCW*, 122; Bayard Rustin interview with WINS of New York, Aug. 21, 1963, tape in MLK(BU); Viorst, *Fire in the Streets*, 199–227.

256   "no way" to "You go on": Fauntroy interview with Oates.

257   "echo": Coretta King, 236; Ralph Abernathy, "Martin Luther King's Dream," in Lynda Rosen Obst (ed.), *The Sixties* (New York, 1977), 94; Walker interview, BOHC.

257–258   "served to strengthen" and "press had expected": *WCW*, 142, 122–24.

258   "tens of thousands": New York *Herald-Tribune*, Aug. 29, 1963.

259   "high on a crowd": Duckett interview with Oates; Abernathy, "Dream," in Obst, *Sixties*, 94.

259–262   King's speech: typescript in MLK(BU). See also the various drafts in MLK(CSC).

262   "that thing": Walker interview, BOHC; Abernathy, "Dream," in Obst, *Sixties*, 94; Abernathy interview with Oates.

262   "most moving": undated newspaper clipping (circa Sept., 1964), MLK(BU).

262   "Farce on Washington" and "That day": Malcolm X (with the assistance of Alex Haley), *Autobiography* (paperback ed., New York, 1966), 281; James Baldwin, *No Name in the Street* (paperback ed., New York, 1973), 140.

262   Meeting with Kennedy: Roy Wilkins interview with Thomas H. Baker, Apr. 1, 1969, and Randolph interview, LBJ; DTTP, 64.

262–263   "totally outside" and "all these years": Rustin interview with Oates.

263   "watch out": Fauntroy interview with Oates; Coretta King, 240–42.

263   "want y'all': Rustin interview with Oates.

263   "morality play": Lincoln, 194.

264–265   Willard Hotel party, Hoover, and FBI: *NYT*, Mar. 9, 1975; Schlesinger, *Robert Kennedy*, 339, 360, 362–63; *FAR*, 531–32; HSCAH, VI, 66, 140–42; Navasky, *Kennedy Justice*, 137, 139, 142 and 142n, 150–151; Demaris, *Director*, 9, 13, 30–36, 44, 96, 231; Sullivan, *Bureau*, 139–40. Garrow, *FBI*, 151–77, argues that Hoover was just a voyeur when it came to King's sexual affairs and that it was William Sullivan, New England born and bred, who reacted to them with a "Puritan's" revulsion. This argument not only betrays a misconception of the sexual attitudes of the historical Puritans, but also disregards a persuasive body of evidence about Hoover's obsession with and repugnance for King's sexual behavior. It is possible, in any case, for a man like Hoover to be both titillated and repelled by the details of King's sex life.

265–266   Kennedy and the wiretaps: Kennedy interview with Lewis, VI, 671–72, JFK; HSCAH, VI, 187, 188, 190, 191, 211–12; Navasky, *Kennedy Justice*, 137–53; Schlesinger, *Robert Kennedy*, 359–61.

266   FBI monograph: Kennedy and Marshall interview with Lewis, VI, 9–10, 687–91, JFK; U.S. Department of Justice, *Report of the Depart-*

page

ment of Justice Task Force to Review the FBI–Martin Luther King, Jr., Security and Assassination Investigations (Jan. 11, 1977), 120, 176; SSCFR, 108, 111–33, 136–37; HSCAH, VI, 68–69, 352; *FAR*, 572–73; Demaris, *Director*, 139, 170; Schlesinger, *Robert Kennedy*, 361–62; Garrow, *FBI*, 73–75.

266–267   "We knew" and "political scandal": Howell, 15; Schlesinger, *Robert Kennedy*, 361.

267–268   "My God," "Dear God," "sin and evil," and "this bestial": PI; King's sermon, Sept. 22, 1963, MLK(CSC); Charles Morgan, Jr., *A Time to Speak* (New York, 1964), 161–63.

268   "poverty of conscience": *WCW*,113.

268   "Every little individual": Raines, 182–83.

268–269   "not for that" and "did not die": Coretta King, 243; King's eulogy, MLK(CSC); also Washington *Star*, Sept. 19, 1963; *NYT*, Nov. 21, 1977.

269   "fullest unity": *WCW*, 115; also King's statement, Oct. 8, 1963, MLK(CSC); Atlanta *Constitution*, Oct. 8, 1963.

269   "men have dreamed": copies in MLK(BU) and MLK(CSC).

270   Kennedy assassination: Coretta King, 243–45; Lee interview with Oates; newspaper clippings, MLK(BU).

270   "I am shocked": King's statement, Nov. 22, 1963, MLK(CSC).

271   "events of those days": quoted in William Manchester, *The Glory and the Dream: A Narrative History of America* (paperback ed., 1975), 1007.

271–272   King on JFK: King, "Comments on John F. Kennedy," JD; *WCW*, 143–47; DTTP, 61, 64; King, "What Killed John F. Kennedy?" New York *Amsterdam News*, Dec. 21, 1963; also King to Henry H. Crane, Dec. 13, 1963, and King's interview for JFK, MLK(CSC).

272   "intellectual involvement": *WCW*, 146; King, "Our New President," New York *Amsterdam News*, Feb. 1, 1964.

273   "kinky sexual preferences," "heard him say," "don't trust anybody": Hugh Sidey, "L.B.J., Hoover and Domestic Spying," *Time* (Feb. 10, 1975), 16; Demaris, *Director*, 170; also Merle Miller, *Lyndon: An Oral Biography* (New York, 1980), *passim*.

274   "pain of injustice," "blot," "had to act": Doris Kearns, *Lyndon Johnson and the American Dream* (New York, 1976), 65–66, 147–48; Lyndon Baines Johnson, *The Vantage Point: Perspectives of the Presidency, 1963–1969* (New York, 1971), 155.

274   "every ounce," "No memorial," "had not died": Johnson, *Vantage Point*, 29, 157; W and M, 155.

274   "college try" and "means business": LBJ, White House Diary and Diary Backup, Dec. 3, 1963, LBJ; LBJ to King, Dec. 2, 1963, King Name File, *ibid.*; MOY, 27.

275   "see Lyndon Johnson": YPI, 75; also Young interview, LBJ.

275   "While boasting": King's speech, Dec. 15, 1963, MLK(CSC); *Time* (Dec. 27, 1963), 19.

page

276   "Dr. King": PI, 66.

PART SIX: LIFE'S RESTLESS SEA

279   "that's Birmingham" and "civil rights issue": MOY, 13.

279   "not going to be the movement" and "have lost freshness": Xerona Clayton Brady in Atlanta *Constitution*, Jan. 14, 1978; Wainwright, "Martyr," *Life*, 132, 134; PI, 77.

280   "empathy": MOY, 14.

280   "pompous arrogance" and "never met a man": Sam Williams in Friends; Walker interview, BOHC; also Gibson interview, *ibid.;* Wachtel interview with Oates; Lee interview with Oates; Rustin interview with Oates.

280   "no messiah": see, for example, King to Jackie Robinson, June 19, 1960, MLK(BU).

280   "His jokes," "tease you harder," "practically fall": Hosea Williams interview with Oates, Aug. 2, 1978; Lee interview with Oates; Young in Friends.

281   "Aw right, Reverend" and "big Negro guy": Wainwright, "Martyr," *Life*, 126; Duckett interview with Oates.

281   "Six, please": Wachtel interview with Oates.

281   "troubled soul": *SL*, 126.

281   "guilt-ridden man": Levison in Stein and Plimpton, *American Journey*, 108–9; Wachtel interview with Oates.

282   "felt that anger" and "basic article": Friends; PI, 73.

282   "deep longing" and 10 percent: *SL*, 60; King to Kivie Kaplan, Jan. 30, 1964, MLK(CSC).

283   "My life": Wainwright, "Martyr," *Life*, 132, 134; PI, 77.

283   "didn't see Martin," "historical obligations," "number of women": Williams interview with Oates; Schlesinger, *Robert Kennedy*, 362; Lee interview with Oates; and confidential interviews with Oates.

283   "tragic lust," "when we yield," "adultery": *SL*, 77, 18, 127; King's speech, Gadsden, Ala., June 21, 1963, MLK(CSC); MOY, 13.

283   "am conscious" and "is two selves": Julius Lester, "The Martin Luther King I Remember," *Evergreen Review* (Jan., 1970), 20–21, 70; King, "The Prodigal Son," Sept. 4, 1966, MLK(CSC). See also King's sermons, "Is the Universe Friendly," Dec. 12, 1965, and "New Wine in Old Bottles," Jan. 2, 1966, *ibid.*

284   "destroy the burrhead" and "excellent data": HSCAH, VI, 104, 193–94, 205–6; Garrow, *FBI*, 106, 109–10.

284   "suffering" and "mistake": King to Lucy Harris, Jan. 27, 1961, MLK(BU); Coretta King, 171.

285   "my doubts," "thrust forward," "quality": PI, 78; Bennett, *Face to Face*, 78; MOY, 27.

285   "power," "core of steel," "truest militant": Dana Swann interview with Oates, Aug. 4, 1978; Sitten, "King," *NYT Mag.*, 10; Williams in Atlanta

page

    Constitution, Jan. 14, 1978, and in Flip Schulke (ed.), *Martin Luther King, Jr., A Documentary . . .* (New York, 1976), 131.

285   "able to find" and "strong-willed": Young and Williams in Friends.

285   "more at home" and "small talent": MOY, 15; Paul Good, "Chicago Summer: Bossism, Racism and Dr. King," *Nation* (Sept. 19, 1966), 240; Rustin interview, LBJ; also Lincoln, 121–22.

286   "say it like that": Walker interview, BOHC.

286   "better job": Wainwright, "Martyr," *Life,* 132.

286   "surrounded himself": Gibson interview, BOHC; C. T. Vivian interview with Oates, Aug. 16, 1978.

286–287   Vivian: Vivian interview with Oates; Vivian to King, Oct. 19 and 23, 1958, MLK(BU); Selby, 351–57.

287–288   Williams: Williams interview with Oates; Raines, 436–45; PI, 236; Schulke, *King,* 130; Williams in Atlanta *Constitution,* Jan. 14, 1978; Vivian interview with Oates.

288–289   King and his staff: Vivian interview with Oates; Williams interview with Oates; Lee interview with Oates; Walker interview, BOHC; Abernathy interview with Oates; Raines, 452; Fager, *Uncertain Resurrection,* 14; Rustin interview, BOHC.

289   "a preacher": Young, "Remembering Dr. King," in Obst, *Sixties,* 232; also Abernathy interview with Oates, and Levison conversation with Oates, May 30, 1977.

289   "Doc really communicated": Vivian interview with Oates.

290   "a tool": Hanes Walton, Jr., *The Political Philosophy of Martin Luther King* (Westport, Conn., 1971), 105.

290   "imaginative artists": Mehta, "Gandhism Is Not Easily Copied," *NYT Mag.* (July 9, 1961), 8–11. See also Lewis Chester, *Martin Luther King* (Geneva, Switzerland, 1971), 293.

290–291   Black Mountain: Raines, 451–52; Wachtel interview with Oates; Lee interview with Oates; Walker interview, BOHC; Young interview, LBJ; Lincoln, 122; also King's remarks at the SCLC Board Meeting, Apr. 16, 1964, MLK(CSC).

291–292   Research Committee: Howell, 18; Wachtel interview with Oates; Rustin interview with Oates; Rustin interview, LBJ; documents pertaining to the Committee in MLK(CSC).

292   "Hammer of Civil Rights": *Nation* (Mar. 9, 1964), 230–34.

293–294   St. Augustine involvement: Robert B. Hayling interview with John H. Britton, Aug. 16, 1967, and Gibson interview, BOHC; PI, 70; Watters, 280–82; John Dillin, "The Story of St. Augustine," *Christian Science Monitor,* July 13, 1964; Kunstler, 289–95.

294   "Negro takes pride": King's letter draft [1964], MLK(CSC); King's telegram to RFK, July 8, 1964, *ibid.;* "wtw" to King, "Suggested Approach and Chronology for St. Augustine," *ibid.;* Vivian interview with Oates; Lee interview with Oates.

295   "quickie" and "many questions": Daves to Gene Exman, Jan. 29, 1964,

page

to Victor Weybright, Jan. 15, 1964, and to Dora McDonald, Jan. 25, 1964, JD; also King to Daves, Nov. 29, 1963, and to Hermine Popper, Jan. 2 and 10, Feb. 3, 1964, and Popper to King, Jan. 14 and May 1, 1964, MLK(CSC). King appears to have had more editorial and rewrite help on *WCW* than on his other books. Alfred Duckett assisted him in the initial stage, when *WCW* was intended as a "quickie." Then Nat Lamar took over as King's editorial and rewrite man, but Daves complained to King that Lamar, instead of editing the manuscript, was recasting it "into a different mold" that King might not recognize as his own. Finally King again prevailed on Popper to edit and polish the text and still preserve his style.

295   "saw this": Vivian interview with Oates; also J. L. Gibson, "St. Augustine, Florida," May 2, 1964, MLK(CSC).

295   "semblance" and "situation": King to LBJ, May 29, 1964, and Lee White memo, June 1, 1964, King Name File, LBJ.

296   "FBI insists," "that man's," "hot seat": Kunstler, 289–94; Miller, *King*, 188.

296–297   King's speech: MLK(CSC); Kunstler, 295–97, Watters, 287.

297   "what on earth" and "opposite sides": DeWolf interview, BOHC; DeWolf to King, July 3, 1964, MLK(CSC).

297   "unusual punishment": Miller, *King*, 189; *NYT*, June 10, 1964.

298   "complete breakdown": King and Hayling to LBJ, June 1, 1964, King Name File, LBJ.

298   King in jail: Hayling interview, BOHC; Vivian interview with Oates, Aug. 16, 1978; Williams interview with Oates; Lincoln, 215.

298   "Tonight": Kunstler, 298–300; Watters, 289–90.

298   "Martin Luther Coon": Lee interview with Oates.

299   "get the hell" and "so calm": Williams interview with Oates; Swann interview with Oates, Aug. 4, 1978; Selby, 88.

299–300   "eerie cry," "mob scene," "see the wounds": Kunstler, 298–303; *NYT*, June 20, 1964; Swann interview with Oates; Hayling interview, BOHC.

300   "had it" and "I'm reluctant": Selby, 285–86; Walker interview, BOHC; King's draft statement, SCLC.

300   "first step" and "good faith": King's statement, June 17, 1964, MLK(CSC); also Lewis, *King*, 244.

301   "toughest nut," "most lawless," "Once he recognized": Gibson interview, BOHC; W and M, 163; Hayling interview, BOHC.

301   "Let us close" and "last vestiges": copy LBJ speech, July 2, 1964, and White House Diary and Diary Backup, July 2, 1964, LBJ.

302   "never have," "What more," "white people": PI, 70.

304   *WCW* sales, foreign rights, and reviews: see the pertinent documents and clippings in JD and MLK(CSC).

305   "Hoss to a mule": Lincoln, 225.

305   "present situation": press release, July 20, 1964, and Farmer interview, LBJ; Kearns, *Johnson*, 192–93.

page

306　"utterly unresponsive" and "shallow rhetoric": King's statement, July 30, 1964, MLK(CSC); King's statement, July 27, 1964, SCLC.

306　"solemnly pledge": King, "Of Riots and Wrongs Against the Jews," *SCLC Newsletter* (July–Aug., 1964), 11.

306　"warn SNCC": Watters, 136–37.

307　"job to do": PI, 71; also DeWolf and Gibson interviews, BOHC.

307　"carried with me" and "Our staff": PI, 78; King's column in New York *Amsterdam News*, Aug. 29, 1964; Lincoln, 224–25; Abernathy interview with Oates.

307　"strong undertow": Lewis, *King*, 248. See also *SCLC Newsletter* (July–Aug., 1964), 1, 5; Carson, *In Struggle*, 111–29.

308　"call me" to "think they started": Wachtel interview with Oates; Walker interview, BOHC; Lee interview with Oates; also Rustin, *Line*, 116–17; Watters, 136–37.

309　"People were bitter": Lewis interview, BOHC.

309　"spiritual capital": Demaris, *Director*, 207; Howell, 16.

309　"will be faced": PI, 71, 72; King, "Negroes Are Not Moving Too Fast," *Saturday Evening Post* (Nov. 7, 1964), 8, 10.

310–311　Democratic convention: King's statements before the Democratic party's platform committee, Aug. 22, 1964, and before the credentials committee in defense of the MFDP, same date, SCLC.

310　"heavy price": quoted in Forman, *Black Revolutionaries*, 392–93; also Rustin interview and Joseph L. Rauh interview with Page Mulhollan, July 30, Aug. 1 and 8, 1964, LBJ.

311　against Goldwater: King's position papers and press releases, July, 1964, MLK(CSC); King's column in the New York *Amsterdam News*, Aug. 1, 1964; PI, 77–78; Young and Rustin interviews, LBJ; King, "Negroes," *Saturday Evening Post*, 10; King, "Let Justice Roll Down," *Nation* (Mar. 15, 1965), 271.

311　"those who assail": undated newspaper clipping (circa Sept. 22, 1964), MLK(BU).

312　"carry your bags," "very humble," "consider this": Wachtel interview with Oates; PI, 78; King's statement, Oct. 14, 1964, MLK(CSC), published in *Christian Century* (Oct. 28, 1964), 1324; also King's exclusive statement to the Associated Negro Press, Nov., 1964, and statement of Dec. 17, 1964, MLK(CSC).

312　"scraping," "Communist influence," "last person": *Time* (Oct. 23, 1964), 27; Demaris, *Director*, 200.

313　"Negro leaders" and "manifestations": *Christian Century* (Oct. 28, 1964), 1324; McGill's column, Boston *Globe*, Oct. 18, 1964, clipping in MLK(BU).

314　"notorious liar," "appalled," "faltered": King's statements, SCLC; *U.S. News & World Report* (Nov. 30, 1964), 56, 58; *Newsweek* (Dec. 7, 1964), 22. "I don't know what everybody got so upset about," Hoover later told Katzenbach about his "liar" charge. "All I said was God's

page

honest truth." Navasky, *Kennedy Justice*, 153.

314   "old and senile" and "pressure groups": Garrow, *FBI*, 124; *U.S. News & World Report* (Dec. 7, 1964), 45.

314   "this story" to "Don't forget it": Farmer interview, LBJ. For Roy Wilkins and the FBI, see Garrow, *FBI*, 128.

314–316   FBI crusade: Washington *Star*, June 20, 1969; *FAR*, 573–74; HSCAH, VI, 235–26; SSCFR, 143, 146, 158–60; SSCH, VI, 210; Sidey, "L.B.J.," *Time* (Feb. 10, 1975), 16; Demaris, *Director*, 196, 199, 322; Navasky, *Kennedy Justice*, 137–38; Sanford J. Ungar, *FBI* (Boston, 1976), 284–87; Washington *Post*, June 11, 1969; *Nation* (Oct. 27, 1969); Raines, 367–70; Jack Anderson (with George Clifford), *The Anderson Papers* (New York, 1973), 196–97; Clark interview, LBJ; Sullivan, *Bureau*, 142–143; Garrow, *FBI*, 125–26.

316–317   New York meeting: Wachtel interview with Oates; Kenneth Clark quoted in Schlesinger, *Robert Kennedy*, 364–65.

317–318   Hoover summit: HSCAH, VI, 167–76; also SSCFR, 163–68; YPI, 75; Washington *Post*, Dec. 2 and 5, 1964; *NYT*, Dec. 2, 1964; Sullivan, *Bureau*, 140; Demaris, *Director*, 200; Garrow, *FBI*, 130.

318   "a circus": Rustin interview with Oates.

319   "built by exploitation": Coretta King, 8; also *Ebony* (Mar., 1965), 38; Wachtel interview with Oates.

319   "Wait a minute": Lincoln, 197.

320   "Congo civil war": King's press conference, Dec. 9, 1964, MLK(CSC); *NYT*, Dec. 10, 1964.

320–321   "quite a time" and Nobel acceptance speech: Coretta King, 11–12; *Time* (Dec. 18, 1964), 21–22; King's acceptance statement, Dec. 10, 1964, MLK(CSC); *Ebony* (Mar., 1965), 38.

322   "past several days": recorded on *King: Speeches and Sermons* (cassette); *Ebony* (Mar., 1965), 38; Coretta King, 16–17.

322   LBJ meeting: see King's comments in Washington *Post*, Feb. 6, 1968; also White House Diary and Diary Backup, Dec. 18, 1964, LBJ.

PART SEVEN: AIN'T GONNA LET NOBODY TURN ME AROUND

325   voting statistics: Lawson, *Black Ballots*, 284; Garrow, *Selma*, 19, 29–30.

325–326   "Our experience" and "Demonstrations": King, "Selma—the Shame and the Promise: the Negroes' Fight for Voting Rights and Human Dignity," *IUD Agenda* (Mar., 1965), 18, 21; King, "Justice," *Nation*, 270; also King, "Civil Rights no. 1—the Right to Vote," *NYT Mag.* (Mar. 14, 1965), 26; Stony Cooks's address, MLK Annual Institute for Nonviolence, Aug. 3, 1978, Atlanta, Ga.

326–328   Selma background: King, "Selma," *IUD Agenda*, 18–21; *NYT*, March 14, 16, and 22, 1965; Fager, *Selma*, 3–21, 41; Marie Foster interview with Oates, June 8, 1977; Garrow, *Selma*, 31–35.

328   "had a Jim Clark," "theater for an act," "tell the people": Lee interview with Oates; Cooks's address, MLK Annual Institute for Nonvio-

page

lence; Schulke, *King*, 131; also Vivian interview with Oates; Williams interview with Oates; Foster interview with Oates; *Time* (Mar. 19, 1965), 23; Raines, 425; King, "Behind the Selma March," *Saturday Review* (Apr. 3. 1965), 57. Garrow, *Selma*, 223–25, also stresses the role of provocation in King's projected campaign, though Garrow deemphasizes its idealistic component.

328–329   "arrests should continue" and "Ralph, I thought": *Nation* (Feb. 15, 1965), 154; Raines, 464; Abernathy interview with Oates; Coretta King, 253.

329   "unreal air": Zinn, *SNCC: the New Abolitionists* (Boston, 1964), 147.

329–330   King's first Selma visit: Fager, *Selma*, 8–11; *NYT*, Jan. 3, 1965; Williams interview with Oates; John Lewis interview, BOHC; Raines, 214.

331   "King, look into your heart": Garrow, *FBI*, 125–26. Some of the language in the letter was clearly Hoover's. Cf "what a grim farce" to Hoover's notation, "what a farce," on the FBI report that no irregularities could be found in King's tax returns (*ibid.*, 114).

332   "What does he think," "much of it unintelligible," "bunch of guys," "toward the end": Howell, 17–18; *NYT*, Mar. 9, 1975; Raines, 428; Lee interview with Oates.

332   "out to break me" and "warning from God": Garrow, *FBI*, 134; also Howell, 17–18; Wachtel interview with Oates.

333   "wild sexual activity": Young interview, LBJ; Howell, 17–18; Raines, 430.

333   King's suffering and determination: Wachtel inteview with Oates, Sept. 20, 1978, and Oct. 7, 1981; SSCFR, 159; Howell, 19–20; YPI, 75; Lee interview with Oates.

333–334   "all life," "Golden Record Club," "Well, J. Edgar": Navasky, *Kennedy Justice*, 150; Raines, 427–28, 430, 454; Rustin interview, LBJ; Young, "Remembering King," in Obst, *Sixties*, 232; HSCAH, 1, 23.

334   informant Jim Harrison: Garrow, *FBI*, 173–203.

334   "King's private life" and "couldn't care less": Rustin interview, LBJ; Arthur L. Murtagh quoted in *NYT*, Mar. 9, 1975.

335–336   "arouse the federal government," "every goddamn one," "out of control": King's speech, Jan. 19, 1965, MLK(CSC); W and M, 166; *NYT*, Jan. 19, 1965; Raines, 198–99; Fager, *Selma*, 31–32.

336–337   "got a *movement*," "ain't nobody scared," "Don't do it," "just what they want": Fager, *Selma*, 33–40, 103; *Nation* (Feb. 15, 1965), 154; Foster interview with Oates; King's statement, Jan. 20, 1965, MLK(CSC).

337   "doohickey": Fager, *Selma*, 44–46.

337–338   "no dinner," "covert contacts," "our good reputation," "honor": Raines, 411–15; *NYT*, Mar. 9, 1975; HSCAH, VI, 102–3; *Life* (Feb. 12, 1965), 4; Mays, *Born*, 271–72; Allen, *Mayor*, 96–99.

338   "what time" and "significant evening": Allen, *Mayor*, 96–99; *Life* (Feb. 12, 1965), 33; Mays, *Born*, 272–73; *NYT*, Jan. 29, 1965.

page

339 "will go down": Mrs. Jackson interview with Oates, June 8, 1977; Lee interview with Oates; Atlanta *Constitution*, Jan. 14, 1978.

339–340 "get down" and "really put something": Williams interview with Oates; Raines, 204–5; Sheyann Webb and Rachel West Nelson (as told to Frank Sikora), *Selma, Lord, Selma: Girlhood Memories of the Civil-Rights Days* (University, Ala., 1980), 18, 47.

340 "Negroes could vote": *NYT*, Feb. 1 and 2, 1965; Fager, *Selma*, 47–51.

341 "tell Dr. King": Fager, *Selma*, 56–58; Coretta King, 256; Lincoln, 211.

341 "madness of those days" and victim of violence: Parks, *Born Black*, 55; King, "The Nightmare of Violence," Feb. 26, 1965, and King to Mrs. Malcolm X, same date, MLK(CSC).

341–342 King's instructions: MLK(CSC).

343–344 King's meeting with LBJ: Wachtel interview with Oates, Oct. 18, 1978; Lee C. White Memoranda for the President, Feb. 8 and 9, 1965, King Name File, LBJ; White House Diary and Diary Backup, Feb. 9, 1965, *ibid.*; White to the President, July 23, 1965, *ibid.*; King, "Selma," *IUD Agenda*, 21; W and M, 167.

344 "wanted to march": Fager, *Selma*, 64–68; Pat Watters, "Why the Negro Children March," *NYT Mag.* (Mar. 21, 1965), 29.

344 Vivian incident: Vivian interview with Oates. Fager, *Selma*, 69–71, and other accounts erroneously claim that it was Clark who hit Vivian in the mouth.

344 "finest tactician": *Nation* (Feb. 15, 1965), 154.

344 "heart attack" and "No, sir": Fager, *Selma*, 68–69; *NYT*, Mar. 16, 1965; Watters, "Negro Children March," *NYT Mag.*, 118–19.

345 "intimidation": King, "Justice," *Nation*, 270; also *NYT*, Mar. 3, 1965; Fager, *Selma*, 31.

346 "on the sidelines": King's eulogy, Feb. 26, 1965, MLK(CSC); *NYT*, Mar. 4, 1965; Jack Mendelsohn, *The Martyrs* (New York, 1965), 133–52.

346 "can't promise": *Time* (Mar. 19, 1965), 23; *NYT*, Mar. 4, 1965; Fager, *Selma*, 81, 86; Selby, 79.

346–347 "whatever means" and Baker's reaction: *NYT*, Mar. 9, 1965; Fager, *Selma*, 86–90; Raines, 201–2.

347 Behind the Sunday march: King, "Behind the Selma March," *Saturday Review* (Apr. 3, 1965), 17; Williams interview with Oates; Lee interview with Oates; Vivian interview with Oates; Abernathy interview with Oates; Lewis interviews in BOHC and in Selby give a somewhat different version of why King wasn't in Selma on Sunday.

347–348 Bloody Sunday: *NYT*, Mar. 8 and 9, 1965; Fager, *Selma*, 92–97; *Time* (Mar. 19, 1965), 23–24; *Newsweek* (Mar. 22, 1965); Garrow, *Selma*, 78–81.

348 "never forget," "taillight," "ministers' march": King, "Selma," *Saturday Review*, 17; Robert W. Spike, "Our Churches' Sin Against the Ne-

page

gro," *Look* (May 18, 1965), 33; King, "A Challenge to the Churches and Synagogues," Jan. 17, 1963, MLK(CSC); King's statement, Mar. 7, 1965, *ibid.; NYT*, Mar. 8, 1965; Fager, *Selma*, 97–98.

349 "direct witness," "couldn't refuse," "agitator": *NYT*, Mar. 11, 1965; Wofford, 178; Spike, "Our Churches' Sin," *Look*, 37.

350 "carpetbaggin'. . . liar": Frady, *Wallace*, 133; *Time* (Mar. 19, 1965), 25.

350 "gone too far," "had the flu," "We're going": *NYT*, Mar. 9, 1965; Lewis, *King*, 276; Watters, "Negro Children March," *NYT Mag.*, 120; also Louis Martin memo for Marvin Watson, Mar. 8, 1965, King Name File, LBJ.

350 strategy session: King's telegram to Dora McDonald, Mar. 15, 1965, MLK(CSC), a statement for the record; King, "Selma," *Saturday Review*, 17; *Life* (Mar. 19, 1965), 35; *NYT*, Mar. 12, 1965; W and M, 170.

350–351 the injunction crisis: *Time* (Mar. 19, 1965), 28; *Newsweek* (Mar. 22, 1965), 20; W and M, 172–73; King, "Selma," *Saturday Review*, 16, 57; King's telegram to McDonald, Mar. 16, 1965, MLK(CSC). Much of the press reported that King had agreed to "a deal" with Clark and Lingo—that he would undertake only a token march if they would restrain their men. King denied any such "prearrangement." I think King right; but consult Garrow, *Selma*, 273–74, for a detailed discussion of this point.

351 "what lies ahead": King's speech, Mar. 9, 1965, MLK(CSC); *Time* (Mar. 19, 1965), 26.

351–352 abbreviated march: *NYT*, Mar. 10 and 12, 1965; *Time* (Mar. 19, 1965), 26; *Life* (Mar. 19, 1965), 32–33, 37; Fager, *Selma*, 103–5; Foster interview with Oates; Wofford, 182–84.

353 SNCC defection: Lewis interview, BOHC; Fager, *Selma*, 105, 140; Renata Adler, *Toward a Radical Middle* (New York, 1969), 16–17; Raines, 213–14; Vince O'Connor interview with Oates, June 9, 1980; James Forman, *Sammy Younge, Jr.* (paperback ed., 1969), 78–79; Watters, 347. After the abbreviated march, SNCC moved its operations to Montgomery.

353 "you niggers": Fager, *Selma*, 108; also *Life* (Mar. 19, 1965), 37.

353 "seclusion": Garrow, *Selma*, 92.

354 "morally inclement climate" to "concerned, perturbed": King's statement, Mar. 11, 1965, MLK(CSC); *Time* (Mar. 19, 1965), 27; *NYT*, Mar. 11 and 12, 1965; Johnson, *Vantage Point*, 162; *WGH*, 39–40.

354 "real hero": Wofford, 186. For a detailed discussion of how events in Selma affected and altered the Johnson administration's plans for voting-rights legislation, see Garrow, *Selma*, 31–32.

354–355 LBJ's speech and King's reaction: copies of the speech in LBJ, published in *NYT*, Mar. 16, 1965; *Life* (Mar. 26, 1965), 33; Mrs. Jackson interview with Oates; King's statement, Mar. 16, 1965, SCLC, pub-

page

lished in *NYT*, Mar. 17, 1965. Johnson thanked King for his "generous comments" about his speech (letter of Mar. 18, 1965, LBJ) and later sent him a published copy.

355–356 "right to assemble," "Communist-trained anarchists," "demagog"; *Time* (Mar. 26, 1965), 19; *NYT*, Mar. 18 and 19, 1965; PI, 77.

356 "gigantic witness" and "will be the people": *NYT*, Mar. 19 and 22, 1965; *Newsweek* (Apr. 5, 1965), 25.

356–358 march out of Selma: Simeon Booker, "50,000 March on Montgomery," *Ebony* (May, 1965), 53, 55, 62; Fager, *Selma*, 150–51; Adler, *Radical Middle*, 7; *NYT*, Mar. 22, 1965; W. C. Heinz and Bard Lindeman, "The Meaning of the Selma March: Great Day at Trickem Fork," *Saturday Evening Post* (May 22, 1965), 90; Wofford, 189.

358 "encampment resembled" and song "Old Wallace": *NYT*, Mar. 23, 1965; Marie Foster papers, Selma, Ala.

358–359 profiles of marchers: *NYT*, Mar. 22, 24, 26, 1965; Booker, "Montgomery," *Ebony*, 47, 56, 58, 76, 80; Spike, "Our Churches' Sin," *Look*, 32, 34, 36–37; *Newsweek* (Apr. 5, 1965), 25.

359 "Aunt Jemima": *NYT*, Mar. 23, 1965.

359–360 Trickem: Heinz and Lindeman, "Selma March," *Saturday Evening Post*, 31–32, 90, 92; Adler, *Radical Middle*, 11; *Newsweek* (Apr. 5, 1965), 25.

361 "trained" and "Communists": *NYT*, Mar. 23, 1965. See also King's speech in Jackson, Miss., July 23, 1964, MLK(CSC).

361 "President's job": Williams interview with Oates; also *NYT*, Mar. 25, 1965.

361 "these segregationists" and "These white folks": *Time* (Apr. 2, 1965), 21; Fager, *Selma*, 152.

361 "a new song": Wofford, 195; Foster interview with Oates.

362 "What do you want?": *NYT*, Mar. 25, 1965.

362–363 To the capitol: Booker, "Montgomery," *Ebony*, 50, 82, 85–86; Wofford, 197–99; Adler, *Radical Middle*, 26, 29; *NYT*, Mar. 26, 1965; Ramsey Clark interview, LBJ.

363–364 King's speech: transcript of the complete text provided the author by David Garrow; incomplete versions in MLK(CSC) and *NYT*, Mar. 26, 1965; Lee interview with Oates.

365 "master organizer" and "from paper resolutions": Washington *Post*, Feb. 2, 1968; Levison to King, Apr. 7, 1965, MLK(CSC).

366 Alabama boycott and SCOPE: documents bearing on both in MLK(CSC) and SCLC; NBC, *Meet the Press: Guest, Dr. Martin Luther King, Jr., March 28, 1965* (Washington, D.C., 1965), 7–8; *NYT*, Mar. 30, 1965; *Newsweek* (Apr. 12, 1965), 29; Fager, *Selma*, 166–70. For a study of SCOPE, see N. J. Demerath III, Gerald Marwell, and Michael T. Aiken, *Dynamics of Idealism* (San Francisco, 1971).

366–367 SCLC Board Meeting: documents in SCLC and MLK(CSC); *NYT*, Apr. 2, 1965; *Newsweek* (Apr. 12, 1965), 28; Raines, 464; Wachtel interview

page

with Oates, Sept. 20, 1978. Even during the Selma campaign, King was contemplating a move north. See King, "'Dreams of Brighter Tomorrows,'" *Ebony* (Mar., 1965), 35.

367 "some of the same things" and "Busing": *Time* (Apr. 30, 1965), 32–33; *U.S. News & World Report* (May 3, 1965), 8; HSCAH, VI, 232–33.

367–368 Airlee House and King's concerns for the ghettos: *Wall Street Journal*, June 7, 1965; King, "Next Stop, the North," *Saturday Review* (Nov. 13, 1965), 33–35; King's column for the New York *Amsterdam News* [1965], SCLC; Wachtel interview with Oates; Cleveland Robinson interview with Oates.

368 "we came South": newspaper clipping dated Jan. 1, 1966, HMB; also clippings dated June 5 and July 7, 1965, *ibid.*; Selby, 344.

368–369 King in Chicago: speeches, summaries, and fact sheets, MLK(CSC); newspaper clippings, July 24–27, 31, Aug. 1, Sept. 2, 1965, HMB.

484 "magnificent": King's telegram to LBJ, June 7, 1965, King Name File, LBJ.

370 "amazing sensitivity": King to LBJ, June 7, 1965, King Name File, *ibid.*; White House Diary and Diary Backup, Aug. 5, 1965, *ibid.*; A. Philip Randolph interview with Thomas H. Baker, Oct. 29, 1968, *ibid.*

370 "a triumph" and "a religiosity": *Time* (Aug. 13, 1965); *NYT*, Aug. 7, 1965; Jack Valenti, *A Very Human President* (New York, 1975), 395.

371–372 "more funerals," "love that man," "Shoes that carried me," "a new Negro": Mrs. Jackson and Foster interviews with Oates; also Garrow, *Selma*, 179–211; Raines, 187, 215, 226; King's report to the Administrative Committee [Nov., 1965], SCLC; Fager, *Selma*, 208–11; T. B. Morgan, "Requiem or Revival?" *Look* (June 14, 1966), 77–78; Hamilton, *Bench and Ballot*, 228–50.

372 "destroy barriers": Sellers, *River*, 165–66.

372 "cannot legislate morality": *Time* (Apr. 30, 1965), 33; *U.S. News & World Report* (May 3, 1965), 8. See also King's speech before the NAACP Legal Defense and Education Fund, May 17, 1956, MLK(BU), and his statement at Abernathy's church, May 21, 1961, MLK(CSC).

373 "True integration": King, "A Challenge to the Churches and Synagogues," Jan. 17, 1963, MLK(CSC); also King's speech at Nashville, Tenn., Dec. 27, 1962, MLK(BU).

375 "not going to sit": King, "Quote and Unquote," *SCLC Newsletter* (June–July, 1965), 4. See also King to Joseph Tusiani, Aug. 8, 1959, and to Ross W. Anderson, Apr. 26, 1961, MLK(BU), for King's hatred of war and his desire to apply creative nonviolence to the world theater. He'd roundly condemned war in a speech at Morehouse College on Jan. 11, 1965, copy in MLK(CSC).

375–376 stand on Vietnam: King's statement at a mass rally, Aug. 12, 1965, during SCLC's annual convention, and his remarks to newsmen the next day, MLK(CSC); King's remarks on "Face the Nation," CBS TV, Aug. 29, 1965, copy in *ibid.*; also Wofford, 222; Lincoln, 215. King

page

conceded that Vietnam was "indeed a complex situation" and that
North Vietnam and Communist China had to drop their demands for a
unilateral U.S. withdrawal from South Vietnam before serious negotiations could begin.

376   "Is he casting" and "They told me": Lincoln, 215–16, 206–7.

376   "nine people": Selby, 343; newspaper clippings, Aug. 13 and 14, 1965,
and Jan. 8, 1966, HMB.

377   "seemed to collapse": W and M, 178; *FAR*, 353.

377–378 King in Watts: *WGH*, 133; King's statement, Aug. 17, 1965,
MLK(CSC); King, "A Christian Movement in a Revolutionary Age,"
Sept. 28, 1965, and "A Cry of Hate or a Cry for Help?" *ibid.*; King,
"Feeling Alone in the Struggle," New York *Amsterdam News*, Aug.
28, 1965; King, "Next Stop," *Saturday Review*, 33–35; Rustin, *Line*,
140–53; Coretta King, 272.

378–379 Decision Chicago: newspaper clippings, Aug. 6 and 21, Sept. 2 and 3,
1965, HMB; King, "Why Chicago Is the Target," New York *Amsterdam News*, Sept. 11, 1965; *Ebony* (Apr., 1966), 100, 102; Bruce Cook,
"King in Chicago," *Commonweal* (Apr. 29, 1966), 176; Meyer Weinberg interview with Oates, Oct. 17, 1979.

379–380 "clean up at home" to "a fiasco": Williams interview with Oates;
Cooks's address, MLK Annual Nonviolent Institute; Rustin interview
with Oates; W and M, 191–92; Fauntroy interview with Oates; newspaper clipping, Aug. 14, 1965, HMB; Rustin interview, LBJ.

380   "nonviolent movement" to "Egypt still exists": W and M, 344; newspaper clippings, Sept. 1, 2, and 12, Oct. 9 and 10, HMB; King, "Why
Chicago," New York *Amsterdam News*, Sept. 11, 1965; also Weinberg
interview with Oates.

380–381 Goldberg visit: Wachtel interview with Oates; Young interview, LBJ;
King's statement, Sept. 10, 1965, MLK(CSC).

381   "most important symbol": Coretta King, 293–94.

381   "confrontation of the big powers": Nhat Hanh to King, June 1, 1965, in
Liberation (Dec., 1965), 19.

382 - "must not allow" and "kooks": *Chicago Defender*, Jan. 1, 1966; Young
interview, LBJ; Wachtel interview with Oates. See also King's remarks
on Vietnam in King's sermon, Jan. 16, 1966, and in Stockholm, Apr. 6,
1966, MLK(CSC).

382   "gravest challenge": Fager, "Dilemma for Dr. King," *Christian Century* (Mar. 16, 1966), 331–32.

383   "wept within": *WGH*, 49–50.

PART EIGHT: THE ROAD TO JERICHO

387   "hit Chicago" to "cooperation and peace": news clippings, Jan. 6, 7,
and 13, 1966, HMB; "Goal of the Project: To End Slums," Dec. 9,
1965, SCLC; "Proposal for the Development of a Nonviolent Action
Movement for the Greater Chicago Area," Jan. 5, 1966, and "Chicago

page

Plan," Jan. 7, 1966, MLK(CSC); King's statement, SCLC Board Meeting, Apr. 14, 1966, *ibid.; Ebony* (Apr., 1966), 94, 95; King, "Nonviolence: the Only Road to Freedom," *ibid.* (Oct., 1966), 30.

387 "trumpet tactics": Morgan, "Requiem or Revival?" *Look,* 72; newspaper clipping, Mar. 24, 1966, HMB.

388 "really get close" and "smell of urine": *NYT,* Jan. 27, 1966; clipping, Jan. 20, 1966, HMB; Coretta King, 276–77; also *Ebony* (Apr., 1966), 95; *WGH,* 136. Barbara A. Reynolds, *Jesse Jackson: The Man, the Movement, the Myth* (Chicago, 1975), 62, cites the same rent differences as King.

389 "get down" and "Many things": *NYT,* Jan. 28, 1966; newspaper clippings, Jan. 27 and 29, 1966, HMB.

389–391 King's tour and study of slums: newspaper clippings, Jan. 28 and 29, 1966, HMB; *WGH,* 134–37; King's speech at the University of Chicago, Jan. 27, 1966, and his speech on his European tour, Mar., 1966, SCLC; "Portrait of a Slum: Lawndale—'Slumdale,' " *ibid.;* King, *The Ware Lecture, 1966* (Boston, 1966), 10–11.

391 "scale so vast": *Ebony* (Apr., 1966), 102.

391 "not impressed": HSCAH, VI, 263.

391 "together" and "organizational undergirding": newspaper clippings, Feb. 6, 12, and 18, 1965, HMB. See also documents on the Lawndale union in SCLC and MLK(CSC).

391 "our problem": Morgan, "Requiem or Revival?" *Look,* 70–72.

392 "really you?": Coretta King, 280–81.

392–393 King and the gangs: Lee interview with Oates; clippings from the *Chicago Defender* about the gangs, Sept. 7–9, 13–15, 1965, HMB; newspaper clippings, May 11 and June 13, 1966, *ibid.; Ebony* (Apr., 1966), 102; Coretta King, 281.

393 "read about," "haven't gotten things," "not perfect": newspaper clippings, Mar. 24 and 25, 1966, HMB; also spring planning and strategy papers for Chicago, SCLC.

393–394 King and Daley: newspaper clippings, Mar. 24, 25, and 31, Apr. 16, 1966, HMB; Lee interview with Oates.

394 "imaginative" and "Negro in 1966": King, "The Last Steep Ascent," *Nation* (Mar. 14, 1966), 290.

394 "should be proud": King, *Ware Lecture,* 15.

395 "rat at night": Lewis, *King,* 312. Documents pertaining to the conference are in LBJ and MLK(CSC).

395 "ugly racism": *WGH,* 29; *Human Events* (June 18, 1966), 387.

396 "southern-honey drawl" and "started screaming": Parks, *Born Black,* 101–8; see also Carson, *In Struggle,* 162–64, and *NYT,* Aug. 5, 1966.

397 "sense of dignity": *WGH,* 29; Adler, *Radical Middle,* 152.

397 "nonviolence stuff" to "some and *all*": *WGH,* 29–31.

397 "naked shit": Raines, 422.

398 "into the Mississippi," "not going to beg," "shameful repudiation":

page

NYT, June 8, 1966; WGH, 31–33; also Sellers, River, 162–63; Williams interview with Oates.

398   "any notions": NYT, June 12, 1966.

398–399   manifesto and "don't see how": ibid., June 9 and 11, 1966.

399   "South you led": Adler, Radical Middle, 159–60; Williams interview with Oates.

399–400   "There he is," "go with him," "grotesque parody," "Jingle bells": Sellers, River, 163–66; Adler, Radical Middle, 157, 162; Paul Good, "The Meredith March," New South (summer, 1966), 9.

400   "Black Power": NYT, June 17 and 21, 1966; Sellers, River, 166–67; WGH, 34; Carson, In Struggle, 209.

401   "Hey! Hey!": Manchester, Glory, 1067; NYT, June 21, 1966.

401   "Some people": NYT, June 22, 1966; King's statement, June, 1966, MLK(CSC); Parks, Born Black, 136–37.

401–402   Black Power debate: WGH, 35–37.

402   "listened and screamed": Adler, Radical Middle, 158.

402–403   Canton: ibid., 159–61; YPI, 74; NYT, June 24 and 27, 1966; Manchester, Glory, 1068.

404   "up these steps": José Yglesias, "Dr. King's March on Washington," pt. 2, NYT Mag. (Mar. 31, 1968), 70.

404   "the murderers" and "brother": King's statement in airplane [1968], MLK(CSC), recorded on I Have a Dream (cassette).

404–405   "think so" and "learned a lesson": The Reporter (July 14, 1966), 12, 16.

405   "No matter," "positively harmful," "Negro who is fighting," "no time": Sellers, River, 170–71; Rustin, Line, 154; NYT, July 3, 1966; King, "Nonviolence," Ebony, 32, 34; WGH, 68.

406   "got to deliver": Newsweek (Aug. 22, 1966), 58; Lewis, King, 331.

406   "just and open city": NYT, July 11, 1966; planning documents for the march, SCLC.

406   "went home" and "balm in Gilead": WGH, 52; King's speech, "Reflections," Chicago, 1966, recorded on King: Speeches and Sermons (cassette). See also King's remarks on black power in SCLC's staff retreat, Frogmore, S.C., Nov. 14, 1966, MLK(CSC).

408   "social disaster" and "seething desperation": NYT, July 12, 1966; also ibid., July 11, 1966; copy of King's Soldiers Field speech, MLK(CSC); Good, "Chicago Summer," Nation, 240.

408   "I realized": WGH, 135.

409   "relieve the tension": NYT, July 13, 1966; Lee interview with Oates.

409   "much more": King's comments, MLK(CSC); NYT, July 13, 1966.

409–410   "conduct violence," "concrete to offer," "sensible and effective": NYT, July 16 and 17, 1966.

410   "midnight in our world": ibid., July 18, 1966; SL, 56–66.

411   "poverty and human misery," "promised land of suburbia," "do not seek": NYT, July 30, 1966; Lewis, King, 338, 350; Good, "Chicago Summer," Nation, 240–41.

page

412 "molotov cocktails": King's speech, misdated Aug. 6, 1966, MLK(CSC), recorded on *I Have a Dream* (cassette).

412–413 Aug. 5 march: *NYT*, Aug. 6, 1966; King's comments recorded on *I Have a Dream* (cassette); King's comments on the march and the inevitability of death, given on airplane ride [1968], recorded on *ibid.*, transcript in MLK(CSC); *Newsweek* (Aug. 15, 1966), 29; *TC*, 58; Lee interview with Oates; Good, "Chicago Summer," *Nation*, 241.

413 "stop marching": King's speech, MLK(CSC), recorded on *I Have a Dream* (cassette).

414 "walk to Cicero" and "scared to death": *NYT*, Aug. 21, 24, and 25, 1966.

415 "most significant program": *NYT*, Aug. 26 and 27, 1966; Good, "Chicago Summer," *Nation*, 238–39.

416 "This agreement," "We told King," "hydra-headed face-saver": *ibid.*; Weinberg interview with Oates; Selby, 347.

416 victory rally: Good, "Chicago Summer," *Nation*, 238–40; also King's remarks about "freedom now" in SCLC's staff retreat, Frogmore, S.C., Nov. 14, 1966, MLK(CSC).

417 Operation Breadbasket: King, "One Year Later in Chicago," SCLC.

417 "frustrates me": Selby, 347–48; *NYT*, Aug. 6, 1966; also Wachtel interview with Oates; Rustin interview with Oates; Weinberg interview with Oates. After Chicago, C. T. Vivian left SCLC and assumed a position with the Urban Training Center for Christian Mission in Chicago.

418 "how to hate": *NYT*, Aug. 6, 1966.

418–419 King's disillusionment with whites: Lincoln, 202; King's remarks on racism, SCLC's staff retreat, Frogmore, S.C., Nov. 14, 1966, MLK(CSC).

419 black anti-Semitism: Good, "Chicago Summer," *Nation*, 238–40; King, "My Jewish Brother," New York *Amsterdam News*, Feb. 26, 1966; *WGH*, 108–9; King's remarks about black anti-Semitism recorded on *I Have a Dream* (cassette).

419–420 Carmichael: *NYT*, Aug. 5, 1966; Stokely Carmichael, *Stokely Speaks: Black Power to Pan-Africanism* (New York, 1971), 17–30, 45–60, 189–90, 192–202; Manchester, *Glory*, 1069. See Carson, *In Struggle*, 215–28, for the evolution of Black Power ideology.

420–421 "not interested" to "wrong way": *WGH*, 63–77; also King, "State of the Movement," SCLC's staff retreat, Frogmore, S.C., Nov. 28, 1967, SCLC.

421 "fearful men" and "come too far": King, "Nonviolence," *Ebony*, 27; King's remarks, SCLC's staff retreat, Frogmore, S.C., Nov. 14, 1966, MLK(CSC).

422 "a decade": *WGH*, 3.

422–426 writing *WGH:* correspondence regarding the manuscript, Dec., 1966, to Mar., 1967, JD; *Ebony* (June, 1967), 112–19; HSCAH, VI, 289. Much

page

of the book grew out of King's speech and discussions at SCLC's staff retreat, Frogmore, S.C., Nov. 14, 1966, SCLC and MLK(CSC). Compare these documents with *WGH*.

427 "been as moved" and "superb": Geneveive Young to Daves, Mar. 9, 1967, and [Canfield] to Daves, Mar. 10, 1967. JD.

428 "can't be silent" and "not centering this": King's address, SCLC's staff retreat, Frogmore, S.C., May 29–31, 1967, MLK(CSC); *NYT*, Apr. 2, 1967; King, "Casualties of the War in Vietnam," Feb. 25, 1967, SCLC; Lee interview with Oates; Robinson interview with Oates; also HSCAH, VI, 289; Lincoln, 205–7; Thomas Edward Offenburger interview, July 2, 1968, BOHC; Young's comments in Friends; Wachtel interview with Oates, Aug. 1, 1978.

428 "great nation": King, "Casualties," SCLC.

PART NINE: THE HOUR OF RECKONING

431 King's speech: *ibid.*, published in a pamphlet entitled *Dr. Martin Luther King, Jr., Dr. John C. Bennett, Dr. Henry Steele Commager, Rabbi Abraham Heschel Speak on the War in Vietnam* (Committee of Clergy and Laymen Concerned About Vietnam, 1967), 5–9.

431–432 RFK and the war: Schlesinger, *Robert Kennedy*, 772–73, 782.

432 LBJ and FBI: Dick Schaap, *R.F.K.* (paperback ed., New York, 1968), 35; HSCAH, VI, 289–90; open letter on King's antiwar stand by William J. vanden Heuvel, Feb. 17, 1967, in King Name File, LBJ.

432 Whitney Young incident: Lincoln, 205–6; Wachtel interview with Oates.

433 "all white people": *NYT*, Apr. 5, 1967.

433–436 Riverside speech: King, "Beyond Vietnam," *Speak on the War*, 10–16; Bennett's remarks, *ibid.*, 19.

436 "belong to us" and "not a mystic": Coretta King, 294; Lincoln, 203.

437–438 critical reaction: *NYT*, Apr. 6, 1967; HSCAH, VI, 296; Lincoln, 213; John P. Roche to LBJ, Apr. 5, 1966, Bayard Rustin Name File, LBJ; *Congressional Record*, May 3, 1967; *Newsweek* (Apr. 17, 1967), 46; *Life* (Apr. 21, 1967), 4; Washington *Post*, Apr. 6, 1967; *NYT*, Apr. 7, 1967; Rowan's column in Akron *Beacon-Journal*, clipping, MLK(CSC), and Rowan's contact with the White House in George Christian memo for the President, Apr. 8, 1967, King Name File, LBJ; Lincoln, 212–18; *NYT*, Apr. 13, 1967. Ralph McGill of the Atlanta *Constitution* also criticized King's stand against the war; he and his wife even wrote King a personal letter expressing their "deep dismay and profound regret" at having to disagree with him. Ralph and Bernice McGill to King, May 1, 1967, MLK(CSC).

438 King's response: Young quoted in Mark Lane and Dick Gregory, *Code Name "Zorro": The Murder of Martin Luther King, Jr.* (Englewood Cliffs, N.J., 1977), 103; Wachtel interview with Oates; Lee interview with Oates. The Johnson White House did in fact encourage the criti-

page

cal response to King's speech, and the list of "secret" FBI reports to the White House, still classified in LBJ, indicates that the administration and the bureau were in close and frequent contact about King's anti-war activities.

438–439   "stand idly by" to "justice everywhere": King's comments in *Speak on the War*, 28; *NYT*, Apr. 13, 1967; King, "Proposed Vietnam Form Letter" [1967], MLK(CSC); newspaper clipping on King's speech in Toledo, Ohio, Sept. 30, 1967, and King, "The Domestic Impact of the War on America," Chicago, Ill., Nov. 11, 1967, SCLC.

439   King's defenders: Parks, *Born Black*, 107; *NYT*, Apr. 6, 1967; Rustin, *Line*, 169; Mays, *Born*, 270–71; *Christianity and Crisis* (May 1, 1967), 89–90; New York *Post*, Apr. 14, 1967; Niebuhr's foreword in *Speak on the War*, 3.

440   "many of these people": Wachtel interview with Oates; Rustin interview with Oates; Lincoln, 207.

440   "just read it": Lincoln, 187; *NYT*, Apr. 16, 1967. King spoke again on "Casualties of the War in Vietnam," copy in MLK(CSC).

440–443   Cleveland and Berkeley: Lincoln, 190–211.

444   "the stirrings": *U.S. News & World Report* (May 8, 1967), 14; King's remarks, July 10, 1967, MLK(CSC). Documents on the Vietnam summer are in the records of Andrew Young, Officer of the Executive Director, SCLC.

444   "substantial number" and "only you could hear": Fred Panzer memo to the President, May 19, 1967, King Name File, LBJ; memo for the President, Aug. 3, 1967, *ibid.;* Sidey, "L.B.J.," *Time* (Feb. 10, 1975), 16.

444   "the nuts" and "possibly survive": Schlesinger, *Robert Kennedy*, 777, 823; memo for the President, Aug. 3, 1967, King Name File, LBJ. For the FBI's COINTELPRO operations against King, see *FAR*, 536, 568–69, and Garrow, *FBI*, 182–88.

445   "chaos and destruction": telegram, July 25, 1967, King Name File, LBJ.

446   "How can the administration": King, "Domestic Impact of the War," SCLC; *TC*, 59.

446   "criminal disobedience" and "outstripped": W and M, 4; *New York Review of Books* (Aug. 24, 1967), 3; also Lionel Lokos, *House Divided: The Life and Legacy of Martin Luther King* (New York, 1968), 342ff.

446–447   "No man," terribly sad, "Supreme Court": W and M, 3–4, 254–55; King's statement, Oct. 30, 1967, MLK(CSC).

447   "seriously question" and "deep rage": Coretta King, 297; *TC*, 15; also Washington *Post*, Feb. 11, 1968.

448   "transitory drama" and "arsenal of nonviolence": King's statement before SCLC's annual convention, Aug. 15, 1967, SCLC; *TC*, 14.

448   "an oppressive society": *U.S. News & World Report* (Aug. 28, 1967), 10; King, "The Crisis of America's Cities," SCLC's annual convention,

page

Aug. 15, 1967, SCLC; *TC*, 15; *NYT*, Dec. 5, 1967. For the origins and background of King's project, see Offenburger's interview and Katherine Shannon's interview with Claudia Rawles, Aug. 12, 1968, BOHC; Coretta King, 297–98.

449 "misguided Moses" and "we don't want": HSCAH, VI, 293–95; W and M, 2.

449–451 planning the campaign: King's remarks, SCLC's staff retreat, Frogmore, S.C., Nov., 1967, MLK(CSC); King, "The State of the Movement," SCLC's staff retreat, Frogmore, S.C., Nov. 28, 1967, SCLC; *TC*, 14–15, 55, 60–62, 77; Williams interview with Oates; Bernard Lafayette interview with Oates, Oct. 19, 1981; Wachtel interview with Oates, Oct. 18, 1978; Robinson interview with Oates; King's statement in Chicago conference, Jan. 5, 1968, and King, "Why We Must Go to Washington," Jan. 15, 1968, MLK(CSC); Bevel interview and Albert Sampson interview with Katherine Shannon, July 18, 1968, and Offenburger interview, BOHC; Fager, *Uncertain Reconstruction*, 15; Lee interview with Oates.

451–452 press conference: King's statement, Dec. 4, 1967, MLK(CSC); *NYT*, Dec. 5, 1967.

452 "international emergency" and "all life": *TC*, 62, 69–70.

453 "bowing to the trend," "peripatetic parsons," "lock up Martin Luther King": HSCAH, VII, 107; St. Louis *Globe-Democrat* clipping, Dec. 10 [18?], 1967, LBJ; L. E. Quarmstrong to the President, Jan. 3, 1968, King Name File, *ibid.*

453 "criminal disobedience" and "whatever form": memorandum for the President, Feb. 14, 1968, and Larry Temple memo for W. Marvin Watson, Feb. 19, 1968, King Name File, LBJ; copy SCLC "staff only" memo, Jan. 1, 1968, in possession of the White House, *ibid.*; Whitney Young interview, *ibid.*; Washington *Post*, Feb. 2, 1968.

453 "preside over": clipping, *ibid.*

453–454 FBI: HSCAH, VI, 72–77, 213, 217–21, 301–6, 321, 338, 366, 374–75; VII, 140–41; FAR, 536, 542, 546, 574.

454 "Mr. Hyde and a Dr. Jekyll": King, "Unfulfilled Dreams," Mar. 3, 1968, MLK(CSC); also Garrow, *FBI*, 186.

455 "big nigger": *FAR*, 470–90; HSCAH, VII, 173–74.

455 "you, Andy," "cannot worry," "strain of wondering": YPI, 74; Coretta King, 304; Gibson interview, BOHC; also Abernathy in HSCAH, I, 21, 22; Raines, 55.

456 "happens to me" and "physical exam": Coretta King, 304; Raines, 431; Young, "Remembering Dr. King," in Obst, *Sixties*, 232; Howell, 19.

456–457 Rustin's objections: Rustin, *Line*, 202–5; Rustin interview with Oates; Washington *Post*, Feb. 26, 1968.

457 "five years wearier" and "merely postponed": Baldwin, *No Name in the Street* (paperback ed., 1973), 141–42.

457–458 "deep apprehensions," "terrible shape," "different person": Rustin in-

page

terview, LBJ; Young quoted in George Goodman, "He Lives, Man!" *Look* (Apr. 15, 1969), 29; Oates interviews with Williams, Abernathy, Lee, Wachtel, and Lafayette; Offenburger interview, BOHC.

458 "Every now and then": recorded on *King: Speeches and Sermons* (cassette).

459 "give us a chance," "areas of agreement," "here to deal": Washington *Star*, Feb. 8, 1968; Washington *Post*, Feb. 11, 1968; King's remarks at SCLC's staff retreat, Frogmore, S.C., Nov., 1967, MLK(CSC).

459 "have not given up": King, "Showdown for Nonviolence," *Look* (Apr. 16, 1968), 25.

460 "ability, togetherness": King's remarks recorded on *I Have a Dream* (cassette).

460–461 master plan: Fager, *Uncertain Resurrection*, 17–18; King, "Showdown," *Look*, 23–25; *TC*, 16; King's speech before the Ministers Leadership Training Program, Miami, Fla., Feb. 19, 1968, SCLC; King, "See You in Washington," MLK(CSC); King, "Conversation with Martin Luther. King," Sixty-eighth Annual Convention of the Rabbinical Assembly, Mar. 25, 1968, 17–19, copy in author's possession; Lafayette interview with Oates. Staff assignments, field reports, and other documents about the poor people's campaign are in SCLC.

461 "mammoth job": Coretta King, 299.

462 "an awareness," "what the powers," "White America": Oates interviews with Lee, Rustin, Lafayette, Wachtel, and Williams; Vincent Harding interview with Vincent Browne, Aug. 16, 1968, BOHC; PI, 194; also King's speech at SCLC's staff retreat, Frogmore, S.C., May 29–31, 1967, MLK(CSC).

462 King on Marx: In a speech at SCLC's staff retreat at Frogmore, S.C., on Nov. 14, 1967, King told his aides and advisers that "I look at Marx with a yes and a no." He liked Marx's "great passion for social justice." But Marx was wrong when, in the process of working out a dialectical materialism from Hegel and Feuerbach, he failed to discern the spiritual in human life and to understand that means and ends must cohere. "The great weakness in Karl Marx is right here," King declared. He went on: "Capitalism fails to realize that life is social. Marxism fails to realize that life is individual. Truth is found neither in the rugged individualism of capitalism nor in the impersonal collectivism of Communism. The kingdom of God is found in a synthesis that combines the truths of these two opposites. Now this is where I leave brother Marx and move on toward the kingdom." MLK(CSC).

PART TEN: FREE AT LAST

463 "Whenever you set out": King, "Unfulfilled Dreams," Mar. 3, 1968, *ibid*.

465–466 Acapulco: HSCAH, I, 25–26, 33–34; Abernathy interview with Oates; Raines, 470.

page
466   "confronted the establishment": *Freedomways* (spring, 1968), 10–11.
466   "God loves us": Testament, 175; King, "See You in Washington," Jan.
       17, 1968, MLK(CSC); *TC*, 76–78. Garrow, *FBI*, 215, argues that "the
       experiences of the 1960s had taught [King] that optimism was unjusti-
       fied" and that "at his death King's optimism had been wholly erased."
       While Garrow is a fine King scholar, his argument does not accord
       with the evidence cited in this reference.
466–467 "a physician's warning" and "This means": *FAR*, 356–57; Schlesinger,
       Robert Kennedy, 846.
467   "devoid of statesmanship": Testament, 234.
467–468 King and RFK: Los Angeles *Times*, Mar. 17, 1968; King, "Conversa-
       tion," Rabbinical Assembly convention, 3–4; Schlesinger, *Robert Ken-
       nedy*, 790, 799, 873, 907; Wachtel interview with Oates; Young inter-
       view, LBJ. For King's and Kennedy's sympathies for one another, see
       King to Kennedy, Mar. 2, 1966, and especially Kennedy to King, May
       4, 1967, MLK(CSC).
468   "racist decision making": Testament, 231.
470   "wanted to escalate": Richard Moon interview with James Mosby, July
       10, 1968, BOHC; also H. Ralph Jackson interview with James Mosby,
       July 10, 1968, *ibid.*
470   "poor folks": Lee interview with Oates; also Offenburger interview,
       BOHC; *FAR*, 359; HSCAH, I, 14–15.
470–471 King's speech: the transcript in MLK(CSC) seems incomplete; *cf.* re-
       corded version on *I Have a Dream* (cassette); also HSCAH, VI, 472,
       571; Offenburger and Moon interviews, BOHC.
471   "talk about fighting": Watters, 354; HSCAH, VI, 574–75; *FAR*, 539.
472   "How do you live?": King's sermon, Washington Episcopal Cathedral,
       Mar. 31, 1968, JD; King, "Conversation," Rabbinical Assembly conven-
       tion, 17.
472   "get the message": W and M, 263; HSCAH, IV, 247–48.
472–473 "sometimes wonder," "You know, Harry," "got scary," "deeper than
       that": Oates interviews with Rustin, Wachtel, and Lee.
473–476 Rabbinical Assembly convention: King, "Conversation," author's pos-
       session; Wachtel interview with Oates.
476   the Logans: Gerald Frank, *An American Death* (paperback ed., New
       York, 1973), 49–50; Lee interview with Oates. Frank misdates the visit.
477   "very unsavory characters": Smith interview with James Mosby, July
       11, 1968, BOHC.
477–478 disrupted march: HSCAH, I, 15–16; VI, 410, 416, 431–32, 451, 473–81;
       FAR, 361–62, 539–41; Smith and Moon interviews, BOHC; W and M,
       263; Selby, 146.
478   "intelligence work": W and M, 264; Lee interview with Oates.
478   "adhere to nonviolence" and "must come back": HSCA, I, 16, 35;
       Raines, 465; W and M, 264.
478–479 Invaders: *FAR*, 362. Testimony varies as to what was said in the meet-

page

ing. Abernathy's version is in HSCAH, I, 17, and in Raines, 465; Calvin Taylor's and Charles Cabbage's versions in HSCAH, VI, 451–54, 510–12, 516.

479   King's press conference: Memphis *Commercial Appeal,* Mar. 30, 1968; HSCAH, I, 17.

479   "had never seen" and "get out of Memphis": Raines, 465; also HSCAH, I, 17.

480   "Dr. King's pose" and "the prelude": Memphis *Commercial Appeal,* Mar. 30, 1968; St. Louis *Globe-Democrat,* March 30–31, 1968; HSCAH, VI, 412; VII, 107; *FAR,* 468, 537–38, 577. The House Select Committee on Assassinations concluded that the FBI was not involved in any assassination plot against King. Hoover did not want him murdered: that would only make King a martyr. No, the director and his men hoped to break and drive King in humiliation from public life. Mark Lane is simply wrong in accusing the FBI of complicity in an assassination plot. For a discussion of the many inaccuracies in Lane's chapters in *Code Name "Zorro,"* see *FAR,* 557n.

480–481   Ebenezer staff meeting: Fauntroy interview with Oates; Selby, 146–47; Raines, 467; HSCAH, I, 18; Lee interview with Oates; Lafayette interview with Oates; Frank, *American Death,* 89.

482   "congratulating me for": Wachtel interview with Oates. King's sermon, "Remaining Awake Through a Great Revolution," given at the Washington Episcopal Cathedral, is in JD.

482–483   "sorry for the delay," "ridiculous," "very well": King, "I've Been to the Mountain Top," Memphis, Tenn., Apr. 3, 1968, MLK(CSC); HSCAH, I, 33, 37; IV, 249; VI, 411–12, 547; Raines, 467–68; Lee interview with Oates.

483   "no police" and "not going to be stopped": HSCAH, IV, 204–8, 257–59; *FAR,* 385–86, 547–51; W and M, 266.

484   "most peaceful warrior" and "Come on, Ralph": this scene draws from Lafayette interview with Oates; Raines, 468; Lee interview with Oates; Dorothy Cotton conversation with Oates, Oct. 19, 1981; HSCAH, I, 18.

486   King's speech: "I've Been to the Mountain Top," printed copy in MLK(CSC), recorded on *I Have a Dream* (cassette); full recording in the National Archives.

486   "almost morbid": *FAR,* 364.

487   "broken the cycle": Lee interview with Oates; also Raines, 468; *FAR,* 364.

487   "Come on now": Abernathy to Gregory in Lane and Gregory, *Code Name "Zorro,"* 117; Abernathy interview with Oates.

487   "cutting up": *FAR,* 364; also Williams in Friends; Offenburger interview, BOHC.

487–488   Invader meeting: *FAR,* 364; HSCAH, I, 27, 28–29; VI, 417, 461, 466–67, 488–90, 512, 518–19; Lee interview with Oates.

488   "doesn't matter": Abernathy interview with Oates; Abernathy to Greg-

page

ory in Lane and Gregory, *Code Name "Zorro,"* 119; Raines, 468.

488–489   "so happy," "magnificent," "home free": Raines, 468; W and M, 269–70; *FAR*, 365–66; HSCAH, I, 19; Lee interview with Oates.

489   "go to West Hunter": HSCAH, I, 19–20, 30–31; *FAR*, 365; Abernathy interview with Oates.

489   "OK, Doc" to "on the balcony": *FAR*, 365–66; HSCAH, I, 20.

489–490   "hurt you," "Solomon," "make sure you play," "Jesse": *FAR*, 366–67; Lee and Abernathy interviews with Oates; Raines, 469.

490–491   the shooting: *FAR*, 367–69, 375–77; HSCAH, I, 20, 24–25, 32; VI, 418–20, 423–27; Abernathy, Lee, and Williams interviews with Oates; Raines, 468–70; Frank, *American Death*, 91–92.

491–492   the hospital: Frank, *American Death*, 110, 113–16; HSCAH, I, 20–21, 58; Lee and Abernathy interviews with Oates; *FAR*, 369, 374; Raines, 471.

492–493   the morgue: Frank, *American Death*, 130; Raines, 472; Abernathy interview with Oates; *NYT*, Apr. 8, 1968; Lincoln, 223; *FAR*, 373; HSCAH, I, 36–37. Abernathy told Gregory that the brown paper bag was hooked to King's toe. See Lane and Gregory, *Code Name "Zorro,"* 121.

493   "in a few seconds": Daddy King, 188–89; also Ivan Allen, Jr., interview, May 15, 1969, LBJ; Sam Williams in Friends.

493–494   "national disaster," "killed Dr. King," "got the s.o.b.": *NYT*, Apr. 5, 1968; Schulke, *King*, 202; Manchester, *Glory*, 1128; HSCAH, I, 107.

494   James Earl Ray: the evidence amassed by the House Select Committee on Assassinations points conclusively, I believe, to Ray as King's lone assassin and to a link between Ray and Kaufmann and Sutherland, the two men who had offered "hit" money for King's life. See *FAR*, 378–83, 423ff.

494–495   world reaction: *NYT*, Apr. 6, 1968.

495   "M.L.!" and "never hated anybody": Daddy King, 190; *NYT*, Apr. 8, 1968.

495–498   funeral and burial: transcript of the funeral service, Apr. 9, 1968, MLK(CSC), partly recorded on *I Have a Dream* (cassette); *NYT*, Apr. 10, 1968; Coretta King, 329–34, 353. In his eulogy to King, Mays mistakenly claimed that King was the grandson of a slave on his father's side. It was his mother's side.

INDEX

About the Author

STEPHEN B. OATES is a professional biographer and historian. He has published eleven books and more than fifty essays and shorter biographical studies in such periodicals as *American Heritage*, the *New York Times*, the *Nation*, the *Massachusetts Review*, and the *South Atlantic Quarterly*. Born in the northern Texas Panhandle in 1936, he holds a Ph.D. in history from the University of Texas at Austin and is an elected member of the Texas Institute of Letters and the Society of American Historians. He has been a Fellow of the John Simon Guggenheim Foundation and a Senior Summer Fellow of the National Endowment for the Humanities. He is currently a Professor of History and an Adjunct Professor of English at the University of Massachusetts, Amherst, where he teaches courses in the Civil War era and the art and technique of biography.